Chir

To Austyn William Follett

Happy Reading - Enjoy this magnificent
book about your old school!

Lots of love
from

Mum

X

PLYMOUTH COLLEGE
THE FIRST HUNDRED YEARS

CHRIS ROBINSON

Pen&inK
PUBLISHING

British Library Cataloguing in Publication Data
A catalogue record for this book is available from the British Library
Robinson Chris 1954 –
Plymouth College – The First Hundred Years

ISBN 0-9543480-2-8

Designed by Chris Robinson
Jacket Artwork Ewan McKnight
© Chris Robinson

First published November 2005

OTHER CHRIS ROBINSON TITLES PUBLISHED BY PEN & INK
PLYMOUTH AS TIME DRAWS ON – 1985
PLYMOUTH AS TIME DRAWS ON vol II – 1988
VICTORIAN PLYMOUTH: AS TIME DRAWS ON – 1991
PUBS OF PLYMOUTH PAST AND PRESENT vol I – 1995
PUBS OF PLYMOUTH PAST AND PRESENT vol II – 1997
UNION STREET – 2000
THE ARGYLE BOOK – 2002
ELIZABETHAN PLYMOUTH – 2002
PLYMOUTH THEN & NOW – 2004

Published by Pen & Ink Publishing
34 New Street, Barbican, Plymouth PL1 2NA
Tel; 01752 705337/228120 Fax; 01752 770001
www.chrisrobinson.co.uk

Printed & bound in Great Britain by
Latimer Trend & Company Ltd
Estover Close, Plymouth, PL6 7PL

FOREWORD BY SIR DAVID SERPELL

My father, Charles Serpell, was one of the first boys to go to Plymouth College – the first of four generations of Serpells (so far) to do so. Some seventy years later he wrote the original history of the School, so it is perhaps appropriate (as well as kind) for Chris Robinson to invite one of Charles's descendants to write the Foreword to this later, and greater, account.

The new history not only covers a far longer period than its predecessor but brings back to life many of those – teachers and taught, governors and governed, scholars and athletes – who have built, guided, changed and made known the School.

Many changes there have been, on all fronts, but the full and enduring picture that Chris Robinson has, rightly, painted is of a fine school, well suited to its time and place; devoted to the education, in the widest sense, of all its students; and contributing, throughout, to the well-being of Plymouth itself – not to mention the ever-widening world beyond.

"Si monumentum requiris, circumspice"

David Serpell

Plymouth College(1919-1930)

David Serpell

Right; David Serpell at School in 1930.
Above; Plate from Greek Prise won by
his father at the School in 1883

Acknowledgements

There are a good many people to thank for their assistance in getting *'Plymouth College - The First Hundred Years'* to this point. Foremost among them OPM Club Chairman Peter Organ, the OPM Committee and Bob Pratt, Ray Pashley and John Mulinder, whose idea it first was to commission the writing of this volume.

I would also like to thank Sir David Serpell for his foreword, and for his helpful comments and observations on the first part of the History. His late brother, Roger, was also helpful, as were Jimmy Woodrow, George Creber, Marshall Ware, SHC 'Bob' Martin, Arthur Lyddon, Tony Greaves and Francis Scott, all of whom, sadly did not live to see this part of the project completed.

Others who have loaned precious photographs and given valuable time include Ralph Hoare, Henry U'ren, Leslie Clemas, Peter Vittle, Cecil Atkey, Michael Clemo, Roy de St Croix, Colin May, John Cundy, David Algate, Rod Fedrick, Derek Pring, Keith Pring, Mike Pearse, Geoffrey Wycisk, Tom Savery, John Stevens, Bob Pratt, Mike Turpitt, Peter Jones (son of Meyricke), Willoughby Cocks, David Cutler, Mike Parker, KE Southwood and Martin Meade-King.

One whose efforts went way beyond the call of duty is Frank Jeffery who not only compiled the wonderful staff register at the end of this tome, but also spent countless hours proof reading and offering valuable suggestions. Proof reading, and correcting is always a far more difficult job than anyone who has never done it can imagine and thanks are due too to good friends and contemporaries, Alan Harris and Rob Warren, my other half, Clare, and my mother-in-law, Trish, for many long days of pouring over the first draft.

The Headmaster - Alan Morsley, the Bursar - Gordon Mills, and various present staff members have also been very helpful with support and sourcing material. And then as the project neared the final stages Ewan McKnight was invaluable as cover designer and computer whizz, while at the print stage itself I am once more indebted to Bob Mills and his wonderful Latimer Trend team at Estover. To them all, my very grateful thanks.

Chris Robinson - October 2005

PLYMOUTH COLLEGE
THE FIRST HUNDRED YEARS

CONTENTS

INTRODUCTION

A rehearsal scene from the School production of the Happiest Days of Your Life (1971) with Doug Martin (headmistress), left, Dennis Collinson (headmaster) and Chris Robinson (vicar's wife) right.

Schooldays ..."The Happiest Days of Your Life" that's what they say and certainly for me they were good times. The memories I have of Plymouth College are all happy ones; the friendships, the teaching, the sport, the army camps ... not that I ever felt inclined to join the services, not that I ever played for the firsts, not that I was ever the most brilliant pupil, but without a doubt I enjoyed the whole experience and even now many of my dearest friends are guys I met at school. Actually some of them I didn't really know that well at school and one or two of them weren't even at school at the same time as I was - but for me that is a good measure of how successful the school has generally been at creating a culture of cameraderie and fostering a certain warmth around Ford Park.

I know many schools have their own Mr Chips, but writing and researching this first hundred years of Plymouth College & Mannamead School I realise that Ford Park has attracted a great number of teachers who have arrived fresh out of college and never felt overly-inclined to see if another school's grass is any greener.

There is something quite special about the place. Much of it, I believe, is down to that great sweep of playing field that frames the frontage of the Main School. So many other city-based schools are hemmed in by neighbouring buildings, making it difficult to get a good perspective on the place. The erstwhile Corporation Grammar School and Sutton High are classic examples of buildings that would look so much better - and different - if they had one or two rugger pitches, or a cricket square in front of them.

At one of the first meetings I attended as a Governor of the School I remember there being a question of the School being offered the chance of a wholesale move to the former Royal Naval Engineering College site at Manadon. There would have been more playing fields, more room and money in the bank as part of the deal. For a variety of reasons, the move, clearly, didn't happen and I for one was relieved; Plymouth College belongs at Ford Park, a move to a different place would essentially mean the creation of a new school with an old name - like St Boniface College, or Notre Dame, or more pertinently St Dunstan's, which somehow was never quite the same after it moved from North Road.

Arguably of course the Prep, or the Junior School, which moved to the new St Dunstan's site at the Millfields, earlier this year, as a consequence of the merger of Plymouth College and St Dunstan's, will never quite be the same again either, but then the Prep had only been at Hartley Road since 1947 and had had several homes around Ford Park before that, so the circumstances are quite different.

The Main School building at Ford Park was opened for the teaching of boys in 1880 and, remarkably, among the first pupils ever to be taught there was Charles Serpell, the father of Sir David Serpell, who, here, 125 years later, provides the Foreword to this volume.

Sir David was also a pupil here, and, briefly, a teacher too. His brother, Roger, also came here and like his father before him, served the School as Clerk to the

Governors for many years. Indeed Roger was sitting in that capacity when the first History of the School was produced. That was in 1950 and it was written by Serpell senior and published the year after his father's death. Sadly Roger too is no longer with us, but I sat with him for a number of years on the Plymouth Barbican Association and I spent many hours with him discussing Plymouth College in the 1920s.

I also spoke at length with Sir David and I'm delighted that he's still with us to witness this publication. After it was first announced, in the OPM Magazine, nearly ten years ago, that I was starting work on this project, he telephoned me with the offer of photographs from his archive. The convivial call ended with a plea from the man who was, even then, well into his eighties; *"For God's sake boy, do get it finished before I die!"*

Certainly it's taken longer than I envisaged, but I hope it's been worth it. I've spoken to countless past pupils and past and present members of staff; I've read every issue of the Plymothian from cover to cover (up to 1955 at least); I've trawled various national archives in London and Kew, the Devon Archives in Plymouth and Exeter and I've scoured the school for pictures and stories.

Sadly a number of photographs were in an advanced state of decay by the time I found them, but happily the vast majority were fine and are presented here in chonological order.

Tantalizingly some of the best early images came from two caches of glass-plate negatives all apparently dating from betwen 1895 and 1910, most without any real clue as to who was in the picture and when exactly they were taken. Perhaps they can be identified yet.

Certainly it was a very pleasant surprise to find that a couple of the mid-1920s photographs in the book, when published in the OPM Magazine recently, were recognised and characters identified, by Ralph Hoare, now well into his nineties and then a sixth-former unwittingly immortalised on film.

This faded and very foxed image of the school (taken outside Shaftesbury Villa) bears the approximate date of 1880. However by that time there were already well over 100 boys on the School role. At the beginning of the previous academic year though there were just over 50 boys - and there are 52 in this picture, so this is almost certainly the first full picture of the school and dates from the first term of 1878. Sadly it is impossible to link specific names to blurry faces, but what follows is a list of the 50 or so boys that were in school at the beginning of that term. The First Fifty ... From the 1877 intake; Harold Alger, Frederick Anthony, Ernest Anthony, Richard Bennett, Henry Bennett, William Cuddeford, William Drury, John Greenway, George Glinn, Edgar Hawke, Howard Heath, Ernest Lewarn, Frederick Mapson,Harold Moon, Charles Prance, George Rogers, Frederick Sims, Charles Stevens, Edgar Stumbles, Charles Trythall, H Turner, CH Whiteford, CJR Wilkinson, Willoughby Wilkinson, Wilson i, Wilson ii, EJM Wood, GR Wood. Arrivals at the beginning of 1878; Thomas Arnold, William Dawe, Edwin Edlin, Barron Haddy, Robert Hutchinson, Frank Key, Charles Lansdown, Matthew Lowry, Henry Marshall, Vivian Millett, Frederick Morrish, Oswald Palmer, Ernest Palmer, Edward Palmer, Richard Popplestone, John Risdon, William Risdon, Desmond Roberts, James Rooney, Harry St George Slight, Arthur Stoneman, Samuel Trounce, Ernest Walters, Joseph Willoughby, William Willoughby, James Willoughby, Richard Worth.

Undoubtedly there are plenty more relevant photographs out there too, but, given that, as late as the 1950s, you were lucky to get even one photograph published each term, the inclusion of around a thousand images in this volume represents a good start.

And that is, I hope, what the chronicle is itself - a good start. Hopefully before too long the it will be brought up to the present day, and then one day perhaps the whole thing can be abridged into a more manageable and possibly more readable form. However, given that the current incarnation of the Plymothian takes the form of an extremely attractive, glossy, and very well-illustrated yearbook, I thought it would be a shame not to try and create something approaching an historical equivalent.

For the most part, the fact that the quotations are mainly taken from the edited and approved pages of the Plymothian, means that the Chronicle is perhaps not as crictical or as colourful as it might have been. Nevertheless I hope what emerges is a picture of a School evolving over 100 years in a City that has seen a great many changes in its own right. I believe it is important to frame the history of the School against both the background of the area it has grown up in, and the context of contemporary culture that society is forever passing through.

In that respect there are a lot of ways in which this could be a chronicle of so many different British schools: look back at the uniforms, the hair cuts, the rugby shirts and shorts, and you will find that only the names and faces are different.

And so, from whatever angle you tackle this tome, I hope there is something here to interest and entertain. Past pupils, staff members, brothers, sisters, sons and daughters, I'm sure will find a great something of personal relevance, but I would hope there is a wider audience too. Plymouth College has played a major role in the modern city's history and so too have many of its old boys ... and these days - girls.

From my own perspective I found it fascinating to try and place the beginnings of the School in a proper Plymouth context and even more illuminating to see some teachers I had only known as curmudgeonly old men as dynamic, athletic, fresh-faced graduates. It was also revealing to read of the exploits of one or two much older OPMs and see their lives in a different light.

On a more sober note however it was harrowing to read through old magazines, in date order, and learn of the academic and sporting successes of first one, and then another generation of young Plymouth College boys, whose names would later fill the obituary columns in the war reports from 1914-18 and 1939-45. Being able to put smiling young faces to so many of the names that were destined to appear on the memorial tablets from those two world wars made the experience even more chilling. It was undoubtedly the most moving part of the whole Chronicle for me, particularly when viewed against the context of the typical young schoolboy's wartime experience; collecting sharpnel, spotting planes, reading war stories and watching morale-boosting movies.

It never does to generalise too much I know, but these were the impressions I formed from the material available. And here, of course, is another area that perhaps needs a little explanation. There can be little doubt that the Chronicle is a little heavy in the bias it shows towards the sporting records of each generation, but that bias largely reflects the emphasis given in the compilation of the Plymothian and in the legacy of the photographs that were taken at the time.

The same is true of so many other school archives: wearing another hat I have been writing about local schools for many years and so far I have only found one photograph, prior to 1955, of a teacher teaching in front of a class. Furthermore I can't ever recall seeing a picture of pupils sitting an examination, or, prior to 1955, of anyone celebrating their exam results. Similarly, photographs of chess matches, school debates, stamp displays and natural history society meetings, are as rare as hen's teeth. However, in readiness for a revised edition I'd be delighted to see anything that anyone has that might be deemed appropriate.

The bias here however is not just a pictorial one as the attempt has been made to focus on those elements of school life that we share most readily with others. Seldom do they include our own examination results, or the activities of the Board of Governors, however important those elements might be. Plymouth College has always enjoyed a good reputation academically and its 'value-added' status is currently as high as it's probably ever been - indeed on hearing the examination results obtained by a wide range of academically-gifted teenagers at the school this summer, a senior HMC Headmaster, suggested that the current head, Alan Morsley, was either performing miracles at Ford Park, or lying about the average IQ of his pupils. In truth the results were just the product of a dedicated, hard-working and happy staff and a dedicated, hard-working and happy band of students.

Alan Morsley, incidentally, is only the fourteenth headmaster of Plymouth College and on his retirement in 2006 will become the fourth longest-serving incumbent since the school's foundation (and that's without counting the six years he taught here in the 1980s). One question he posed as I neared the end of this first part of the chronicle was *"who do you think has been the greatest head?"*

It's a difficult question for a number of reasons and clearly longevity, both in life and in post, plays a part in the final analysis (otherwise it is quite possible that the likes of Lockwood would have been a candidate). Colson's role (1889-1908) was a crucial one, both in terms of the School's early survival and then its effective takeover of Mannamead School; Ralph's reign (1929-45) was key in obtaining improvements in facilities, improvements in staffing and in keeping the School functioning in the City throughout the difficult years of war and the Blitz; while Meade-King (1955-73) sailed a steady path through the turbulent times of the late-fifties and sixties when young people set about re-evaluating their role in society. The school also grew and prospered during his time. More recently Morsley himself (1992-2006) has guided the School safely and smoothly through some of the most momentous changes of all; the scrapping of Saturday morning school; the loss of the Government's Assisted-Places scheme (which affected all independent schools); the introduction of co-education throughout the whole school and the amalgamation with St Dunstans Abbey Girls' School, the only other remaining independent secondary school in the City.

It is largely to these men that the current generation must look and be grateful, but equally it would be unfair to overlook the contribution of certain other heads, the many capable deputies and the long-serving stalwarts whose contributions all too often are overlooked.

Then there is the pivotal role played by a worthy succession of Governing Body Chairmen, many of whom have brought considerable influence and expertise to bear on the School's continued success.

It's a tough call and doubtless each generation will have it's own view on the answer, and so I'll leave it to you to express your own personal opinion.

Under Dr Simon Wormleighton I have no doubt that the School will continue to flourish and would anticipate that when the second part of the Chronicle is completed that he will still be at the helm!

In the meantime I hope you enjoy this installment and trust that maybe in another fifty years or so it may provide some future historian with a useful platform.

Chris Robinson - September 2005

Who are these boys? This image is taken from one of a number of glass plates found at Ford Park after it had spent a hundred years on site without seeing the full light of day. There is no date. There are no names - but surely here we have an invaluable picture of someone's father, grandfather, great-grandfather .... Even if we had (as we do) a list of names of boys at school at that time, we have no means of marrying the two together. Just as we don't for most of the whole school photographs and, indeed, most of the pictures that have ever been taken! Such a pity!

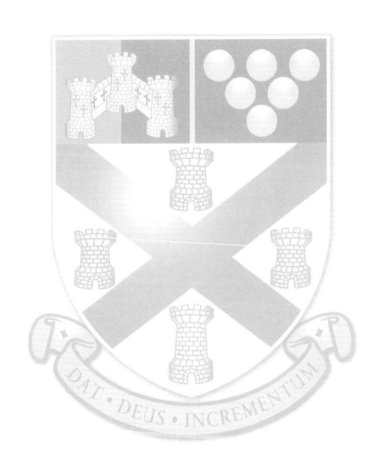

DAT · DEUS · INCREMENTUM

THE OLD SCHOOL TIE

In 1896 Plymouth College and Mannamead School were united on one site - Ford Park. The union between these two traditional adversaries had been the subject of behind-the-scenes negotiations for some time, but to parents and pupils alike it generally came as a great surprise.

The relative pupil numbers at the two schools at that time was about as even as it ever had been, with both around the 150 mark, but, at that stage, Mannamead was going through a difficult phase, and had been since the sudden departure of Theobald Butler in 1893. Plymouth College, on the other hand, was entering a period of steady growth under FH Colson.

Generally though both schools were of a size that made them vulnerable to quirks of fate, and probably the biggest single influence over the success of any school in the nineteenth century was the quality of the headmaster - as the records of many other independent schools that were set up in the Three Towns in that period bear witness.

Until the Education Act of 1870 local schooling had tended to be a very haphazard affair; it was not compulsory for children to attend and many parents could not afford either to send their children to school or forsake the meagre amounts their young offspring might be able to earn. Contemporary records suggest that more than 2,000 children in Plymouth in 1870 were receiving no schooling whatsoever, that at a time when the population of Plymouth - the town rather than the modern city incorporating Devonport, Stonehouse, Plympton and Plymstock - was a quarter of what it is today.

Nevertheless there was a demand for education and by 1840 there were fifty-six private schools operating in Plymouth, most of them *"ill-equipped, badly-staffed, and inadequately- housed"*.

Among the most promising schools in Plymouth at that time was the "Publick" School established in Bedford Street in 1809 (moving three years later to new purpose-built premises *"in Old Town Without in the suburbs beyond the Gate"*, as the rurally-situated Cobourg Street then was) and, standing *"under the shadow of the stately tower of St Andrew"*, deep in the heart of the old town - Plymouth Corporation Grammar School.

An early nineteenth century view of St Andrew's Church tower from Bedford Street. The old Grammar School was just beyond the tower on the other side of the steps.

Public School was founded *"to provide education for the children of such persons as are unable from their indigent circumstances to provide for them"*. Soon after the terrible cholera epidemic of 1832 the school was obliged to start charging fees; initially one penny per week, later increasing to tuppence. Still the school struggled though and it was a happy appointment in 1842 when the great educationalist George Jago took over the then dwindling establishment. Over the next forty or so years under his headship Jago managed to turn Public around and make it one of the three largest schools, in its day, in Britain.

Not such a rosy Victorian picture can be painted of the Town's oldest academic institution, the Grammar School.

It was back in 1561 that the Corporation *"determined that one Thomas Broke should supply the office of a Schoolmaster within this town so long as he shall decently behave himself, and, for an annual stipend of £10 to be paid quarterly, he shall freely teach all the children, native and inhabitant, within the town and that for his lodging he shall have chambers over the alms house chapel, and the said chapel for his schoolhouse"*. Furthermore it was decreed that he should *"teache no other but gramer and writinge"*. An earlier Act, of 1548, had dissolved chantries, colleges and guilds, theoretically that they might provide endowments for new Grammar Schools.

The Alderman, the Mayor, the Councillors, and the townspeople all subscribed to the arrangement. Eleven years later Elizabeth I, as part of a national initiative, gave the Corporation the advowson of St Andrew's and a pension of £8, on condition that they *"maintain for ever a free grammar school"*, which effectively gave the local authority support for running the school they had just established.

Little is known about the success or otherwise of the school over the years, but we do have a continuous list of headmasters from Brooke onwards. Andrew Horsman was the last master to teach in the old chapel building and in 1658 Nathanial Conduit succeeded him in a new building, erected in the in the quadrangle of the then forty-year-old Orphan's Aid Charity, in Catherine Street.

For the next two hundred years this was the school's home. *"The whole of the building is substantially erected in stone. The school room is a long narrow room fitted up for seven classes of ten boys each; the rooms are all gloomy partly owing to the situation and partly from the walls being very thick and the windows narrow. There is a garden for the schoolmaster and a playground for the boys of the Orphans' Aid as well as the Grammar School separated from one another* (Woollcombe *'Picture of Plymouth'* 1812). Looking back on it in 1871 one old boy was moved to remark that *"there are few school-houses that I have seen that looked more fitted for their purpose than did the Plymouth Corporation Grammar School buildings".*

The old Orphans Aid building in Catherine Street with St Andrew's tower on the other side of the road.

This was the school that twenty-four year-old Oxford graduate Peter Holmes took over in 1840. With its long tradition the old Grammar School no doubt seemed like a good move for the young man. The prospects were all there; the rival "New Grammar School" was not fulfilling its perceived potential and yet education - and the idea of boarding - were becoming increasingly popular. Furthermore Plymouth was just entering its greatest ever period of growth, so the old school would appear to have had everything going for it. There can be no doubt that Holmes knew exactly what he was taking on as he had been a pupil there himself, under the Reverend John Henry Coates Borwell, whom he succeeded.

Entrance to the old Grammar School in Catherine Street

After a few years, however, Holmes doubtless saw a different future unfolding. With the increase in population, the improvement in road transport and with the introduction of rail travel in 1849 there came a move away from the centre of town. The better-off members of the local community started to move out as new and impressive houses - villas - were built in the fields of Mutley and Mannamead.

The Catherine Street area was by now decidedly unfashionable. When wealthy local merchant Thomas Yogge had built his great house across the road (known today erroneously as the "Prysten House") in the late fifteenth century, this site was on the edge of the town … four hundred years later the streets around here were old, dark and narrow. In the 1860s most of the area around the school and the school itself would be pulled down as the Corporation cleared the way for their new Guildhall and Municipal Buildings.

Holmes would have been aware that the lease of the school building by the Corporation from the Orphans' Aid Trustees was due to expire in 1860 - the writing was truly on the wall and it didn't look all that promising.

Another important element in all this is that the Reverend Holmes (as he now was - his clerical appointments included the curacy of St Edward's, Egg Buckland and the living of St Pancras, Pennycross) must himself have been a man of some means, otherwise it is hard to see how he could have made his next move, which was to acquire one of the largest of the newly-built houses in Mannamead - the well-disposed double-fronted Wellington Villa.

Here it was that Peter Holmes set up his new school - Mannamead School - at the beginning of 1854. With him he brought a number of boys from the Grammar School, including the thirteen-year-old Roper Lethbridge (later Sir Roper Lethbridge, MP and Deputy-Lieutenant of Devon).

For the old Corporation Grammar it was a blow from which it struggled to recover. One of the pupils arriving there late in 1854 subsequently recalled;

"The fortunes of the school had ebbed before I joined it. There were no boarders to fill its ample dormitories, which the master declared too damp to permit him to think of using them, and there was no dinner-bell to summon hungry scholars across the little quadrangle to the room which would have formed so fine a dining-

hall if there had been diners to make use of it; the only demand on the roomy kitchen was to supply the limited wants of a bachelor's household".

"Only a moderate proportion of the desks in the long school-room were used, and the headmaster was unsupported by assistants - though two empty desks, grim and lonely at the untenanted end of the chamber, shewed that the founders had hoped for a body of scholars sufficient to find employment of a moderately strong staff of teachers, and our small numbers would have seemed half lost in the great play-ground, if our activity had not atoned for our fewness."

The advertisement looking for a successor to Holmes at the Grammar School was not posted until June 1854 and the eventual successful applicant, William Clase, was to stay only four years before resigning his post.

"I left that school or rather the school left me, for no successor to the gentleman (Clase) appeared for some considerable time, and even then he started in another part of town with little beyond the foundation boys to connect his academy with the original institution."

So it was, that in 1858, the Corporation Grammar moved to Alfred Place, then in 1866 to Princess Square, then in 1885 to Park Street. In the course of the last two moves the school joined with and nominally took over the New Grammar School and Park Grammar School. In 1909 it moved again, and was briefly located in the old Plymouth Technical College before coming to rest in North Road West where it remained until its closure in 1937.

These later changes were also accompanied by great changes in the constitution of the school - the only real consistent thread being the name itself. There is therefore a vague sense in which part of the original spirit of the sixteenth century Grammar School actually moved with its headmaster, Holmes, to the new Mannamead School. On the final closure of the Grammar School in 1937 it is interesting to note that the headmaster of Plymouth College succeeded the headmaster of the Grammar School as a trustee of the old school's Kelway Trust, a trust which had been established back in 1737.

Messrs. Crisp, Fowler and Bennett were the developers who had acquired, in the early 1850s, from the Seymour Trust, the two green fields known as the Mannameads. Then, having completed the purchase of East and West Mannamead these gentlemen *"had the two fields laid by Mr Damant for a series of villas"*. One of the first of these villas was Wellington, in what was originally known as Second Avenue (now Seymour Road) - all the new houses in this new area having the collective address of Mannamead.

And Wellington was where Holmes and his boarders were to move on 25 March 1854.

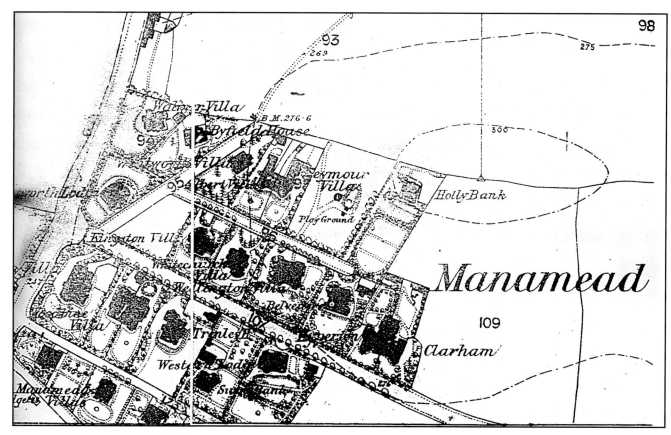

Mannamead School

Wellington Villa, Mannamead, where the new school began.

March 1854 was a strange time in British history, the country was in the grip of an almost hysterical clamour for war. The Prime Minister, Lord Aberdeen, and his cabinet were not really in favour of it, neither were a small group of Liberal pacifists nor the Quakers. Public opinion, however, was unequivocal, the majority of Britons, whatever their class, wanted war.

There had been almost forty years of comparative peace and it was felt that a test of the nation's manhood was long overdue, it was time to push profit-seeking aside, forget comfort and consider instead self-sacrifice and heroism. War was not seen as bad but rather something that generated excitement, great deeds, much glory and national pride. There were it hardly needs to be said, no thoughts of losing or even of losses.

So it was that, primarily on the pretext of asserting public law against a transgressor, Aberdeen and his chancellor Gladstone, took Britain into a war, over three thousand miles away by sea, in support of Turkey, who had actually turned down terms we had agreed with their aggressors, Russia. In addition to this we were to fight alongside the French, our old adversaries, who only a year earlier had been generating rumours that they were to invade Britain.

But it was what the people wanted, the working classes clamouring for comic-strip style heroes, the officers themselves looking towards a great jamboree, a military picnic in some exotic far-off place.

Thus, on 26 March 1854 Britain and France, allies now of the Ottoman Empire, declared war on Russia. Had those involved known anything of the real circumstances that they would find themselves in it is doubtful that so many would have been quite so keen. It is also doubtful that they would have allowed their wives, together with their personal maids, to accompany them to the war zone. Incredibly, however, they did, and even more incredibly there were wealthy civilians who cancelled their holidays to follow the army and see all the fun!

It was in this climate that, on the very day before war was declared, Peter Holmes started Mannamead School.

THE REV. PETER HOLMES, M.A., F.R.S.,
(of Magdalen Hall, Oxford)
HEADMASTER OF PLYMOUTH GRAMMAR SCHOOL

BEGS to announce to the Nobility and the Gentry of the West of England, his resignation of his present office and the removal of his residence to

WELLINGTON VILLA, MANNAMEAD, NEAR PLYMOUTH;

Where he proposes, at and after Lady-day, to educate a number of Young Gentlemen preparing for the Public Schools, the Naval and the Military Colleges, or the Universities. Mr Holmes will be assisted by an efficient staff of Masters and trusts that his own long experience in tuition, and the salubrity and beautiful situation of his residence, will procure for him a continuance of that support, the favour of which during nearly 14 years, he takes the opportunity of thankfully acknowledging.

Programmes of the terms to be had at the GRAMMAR SCHOOL , or at Mr Lidstone's, 16 George-Street, Plymouth; and (after Lady-day) at Wellington Villa.

Pupils destined for the Indian Service, instructed in Sanskrit and Hindustani by the Head Master, formerly a student of those Languages at the University of Oxford.

March 10, 1854

As of 10 March 1854 Holmes was still at the Grammar School, and it is hard now to imagine the feelings of those responsible for the school and their attitude to the head for not only leaving but distributing the prospectus for his new venture from inside the old school.

Holmes' last function as Head of the Grammar School would appear to have been the Prize-Giving that term.

The event was held on that very same day, Lady-day, 25 March 1854, that the new school began. It was held in the Guildhall (the old one in Whimple Street). Holmes was there, as was the head of the corporation, the Mayor, Copplestone L Radcliffe, indeed it was he who presented the prizes.

Clearly the situation must have been a little tense, but our only clue as to the nature of the proceedings was a line in the *Plymouth, Devonport and Stonehouse Herald*, which noted that *"the proceedings were of a very interesting character"*- a classic piece of journalistic understatement, but then Holmes was a man of the cloth and no-one was going to slight his reputation in print; similarly the local press were unlikely to criticise the local authority so we can only guess at what was meant by *"very interesting"*.

Whatever Holmes' final motivation for leaving the school we do know that he was not alone in his thinking: there were plenty of other similar ventures advertising themselves in 1854.

"Married clergyman, graduate of Oxford, residing in a most healthy and pleasant situation in the country, receives a limited number of pupils who will be treated as members of his family"

This could have been Holmes, but it wasn't, for this January 1854 advertisement was placed by Rev. M Gueritz, Bigbury Rector, Modbury. Fees were fixed at 40 guineas for under twelves, 50 for over twelves.

The same paper, later that year, carried a similar advert from the Rev WJ Coppard of Plympton.

The idea of these learned gentlemen passing on their knowledge to the sons of the wealthy was becoming increasingly popular, particularly in the absence of a satisfactory state system. Remember, too, that in those days both the major Universities, Oxford and Cambridge, were still refusing to admit non-conformists up to degree level, and there was, as yet, no question of young women being admitted to either institution on the same basis as men.

The seeds for change were being sown here too however: Cheltenham ladies' college, the first boarding school for daughters of the wealthy gentry, was founded in 1854, as was the albeit comparatively short-lived school founded by the Misses Lott in Wentworth Villa, Mannamead. This school was in the villa at the entrance to Seymour Drive.

Other new small schools in town advertising for pupils included the South Devon Collegiate School, North Hill; the Mount Pleasant House Academy (where the Duke of Cornwall was soon to be built); a "Boarding and Day School" in George Street, plus the Grammar Schools old and new and doubtless others. There were also the new Plymouth Ragged Schools (based in then very crowded areas of Octagon Street, Foundry Ope and Catte Street), which celebrated their fourth anniversary in March, 1854.

Survival of any one of these schools was dependent on a number of factors, paramount of which was undoubtedly the quality and reputation of the headmaster, and it is a testament to the ability of the Reverend Peter Holmes that the Mannamead School prospered.

When the school opened there were only a handful of villas on either side of Second Avenue, a few in Mannamead Avenue and another two or three in Seymour Avenue (now Seymour Drive), including the semi-detached Seymour Villa which was to become the home of the main school itself. Apart from these impressive new villas however there was little or no housing until the outskirts of Compton on one side and green fields of Mutley on the other, where the big new houses of Ford Park represented the largest new development. There were only one or two houses in Hartley and none in Peverell, other than Burleigh Manor House and Pounds House.

From upstairs in Wellington Villa the boys and their headmaster would have looked out over acres of green, Plymouth Sound sparkling ahead in the distance, with the undeveloped expanses of Lipson, Efford and Saltram to the east and Cornwall and Mount Edgcumbe to the west.

View from Mannamead, looking out to the Sound, the heights of Mount Edgcumbe rising high in the distance.

Holmes' move was very bold but also, given the size of the new houses and the families that filled them, very sensible. Carrying forward the traditions of Plymouth's oldest established educational establishment he was bound to appeal to the wealthy merchants with young families who also moved out here in the 1850s.

Such names consistently appear in the school records, brothers from the same families being referred to as Wolferstan ma. or Wolferstan mi. (major/minor or maximus/minimus) or using numbers - Brown i, Brown ii and Brown iii.

Of those very early years little is known. The only evidence that we do have suggests that Holmes probably carried on with much the same syllabus and continued to use the services of some of the members of staff from the old Grammar School and in Holmes' last term there the staff list was as follows: Rev. J Gill, second master; assistant masters Mr T Peters and F Nixon; German master Dr J Kestenberg; drawing, Mr Penson; lecturer in experimental science was Jonathan Hearder, Monsieur Onfroy was the French master, Mr Beedell taught writing and Mr Burke, drilling.

The last three were also mentioned as teaching at the New Grammar School in July 1854 and it is quite likely that, apart from the assistants and the second master, the other teachers taught at more than one school.

How many of them taught at Mannamead we don't know, but we do know that it wasn't long before they had outgrown Wellington Villa and the main school had moved into Seymour Villa, across the road - Seymour Avenue/Drive - from Wellington Villa.

The then sloping plot immediately to the east of Seymour Villa was the playground. Most of the recreation then would have been fairly ad hoc, the academic aims of the school being closely bound up with the hoped-for destinations of the scholars - any extra-curricular activities then were quite limited.

"In the old days football was unknown, and cricket used to be played in a somewhat primitive manner in the school playground and on the Hoe", according to Thomas Wolferstan, solicitor, said to be then the oldest Old Mannameadian in town, who was speaking in 1891. His brother, Dr. Sedley Wolferstan, talking the following year at an old boys' dinner, confirmed this: *"In those days a professor of cricket was unheard of, and the boys had to learn the best way they could, and even roll their own ground, and cut their own grass"*.

Although it was, in essence, the same game as that played today, the kit tended to be pretty basic and there were even those who thought certain items weren't even necessary ... *"Some persons laugh at the idea of putting on pads and gloves, but prevention is better*

1854

5

than cure ... and not only this but when one feels that he is well-protected, he is embued with a greater amount of confidence and assurance".

So ran part of a letter "Hints on Cricket" from RA Rundle to the school magazine in 1869. The writer was also keen to point out that *when you are batting, play as easily as you can, and do not put yourself into what you imagine are becoming postures, but which only render you ridiculous in the eyes of others."*

CORRECT POSITION (*side view*).

It is worth remembering that although the game had been played in select circles for a number of years, by this time it was only really just starting to enter the public awareness, thanks essentially to the prowess of one man.

"It is doubtful if anyone in the history of sport has had quite such a popularising influence as W.G. Grace. When at the age of fifteen, he scored 170 and 56 not out in his second 'first-class' match, for South Wales Club against Gentlemen of Sussex at Brighton in 1864, cricket was a game steadily increasing in public affection as both a participant and spectator sport. In the next generation the game became a national institution, widely reported in the newspapers, a part of every boy's education." (Christopher Martin-Jenkins, *Cricket a Way of Life*, 1985).

1864 incidentally was also the year in which the last major refinement of the old game took place, effectively creating the game as it is played today. That refinement was the acceptance, after much fuss, of the overarm bowling law, which permitted bowlers to bowl with the hand at any height provided that the ball was not thrown or jerked.

As cricket, and sport generally, became increasingly regarded as an important adjunct to the academic syllabus, Mannamead School, from the very first, led the way locally. There weren't many other teams around to play and Mannamead won most of their encounters. In the 1869 season they beat old rivals Plymouth Grammar School convincingly at the South Devon Ground (Prince Rock, where the Astor Playing Fields are today - the infant Plymouth Cricket Club had set up home there in 1862). Another victim that season was the comparatively short-lived North Hill Grammar School XI, while additional opponents included Plymouth New Grammar School, Devonport and Stoke Grammar School (the local equivalent there almost of Mannamead School, mainly populated by sons of the senior Servicemen and wealthy Devonport merchants who filled the new villas of Stoke), Tavistock Grammar and the Eleven of North Hill, the Hyde Park Eleven and the Ford Park CC.

Football was an even newer sport. The first rules were formulated at Cambridge University in 1846: Sheffield, the oldest club still in existence, was founded in 1857, just three years after the foundation of Mannamead School, while the Football Association didn't come into being until 1863 - the FA Cup following eight years later. Small wonder therefore that in the October 1869 edition of the school magazine someone was prompted to ask - *"Can any of your readers inform me , whether, if a player in Foot Ball kicks the Ball through his own goal, it counts as a goal to his opponents?".*

Clearly the fixtures alone do not tell us the whole story. School games were a little different then; in an account

of the game against Plymouth Grammar School - the old rivals again - in November 1869 we learn that *"the school sixteen consisted of ... "* - the theory being that numerical advantage was fair when boys played against men - and that the game only lasted half an hour. There were no proper changing facilities, boys walked to the games, from school, in their kit, which was by no means uniform. Regular correspondence suggests that many boys wore the wrong items, but at least that was better than not turning up at all. One letter writer bemoaned those *"who agree to play* (in this instance cricket) *then find something better to do ... like going into Plymouth for a row, or some such paltry affair".*

Sport was clearly not as high on the agenda then as it was soon to become. Another letter in the same year, this time from EM Hancock, an old boy, spoke about athletics: ... *"these sports are held annually at all schools of note, but the schools of Plymouth and its neighbourhood seem to be an exception to the rule ... why shouldn't Mannamead set an example?"*

It wasn't to be too long before it did, and soon there were more than 30 events competed for each year by the boys of the school. Included among them were throwing the Cricket Ball (traditionally the first event), the 100 yards, quarter mile, mile, long jump, high jump, fencing competition and the egg and ladle open event. It was always a joyful occasion, particularly when

1869

the sun shone: *"very few schools can possess a field more happily situated than ours. Hills and moorland stretch all round us, and are swept by the breezes of the most historic of English waters"*. In addition to the playground between Seymour Villa and Holly Bank, the school also used a playing field at Hartley, in the otherwise undeveloped land around the reservoir.

Here, each year, weather permitting, the school would assemble, the head would provide a "pavilion", and a healthy crowd would arrive - *"very few schools can be happier in the number of their friends,"* and across the course of the day the Band of the Royal Marines would play a selection of waltzes, gavottes, gallops, polkas and the odd quadrille and march; a bright and glorious occasion and an undoubted highlight of the school calendar.

Swimming was another activity being encouraged within the school, although, with no school pool, there were those who *"living at such a distance from the water find it rather gloomy doing three miles by ourselves in the morning before breakfast"*. It's difficult to imagine many of today's boarders relishing the prospect of a pre-breakfast sea-dip, even if transport were provided both ways!

Sport was not the only extra-curricular area being developed then for the benefit of the boys rounded education; there was also the Glee Club and the Debating Society.

Subject to lapses, depending on the strength of the characters running these bodies at any one time, these clubs were good for promoting self-confidence and social skills. The Glee Club brought boys together to sing glees - musical compositions for three or more voices, usually unaccompanied, one voice for each part. These could be *"gay or grave"* and more often than not consistited of two or more contrasting movements.

Meanwhile the Debating Society was there to promote discussion on the various contentious issues of the day and in the late 1860s these included Trades Unions and

Smoking, while the magazine was there for anyone who wanted to provoke thought on an issue outside the debating society.

The first printed edition of the magazine (there is a reference to earlier manuscript issues) was introduced with a fairly long and very one-sided political piece, prompting one correspondent to write that *"I think it would perhaps be much better for the peace of the school and the prosperity of the magazine itself if politics were left altogether unnoticed by it"*.

The editors however didn't agree; they saw it as a political vehicle - and a conservative one at that. Undaunted they carried on for the next three monthly issues, the second containing an attack on Mr Gladstone.

By October 1869 however the magazine had passed into other hands and the new editor was determined to *"abolish Politics from its pages, as such a number of our subscribers think them out of place in a school periodical, and other persons have refused to advertise on account of a too strong partiality in this respect"*.

Nevertheless there was a very partisan piece that month (October 1869) on the designs for the new Guildhall, designs which the corporation had put on show in the Tea Rooms of the Royal Hotel.

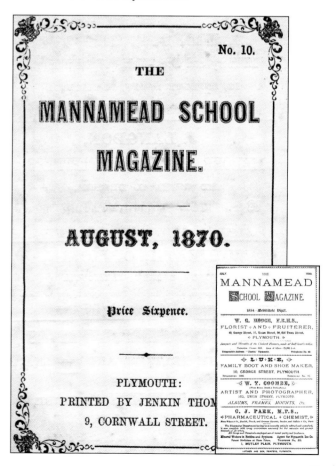

Undoubtedly one of the most interesting entries in the early Mannamead School Magazines (their production was suspended for some reason between 1871 and 1881) was the account, in the May 1871 issue, of the establishment of the Mannamead Cadet Corps, prompted, in all probability by the recent Prussian successes against France.

Brigade Order, No.333, 4th May 1871

Her Majesty has been graciously pleased to approve the following appointment in the Cadet Corps, attatched to the Second Administrative Brigade Devon Artillery Volunteers.
Henry William Freeman, to be *Honorary Lieutenant.*
By order,
(*Signed*),   Ed. Palmer, (Lieut-Col.),
                                                Adjutant

There will be drill on
                  TUESDAYS, at 4-30 p.m.
                  FRIDAYS, at 5-30 p.m.
until further notice.

Mannamead School was clearly ahead of its local rivals in taking this initiative. Indeed it would appear to have been one of the first schools in the country to establish such a body. But like that of the magazine itself, its early survival was by no means certain and a letter from the Hon. Lieutenant H.W. Freeman highlights one or two of the problems - *"serious laxity of discipline amongst some of its members"* being at the heart of the trouble.
"That a member should turn round to argue a point with his officer; that members should put out their legs for the sake of tripping other members up; that there should be unlimited laughing and talking in the ranks, are facts which will tend to disgust those amongst us who take this matter, as indeed all should do, as an earnest and real enterprise, and will also deter others from joining who would otherwise feel inclined to do so ...."
"I make this most earnest appeal to the Corps to support an institution which will render the Mannamead School a leading one of the West ... I am loath to believe that this Corps, launched under such auspicious circumstances, will sink and expire through neglect."
Quite when it did sink we don't know but it wasn't until 1885 that it was successfully revived, by which time the school had gone through a number of changes, not least of which was the loss of its founding headmaster Dr Peter Holmes.
"Dear old Dr. Holmes" as Sir Roper Lethbridge was later to describe him, died early in the Christmas term of 1878. He was sixty-two and had seen the school through its first twenty-four years. He was buried in the churchyard of St Pancras, Pennycross, the church of which he held the living. The whole school attended the service, as did many of his former pupils from the Corporation Grammar School. His gravestone can still be seen today.
Although no picture of the man survives today one can but wonder about the authenticity of the pen-portrait of the man painted by Eden Phillpotts in his novel *The Human Boy*, published in 1896.
Phillpotts was undoubtedly the most famous old Mannameadian of them all. The eldest of three brothers, all of whom went to the school, he was born in India in 1862 and came to the West Country with his mother and two brothers after the sudden death of his father, in the early 1870s.
The book, *The Human Boy*, one of almost 300 of his published between 1890 and his death in 1960, chronicles the school-life at Merivale (Mannamead?) School through the eyes of various pupils and it was one of five that Phillpotts wrote about boyhood (there was also *The Human Boy Again*, 1908, *From the Angle of Seventeen*, 1912, *The Human Boy and the War*, 1916, and *The Human Boy's Diary*, 1924).

Eden Phillpotts based many books on his Mannamead experiences

The description of Merivale's headmaster Doctor Dunston fits Holmes rather well, in as much as he is described as a *"Rev and a DD"* and *"sixty-two years of age"*, which is the age that Holmes was when he died, in harness, around the time that Phillpotts left the school. By making him that age the writer not only keeps his memories intact but also confers some kind of immortality upon the man, a man that Phillpotts clearly had happy memories of ... despite his *"solemn nature"*.
The fact that the school is referred to as Merivale one minute and Dunston's the next, also tends to suggest a strong link here between fact and fiction. There can be little doubt that, as its head since its foundation twenty years earlier, the school would have been popularly known as Holmes's School and/or Mannamead School during Phillpotts time.

Juvenile sketches of Mannamead schoolmasters made by a young Eden Phillpotts while still a pupil at the school in the 1870s.

As for the rest of the staff, there is Mannering, the classics master, Thompson, who takes maths, Briggs who takes writing and drawing, Monsieur Michel, French and finally Browne and Stoddart - who came up once a week to take chemistry. No other staff members are mentioned in this first book and certainly that would be about right, including the headmaster, for the size of the school as it was in Phillpott's day - although Phillpott says that Merivale itself had about 225 boys. Phillpott's fictional staff members also, doubtless, bore some relation to his own teachers and the glimpses we have of these characters are quite fascinating. Browne, for example, was a young man in his very early twenties, with a modest "whiteish" moustache, a poet who fell for one of the Doctor's daughters. Stoddart, on the other hand, was only brought in because Nubby Tomkins' father was only prepared to send his son to the school if chemistry was taught there - there were only four or five in the class.

Thompson was another new teacher whose perceived unsuitability by certain older boys led to a minor school revolt - *"he left out his h's and stuck them in with awfully rum effects"*.

The younger boys didn't have a real problem though - *"Thompson meant so jolly well that nobody could get in a wax with him personally, and the kids, who didn't see the "unholy bounder" side of him, and only knew he stood gallons of ginger-beer on half-holidays in the playing fields, liked him better than anybody"*.

Monsieur Michel, *"Frenchy"*, on the other hand was different, *"a rum oldish chap"*, he was fifty-three, *" nearly cried sometimes"* and *"told us his nerves were frightfully tricky"*: *"He would slang a fellow horribly one day, and wave his arms and pretty nearly jump out of his skin; and the next day he would bring up a whacking pear for the fellow he'd slanged, or a new knife or something ... He didn't entirely belong to Dunston's but lived in Merivale and came to us three days a week, and went to a girls' school the other three"* - note the six day week.

One whole chapter was written about *"Frenchy"* and how one boy, Steggles, ended up trying to *"stick him up"* on his way home late one night. There was also a chapter about old Briggs, or rather what happened when Briggs asked the Doctor if he might *"instil the lads with a wholesome fondness for natural history"*. *"The Doctor said it was an admirable notion, and would very probably keep some boys out of mischief on half-holidays"*.

Illustration from Phillpott's The Human Boy Again.

The upshot of these early biology lessons was that *"one or two chaps really got keen about natural history and even chucked cricket for butterflies and beetles"*.

Things started to get a little out of hand though when one boy *"let it be generally known that he had two live lizards in his desk ... and the idea really caught on"*...

Before long Ashby minor a dormouse, Freckles Maine two guinea pigs, Fowle, tadpoles in a jar, Morrant, sparrows, the wings of which he'd clipped himself, Ferrars a piebald rat, Playfair a mole and Corkey minimus a hawk moth.

That these stories were at least loosely based on fact we can be fairly certain and Corkey minimus would appear to be a reference to his youngest brother. Interestingly enough the book itself is dedicated to Phillpotts *"minor"*, the middle brother *"as a trifling tribute of fraternal regard and in green and grateful memory of our boyhood"*.

Then, as now, it would appear that a young person's memories of their schooldays became more rose-tinted as the year's passed. In the *Human Boy Again* we read of Johnson maximus, Corkey's cousin who went into *"what is called the mercantile marine, which means liners, and not battleships or destroyers; still you see a great deal of the world, and have not got to fight for your country, but only for yourself"*.

Johnson maximus - Joe Johnson - who was some years older than young Corkey, brought a parrot and a very fine tiger skin home for Dr Dunstan and *"when Corkey*

reminded him very naturally that he had always hated Dunstan as much as anybody when he was at Merivale, and had been jolly thankful to leave, Johnson maximus admitted it, but confessed that, looking back, he had found it different, and felt that Dunstan was an awfully good sort and that he owed him a great deal". A change of heart that doubtless countless schoolchildren have experienced over the years.

There are one or two other illuminating insights into Merivale school-life in the 1870s as Phillpotts portrayed it. Clearly many schools these days hold annual firework displays, and certainly from the pages of the Mannamead School magazine we can hazard a guess at Mannamead being one of the first in the area to do so. But if we can accept that many of Phillpott's stories are based on fact, these displays had their beginnings in the show that "Nubby Tomkins" put on. Nubby was the one whose father had insisted on Chemistry lessons at the school and Nubby it was who persuaded the head to let him buy materials for and manufacture his own fireworks. Health and safety legislation today simply wouldn't allow it. The evening was marred incidentally by someone re-arranging the lay-out of the final part of the display - a message was supposed to light up in fireworks saying *'Dr Dunstan is a brick'* - *"Excellent! Pithy and concise, if a little familiar."* Unfortunately for Nubby it was made to read *'Dr Dunstan is a brute'!* Various references to licking, roughing up, fighting and fagging also conjure up a much changed picture of school … *"Tomlin (the fag) was cooking a sausage for me in the sixth's classroom"*.

One final episode from *The Human Boy* serves to illustrate a point about school uniform in Phillpott's day. It's another chapter written around Corkey minimus (the author's youngest brother?) and concerns Corkey's competition with his chum Bray in the necktie department. As the story unfolds we are led to the inevitable conclusion that there was no clearly defined style, pattern or colour for the school tie in those days.

Dr Dunstan of Merrivale School (from A Human Boy)

Bray and Corkey, we are told *"used to be awfully swagger with their neckties, and each fancied his own. So one bet the other half a crown he would wear a different necktie every day for a month. The month being June, that meant thirty different neckties each, and the chap who wore the best neckties would win. A fellow called Fowle was judge, being the son of an artist; and neither Bray nor Corkey was allowed to buy a single new tie or add to the stock he had in his box. At the end of the first fortnight they stood about equal, though Corkey's ties were rather more artistic than Bray's, which were chiefly yellow and spotted. But then came an awful falling away, and some of the affairs were simply weird. The test for these was if a tie passed in class. Then the terms of the match were altered, and they decided to go on wearing different things till one or other was stopped by a master. Any concern not noticed was considered a necktie "in the ordinary acceptance of that term."*

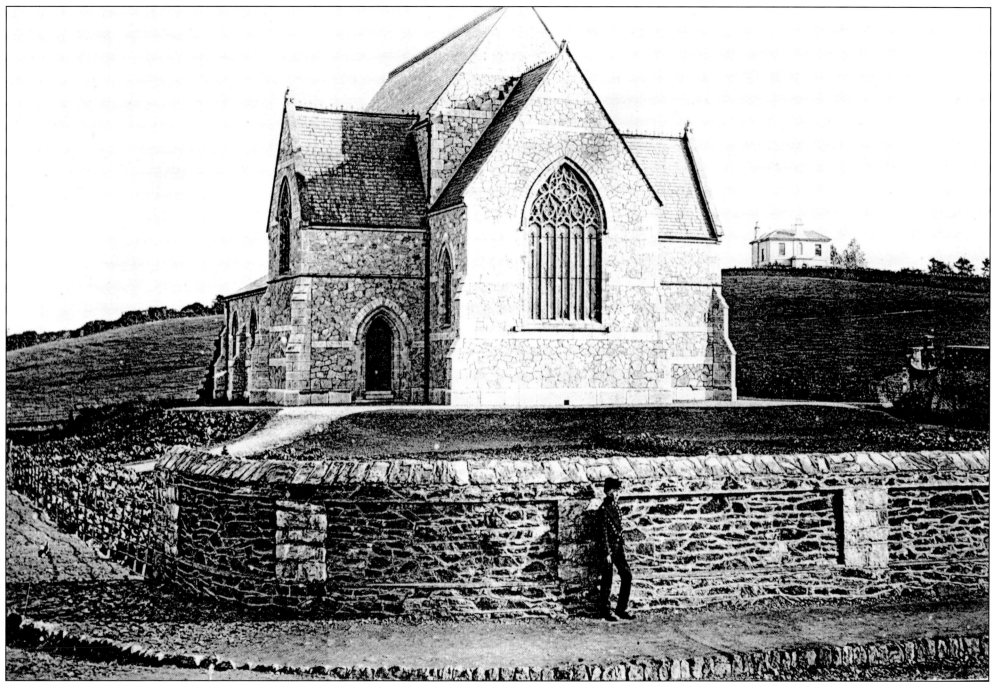

The first phase of Emmanuel Church is completed, surrounded by open spaces, with Holly Bank, soon to be obscured by Compton Park Villas, just over the brow of the hill.

1878

At the end of the third week Corky minimus came out in an umbrella cover done in a sailor's knot, but nobody worth mentioning spotted it; the next day Bray wore a bit of blue ribbon off a chocolate box, which also passed. They struggled on in this sort of way till Bray got bowled over. I think Corky was wearing a yard-measure dipped in red ink that morning, but it looked rather swagger than not. Class was just ended when old Briggs, of all people - a man who wore two pairs of spectacles at one time very often - said to Bray:-

"What is that around your neck, boy?"

And Bray said:-

My tie, sir."

Then Briggs said:-

"Is it, sir? Let me see it please. I have noticed an increasing disorder about your neck arrangements for a week past. You insult me and you insult the class by appearing here in these ridiculous ties."

"It shan't happen again sir," said Bray, trying to edge out of the classroom.

"No Bray, it shall not," said old Briggs.

"Bring me that thing at once, please."

Bray handed it up, and Briggs examined it as if it were a botanical specimen or something.

"This," he announced, "is not a necktie at all. You're wearing a piece of Brussels carpet, wretched boy - a fragment of the new carpet laid down yesterday in the Doctor's study. You will kindly take it to him immediately, say who sent you and state the purpose to which you were putting it."

So Bray by the terms of the match, lost, and Corky minimus won with the yard measure.

Then the feeling between them grew, especially after Bray said that he could only pay his half-crown in instalments of a penny a week."

Eden Phillpotts would appear to have left Mannamead School just before his headmaster, Dr Peter Holmes, died, in 1878.

It must have been a very difficult time for the school; not only was it faced with the daunting prospect of replacing its founding head but it was also faced with the foundation the previous year and less than half a mile away, of another new educational establishment - Plymouth High School for Boys or Plymouth College as it would become a few years later.

The man who found himself with the task of taking Mannamead School through its first period without its original guiding light was the young man who had arrived seven years earlier to teach mathematics - Adam Pollard. *"A delicate man"* … and *"a brilliant teacher"* is how Eden Phillpotts was later to describe him, and the results he achieved for the school, particularly in the mathematics department, suggest that he was indeed truly gifted. There were excellent results in the Cambridge Local Examinations, with one year two pupils finishing in the top twenty of the all-England lists, another pupil topping the mathematics results for entry into Dartmouth and with a fourth place for entry into the Civil Service.

Pollard was also a keen sportsman and, along with one or two other members of staff, played for the school both at Cricket and Football soon after his arrival from Cambridge as a twenty-two-year-old in 1871. From the pages of the school magazine, which was revived in 1881, we find that the annual fixtures with the High School (Plymouth College) had already become the most keenly fought highlights of the sporting calendar.

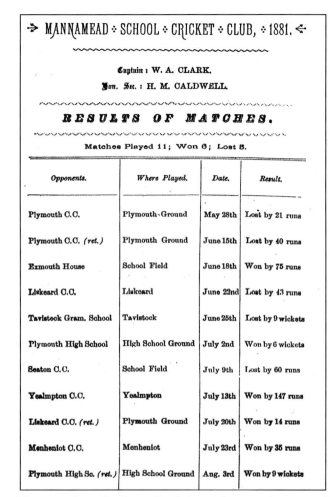

MANNAMEAD ⸬ SCHOOL ⸬ CRICKET ⸬ CLUB, ⸬ 1881.

Captain : W. A. CLARK.

Hon. Sec. : H. M. CALDWELL.

RESULTS OF MATCHES.

Matches Played 11; Won 6; Lost 5.

Opponents.	Where Played.	Date.	Result.
Plymouth C.C.	Plymouth Ground	May 28th	Lost by 21 runs
Plymouth C.C. (ret.)	Plymouth Ground	June 15th	Lost by 40 runs
Exmouth House	School Field	June 18th	Won by 75 runs
Liskeard C.C.	Liskeard	June 22nd	Lost by 43 runs
Tavistock Gram. School	Tavistock	June 25th	Lost by 9 wickets
Plymouth High School	High School Ground	July 2nd	Won by 6 wickets
Seaton C.C.	School Field	July 9th	Lost by 60 runs
Yealmpton C.C.	Yealmpton	July 13th	Won by 147 runs
Liskeard C.C. (ret.)	Plymouth Ground	July 20th	Won by 14 runs
Menheniot C.C.	Menheniot	July 23rd	Won by 35 runs
Plymouth High Sc. (ret.)	High School Ground	Aug. 3rd	Won by 9 wickets

Mannamead's cricket fixture list, below right, an early scorecard from the game with the High School (Plymouth College - 1883).

MANNAMEAD SCHOOL v. HIGH SCHOOL, (ret.)

We also learn that the cricket pitch had been levelled and re-turfed, a pavilion had been erected in the school field (at a cost of 10 guineas) and *"the football team have made an alteration in their uniform, which is also an improvement. They have discarded the dark blue jersey and adopted in its stead a parti-coloured shirt of dark blue and crimson"*. Things were also picking up on the athletics front, although the weather for sports day was often abysmal.

1881

In the summer of 1882 the *"Athletic Sports were held in a down-pour. The original fixture was June 8th, but June 8th was probably the worst day we have had this year. It was decided to postpone them till the 13th. During this interval the weather was fine. The eventful day dawned bright and beautiful and we were informed by a weather-wise friend that it could not possibly rain ... When the sports began the rain began, and while the sports lasted the rain lasted"*.

The wet and greasy conditions were not without their effects on the proceedings; with no spikes there was plenty of slipping and tripping, but all the events, including Putting the Weight, the 100 Yards, Broad Jump and Strangers Race, were held and Eden Phillpotts, now described as *"an old Mannamead boy"* returned to assist in the prize-giving.

1884 was to be a year of mixed emotion at Mannamead. The magazine published that summer acknowledged the school's thirtieth anniversary and introduced us to the school motto *"Mobilitate Viget"* - *"Strength through activity"*. And as the school moved on so too did the headmaster, as, sadly at just thirty-five years of age, Adam Pollard - *"after many weeks of deep and patient suffering"* - died of consumption on Ash Wednesday.

The premature demise of Pollard was accompanied by another loss for when he went Mrs Holmes, who had stayed on after her husband's death, to look after the boarding house, opted for retirement and was succeeded by Mrs Butler, the wife of the new man at the helm of Mannamead - Theodore Butler.

Mrs Butler soon introduced a brand new boarder as their son, Theobald Stuart, was born on 26th June that year. Other new arrivals included staff members J Vivian Thomas, Francis Simpson and CS Hervey, who more than filled the gaps left by the departures of Mr Rowles and Mr Carpenter.

Theodore Butler himself, however, was not a new arrival at the school, rather he had been at the school since 1881 when he had been appointed to teach modern languages.

By no means a teacher of the 'old school', Butler was eminently suited to his original post as he had evidently been educated in Paris, taken a French degree and entered the Diplomatic Service. It was in that guise that he found himself in St Petersburg where, for reasons lost in the mists of time, he ended up fighting a duel with a Russian. A dual, moreover, in which the Russian was killed and Butler was badly injured in the foot and left with a permanent limp.

After that little incident our man left the Service and became a tutor to a family in the Baltic. He then spent another few years working his way around Europe, acquiring in the process a remarkable facility in languages. Clearly he was not a man entirely without means either and so when Pollard died, young, but not altogether suddenly, Butler bought Mannamead School - presumably, as Pollard was unmarried, at quite a reasonable price.

On his succession to the headship then, Theodore Butler immediately set about launching Mannamead School into a new phase of its development.

The School Library founded by Mr Pollard, shortly before his death, was one innovation that year as, more significantly perhaps, under the duelling Mr Butler, was the introduction of fencing to the list of in-school activities available thanks to Mr Bain.

Mr Bain it also was who was given the responsibility for re-establishing the School Cadet Corps *"on a war footing"* the following year. Again there can be little doubt that Theodore Butler was the prime mover behind this. The Corps had lapsed some six or seven years earlier, around the time that Pollard had taken over. Quite why that should have happened is unclear but given the numbers of boys that were being sent here with a view to careers in the Services, the move to revive that body was an entirely logical one.

By the mid-1880s though it was undoubtedly in the sporting life of the school that most changes were apparent. More and more, not just here, but across the country, sport was becoming an ever-increasing part of school and social life. Two fields adjacent to the existing field were acquired to meet the increased demands, and a new sport entered the agenda - lawn tennis:

"It has passed through the stages of probation and its merits have lived down the opprobrium, once launched against it, of being a game fit for ladies and dandies. It has won a standing homage at the Universities and most of our large public schools, and, as long as it does not seek to usurp the royal supremacy of cricket, deserves the support of all schoolboys."

There was also a revival of early morning bathing, *"with a much appreciated addition of an instruction class for non-swimmers. Three times a week are we to be seen 'tooling' down in a special bus to the West Hoe Baths - reserved at these times for our use."*

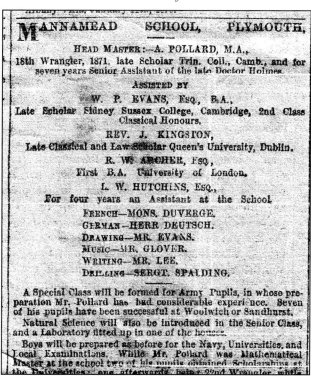

One of Pollard's advertisements for Mannamead School.

Whatever the situation with its young neighbour, Plymouth College, these were good times for Mannamead.

When Butler had arrived in 1884 there had been 110 boys on the school roll and before the decade was out he had increased the size of that roll by over 50%. And increases in the number of boys meant it was necessary to increase the amount of space available for the boys. The school field was developed further and the nursery at Hartley which had been used by the school so much over the years was now *"a thing of the past... Old landmarks are swept away forever. The wire fence on the eastern side* (of the school field) *is wire fence no more, and from the well-laid square the ground slopes very gently down."*

In the summer of 1886 we also learn of good news for the boarders - *"our headmaster has succeeded in securing Albert Villa, which adjoins Seymour, and which it is hoped, will be ready for occupation early in January ... we trust too to see a good tennis court on the combined lawns of the two houses."*

The improvements were by no means confined to the sporting, academic and domestic fronts either; the spiritual side of school life also received a boost as the same report speaks of *"a harmonium of look and tone ecclesiastical"* which had been placed in the chapel, with the result that *"morning and evening prayer is now of a musical character"*.

Clearly the school was thriving under its new head: *"scarce twelvemonth has elapsed since Hollybank was added to our school premises, a fifth School-house was found necessary at the beginning of this term and we entered on possession of Compton Villa, a pleasant house about five minutes walk from the school"*.

Such was some of the good news on the first page of the July 1887 Mannamead School Magazine. A page that started with "Mobilitate viget" and ran on *"No one can deny that our school has amply justified its founder in the choice of its motto, and at no time more truly than*

today could it be said of the School that like the ancient poet's description of Fame,

'Mobilitate viget, viresque adquirit eundo.'

Last year our numbers were 142; this term our muster-roll contains 162 names. At the same time our Head Master has been fully alive to the changes and extensions which these increased numbers entail."

The problem of space did not simply confine itself to boarding accommodation and *"So ... a convenient site was chosen in the grounds of Seymour Villa, and an army of masons, carpenters, etc., set to the work; the early stages of the building were watched by us with great interest, and now that it is complete and we have tested it by a term's work in it, we can pronounce a verdict wholly favourable on the result. Considerable ingenuity has been shown in the construction; no less than six large class-rooms have been provided, but five of these are partitioned off from one another by strong wooden curtains, which can be made, as it were, to disappear into the roof with the result that we get one large hall, likely to accommodate the School for several years to come even with its present rate of growth."*

Horse tram to Mannamead from the Theatre Royal

Late-nineteenth century rural Compton

Mannamead School started in Wellington Villa, between Seymour Road and Seymour Avenue and gradually expanded into neighbouring properties, including Albert Villa and the adjoining Seymour Villa (below) and Holly Bank (right). Note on the map the area to the right of the building labelled 'School boys' which served as the Mannamead playground.

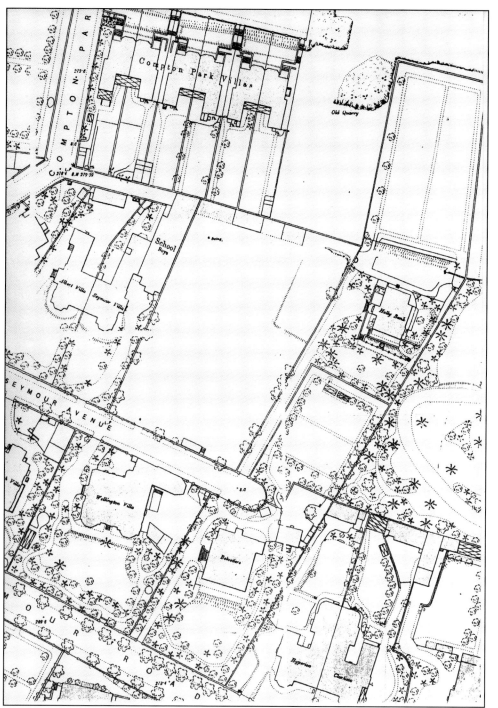

With desks that converted readily to benches and a continuous skylight in the roof to light the building, this was a major new addition to the school's facilities and one which was accorded a truly splendid christening.

"Our Headmaster and Mrs Butler invited a large and brilliant company of guests to enjoy 'the mazy windings of the merry dance' in the new Hall. What a feast did it present on that night with its flags and flowers and fans and drapery. A covered way connected it with a suite of retiring and refreshment rooms extending through Seymour and Albert Villas and equally tastefully decorated. What a house-warming that was!"

Clearly the impact of the neighbouring Plymouth College, now ten years old, was minimal on the success of the old school under its dynamic new head. As shrewd commercially as he clearly was academically, Butler's successes came largely on the back of his directing the school more towards the preparation of students for entry into the services; hence the revival of the Corps and hence the decision later that year to make the *"next far-reaching and important extension... The Army work of the School has developed to so great an extent and has attracted so large and ever-increasing a body of Students, that the Head Master has felt himself justified in opening a separate Army Establishment at Thanckes, the late seat of Lord Graves, which will be known as the Devon and Cornwall Military College. As Resident Principal, he has secured the services of his brother, Mr Walter Butler, B.A., who is resigning his instructorship on board H.M.S. Britannia to join us, and who was previously on the staff of the Royal Naval Academy, Gosport."*

"That this change will have a most beneficial effect alike on the Army Department and on the general work of the School, will be obvious to all. We have no doubt the inhabitants of this part of the West of England will be quick to recognise the advantages thus offered close at home for the training of their sons for the Army and other Service Examinations."

On the 19th July 1888 the Mannamead Corps was allotted a place of honour, between the representative detachment of Royal Artillery and the Line of the Honourable Artillery Company, in the Armada Tercentenary celebrations on the Hoe, a glittering occasion all round and a proud moment for the the school.

That same summer a Preparatory Department was started at the school under the superintendence of Mrs Butler, and a governess - and the headmaster and two other masters. There was no home work for these younger boys who were kept well apart from the boys of the upper school. By the summer of '89 there were already eighteen boys in the Prep, ten of them boarders.

Mannamead was booming and as if to celebrate, the whole school was photographed (a great novelty at the time); form by form, the Cadet Corps, the whole school, the masters, the boarders *"according to every imaginable principle of division"* … and *"finally a detachment of us went over to Thanckes, to give life to a photograph of this latest addition to our establishment."*

Within two years of Thanckes being established Mannamead School was rated ninth in a national league table of schools supplying successful candidates for entry into Woolwich and Sandhurst and their figures for Dartmouth appeared every bit as impressive. One particularly outstanding candidate, RNB Thompson, not only topped the Woolwich list in 1890, but the margin in marks between his score and that of the second candidate was greater than that between the second candidate and the sixtieth!

These were heady days at Mannamead, their sporting records matched and bettered those of their rivals:

"Most of our elevens have met the corresponding ones of Plymouth College, and all matches have resulted in our favour. It is worth mentioning that we have scored over 60 goals against them, while their record against us may be put down with a single figure …"

Many of the fixtures were played against older boys too, young servicemen and the infant Argyle team. The same was true of cricket as the school magazine became increasingly dominated by match reports and scorecards.

But it wasn't just in the academic and sporting areas that the school was flourishing; we read of the many and lively meetings of the Debating Society - the subject matter here again giving us the odd insight into the school's agenda in the late 1880s early 1890s.

"War is necessary for the settlement of international quarrels" (ayes 15-2)

"The Navy is superior as a profession to the Army" (12-12 motion carried by the chairman)

"Capital punishment ought to be abolished" (noes 5-12)

Opposite page: Mannamead Corps 1890. Left: Mannamead's military academy which brought the school national recognition.

1889

"England as a nation is on the decline" (noes 4-19)

"Classics is superior, as an instrument of education to mathematics" (noes 7-14)

"Football is superior to cricket" (11-11, chairman carried the motion)

"System of compulsory Cricket and Football in schools is beneficial" (noes 2-11)

"Lawn Tennis has won a place beside Cricket and Football" (noes 5-7)

"Football as played under the Association Rules is superior to Rugby Union games" (ayes 23-15)

"The old system of entering the Army by Purchase was preferable to the present system of competitive examination" (noes 5-8)

Some of the debates had a curiously contemporary ring;

"The Channel Tunnel scheme is detrimental to the best interests of the Nation" (noes 8-13)

"Field Sports should be discontinued on the grounds of their cruelty" (noes 2-12)

"Man was intended to subsist entirely upon Vegetable Food" (noes 9-19)

…And finally one that sounds a little more contemporary than it was;

"Town life is more enjoyable than country life" … the giveaway here being the rider - *"exhibiting a supreme contempt for the modern conveniences of telephone exchange, electric lighting & c.,"* The noes, incidentally, carried the day by a substantial margin.

Life, even town life, was so much more simple then, as was perfectly illustrated in the account of the School Picnic of 4th August 1885 (the last day of term).

"The meet was at the bottom of Seymour Avenue, and there assembled stood drags and brakes, each burdened with a goodly load of boys. I was pleased to see that, immediately before starting the head master had confiscated a formidable array of pea shooters … I mounted one of the drags, therefore with a feeling

somewhat akin to security, which lasted some minutes … Might I suggest that next year the head master confiscates the peas as well as the pea shooters?"

"However no harm was done; to be sure a rustic and the cow he drove were alike goaded to madness by three or four well directed broadsides; and death was threatened to one and all of us: but on reaching our destination our roll was found to be complete. But as a general rule the passers by seemed to enjoy the pleasure of being pelted by these harmless missiles, and we rolled on without mishap through Knackersknowle and up Crown Hill to Tamerton. At this point we were attacked by about twenty children with cries of "Plaize to haive's a copper" sung to a sort of wild Gregorian chant, and in truth they reaped a golden or rather a copper harvest."

And so the day unfolded and the privileged boys of Mannamead had a thoroughly enjoyable time communing with nature at Shaugh Bridge, by the banks of the Cad and the Meavy … *"Many bathed in the clear pebbly stream; others idly strolled among the trees".*

It is hard to picture just how rural everything between Mannamead and all points north of it were back then, although an account of a school paper-chase paints a very different picture to the one we know today:

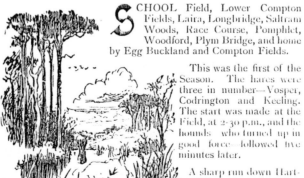

No. 1 Run.

SCHOOL Field, Lower Compton Fields, Laira, Longbridge, Saltram Woods, Race Course, Pomphlet, Woodford, Plym Bridge, and home by Egg Buckland and Compton Fields.

This was the first of the Season. The hares were three in number—Vosper, Codrington and Keeling. The start was made at the Field, at 2-30 p.m., and the hounds who turned up in good force followed five minutes later.

A sharp run down Hartley Hill to the end of Seymour Avenue, where the

A sharp run down Hartley Hill to the end of Seymour Avenue, where the fields were entered, was followed by a break-neck race down the steep slopes of Lower Compton Fields. The opposite slopes being surmounted, a brisk run was taken through Laira to Longbridge …."

The area was ideally suited to these country runs, both for Mannamead and Plymouth College; indeed on occasion, the two schools would be out on the same day, following a similar route *"…owing to the fact that names of boys of Mannamead were on parts of the scent, we kept on the right track, but the College boys were somewhat confused".*

You wouldn't expect them to appear otherwise after all, not in the pages of the Mannameadian. The rivalry between the two schools was intense. When the firsts met on the pitch for either football or cricket, the whole of both schools would turn out to cheer their teams on. The boys of Mannamead, with their greater number of boarders, tended to come from even wealthier families than the boys of the College and to Mannamead boys the initials 'PC' stood for 'Plymouth Cads'. The College boys in turn translated 'MS' as 'Mud Scrapers'. Each school stood steadfastly in the other's way in their claims to be the top boys' school in the region.

Butler at Mannamead thrived while Batten at the College struggled, then in 1889 with the appointment of Colson at the College the latter started to pick up again. That year the numbers at the College were around the 100 mark, a fall of around thirty, while Mannamead was around its peak of 170 boys. It all seemed so very rosy for Mr Butler, too rosy, too cosy perhaps, no longer enough of a challenge for this well-travelled and, we must assume, impetuous and atypcial, Victorian gentleman.

As the so-called Naughty Nineties dawned numbers at Mannamead fell slighty, while at the College under Colson they started to rise again, nothing that gave too much cause for concern, though, or did it?

Quite what was going through Mr Butler's mind we will doubtless never know, but in the Mannameadian, published in April 1893 we learn of an *"important change which has taken place in the management of the school since the last issue. It is probably well known to all our readers that after more than ten year's labour at Mannamead, during the last ten of which he was Headmaster, Mr Butler has given up his work here to enjoy well-earned repose."*

The account then went on to say;

"During the years of his Headmastership Mr Butler worked indefatigably for the interests of the School, and his efforts were crowned with remarkable success. When he became Headmaster the school numbered 110; during his years of office the numbers rose at one time to 170, and the normal number was regarded as 150. Beside his work at the School, Mr Butler's energies found a vent in promoting education generally in Plymouth. It was due to his initiative that the Commercial Classes, now merged to the Technical Schools, were started. He was also instrumental in making Plymouth a centre for the London Matriculation Examinations, and was a most energetic member of the Local Committee."

What the report didn't tell us, and yet what we can be certain that just about everybody at the time knew anyway, was that not only had Theodore Butler left, but so too had his son's German governess … but not Mrs Butler or his eight year-old son.. Mannamead School suddenly found itself at the centre of a major public scandal.

But as there were no tabloid newspapers in those days, whatever gossip was flying around has almost all been lost in the wind. Newspapers, particularly local papers, then were extremely dull affairs by modern standards. There were no banner headlines, front pages were invariably entirely taken up with classified advertisements and inside information was presented in great grey slabs of text, unbroken by photographs or engravings. The dastardly doings of the working

classes might occasion the odd lengthy story but an upper-middle class social scandal was unlikely to generate much in the way of column inches.

So it was that Butler simply disappeared from the local scene and his successor at Mannamead was Mr FL Griffiths … *"formerly scholar of Magdalen College, Oxford, afterwards a Master at Portsmouth Grammar School, until he started a school of his own at Southsea."*

"Mr Griffiths", the Mannameadian informed us, *"does not come to Mannamead as a stranger; for curiously enough, in his earlier years he lived at the house which is now Albert Villa, and he was for some time at Mannamead School, until he gained a scholarship at Winchester."*

The account, again taken from the April 1893 magazine, then went on to say; *"Mr Griffiths has already been here long enough to evince the great interest he takes in all our School institutions, and everyone who knows him will feel sure that the fortunes of the School will prosper in his keeping."*

Griffiths clearly threw himself wholeheartedly into his new school - he instituted games for those not playing in matches and he "seldom failed to occupy the position of centre half-back throughout the season".

His report later that year was very positive and the vicar of Emmanuel, the reverend GB Berry, was prompted to say that Mannamead School was *"no longer a thing of yesterday"*.

Sadly however its days were numbered.

Thanckes, one of Butler's many innovations, was closed down under the terms of the arrangement reached between Butler and Griffiths when the latter bought the school … *"a special and distinct army class"* was organised back at Mannamead for all those *"to whom the army is the goal of their hopes"*.

Griffiths however was looking to broaden the academic horizons of the school, for he hoped to achieve Public School status for Mannamead.

Chemistry, *"hitherto somewhat neglected at the school, is now being taught in the upper forms"*. The Science Department was further extended by the addition of a Physics Laboratory and the school library was upgraded.

Emmanuel Church after the extension work which started in 1887.

In the summer of 1894 "Mannamead Week" was inaugurated. Hailed as a *"brilliant first of a long line of successors"* there was, within the week, a special service at Emmanuel, the annual school sports, a Past versus Present cricket match, a dance, a concert and an old boys' dinner at the Duke of Cornwall. Among those old boys in attendance were Sir Roper Lethbridge, Sir Alfred Croft and Colonel Carlyon, said to have been the first pupil to have arrived at Mannamead on its opening day, Lady Day 1854, forty years earlier.

Everything looked extremely rosy, but clearly it wasn't and clearly there were those who were already working on a new future for the school, one that involved amalgamating with the old enemy - Plymouth College. Less than eighteen months after Mannamead Week had been held, letters went out to the parents of both schools in which reference was made to *"negotiations extending over several years"*.

If we are to give any credence to the use of the word *"several"* here, we can only assume that, as these letters were sent out in December 1895, and as Griffiths only arrived at Mannamead in the early part of 1893, either overtures had already been made before he arrived, or they started almost as soon as this former pupil took the old school on.

Three letters were sent out - two of them to the parents of pupils at Mannamead:

MANNAMEAD SCHOOL

"Dear Sir or Madam,
I have to announce that arrangements have been concluded whereby the Mannamead School and Plymouth College will be in future carried on under one governing body and one head-master. The attainment of this object has been the subject of negotiations extending over several years, but it is only recently that we have been able to bring them to a successful termination.
In informing you of the arrangement, I wish to give special prominence to the fact that my chief aim and desire has been to make sure that the special characteristics and traditions of Mannamead School are to be preserved, and that what is contemplated is a UNION of the two Schools, with all the advantages which co-operation affords, without the attendant disadvantages which might ensue from either establishment being absorbed in the other. The important members of my old staff will remain, and classes and boarding houses at Mannamead will be carried on as heretofore. The Army and Navy classes, which have been such a successful feature in the past, will be continued on the old lines.
I wish to assure parents and the many friends who are interested in the School that the new scheme has my hearty approval.
I earnestly wish that any parent or guardian who would like to be further re-assured will communicate with me, or call upon me, as I am most anxious to afford every assistance and information. The wishes already expressed to me by parents will be strictly respected in the future and I shall continue to be available in all matters pertaining to the welfare and interest of the Mannamead section of the boys.
I remain,
Yours faithfully,
LF GRIFFITHS
Head-Master of Mannamead School

On the same sheet of paper was the following letter:

PLYMOUTH COLLEGE

Dear Sir or Madam,
I wish to express my most hearty approval of the step which the Governors have taken, and I shall make my every endeavour to carry on the work on the lines which they have laid down, namely that the two schools are to be united, not one absorbed in the other.
Mr Palmer, who has been for 17 years a Master at Mannamead and 12 years 2nd Master and also House-Master, will take charge of the Boarders at Wellington Villa, and the other houses will be utilised as required under suitable management. The two next Senior Masters of the Staff who have served for 8 and 7 years respectively, will also join the combined Staff.
Examination of the time-table has shewn that the curricula of the two Schools are substantially the same and I am confident that no dislocation of work will result from the change. Classes will be held in the Buildings at Mannamead on the same lines as before. Army and Navy Classes will be made a special feature of the work.
The Cadet Corps will still be carried on, and Captain Munro has consented to continue his invaluable services.
Mr Griffiths has promised me his hearty co-operation in carrying out these arrangements; and I shall be sincerely grateful for advice and suggestions from parents and all others who are familiar with the working and traditions of the School.
I remain,
Yours faithfully,
FH COLSON,
Head-Master of Plymouth College.

Additionally a third letter was sent out - the two above enclosed with it - to the Plymouth College parents:-

PLYMOUTH COLLEGE

Dear Sir or Madam,
We beg to inform you that after long deliberation on both sides we have arranged with Mr Griffiths to take over Mannamead School and incorporate it with Plymouth College.
It has often been the wish of the authorities on both sides that the schools could be united and one large school do the work. Circumstances have now favoured the amalgamation with the hearty good will of Mr Griffiths and the principal Masters, and as from Christmas the schools will be conducted under one authority, and known as Plymouth and Mannamead College.
Our aim will be to unite the two schools, not to absorb one in the other.
We are fully conscious that Mannamead School has a long and honourable past, a worthy record of successes and many valuable traditions. It has many loyal sons in all parts of the world, and we hope they understand the arrangements we are making, that they will be able to feel that their old school still exists, on a surer basis, and with a doubled prestige.
With the advantage of one large school many things can be done which separately are impossible.
There seems to be no reason why the schools now combined should not before long take foremost rank not only in the West of England, but amongst the first Public Schools of the Country.
In inviting the support of those who have hitherto looked to Mannamead for the education of their boys we can with confidence call attention to the record of the Plymouth College.
Our Head-Master, Mr Colson, is well-known as a gentleman of high scholastic attainments, with an exceptionally brilliant University career, and is supported by a strong and able staff. Since he has been Head-Master the work of the school as shewn by the Cambridge Local Examinations, the Oxford and Cambridge Joint Board, the Naval Clerkships, and University Scholarships, has reached a higher standard than has ever been attained before in Plymouth, and the numbers of the school have been and are steadily increasing.
With this record we venture confidently to appeal to your support. The present step is a most important one educationally for the West of England, and we believe will ultimately meet with abundant approval.
Referring you to the annexed circulars of Mr Colson and Mr Griffiths.
We remain,
Yours faithfully,
MORLEY, Chairman
C.T. WILKINSON, Vice-Chairman
J WALTER WILSON, Secretary
for the Governors of Plymouth College

Clearly as two of the top schools in the county, it made good sense in many respects for the two to join forces and thereby become an even more potent educational establishment within the area. However, if it is at all possible to see a hidden agenda in all this we must look to the ramifications of Butler's sudden departure and, despite all the talk of a *"union"* and an *"amalgamation"*, the telling expression used by the Governors in their letter where they talk of a *"take over"*. The other significant passage, of course, in that letter is where the Governors say they hope all old Mannameadians *"will be able to feel that their old school still exists, on a surer basis …"*

Had the union not occurred would Mannamead have struggled to survive, would it have gone the way of so many other comparatively short-lived schools in the area or would it have come through any difficulties and caused a longer term downfall of its old rival Plymouth College?

Alternatively was it one of those mergers that, after so long, was just waiting to happen and, given that Plymouth College had the greater land, and the more impressive school building, the move down the road from Mannamead was always going to be inevitable?

We shall probably never know the full story, but whatever the answer there is a very real sense in which the history of Mannamead should always be the first chapter of the history of what after Christmas 1895 became known as Plymouth & Mannamead College - PMC - and although the Mannamead element has now dropped out of common usage the full name is still perpetuated by the old boys who, since 1896, have styled themselves OPMs - Old Plymothians and Mannameadians.

In the event sixty-two Mannamead boys became part of the new, joint school in January 1896. For the boys it would appear there were no great problems adjusting - the only difference between the two in those early days being the colour of their caps. The College boys wore red and black, the boys of Mannamead green and magenta (Mannamead's junior football colours incidentally were red and green which logically suggested the red, green and black eventually adopted for the combined school).

The teachers on the other hand did not adapt as easily to the new situation and it was some months before the tact and diplomacy of Mannamead's Mr Palmer could get the two groups to speak to each other. However, once they did, the united school began to build most successfully on its new broader base.

Francis Palmer of Mannamead School and Plymouth High School and first OP & M Club Chairman

21

PLYMOUTH HIGH SCHOOL

In 1848, the so-called year of Revolution across Europe, two young ladies, Dorothea Beal and Frances Mary Buss, aged 17 and 21 respectively, were among the first ever pupils of the newly opened Queen's College in London's Harley Street. The following year, Bedford College, part of the University of London, became the first such college to admit women - although it was to be another thirty years before women were allowed to study for degrees. Miss Beale and Miss Buss both went on to study at Bedford College, after which the two went on to become great pioneers in the education of women.

In 1857 Dorothea Beale was appointed head of Cheltenham Ladies' College. Established in 1854, the same year as Mannamead School, this was the first great secondary school for girls and as its head Miss Beale's achievements were considerable. After fifteen years at

the school she published the report of the "Commission on the Education of Girls", the following year, 1870, meanwhile saw Miss Buss hand her North London Collegiate School over to a trust so that it might serve as a model for others. This action marked the beginning of the Girls' Public Day School Trust.

Two years later, the Devonport Branch of the National Union for the Education of Women held a meeting at which the treasurer, Mrs Metcalfe, suggested that a school should be established in Plymouth by a Public Trust, on exactly those lines. So it was that in February 1874 the Devon and Cornwall Girl's School Company was formed under the presidency of Frederick Temple, the Bishop of Exeter, who became the first chairman of the new school council.

Sherwell House - first home of Plymouth High School for Girls

The new school began on 14th September 1874; Miss Kendal was its head and initially its home was Sherwell House - then just up from and opposite, Sherwell Church. In the meantime a fund had been set up for the building of a new school and the purchase of its site. Within three years Plymouth High School for Girls had been completed. The cost of the new building was £10,000 and the cost of the site, a Jacobean dwelling known as "North Hill", together with its adjacent land, was £3,000 (the old building incidentally stood until 1939 when it was demolished to make way for a new wing - for most of that time it served as the headmistress's house).

When the school was opened there were but a few major buildings on Tavistock Road above Sherwell Church; Sherwell House itself (where Queen Anne Terrace now stands), Mount Drake House, North Hill Cottage, North Hill House (where now stands the masonic building next to Charles with St Matthias), a few shops, "North Hill" and the Blind Institute, completed just a year before the school. Beyond this point there were even fewer buildings, although the western side of Mutley Plain was beginning to fall, plot by plot, to the developer.

The green fields of Mutley and Mannamead start to disappear.

At the opening of the new school, Bishop Temple addressed those present with the words *"School must be the anticipation of practical life"*, and in this he echoed Cicero's saying, later adopted as the school motto, and also used by Queen's College, Taunton, *Non Scolae sed vitae discimus* - *"we learn not from school but from life"*.

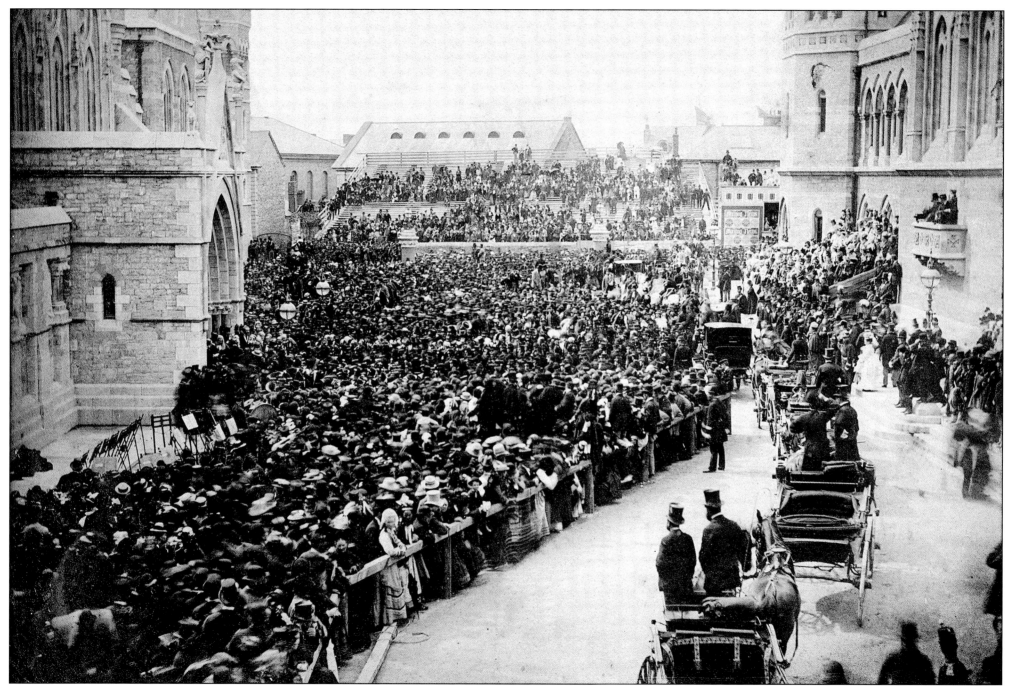

Thursday 13 August 1874, Prince of Wales opens the new Guildhall with music specially composed by Frederic Lohr, organist of Sherwell Church and future composer of the music of the School Carmen.

It wasn't just for the foundation of a girl's high school though that Bishop Temple's expertise was called upon in Plymouth. While Mrs Metcalfe may have been a guiding light in the foundation of that establishment it was Mr Metcalfe, who, together with Charles Wilkinson, had first had the thought that it *"would be desirable that they should establish a high school or high schools in the town"*.

An early view of Plymouth High School for Girls

The quote is from Venerable Archdeacon Wilkinson, as he later became, looking back on the early days, in 1908, at FH Colson's last speech day as headmaster of Plymouth College.

Clearly the role of the clergy in the development of education in the nineteenth century should not be underestimated, particularly in Plymouth.

In 1870 Charles Wilkinson was appointed vicar of St Andrew's Church. Mr Metcalfe, the Reverend J Metcalfe, meanwhile, was incumbent of the comparatively newly-established Christ Church (built in 1845-6 it stood, until the Second World War, in Eton Place - just off what is now Western Approach).

Wilkinson together with two ministers of dissenting congregations, Charles Wilson and Benwell Bird, were three of the original list of nine subscribers to the Articles of Association of the "High School for Boys Plymouth Limited". Thirty-five year-old Bird had been

educated in Hammersmith and came to Plymouth, to Mutley Baptist Church, in 1876. The other names were those of prominent local figures, Judge Montague Bere, the wealthy merchant William Collier, Professor FE Anthony, a leading non-conformist and educationalist, Robert Bayly, a leading townsman, Dr. Charles Rooke Prance (a forty-four year-old medic and deacon of George Street Chapel, who like Professor Anthony contributed two sons to the new school) and, at the top of the list, William Temple.

Charles Wilkinson - Vicar of St Andrew's Church

Temple was at that time Bishop of Exeter, he had earlier been headmaster of Rugby School *"in the direct line of inheritance from Arnold"*, and he was to go on to become Archbishop of Canterbury. In the early days his input and experience was obviously invaluable, but primarily, it would appear, his role was as a consultant and as a source of inspiration.

At that same speech day in 1908, headmaster Colson was prompted to recall the story of how he met the Archbishop in Exeter, in 1891, two years after he, Colson, had arrived at the school;

"When he heard that I was headmaster of Plymouth College, he said in his gruff way, "Oh that place has never succeeded", so I remarked, humbly, to Dr Temple that perhaps it was due to the frequent changes that had taken place, and the reply was that that was

only another way of saying the same thing, and that the school did not fail to succeed because they went away, but they went away because the school did not succeed."

Dr Temple clearly had no long-term involvement with the school himself, despite nominally being a governor, and when Colson wrote to the Archbishop ten years later, in 1901, asking for a subscription to the Bulteel Fund he said;

"I was surprised to get a letter from his Chaplain, enclosing indeed a very small cheque, but saying that His Grace would like to know how he became a Governor of Plymouth College".

(It is perhaps worth pointing out that Temple renewed his connection with Rugby while still at Exeter, becoming a governor of that famous pile and indeed was chairman of the governors there for the last ten years of his life 1892-1902. He was also a governor of Sherbourne School).

But to further quote Archdeacon Wilkinson; *"The Three Towns were indebted to Dr Temple for assistance rendered in various ways and on various occasions; but especially the committees of the two colleges (boys and girls) were very much indebted to him because he was not only an eminent scholar, but had also been master of Rugby School, and they had the advantage of his assistance and knowledge in directing them."*

Rugby School, established in 1567, just a few years after Plymouth Grammar School, came into its own in the early nineteenth century; here it was in 1823 that William Webb Ellis inadvertently invented a new game of football, when, during a game, he picked up the ball and ran with it, "with a fine disregard for the rules of football". The next thing to happen was that all the other boys chased after him and from then on in were as likely to carry the ball as they were to kick it. Such is not to suggest that the rules for football were all that formal in those days though, it is just that this is the incident singled out as the beginning of the handling code in what came to be called Rugby Football.

Five years later there was another major development at Rugby, one that was to have an even greater impact on the everyday life of the English Public School and that was the appointment of thirty-three year old Thomas Arnold as Headmaster.

Rugby School, Warwickshire - a model for Plymouth Collge?

Arnold arrived to find a school where prefects were more likely to incite younger pupils to rebellion than they were to set a good example and so he set about reforming and institutionalising a prefectorial system where boys were encouraged to take more personal responsibility, where bullying was frowned upon and self-discipline and self-respect promoted in its place.

His piety was infectious and the school became noted for its so-called "muscular Christianity" - boys were encouraged to ask questions and new subjects were introduced into the curriculum. French, Maths and Modern History all became regular subjects as Arnold looked to prepare boys who were well equipped to serve the Church and State in nineteenth-century Britain, and its Empire.

In 1842 Arnold, who was both loved and feared for his reforming zeal, met with an early and sudden death through angina - but the die had already been cast and Rugby became the model for the Victorian English

public school. Holmes would have been aware of it in 1854 when he abandoned the Grammar School to set up Mannamead School and public awareness would have been even greater, three years later, when Thomas Hughes published what amounted to a eulogistic record of Arnold's achievements in *Tom Brown's Schooldays*.

Thomas Arnold, Heamdaster Rugby School 1828-42
Frederick Temple, Headmaster Rugby School 1858-69

Frederick Temple had been offered a mastership at Rugby in 1842 by his Oxford colleague Tait, who succeeded Arnold at the school (Arnold's son Matthew was another of Temple's Oxford contemporaries), however it wasn't until 1857 that he did go there and then it was as head himself.

In the meantime the former Blundell's schoolboy had written a number of important papers on education and was very much perceived as a national authority on the subject.

Temple's main achievements at Rugby were to increase the number of staff, expand and systematise the teaching of history, make English language and literature a "form" subject and to introduce natural science, music and drawing into the regular curriculum. While there he also managed to raise funds for the building of a new quadrangle, complete with a music school and a drawing school, two science lecture-rooms and half a dozen classical rooms. The chapel was also enlarged.

Throughout the 1860s Temple continued to be a major player in the various bodies established to look at education in this country, most notably the Popular Education Commission, or the Public Schools Commission. In 1869 the newly-elected Prime Minister, Gladstone, offered Temple the deanery of Durham, which he turned down, but then later that year he was offered and accepted the see of Exeter. Having been brought up in Devon it is easy to see why this offer might have been more favourably received.

No sooner had Temple taken up his new appointment than the Education Act of 1870 was passed. William Forster was the parliamentary promoter of the bill, the terms of which were to provide an education for every boy and girl in England and Wales. The Act was the climax to series of measures and steps taken by the government since 1833 and Temple had clearly been one of the most listened to voices over the previous three decades.

So it was then that in 1870 it became incumbent on church people to improve and add to their schools. In Exeter Bishop Temple set to work immediately and through his words, and his example - he subscribed £500 to the project - the task of raising money for new schools was begun. The city was clearly very fortunate to have this great man working in their midst. A royal commission reporting some thirty years later said it all; *"there are more boys and girls per thousand of population receiving secondary education in Exeter than in any other city in this country, due in no small measure to the improvements carried out largely under Dr Temple".*

But it wasn't just Exeter that benefitted from the temperate Doctor's good offices, without him Plymouth High School for Girls and Plymouth High School for Boys might not have been started when they were, or on the scale that they were.

There was, it should perhaps be noted, nothing unusual in teachers, even head teachers leaving a school and going into the church. To quote Phillpotts again, who was at Mannamead in the 1870s - *"Many of the masters at Merivale (Mannamead?) used to read for the Church while they taught us; and when they had read enough, they went away and became curates, as the next stage in their careers" (From The Angle of Seventeen).*

It was doubtless Temple's Rugby experience that influenced those involved in setting up the Boys High School to make adequate provision for playing fields - when first established the school had a good eight or nine more acres of playing field than it has today.

"To do this they landed themselves in great financial difficulties and yet even financially the set had its advantages, for the property, though mortgaged to the full extent rapidly appreciated as potential building land. Still on the whole saddling the new School with a heavy mortgage instead of an endowment, the Governors were asking for trouble - and got it" (FH Colson).

But all this is to jump forward in time; following a series of meetings that had started in 1875, in the home of Judge Montague Bere, Articles of Association were drawn up and signed on 10th February 1877. Bishop Temple's name headed the list of the nine original subscribers, and work, it would seem, was swiftly begun on building the new school.

Mutley Station, just yards away from Erme House.

George Bennett - first headmaster of the new Plymouth High School for Boys.

In the meantime George Lovett Bennett was appointed headmaster of the new institution and with 28 pupils (several of them from the families of the eight other original subscribers) and a handful of staff, the school was started in a large private house, Erme House in the then comparatively recently-built Ermington Terrace, just above Mutley Station (which had brought new development to this area after its completion in 1849).

Erme House, first home for the new Boys' High School

Bennett was another who was no stranger to Rugby, he had been headmaster of an important Preparatory School there and was closely connected with the great school itself. It would seem therefore that he almost certainly knew Dr Temple before coming to Plymouth and may have even been "head-hunted" for the job.

A former scholar himself of St John's College, Cambridge, with a fine reputation as an author of Latin school books, and as a teacher of French, Bennett opened Plymouth High School for Boys, with 28 pupils, in Erme House in September 1877.

"Is there any one of the twenty-eight who joined the School at the commencement, who will ever forget the impressions of the first day. To a boy fresh from a dame's school - and I must confess to a lingering attachment to mine - a being in a cap and gown is an awful thing when viewed for the first time. The most trivial incidents of the first day are still fresh in my memory. The polished desks were worthy of better treatment than they received at my hands; for barely had an hour passed when it was my ill-luck to upset a large ink-pot over the spotless bench. And then the sense of impending punishment which never came!" So recalled an anonymous and original old boy in an 1889 Plymothian.

Meanwhile Charles Serpell in *Plymouth College An Historical Sketch,* a booklet published in 1950, the year after his death, Charles Serpell wrote;

"Those temporary quarters were inconvenient for future purposes, though they well suited the convenience of boys who arriving late for prayers were enabled nevertheless, by the benevolent connivance of the porter, to enter by a back door in time for call-over and so to escape the more or less painful results of being technically late."

Charles Serpell served the school as Clerk to the Governors from 1908 through to 1946 (when he was succeeded in the post by his elder son Roger); his involvement with the school however goes back to

those early days in Erme House - he joined the school in September 1879, when he was nine years old.

"Plymouth in those days was a simpler place to live in. The road in front (of the house) became perforce a sort of playground and was then decorated with an avenue of young trees. Three only remain (this passage was written in 1927), doubtless the fittest. The human atmosphere was not congenial to the growth of saplings."

"At the top of Ermington Terrace was a blacksmith's forge at the open door of which boys going home from school would stop to look in and see the shoeing of horses, the mounts perhaps of some of the six or eight of their school-fellows who used to start off in a cavalcade of ponies along Mutley Plain to reach home on the outside borders of the town. Regular public road-transport hardly existed. Mutley was close to fields and country roads ... Masters were accustomed to walk to school in cap and gown, even I think from so far off as Hill Park Crescent, where lodged, for instance, Mr Logan and Mr Field."

Of course when the school was based in Erme House, Hill Park Crescent was not so far away and the head had but a short walk from No.3 Shaftesbury Villas, where he was living.

Messrs Logan and Field appear not to have been the earliest members of staff here though, that distinction rather being shared by the Reverend Frederick Sparks, who taught mathematics, JS Norman and F Ritchie, both of whom were to leave for prep schools in Kent in 1882 and, as a writing and arithmetic teacher Mr Botheras. Sparks, *"a kind-hearted man who was almost as ready to forgive and.remit an imposition of a thousand lines as he was prone to set it"*. His life *"was devoted, with all due allowance for his other teaching and the calls of the Church (he was a "part time curer of souls"), to the production of his* **magnum opus**, *an arithmetic on the unitary method. The method may have been sound enough but it never won the sympathy of victims who spent hours in working out answers labelled "nearly" right and left at that. We felt, I believe, that in an exact science we were being cheated.. But he was a kindly old man - and probably not old at all."*

Ritchie was another writer of school text books, one or two of which were still in use fifty or sixty years later. The latter clearly cut a very serious figure - *"I cannot conceive the gravity of Mr Ritchie as ever shaken"*. On the other hand the impression we have of Mr Botheras is that he was perhaps not as effective a communicator as he might have been;

"Do many yet recall Mr Botheras, who taught ... I am not sure what he taught, or at least what we learned from him."

As for the headmaster himself, Serpell conjures up a marvellous image of GL Bennett whom he says was universally liked and trusted; *"Boys responded to his evident liking for the work they and he were doing ... He read with us Erckmann-Chatrian's "Waterloo", and rode a classroom chair into battle against a British square ... His French was good and his enthusiasm a fine stimulus to appreciation of a great story."*

Under Bennett in those early years the school grew quickly and by 1880 there were about sixty boys bustling around Erme House, too many, it was felt, for the shored-up staircase there to cope with, and the decision was taken, mid-term, to move into the as yet incomplete new buildings at Ford Park.

Charles Serpell was by now ten years old and as he later recalled the assembly hall, the southern half of Big School, was not then ready ... *"Prayers were read in the lower corridor (which did not extend beyond the third class-room), the Headmaster standing at the top of the lowest flight of stairs from which his eye commanded the school drawn up before him by form"*

In saying that the school was incomplete we need here to qualify what that meant in 1880;

The original plan, based on the surviving architectural vision of the school, was that the main entrance to the old block would, in the fullness of time be the central point of a much greater edifice, with another, even more substantial block to its left and a large chapel to its right. The overall style of the whole building is very much reminiscent of parts of Wadham College, Oxford, established during the reign of James I, more than 250 years earlier, at the beginning of the seventeenth century. The layout, the castellations, the entrance, the chimneys and the chapel (as planned) are too similar to have occurred coincidentally but we do not know what the connection between the two was. Temple was an Oxford scholar of course, a Balliol man, could his influence have had some impact here as well?

Above Wadham, below original plans for Plymouth High School.

Plymouth High School outside No 3 Shaftesbury Villas - 1880

Whatever the answer, one thing is for sure, the grand original vision was never fulfilled and certainly in the early days it is hard to see how it would have been. When what we now know as the main school was completed, within a year or so of the boys moving in, there were still only around 60 in the school, and they would have rattled around quite freely in the eight large classrooms there.

Given that the school had also been established with a generous amount of land it was clearly going to be some time before phase one had been paid for and the numbers would have to be very good indeed to justify further building works.

The plans were clearly not abandoned however and for some fifty years the eastern end of the school was left slate-hung, the corner stones unturned in readiness for the next stage. In the event the next stage did not come until the 1930s when a new eastern wall was built and a new gymnasium with changing rooms constructed onto the back of the old building and then, above that, three extra classrooms and an extension to Big School. Some idea of the original northern aspect can still be gained walking along the corridors upstairs and downstairs and looking through those windows that once looked out over Hyde Park and now just look into those 1930s extensions to the main school.

So that was the extent of the school in the 1880s and for many years afterwards - the southern half of main school. The Headmaster, Mr Bennett, tenanted No.3 Shaftesbury Villas, which was not then part of the school's estate, nevertheless the school's first football pavilion was soon afterwards built against the garden wall of that property, while a cricket pavilion was put up at the lower end of the school field (on a site later to be buried beneath the developments of Devon Terrace and College View - land the school would be forced to sell to help remain financially viable).

That football was the preferred game to rugby appears to have hinged on a chance incident;

"We hesitated between the Rugby and Association game ... a serious accident which happened whilst we were playing the former game, decided us in favour of the latter."

(anon - "Reminiscences" Plymothian 1889).

Games were on a very rough and ready footing in those days though, and we shouldn't think of them as being organised in the way they are now and the same applies to the teams. Indeed the first cricket team chosen to represent Plymouth College (Plymouth High School for Boys as it then was) *"was composed of the eleven biggest boys. The Captain was elected, because, in addition to other habiliments universally regarded as part of a cricketer's outfit, he possessed a white flannel coat. Of course his claim to supreme authority was incontestable. At the end of the term, the second XI played and easily beat the first team, and a considerable change was made in the composition of the following year's eleven."* (Anon - 1889).

More substantial than even the football or the cricket pavilions were the fives courts, the use of which has been a matter of some concern at various times over the years. Contemporary with the main school itself it was not long before we first find evidence of apathy in respect of these fine limestone structures;

"Sir ... I am surprised that so little attention has been paid to Fives this term. It cannot be the expense attached to the game that prevents those who like the game from playing; for it is the least expensive amusement we have. It is a pity when we have such splendid courts, pronounced by some to be the finest in England - that so little interest is taken in the game ... Hoping that this letter will not be unheeded, I remain, Yours truly QUADRANGLE."

Quadrangle, whoever he may have been, was addressing his comments to the editor of the first ever edition of the *Plymothian*, published on 1st December 1883. The inference we can draw here is that fives quite clearly was one of the sports the school's founders must have been keen to promote, why otherwise would any money have been spent in this direction.

Here again we must look to the Rugby connection, for it was there that the version of the game played at Plymouth College - "Rugby Fives" - was developed in the 1850s. "Tom Brown" refers to the game in "his schooldays" at Rugby. That book written by Thomas Hughes, himself an old boy of the school was first published in 1857, the year that Frederick Temple took over there as Headmaster. So was it Temple's influence again or was it that of Bennett himself, who had come from the Prep School in Rugby or even a combination of the two?

Whatever the answer the sport has undoubtedly had its moments here over the years and in March 1884 it was noted in *Plymothian* No.3 that *"One of the best events this term has undoubtedly been the Fives competition"*.

Two of the five Whiteford brothers (of the family whose name is remembered in Whiteford Road) entered; the older brother lost the Senior Cup he had also lost the previous year, but the younger brother won the junior tournament. The youngest of the Whiteford boys, incidentally, was later responsible for setting up Hill

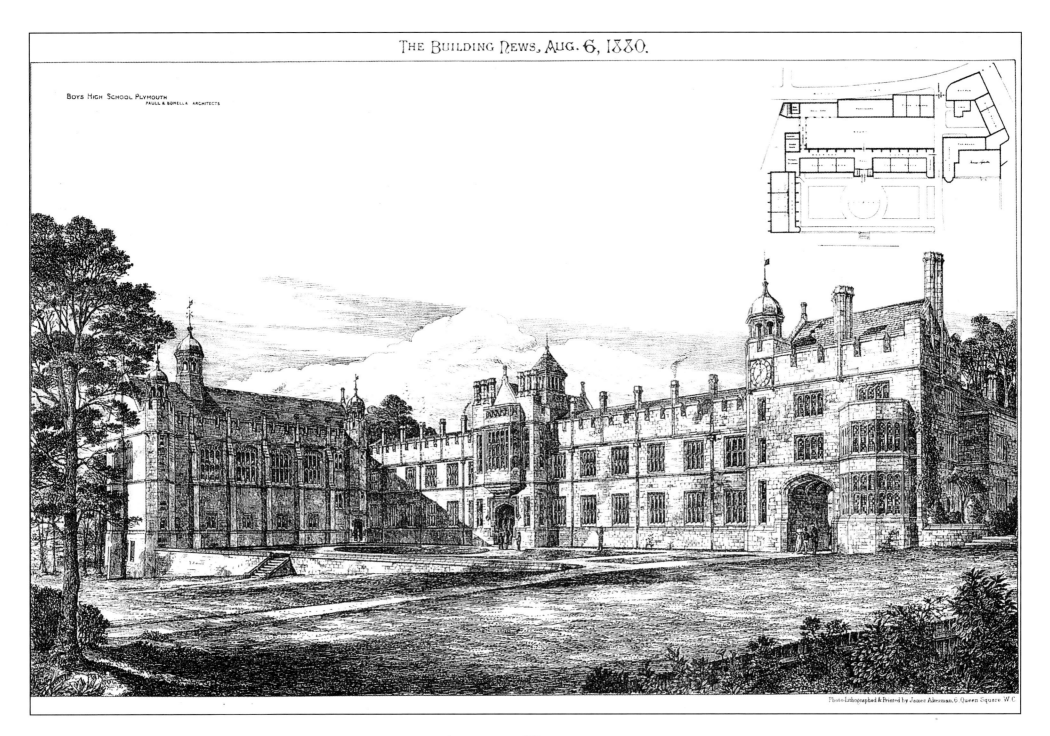

BOYS HIGH SCHOOL PLYMOUTH
PAULL & BONELLA ARCHITECTS

Photo-Lithographed & Printed by James Akerman, 6, Queen Square W.C.

Lane Tennis Club and just as tennis had originally grown out of hand-tennis, it would appear that the origins of squash are to be found in fives. But that is to pre-empt later developments here.

To return to the early 1880s, it would appear that sometime around 1881-82 a corrugated iron gymnasium was erected immediately to the east of the fives courts. *"Gymnastics in those days were a discipline applied with rigours now much modified"*, wrote Serpell in 1927. He continued, *"Because the appliances were there big boys and little boys alike were put through the mill"*. The highlight of year in those early days was the grand Assault-at-Arms gymnastic display staged annually in the gym, the highlight of which the boys were thankfully spared;

"Sergt. Fitch used to bring the house down by cutting in half with a sword-stroke the carcass of a sheep. It never seemed to occur to him, to have a whole class of boys hewing lambs in pieces by numbered motions."

The absence of the kind of Cadet Corps that was in place at Mannamead School did not mean there was no attempt to provide the boys with some regimental discipline here and Sergeant Fitch was presumably also one of the men employed by the school to drill the boys on the playing fields; *"It was a barren sort of performance, infantry drill without arms, and dull unless the cane, carried by a somewhat irascible instructor came into play, or unless, as happened in 1881, there was heavy snow and cold weather kept it lying."*

The weather during the winter of 1881 was clearly quite exceptional and Serpell made reference to it again in his *"Historical Sketch"* of 1949; *"In 1881, while we still occupied wide spaces, came the great frost and heavy snowfall of that hard winter. The old open leat was blocked and the water supply of Plymouth would have ceased had it not been maintained from long disused wells. This not inconsiderable inconvenience to the population at large was compensated - at any rate to*

the boys - by the fact that solid snow forts could be built, attacked, and defended, with unlimited ammunition on the school field."

Meanwhile one of the other items gleaned from the pages of the first Plymothian is that, at the suggestion of TW Lansdown, a parent, on Speech Day in 1883, it was decided to change the name of the school from Plymouth High School for Boys to Plymouth College. No one quite knows why but of the fifty-four other Headmasters' Conference Schools established between 1840 and 1882, just before Plymouth High School for Boys changed its name, exactly two-thirds of them are today called Colleges rather than Schools. So perhaps it was as much a fashion or vanity thing as anything else. Whatever the reason, though, the new name stuck.

As well as the name the school also had its colours, red and black (as opposed to the green and black of Mannamead), colours which were worn on the hats and caps as well as the playing fields. One piece of correspondence in the school magazine even bore the suggestion that the school colours ought perhaps to be worn on bowlers as well as straw hats. While another missive, written around the same time by "J.G.", was a little more guarded on the subject of colours;

"I have noticed, especially during the last vacation, numbers of ill-dressed, disreputable street boys with the Plymouth College colours on. I think we lay ourselves open to this sort of thing by allowing any and every hatter to sell our caps and hats. I have a vague sort of suspicion that charitably disposed fellows are in the habit of giving away their hats, when done with, to street boys; thus the misdeeds of these frequenters of the gutter are very naturally put down to us. The obvious remedy to all this is, that only one hatter should be allowed to sell our colours, and that when a fellow wants a new hat or cap he should apply for an order to one of the masters. Fellows should also persistently refuse to give away their school hats unless they previously tear off the ribbons. If this were done, I

The letter is illuminating in a number of ways, not least of which is the implication that the cap or hat ribbon was the main distinguishing feature of a chap's apparel - no stripey blazers, or other obvious uniform garments although it is likely that neckties had to conform to the basic colour scheme.

The major event of 1883 however was the departure of the school's first headmaster George Bennett, who accepted the headship of the sixteenth-century Sutton Valence school in Kent. Many were disappointed to see him go but FH Colson said having spoken to the man many years later, that it was his wife's health that was the main consideration in his moving.

Of Bennett's successor, Colson noted that *"Mr (afterwards the Rev.) J.R. Cohu was an exceedingly young man when appointed, and went after something*

under two years to the Headship of Richmond Grammar School. He was a fine scholar, and has since made a considerable name in theological literature".
No mention is made by either Colson or Serpell, in print at least, of the story that young Cohu's very early resignation was allegedly prompted by his being caught in a compromising position over the kitchen table with one of the maids, however Charles Serpell's son, Roger, who succeeded his father as clerk to the governors, assured me that this was how his father recalled the affair.

Educated at Queen Elizabeth School, Guernsey, then Jesus College Cambridge, where he secured a double first and an MA, Cohu came to Plymouth College from Dulwich, where he had been sixth-form master. His stay here was particularly brief, just four terms. Curiously enough he was ordained the year he left the school, 1884, and as well as gaining the Headship at Richmond he went on to become a parish priest and a writer of nine theological books.

Perhaps the most notable event to take place in Cohu's short spell at the school was the publication of the first-ever edition of the Plymothian, from which we learn that the headmaster clearly possessed some athletic ability as he and his partner won the school tennis tournament. Other insights into school life gained from that first school magazine, include the fact that there were two Ist XI's, cricket and football and a newly formed Debating Society.

The soccer team were unbeaten that term and one assumes that the game at that level was played with a little more sophistication than the game described by Serpell; *"How many boys would take part in one game of (Association) football was not prescribed by any law. Youngsters were told off to follow in a sort of queue some more or less good-natured senior and snatch a kick whenever they had the chance."*

Such a view is endorsed by the anonymous OP account in an 1889 Plymothian;

"None of the boys now at School will remember the "League", it was found of great service when there was a premium on individual dribbling; the whole school would turn out at 12-30 or 5 o'clock, and play against the XI."

Plymouth College football team 1883-4

But to return to The Plymothian No.1 of December 1883, it contained a plea from the music teacher, Mr Lohr, for suggestions for a school song. Little could he have thought that within a matter of months such a song would be supplied by a new headmaster.

Following the sudden resignation of Cohu, the governors appointed, without advertising the post, J.M. Batten. In his review of the various headmasters of the school, John Spear made the observation that although there were no apparent problems internally with the school "folk from the outside may have drawn the wrong conclusions about a school that had two headmasters in seven years".

Jean Rougier Cohu - Headmaster 1883-84

Certainly if the governors were looking to inspire confidence in the school, James Maxwell Batten was an admirable choice. A westcountry man, Batten was educated at Hailebury School, then St John's College, Cambridge. He then went on to become one of the original masters at Kelly College before taking up a position as second master at Newton College. An extremely able young man, Batten had been head-boy and captain of both cricket and football at his old school and at Cambridge he was rackets champion and captain of the Rugby Ist XV. He also came away from there with a first class Classics degree.

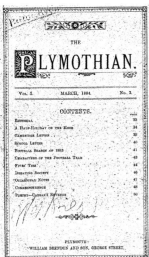

Cover over Plymothian Issue No.3 March 1884
James Maxwell Batten - Headmaster 1884 - 1889

Batten was still only thirty-one when he came to the College, young enough to participate fully in all sports and he played cricket, fives and hockey here. In his second year he had the school field levelled for a square and a football pitch, at a cost of £5.8.6d (the bulk of which - £2.15s.0d - was raised by the Old Boys), and in February 1886, doubtless also at Batten's instigation, the first game of hockey was played at Ford Park.

The school by this stage was coming up to its tenth anniversary and clearly by now would have had a small but significant body of old boys. Clearly they were one of the driving forces behind the creation of the new pitches at the school and it is no surprise to find that following the creation of the square an Old Plymothian cricket team was formed in May 1886, and later that year an OP football team.

It had been back in December 1884 that the first Old

Boys dinner had been held and building on the success of that, and the sporting sides, it was no great surprise to find the idea of a proper Old Boys Club being raised in 1887 (annual subscription 2/6d - 12p), with the suggestion that there should be a black OP blazer with maroon stripes and the college arms on the pocket.

WS Picken and JB Greenway were two of the guiding lights in those early days of the Old Boys club and although that first OP sporting side, the cricket team, did not exactly get off to a flying start -seven matches lost, two won - they did not disgrace themselves; *"our bowlers equal, if not surpass, those of any in our neighbourhood, but our batting is decidedly weak".*

The same "Old Plymothians" report in the autumn 1887 edition of the school magazine also contained the first of many thank-yous to members of the various school XI's who helped make up the OP XI numbers from time to time, and the annual thank-you to the headmaster *"for his kindness in lending us the college ground".*

As for the football team, it was noted that *"we have some of the best known players in the county, and without being boastful, we mean to give a good account of ourselves during the winter vacation".* The anonymously produced piece then concluded on an equally positive note … *"Let us look back on the cricket and football records of the College in its infancy, and*

then examine the records of the last six years, and if the analogy is any guide, we have a brilliant and glorious future before us".

The optimism wasn't misplaced and in the next magazine we find that the football team *"gained an easy victory over the Argyll Club".* Football then was a much newer game than cricket and Argyle Athletic (as the infant Plymouth Argyle FC then was) had itself just been formed the previous season by a nucleus of old boys from Launceston (then called Dunheved) College, who were based in Plymouth. Their first meeting was in the newly-built Argyll Terrace, off Houndiscombe Road, not far at all from Ford Park.

If local football was in its infancy though, hockey was even more so. The first school game was played on Wednesday 3rd February 1886 and *"considering not more than four or five fellows had ever played the game before under proper rules, it may be considered on the whole a success. It resulted in a win for Mr Moore's side by 6 goals to 4, chiefly owing to the good forward play of the captain, well backed up by Bridgman i., while Mr Batten and Prance i. (forward) and Lewarne i. (back) strove hard to avoid defeat".*

The match report then launched into a brief appraisal of why some of the rules of the game were in place … *"one or two points which gave rise to dispute ought* to be noticed, namely the dangerous habit of raising the stick above the shoulder. This rule, unlike "hands" in Association, was made simply to lessen the danger which certainly exists in the game".

Little else was said about the match itself, save to record that "Ryall showed promise behind, as did also Palmer, but he should avoid being so dangerous."

There then followed "The Rules of the Game of Hockey" which included;

"5. The ball shall be an ordinary cricket ball painted white".

"11. A goal is scored when the ball has been driven between the goal posts under the bar or tape ..."

"13. ... The ball shall be played from right to left only, and no left or back-handed play, charging, kicking, collaring, shinning, or tripping shall be allowed."

And finally ..

"19. Should there be no umpire or umpires appointed by the Captains, the Captains shall be arbitrators in all disputes, and should two umpires or arbitrators fail to agree they must appoint a referee, whose decision shall be final."

One supposes that this was one of the reasons at least that in that historic first game the captains were members of staff - the newly appointed Mr Moore and the headmaster, Mr Batten, himself.

It's hard to imagine the staff taking quite such a formal part in school games today, but then it was very much the done thing, as is more than evident from the school Paper Chase held that year;

"On Saturday, February 6th, we had a big paper chase, the first for three years. CV Bellamy and F Lewarne were "hares" and a capital run of some 16 or 17 miles they gave us. They left the College at 2-22 p.m., first made for Egg Buckland, then to Cann Tunnel. From this point they started off across country and finally reached Bickleigh Vale; crossing the Plym they then zig-zagged up and down through the woods, which part of the course was very trying, and made for the top of the

train incline. They went down here on the trucks, thus gaining on the "hounds," and, leaving Plym Bridge and Marsh Mills behind, ran home by way of Lipson, reaching the College at 5-18."

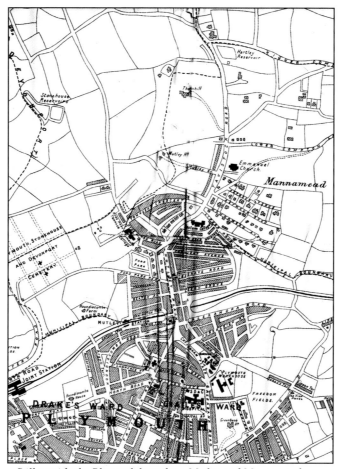

Still outside the Plymouth boundary, Mutley and Mannamead grow

This delightfully rural romp around land that was all, in the late 1880s, still outside the Plymouth boundaries, was entered into by over forty "hounds", a significant number considering there were probably a little under a hundred boys in the school at the time. The first "hound" home clocked in four minutes after the "hares"... "in the person of Mr Thompson" - another new member of staff who had joined around the same time as Mr Moore.

Thompson therefore completed the course in an impressive straight three hours and was followed by two boys, Ryall and Bridgman eighteen minutes later, who were just ninety seconds ahead of the Headmaster and that dangerous hockey player EA Palmer. Serpell, Prance, Brendon and Weekes were five minutes behind them but no other boys managed to finish within half an hour of the athletic Mr Thompson, while the twelfth hound back, H Moon, an old boy, was more than a quarter of an hour behind the Headmaster.

Clearly then there would have been a lot of respect and admiration for this energetic breed of educators and it was undoubtedly a great loss when Messrs Moore and Thompson left in 1887 to start a prep school in Kent: The Headmaster referring to their "joint venture" on speech day that year. The greater loss, though, come two years later when the athletic Mr. Batten himself announced that he was leaving to take up work as the representative in the British Isles of the European manager of the Equitable Life Assurance Society of the United States - "one of the largest and most progressive offices in the world".

Insurance was very much a growth area around this time and interestingly enough when Eden Philpotts, in the literary alias of Corky major, left Merrivale (Mannamead) School, he went straight to an insurance job in London.

At Batten's leaving presentation in the school Lecture room, in the presence of all the boys, the Reverend Benwell Bird said the duty which he had to perform was "at once painful and pleasant - painful because the act in itself showed that Mr Batten was going to leave them and that they were going to be deprived of an excellent headmaster, and pleasant because it afforded them an opportunity of shewing in a humble way how much they prized and esteemed his high character and manly spirit, his just and considerate government of

the school. His (Mr Batten's) sympathy had always been with the boys alike in their work and in their play, and his skilful and interesting teaching had won their warmest regard and admiration. They all cherished very pleasant memories of Mr Batten's head mastership of the College, and earnestly desired for him and Mrs Batten great happiness and prosperity in their future career. They begged Mr Batten to place on his table that small token of their regard, and hoped that as often as his eye rested on it, it might awaken memories of a period not the least pleasant in his life."

The present in question was a silver centrepiece with spoons to match and gift bore the following inscription:-

"Presented to J.M.Batten, Esq., M.A., by the boys of Plymouth College, in grateful remembrance of head mastership, April, 1889."

Why did he go? Was it perhaps as John Spear suggests because of the success Theodore Butler was having at Mannamead School. Butler had arrived here in 1884, the same year as Batten, and through his various measures had seen numbers there rise from around 110 to 170, at Plymouth College however numbers had if anything fallen. Here the roll of around 100 had been supported by an annual intake of about 40 pupils but by 1888 this had dropped to an intake of 26 and then, in the year Batten left, to just 21. The lure of a lucrative post in London was clearly that much stronger than what may have been an uncertain future at Plymouth College - remember many of the schools started around this time did not make it into the twentieth century. Again was it just Butler's ambitious plans at Mannamead that made the school so attractive or was it a lack of charisma on Batten's part. It is hard to read too much between the lines in Serpell's brief account of Batten's headship:

"He was a teacher who did not shun liberal discursiveness, and was well liked by the boys, especially the Classical VI, whose literary tastes he cultivated."

Then comes a line not without some implied criticism ... "Discipline was not, as one suspects in retrospect, too rigorous, but he did nothing to let the school down." Whatever else Batten left behind him though there is one gift to the school for which he will always be remembered, and that was the School Carmen. Responding to FN Lohr's plea for a song Batten composed the words which have since struck a familiar chord in the heart of every old boy from that day to this. Written in his first term at Plymouth College the full text appeared in print for the first time in December 1884, "and will before long, we hear, be set to Music by Mr Lohr".

Frederick Lohr - Composer of the School Carmen

Mr Lohr had been choirmaster at the school since it had opened, he had come to Plymouth via Norwich and Leicester as a young man of twenty in 1864. In addition to his duties at Plymouth College he was also choirmaster at Plymouth High School for Girls and a number of other schools. Exceptionally gifted and hardworking he founded the Plymouth Vocal Association, (it later became a Choral Society), and he wrote a "large number of most popular songs and the marked originality of his genius had during the last few years ripened into a strength which was rapidly bringing him into the front rank of English composers".

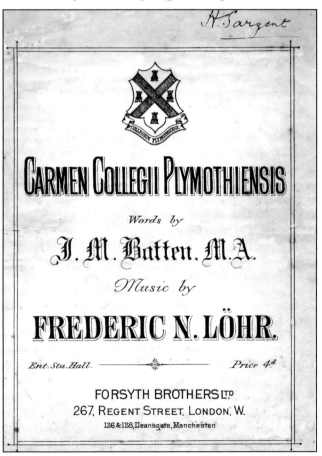

CARMEN COLLEGII PLYMOTHIENSIS

Words by

J. M. Batten, M.A.

Music by

FREDERIC N. LÖHR.

Ent. Sta. Hall.   Price 4d

FORSYTH BROTHERS Ltd
267, Regent Street, London, W.
126 & 128, Deansgate, Manchester

Bert Sargent's Copy of the School Carmen

1887

Plymouth College in 1887 with, presumably, the now-bearded Batten in the middle of the group.

Tragically those last remarks appeared in Lohr's obituary, for he died, aged just 44, on December 18th 1888. It was truly a great loss, Lohr was *"beloved by all who knew him"* and was *"perhaps the most popular man in Plymouth"*.

"Apart from the excellent work which he did with our choir, his visits every week were a periodical source of enjoyment to those who came into contact with him, and there never was a man of whom it could be more truly said, that it was like a breath of fresh air or a tonic to meet him. His simple, hearty, cheery nature seemed to spread gladness wherever he went, and to know him was to love him."

Lohr's obituary was several times the length of the aritcles given over to the departure of any one of the three headmasters the school had had by April 1889 and it spoke volumes in every sense for the high esteem in which he was held. There weren't many members of staff at the school in those days of less than 100 pupils and his impact among them would have been that much greater, particularly as singing was a far bigger part of daily life then than it ever is now.

Then almost any formal social gathering would have had a musical section, with no radio, television or recorded music available, everyone was, to a greater or lesser extent, more musically literate than the average person is today, despite the fact that more people today have access to music one way or another. Good singers were especially valued and many would stand up and sing at luncheons, dinners and teas.

Reading the tribute to Lohr now, though, it is remarkable how true one passage remains, whatever social changes have occurred in the intervening years; *"our own School Song has a swing and vigour about it, that will make it stand comparison with any composition of the kind"*. Undoubtedly those qualities have conspired to make the song, even now a highlight of any Old Boys reunion and any formal school function.

In drawing attention to one or two of the differences

between then and now though, one is prompted to think about just how young boys did spend their days in that pre-electric world, and happily for us the Plymothian No.27 of June 1888 opened with a day in the life of "Examinatus". Title *"A Hard-Worked Youth"* it bears reproducing in its entirety, not just for the insight it gives us into life at Plymouth College in late-Victorian times but also for those elements that sound as pertinent today as they did then;

Plymouth Hoe and the first phase of the Pier - 1889.

"It is an astounding fact that in the face of every proof to the contrary, there are some papas and mamas of the present day who have the audacity to say that boys do hardly any work at school now; at any rate not half what they used to do. Now in case any poor innocent person should be taken in by these poor deluded people, I now venture to expose to public view the real state of the case. Our school, that is to say Plymouth College, is an average school for work I should say, and I myself am certainly a fair instance of a hard-worked boy belonging to it. How then can I do better than by giving a true record of one day's work, and play (which is really very hard work indeed). Thursday is the day I choose. At 6-40 I am half awake. Can I get up? No, it's too wet for bathing. Just then a stream of sunlight takes

away that hope. 6-42. I heard whistle in the street. In half a moment I am dressed, having dispensed with all such unnecessary things as buttons. 6-42 3/4. I am in the street being jawed for coming out late. 7-30. Home from bathing. I remember that I have some Latin to prepare; which I do. Notice please that at this hour I have to begin drudgery. 8 a.m. I have to undress and dress again, this time less quickly and with more care. I have lost my stud. Where on earth is it? Ah! In my boot, but in two pieces. 8-20. I have borrowed a stud and am dressed all right I believe, can't help it if I am not. Now I have five and twenty minutes for breakfast, which I decidedly need after bathing. Bother! I have left my Latin Primer somewhere. Had been trusting to this time to prepare it. By 8-43 I have found it, and am ready for breakfast. 8-45. Breakfast done. 9-10. At school after a mile's uphill walk. I think I must have eaten my breakfast too quickly, for I ache. And now from 9-15 to 12-30 I have to sit with only ten minutes break. In my opinion it is cruelty. Am accused of not having done my Latin, which as you all know I prepared after bathing. 12-30. Free!! I wonder if there is a stray cricket practice for me. I go to the notice board. A mass of notices on it. The secretary wants to sell old cricket cards at half-price. How kind of him. Contributions for the Plymothian must be sent in before Saturday. The editor might have saved himself the trouble of putting that up. Second XI. Fixtures, from which I gain that their captain is energetic. Triumph! On 1st board, third layer, I find 1st XI. Cricket Practice. There is one likely to be vacant. 12-45. First man has been in five minutes. I get a ball and bowl. My first ball is straight, of which I am proud, as I am not a first-rate bowler. I continue with varying success for a little while until alas! the ball goes twice outside the net. I say the ball is so slippery. I see they are not taken. R-ckl-y laughs. I wish he would not. Next attempt I am hit to the wall. "Thank you," I yell to a fellow close to where it has gone. Poor chap he is deaf. "Thank you, boy," says a master who has just been hit to the same place."

"It is instantly sent in. Mine follows. Alas! it pitches a half-volley and goes far to the other side. I look around to see if any one had heard my remark when it did so.

Only Smith, who of course thinks it nothing out of the way, so I feel safe. My turn to bat. "Get your pads on," are the welcome words. I have them on, but the fellow batting wants one more hit. He has three. He asks me to let him finish the round, which I do; after which he goes out looking as if I had cheated him of some time. I am bowled. "Play forward to it." I follow the advice. Am bowled again. "Play back." I can't do both so play between the two. I don't get out again. 1-32. Late for dinner, having had to run. I wish I hadn't had that breakfast this morning. 3 o'clock. In school. My back is tired, so I lean back. "Sit up, please." I do, but my back goes back with a crash in two minutes. What am I to do with my legs? Happy thought. The desk in front. Dash you. The cad has run his pen into my calves. And so I get through the rest of the two hours. Space fails me. Out at 5. Field out till 6-15. Mile home, and work until I choose to stop. I don't think anyone, however learned, can say that it is not a long day."
EXAMINATUS

The account is fascinating for a whole number of reasons, not least of which being that it was written as a single paragraph. But what can we learn from it? Our writer appears to have been a senior boy, otherwise he probably wouldn't have been entertained in the 1st XI nets, he seems to have lived somewhere between the school and the Hoe, this would explain the mile uphill walk and the fact that he could get to the sea and swim in it, in just over 45 minutes (there were no other bathing facilities in town at that time).

We also learn that the basic school day is roughly 9 till 5 with two and a half hours for lunch and a ten minute mid-morning break. It was indeed a long day, and one where, for our writer at least, cricket was deemed to be far more important than the content of the lessons and certainly in the context of the Plymothian this comes as no great surprise for seldom do we find any reference to what is actually taught in school. Traditionally that would appear to be what a prospectus is for, as school magazines generally never appear to serve as a forum for any sort of debate, discussion or even comment about syllabus. The odd report on this or that society, the odd poem or piece of prose and sport, plenty of sport.

Interestingly enough soon after Examinatus' item on the Hard Worked Youth appeared in the magazine there was a poem published - *"with apologies to Longfellow"* - in the Plymothian, entitled *"The College Schoolboy"*.

"Under a spreading chestnut tree,
The College schoolboy stands:
Full four foot six in height is he,
With small and inky hands;
And the wrinkles in his collar white (?)
Are black as iron hands.

His hair is thick, and black, but short,
His face is like the tan,
His coat is muddy on the back,
For he plays whene'er he can;
And looks the masters in the face,
For cheek them that he can.

Week in, week out, from nine to five,
You can hear his shrill voice yell;

You can hear him slam his locker up,
At the joyful sound of "Bell";
But to stand upon the form again,
The master doth him tell.

And on his way back from school,
He looks at the chestnut tree,
And tries to find out in his mind
How many nuts there'll be;
And also when that he gets home,
What grub he'll have for tea.

He goes on Sunday to the church,
And he sitteth in his pew,
But ears, they hear no parson's voice,
For the cushion's soft and new,
And the bring him to a soft repose,
That beholds him as if glue.

Swotting - cheeking - humbugging,
Onward through life he goes,
Each day, it sees some task begun,
But seldom sees it close.
Something accomplished, though not done,
Has earned a night's repose.

Here again our writer ("D.N.L." this time), albeit tongue in cheek, highlights the long hard day of the late-Victorian schoolboy, an interesting reference here being to "grub" - just what did the average Plymouth College schoolboy eat? Here again we find a partial answer in the pages of the Plymothian. The relevant passage appears in a piece entitled "Hints on Training";

"In diet, great care must be used. Beef and mutton, but not pork and veal, may be taken in the ordinary quantities. Pastry of all sorts should be avoided, and milk puddings substituted in its place. Fruit is not injurious, though jam should not be taken. At breakfast, oatmeal porridge is very good, and eggs may be eaten with advantage, though not too often, as they are liable to produce biliousness. Meat should be eaten twice or even three times a day. The best and safest drink is water, or milk and water, though coffee in small quantities does no injury."

The article concluded with the advice *"be moderate and abjure the tuck shop"*, but it should be remembered that this was written for the benefit of those in training and was not a piece on general health. To that end it also recommended nine hours sleep and that the *"time for rising should not be later than from 6-30 to 7"* and added that *"a cold bath on rising is extremely beneficial"*.

School numbers around this time were about 100 and doubtless life at Plymouth College was much like life at any similar school across the country. Certainly if the Headmaster had any great influence on school life, based in part on experiences gained during his own school days, then the hand over in 1889 from Batten to Colson should have been a remarkably smooth one, for both men were educated at Haileybury in Hertfordshire, a school that itself was only founded in 1862. Colson had been there when Batten was head-boy, and coincidentally both had then gone on to become Classical scholars at St John's College, Cambridge.

1887 - 11 year-old George Poole David Hawker and his 12 year-old brother, Robert Samuel John Norris Hawker, of Mutley House, on their way to Plymouth College through the grounds of the house (now Mutley Park) with the lodge behind them..

Just beyond Mutley Park - Thorn Park with its original railings soon after being laid out.

Plymouth College viewed across Ford Park Cemetery - 1885

1885

THE COLSON ERA

F. H. Colson

While Mannamead School was manifestly thriving under the dynamic Mr Butler, Plymouth College was clearly struggling when the thirty-two year-old Francis Colson assumed the post of headmaster in May 1889. One can but wonder what attracted him to the post. The school had a bank overdraft of around £15,000, numbers were falling and as the school's fourth head in twelve years there can't have been many who would have tipped the College in a two horse race, with its school roll of 100 and falling, against Mannamead with 170 and rising.

First impressions of the man himself would perhaps not have helped find in his favour either; *"He was short of stature and rather abnormally constructed about the knees, and with a sometimes unduly comprehensive indifference to the normal uses of buttons"* (Wilson Harris).

Colson had previously taught at Clifton School, in Bristol, but came to Plymouth College from Bradford

Grammar where he had been sixth-form classics master. An academic of the old school he was a classic classicist and in addition to his given subject he taught the Greek Testament and a certain amount of English Literature.

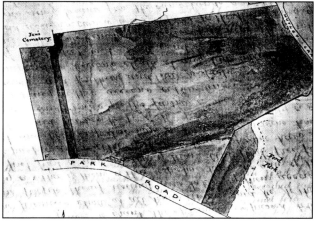

Top; the School and 'the solitary tree of trees'. Middle; the original extent of the School grounds. Below; The site is significantly reduced in size as grounds are sold for development to meet debts.

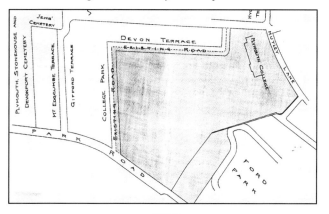

In his first year Colson saw a slight improvement in the school roll but the financial position was hardly any better, the school was running at a loss of around £455 per annum and so the decision was taken to sell off some of the playing field in order meet the most pressing debts. Originally the school land had run down to the eastern corner of the cemetery, but in order to raise funds something like 40% of the site was sold and Gifford Terrace and Mount Edgcumbe Terrace (now all Gifford Place) were cut through one part and around the edge of the rest of the site College Park Road (now College View) and Devon Terrace were constructed. Interestingly enough the school had to half fund the cost of the new road running around the field.

Given the number of boys at the school then the amount of playing field left after the sale appeared to be more than adequate and the only tears shed appear to have been for one particular loved one;

"By-the-bye, Op's who have not visited the school for some time will be sorry to hear that with the surplus land lately sold has gone the tree, the solitary tree of trees" (Plymothian December 1890).

Perhaps the brightest note of that year in retrospect however was the planting of a little acorn that gradually grew to be an extremely important part of Plymouth College, namely the establishment by Colson of a *"preparatory class for little boys, held under a lady at the School-house."*

"The experiment," said the Headmaster at Prize Day, *"has been thoroughly successful. Little boys,"* he added, *"up to a certain age thrive best under a lady of tact and firmness, and the class, while isolated from the bigger boys, is generally supervised and occasionally examined by ourselves, and has the use of the school playground and gymnasium, with other advantages."*

It started out as a room in the headmaster's house, a large house, south of the south gate, on the northern corner at the top of Pentille Road. By all accounts the Prep grew fairly rapidly.

1889

In 1891, when he was six years old Charles Brown was a new boy there; *"the Prep was kept by the three Miss Stonemans, sisters of the Walter Stoneman who became the famous Court photographer (Heath and Stoneman was his firm), but the Prep was only in one room; there were eight of us boys."* There were a number of boarders living in the house too and *"soon after the Headmaster moved to Ford Park, where, of course, the Head's house still is."*

Valletort Villa, from the west.

Valletort was purchased in 1893 but in 1890 none of the villas to the east of the school site were anything to do with Plymouth College. Known collectively as Ford Park this was one of the most upmarket developments in and around the Three Towns of Plymouth, Stonehouse and Devonport. Then, as now, gates ran across the entrance to the private road and the small cruciform-shaped lodge, Ford Park Lodge, still standing, had stables and a coach house immediately behind it, to the right of the entrance, also still there today. Fifteen substantial properties made up the estate and they were inhabited by wealthy merchants, solicitors, doctors, naval officers and widows, several of whom gave generously to the headmaster's 1890 appeal to raise funds (£40) for the Carpenters' Shop. George Rogers of neighbouring Seaton Terrace, presumably

a parent, and Colson himself were the most generous subscribers, each contributing three guineas (£3.15p). Undoubtedly the school's greatest benefactor for any scheme however arrived the following year, his name, Joseph Thompson. *"What differentiated Thompson from his colleagues was that he was a man of means, and being unmarried, he had no-one in particular to bestow them on. The school benefitted by that in various ways, most of all when he provided funds for the construction of an open-air swimming bath"* (Wilson Harris).

Joseph Thompson had arrived in the early part of 1891 "filling in" temporarily for Mr Greenway and thanks to yet another rise in numbers that year (29 excluding the prep class, as opposed to 21, 19 and 21 for the three previous years) Colson was able to offer Thompson a permanent post that September - it was to be a fortunate appointment for the head and the school.

Having previously worked as a barrister in Truro, Thompson was just thirty-one when he came to teach Latin and Modern Languages at Plymouth College and according to Wilson Harris *"he was no more than a fair teacher and a fair disciplinarian ... He had a high colour, so that the close-cropped reddish beard which he cultivated was inconspicuous. His voice was curiously throaty. But he was an essential gentleman, and we realised it. He was keen on fives, and always ready to make up a four with three boys, or another master and two boys; and on the last Sunday of term he always read, most impressively, as First Lesson the twelfth chapter of Ecclesiastes at the service that was held every alternate Sunday evening and attended by the boarders and a sprinkling of day-boys and their parents."*

He was also, along with Colson's first appointment, George Gwyther, a keen member of the debating society. Twenty-two year-old Gwyther, who came from Oxford University and was a graduate of Cambridge, *"taught English and Latin and I fancy some history, but his chief value was as guide and stimulator of the*

debating-society, organiser of Speech Day Greek plays and like diversions and supervisor of the very poor sixth form library"(Wilson Harris).

Colson was clearly shrewd in his appointments and more successfully than any of his predecessors he managed to choose men who in turn chose to stay at Plymouth College.

Perhaps it was a reflection of Colson's own commitment to the place, but of the twenty or so staff that the school had seen prior to his arrival only two had stayed for more than ten years - the celebrated music teacher Frederick Lohr, who died in his post and WH Logan who had arrived in 1879 and who left as Colson arrived in 1889.

By comparison of the twenty appointments Colson made, over half of them stayed at the school more than ten years and six of them were here more than twenty years, most of them leaving only to retire. This alone gave the school a remarkable sense of stability and must have done a great deal to boost confidence in Plymouth College within the local community.

One of the longest serving of Colson's appointments was the successor to Frederick Lohr, Carl Kuhne - *"commonly rendered, and not so inaccurately, Cooney"*. A graduate of Cologne, forty-one year-old Herr Kuhne was *"a rather attractive German"* who eventually retired after twenty-eight years having, interesingly enough, served right through the First World War.

Clearly the atmosphere at the College was changing - very much for the better. By the end of 1895, just six years into his headship, there was not a single member of the pre-Colson staff left at the school.

The maths teacher, Bere, had been the last to leave and his replacement, FF Southby came to the school in the same term as the Reverend KA Lake *"both were substantially built, one endowed with a considerable corporation, the other with a large, clean-shaven visage. Before they had been there a week they were universally known as - but on the whole what they were known as is better undisclosed. Boys can be wickedly apt, but not always scrupulously delicate, in nomenclature"* (Wilson Harris).

It was not just in the staffing of the school that Colson improved the local perception of the College, at the Prize Giving in 1891 the proceedings were enhanced by the presence of the Duke of Edinburgh. After the formal handing out of prizes his Royal Highness spoke about the boys and the school, which, as he understood;

"although principally a day school, is one carried out on the lines of what we call in England a public school. Now I think nobody will contradict me that the public school, so-called, is one of the grandest institutions which we have to be proud of in this country - (applause). It is one which, though principally intended for education proper, and learning, also brings out everything that is noble and manly in a boy - (applause). But having been placed in such a school, he must look to himself for a good conclusion."

In the various votes of thanks that followed, the speakers were keen to express not only their gratitude to the Duke for attending the Prize Giving but also to the Head Master who *"was throwing himself entirely into the work of the School, and it was prospering largely under his head mastership".*

At last Plymouth College was starting to find its feet and if any one ingredient was responsible for increasing its appeal that was Colson himself and in his report that day the Head not only acknowledged a substantial overall increase in numbers, but a rise in the boarding population from 6 to 20 and success for one boy, Bird, at Exeter College, Oxford and another Walter, at Middlesex Hospital. In the only direct reference to the content of the school's academic syllabus, the head spoke of developing the *"our work in natural science".* Mr Rudge, Colson's third appointment in 1890, had been the school's first specialist science teacher.

Mr Colson also noted a number of achievements by old boys, including a couple in Army Preliminaries,

but he made much of the fact though that *"far too few boys from these towns gain scholarships to Oxford and Cambridge"* and announced his intention to address the situation. Notwithstanding scholarships though the school regularly sent boys to both Oxford and Cambridge.

Outside of those two great medieval institutions of course there were only a handful of English universities for those considering further education to choose from, and by comparison, they were all rather modern - Durham and London, early 1830s and Manchester and Newcastle early 1850s. A good many school leavers went straight into work or the services and many of them stayed in the Plymouth area. Such was their enthusiasm for Plymouth College though that within seven years of the school opening the first "Old Boys" dinner had been held and by the end of that first function a committee had been formed with a view to making it an annual event. Before the second annual dinner had taken place though an Old Plymothian club had been formed with WS Picken and JB Greenway, captain and secretary of the team.

By the time the formation of the club had been noted in the Plymothian nine games had been played of which only two had been won, however, a report six years later noted that the record of the OP team, *"since the club's formation, "* has been *"76 matches played, of which 59 have been won, 8 lost, and 9 drawn".*

Small wonder therefore that when the club embarked on what was only their second tour (1st January 1892) one local paper was moved to refer to them as the *"leading club in the West of England".*

They set off for Truro from Millbay Station with barely eleven players - at one time there had been many more *"however as the time for the tour grew nearer some had lost their enthusiasm and others had engagements which could not be put off. "Beastly sorry, old chap," they wrote "I would have given worlds to go but I can't possibly get off"."*

Millbay Station and the Duke of Cornwall Hotel, 1890s.

They arrived in Truro in plenty of time for the game but with *"no time for a square meal, we foraged for a tavern in town where we regaled ourselves of beer, baccy, buns and bovril".*

Truro *"a better team than we had expected"* were beaten 4-2, but they lost 2-1 to Cornwall at Redruth on the Saturday. It was, though, the only setback of the tour, Penzance fell 6-0 on the Monday, Penzance & Porthcurnow 3-1 on the Tuesday, and East Cornwall 5-1 on the Wednesday. Clearly the OP's were a formidable footballing side - on the pitch and off it.

Old Plymothians Football Club 1891-92.

And remember Football was still in it's relative infancy in those days; *"Hacking was just then being ruled out, but tripping was still allowed. The style of play was entirely different from what rules now. When a forward got the ball he kept it, making as much ground as he could until intercepted. He would have a man "backing him up" who would hope to take the ball from the man who had robbed his pal ... There is only one certain method of obtaining possession, and that is by barging the man off it, in fact "going for the man" ... "when a half-back sent a speedy forward head over heels with a shoulder charge, he was rewarded with shouts of "well played", "good charge" and I should here say that the rule regarding the charge was most particular as to how the charge was made, and a free kick would be given if it was at all from behind or too low or in the nature of a push* (Herbert Prance, Memories of The Three Towns).*"

All part of the rough and tumble of the game and of course, like any sporting club through the ages though there was, inevitably, more to the touring than the games themselves and it's hard to imagine a team today being any more disreputable than this late Victorian collection of old boys - it's also hard to imagine that the Plymothian would be allowed to carry an account such as this - even if it were true. To return to the report;

"I should have mentioned that on Monday morning we left the Queen's (Penzance) intending not to return. A little difference between the hotel manager and ourselves as to the latitude to be given to football players, decided us to withdraw to the less pretentious but more homely Western Hotel. This arrangement commended itself to all parties. I should like to give a few words of warning to football teams who intend to stop at the Queen's. Don't play football in the smoking-room, don't play the piano in the ladies' drawing room, don't rush about the corridors at two o'clock in the morning, and don't attempt to stave in the bedroom doors with boots and sticks. If you resist all these temptations you will be made most welcome at that very desirable hotel."

Clearly a good time was had by the tourists - there was a great deal of drinking and smoking and singing, and plans were mooted for a tour of London or Somerset and Gloucester the following year.

Whatever sort of figure they cut these high-spirited old boys were passionate about the school. They played all their home matches at Ford Park, and they were of great assistance when it came to fund raising and generally promoting the name of the school, and when all is said and done, times were just a little different then. If the old boys sounded as though their behaviour left a little to be desired, then so did the shenanigans on the school field. In 1895 matters came to a head and the system of school games was altered; *"The present arrangement, by which our lower elevens are entitled to invite foreign teams to our ground is open to several objections. First, the said teams are often of a strange*

and uninviting appearance, and, we shrewdly suspect, initiate our small boys into hitherto unsuspected possibilities of the native English tongue."

"Furthermore, these teams bring their friends, and these friends bring their friends, one of whom brings a ball and thus a friendly game is begun in another corner of the ground. The field must present a motley sight on afternoons when two or three of these visiting teams are in evidence, - a sight not often seen on the playgrounds of public schools."

Consequently it was decided that only the first and second elevens would play outside matches other than against school teams. An advantage of this being that henceforth smaller boys at the school generally would have more opportunity to play form matches; *"This ought to lead to keener competition among the players and certainly have the good result of making the field our own property."*

It may seem difficult to us now to appreciate that this was ever in dispute, but there were several incidents of "trespassing" reported, notably around the old gymnasium and on one occasion there was talk of *"intruders on the 1st XI pitch after school practice was over"* and there were occasions when *"half the riff-raff of Mutley are there, and the place looks like a board school"*. Consequently there was a plan suggested in the school magazine to *"rush them and wound them"*.

"We would suggest that a picked body of the bigger and heavier boys, and those skilled in the noble art of self-defence, might under cover of the pavilion or by other unsuspected paths, circumvent the intruders and "signo dato" rush upon them from all sides. This having been done, the enemy would not be able to bear up against the charge of our men, but, many having been wounded, would retire their feet each unto his own home."

So ran a piece in a Plymothian that *"with the exception of the Athletic Articles"* is the production of the Masters and Old Boys only.

"This is strong language, but no stronger than the occasion merits. These louts must be kept out, and for that purpose prompt and combined action of every boy of decent size in the school is necessary. It is no use depending on the police. A policeman cannot always be on the spot. The defence of our field lies in our own hands, and it is our own disgrace is we allow it to be polluted by the feet of rank outsiders."

Once again while we may accept that this is the way things were it is not so easy to believe that the school magazine was able to incite the pupils in this way - imagine the local press getting hold of material like that nowadays - but life was that much different then and as if to confirm that it was not all just hot air we have this first hand account;

"We were plagued at that time by what we called the "cads", a rough element in the town who would beset us on the way home from school or from football matches. Sometimes they would invade the playing fields and and then the whole school would turn out to repel them. I remember once the Head (FH Colson a small man in a bowler hat - a great character and a great scholar) advancing quite fearlessly with a stick or an umbrella in his hand to reprimand these invaders and getting his bowler hat knocked off for his pains ... There was an older prefect then named Shanks who went into action with his fists."

Memories of Charles Brown again, his recollections of life in the 1890s giving us an insight into a world that is both familiar and yet somehow quite distant.

Clearly there were a number of problems besetting the sportsmen in those days, the sale of a large part of the field, the complaints from the occupants of the new houses about cricket balls, the complaints of the cricketers that the footballers were spoiling their pitches, the complaint about *"the trench running down the back of the pavilion down to the railings at the bottom of the field - a considerable hindrance to boundary hits"*.

And then there was the shed near the gymnasium - could it please be used as *"a satisfactory place for the bestowal of Cricket paraphernalia rather than a sheep shelter"*.

The School's four-legged lawn-mowers, note the unfinished wall.

The footballers had problems too; holes in the 2nd XI goal meant that *"the goalkeeper has often to take three or four cold baths during the course of a match"*.

It wasn't all bad news though; in the summer of 1892, helped by the good offices of an old boy, architect M Alton Bazely, who gave his services free, a new pavilion - *"a joy forever"* had been built and the following year *"a large number of trees were planted at short intervals around the field ... many of them presented by members of the council"*.

The decision to sell the surplus school land had obviously been well-timed, the development of the Peverell Estate was just about to start and local land prices must have been at an all-time high, particularly as the site that was sold represented the only access to that area between the main school itself and Alma Road, there previously being a solid green belt from the school playing field, through the cemetery and across the fields of what was to become Central Park.

View across Houndiscombe Farm to Ford Park Cemetery

The sudden housing boom in the area had another unforeseen repercussion, there was no Anglican church in the immediate neighbourhood until you got to Emmanuel one way and the even-newer (1887) St Matthias back towards town. Consequently, in conjunction with Emmanuel a Mutley Mission was established. For a few weeks meetings were held in the premises on the southern corner of the junction of Mutley Plain and Ford Park Road and then, by arrangement with the School they moved into the Plymouth College gymnasium. For the next fifteen years, until the opening of St Gabriel's in Hyde Park Road, regular services were held there. Every Saturday night the gym would be converted into a church, then, late on Sunday night, it would revert to being a gymnasium again.

The School Gymnasium and temporary chapel.

The biggest service undoubtedly being one of the last; on 29 January 1907, the Bishop of Exeter, Dr Robertson, came down to the gym and, in the presence of a large congregation, including Thomas Lockyer, Mayor of Plymouth, and his Deputy, he publicly licensed the Rev JL Nightingale as curate-in-charge of the new district to be known as St Gabriel's.

Plymouth was undergoing a rapid phase of expansion, in a thirty year period straddling the end of the nineteenth century and the beginning of the twentieth century the population of the Three Towns, Plymouth, Stonehouse and Devonport, increased from 80,000 to over 220,000. During that time Plymouth College went from being outside the boundary of Plymouth, outside of any great built-up area, to being within the expanded boundary of the town and surrounded by development.

Nevertheless there was still a different flavour to the area - Charles Brown again;

"We used to buy hokey-pokey through the railing of the College, the Italian hokey-pokey carts selling that early version of ice-cream for a halfpenny a slab. I am sure it was most unhygienic and unwholesome, and how we kids were not striken with every kind of infection I do not know. Then to cheer up the streets, there were barrel-organs with their monkeys and German bands."

Horse tram on Mutley Plain - below, Crownhill Fort in the snow

There was of course very little traffic on the streets then; *"If we went into town, we walked, in fact we walked everywhere. If you wanted to cut a dash you might go by wagonette or by train. Stonehouse and Devonport were practically unknown towns to me as a boy. Manadon Hill was a narrow road between high hedges ... there were few houses at Crownhill apart from the Barracks. It was then called Knackersknowle."*

Closer to the school, work on the Peverell estate had only just begun and Compton was still an isolated village, as indeed was Eggbuckland. Consequently the paper-chase from the school out to Plym Bridge and back was still very much a rural, green-fields-and-hedges affair and a very popular one too.

Compton village late 1880s, below Eggbuckland Church, 1889.

"Monday, March 20th (1893), an extra half-holiday was given us and the weather being fine a paper-chase was got up. The hares were Lobb i., Hughes. The hounds were about the number of forty."

Forty was a good number for a voluntary activity, getting on for a third of the school. There weren't many boarders then, and given that there were one or two OP's and members of staff who joined in, it was obviously a happy event.

Most of us, of course, have a tendency to look back on our school days and see them as being not only happy ones but also somehow happier than those that are the lot of the current generation. Older members of staff also often succumb to the rose-tinted spectacles view of the past and reading the back pages of the Plymothian it is somehow quite reassuring to note that it has always been that way.

A letter written to the editor just a few months before that paper chase sums up the situation;

"The Good Old Days" ... *"I am getting quite tired of hearing the above expression used. Those who have been at the School for some years seem to think it their right to run down the present and praise up the past at every possible chance. I do not like it, and though I may not have been at the School so long as some, still, I do not believe those of the past were better all round than we"* .... *"I remain, yours truly, H.P.T."*

Further insight to those times is given to us, once again, from the reports of the Debating Society, where both Mr Thompson and Mr Gwyther were on good form. Addressing the proposition that the *"Modern Style of Dress is Absurd"*, Mr Thompson was reported as suggesting that *"men have no taste and wear colourless garments to hide the fact ... Boots if comfortable, look ugly; if neat cause corns ... the top hat is very inconvenient, especially in church - always wore a soft hat himself and found putting on a dress shirt very trying to the temper ... Aggravation caused, only surpassed by that of putting on collar".*

Mr Gwyther for his part *"did not see why he should not be allowed to wear colours, as much as the ladies ... Only chance men had of making their appearance attractive was in the tie. Modern dull attire prevented the masculine mind from soaring to higher things. No man could perform glorious deeds if attired in a* "bowler" *and a pair of baggy trousers. Soldiers dressed in red to stir up their valour."*

Among the boys there was much discussion about top hats and *"with regard to evening dress, irritating to be mistaken as a waiter"*. Uncomfortable *"Sunday clothes"* for church were singled out for attack and the long and colourful dresses of the fairer sex also came in for much comment; *"owing to length, spoilt by muddy weather, and had to be replaced by new ones; therefore expensive."*

On the current vogue for the tight lacing of the bodice - this was said to be not so objectionable *"as it killed off all foolish and frivolous girls and left the field open to the staid and sensible."*

It should be remembered that generally the attitude to the "fairer sex" was quite different then. In September 1893 the self-governing colony of New Zealand stunned the world by passing the Electoral Reform Act and thereby became the first nation to grant its female citizens the right to vote, a right that they exercised for the first time in the General Election of November 1893. That same month the school debating society met to consider a motion condemning the idea of Woman's Suffrage.

Upstairs, Downstairs: The staff of Mutley House outside the lodge.

Fouracre spoke first suggesting that ... *"domestic strife was rampant enough already"* and that a *"woman's brain was smaller than man's"* and that he had consulted *"many lady friends and found that they did not want suffrage ... Some had joined the Primrose League, but only for fun ... Women's province was to comfort and caress (approvement of House shown by tumultuous applause)."*

There were voices supporting the feminist cause but they were few and poorly reported and included Brown ii who pointed out that *"ladies were successful canvassers - why not voters."*

Then there was the compromise suggested by Brackenbury who thought that *"unmarried women only should have the vote; married women had enough to do at home".*

The unmarried Mr Thompson picked up on this stating that *"the only women keen on franchise were unmarried women of a certain age (laughter)"* and added that women are *"too much ruled by passionate feelings. Virtue of most ladies of his acquaintance was lovableness. (Wild applause)."*

An old boy, Peake, spoke next and entertained the House with *"description of rich widow of education without vote, but possessing gardener and boot-boy with votes. Gross injustice."*

But another teacher, Mr Gwyther again, added his voice to the proceedings and not only supported the motion heartily he also proposed a rider that the *"House express its horror at any proposed increase to scope of female garrulousness."*

Crowther i brought a new slant to the debate suggesting that no-one ought to have the vote who could not carry arms, to which Jeffrey i replied that there were many Members of Parliament who could not be trusted to carry a gun. Finally Fouracre had the last word by saying that he didn't see why a husband need tell a wife how he was going to vote - He wouldn't!

The motion was then put to the vote and was carried by 17 votes to 4 ... *"which ungallant proceeding the House immediately capped by passing Mr Gwyther's rider by a majority of 11 votes."*

With such sentiments deeply ingrained among the staff and students alike it's small wonder that it was another twenty-five years before women got the vote in this country, although perhaps even the minority of four voices opposing the motion had it's influence in time, given that the first woman Member of Parliament to ever to take her seat in the Commons was Nancy Astor - MP for Plymouth Sutton!

The concerns of the debating society and the way those concerns were expressed give us a great insight into the culture of the school in the 1890s. The House was divided on the somewhat admirable, but perhaps implausible, motion that *"War should be abolished and replaced with International Arbitration"* and the suggestion that proposed *"Temperance Legislation did more harm than good"* was defeated by five votes. Interestingly enough this last debate saw the two teachers Thompson and Gwyther at odds with one another.

Following up a suggestion that it should be illegal for a publican to allow a man to be drunk on his premises Mr Thompson suggested that a publican need only use his nose to find out whether a man had been drinking already. Whereupon Mr Gwyther rounded on the wealthy, former-barrister and said that the *"shutting of public houses did not affect private drinking of upper classes - therefore unfair to lower. All class Legislation unqualified curse. Silly faddish cliques would deprive human race of all innocent enjoyment, and should be rigorously suppressed. Did previous speaker intend landlord to sniff around each customer before serving beer?"*

Drunkenness was a general problem though and the local papers were full of accounts of men, and women, being found much the worse for drink, including many tram and wagon drivers.

Happily it seems not to have been a problem in school, young boys finding plenty of other extra-curricular distractions to keep them occupied.

Head and shoulders above some of them was the domestic pet;

"Witness last year's (1892) menagerie race, when an agile goat was followed home by a self-opinionated bantam and a guinea pig which sadly showed the want of previous training in athletic sports."

However at least Walter's goat had serious competition that time, the previous year the goat had been the only creature to finish.

After the household pets ... *"the most popular hobby among boys seems to be that of Practical Chemistry, although (or ought I to write, because) this is also looked upon askance by the class of parent, cousins, uncles and aunts."*

"Chemistry", wrote an anonymous contributor to the Plymothian, *"is rather the more expensive of the two, because you have to buy your own chemicals, while in the case of animals your parents will provide food rather than let them starve, but it is infinitely more exciting. It also adds to a boy's dignity. He feels that he is master of the situation when he is armed with a bottle of an evil-smelling compound with which at his own caprice he may drive the whole family out of doors. This gives him a sense of importance and authority otherwise not easily attainable."*

"Electricity offers almost as much scope for enjoyment as chemistry. True, it does not produce any odours to speak of, but there are compensating advantages in other ways. Its capabilities are infinite. You may persuade your father, or more likely, mother, to let you put up an electric bell, and consider what chances that gives you of knocking the wall to bits."

Mains electricity as, we know it, was not available in Plymouth when that was published in December 1893, but it was on its way. Instituted under the Plymouth Electric Lighting Order in 1894, it was originally designed for lighting and tramway purposes but by the end of the first year some 82 private consumers had been connected.

Telephony was another novelty of the age;

"A telephone is not a bad amusement, and can be turned to profit by allowing friends to speak through it at a penny a head."

Back l-r: PL Coleridge, GGH Reade, HH Butcher, RJP Thomas, HC Paige, RHS More. Middle: AWS Brock, G Tucker, HA Brown. Front AJ Ellis, DH Magnus

And then there was amateur photography - kits available, complete with chemicals. Plym Woods was a favourite haunt for the School Photographic Society and the ever enthusiastic Mr Thompson was its President for several years. Science teacher Mr Rudge gave the group one of his most successful lectures on making "lantern slides".

In the playground "prisoner's base", leap-frog, marbles, balls and tennis were among the popular pastimes.

And then there was entomology or butterfly chasing. To this latter end the school had a Natural History Society, but as of the summer of '93 it seemed to have fallen entirely to pieces, the Annual Excursion had become little more than a school picnic. An amusing account of a "bug hunt" appeared in the Plymothian and in the winter term of '95 the Entomological Prize was awarded to Rogers for his rounding up of 36 different species of creepy crawly. All in all *"the number of captures by boys reached the respectable total of 98 different species"*, many of them obtained "by sugaring" nevertheless it had earlier been noted that the proposed Museum had amounted to no more than a *"case with a few butterflies in one of the shelves of the library"*.

Ah, the library! *"There was, of course, no wireless and there were no cinemas. It is true that, some time I suppose in the late 'nineties, a local firm of opticians exhibited a few flickering pictures which represented the first efforts of what was then known as the bioscope (or was it biograph?), but it was an example of the latest achievements of science or invention, not at all as a form of entertainment."*

"I did not care for concerts and my parents did not approve of the theatre, so for the rest there was the countryside and there was reading."

"I read, of course, the usual boys' authors, Ballantyne and W.H.G. Kingston and the writers of school stories like Talbot Baines Reed"

A few years later, incidentally, it's interesting to note that *"an analysis of the borrowing from the Junior Library (which is open to the V., Remove and IV. Forms) shows that since the opening of the Library Henty's books have been taken out 410 times ... Rider Haggard 63, Stevenson 53, Conan Doyle and Gordon Stables 45, Marryatt and Kipling 43 ... others are nowhere, although the popularity of solitary books by Stanley Weyman and Crockett would seem to show that more works by those writers would be acceptable"*.

To return to Wilson Harris;

"I took in The Boys Own Paper, the monthly edition with a yellow cover and a rather good coloured plate in each issue, but preferred on the whole the slightly more plebian Chums, which has, I believe, ceased to exist. Then there was, in other categories, Comic Cuts and Chips on pink paper, and Ally Sloper's Half-Holiday; of these my selective taste favoured Chips. Of a still different order I read impartially Tit-Bits, Answers and Pearson's Weekly and Cassells Saturday Journal. There were odds and ends and interesting bits of information in all of them."

"When I began to read the local papers, the Western Morning News and the Western Daily Mercury, both good ... the former came into the house regularly ... I preferred the then inferior weekly, The Western Independent, with its entertaining gossip column about local celebrities (Wilson Harris).*"*

Newspapers were becoming increasingly popular, the illustrative content was rising and gradually the great grey slabs of copy were being broken up with bolder headlines and livelier advertisements, although front pages still tended to be just a mass of classified ads.

"... the Library Committee have agreed to discard the homely Tit-Bits and Illustrated London News in favour of the Times - such has been the intellectual improvement of the upper forms of late (June 1896).*"*

Nevertheless the changes in that field again prompted the debating society into action, the motion this time being that *"Newspapers exercise a demoralising influence over the public ... First condemned publication of crime, which lead to imitation ... Sad fact but true - Police News most popular literature among young England - excepting such ingenuous individuals as all hon. Members present."*

The activities of the debating society were not just restricted to the constructive presentation of arguments though - they also produced regular entertainments, generally in the Big Room.

It was around this time, incidentally, that the Big Room was rechristened Big School - *"a much better name and one generally used in public schools"*.

Big School laid out as a chapel - 1896.

At the same time there was a suggestion that oak boards should be made to record the names of those achieving scholarships and one to set out the words of the school carmen - *"scarcely one person in the school knows the words ... when it is sung, everyone tries to hear what his neighbour is saying and the result is a series of inarticulate grunts, or (in the chorus) yells"* - Nothing changes there then!

Allied with the complaint about the Big Room there was general criticism of the lack of interesting material on the walls of the corridors and classrooms. There was but one exception;

Big School, 1896, with the curtains open.

"We congratulate the Remove on the appearance of their Class Room. Some handsome pictures have been presented to the Form by Mr Gwyther, and the Class itself has subscribed to add to the number".

Clearly on a number of counts what happened in school fell short of desired standards ... *"May I suggest that our cricket team should all turn out in white and not grey flannel, which is now worn by several of the team ... no self respecting club should tolerate such a want of taste (Plymothian June 1895)."*

Back row: VK Shanks, G Tucker, JL Fouracre, GL Barley, BH Whiteford, HH Butcher. Middle: GH Pethybridge, AP Hughes, C Peters. Front; WD Martin, PC Barley, PL Coleridge.

Uniformity was a major issue that summer and was directed not only the whites of the cricketers but also the colours of the footballers for it was then that the 2nd XI colours were changed from the old chocolate and blue to the old 1st XI colours - red and black in narrow bands, the new 1st XI strip being broader bands of the same colours. There were, evidently, two reasons for the change; one the chocolate and blue dyes faded too quickly and two, *"because red and black are the school colours, and all caps should therefore be of them".*

But not for much longer, because, the following year, all was to change again after the amalgamation with Mannamead School.

Not that there was any hint of this momentous change in the school journal, there was absolutely nothing until the announcement was formally reported in the Plymothian of February 1896. Indeed in the previous issue, December 1895, there was the usual report on the main fixture of the season, Plymouth College v Mannamead School; *"We met our old rivals on*

November 2nd on our ground ... The kick off was at 1 o'clock so as to allow the boarders to get away early, it being the half-term holiday on Monday".

The College started well and were 4-0 up when the visitors began to play with *"great determination and good shots were put in and at last, after Serpell had saved splendidly several times, Powell scored with a fine shot. Time was called shortly afterwards."*

All in all the report occupied more than a page of the magazine and was at least twice the length of any other match account, as was usual for this annual encounter - and no-one reading it would have guessed that just a few weeks later the two schools would be one.

With the benefit of hindsight it's interesting now to note how the fortunes of the football rivalry between the two schools had mirrored their fortunes off the field.

"When the games were first started at a very prehistoric period, the College were certainly not much of a match for their opponents. The first match they lost by 15 goals to nil. The second they reduced the score by 2 or 3 goals, and continued to do so until they drew with them. At this point the ill-feeling grew to such a pitch that the matches were discontinued for several years. When the rivals met once more in the football field on November 12th 1884, the College won for the first time by 2 to 1, and again in the return match by 3 to 2. This was the last win for the College for five years."

"Out of the 19 matches recorded since 1884, Mannamead has won 10, and the College 8, 1 being drawn; and the School have kicked 39 goals against

Right: Lower corridor 1896, note light coming n from the north.

50

the 32 of the College. From '85 to '90 the College were the weaker, and Mannamead from '90 to '95" - so ran part of the text of the history of the "Cricket and Football Matches" between the two schools in the magazine of February 1986.

There was no attempt to account for the changes but significantly the footballing fortunes of the College improved after the arrival of Colson in 1889 and Mannamead managed only one win in seven matches after the departure of Butler in the early part of 1893.

And by 1895 the success was right across the board;

"Once more we are able to rejoice in a complete victory over Mannamead in Football. While the First XI won by 4 to 1, the Second won by 3 to 2, the Third by 6 to 1, and the Fourth by 13 to 0."

There was a similar story on the Cricket Pitch the "turning point" there had come in the summer of 1890 when *"it had begun to seem almost impossible for the College to defeat their rivals, so that there was a good deal of excitement when in '90 the College defeated their opponents by 143 to 132"*

As we have already seen, the relative numbers of boys in the school was also fluctuating in the College's favour, such that in his annual report in 1895 he was able to state that *"for the fifth year in succession I have to report an increase ... the increase has been most marked in the Preparatory Class which has doubled during the year."*

Giving his report at the July 31st Prize Day, he further stated that *"last year we won our first scholarship at the Universities (R Nettell - Oxford). This year we have added two more* (Treleaven - Oxford and Brackenbury - Cambridge).

The head was ringing the changes and the school's status was rising accordingly, of that there could be no doubt. 1894 had seen a major change in the school's examination proceedure as Colson adopted the Oxford and Cambridge Certificate Examination - *"though not so well known in this part of the country as the Oxford*

and Cambridge Locals, represents in many way a higher standard".

It was also the year that the headmaster was elected *"to the society of head-masters of the great schools of England ... a somewhat rare distinction, which he* (the Rev Benwell Bird, quoted here addressing the 1894 Prize Giving) *believed was only enjoyed by two head-masters west of Bristol".*

Colson was consolidating the position of the College after those first twelve years of regular upheavals and he clearly had a loyal team around him. And team work was equally clearly a key element in all this. It wasn't just the boys on the cricket and football field - a careful look at the school fives competition in 1895 shows more than half the staff taking part, Messrs Lake, Thompson, Southby, Haywood and even Colson himself all entered the Senior doubles competition, each master partnering a senior boy. Mr Lake, incidentally ended up winning with a boy called Lovell.

Staff and boys playing together, with Mr Gwyther second from left in the back row.

Occasionally too the masters would join in the school football and cricket (notably Lake, Gwyther and Bere) and all seemed to be involved in one or other extra-curricular activity, Colson, Thompson, Haywood and Bere all preached at the Sunday services held in Big School and Thompson, Gwyther, Lake and Kuhne were all in the Choir. Therefore, one can assume that after so many staff fluctuations in the past, Colson's team were quite a close knit group. Indeed on 29th June 1895 Mr Haywood married Mr Rudge, the former being a man of the cloth, the latter, who left later that year, tying the knot with Miss Margaret Brown.

Rudge (whose *"Oxy-Hydrogen Lime Light Lantern was bought at a very low price for the school"*) was one of two staff to leave that year, the other being the only pre-Colson appointment still on the staff - Mr Bere. It's never an easy thing to read between the lines and Bere was evidently a popular figure around the school, his singing at various Glees and Concerts alone gave him great status, nevertheless there are one or two odd remarks in the Plymothian piece on his retirement;

"He had always had the best interests of the school at heart, even though there might be some who thought him harsh and unkindly " and *"it was the source of the greatest gratification to him to receive evidence of good faith towards him - evidence which would show unkindly critics that he had not deserted his profession because of ill-success."*

Quite what was meant we shall probably never know but for at least a year or two after his "departure", he was still to be seen and heard at entertainment evenings. It did mean, however, that all of the staff (albeit only eight or nine of them) were now Colson's men, a situation no subsequent head has ever found himself in.

Plymouth College was on the way up and Mannamead, looking so promising just five or six years earlier when the College had been struggling, was now struggling itself. Therefore when the amalgamation did come, it was little surprise which of the two was dominant.

Palmer's House, 1896. Palmer is standing behind the boy in the straw boater.

Attempts were made to keep the union as trouble-free as possible and, it would appear, the transition was largely successful as far as the boys themselves were concerned. Indeed, after years of intense rivalry, first impressions of the amalgamation suggest that is was remarkably smooth;

"Those croaking prophets of evil, who foretold a school divided into two camps, and sanguinary pitched battles in the playground, relieved only by a regular series of single combats in the task-room, have only to walk along the Plain at half-past twelve or five to be convinced of the emptiness of their forebodings. The red and black, and the green and magenta are seen in pairs along every street, covering heads engaged in friendly and even loving conversation."

However it would appear that not all the Mannamead boys came down the hill, and certainly not all the staff, among whom it has been suggested the amalgamation was not quite so well-received. The evidence available doesn't quite bear that out though; three teachers, Murch, Woodcock and Palmer, made the move and they seem to have got stuck in soon enough. Francis Palmer had been the second master at Mannamead and was appointed to the same position at the joint school and along with Mr Woodcock made an immediate impression on the school cricket team. Along with Allen, the professional, Messrs Woodcock, Palmer and Lake headed the batting averages that summer for the Plymouth and Mannamead College 1st XI. Frank Woodcock also threw himself immediately into the Debating Society and Glee Club (at the March Entertainment he gave a reading from Arthur Quiller-Couch's "The Affair of Bleakirk-on-Sands).

Francis Palmer, meanwhile, in addition to his other duties, was made Master of the Boarding House. At the same time the increase in the number of day boys at the joint school made possible the reversion to *"a common public school system"*, the regular *"inter-house competition"*. Accordingly Mr Thompson was

made head of the new South Town House and Mr Haywood, North Town, the boys, as you might surmise, being separated out on a local, geographical basis. It is, incidentally a matter of no small coincidence that the same year that the two schools amalgamated so the area of Mutley was absorbed in the new boundary extensions of Plymouth.

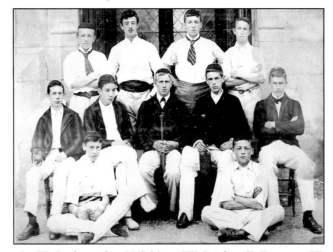

1st XI: Back row l-r; RHS More, HH Butcher, JL Fouracre, HL Stephenson. Middle; PL Coleridge, G Tucker, UK Shanks, WK Legassick, CD Back. Front; D Cornish and DH Magnus.

Plymouth was expanding rapidly and whereas Ford Park had been relatively isolated when the school was first built, now it was at the heart of an area of great development. The division of the day boys into town houses though, wasn't anything to do with this, rather it was an attempt to promote competition in an area which had now been deprived of the great sporting challenge of the year - that is any sporting fixture, at any level, between Mannamead School and Plymouth College. That was the main reason given, it wasn't the only one though, for there had also been a *"feeling for some time that the list of foreign matches played by the school might be reduced. Especially as regards football. At cricket regimental matches are very valuable, but at the more violent game, there are obvious objections to*

our lighter teams contending with powerful elevens, consisting mainly of non-commissioned officers and men". Regimental sides were also notoriously fickle when it came to adverse weather conditions - *"a wet day does certainly cause them to cancel matches with more frequency than is desirable"*. Furthermore *"with regard to the other teams we play there are even more forcible arguments to be adduced for the discontinuance of our meetings."*

Clearly the still-legal charge tackle could be a rather one-sided affair against heavier, rougher, bigger sides.

There was however yet another side to the football debate. Now that the inter-school football fixture had gone there were no significant school sides available to play. The Corporation Grammar fixture did not have the aura of a great match therefore *"We must look further afield, to those schools which, though it may not always be recognised, are now our real rivals: and I am sure, that in Kelly, Newton, or Exeter, we shall find something which will take the place of the Mannamead match, and will bear the good fruits that that has borne in the past. But these schools play Rugby, and sooner or later we shall have to change"*.

Above, from undated glass plate negative, right the School - 1895.

The first amalgamated School football team - Plymouth and Mannamead College 1896-1897: Back; DL Serpell (PC) goal, G Tucker (PC) Inside Rt Forward, P Anderson (MS) Rt Half, D Spearman (PC) Centre Forward, B Bird (PC) 12th Man, EC Pitt-Johnson (PC) Lft Half. Front; W Stanhope-Lovell (PC) Centre Half, HH Butcher, Captain (PC) Rt Back, AW Brock (MS) Lft Back, CV Hunt (MS) Outside Rt Forward, FG Powell (MS) Inside Lft Forward. Absent B Spooner (MS) Outside Lft Forwd.

1896

So wrote R Nettell, in the April 1896 Plymothian, the same Nettell who three years earlier had become the first Plymouth College boy to get an Oxford scholarship. He continued;

"At the 'Varsities a good Rugby player is thought more of than a correspondingly good "soccer" man, and brings far more honour to his old school. With all due respect to the Old Boys' Club, a few good Rugby players at either of the Universities would do much more for the School than the Xmas tour of the O.P.'s."

He then added *"It is a common mistake to suppose that if Rugby were instituted nobody would be able to play at odd moments. I have questioned men from the great public schools, and everywhere I find that boys practice without changing, just as we do now. Of course no one can play either game properly without tumbling into "footer" clothes."*

Plymouth and Mannamead College, was now *"the only first-class school in Devon that plays Association"*, and with an eye on the future, they played their first game of Rugby on 28 March 1896, against the Royal Naval Engineering Students - *"In consideration of our inferiority in weight, the Students generously allowed us the advantage of the wind for both parts of the game"* .... *"the game ended with the score:- 1 goal 2 tries (11 points) to 1 goal (5 points), in favour of the Students"* ... *"Altogether the school is to be congratulated on its first attempt at Rugby Football"*

Football continued to be the main game but *"after the half-term, a few games of Rugby were played, which proved to be a very nice change from Association"*.

Predictably resistance to the new incentive came principally from the Old Boys, notably EH Babb who failed to understand why people couldn't appreciate, now that the two schools were one, that the footballing prowess of the school and the new joint old boys club would increase and take them to even greater heights. *"All interested in Association in these parts know how much the two Schools have done for the game in the*

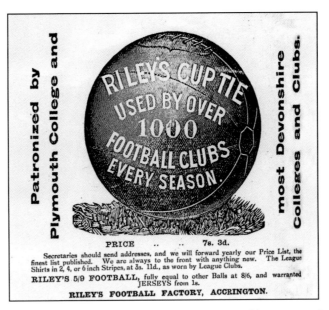

past. Therefore I look upon it from a public point of view. If the game at the College were changed, the two clubs, at any rate, would fall to the ground. How could Plymouth F.C. live, for it has always relied on Plymouth College and Mannamead School for it recruits? Where would the newly formed Old Plymothian and Mannameadian F.C. which promises such great things, be? We are entering for the English Amateur Cup next season, with the desire to encourage the game in our midst. Last, but far from least, from a public point of view, where would our County team be, which is this year Champion County of the South Western group, mainly through the efforts of Old Boys?"

"....My aim in writing is to try and get the present boys the more thoroughly to realise what any change would mean to West Country Association Football".

It should be remembered here perhaps that within two or three years of that statement, Plymouth FC had been eclipsed locally by the Argyle team who played their first match at Home Park on 22 September 1900 (against the Welsh Fusiliers) and who consolidated their status as the top local team by turning professional in 1903.

Might things have turned out differently had Plymouth College not forsaken football and not cut off their supply of talented old boys to Argyle's main rivals?

The football/rugby issue dominated the pages of the Plymothian for some time and here it is perhaps worth noting another small, but significant, element of the amalgamation and that is the fact that the magazine of the new joint school continued to be known as the Plymothian and not the "Plymothian and Mannameadian" or any such other combination. Furthermore, as if for the benefit of the new boys from Mannamead, the July '96 Plymothian carried a full transcript of the words of the "Carmen Collegii Plymothiensis". A none-too-subtle way perhaps of saying this is the school song chaps, you might as well learn it now.

Perhaps it was the way such seemingly minor aspects of the Union were tackled that ruffled a few feathers of the Mannamead staff and students, but generally the move appears to have been amicable enough and one area where Plymouth College did undoubtedly benefit from amalgamation was in the ranks of the Cadet Corps.

The Mannamead Cadet Corps was one of the earliest in the country (1871) and although it had a somewhat chequered history, it had been operating on a sound footing since a major revival in 1885. In the first Plymothian after the amalgamation we find the first reference to the Plymouth and Mannamead Cadet Corps and a note to the effect that *"we hope in our next issue to give our readers some entertaining details of the history of our own School Corps which is attached to the 2nd Devon Volunteer Artillery, W.D.R.A., and also to record some of its recent doings"*.

Sadly that account doesn't seem to have made it into the magazine. It is interesting, though, to read the opening words of that first Cadet Corps report; *"Prominent among the many improvements and advances which have been effected in the English Military System of recent years, stands out the development of Military*

Part of the newly-combined ombined Cadet Corps at the back of main school.

"The long-expected performance of the Mandarin took place on Tuesday, March 2nd (1897), in the stormy and boisterous weather which has long-associated itself with College Entertainments. Too much praise cannot be awarded to the boys who took the ladies chorus, viz.- Watts, Roberts, Brown iv., Sansom ii., Emerson, Anderson iv., Blackwell i., Blackwell iii., Foord ii., Mackenzie i., Moule, Poyneter, Stephens and Brook. To come to the individual performers - first of all, we must acknowledge ourselves most fortunate in having secured such talented assistance as that of Miss Blackie and Miss Carter - the duet between them was perhaps the best piece of the whole opera."

"The leading part of the Mandarin was taken by Mr Gwyther, the twin parts of Chung and Chang were excellently rendered by Mr Woodcock and Mr Burgess (O.P.). Spooner let his excellent tenor voice be heard to advantage, and also, unexpectedly, gave us a taste of his acrobatic pwers. Mr Lake, as Foreman of the Jury, and Mr Powell, as Captain of the English Forces, completed a most powerful cast. The piece (originally written for Brighton Grammar School) was suitable for us, as it gave an opportunity to the Cadet Corps to show in public how they behave under fire."

The costumes and groupings were carefully arranged and most effective - to quote from the Local Press, 'the bewildering array of jurors, Chinese ladies and English soldiers made up a most picturesque ensemble.' We must not omit from the general congratulations Mr A Groser (O.P.) who shared with Mr Gwyther (in the middle of the back row with the Madarin hat) *the task of practising the choruses last term, before Herr Kuhne took over the superintendence and without whose valuable aid the performance could not have taken place. Finally our thanks are due to W.M. Opie (O.P.) who, as usual, kindly painted our scenery; to Sergeant Smith of the Marine Theatre, who did the 'make-up' for the men; and to Pitts who performed great things behind the scenes on a kettle drum. The whole performance was such a success that we have been asked to repeat it at the Girls' High School at the beginning of next term.*

training in the great schools of the land. Cadet Corps raised under the Authority of the War Office and attached to the various Volunteer Corps have received an amount of encouragement from the Government and of favour from the public at large which has rendered them an almost indispensable adjunct of important schools."

If this begins to sound like an attempt to justify what for many parents and pupils was a sudden and new departure for Plymouth College then what followed only serves to emphasise that feeling;

"In earlier days of the movement, a certain amount of feeble opposition was raised to these schoolboy armies by unenlightened parents, and elder boys who characterized their efforts as "playing at soldiers." Thanks, however, to the unwavering support of the War Office and the remarkably increased efficiency of the Corps themselves, sneers of this description have long been regarded as mere tokens of the ignorance of their authors, and it is now considered a matter of reproach when boys of the necessary age and physique make such unpatriotic sentiments and excuses for their innate laziness in neglecting to train themselves when young to bear arms in defence of their country."

There can be no doubt about it. This was a sales pitch for the Corps and one that must be understood not just in the light of the amalgamation, where Mannamead's Corps was being brought in and presented as an established body within the joint school, but also within the context that Plymouth is, and has been for hundreds of years, one of the country's principal Services towns. Hence all the Regimental and Naval sides that had traditionally supplied opposition on the sporting field. Then there was the prevailing climate of the day - just a few weeks before the publication of that piece Dr Leander Starr Jameson had led a reckless and unofficial attempt to seize the Boer republic of the Transvaal, thereby heightening the tension and the threat of war in an already fevered South Africa.

Jameson's surrender.

Jameson surrendered on 1 January 1896. On 21 February, the Debating Society considered the motion that "Jameson's raid on the Transvaal was unjustifiable and punishable by death".

Interestingly enough, the former Mannamead master, and Commanding Lieutenant of the Corps, Mr Woodcock, spoke for the majority in condemning the man - "Jameson must be mad". Mr Thompson agreed, saying Jameson had to be condemned, "if only for one thing - he, a subordinate officer, had disobeyed his superiors."

And so the Corps became a significant element of the new school and by the end of the year over fifty of the boys, that is a quarter of the whole school and only recruited from those over twelve, had been enlisted.

The Plymouth and Mannamead College Corps were, at that time, affiliated solely to the Artillery and they were armed with a 9-pounder R.M.L. Field Gun and by the end of the winter term of 1896 they had been "supplied throughout with Government Martini Carbines ... When the corresponding Sword-bayonets arrive, we flatter

ourselves that our appearance as a Corps will strike the popular eye."

Clearly they were very concerned to look the part but there was, of course, much more to it than that;

"By instilling prompt obedience, punctuality and smartness into its members, the Cadet Corps training is useful in after life to all, no matter what career they choose."

The Cadet Corps wasn't the only "new" body to appeal to the readers of the February 1896 Plymothian, there was also the Old Plymothian and Mannameadian Club "now an accomplished fact under the above title".

By the time the Old Plymothians and the Old Mannameadians met for their annual football fixture on Christmas Eve 1895, the news of the amalgamation had already been circulated and so it was, that when the OP's and OM's met at a Smoking Concert held that evening at the Globe Hotel in Bedford Street "the matter was talked over and it was suggested that the two clubs should amalgamate."

After a few preliminary meetings a General Meeting of OP's and OM's was held, again at the Globe, with "Mr FH Colson, Head-Master of the newly formed Plymouth and Mannamead College, in the chair."

Inside the Globe Hotel, Bedford Street

"Things were then placed on a firm basis, and it only remains now for the Old Boys to work together in real union, and have the interest of the old schools truly at heart, to make the club a big success, and most considerably further the ends of the College."

The account of the formation of what is now known more simply as the OPM club then went on to speak of past rivalries.

"We can recall the times, many of us, Old Boys of both sides, when we have met in the keenest rivalry on the playing fields. Whenever Plymouth College met

Mannamead School at any game, it was a time to be remembered by all concerned. Many deadly struggles have ensued, and, if the slaughter has not been great, feelings have run high. There is no reason why the rememberance of the past should make our union now any the less real and sincere. On the contrary, we believe that, being Englishmen, and having tested one another's steel, we shall be all the better and truer friends on that very account."

Thus the OPM club was born and an annual subscription fee of 5/- (25p now but a considerable sum in real terms) was agreed entitling members to take part in all club affairs.

"It was decided to have a President, 4 Vice-Presidents and 2 General Secretaries, together with the Captain and Secretary of each of the branch clubs (football, cricket, tennis), as a ruling body for the club. The officers were elected as follows;
President : - Mr F.H. Colson
Vice-Presidents : Sir Roper Lethbridge, C.S.I., Mr J.B. Greenway, M.A., Colonel Carlyon, Mr M.A. Bazeley.
Hon. Gen. Treas. : - Mr F.B.Palmer
Hon. Gen. Secs. : - Mr E.H. Babb and Mr H.W. Webber, M.D."

A number of familiar names were among those elected officers of the various sporting clubs; Conry, Pethybridge, Babb, Jackson and Cridland (football), Whiteford, Conry, Jackson, Greenway, Roe and Webber (cricket) and Bazeley, C. Whiteford, B. Whiteford (of the Whiteford Road Tennis Club family) , Weber, Groser and Palmer (tennis).

The exact arrangement of the football shirt, halves, stripes etc. had yet to be decided, but the now familiar OPM colours had been chosen - chocolate, red (maroon) and light blue.

It was further decided that the new club should be "At Home", on the occasion of the Past v Present cricket match in the Summer term and that they might have a cricket week, playing all the best teams in the area.

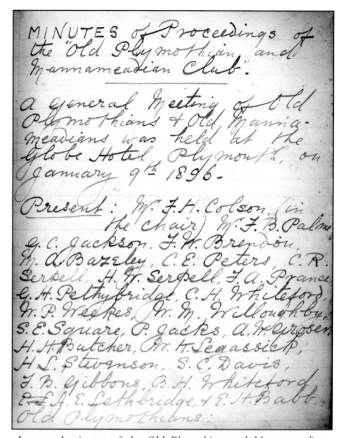

Inaugural minutes of the Old Plymothian and Mannameadian Club. Note the wording O.P. & M Club.

The footballers meanwhile proposed a tour of Dorset and entry into the Amateur Cup.

And so the joining of the two institutions was completed at all levels and the school set about its usual business. At the first Speech Day of the combined schools held that July in the Gymnasium Mr Colson was able to report that the amalgamation had proved to be a great success and that there was now *"nothing to beat the school this side of Tiverton"*. The Reverend Philip Williams, vicar of St Matthias, then a relatively new church itself (1877), said that the success of the amalgamation had been due to the *"tact and wisdom"* of Mr Colson.

Plymothian, June 1896, note the small print "Being the Magazine of Plymouth and Mannamead College".

With the excitement of the great union now behind it, even the correspondence pages of the Plymothian were back to dealing with the everyday minutiae of school life; *"Dear sirs, I would like to call the attention of the authorities to the state of the ink provided in the school this term. It seems to be composed mainly of gum. I did three exercises the other night, and in the morning they had stuck fast together, and I lost my marks for all except the top one."*

And in the even messier stakes.

"Dear sirs, I wish to call attention to the disgusting state in which a great part of the field is now on account of the sheep's dung. Surely the field could be cleaned to a certain extent every week. In fact why should not the butcher, who keeps the sheep on our field, have to send somebody to do this each week?"

Clearly not a lot was done about it, not in the short term anyway, for a couple of years later another letter to the school magazine complained about the number of sheep and added that the *"state of the field at present is anything but pleasant"*.

Above - looking sheepish, the butcher's stock fail to find friends on the playing fields. Below - lads lounging on the railings.

It may seem hard for us to imagine the situation now but the last correspondent gives us some idea of the scale of the problem when he suggests that *"considering there are 120 sheep in the field as I write this letter, surely the number could be diminished to much less"*.

Doubtless though this unhygienic situation had nothing to do with the two epidemics that attacked the school that summer - Examination fever and Mumps. Happily the latter passed off quickly; the former, however, has never entirely been cured.

The tail end of the nineteenth century saw the school beset with any number of problems that might seem strange to us now and the magazine provided a relatively censorship-free forum for complaints, not all of which were acted upon, as correspondents were often quick to note. However, from time to time, issues raised in those pages were addressed; like the introduction of putting the weight; the lowering of hurdles; the provision of a running track; the taking of a school photo; the introduction of more paper-chases and the provision of a tuck-shop.

1st XI, 1897: Back; HA Brown, R Walkey, RHS More, C Basden-Smith, EC Pitt-Johnson, AC Magnus, CRB Lane. Seated; WP Anderson, GWl Lovell, J Bennetts. Front; JR Walkey, LW Walters.

The tuck-shop, clearly a welcome addition to the school campus, was nevertheless not without its critics. It was evidently dark, damp and only offered a limited range of goodies ... and no bags - *"At present"*, wrote "Grub", *"when one buys biscuits and such like, one has either to put them loose in his pocket or carry them in hand, neither of which things are pleasant, especially when the biscuits have jam in them"*.

The Plymothian generally affords us fascinating insights into school life. Dominated by sports reports, notably Football, Cricket, Fives and the Athletics, there were a number of other regular features: Society Notes, mainly the Debating Society and Glee Club around this time, although there was a relatively short-lived period when La Societe de Controverse Francaise thrived (a spoken-in-French-only debating society, that Messrs Thompson and Gwyther again seem to have been responsible for); major examination results for all boys were generally printed in tabulated form, there were correspondence pages, OPM notes, a Corps section and a regular Oxford and/or Cambridge Letter.

This latter section was generally written by an old boy who had managed to get a place in one of the 'Varsities and they were generally quite reluctant and recruited-at-the-last-minute scribes who were seldom very confident about the literary merit of their missives ... *"I have cheerfully been told that any drivel will do"*, wrote GF Forrest from Christ Church, one year. *"And if you are dissatisfied with my letter, as, I grant you, you have every reason to be, propel it, sir, into the editorial waste paper basket, with the scorn it deserves: Cheap cynicism and a blase ennui, especially in the young and foolish, are rightly viewed with disgust"* but ... *"Nobody shall ever accuse me with impunity of having failed to fulfil my instructions. For I have drivelled like a man"*.

Encouraged, one imagines, by the member, or members, of staff responsible for overseeing the magazine, its function was presumably to say, in a subtle kind of way - look boys, Oxford and Cambridge are well within the reaches of some of you, here's one old boy who is there now and see, he mentions one or two other OPMs there - in a year or two's time it could be you.

There were times though when the pieces were of general interest. Like the time the Cambridge letter was published anonymously and the editors prefaced it with the disclaimer - *"we do not hold ourselves responsible for the views expressed by our correspondent."*

It was in the June 1897 Plymothian and it opened thus; *"Cambridge has made a fool of herself. Cambridge has shown that she cannot see further than the end of her nose, if indeed that far."*

The reason for this impassioned outburst was that there had just been an extremely well-publicised vote at Cambridge on the subject of awarding degrees to women. And, according to our man at the scene; *"Far from behaving in a way worthy of one of the chief seats of progress and enlightenment, she has behaved like a stronghold of bigotry and prejudice .... Unworthy of her former fame as the leader of women's higher education, she ignores all British principles of right, and makes and fosters artificial differences."*

And then for the benefit of any who may not have been aware of what all the fuss was about our writer explains thus; *"If Mr Jones and Miss Brown each get a first in their Tripos, Miss Brown has just as much right to call herself B.A. as Mr Jones, and any difference made between them is an artificial difference. Indeed the granting of the B.A. was going to perform marvellous things. Women being inferior to man, it was going to make her equal to him; it was going to bring hundreds of women swarming up to Newham and Girton, all as venomous and terrible as serpents; it was going to put male and female education on the same lines."*

"Most of the undergraduates are labouring under a great delusion, namely that women are here by courtesy, and that it is very gracious on our part to allow them here at all; this permission is named, "the thin end of the wedge." They do not see that women's advent to the 'Varsity was an experiment, and that the experiment having succeeded the women have a right to claim degrees. They take their stand on an artificial sexual difference - a person may come here and study (or play the fool) by right if he is a man, if a woman, only by a great favour."

It was a very emotive issue at the time, even evidenced by the editorial disclaimer - remember the debating society had shown that there was little support for the status of women among the pupils and staff of Plymouth College and indeed at Cambridge it was a similar story. *"On poll day the whole place was decorated with female effigies in cap and gown, usually in knickerbockers as well, - one being perched on a bicycle."*

Cambridge votes against women and creates an effigy on a bicycle

The voting 1,735-666 against the female cause, was pretty clear and great were the celebrations among the majority and although the whole thing could put down as being merely a "rag" it didn't become a forward thinking institution; particularly when there were *"dons making speeches from the windows, in congratulation of the 'manly' spirit of Cambridge, and in exultation of the defeat of those 'effeminate and sexless' men"*.

All of which clearly riled our Cambridge correspondent who concluded by writing;

"I am constantly assured that if women had degrees, many men would go to Oxford. Well if they really are men (and I am loth to think it) who are afraid of women ... who dread being beaten in the tripos by their "mental inferiors," and who fear to prove their superiority by deeds as well as words, if there are such men in existence, by all means let them go to Oxford! It is all they are fit for."

The Oxbridge grip on higher education was slackening however and it's interesting to note that in the June 1901 Plymothian there was an Oxford Letter and there was a Victoria Letter. *"I don't believe you knew that there were other Universities in England besides Oxford and Cambridge. I didn't before I became part of the Victoria 'Varsity. We only boast three Colleges - Owens, Manchester, University Liverpool (by the way, I have heard some people talk of Liverpool University, there is no sich pusson (sic); but University **College**, Liverpool), and Yorkshire College, Leeds."*

The writer then went on to talk about Owens' Jubilee, the college was founded in 1851, celebrated with a *"gorgeous smoker"* at St James' Hall, Manchester where four thousand past and present students sat in companies of five to ten around tables and drank and spoke and smoked and sang.

He then continued; *"I hear on fairly good authority that science is now a general subject at the College. Well, that's very nice, for surely a few will become sufficiently interested to want to pursue the recreation after leaving school. Allow me to recommend Owens College - all the modern improvements, laboratories a trifle more commodious than your own ..."*

"Though the work (but who would call chemistry work) is a trifle stiff in the winter, it becomes delightfully lax in the summer, and cricket becomes quite a recognised feature of the College course, that is for those who do not play tennis. On the whole, chemistry is quite an attractive subject to pursue for those inclined that way."

He then concluded thus;

"As another attraction I may mention that Owens College is open also to the Students of the fair sex, laboratory work becomes so interesting when done in partnership."

Outside of Oxbridge the openings for women were improving all the time as indeed were the opening for those of scientific frame of mind, but they were too late for Wilson Harris who left the school in 1901;

"Science was, of course, taught, but not to boys on the classical side. One term, indeed, the chemistry master did take a voluntary class for an hour a week after morning school. I joined it, but if I learned anything beyond the meaning of H2O it has left no deposit in my mind. I certainly never learned the difference between organic and inorganic chemistry, between chemistry and physics, between biology and physiology."

Mutley Chemist of 1896 - The chemist's art was increasingly a source of fascination for young boys.

The science lab was an innovation in the early part of 1900, the editors of the school magazine noting that *"The school is now in possession of a Laboratory worthy of the name. Not being of a scientific turn ourselves, we cannot dilate upon the details but ... all the Apparatus and Fittings have been radically improved. One glance into the room will show that the whole subject has been put on a different footing ... Another external proof is the appearance of a Barometer and Thermometer in the Front Hall. Soon, we hope, a further result will be seen in Science successes at the Universities and elsewhere."*

There was no doubt about it, Plymouth and Mannamead College had to keep moving with the times and looking to provide the sort of education that would equip its pupils for a suitable career. Increasingly there was the threat of competition from the new government-instituted secondary schools and the College had to show its worth in the community.

Neigbouring, late-Victorian competitor - Mutley Grammar School

At the 1897 Speech Day, Sir Henry Norbury, whose son had been to the school, addressed the assembled body on the subject of public schools;

"Some people," he said, *"thought that a public school was a school where everybody had a right to go - like a public-house. I do not think that is the case. Every*

school, public or private, had a right to exclude those who could not profit by the education given. A public school meant a school under public control, the essential difference being that the headmaster was appointed by the governors, and did not buy it from his predecessor. If this school were his own, and he was offered £5,000 for it by a competent man, and £6,000 by an incompetent, he might be tempted to sell it to the incompetent one. Thus, although private schools might do excellent work, there was no guarantee of continuity, and therefore," he said, "it was the job of every community to maintain at least one public school."

Essentially Sir Henry was promoting the cause of the public school as epitomised by the "great public schools" like Eton and Harrow and as opposed to the new breed of schools under public control that the Government were seeking to establish. Knowing that he was likely to be quoted in the local press and elsewhere he was emphasising the worth of the College and in talking of potential problems of continuity we have to assume this was a veiled reference to what had been the privately run Mannamead School.

Still, if the success of either institution was to be measured in terms of the success of its past pupils both separately and together, Plymouth and Mannamead College had reason to proud of its achievements. With or without university education OP's and OM's were scattered all around the world. Many were in the Services, serving their Queen, while many others were serving the nation in *An Outpost of the Empire*.

Such was the title of a Plymothian piece in July 1900 from J Owen Webley Hope, who had left England in July 1899 and been appointed *"Assistant District Officer to Taveta, a district at the foot of Mt Kilimanjaro."*

It is worth remembering at this point that the British Empire was, at that time, the largest empire that the world had ever known. One in four human beings then populating the world were living within its boundaries

and those boundaries encompassed a fifth of the earth's land mass - and then there were the oceans for few were prepared to dispute that Britannia ruled the waves.

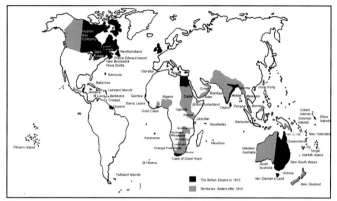

The British Empire: grey pre-1815, black post-1815.

Nevertheless for these tiny islands to reach that level of world domination the nation's most capable and willing young men were at times very thinly spread;

Webley-Hope had had a long march from Ndi, where the train line terminated, to Taveta and had to take a few months supplies with him. Consequently his marching party was made up of *"35 porters, 1 headman, 3 askaris (policemen), my cook, boy and my plucky fox terrier puppy ... No one knew English, and my Swahili was limited ..."*

Clearly however his Swahili improved rapidly for in no time at all he was able to converse with his German neighbours - in German territory - in that language.

"I am", wrote Hope, *"the sole representative of H.M. Government in Taveta, and have under me a native officer and 20 men of the East Africa Rifles, 5 customs police and 5 station police. They are employed at present in building a bridge on the cantilever system. The place is fairly busy, as Greek or Italian traders' caravans pass through almost every day. The only other Europeans on the station are five CMS Missionaries, three men and two ladies."*

"The day after my arrival the wazee or chiefs came

to welcome me, and brought me some goats and a cow. The goats I put in the Government pound, as, of course, I may not receive presents. The cow I sold for the benefit of the Settlement."

"I have not very much work, but critical things may arise any day. The natives round here are very quiet, and I have not many cases to try. The life out here is really ripping, but is of course lonely. Strangers are always welcome."

Other Empire-building old boys were not so isolated; *"Ratnapura, Ceylon, 26th June 1899"* was where AR Tothill (OM) sent his missive to the magazine. He wrote, *"As OM's and OP's are fairly well represented in this spicy Isle, perhaps a few lines as to their doings will not be out of place. There are some five or six OM's and the same number of OP's ... tea planting has claimed most of them, and amongst these will be found such well-known names as Picken, Brock, Burnard, etc.".*

Tothill then went on to list the various old-boys in question, including W Brock OPM who *"only came out in October, and after "creeping" (slang for "learning tea-planting") for a few months has been successful in obtaining a billet as "Sinuai Dorei" (Assistant Superintendent) on an Estate in Matale, not far from Worth's (OM) place. Brock has been wonderfully successful at Cricket, especially in the bowling line. He plays for the "Kandy Sports Club" and the "Matale Cricket Club"."*

Ceylon clearly offered a better social life than many Empire outposts and there were evidently a good many public schoolboys out there;

"... we get a lot of Football (soccer and rugger) and Hockey in Columbo ... a proposal is afoot to get up a "Devonian" team to play Footer, Cricket, etc., against any other School in the Island. I fancy we shall have a very good chance as Newton, Mannamead, Plymouth,Kelly, Blundells, etc., can all boast of good men in the various games."

Tothill signed off with a cheery - *"We are always getting additions to our ranks, and OPM's are always welcome in the Island. Let 'em all come!!"*

The pace of life was clearly quite different out there in Ceylon, quite literally - *"most of the travelling has to be done in bullock bandies or on "shanks' pony"..."* - and indeed all other parts of the Empire, but, it seems when it came to sport, distance was no problem. Another 1899 Plymothian correspondent was EFH Edlin, who noted that there were *"no less than five OP's in Singapore at the present time"* ... *"All five are members of the Singapore Cricket Club, and we constantly meet at Cricket, Football or Hockey."*

One of the five was Charles Ryall, who was stationed there with his Regiment, the West Yorkshires. Ryall was then just thirty, and was therefore among the older generation of OP's (he joined the school when it was in Erme House in 1879), a regular of the cricket and soccer elevens at school he'd gone to Germany at the end of the Easter term 1888 and had passed into Sandhurst six months later. His posting to Singapore came after stints in Gibraltar and Hong Kong. Promoted to the command of a company in 1899 he spent several weeks that summer in Plymouth before being summoned to join his Regiment in the Cape. It was there, in the early stages of the war in South Africa, that he met his untimely end - *"at the hands of the Boers at Potgieter's Drift"*.

Ryall was not the only casualty *"In common with many other Public Schools we have to mourn the loss of Old Boys at the War in South Africa"* (it wasn't called the Boer War until later); Eustace Le Sueur (Ladysmith), Charles Martin, 24, Vincent Drury-Lowe (shot accidentally at Klip's Drift), Charles Fortescue, 27, and William Creak, 25, were among those who died out there, while J Conry was among the wounded.

It was not all bad news, though, and a number of old boys distinguished themselves in the conflict. Captain's Conry, Vawdrey, and Grepe were all mentioned in Lord Roberts' final despatch - the aforementioned Conry also receiving the DSO, along with Lieut. EN Buchan, of the 1st Manchester Regiment, who served right through the Campaign. While various others were honoured with medals and other trophies. *"Trooper CA Loveys, who lost a leg in the Transvaal, was presented with a Silver Loving Cup"*

Ladysmith.

A by-product of the European scramble for Africa - between 1880 and 1899 only four of the forty units that the continent had been carved into had not fallen under the control of a European country - the war in South Africa had not started well for the British. The Boers, or Afrikaners, had first rebelled against British rule in 1880 and having regained independence were now, under the president of the Transvaal, Paul Kruger, reluctant to allow British workers there any voting rights. With a view to aggressively asserting their independence from any British influence Kruger had been building up their military strength and were initially successful in keeping British forces at Ladysmith and Mafeking, under uncomfortable siege. Buller's early request to surrender had been countered at home by the Queen entering the debate with the words; *"We are not interested in the possibilities of defeat. They do not exist."*

For schoolboys it was of course all stirring stuff ... *"I remember well the first bulletin, issued by the principal local paper about mid-day and posted up in a newsagent's shop near the school, to the effect that an armoured train had crossed the Natal border the previous evening, and - the phrase sticks in my memory - fighting began shortly afterwards. (Wilson Harris)."*

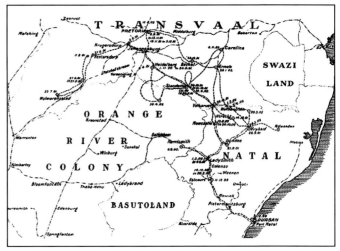
Publication of maps of the area allowed people to follow the war.

"I bought war-maps and moved little flags over them (by no means always in the direction one would wish)" ... *"got familiar with hitherto unknown military names (not quite all unknown, for Sir Redvers Buller was a Devon man and Sir Reginald Pole-Carew came from just across the Tamar) like Methuen and Gatacre and Hector Macdonald and French; later on argued earnestly with the second master, who for some reason was in charge of the school at the moment, as to whether the capture of Bloemfontein provided sufficient occasion for hoisting the school flag; had my first sight of khaki - the soldiers in garrison at Plymouth were redcoats till then - when a detachment of local recruits to the City Imperial Volunteers paraded on the Hoe and fought their way through the cheering crowds down Lockyer Street to entrain."*

There could be no doubt about the scale of interest in this conflict. Partly it was fuelled by the improvements in communications and certainly it was the making of the Western Evening Herald. Newspaper readers were not used to up-to-the-minute information about anything that happened outside the immediate area. Thanks to the recent development of the land telegraph and the deep sea cable distances had been annihilated.

"Thanks to these wonderful inventions, conjoined to the enterprise of newspaper owners and the daring of newspaper correspondents, we survey the campaign in South Africa as though through a telescope ... From the outset of the war we resolved to supply our readers with a service of war intelligence which would be second to none in the kingdom. The cost has been considerable. War is a costly thing to a newspaper as well as to a nation. Our service of war telegrams in twelve months cost us over £3,000 ... this expenditure for a provincial newspaper was on a grand scale ..."

But it paid dividends, and the Evening Herald, published for the first time in 1895 *"substantially increased its circulation"* thanks to its coverage of the Boer War.

"When a great event occurred we were reading an account of it almost before the echoes of the guns had died away."

Buller's final advance on Ladysmith

"When we advanced to Ladysmith with Sir Redvers Buller, thrilled by the spectacle of the Devons and the Irish and Welsh Fusileers literally hewing their way over kopjes, spruits and dongas on their irresistible advance towards Ladysmith, and the British People learnt almost simultaneously with its own inhabitants that the beleaguered city was at length relieved."

This was why, from a propaganda point of view, the war became so important. This is why the relief of Mafeking led to such rejoicing and the name becoming a verb - to maffick, to make merry, to wildly celebrate. However, on a down-to-earth-note, at Plymouth and Mannamead College there was another lesson to be learnt from the Boer War *"thanks to the wisdom and mental integrity of my headmaster"* - Francis Colson.

Mafeking is relieved.

"Himself a Liberal, he was scrupulous to avoid intruding any political opinions into his class-work, or even into casual conversation with boys. But in the case of the South African War he saw the situation steadily and saw it whole, and with great discretion he moderated our youthful ebullience by pointing out that in this, as almost every, quarrel, there was something, even if not much, to be said for the enemy's point of view as well as our own. While he said nothing particularly memorable his words had the effect of pulling us up and making us think. There can be no more salutary

experience, and if I were asked to name the best thing that my years at school did for me I should instance this (Wilson Harris)."

Stirring sentiments from a man who was to later serve in Parliament as an Independent MP for Cambridge University. Clearly not everyone at Plymouth and Mannamead College was blinded by the jingoism of the Empire builders, and if the Head wasn't, one can only wonder at how far and how subtly his influence was spread.

But we must remember that our social climate and global understanding were very limited then and even before the "Letters from the Empire," there had been less-than-glowing articles on the "Japs", "Johnny Chinaman" and a piece on Charles Slaughter OM, who described Australian Aborigines as *"degraded specimens of humanity and very treacherous"*.

The world was indeed very different then and Charles Ryall was not the first OP to have lost his life serving his country - that dubious honour fell to Nicholas Lewarne.

Captain Nicholas Lewarne OP, killed in action, 1897

"Nickey, as he was called, was deservedly popular ... He carried off the "Victor Ludorum" Cup in 1883, the first year that one was given, he was the most dashing centre-forward the school has ever had .. and he made an enormous number of runs in 1884."

In 1885 he passed into Sandhurst *"where he distinguished himself in every way"*. In 1897 he was *"ordered to the North-West Frontier of India, and it was whilst gallantly leading a company of his regiment (15th Sikhs) in an attack on the enemy's stronghold that Captain Lewarne met his death."*

Among those monitoring events on the frontline with the keenest interest back home were the various members of the Cadet Corps. Ironically of course Lewarne's fateful year had already seen *"the greatest day in the history of Corps - Tuesday, June 29th, 1897"*.

Jubiliee celebtrations on Plymouth Hoe

It was the year of Queen Victoria's Diamond Jubilee and among the many events organised to celebrate the occasion was a *"Review by Her Majesty The Queen of the Cadet Corps of the Public Schools"*.

The Press subsequently hailed it as being *"perhaps the most picturesque event of the Jubilee Celebrations"* and in order to take part a way had to be found of transporting the school Cadet Corps to Windsor and back in one day.

A special train was timed to leave Mutley Station at 5.10 am and Colson was there on the platform to wish the boys "bon voyage". *"Most of us had had quite sufficient of the Great Western Railway by the time Windsor Castle was sighted, and then within a few minutes of half-past twelve our journey was at an end."* Mr. (Lieutenant) Woodcock was in command and an unprecedented six pages were given over in the Plymothian to an account of the day. In all some 3,600 cadets appeared before the Queen and *"as the royal carriages drove slowly past at only a few yards distance we were all enabled to get a good view of both Her Majesty and of the Princess Beatrice who accompanied her."*

Hopefully Her Majesty formed a good impression of the school too;

"It is a very invidious task to pick out any school for special mention, when there are so many which deserved it; but among the rest, one may select schools which caught an individual eye, and pleased an individual taste, the Dulwich boys in the neat uniform of the King's Royal Rifles, the grey Eton boys, and the Scarlet Winchesters, the Mannamead (Plymouth) Artillery, and the Malvern busbies and the dark green of Charterhouse", were all singled out in the account that appeared in the Graphic on July 3rd.

Public Schools Review from 'the Graphic' July 3rd 1897

The Cadets were undoubtedly a credit to the school, but there were others who, individually were doing much to enhance the reputation of Plymouth and Mannamead College in the eyes of the "Establishment", not least among them HA Brown.

Captain of the School in 1898, HA Brown *"had been at the College 11 years - longer than anyone else connected with it even among the masters ... He was a thorough all-round man, giving conscientious attention to everything he took up, and having a high sense of school patriotism."* A great scholar as well as being a first eleven footballer and cricketer, Brown was the 1898 Victor Ludorum and set a new school record for the mile, he also won a Senior Mathematical Scholarship to Caius, Cambridge ... *"where we hope to hear of his continued success"*.

And so they did, in April 1901 he beat all the Oxford runners in the Inter-Varsity mile, unfortunately though he lost out again to Cockshott *"an exceptionally good man"* who twice deprived him of a full Blue. However there was further cause for celebration a few months later when the school was given a *"whole holiday in honour of the recent successes of HA Brown (3rd Wrangler) at Cambridge , and A Maxwell (1st Class in Classical Moderations) at Oxford"*.

HA Brown with his family (his four brothers also went to the school) on a family picnic at Bull Point - 1898

1898

1897 1st XI Back row l-r; EH Watt, CRB Lane, AC Magnus, GWLS Lovell. Middle; AG Thomas, RHS More, PL Coleridge, AJ Ellis, H Brown. Front; HN Millett and EP Cudlip.

1897/8 1st Back row; RHS More, PL Coleridge, AG Thomas. Middle; FE Bowden, GWLS Lovell, R Milnes. Front; HA Brown, CB Smith, WP Groser, GD Brook and CRB Lane.

Small wonder therefore that around this time there were letters to the magazine suggesting that the school should have an honours board *"filled up with the names of those who have won honours for the School at the Universities and in both the Services"*. There were such lists already in the Chapel at Palmer's House (i.e. what had been Mannamead School). One letter making such a proposal was signed "A.B." (as in H.A.Brown

perhaps?), whoever wrote the missive though it's sentiments did not fall on deaf ears.

February 1899 ... *"The aspect of Big School has been much improved by the appearance of a handsome board inscribed with the names of winners of University Scholarships. For this the School is indebted to the generosity of Mr Thompson".*

Joseph Thompson was also among the leading contributors to the "Railing" or "Permanent Enclosure Fund". Colson himself though was the largest single donor and in his Summer 1899 account he was able to report that two sides of the fence had been put in place and the *"additional piece of fencing in what is now the vegetable garden"*, together this came to over £300, then there was the estimate for the *"stone wall and putting in the corner by the lavatory"*, all of which still left the *"side of the field adjoining the Cemetery Road ... This is not quite so pressing, but still I think every one will agree that the work will not be satisfactory until it has been dealt with"*.

The head said he favoured a dwarf stone wall surmounted with an iron fence, *"but if it is thought that a plain iron fence to match the rest would be satisfactory, the cost is not likely to be more than £100"* - about half the cost of the stone plus fence option.

"I think I may say that scheme of building a caretaker's cottage on the waste piece has been practically abandoned, at any rate for the present. When this scheme was in favour the idea of using this piece as a vegetable garden had not been suggested; and anyone who sees the rich and well ordered fertility which our tenants have created so quickly, will probably agree that we are not likely to improve on the present arrangement".

The fact that the pitch was now more effectively cordoned off had resulted in an instant improvement in the amount of trespassing, however it had little immediate effect on the quality of the pitches themselves.

1st XI Back row; AG Thomas, C Basden-Smith, EP Cudlip, FE Bowden. Middle; AJ Ellis, PL Coleridge, RHS More, HA Brown, CRB Lane. Front CH Watt, GD Brook.

As R.O.L.Ler noted in the July 1899 Plymothian;
"Dear Sirs;
Could not more trouble be taken about making the pitches level on which the 2nd XI House Matches are played, as usually they are hardly fit to play on."

And apparently it wasn't much better for the 1st XI, from the following summer we read a similar sentiment in Giglamps letter;
"Sirs,
May I suggest that during the football term the cricket square be enclosed. I find that it would not interfere with any football pitch, and would vastly improve the wickets next season."

Perhaps it was on account of all this pressure that extra steps were taken and perhaps it was because of the primitive DIY system then in place that one of the most costly accidents occurred on the school field.

The incident in question was the subject of the famous Bulteel trial, a trial that caused the school and particularly the headmaster a good deal of grief. Who better therefore to give an account of it?

1899

"Probably to most readers of this (wrote Colson in 1927) this trial is a mere name, if that. The school had always, like the great majority of Public Schools, been accustomed to enlist parties of boys to roll the cricket pitch. In March, 1899, it was found necessary to roll part of the running track. A party was organized and in the course of a moment's "ragging" Walter Bulteel fell in front of the roller, the edge of which passed over his head. His life was saved through the facts that the ground was soft and that the roller had not been filled with water, and as a matter of fact his injuries were in no way permanent. His father however held the School responsible, and after two years discussion the trial was held in London. Our Counsel was Mr. Duke, now Lord Merivale. We had obtained ample evidence of the commonness of the practice, and masters from well-known schools were in attendance to give evidence to this effect. It seemed, however, that the method of drawing the roller employed by them and us was not exactly the same, and Mr Duke, rightly or wrongly, did not call them. Mr Bulteel obtained damages of £380, and our costs were about £1,000, though happily a considerable part of this was obtained by subscription from the public, whose sympathy was mainly on our side."

"Though one could not feel culpable negligence with regard to a practice so long established and so widely used, experience had proved that it was dangerous and I think that the father had a right to some compensation, if he cared to claim it. In fact we had "without prejudice" offered him a larger sum than he actually obtained. Walter Bulteel went to Newton, and our chief score in the trial was obtained by extracts from the Newtonian, which extolled his prowess on the football field, and formed an amusing contrast to the sombre description of his injuries given by his counsel."

The method of pulling the horse roller in question incidentally was by ropes and although little reference was made to the incident itself in the Plymothian, one aspect of the matter was not missed, and that was the fact that at the actual scene of the accident the ground was mercifully soft;

"We cannot refrain from some allusion to the "ditch" which has been discovered, after twenty years of obscurity, at the bottom of the field. No doubt it will afford as much gratification as astonishment to the heroes of the Athletic Sports during the last twenty years to discover that their records have been established on a track intersected by "a furrow 18in deep and 9ft 6in broad at its widest part"."

Copies of the trial reports were freely circulated and Colson himself had printed *"a few notes elucidating and correcting"* other accounts. Apparently one of the best versions of the case appeared in the Times, but the newspaper refused to allow it to be reprinted.

Colson's home and the boarding house - Valletort 1897

Clearly it was a big case and a very expensive one for the school and a great relief when it was all over. To put the matter of £1,000 costs in some sort of context the total expenditure for the new swimming pool was only £900, so clearly, with the damages added on, the financial implications were substantial.

However Walter Bulteel seemingly prospered and the school survived. Other pupils were not so fortunate, however, and although the causes were generally natural ones, death was not an infrequent visitor to the school at this time.

On 14 June 1899, *"Adams ii, died from peritonitis"*, two years earlier, H Roberts *"lost his life while bathing ... Roberts had been among us three years and was one of the most promising boys in the School"* - his father incidentally *"also lost his life in a vain edeavour to save his son"*. Also that year nineteen year-old CF Phillips died at his home in Falmouth. In November 1898, the school's geography teacher Mr Murch died of a heart attack and in the early part of 1901 the peripatetic business teacher Mr Prior fell victim to influenza.

In 1902 *"owing to a scarlet fever scare (to which are nerves are now getting quite accustomed), the School for a week found itself divided into three - each House, confined in quarantine, being transformed into a small private school, so to speak and working as usual, under the House-masters, who to the obvious disappointment of the boarders, were quarantined as well. Meanwhile, in the school buildings, a day school of some 130 boys was being carried on by the six available masters"*.

And of course it wasn't just the boys who suffered, in 1906 the School was again visited by the scarlet fever and that same year several teachers, Messrs. Gwyther, Palmer and Gardiner had long absences through illness. In July 1906 thirteen year old RW Wagner, a doctor's son who had only just joined the School, died and the following year the Captain of the School, RC Crews, a very talented young man who had just won *"an open Demyship at Magdelen, and was apparently on the verge of a successful future"*, died, *"when a sudden relapse after an attack of scarlet fever proved unexpectedly fatal."*

Illness was another sad fact of life and in 1901 another virulent outbreak of measles stopped concerts, caused havoc with the examinations and led to the cancellaton of a good many sporting fixtures at the school and outside it. The outbreak *"satisfied apparently with the alarm it inspired in the school, and the still greater sensation which it seems to have caused in the town .. then relaxed its efforts"* - but not before Kelly College had also fallen prey to the affliction and a combined Field Day had to be postponed.

Kelly may well have been relieved by this for their encounters with the school that year were not always happy ones for them. It was the year that the Blackwell brothers dominated the school sporting records, particularly on the cricket pitch, and in the home fixture against Kelly the school won by an innings and 78 runs. The three Blackwell brothers then in the side top-scoring for their team and logging over half the school's runs. WG and H Blackwell twice bowling Kelly out for just 25 - the two brothers each claiming ten wickets. In the away match it was much the same story: H Blackwell scored 122 of the school's 301-9 and took 5 wickets for 31 as Kelly were skittled out for 120.

Come the end of the season H Blackwell *"not only obtained the best batting and bowling averages in the*

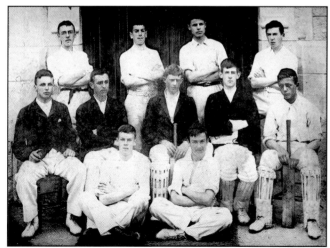

st XI Back row; LS Samson, ES Coppin, CL Spalding, N Maxwell. Middle; H Blackwell, WG Blackwell, GD Brook, GE Berry, HC Pinsent. Front HBI Pocock, EG Mackenzie.

history of the School, but also the highest aggregate of runs and wickets". Small wonder therefore that a picture of H was published in the "Public School Magazine" and subsequently reproduced in the Plymothian earning the distinction of being the first ever photograph to be printed in the School magazine.

H. BLACKWELL,
Captain of Cricket.

It was around this time incidentally (July 1901) that, some sixty or so years ahead of the event, the OPM Club resolved to publish an annual magazine *"at the end of each year or the beginning of the next"*.

The OPM Club was entering a very healthy phase at this point, membership had just risen from 96 to 120 and a Chess Club had been added to the list of OPM offshoots, sadly for us however, *"a proposal for the compilation of a History of the School was dropped"* ... however ran the report *"this may be considered on another occasion"*.

The proposal for issuing an Old Boys Annual was also withdrawn *"for financial reasons"*. Overall though the Club was clearly growing all the time and in response to a suggestion for a Club motto the Headmaster proposed *"Juvat Meminisse"* - *"It is pleasing to remember"* and the motion was unanimously approved.

Such is not to say that there weren't problems in the ranks; for a start it seemed that many OPMs *"prefer any football shirt rather than the OPM colours? These colours are indisputably the prettiest in the neighbourhood, and yet we believe only two players possess them ... The shirts may be obtained from Messrs GS Evens, Oxford"* (but not anywhere in Plymouth!).

Secondly there was, even then, the problem of *"Old Boys playing for other clubs"* (March 1901).

However this did not deter efforts to increase the scope of the OPM sporting sections and later that year B Hamilton Whiteford announced his intention of putting together an OPM hockey team.

At that time the School were not playing hockey themselves, officially, but the following term we learn that the games committee had decided that *"Hockey is to be played next term (January 1902) ... with some possible restrictions as to age and size"*.

1901 Football XI Back: T Hudson, EG Mackenzie. Middle; GH Thomas, RGF Foord, RS James. Front; FE Weekes, HF Glanville, HBI Pocock, HB Blackwell, ES Coppin.

!901 Cricket XI. Back T Martyn, K Burns, TNL Barber, HM Blackwell. Middle; EG Mackenzie, HC Pinsent, H Blackwell, N Maxwell, LS Sansom. Front; HF Glanville, FJ Hicks.

It's worth noting perhaps that it was also around this time that what now passes for the OPM badge was adopted by the school as its new crest. Prior to 1898 the title page of the Plymothian had been adorned with

a version of the Plymouth crest - a simple saltire with the four towers of the town's medieval castle in each division - and although there had been suggestions that there should be a new school crest ever since the amalgamation, nothing was formally done about it until *"the necessity of framing a joint shooting trophy with Exeter and Kelly", forced matters on in the summer of 1898. From then we read that "a neat design has been decided on, representing a ship with lighthouse, surrounded by a joined band, with the dates of the formation of Plymouth College and Mannamead School together with that of the amalgamation. The motto, "L'Union fait la force," had already long been decided. We hope all necessary arrangements will be completed, so that the crest may be used for stationery, &c., by all who wish."*

In July 1898 the crest made its debut on the front page of the Plymothian. *"Strength in union"* and with the consequences of that union still under review, before the year was out another item in the magazine raised the football/rugby debate ... *"there seems to be a strong desire for change in the School itself, and it appears likely that Rugby will at any rate be given a trial".*

And so it was, viz. Plymothian, April 1899;

"The Rugby game has had a fair trial, and it is remarkable what a fatality there seems to be about the game with us. Three injuries in the dozen or so games played is a rather large proportion. It may not be generally known, too, that Rugby was the original game of the School, and was given up partly because of an accident that occurred in it. For ourselves, we do not think that Rugby is a particle more dangerous than Association, and no doubt those accidents were caused by the want of experience of the players, but the very fact of their occurrence will naturally not prejudice the minds of parents in its favour. We are therefore inclined to think that the supporters of Rugby are wise in not bringing the question definitely before the authorities".

Eight of this eleven played Argyle on 15 October 1898 at Ford Park. The School team lost 8-1. Team, back row: RHS More, WG Blackwell, JM Hodge. Middle; T Hudson, G Thom, Heard. Front; C Basden-Smith, AJ Ellis, GD Brook, HBI Pocock and ES Coppin.

Fate is a funny thing and looking back now it is strange to see just how circumstance played such a large part in the history of the School. It was very much the same with the swimming pool, news of which was announced thus in the Plymothian of June 1901;

"It is our pleasant duty to record what is no doubt familiar to most of our readers, the munificent gift to the School of a Swimming Bath, at a cost of £900. The donor of this generous gift wishes to remain anonymous, for the present, at any rate, but we can assure him, if he reads these lines, of the deep gratitude felt by every member of the School. The plans of the bath are already prepared and it will be ready for use next Spring. It is to be built on the disused tennis court by the gymnasium and will be unroofed, but surrounded by closed dressing sheds."

A few months later the editors were able to report *"substantial progress towards the construction ... the excavations at present in progress are arousing much interest from the admiring crowd to be seen there during the day."*

They added; *"We are also happy to draw attention to the state of the Lavatory - now. No longer are the names of its former frequenters handed down to an admiring posterity!"*

Plus ca change!   The next few lines are interesting too as we learn that *"The quantity of earth put at our disposal by the digging of the bath is being utilised for the levelling of the corner of the field near the gate. Solemn and unbroken processions of heavy carts drawn by stolid horses with feet of the type known as "useful" have converted our "path" into a rutty quagmire ... We may take this occasion to warn visitors to go round to the top gate on the Concert night ... Could not the opportunity be seized, and our path made a little more serviceable than hitherto."*

There was, it seems, danger on every corner, such were the hazards of life in late-Victorian England, only by this stage Victoria was no longer Queen, for, on 22 January 1901 the great lady had passed peacefully away at her seaside home at Cowes on the Isle of Wight.

"We first knew" wrote Wilson Harris again in Life So Far, *"by hearing the boys with late editions of the evening papers crying up and down the roads near my home "Death of Queen Victoria"."*

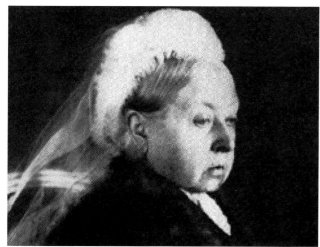

The late Queen Victoria

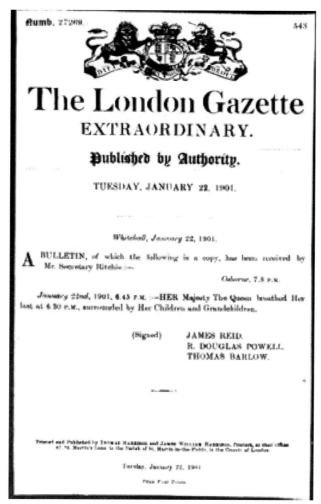

The big news story of the day knocks all the advertising off the front page of all the daily papers.

Wilson Harris was at that time Captain of the School - Head Boy - and ex-officio head of the Games Committee, and by his own admission rather hoped that the Headmaster *"if he had any proper feeling ... would arrange it for him to be the first boy in the bath"*, but he didn't.   The bath here being the new swimming pool, which, interestingly enough *"was not to be opened formally"*, rather it was *"to be made available to the rabble after school on a certain morning."*

"That kept my chances of priority pretty low. But it happened that during one period that morning I was working, alone and unsupervised, at Latin verse or something, in an alcove in one of the corridors. Occasion is meant to be taken by the hand, not neglected. I nipped out to the changing-room, stripped and donned a bathing slip in several seconds less than no time, dashed over to the bath, swam a length and was back in my alcove clothed and contented and unashamed after roughly five minutes' absence. It was all, as it turned out, barely necessary, for when the authorized rush came at 12.30 I was only beaten by a split second for the first dive by a boy from Palmer's House called Mackenzie."

By this stage the identity of the anonymous benefactor who had entirely funded the swimming pool project had been revealed - it was none other than the assistant master, Joseph Thompson, as we learn from the foundation stone of the baths which was laid by Mrs Colson on 14 December 1901. At the same time Mr Thompson also defrayed the costs of having the fives courts relaid, making the total value of his gift to the school that year in the order of £1,000, an enormous sum when you consider that most teachers then were earning less than £100 - per year!

Joseph Thompson - teacher and benefactor.

While Plymouth College staff may undoubtedly have been in receipt of above-average salaries it is interesting to note that, at the end of 1900, a report on Education in Plymouth's fifteen Board Schools revealed that there were a total of 323 teachers (58 more than in 1897) in service but only half of them had teaching certificates. A quarter of the Board School teachers were paid over £100 but most, 46% received between £50 and £100, while 30% earned less than £50.

Joseph Thompson was clearly then a man of very substantial means and although *"he was himself giving back to the school in one way or another the whole of his own salary ... he strenuously insisted on adequate salaries and was a protagonist for improvements in rates of pay* (CR Serpell in his History of Plymouth College)".

The swimming pool was neither the first nor the last of Thompson's great contributions, it does however remain the most conspicuous and in those early days of the twentieth century where such baths were few and far between, it was an instant success with the boys.

It was also undoubtedly looked upon by the wider community as a sign that the school was prospering and it's no wonder that, despite the adverse publicity surrounding the Bulteel case, in the Christmas term of 1901 the school increased *"by over 8%., the largest in any single term since the amalgamation in 1896"*.

Happier times for headmaster Colson and one can only guess at what he thought when Archbishop Temple, a founding father of the school and still nominally a governor, who had said to him ten years earlier *"Oh that place has never succeeded"*, sent *" a very small cheque"* towards the Bulteel fund. Reading between the lines we can be sure that Colson was deservedly proud of having pulled the school around and one suspects he would have relished rewriting Temple's perception of the place.

Incidentally Temple himself made the newspaper headlines later that summer (9 August 1902) when he

had to be helped from his knees at the coronation of Edward VII at Westminster Abbey. It was the King himself who lifted the frail archbishop after the ageing cleric had sworn allegiance to the new monarch on behalf of the church.

There was no such frailty in evidence at the opening of the school pool however. Opened officially on 6 May 1902, it had been the original intention to hold an aquatic display that day but the headmaster in his introductory remarks *"explained that it had been found impracticable, owing to the coldness of the weather ... and so the afternoon's ceremony would simply consist of the formal opening by the Mayor"*.

Diving in the deep end. The new pool is the envy of Plymouth.

For his part the Mayor, Henry Hurrell (or possibly still Joseph Bellamy) said that the swimming bath was *"a splendid institution"* and looking at it *"he could not help hoping that before long they would have a similar one for the rest of the boys of Plymouth. They were proud of the College, and there was no doubt that the masters had devoted themselves to bringing it to the premier position in the West of England"*

The Chairman of the Governors then thanked Mr Thompson for his munificent gift and Thompson, replying, said he *"was very glad to see the bath completed, and he hoped the boys would make good use of it."*

He then added that *"one of the chief motives that had prompted him in presenting the bath was finding how many boys in the school were unable to swim. Swimming,"* he said, *"was as important as any lesson in the school curriculum, and the boys could express their thanks to him in no better way than by enabling him to say at the start of the term that not a boy was unable to swim."*

The concern was a real enough one too, for almost every month it seemed that the local papers carried stories of boys drowned. The Hoe, Mount Wise and the Plym Estuary being the most common scenes of such tragic fatalities. Indeed in the November magazine one OPM, CD Back, writing from Singapore, offered a Silver Cup for the most expert *"man in the water"*. Mr Back, now a British Indian Marine, said he didn't just mean swimming to keep afloat either, *"but also the ability to swim in a full suit of clothes, and to render aid to a drowning man or woman when necessary."*

Within six weeks of the pool opening about a hundred boys had joined the baths and although at first only 35 could swim the test of two lengths (50 yards), another 30 soon qualified *"a good testimony to Mr Searl's tuition."*

"It is perhaps too early to judge", wrote the editors of the Plymothian in the July edition, *"but it has several*

times struck us that as affording a new field for keenness and espirit de corps, the bath is already providing itself invaluable, and if this is really the case we are confident that it will have a more beneficial effect on the School than any quantity of centuries or record-breaking."

Enjoying the new facility.

It was also recorded that a number of OPMs were taking advantage of the bath, although there was a certain amount of dispute about the charges. Initially there was an annual subscription for OPMs of 7/6d, with hours of use for them restricted to 6.45 to 8am, 12.30 to 1.20pm and 5 to 7.30pm. The hours for Wednesdays and Saturdays being slightly different, still 6.45-8am but no midday session and an extended afternoon/ evening period of 3 to 7pm.

In the first ever annual Aquatic Sports, incidentally, held on 26 July 1902, Wilson Harris proved himself quick off the mark once more, winning the senior 50-yard race and coming second to H Blackwell in the 25-yard sprint. FL Cunningham won all three of the junior races.

Back in May, Blackwell had just pipped Harris for the title of Victor Ludorum at the school sports. Harris won the mile and half mile and set a new school record for the long jump along with Blackwell, both jumping 19feet 10inches. Blackwell, meanwhile, set a new record for the hurdles; was just an inch short of the record high jump at 5ft 1½in and threw a cricket ball further than anyone other than his elder brother had ever done before.

May 1902 Harris wins the mile race

With around 150 boys at the school, including the Prep, there was clearly less competition in those days. Nevertheless certain young men were clearly outstanding and H Blackwell and his boarding brothers from Helston played a major part in all aspects of the school; they sang in the concerts, they played in the bands ... H - a fine clarinettist and keyboard player and was "*musician-in-general to the school in his last*

two years" ..."*it will be a bad day for music as for the cricket of the school when they disappear.*"

There were five brothers in all and they appeared in the speech day plays, they were in the cadet corps - H was the Company Sergeant Major, H and HM proved to be an unbeatable combination in the inter-house fives competition and they also beat Kelly as the school fives team in 1903.

June 1902 Cricket XI. Back; K Burns, IS Watts, MH Langford, MH Kingcome. Middle; TN Barber, HBI Pocock, H Blackwell, HM Blackwell, EG Mackenzie. Front; GAVN Thomas, R Barber.

That same year HM Blackwell was selected to play for the Cornwall County Cricket side while H took 6-15 against the Lancashire Regiment (including 4 wickets in 4 balls), and later 8-31 against Argyle at Home Park on coconut matting. H was also described in his valedictory report as being a "*fine boxer, and altogether the sort of person to have on your side in a row*". Clearly though he wasn't a victim of his own success "*In spite of the many triumphs which his varied talents won him, Blackwell always conducted himself with a modesty which was not the least becoming of his attributes. Perhaps this is the most valuable lesson that his brilliant career should teach his juniors.*"

May 1902 Victor Ludorum Blackwell competing in the High Jump. Note the scaffolding in the background on the left, as Hyde Park School starts to take shape.

Needless to say he *"passed triumphantly at the first attempt into Sandhurst"*.

1903 Cricket XI Back row: l-r PD Stuart, GR Heard, D Paige. Middle; R Barber, HBI Pocock, H Blackwell, HM Blackwell, GAVN Thomas. Front; FG Cooper, CHA Crouch, TF Coke.

As well as being captain of cricket Blackwell also enjoyed the distinction of being one of the last football captains the school has ever had. The round ball game was undoubtedly on the wane by this time and there appeared too little enthusiasm for either playing or watching on Wednesday or Saturday afternoons, as a leaver of some 5 or 6 years observed in the July 1902 Plymothian; *"when I was at the College the option used to be given to us of either playing in any game or watching the 1st eleven play, and unless a boy had a feasible excuse his absence would not be permitted"* and the *"football or cricket field was surrounded by a group of enthusiastic fellows, but now a good tackle or a fine stroke goes practically unnoticed."*

In this same season the OPM XI played the fewest number of fixtures yet - four - and, for the first time ever, all of them were lost. There was talk of blacklisting any OPM's playing for other teams, particularly against their own colleagues, but the agenda was changing and even the school had but a few fixtures and most of them against Service sides, although they did secure an honourable 4-4 draw with Argyle's Wednesday side. The return match was not so successful, the school led 3-2 at half-time but Argyle posted eight goals past the hapless school keeper in the second half, with hardly any opposition.

This was, though, 1903, the year that Argyle went professional and this appears to have been the last formal fixture between the two sides. In the 1903/4 season the school played instead the newly-formed Plymouth Wednesday team. So newly-formed in fact that the first encounter was Wednesday's first full match and the school won it 5-0. However in the return, played at Oreston, the new side, strengthened with a couple of Argyle reserves, finished 2-1 victors.

Clearly apathy for the old game affected other aspects of the match too as another correspondent to the magazine noted in December 1903;

"Dear Sirs, May I venture to ask what has become of the old custom of serving out lemons at half-time to the 1st XI and their opponents? Cannot something be done to revive the custom? In two instances I have seen our opponents produce their own lemons."

However the issues surrounding association football had, by this stage, been rendered largely irrelevant as earlier that term, on the 9th October 1903, Mr Gwyther put the proposal to the Debating Society that *"Rugby Football should be introduced into the School"*.

It was, though, no ordinary meeting of the Debating Society as *"the object of the motion was to find out the feeling of the School as to a possible change, owing to the steady diminuation of the school games, and our inability to secure an inter-school fixture ... Accordingly the whole of the Upper School was admitted, and the question fairly argued out before a large and interested audience. The mover was seconded by Mr Thompson and opposed by Mr Woodcock and Mr Gardiner. No spirit of prejudice was shown by either the speakers or the audience, who had evidently come ready to give the question a fair and impartial hearing"*. In the event the motion was carried *"with most unexpected unanimity, the minority consisting of one only"*.

Mr Gwyther, who had come to the school from Oxford University and had a Cambridge degree was clearly a full-blooded rugger man and must have been delighted with the result.

His case was perhaps in no small measure helped by the fact that a few months earlier JR Walkey, of Christ's College, Cambridge, *"won the first full Blue ever obtained by an old College boy"*. An auspicious day for the School except that bizarrely it was for Rugby and as the magazine editors noted *"as an Association school, we can hardly share the honour ... But Walkey took a prominent part in the games organised after the Amalgamation"*, games that, doubtless, George Gwyther played a large part in too.

Fixtures of course were already in place for the current season and as it transpired the 1st XI had a reasonable time of it, with 15 fixtures, winning six and losing six, drawing the rest with a positive goal tally of 38-29.

Football XI 1902. Back FG Cooper, MH Langford, EG Mackenzie. Middle; EG Cullum, HM Blackwell, R Barber. Front; WE Law, HM Legassick, HBI Pocock, H Hancock, HL Davis.

Messrs Gardiner and Pocock both turned out for the School and Messrs Woodcock and Sargent refereed. Ernest Gardiner and Bert Sargent were both new to the staffroom in 1903 and as junior members were doubtless quite prepared to go with the flow.

The last association game against OPMs was played on 12 December 1903 and ended honours even, 2-2. Four days later, in one of the last-ever scheduled football matches, the School beat the Avenue 3-2 at Vinstone Park.

The last School Football XI ? 1903. Back; FG Cooper, EL Blackwell, GA Thomas. Middle; CHA Crouch, R Barber, CD Kerr. Front WF Rice, HM Shapcott, EB Champerowne, D Paige WU Broad.

The change of the main game thereafter was swift and on 5 March 1904 the School 1st XV played a practice game against Argaum Reserves. Argaum fielded several of their first team players though and not only outmanoeuvred their younger opposition they also substantially outweighed them and scored an easy seven tries, two of which they converted, while the School failed to score. There was an even greater tale of woe against *"our future rivals"* - Kelly - on 16 March. Seen as being the footballing fixture that would replace the old bi-annual contest with the now long-since-amalgamated Mannamead School the first blood

went convincingly to Kelly by *"6 goals 8 tries to nil"*. Small wonder therefore to read that punch-drunk members of the 1st XV wrote, in an unprecedented three page post-match appraisal *"we have gratefully accepted the kind offer of the Argaum team to send up players regularly every Wednesday next Christmas term to play, not against us but among us and so raise the level of play generally"*.

Small wonder too that the following ode was submitted and printed in that term's magazine;

"There is blood on his beetling brow,
There is blood in his glaring eye,
And he walks with the grace of a drunken cow,
And a buccaneer's modesty.
Tell me, tell -
(Though I know full well)
What does it signify?
You'll murmur it low,
Of course, just so,
"Rugger! old man! That's why."

Nor was it just the 1st fifteen that had been introduced to the game by this stage. Throughout February and March almost fifty boys - a third of the school - had been involved in a 12-a-side, inter-house, senior competition which was won, quite convincingly, by North Town House who together with Palmer's House had most of the 1st XV players.

In October *"the opening match of the season set at rest any doubts we may have had before as to the great improvement of our team since last spring"* and although the Arguam side that played that day was markedly weaker than the one faced that spring the fact *"we only had one try scored against us, was very encouraging"*. Particularly, it must be said because Mr Pocock (who had himself originally joined the school in amalgamation year - 1896 and had completed his schooling the previous year), had scored for the School and that try had been converted giving the side their first victory with the oval ball.

The first 1st XV: Back WU Broad. Third row; PD Butcher, H WInnicott, GS Maginness, GT Broad. Second row; RC Crews, J Brown, SL Heard, LN Brown. Front; JS Nias, CH Sansom, FG Cooper, HG Tennison, FH Lane.

Later in the month a Wednesday game against the Border Regiment was a slightly different story *"their arrival at our ground somewhat appalled us, as they averaged some two stone per man more than our team"*. Inevitably it was another heavy defeat for the inexperienced boys (46-0) but there were encouraging signs and there was an interesting footnote from the match reporters;

"Our heartiest thanks are due to the Officers of the Border Regiment for the interest they afterwards showed in our team."

The true test of the new sport however came on Saturday 22 October 1904 - *"The first real match in football against a rival school that we have enjoyed since the last College v Mannamead match in November 1895, and was looked forward to with great anticipation. Our determination was to wipe off as many points as possible from the score which Kelly had run up against us in the friendly game they had given us last spring."*

In the event a 51-0 deficit was reduced to a margin of 20-3. FG Cooper it was who became the first boy at the school to score for the 1st XV.

It was enough to inspire the editors of the first Plymothian of 1905 to wax thus;

"Whatever difficulty Editors of this Magazine may sometimes find in distinguishing any event of the year which they are reviewing as of unusual importance, there can be no doubt that on this occasion at least we do not err in so distinguishing the appearance of our first Rugby XV. It was during the year 1904 that we won our first Rugby victory, that we scored our first try against Kelly College, that we first afforded more than one Devonshire school a hard-fought game of football; and these facts will assuredly be remembered by the future historian of the school."

They then speculated about the prospect of beating a fellow Devonshire school in the coming season and followed it with a eulogy to the thirty-six year-old man most responsible for the change - George Gwyther;

"The really great advance made by the school in the knowledge of the Rugby game, is due, to an even larger extent than most of us realise, to the great interest shown by Mr Gwyther in our progress. His self-sacrifice in giving up his spare time, both to coaching the xv. And refereeing in the games, and to attending all our matches at home and away, must raise a feeling of gratitude, especially of course in the xv., but also in the whole school."

Again there was a note of optimism for the coming season and after years of sporting fixtures against Service sides it was a healthy move to see Kelly, Newton College, Allhallows' School and Exeter School among the forthcoming encounters, including a 2nd XV game against Kelly.

Argaum were still on the list though and again they trounced the lighter boys (63-5), but come November 1905 Newton College became the first school scalp claimed by Plymouth College. They also beat the Three Towns Law Students, in very poor weather, *"by 4 tries to 1 ... Owing to the heavy ball no tries were converted"*. Meanwhile the seconds beat Kelly 11-9.

Kelly were undoubtedly the principal "enemy" - for the Cadet Corps in their regular moorland battles, for the fives teams (such as could be raised by the School), by the cricket XI and now, at last, by a rugby XV. In 1906 we find two pages given over to this fixture and clearly it had been well promoted around throughout the School;

"This is the first time since the old College-Mannamead days that the school has turned up in such numbers to watch a football match, and we won; the moral is obvious". The scoreline was less so; 8-3, in favour of the School, but it was a notable victory and one that meant the encounter was destined to be a major fixture for many years to come.

Rugby XV 1905/06 Top; GT Broad. Back row; RC Weeks, GS Maguinness, HP Hodge, AB Norman. Third, row; J I Stuttaford, HD Hodge. Second row, JS Nias, AC Hancock, HG Jennsion, RC Crews. Front; LE Morgan, AH Macklin, CC Langford.

The following season the place of the new game was well and truly consolidated as the 1st XV won 11 of their 14 encounters, including their game against the newly-formed OPM XV.

The switch from football to rugby followed inevitably on from the change at School. With no "Past v Present" football encounter in the 1903/4 season and another date being scratched there were only 3 OPM matches - Christmas Eve against the Border Regiment at Crownhill (lost 5-4), Boxing Day against St Austell (lost 2-1) and finally at Launceston (lost 3-1).

"There is one redeeming feature in the above rather poor record, namely, we always turned out with a full team! That in itself almost constitutes a record. Sooner or later Old Boys will have to consider the question of following the School's example and changing to Rugby, and the Secretary who undertakes to place fifteen OPMs on the field will have my heartiest sympathies. Although the changes will be regrettable, it will be unavoidable. Even playing members of the Club are not endowed with perpetual youth, and one of our most regular players was referred to at the Club Dinner as an "hoary headed old man"! Unless new blood is infused into the team it cannot exist many years more."

It was no surprise therefore when at the Annual Meeting of the Club, on 21 December 1906, it was decided to adopt *"the Rugby instead of the Association game in consonance with the same change at the school"* (WMN 22.12.06). The meeting was held at the Plymouth Law Chambers and the Headmaster presided. Mr EE Rogers was elected the first OPM Rugby captain, with ES Griggs, vice-captain and JA Brown, secretary. Officials of the OPM Cricket, Hockey, Tennis and Chess Clubs were also elected and it was reported that overall membership of the Club had risen from 183 in 1905 to 203 at present. Financially the club was reasonably healthy with £29.6s.2d and a further £9.9s.0d in pre-paid subscriptions to be added. Interestingly enough though it was noted that there were also *"many subscriptions in arrears"*.

Mention of the hockey and tennis sections suggests that here, as with the other sporting sections, there was perhaps a direct feed through of boys from school.

However early in 1903 we learn that "*the experiment of playing Hockey during the Easter term, has been discontinued ...Fives, Shooting, and Paper-chases, have been arranged for the Upper School.*"

The decision appears to have been a fairly arbitrary one and one that didn't meet with universal approval;

"*Many boys last year supplied themselves with sticks, which are now useless. Many of us were anticipating Hockey Matches against other schools this year*" wrote "Blue Bottle" in the March 1903 Plymothian, to which the editors replied;

"*We have received several letters on this subject, but can assure our Correspondents that there are excellent reasons for discontinuing Hockey in the School. There is no doubt that shooting and fives must inevitably suffer, if it is played, and this alone is sufficient reason for giving it up.*"

The renewed attempt to promote fives seemed to meet with little more success than it had in past years though. The 1904 fives fixture list featured only the OPMs and Kelly and even there the return match was scratched due to a fresh outbreak of chicken pox. An unusually full Inter-House competition that season seems to have forced a little more interest in the game and two years later we find the RNE College and "Mr Cohen's Team" fattening out the fixture list. But more fixtures did not mean more success and all the scheduled games were lost.

According to "Blackguard" (Plymothian April 1906) this was due to two things;

"*firstly, the game under present conditions is too expensive and secondly the game cannot be played in bad weather.*"

With the benefit of modern materials you could be forgiven for wondering what was so expensive about fives, happily for us though Blackguard supplied the answers;

"*The expense is caused by the number of shoes and balls that are used. As a rule, a pair of shoes will rarely last a hard player more than four afternoons, although of course there are two or three exceptions. Now, is it likely that a boy's parents will be willing to provide him with a new pair of shoes every fortnight?*"

"*A fives ball costs 2½d., and in some cases three balls are necessary for one single game.*"

Blackguard felt that the condition of the School fives courts was to blame - "*the same make of ball is used in other courts and one ball usually lasts through at least two games*" ... "*Surely there must be some cement which has a smoother surface than that which is used for our courts?*"

Unusually a reply was published to this letter - it was signed JT, whom we can doubtless assume was the teacher/benefactor Joseph Thompson, himself.

Thompson, who had contributed substantially to the improvement of the fives courts just a few years earlier was unconvinced by the arguments put forward;

"*As a matter of fact*", he wrote, "*the main cause of the relative badness of the Fives is the attention which has to be paid to Football.*"

JT's solution was to afford the game more time in the Autumn Term.

Mr Gwyther had got his way at last on the Rugby front, Mr Thompson, it would appear, was now trying to keep Fives alive. Hockey had already fallen prey to the efforts and judging by a report in the June 1907 Magazine, tennis suffered a similar fate. Following a suggestion that the school should make tennis courts in the field in front of the School House the editors noted that;

"*The field does not belong to us, and it is, rightly we think, an axiom that lawn tennis should not be encouraged at Public Schools.*"

Later in the year the editors were a little more charitable with a suggestion that "Diabolo" - "*we wondered how long we should be spared this suggestion*" - be introduced. This idea they ventured "*should be taken to some member of the games committee.*"

Cricket XI June 1904. Back row; RE Mercer, EB Champerowne, CH Sansom, JR Baker. Middle; CHA Crouch, GAVN Thomas, R Barber, D Paige, FG Cooper. Front; EL Blackwell, AC Hancock.

Cricket meanwhile seemed safe in its status as the traditional summer game - it was not without its minor problems though; "*Dear Sirs. I should like to propose that two boys (in the VIth or Vth form) be appointed as Umpires for House Matches (Senior) right through the Term. This would be a great benefit to all players, as now no suitable boy can be found to Umpire, and in consequence two players are sent out, who have to be continually changed in order to get their pads on*", wrote Bill Stumps.

While later in the year "Disgusted" complained that no umpires' coats were provided for the Second XI;

"*the excuse is that if used they would be left about on the field and get dirty ... The second XI have not a chance to prove their carelessness, for they have not had the coats once this term ... It is not a very satisfactory spectacle to see umpires, in a school match, without white coats.*"

Evidence did however suggest that not all equipment was properly looked after across the school. According to "Fish's Ear";

1903

"when one of these youthful C.B.Frys is bowled with a full-pitcher, he usually signifies his disgust either by knocking down the wickets with his bat, or throwing his bat violently against the wall or railings".

There were, incidentally, new railings in place by this time (April 1904), along the bottom of the field, but the sheep were still there;

"Might I", said the Voice of the Turtle, *"with all humility be allowed to protest against the presence of a Ram in the field. It is certainly very annoying when talking seriously about the discipline and management of the School, to be interrupted by feeling the horns of a ram butting one on the knees from behind - I know that it knocked over some lower school boys and I heard of attacks on Masters ..."*

Masters continued to dominate the batting and bowling averages of the school XI when playing non-school sides, particularly Messrs. Sargent, Gardiner and Pocock (in the 1905 season Mr Pocock enjoyed consecutive scores of 76, 76 and 67). A succession of professionals also performed well for the school.

Generally though, if the opinions of the debating society were anything to go by the school did not approve of the growth of professionalism in sport (it should be remembered that footballing rivals Argyle, turned professional as Plymouth Argyle in 1903).

As ever the topics brought before the School Debating Society continued to highlight the prevailing culture of the day.

With attendances averaging around 16-17 per meeting, with each debate having around five speeches, both for and against, usually with a least one or two each side from a master, the Debating Society was a relatively-healthy institution and its records make interesting reading now.

In March 1903 the house condemned the development of Esperanto. In October 1904 a motion to tax bachelors was thrown out, despite its protagonists arguing that it would; *"put gentle pressure on them for the benefit of the other sex, and a little gain put into the exchequer."* Mr Thompson, as one might expect, *"remarked that he was a bachelor and was taxed already".*

The votes-for-women issue was again raised, in March 1905, and this time was only defeated by the casting vote of the chairman. Later in the year *"Crews endeavoured to convince the House of the general undesirability of India as an Imperial Possession, but was defeated 17-4."* A few weeks later Parsloe urged the necessity of conscription and lost narrowly 11-10 and then on 17 November *"the Society discussed the expediency of keeping domestic servants"*;

"Austin upheld the institution as a necessary evil: if we had no servants we should have to eat our dinners cold or dine at our clubs. Crews proposed a lockout to bring our menials to their senses ... Norman proposed that we should employ the Heathen Chinee; and Hancock declaimed against education as the root of all evil. The commiseration of the Society was called on behalf of boarders who would have to make their own beds and black their own boots. Messrs. Sargent and Thompson both thought it was a good thing to learn such matters, but the House preferred that others should do the work".

Cricket XI 1905. Back row; GS Maginness, D Blackwell, G Underhill, PN Sansom. Middle; SL Heard, RE Mercer, CH Sansom, AC Hancock, JR Baker. Front; GT Broad, JI Stuttaford.

July 1905 - Above (Bellamy batting - without gloves) and left, cricket at Ford Park - note the new railings, the ivy-clad houses at the top of Kingsley Road and the open fields where the bungalows were later built.

The following year the House narrowly voted in favour of the Russian Government suppressing the revolt of the Russian peasantry. In the early part of 1906 a proposal to abolish war was overturned largely for fear of the increase of the unemployed

In March there was an impromptu debate about *"whether the fagging system should be instituted in the School"* ... Hancock vigorously asserting that such *"system already existed"*. It was then proposed that submarines should be abolished (the previous summer fourteen sailors were drowned when their submarine sank in Plymouth) - the motion was rejected.

The abolition of Street Music was discussed on another occasion and Parsloe pointed out *"that if the Italians were not allowed to grind organs and mechanical pianos, they would turn vendors of ice cream and poison us all"*. The next debate proposed a *"scheme of vegetarianism in order to improve the English race"*, against which Crews appealed to *"History and showed that it was beef that won the Battle of Waterloo."*

On the 9 March there was a joint debate with the Law Students, but only one Law Student and one Solicitor appeared and they were both OPMs.

There had been, by this stage, many strong links forged with the school. OPMs regularly took part in the School Concerts and Glees and there was even an OPM Debating Society, although attendances often left a little to be desired. Dinner numbers were better however and although the annual event had lapsed for a few years, the dinner held at Chubb's Hotel, on 30 December 1903 attracted 38 Old Boys (over a fifth of the membership) and the following year over 40, a club record, were in attendance at the Duke of Cornwall. All this hot on the heels of the first - *"but by no means the last"* ever London OPM dinner held at the Holborn Restaurant, on Saturday 12 November 1904. RH Brent Clark, then based at the Royal Artillery Barracks at Woolwich, was the co-ordinator of the affair and tickets were 6/- (30p).

Sixteen OPMs attended plus two guests. AP Roe presided, John Fouracre proposed "The School", CP Brown, replied and a telegram was sent congratulating Mr Colson *"on his fifteenth year of head-mastership"*. "Members were then regaled with the delightful and fluent discourse of WP Groser *"There are some, "* he remarked, in proposing the toast of the club, *"who asked what was the use of the Club - what did it do?"* He would like to remind them that it was not what the Club did so much as what it was - its very existence, which was important," a sentiment which was entirely endorsed by those present."

A committee was formed to arrange a similar re-union the next year and in the *"impromptu "Smoker" that followed, S Morris delighted the assembly with his excellent recitations in dialect".*

c. 1905, unidentified team with trophy, from an old glass negative.

Two years later we find Oxford OPMs staging their first Annual Dinner - in Buol's Cafe on Saturday 15 June 1907. HEM Icely, the senior OPM "up" and a former editor of the Plymothian, took the chair and at least seven OPMs were in attendance and it was deemed a great success.

"In the intervals between speeches, recitations and songs were given. GR and EB Champernowne (Christ Church) were both encored, the first for his "Glorious Devon", the second for "Widdicombe Fair" ... "Many other songs were sung, the choruses of which were taken up with such fervour, that two "bullers" thought it worthwhile to keep an eye on the door of the Cafe."

There appears to have been no formal proposal at this stage for a Cambridge Dinner but there must have been many OPMs dotted around the globe who looked longingly on these accounts.

Not FJ Tothill though, late in 1902 he had already set to on such a project out in Ceylon;

"HB Daniel (an Old Newtonian) and I are now collecting names with a view to having a dinner in Kandy next January, among the Old Boys' of Devon Schools. At present we have about forty or fifty names, so the dinner is pretty certain to come off and you may be sure it will be a great success ... You will be pleased to hear that Old Mannamead-Plymothians head the list so far sent in, with sixteen names."

All the Old Boys incidentally were members of the CPRC (Ceylon Planters' Rifle Corps) - *"we are over 1000 strong spread all over Ceylon"* ... *"the chief object of the Corps is to make every member efficient at shooting so that in case of emergency Ceylon can turn out a number of good shots to assist the Mother Country in time of war."*

Britain's great Empire of course was not won freely and on 23 April 1903 another Old Boy paid the ultimate price for his Country as Captain Charles Godfrey, 31, was killed in battle in Somaliland. Two months later John Grant, an assistant-paymaster with the Royal Navy, died of enteric fever at Trincomalee.

Certainly the OPM notes section of the Plymothian was still regularly visited with letters and reports from past pupils scattered in the far corners of the Empire. Including LJG Anderson, who wrote on 27 January 1904 from HMS Odin *"at sea"*;

Old Town Street, with Chubb's Hotel, venue for the OPM Dinner 30 December 1903, on the left.

"We anchored at Tristan da Cunha, about 10am on January 23rd, about three quarters of a mile from the shore, and were at once besieged by the men of the island, who came off in their boats with their "trade" articles, consisting of sheep, geese, fowls, milk, albatross, and penguin skins, and shoes made of raw oxhide" ... "most of the women and children are fearfully shy, but that is not to be wondered at, considering how seldom they see strangers ... They are all painfully ignorant, though an old grey beldame teaches them all she knows. Crime is unknown, though they have no Governor or laws and they never quarrel. If there is anything made in "trade" it is divided in shares according to the size of the family."

"The people are contented and happy, and the majority of them have no wish to leave the island. They have all they want except education for their children. The principal thing they want and desire is a clergyman or someone to teach their children."

"We sailed on Tuesday, the 26th, for the Cape again, calling at two other islands en route, the Inaccessible and Nightingale Islands. We lowered a boat and collected a specimen of guano from each. We have six passengers from the island who wished to go to Capetown. This yearly visit of a man-of-war is the only regular means the people have of communicating with the outer world."

In 1904 these tales were of a world beyond most schoolboys' range of experience, maybe the odd written account or a rare black and white picture in a book perhaps, but it's hard now to imagine the impact such stirring letters would have had then in the pages of the Plymothian.

Another good example came in from Hong Kong in October 1906. In it the sender, Philip Jacks, spoke of having met a number of OPMs out there and a number of "Old Newtonians, Old Blundellians, Old Exonians and some Old All Hallows' boys; there are crowds of other Old Public School Men here ... We are now looking forward to our cricket season here ..."

Then he added;

"Before closing, I ought to say somewhat of the never-to-be-forgotten 18th of September, when we were visited by one of the most awful disasters in the history of the Colony, the typhoon ... the worst since 1841."

"Coming as it did, very suddenly and with scarcely any warning, the consequences were terrible, it is difficult to realise that it lasted only three hours when one sees the damage done, the loss of life among the Chinese will probably never be accurately known, as thousands were carried out to sea, and bodies decompose very rapidly in these climes. The Chinese place the loss about 10,000, and I don't think they can be far out when one considers that there is a boat population of about 30,000 here, that 1,400 big junks have gone, and no one knows how many sampans. The loss of life among other nationalities was comparatively small ... One of the saddest consequences of the storm was the death of Dr JC Hoare, Bishop of Victoria, who was out in his cruiser yacht."

Much to the fascination of all schoolboys, the motor car comes to Plymouth courtesy of one of its better paid citizens, medical man Dr Pearce.

Perhaps one of the best OPM pieces posted in the Plymothian around this time, however, came anonymously and was titled, simply "The Hospitals". Reading it now, in these days of a National Health Service, we find not just a delightful picture of the past, but also many accurate insights into those rather more timeless aspects of medical study.

"Considering the number of boys who are constantly passing on from School to one or other of the hospitals, the following hints sent us by a medical OPM should prove valuable;

"Choose a big hospital unless you have special reasons for entering a small one."

"At a big hospital the teaching is usually better, and the hospital is less likely to be rendered inefficient from want of funds."

"Nowadays there are people who do not smoke and even more who are teetotallers and are none the worse for it. Therefore do not think it necessary to get a pipe at once on leaving school (if you haven't one already)."

(It's interesting to note that although smoking was massively popular one or two voices were starting to speak out against it - including Devon GP Dr Herbert Tidswell, who condemned the habit as evil and claimed that it was damaging the health of the nation. Cigarette advertising however was enormous and many firms claimed that smoking was actually good for you. A set of Boer War cartoons depicted all the great Army heroes smoking although curiously enough two out of every five men who applied to enlist were declared medically unfit)

"Don't extort too big an allowance from your people. No really successful student was ever cursed with too much per quarter."

"Have a clear idea before you start what degrees or diplomas you are going in for. There are about thirty different ones. You can get through any exam with steady work. With a fair amount of perseverance any one can get through in five years."

Below right JP Brown's children photographed in 1903, all five boys passed through the school. Standing l-r; Ralph and James, seated; Charles, Muriel, Kenneth, Dorothy and Harold.

Below, wedding of Harold Brown and Margaret Brooke, 1903; l-r Muriel Brown, the groom and bride, Kenneth Brown (best man) and Aline Brooke.

Above the first full school photo since 1893 taken in the summer of 1902, on the darker, northern side of main school in the rear quadrangle. Below, 1903 quarter-mile handicap.

"Nine-tenths of all medical students have no definite idea what they intend doing when they get qualified."

"Once you get qualified there is no difficulty whatever in making a living."

"Personally I am convinced, and nearly all I have met agree, that the earlier one starts, if the character be sufficiently formed, the better."

"As a student it is the easiest possible thing to keep "respectable" in word and deed; but the hardest possible to retain the pre ideals one ought to have on starting."

"Enough German to make oneself understood and to be able to read is more useful than an equal amount of French. More scientific books are written in German than French. Apart from the training and general knowledge it gives one, the most elementary knowledge of Greek is all that one requires in medicine."

"Cultivate many hobbies. In no profession is a good all round man at a premium."

"Get to know everybody at the hospital from the head surgeon to the hall porter. All or each may be useful to you."

"One hears a lot about cliques at big hospitals; the biggest and most compact is the 'Varsity clique, usually sub-divided into two - the larger, better dressed, athletic and slacker portion; the smaller shabbier, non-athletic but more hard working."

"Other sets more or less distinct are the cricket, rugger, soccer, and London M.B. All comprise all sorts and conditions. You can be equally happy by belonging to any. It is not worth while playing cricket, as besides being expensive it takes up a lot of time."

"Footer, hockey and tennis are cheaper and take up less time."

"Anybody well up in the School XI will get into the Hospital XI's with luck. It is usually easier to get in the team the first year you are up."

"About three in seven medical students are from the big public schools."

"In the first two, or three years, you can get about ten weeks holiday in the year without missing anything; later every week's holiday is taken at the expense of your practical work."

"I don't know why but fellows living in college are usually (not always) slackers."

"Work at the hospital is, to a great majority, intensely interesting. Reading at home is the drudgery, but is essential to success."

"Take as large a share as you can in the public life of the hospital, all will help in realising your dream of becoming a house surgeon."

"It is fashionable to dine in the evenings, but from the point of view of work, a mid-day dinner is infinitely more satisfactory."

"For extras, in the way of instruments, &c., add 20 per cent to your calculations, your estimate will then be near the mark."

"Beware of buying second-hand books, &c., before doing so consult someone beside the seller or his friends. Money is not wasted on a good microscope."

Mutley Plain ,looking south - 1904

While Plymouth College may not have been classed as one of the big public schools, it is none the less apparent that a number of boys left bound for a medical career and in those days the school curriculum was far less geared towards the sort of background that would have been useful to such prospective students.

Nationally, however, various authorities were taking an increasing interest in the curriculum debate and interestingly enough one of the most glaring criticisms thrown up by the school's first ever inspection was the lamentable provision of science facilities, hence the decision to re-fashion the old drill hall in 1905;

"The buildings, which have been adapted at a cost of about £400, consist of a Chemical Laboratory for 26 workers, a Physical Laboratory, capable of holding 14, and a Balance and Store-room".

The school did, however, cater well for the future Military men. While the South African War had witnessed a number of tragic losses among the ranks of the OPMs it had provided a substantial boost to recruitment for the Cadet Corps; as, doubtless, did the gung-ho piece from AP Hughes in the November 1900 Plymothian. Hughes was serving with the Naval Brigade in China and was, in June of that year, besieged in Tienstin;

"To say that I didn't mind it would be untrue, for I often felt in a blue funk, but now that part is over, I am glad I went through it. For ten days I never went to bed or had my boots off more than twice - and then only for five minutes. We had hard fighting for a whole week. One of our lieutenants was on the top of the Consulate with me, directing the fire of a 9 Pounder Gun at two of the enemy's field guns, when a shrapnel crushed his head and left me untouched. That morning I never expected to live more than five minutes longer at any time ... On the next day I was tethering my horse to a gate, when a piece of shell took off a lump of the wall within six inches of me, scattering mud and dust all over me and sent my moke off at double quick time. Heaps of our poor fellows have been killed or wounded."

Things are improving since the siege has been raised, and the country between here and Taku is fairly clear. The Russians see that there are not too many Chinese left wherever they go."

A selection of photographs from the summer of 1905, detailing various aspects of poolside activity; diving, lifesaving, resuscitation and recreation. With no other fresh water public swimming facility in the Three Towns, the pool was undoubtedly a great attraction and a great asset. Few individuals are named but the solo portrait (middle row, three from the left) is captioned Bellamy.

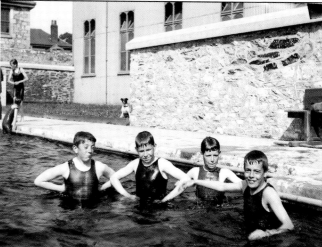

This was gruesome but beguiling for many and the Cadet Corps were enjoying one of their most buoyant periods when they were photographed for the *"Army and Navy"* in the summer of 1902 (incidentally the school was photographed around the same time and for the first time since 1893).

The Royal Review in Windsor Park however, to which the Corps would have gone that year, was cancelled due to the King's illness. Happily there was no illness in the wind when the Cadets went for their march out and mock battle with Kelly the following year. Unfortunately though, bad weather prevented the full programme being carried out. Nevertheless the two Corps ended up having a fine sing song in Baron's Hotel, Dousland with both sides joining in.

"On conclusion of the Concert we marched together as far as Yelverton, when the Kelly Corps turned off for Tavistock, and we unanimously decided to march to Plymouth. Our band played vigorously, and though the night turned out particularly dark we none of us regretted our march, when soon after half-past nine we reached our head-quarters. We all voted that the day's proceedings were amongst the most enjoyable of the whole series of marches that the Corps has ever had."

There was a certain amount of unhappiness in the ranks though and principally it centred around the shooting arrangements. The Corps crack shots were clearly disadvantaged by the lack of proper opportunities, Kelly had *"unlimited opportunity for practice on an easily reached range, whereas our practice has been mostly at the Morris-Tube".* Furthermore the Morris-Tube itself was still somewhat inconveniently situated in Palmer's playground on the old Mannamead site. It was hoped, though, that the use of the Staddon ranges would soon make better marksmen of our boys and that one day the School would have a fairer chance of winning a shooting trophy.

The highlight of the following year for the Corps, however, was to have been the Battle of Sheepstor.

Here, once again, *"the combined meddling of the weather office and the Measles Department"* thwarted four attempts at arranging a clash with Kelly and it wasn't until the summer of 1905 that such an action took place. When it did, it swiftly entered the realms of the great days of the Corps and *"the glowing accounts, published and narrated, induced a few of the bigger boys in the school to join the Cadet Corps."*

"It was then an excellent day, and a most enjoyable one. The weather was perfect, unless perhaps it was too hot; for a day or two afterwards it was possible to pick out the members of the Cadet Corps from the rest of the School by their sunburnt faces. Moreover, we Cadets were left in the possession of an abiding pity for the rest of the School. Poor creatures, they will never know what they have missed until they join the Corps, and have another such glorious day."

In spite of this though the Corps was *"as small as it has ever been ... We are afraid it will never reach proper numbers until every boy of a fixed height and age is forced to join, as every boy now is forced to attend the gymnasium."*

Cricket XI 1907; Back row; HP Hodge, J Woolland, H Littleton, GL Pearce. Middle; P Wallice, GS Maginness, AC Hancock, AH Macklin, JM More. Front; HD Norman, S Trust.

So said T Austin and RC Crews, March 1906 editors of the Plymothian. They then added;

"We should like to say a few words in praise of the instalment of a Morris-tube range in the Gymnasium, as arrangement which has been advocated more than once in our correspondance columns. Not only should this afford agreeable employment for many on wet half-holidays, but it should also increase the popularity and efficiency of the shooting of the corps."

The following year there was even more promising news on that front as the *"long-looked for answer to our application for transference from an Artillery Corps to a Corps of existing establishment attached to a Rifle Battalion has been received from the War Office."*

"Our new name and title is "Cadet Corps, attached to the 2nd (Prince of Wales) Volunteer Battalion Devon Regiment ... The main reason for the reconstitution of the Corps was that the Corps being formerly armed with carbines only, were prevented in taking part in rifle competitions from other schools who were supplied with service rifles."

"Cadets of sufficient physique will now be required to fire at ranges varying from one to five hundred yards, at least sixty rounds, with full charge ammunition, in the course of the year. This new practice will give added interest to the work of the Corps, and ought to be of service as a recruiting agency."

And with the change in constitution came a change in uniform; *"The new uniform, consisting of drab serge tunic, knickers and puttees is already on order."*

"We have already had two drills with our new arms, and judging by the interest already displayed in the acquisition of knowledge of the intricacies of the Mechanism of the rifles, there is every reason to believe that the new system will prove eminently successful."

There then followed a note of thanks to the old unit; *"In taking leave of the 2nd Devon RGA (Vols) I am sure that all ranks will retain happy recollections with the Artillery Volunteers."*

1905

Sports Day 6 April 1906. Above; end of the junior sprint. Right; climax of the junior half-mile. Below Macklin completes in the high jump. Note newly-completed Hyde Park School in the background.

The new uniform duly arrived in the summer and was indeed perceived as a drab mixture - "*serge tunic, knickers and putties, new service forage cap, brown pouches, enamelled iron water bottles covered drab, and drab haversacks ... Though some of us may regret the picturesque appearance of our old Red and Blue, sharply picked out by the white haversacks and white leather bottle straps, yet we shall feel the greater safety of the drab, as offering a less conspicuous target to the vision of our enemies.*"

The new look School OTC

It was of course the South African War that had seen a general move away from the colourful and conspicuous British Army uniforms towards the more easily concealed khaki and it was fairly inevitable that the Corps should change at some point anyway. Indeed, there had already been a cap change back in 1905 when the "pill box" style headpiece was replaced, by decree, with a Field Service cap.

The status of the Corps was undoubtedly improved by all these changes and at 1906 Speech Day, Francis Colson was able to report that in consequence of the inspection of the Army Council, Plymouth College had now been added to the Army Council's list of approved schools, of which there were then fifty ... "*including Eton, Harrow, Rugby, Winchester, Charterhouse and other famous schools*". Colson's speech of that day was one of the longest, and probably the most important he

had yet made since becoming headmaster, as he had felt it incumbent upon him to address an important subject "*which had been a good deal misunderstood in Plymouth, namely, the proposed conversion of the School into an Endowed School or Public Trust*".

It was not just the constitution of the Cadet Corps that was changing - out of necessity the constitution of the school was changing too.

The impact on the school, as perceived by the boys, was to be almost imperceptible and doubtless not much greater for the majority of the staffroom. For the Headmaster, the governors, the hitherto little-mentioned shareholders and a number of misinformed parents however the issue was of paramount importance. Consequently the topic dominated the Head's annual speech day reports for the next four years.

It had all started with the education bill that had been outlined in Westminster in March 1902. Under its terms County councils and the larger urban authorities were to take over responsibility for all secondary, elementary and technical schools in their areas, bringing to an end the powers enjoyed by thousands of school boards up and down the country and eliminating the managers of the various voluntary schools. Public money was henceforth to be made available for the education of children in all schools in an area.

Behind the promotion of the bill was the government's desire to see an improvement in standards and a more regulated approach towards the provision of education generally.

The first, albeit indirect, reference to the Act in the Plymothian gave it a guarded welcome; "*The School is watching with disgust the erection of a stately Board School within an easy stone's throw of our windows. We anticipate much trouble from such an unfortunate juxta-position - especially when there is snow about ... If the new Education Bill and the establishment of the single authority will render such blunders impossible in the future, it deserves a hearty welcome*".

Main school overlooking the newly-erected Hyde Park Schools.

Non-conformists, however, were less than enthusiastic about the new bill, as they saw it as using taxes and rates to fund various Anglican and Catholic schools; schools which would still retain a considerable amount of autonomy from local authority control. This latter point was missed by many Plymouth College parents who imagined that, by surrendering its proprietary status and by becoming an endowed school and accepting an annual grant from the government, the School would lose its identity and its independence.

Essentially, though, all that was to happen was that the School would have a few governors appointed for it by the local authority and it would be obliged to take in a small number of bright boys from the elementary schools. In order to pacify the doubters and in order to win over the shareholders - who had to, one way or another, surrender their shares - Colson published a letter in the Plymothian. Written the day after Speech Day (28 September 1905) the letter followed straight on from the Speech Day report in which he had outlined the proposal to change from being a proprietary school, free from inspection, to one with a small element of local authority interest where they would be open to a regular inspection. Presumably he was prompted to write it in response to a number of parents who expressed their concerns to him at the conclusion of the formal speech day agenda.

From the contents of Colson's missive we learn much, not just about the standing of the school locally in 1905, but about the provision of higher school education generally at that time and about the financial history of the School.

"Plymouth College is one of the very few first-grade town schools which are "proprietary" instead of "endowed". By "town school" I mean a school which, even though it may have a considerable mixture of boarders, exists primarily to meet the needs of a particular town. In the word "first-grade" no superior efficiency is implied, but merely that it is a school which caters for those who are willing to keep their boys at school till seventeen or eighteen, and acts as a direct avenue to the Universities, services and professions. It is a practical necessity in such schools that they should be more expensively staffed and equipped than schools of the second grade, and altogether the cost of education works out at a higher figure. Professor Sadler estimates it at £23 a head, though I think myself that this is somewhat excessive."

"Now all towns in England of the size of the Three Towns (Plymouth, Stonehouse and Devonport) possess a "first grade" school, but the vast majority are endowed. In fact, I think the only exceptions are the twin cities of Liverpool and Birkenhead, and the Three Towns."

"Most first-grade schools, therefore, start with a considerable income of their own, and are able to provide an education costing £20 a head without charging more than £15, or in some cases £10 a head. The "proprietary" school, on the other hand, must charge a higher fee, as it rarely, or never, starts with an income of its own, and generally with a debt. As many of your readers know, the founders of Plymouth College subscribed £12,000, but borrowed another £15,000."

"Paradoxical as it may seem, the fact is that the management of Plymouth College has been, in a sense, a great financial success, if - that is - financial success consists in making a great deal out of a little. Without

sacrificing any of the essentials of a first-grade school, it has paid its interest and paid its way - done, in fact, the same work which other schools do with £1,000 or even £2,000 more a year. It has been able to do this largely because in spite of its high fees its numbers have been exceptionally high."

"Here again there is some misapprehension. If higher education were better valued the numbers might no doubt be larger still, both here and elsewhere. But as a matter of fact the numbers attending first-grade schools are very small all over England. With us, taking Plymouth and Devonport as one place, they are about 1 in 1,000. In Liverpool and Birkenhead, where the schools being like our own, proprietary, the fees are over £20 a year, the number attending the first-grade schools are only 1 in 1,800. In some large towns, where, owing to a large endowment, the fees are small, the proportion may be larger. Thus in Leicester, where the fees of the school range from £5 to £9 a year, it is about 1 in 500. On the other hand, in Leeds, where the fees are also quite small (10 guineas a year), it is 1 in 1,700."

Mutley Plain looking north.

(One hundred years on, incidentally that figure for Plymouth is a little under 1 in 15, as the school leaving age has been

long since raised and almost all schools offer teaching for 17 and 18 year-olds. But back then the fact that the number was more like 1 in 1,000 and the fact that Plymouth College, locally, was the only one to offer such a facility, makes it easy to see why the old boys of these rare "first-grade" schools played such a large part in the country's Empire building.)

"We claim, then, to have carried out successfully a very difficult task, to have done, in fact, what many people who know the educational resources of other great towns would have thought an impossibility. Still, the difficulties are obvious. So long as the town calls upon us to do with a debt of £15,000 what other schools in great towns do with £15,000 to the good, the position is not a stable one nor, I think, quite creditable to the town. The Board of Education quite appreciate our difficulties, and are willing to give us help, but they insist on our coming to an arrangement with our shareholders by which the school will cease to be their private property. The help which the Board will give us, assuming it to be permanent - and we have no reason to think the contrary - is practically equivalent to an endowment, and will very much improve the situation, and moreover it may be hoped that possible benefactors may feel differently disposed to the school when they realise that it is in the fullest sense public property."

In other words Colson was hoping that a school without shareholders might be looked upon more favourably by potential benefactors than one where there was a possibility of profits going into private hands - not that there had ever been any profits to date ... *"the parents who ever expected a dividend must have been as sanguine as they were rare"* (Serpell). In the early days however there had been advantages, most notably reduced fees for children of shareholders, but even that privilege had long since been waived.

A bigger threat of course was the chance that one day the shareholders might have been driven to say *"Let us sell up the thing, and put the proceeds in our pockets"* ... and as Colson reported at the 1907 Speech Day, there had been times when that was very near;

"When I first came here, I was a little surprised to find they were £400 out of pocket at the end of the year, besides being £15,000 in debt on the capital. If things had not changed I have no doubt that that in a year or so the place would have been closed and the property sold. Now this can never happen".

However, if the change in the school fortunes nineteen years earlier had been due to a combination of Colson's determination and the failure of Mannamead School, there could be little doubt who was largely responsible for this latest move;

"The town of Plymouth owes this gift almost entirely to the munificence of Mr Thomspon".

Joseph Thompson was undoubtedly not only the driving force behind the move to eliminate the school's private company status he was also the one that made it possible financially. For although both he and Colson used their own monies to buy out those shareholders who were reluctant to simply surrender the shares free of charge, there was no question as to who bought the lion's share. Happily for Plymouth College, Joseph Thompson was a very wealthy man and one who held the school very dear to his heart and as the person who had gifted so much already it is easy to see why he was so keen to put an end to the possibility that the school might one day be sold and, in the process, that someone else would profit from his investment.

Nominally, around that time, the school appears to have been valued at around £50,000; held in 2,000 shares each worth £25, originally to raise the £12,000 subscribed at the time of the school's foundation 501 shares were actually issued. By 1900, 33 share certificates had already been surrendered voluntarily and a further 12 had been bought in for £35 "as consideration money". That still apparently left some 115 individual shareholders *who sold and bought their £25 shares for 10s (50p), and might at any time sell the place"*. Whatever their number and value, however, it was essential to round them all up if the scheme to re-found the school was going to succeed.

The School's first mortgage - £12,230 at 4% - was, in fact, paid off in 1900, but only by securing a second, larger mortgage at a better rate - £14,500 at 3%. This was done to enable the High School For Boys, Plymouth, Limited (the official name of the company - for that is how the business that was Plymouth College was then constituted) to not only pay off the existing mortgage, but also *"the special loans of £1,000 which were raised in connection with the purchase of Mannamead School; a sum of £709.18s.6d. due to the Plymouth Urban Sanitary Authority for paving expenses; legal and other expenses incident to the new Mortgage, - and ... a small balance left available for school purposes"* (Report to the Board of Governors 1899).

1903 High School for Boys share certificate.

A little over three years later, on 27 November 1903, an arrangement was drawn up whereby the High School for Boys Limited, *"hereinafter called "the Company"*, conveyed to Francis Henry Colson and Joseph Thompson *"the pieces or parcels of land messuage and buildings known as the Plymouth and Mannamead College by way of mortgage to secure the principal sum and interest"* ... subject to their mortgage thereon.

Colson and Thompson, by thus acquiring the school, apparently for themselves, were in fact clearing the way to free the school from private hands so that they could

become an endowed School. Had they not managed to effect that change then they would have lost the Government Grant they had had for some years and this, combined with the burden of the original debt, would have put the School in a difficult financial position. It would also have meant that the local authorities would have looked elsewhere for a first-grade education. As Colson pointed out in his 1906 Speech Day address, the School was fortunate that the local authorities had *"lost its old Grammar School ... which probably would have developed, like Exeter School, into a school of this kind"*.

The Headmaster then proceeded to entertain his audience with a brief discourse on the old Grammar School, the very school that Holmes had left to establish Mannamead School over fifty years earlier;

"How they (the Corporation) came to lose the Grammar School I hardly know. I have heard extraordinary stories. The general belief is that at one period Plymouth Corporation thought they would rather manage a church than a grammar school; accordingly they sold the grammar school and bought the advowson of St Andrew's ; then thinking they would rather manage a hotel, they sold St Andrew's and built the Royal Hotel (Laughter.) How this was done and why they were not all sent to prison for it were mysteries too profound to be inquired into. (Laughter.) They must accept the fact that they had here no endowed first-grade school, and when they needed a first-grade school it had to be founded on a proprietary basis, endowed by subscribers or shareholders. Now they wanted proof that the change to a public trust was a good one."

(nb. It is true that in order to part-fund the Royal Hotel the council decided to sell its advowsons - its rights to appoint the vicars of St Andrew's and Charles Church - in order, as one cynic put it, to appoint a landlord and a manager.)

Once again therefore we see that the failure of the old Corporation Grammar School, although still operating in name, still had a part to play in the ongoing story of the success of Plymouth College.

Fate continued to smile on the School, although such is not to belittle the contributions and determination of both Colson and Thompson. Plymouth College was but one of several independent schools in the Three Towns at the time, but it was the biggest and the most successful and the one that the local authorities looked to first. Both in Plymouth and in Devonport, picking up Colson's account again, we learn that; *"there (Devonport) the Municipal Authority had bought the High School and were going to administer it as a second-grade school. We, on the other hand, are to be a first-grade School, not only for Plymouth and Devonport, but for the two adjacent counties, and the fact that we receive representatives from these two County Councils on our council will by no means put the School under their control"*.

This was another popular fear that Colson was anxious to allay. Under the terms of the new constitution of the School, six of the fourteen governors to be appointed would be local authority nominations;

"ONE by the Devonshire County Council;
ONE by the Cornwall County Council;
TWO by the Plymouth Town Council;
ONE by the Devonport Town Council; and
ONE by the Governing Body of Exeter College in the University of Oxford."

"Some of our friends," said Colson (Speech Day 1908), *"thought we would get a man in the street, who would work mischief in the Governing body, and lower the status of the School"*. He then went on to describe the new Governors appointed in this way;

"The man in the street sent by Cornwall was Mr Quiller-Couch. Devon was represented by a Fellow of the Royal Society, and Exeter College by Canon Hammond. Plymouth had sent Sir Charles Radford and Mr J.Y. Woollcombe and Mr Littleton came from Devonport ... None of these will be in the least anxious to lower the status of the School."

Arthur Quiller-Couch ("Q"), who had given away the prizes at the 1903 Speech Day, was the celebrated and later-knighted novelist and short-story writer, then resident in Fowey; Sir Charles Radford had just taken up office, for the second time as Mayor of Plymouth and in 1909, the Devonport Governor, William Littleton, became one of the last Mayors of Devonport. A more distinguished local group at that time it is hard to imagine.

The eight other School governors, incidentally, under the new set up were;

Sir Alfred Croft, an old boy of Mannamead School; the Reverend Benwell Bird, a founding governor who had been on the board since 1877; John Greenway, solicitor and OP; Joseph Brown, a successful merchant, who had put his various sons through the school; Dr Charles Hingston; the Reverend Stewart Ponsonby, Rector of Stoke Damerel; Montague Bazeley, architect and OP and Charles James (Charles Serpell, incidentally, had been the first old boy to be appointed a governor - in 1905).

Two of the new governors; Sir Alfred Croft an old Mannameadian and Dr Charles Hingston.

This then was how Francis Colson left the school - re-constituted and, hopefully, soon to be free of the debt that had hampered its development from day one. In order to court that gesture, whereby the local authority might absolve the school of that burden, his farewell Speech Day speech of 1908 carried this delightful piece of goodwill propaganda;

"My chief wish is to have been regarded not so much as a servant of the School but as a servant of the town. Nineteen years ago the School was not merely a High School for boys, but one of the most precious assets of the town. I trust in the future the people of Plymouth will realise that more and more, and that they will take the practical step of wiping off the debt, which has been such a drawback, and that I might then feel from a distance that what I was able to do here was going forward".

At that point Bernard Thomas, Secretary of the OPM Club, on behalf of the Old Boys, asked Mr Colson to accept a complete set of the Encyclopedia Britannica and a silver salver, and presented Mrs Colson with a diamond pendant. He also paid a warm tribute to the *"esteem in which Mr Colson was held by Old Boys, now scattered over the world"*.

Mr Colson, in reply, expressed his gratitude and affection to the Old Boys.

"I have always felt that the future of the School depended very largely on the good-will of the Old Boys, more than on that of the Masters, or the present boys, or the parents. They spoke with more knowledge of the School than the parents, with more weight than the boys, and with more impartiality than the Masters, and therefore what they said and thought of it was always listened to with respect".

Mr Colson said he was also grateful to the Old Boys for their delightful present to Mrs Colson; *"I wouldn't like to say that either of us deserved such kindness ... but if anyone does, she does. A Headmaster's wife stands, I think, in a particularly difficult position. Not only has she the weight of the boarding house on her shoulders, and to be responsible for the health of other people's children was no small burden, but in the management of the Day-School her help was most useful."*

"A Head-Master must always bear in mind the mother's point of view, and to ascertain this I needed a wife's advice. At the same time she must not be the Head-Mistress. A School like this was in the hands of men; the assistant masters were men of ability and standing, the Headmaster's colleagues rather than his subordinates, and her advice had to be used with tact, and indirectly; I think Mrs Colson has steered her way very well through these difficulties."

Then he checked himself;

"I must apologise for these personal remarks; I have never made them before and never will again."

It was to be Colson's last major, formal speech to the school. Three days earlier, however, he had given a very personal address at his last College Service. It was almost indirectly personal ... *"as I feel that I'd rather say as little as possible of my own ... I would rather leave you with some thoughts and words of great and wise men, that have helped me in the past and may, perhaps, remain with you."*

Matthew Arnold was the source of much of his text as he elaborated on the stanza:-

"Children of men, not that your race excel
In pride of life, the ages of your sires,
But that ye think clear, feel deep, bear fruit well
The friend of man's desires."

Colson's interpretation of the above then confirmed the balanced and reasoned approach that made such a lasting impression on Wilson Harris and, doubtless, was the reason that the Headmaster and his wife were so heavily laden down with leaving gifts - not just from the Old Boys but from the school, the staff and the Governors.

"To think clear - to have the love of truth for truth's sake - to see both sides of a question - to sift evidence - to use your reason - to be able to discriminate between what you know and what you merely think. This is a gift, which a good school, with a liberal education will give if it gives anything."

"To feel deep. Perhaps it may be thought that this is given us not so much by the associations of school, as by those of home and church. And yet a good school can do much for this also..."

"Thirdly, to bear fruit well - to despise mere sentiment - to fight against dreaminess - to value hard facts - above all to prize at its true value the unspeakable treasure of hard work - to hold it as a privilege and not a grievance. These are things which the school if it performs its true functions will continue to teach."

"... This then would be my parting wish and prayer for the school, with which I have been identified for so many years and which I can never think of as a thing apart from myself, that it should be a place where boys learn to think clear, feel deep, and bear fruit well."

1908 Ist XI Cricket: Back row; HL Heal, DGC Murphy, EAR Nepean, AR Coppin. Middle; HD Norman, JM More, P Wallace, J Wolland, JC Butlin. Front; CGT Colson, RW Macklin.

And so, at the age of 51, Francis Colson left Plymouth College almost instantly receiving what we are told was the *"spontaneous offer of Classical Lectureship by his old College of St John's, Cambridge".*

As one old boy was later to write;

"Mr Colson will be remembered not only for his scholarship but also as a teacher who exercised a profound influence on his pupils. His erudition was never dry; it was full of sap and gusto and often found such homely and humorous expression that even schoolboys could appreciate its fine flavour. Perhaps Mr Colson's chief power lay in the penetrating honesty of his thinking. His fierce scorn of shams and his contempt for all woolly statements made a lasting impression on all his pupils. Whatever subject he taught became an instrument for developing in the student a capacity to detect sophistry. To learn Latin or Greek grammar accurately and to construe an ancient author intelligently were first steps towards recognising inaccuracies, half-truths, exaggerations, confusions and the deceptive power of words in contemporary speakers and writers. "Some people," he said in the course of a Scripture lesson, " think it blasphemous to "make sense" of the Bible, but that is a mistake," and his imperious insistence that his pupils should "make sense" of everything they read was an unforgettable lesson."

1907/08 Ist XV: Back row; JA Butlin, SGK Beer, WD James, HL Heal, PT Satterford, LE Sanders, DGC Murphy. Middle; JC Hawk, P Wallice, HD Norman, S Trust, JM More. Front; AH Ward, GH Lane, A Letherby.

In considering Colson's replacement the Board of Governors had more than a dozen or so candidates to chose from, however following a Board resolution that *"the post should be held by a married man"* – a short list of six candidates were *"chosen to appear before the Council at the School, on Wednesday 15 July"*. The list comprised Messrs, SE Winbolt (Christ's Hospital, West Horsham), Rev HJ Chaytor (King Edward VII School, Sheffield), JAH Johnston (Tonbridge School), A Jagger (Queen Elizabeth's School, Mansfield), Rev. S Longland (Wellington College, Berkshire) and the Rev. RS Moxon (King's School, Canterbury). Only one of them, Arthur Jagger, was already a Headmaster. The list was drawn up on Wednesday 8 July, so with the interviews just a week away *"Mr Serpell, on behalf of the Secretary, was asked to communicate with the gentlemen named by telegram the same evening in order that they might have due notice."*

Of the six, only four appeared for interview the following Wednesday; Jagger, Moxon, Winbolt and Chaytor and Mr Chaytor was elected and duly informed that *"the services of the Teaching Staff should be retained until at least the end of the 1st term 1909 and he expressed his assent to this arrangement."*

Postcard of Plymouth College dated 1908

Scenes from around Ford Park from the first decade of the twentieth century. Above left; Mutley Plain. Above, Mutley Station with the familiar outline of the Baptist Church in the distance. Left; Outside the Co-operative Stores at the top of Peverell Park Road. Below; Plymouth College - its temporary eastern wall still awaiting development.

1908

THE CHAYTOR YEARS

The Plymothian of November 1908 opened with the simplest of statements;
"The School most heartily welcomes Mr and Mrs Chaytor."
Little could anyone have been aware of just how momentous, for a variety of reasons, the next ten years or so - the 'Chaytor years' - were to be in the history of the school and indeed the history of the country.
Let us briefly imagine ourselves back in 1908. Fifty-six year-old Liberal Henry Herbert Asquith is Prime Minister and Queen Victoria's elder surviving son, Edward VII, aged 67, is King. Curiously enough one of Sir Edward Elgar's marches, which was set to words in the coronation year by AC Benson, looks set to rival "God Save The King" as an English national anthem. Patriotism is running high with the staging, this summer, of the Olympic Games in London - most events being held in the new sports stadium at Shepherd's Bush, opened earlier this year. Built as part of the 200-acre site commemorating the Franco-British exhibition, the stadium has been nicknamed the White City on account of the pale, fresh-faced stonework of many of the buildings. If Anglo-French relations are particularly healthy though those with Germany are becoming increasingly less so in the wake of Kaiser William's anti-British remarks made in an interview in the Daily Telegraph (31 October).
Meanwhile Mafeking hero, Sir Robert Baden-Powell, has begun consolidating the experimental scout "troops" he set up last year. WG Grace has just announced (in September), his retirement from cricket and former American cowboy, Samuel Cody, has made the first flight in Britain (16 October). "British Army Aeroplane No.1" completed a quarter of a mile flight at a height of no more than thirty feet before crashing back down to earth. A bleeding Mr Cody emerged undaunted, from a plane financed by the war office in Farnborough. He had, he said, *"constructed a machine which flies"*.
At school these various events were highlighted at a meeting of the Debating Society, on 6 November, during which Saunders brought forward a motion on the necessity of compulsory military training and W Stoneman, OPM, *"once more terrified us with the prospects of aerial warfare"*.
If it is perhaps hard for us now to imagine the sense of awe and wonder generated by futuristic images of the aeroplane in 1908. Consider another technological wonder that we all take for granted today (and which will almost certainly, in years to come, be superceded by another form of transport) – the motor car.
Speaking at the 20 November meeting of the Debating Society, Ward i. Condemned motor cars, *"the modern Juggernaut"* and *"thought that all drivers should be subjected to a strict test of moral character before being allowed to imperil the lives of others"*.
Murphy and Simpson replied, abusing the *"dangerous and microbe spreading horse ... no-one knew what a horse was going to do next"*. Furthermore, he suggested, the *"dust nuisance and smell"* of the motor car *"were mere trifles which would soon be done away with."*

Heavy traffic on Mutley Plain

In what became quite a heated discourse, W Stoneman thought that *"something might be done to make motor-horns more attractive, - why not orchestral overtures, and songs a la gramophone, varied with hymns on Sundays?"*
Mr Gwyther on the other hand, while clearly understanding certain benefits of the motor car, nevertheless suggested the *"hanging of a few of those who did not give a sporting chance of escape"*. Road rage in 1908?!
All in all some 13 members spoke and *"the motor car escaped anihilation by 5 votes"*.
As for the idea of getting yet more young boys in

uniform, a letter in the same issue of the Plymothian asked "*Could not Baden-Powell's scheme "Scouting for Boys" be taken up next term as an alternative to Paper-chases?*"

"*There is*" the correspondent continued, "*already one Patrol formed in the School and is at present doing well, and if anyone wished to learn more about this scheme, they should ask one of the members of this Patrol or else buy a shilling book on it. It teaches a boy to be observant, accurate and reliable.*"

"*Scouting*" we learn was quickly taken up "*with great enthusiasm*", much at the expense of paper-chases. Which leads one to wonder exactly what form this "scouting" took, particularly when we read that several great scouting expeditions were "*somewhat marred by the vigilance of various game-keepers (which, however, affords excellent practice) ..*"

And further Scouting has now "*been recognised as a school game, and is represented on the Games Committee by C Davis*".

It was also around this time that another school popped up in the area. Based in one of the large houses on Townsend Hill it immediately aroused the wrath of a number of OPMs by proclaiming itself "*Mannamead School*".

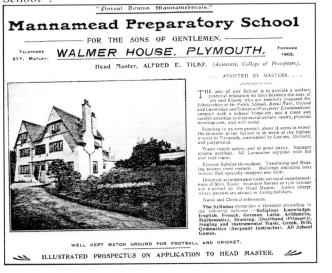

"Floreat Domus Mannamedensis."

Mannamead Preparatory School

FOR THE SONS OF GENTLEMEN.

TELEPHONE
37Y, MUTLEY.
WALMER HOUSE, PLYMOUTH. FOUNDED 1903.

Head Master, ALFRED E. TILBY, (Associate, College of Preceptors),

... ASSISTED BY MASTERS. ...

THE aim of this School is to provide a modern practical education for boys between the ages of six and fifteen, who are carefully prepared for Scholarships at the Public Schools, Royal Navy, Oxford and Cambridge, and College of Preceptors' Examinations; coupled with a refined home-life, and a close and careful attention to their moral welfare, health, physical development, and well-being.

Standing in its own ground, about 1½ acres in extent the situation of the School is on some of the highest ground in Plymouth, surrounded by Garden, Orchard, and playground.

Water supply ample, and of great purity. Sanitary system certified. All Lavatories supplied with hot and cold water.

Electric lighting throughout. Ventilating and Heating system most modern. Buildings including lofty School Hall specially designed and built.

Domestic arrangements under personal superintendence of Mrs. Tilby. Boarders limited to ten in number are received by the Head Master. Entire charge where parents are abroad or during holidays.

Naval and Clerical references.

The Syllabus comprises a thorough grounding in the following subjects :—Religious Knowledge, English, French, German, Latin, Arithmetic, Mathematics, Drawing, Shorthand (Pitman's), Singing and Instrumental Music, Greek, Drill, Gymnastics (Sergeant Instructor). All School Games.

WELL KEPT MATCH GROUND FOR FOOTBALL AND CRICKET.

ILLUSTRATED PROSPECTUS ON APPLICATION TO HEAD MASTER.

"*I had been under the impression that at the amalgamation, the title of Mannamead School passed into our possession; how is it that the School authorities allow it to be usurped by another?*", wrote "Mannameadian".

Meanwhile on the same letters page "Apex" suggested that it was time that a satisfactory School cap was devised.

"*The present ones are imitated all over the town, and some of the wearers of the imitations are likely to cause mistaken impressions as to the class of boy that attends the College. Also, the green of the North Town cap fades like the grass. Could we not have some design that could be registered and not imitated? Surely now, too, is the time to settle on a real School crest; the caps could then all have the crest, with some variation in the colours black, red, and green, to mark the different houses*".

Apex's letter was clearly a timely one, the arrival of a new head is always a testing time and Henry Chaytor seemed to be passing through this phase with flying colours;

The Plymothian, March 1909 - "*The success with which Mr Chaytor has made his mark and won popularity within the School, among the Old Boys, and in the town generally, is a matter of common knowledge,*" ran the editorial. It continued;

"*There was no general upheaval of School traditions as some had feared, but two changes of great moment were introduced.*"

In setting out those changes the editors then give us a rare glimpse into the nature of the school day and the curriculum.

"*School periods*", they explained, "*have now been made shorter and more numerous. The school day is now divided into seven periods of three-quarters of an hour each – four in the morning and three in the afternoon.*"

In consequence of these changes dinner break was now from 1pm and afternoon school from 2.30 to 4.45pm, prompting "A Sinking Void" to complain that if he had cricket after school in a house-match he might not get home until 7.30, "*very tired and hungry*". "*I think this might be less the case if I could get some tea before the cricket, after afternoon school. A cup of tea and a bun would make all the difference and retailed at 3d. a head, ought to bring in some profit to the tuck shop.*"

The School Dining Room

For the record school holidays were then six weeks in the Summer, four at Christmas and three at Easter, a situation "Vacatio" thought could be improved by having only two weeks at Christmas "*when Nature is asleep and the days are short and cold*" and having five instead at Easter.

By the other Chaytor change we learn that "*the old "alternative system" (Greek, Science and German) has been done away with, and all boys in the Upper School who do Science also do German. There are now three choices for a boy to make on entering the Vth – (1) Classics, (2) Modern Languages (with Latin), (3) Science (with French and German); Mathematics and English are done by all*" (Greek, incidentally, was then still required for Cambridge or Oxford).

"These changes have met with universal approval, and work with the utmost success."

They weren't the only early modifications that Chaytor oversaw … *"The abolition of Saturday afternoon detention was also welcomed, and we seem to get along very well without it."*

"A last change is the taking of all external school examinations (Joint Board and Cambridge Locals) in July."

There was one further change and in some respects it was most major of them all, however it's likely that it was the one least noticed by the boys. This was the *"great Scheme"* which after years of planning and paper work was now *"a thing accomplished and will come into full force next term"*.

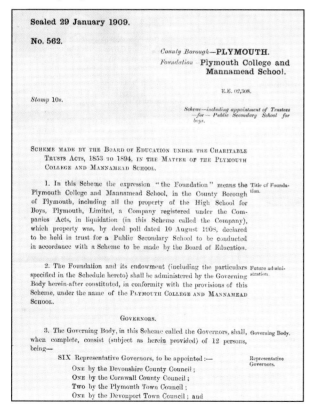

The 1909 School Scheme.

All in all there could be no doubting that the new, thirty-seven year-old head had thrown himself wholeheartedly into all aspects of school life;

"The interest taken by Mr Chaytor in the games, and above all, his personal participation in them, has been most inspiring to all concerned."

Mr Chaytor was clearly a keen sportsman and played for both the School 1st XV on the rugby pitch and 1st XI on the cricket square. The school teams, were generally short on inter-school fixtures, there not being many schools they could reach easily and compete with.

Cricket on the School field - from a contemporary prospectus.

The revived Corporation Grammar School, Kelly, Exeter and Newton College were the principal local opponents and apart from them the fixture lists were still largely filled out with Services sides. In the school v school encounters only boys played, but against the other sides it was common for the odd member of staff and the school pro to beef up the side.

In his first season, Mr Chaytor scored a fine fifty against Tavistock, taking four wickets for sixteen runs in the same game. Over the season he took 39 wickets and finished second in the bowling averages to Moore, the school professional. He also scored 230 runs at an impressive average of 18, but some way behind Wooland, the team captain *"the most effective scorer we have had for years"*, who posted an excellent average of over 40 across 21 innings.

Bert Sargent and Ernest Gardiner were other staff regulars around this time and Francis Palmer still managed the odd game.

Another master, George Gwyther, who had done so much to revive rugby football at the school, also continued to make his presence felt. Turning his attention to the imminent 1909 Sports Day he complained, via the Plymothian, that the Sports Secretary was once again *"going through the humiliating process of begging the friends of the School (for whose generation we are most grateful) to provide us with prizes for the events."*

"No other School sport compels us to take the position of beggars, for in all others the aim is not personal profit or glorification, but the increase of the honour of House or School. Why cannot this principal be extended to the Sports also, especially as the sports themselves are now arranged in the House system?"

And then he asked; *"Do boys really go in for Sports in order to win tennis-rackets and biscuit boxes?"* … *"I do not believe it, they think first of the honour of the House. If any boy does not, we can do without him, - if all do, where is the need of prizes and their unpleasant accompaniments?"*

Gwyther went on to point out that *"the Victoria Cross, I believe, only costs a few pence, and for a little more than that, a bronze medal, as a memento, not as a prize, could be given to the winners of events."*

He was not, he claimed, against the presentation of Challenge Cups but *"in the system I have in mind, - one which worked with great success at Manchester Grammar School – marks would be given to all Competitors who reach a certain standard, as well as to the actual winners."*

He concluded his case with an impassioned plea; *"When it is a lamentable fact that throughout England we find sport being more and more degraded to mercenary and commercial uses, it is all the more desirable that any contamination of pure sport with selfish interests should be kept from our public schools"*.

One wonders what he would have made of the level of commercial contamination in sport today, although happily schools have largely managed to steer clear of it.

Curiously enough a debate the following year on the increase of professionalism in athletics found the house very much against such a trend. The main speaker urging that *"the attendance of vast crowds at professional matches had a bad influence on the players, and attracted people that ought to be developing their own muscles by exercise of some kind."*

Incidentally, it may just have been a coincidence, but it's a very curious one if it was, but the very Plymothian that carried Gwyther's anti-commercial cries was also the first to carry a page of advertising!

On the subject of prizes though it is interesting to note that Gwyther prizes for Classics and History are still awarded today.

Still with George Gwyther, he would undoubtedly have been pleased to see that year a revival of Junior matches with other schools for it had been three years since the last game. Illness undoubtedly played some part in this though, as, even above weather, it appears to have the most frequent cause of cancellation of sporting fixtures.

Fives was hit by both. *"Once more the absence of covered courts was felt, when the beginning of Fives had to be postponed on account of the snow and rain until several weeks from the beginning of term ... It was unfortunate that we were prevented from playing Kelly by the epidemic of measles in the College and by a counter attack of mumps at Kelly."*

The cricket team had a similar problem – *"The strongest team that we have had for some years were unable to show what it can do against either Kelly or Newton owing to slight epidemics at both these Schools."*

School services were also *"interfered with"* by the measles epidemic and the Corps march out had to be cancelled *"owing to the respective outbreaks of measles and mumps here and at Kelly."*

Officers Training Corps Band

"As far as can be ascertained at present, it will take place about a week later, when the combatants will be prevented from coming into contact with one another, for fear of producing a hybrid ailment such as "measumps" or "mumpsles".

There was an even bigger blow in store for the Corps though, later in the year, with the retirement, through ill-health of the OTC commander Captain Woodcock.

Francis Woodcock had of course brought the successful Corps unit from Mannamead School with the Amalgamation and the summer of 1909 was to have seen him lead his troop to their first Public Schools Camp at Tidworth, Salisbury Plain. However, he was taken ill shortly before the train was due to leave Mutley and was unable to go. Woodcock had suffered a nervous break-down, seven years earlier, and many of his friends and colleagues had hoped that he had fully recovered, however, the previous year it became apparent that *"the same conditions were developing in a still more serious form ... He continued to grow steadily worse until it had reluctantly to be recognised that he was unable to bear the strain of school work."*

He retired early in 1909 and sadly died, *"with almost startling suddenness"* on 1 August 1910, leaving behind a wife, a very young son, and a wealth of happier memories for many old boys.

Francis Woodcock had only just turned 47. His place on the staff was taken by 21 year-old Charles Dodson who had a degree in History from Oxford and who was a Lieutenant in the Royal West Surrey Regiment (The Queen's).

Dodson arrived too late to help with that first camp at Tidworth, which, incidentally was deemed to be a great success, but his influence on the OTC was quickly felt.

Dodson was Chaytor's first appointment at Plymouth College; the first appointment of his predecessor, Colson, had been George Gwyther. Like Woodcock, Gwyther was also suffering from a nervous disorder and in the early part of 1910 he was forced to take time off school at home, following *"a severe attack of neuritis"*. *"We wish him a speedy recovery and hope he will be back before this magazine is in our reader's hands"*.

George Gwyther 1868-1910 - the man who introduced rugby.

Sadly however he didn't return. Gwyther was to follow Woodcock to an early grave, he died just before Christmas and was buried on Christmas Eve. He was 42. Colson, who not only appointed him, but had also taught him (in his previous post at Bradford Grammar School) described him as *"something like a genius"* when it came to *"coaching boys for singing, acting, recitations and the like."* While his *"knowledge of English Historical Grammar was considerable and his knowledge of English History was something more than considerable."*

The impression left after reading the generous obituaries

from both Colson and Thompson is that here was a man who gave his all and more to the school, both in and out of term time. Indeed one line from Colson is perhaps particularly telling;

"The exertions when he spent his summer holidays (1904) at Oxford attending lectures on the science of teaching, and at the end obtained a diploma with distinction, though, I fear, they cost him dear, were a very fine achievement."

Clearly a teacher's teacher as well as a fine academic, he was not only responsible for setting up the South Western Branch of the Assistant Master's Association but he also wrote three school text books and was the strength behind a number of school bodies, including the Debating Society, the Library and the Plymothian.

Among the last debates he addressed were a number that gave us a delightful insight into the time. The question of a proposed Wembury Dock scheme (it never came to pass), the future of aerial warfare (*"not much to be feared in war"* said Mr Dodson) and the issue of daylight saving.

Prompted by the Government's Daylight Saving Bill, this matter was one that speakers found difficult to take seriously;

"Icely could not get out of bed an hour earlier without an electric heater, which he wished the House of Commons to supply, Ward was aghast at the prospect of breakfast before the milk had come, Mr Gwyther prophesied that the ladies would be recalcitrant", while *"Chegwidden horrified the socialist members by not wanting the working man to have too much leisure"*.

This meeting, we read, was *"honoured by the presence of Mr and Mrs Chaytor"*. Like his most active members of staff, Chaytor breathed fresh life into a number of extracurricular activities, not just sport.

The Opera was revived in his first year and Mrs Chaytor sang in the Christmas Concert and the April production of the Comic Opera – Don Quixote. This latter show was in some respects George Gwyther's

swansong and in the five page report that appeared in the Plymothian we gain an interesting insight into his involvement and his modesty. *"Miss Robinson and I did our best with the somewhat insipid parts of Duke and Duchess,"* he wrote, in a piece where praised was heaped upon everyone, including Mrs Gwyther for designing the dresses and arranging them on the night (*"I dare not think of the ludicrous mistakes I must have made in this direction, in the days before there was a Mrs Gwyther"*). Mr Gardiner incidentally was Don Quixote and the genial Beer, Sancho Panza.

Also thriving under the new regime were the Glee Club, the Debating Society and the Natural History Society – Mr Chaytor kindly consenting to take the chair at a number of the popular weekly meetings.

The Natural History Society now, in fact, had its own library with 61 books. The VIth form library on the other hand then numbered 318 volumes, while there were 374 in the Junior section.

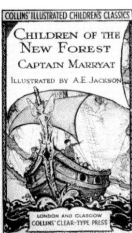

Here again its interesting to look back on what the boys were reading and an analysis of borrowing of the previous two years showed that the most popular authors were then *"Conan Doyle, Rider Haggard, Seton Thompson, Brereton and of course, Henty among the younger boys"*. *The book most taken out has been the*

Adventures of Sherlock Holmes. Books that we think have been unduly neglected are Owd Bob – perhaps the finest dog story ever written, which has only gone out once; The Maid at Arms and Cardigan; Marryat's books (surely English boys will never allow Marryat to fall into neglect?); Boldrewood's Robbery under Arms; and the delightful works of Mrs Nesbit, which only a person utterly devoid of humour would call "childish"."

Such were the editor's views on the book-reading habits of their peers. As for magazine reading, what little we learn of that comes from the letters page;.

"The magazines provided are few and of an uninteresting nature," wrote "Bookworm", adding; "The average person prefers the "Railway Magazine" or the "Illustrated London News" to "Truth" or "John Bull". Nor is this the worst. Such few papers as are readable, such as "Punch" disappear after a day or so for a destination unknown. Surely this is hardly fair on members who regularly pay their subscription."

Whatever its shortcomings, though, the library was one of the more successful school bodies at that time. The Chess Club and Photographic Society, meanwhile, seemed to be struggling and although the Cadet Corps was reckonned to be of "about usual strength" it was nevertheless deemed to be "considerably below what it should be"... "The number of boys who, though fully qualified physically and otherwise, still refuse to recruit, is proof of a regrettable lack of the public spirit which is so essential to the School's success."

A number of letters were fired off to the Plymothian bemoaning the same thing. "Making military training compulsory" was the common theme. However, as of March 1910, the strength of the Corps was still only 55 "which is not as it should be in a School numbering 161".

Such was the social and political climate though that by the end of the year the then magazine editors, Cumming and Reed, were reporting that "universal compulsory training seems imminent".

The school number had by that stage risen to over 170, an increase of almost 25% since Chaytor had arrived and as the head himself said; "Coming at a time of commercial depression, and when many other schools were complaining of a decline in numbers, they had no reason to complain of those figures."

Furthermore, added the head at Speech Day, "the preparatory school under Miss Robinson has overflowed into a building of its own, and I have no doubt it will still further increase."

And with the growth in the number of boys at the Prep came an increase of its staff; "the appointment of Miss Lethbridge, who for some years has been the chief assistant mistress under Miss Tubbs at Alton House will give universal satisfaction" ran an earlier announcement.

Coincidentally the Miss Tubbs in question - Miss Foulger Tubbs - had been born in Mount House and in later years was to relocate her school from Alton Terrace back to the place of her birth; the coincidence being that Mount House School moved out to Tavistock during the Second World War never to return and Plymouth College Prep later (1947) came to occupy the same premises themselves, renaming Mount House, Munday House in the process.

But to return to 1909 and if the young boys of Plymouth College were in good shape so too were the Old Boys. Nineteen attended the London dinner that year at the Holborn Restaurant, Colson was in the chair, and thirty-six (out of a membership then of around 200) made it to the Plymouth Dinner, where Chaytor was in the chair. Interestingly enough the local dinner was held on the eve of New Year's Eve and the Club AGM on Christmas Eve.

There, Club Secretary, B Thomas' acknowledged to the members that "at successive Annual Meetings for years past a consensus of opinion has prevailed as to the desirability of obtaining Headquarters for the Club,

and at last realisation is at hand". Only it wasn't to be, the 1909 report runs "in regard to head-quarters we are no further forward than we were twelve months ago ... Everyone knows that the scheme for rooms in connection with one of the hotels became impossible owing to the legal difficulties of the Law Guarantee, etc, Society".

Also at the 1908 meeting, incidentally, it was decided that a Golf Branch of the club should be formed;

"The Hon.Secretary already has the nucleus of a very fair golf team, and the game is now so widespread that there are probably many other Old Boys who can assist in this branch if they will only send in their names (and Club handicaps)."

Golf was another developing sport around this time, the hard rubber balls had not long come into the game but there were, as yet, no tees; players instead making little mounds for their balls.

Cricket on the other hand was now well-established and Messrs Chaytor, Sargent and Gardiner didn't just play for the school they also turned out for the OPMs a number of times; Mr Chaytor winning hearty OPM thanks for allowing the Old Boys the use of the school nets on two evenings a week during the summer … *"a privilege which has been granted us after years of weary waiting"*.

This was undoubtedly one of the *"golden laurels"* that the OPM secretary spoke of when he praised the new head in his AGM report of 1908 … *"we are fortunate indeed to have such a delightful gentleman and thorough sportsman to succeed Mr Colson as our President"*. Chaytor and Gwyther were present at the 1909 AGM and dinner, but the 1910 dinner was cancelled due to the sad loss of the latter only days before the meeting. Cricket clearly meant a lot to the new head and in his second season he took over fifty wickets for the school and knocked up at least one score of fifty. Bert Sargent recorded 256 runs and Mr Dodson proved to be another useful all-rounder; as indeed was young W Douglass-James, who appeared in the first two team photographs to be published in the Plymothian.

W Douglass James. Victor Ludorum 1910.

Described by his captain, JA Butlin (who led both the cricket and rugby teams - and the shooting eight and the fives team), as a *"good ground field with a good return"* who, nonetheless, *"pokes too much"* and *"should try to get a better length with his bowling"*, Douglass-James was clearly one of the more capable sportsmen in the school. He won the Victor Ludorum of the 1910 Sports Day, was a leading fives player and was one of three cadets to obtain a Certificate A on the first occasion that the school OTC aimed at such a qualification. A promising career ahead of him, he left for Cambridge that year. Sadly, however, like a number of the others he was pictured with in those teams he was to become one of 100 or more OPMs to lose their lives in the Great War. Along with his younger brother, Douglass-James was killed at the front in September 1915.

The first school team photograph to appear in the Plymothian, the 1909-10 "Football XV". Back row, l-r; G Simpson, GRT Kennedy, FW Ford, FS Morrish, H Sturdy, W Hosking, MG Hele. Middle; WA Wroth, WD James, JA Butlin (captain), HL Heal, JC Bullock. Front; R Coyte, G Woodland, CD Hambly.

But all this is to jump forward too far. The school had other losses to cope with back in 1910 – and the death of the 59 year-old King Edward VII was not major among them.

"It would ill become the magazine of a school conspicuous for its loyalty, were no expression of sorrow to appear upon the occasion of our national loss. We have taken our part in the public lamentations for King Edward VII's death, and for us this has been no mere formal or outward manifestation of grief. Kings may die but the throne never dies, and in the same breath with which we record our sorrow we express our loyalty and devotion to His Majesty King George V."

King Edward VII postage stamps.

The departure of Colson and the deaths of two of the school's longest-serving staff members must have had a profound effect on the mood of the school and the sadness would only have deepened in March 1911 when the Reverend JM Hodge also passed away. Mr Hodge was considerably older than the other two, however, and had taught at Mannamead School many years earlier under Dr Holmes. Mr Colson had brought him back to the school in 1906 as a visiting master, in which capacity he continued until his health forced him to retire three years later.

To appreciate the full impact of such losses it should be remembered that there would only have been a dozen or so full-time members of staff at this time, so the atmosphere in the school rooms and the staff room would have been significantly affected. Likewise for the growing Preparatory department, for in the summer of 1911 Miss Robinson also left the school, again for reasons of health. In the previous three years the Prep had grown in number from eight to thirty pupils and the previous December had been sufficiently strong to stage their own entertainment *"on their own premises and from its own resources"*. Mr Palmer and Mr Gardiner helped out and most of the boys took part.

Whatever the impact of these events though they weren't the only conditions affecting the atmosphere within the school and as the nation gradually geared itself up for another international confrontation, so a number of boys were encouraged to indulge in individual confrontation – boxing.

"At many schools they have boxing at least eight times a week during all terms, yet here we have it once a week during one term only . We sincerely hope that the reason is not that English boys are afraid of getting their beauty temporarily spoilt. Cannot something be done to encourage these weaklings to join next term, and also allow us to indulge for two terms at least instead of one? ... We might also remind the above named weaklings that boxing is splendid training for football."

So wrote two of the six great enthusiasts for the sport in the Plymothian. The activity was still, in certain respects, in its infancy back then though. Indeed, speaking at a Big School debate in November 1911, CH Akaster (OPM) confessed a total ignorance of the sport of boxing, *"but regarded boxing as disgraceful as bull-fighting"*.

Akaster was by no means typical of his peers though and the debate was principally around the question of professionalism in the game, with the issues of race and "cinematograph rights" thrown in for good measure. Concerns were expressed about the screening of such professional bouts having a "bad influence upon frequenters of picture palaces."

Picture Palaces themselves were the subject of many mixed opinions. Another debate, this one in February 1912, the year that the Belgrave Cinema opened on the other side of Mutley Plain, Morcom *"tried to persuade the House that Picture Palaces were demoralising the youth of the country on the grounds that they were not an educating influence and they taught young people to read novels, to smoke and to steal!"*

In a fairly even debate it was argued, on the one hand, that such places were *"bad for the eyes and took people into stuffy rooms instead of the open air, and on the other that they kept people from worse places, and caused boys to spend money on pictures instead of cigarettes"*.

The comparison is an interesting one, but then it should be remembered that there weren't anything like the number of diversions for boys to spend their money on then as there are today. And what was true for the pupils was also true for the school. Nevertheless the head had a large shopping list coming up to Christmas 1911, including a number of what he termed luxuries;

"There are a number of improvements which most of us would like to see effected; the seating and extension of the Gymnasium, the extension to include a cloak room, the roofing in of the Fives Courts, a new Organ in Big School, and an improved Cricket Pavilion ..."

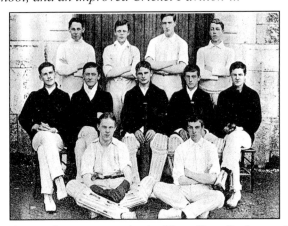

The first cricket team seen in the Plymothian: Back row; RK Marwood, PG Fraser, WD James, KH Jones. Middle; CH Sturdy, CGT Colson, JA Butlin, R Coyte, GRT Kennedy. Front; CHNJ Kennedy, CG Bellamy.

"But these improvements cannot be termed vital, however desirable in themselves."

What prompted the list was the notion, albeit mistaken, that many clearly held regarding the question of the grant from the local authority. A part of the Great Scheme, the grant had at long last, just been decided in the School's favour, but all this did was to *"guarantee the necessaries of existence ... these grants will not provide luxuries."*

Just how close the question of survival had been is hard now to determine. However, a number of remarks made that year at Speech Day, in a Gymasium that was so crowded there was not even any spare standing room, give us some insight into the situation.

The ever-photogenic Main School building.

One of the Governors under the new scheme was the Mayor of Devonport, who in seconding some comments of the headmaster, said;

"Whether it was £500 a year or even more, the Town of Plymouth would do its duty and see that such a school as Plymouth College, which had such a record, was permitted to continue its excellent course".

"It would be suicidal policy," he said, *"to allow such a school to go into disuse"*.

Later Mr Thompson, replying to the many plaudits for his continued generosity, *"expressed the hope that he would live to see the School a permanent institution in the town."*

Saturday, September 17 1910, PMC v Butlin's team.

Had the school not been successful in its Great Scheme bid and had the local authority looked instead to further enhance the long-struggling Corporation Grammar School, would Plymouth College have failed generally? We will never know. We can only assume, from the gravity accorded the situation at the time by all who were concerned for the school's future, that it was a Great Scheme in more ways than one.

A SCHOOL FOR BOARDERS.

PLYMOUTH COLLEGE

One of the leading S.W. England
Public Schools.

COLLEGE HOUSE KITE.

THE MAIN SCHOOL.

THIS BROCHURE IS ISSUED BY THE HOUSE MASTER, WHO INVITES YOUR KINDLY PERUSAL.

A new era and a new prospectus for the School

Its success clearly inspired others to step up their commitment to the school and a fund to improve the Gymnasium was soon well under way. Both local MPs, Waldorf Astor and Mr Shirley Benn. sent subscriptions and the work, drawn up by M Alton Bazeley OPM, which saw the provision of 100 additional seats was completed during the summer holidays. Waldorf Astor, incidentally presented a further £5 for the School Libraries.

Another OPM, JL Fouracre, meanwhile, *"kindly provided plans for a new Pavilion ... which will include proper lavatory arrangements and more comfortable accommodation for our lady spectators".*

"The present structure is not entirely weatherproof, and some expenditure either upon repairs or upon reconstruction is inevitable".

Big School photographed for the Prospectus

OPM input to the magazine was still a regular feature and a number of the letters written back to the school give us a fascinating insight to the period.

Having earlier seen how various old boys did their bit for Britain's Empire-building it's interesting to note Madrassee's letter of June 1912;

"Dear Sirs. I think it was Lord Selborne who, some time back, expressed surprise that the competition for service in India and the Colonies was becoming less keen every year: perhaps he thought Sir AC Lyall's little poem, addressed to the Land of Regrets, was being

taken too seriously, and people thought that all Anglo-Indians were of the same opinion as the young civilian of whom the writer says: -

*Has he learnt how thy honours are rated?
Has he cast his account in thy school?
With the sweets of authority sated,
Would he give up his throne to be cool?*

*Doth he curse Oriental romancing,
And wish he had toiled all his day
At the Bar, or the Banks, or financing,
And got damned in a common-place way?*

*Hath he come now, in season to know thee?
Hath he seen, what a stranger forgets,
All the graveyards of exiles below thee,
O Land of Regrets?*

To which our correspondent then adds – *"I suppose India has its drawbacks, but snakes and scorpions, cholera and enteric, bombs and conspiracies, are not really so general as some people think: and it's a country which certainly provides for all tastes".*

"Are you", he asks, *"fond of your own company? You may go to where you may never see another white man for months on end. Are you fond of other people's society and good living and gaiety? You may be sent to a big Military station, where you will dance and act, flirt and hunt, and do all sorts of nice things. But the majority of stations are quite small, with just enough people to make up games of bridge, billiards and tennis, each evening ... The sportsman will find tennis and golf everywhere, and in big stations, polo, football and cricket in addition. As everyone in India plays bridge, the gambler will not suffer from boredom. A mighty hunter will be able to adorn the drawing room at home with the skins of tigers and bears and the heads of deer".*

March 1910 Scrapbook. Clockwise; Above Under-12 100 yard sprint. Far right; Blofield ii jumping and below that, Winnicott winning the junior quarter mile. General swimming pool shots ... top view from the new prospectus, other two taken June 1910.

"Are you a naturalist? We could well dispense with several of the weird and fearful insects that India breeds."

"Those who want a position of power and responsibility should know that in India the responsibility for everything falls on the Englishman's shoulders, and that seems to be why we are here!"

"Finally, where but in India are there more problems for the student of humanity? It would take more than our life-time out here to understand the Indian mind."

Madrassee then launched into a series of questions designed to highlight the cultural differences between home and the impoverished country he found himself in and, after gving a little news on his fellow exiled OPMs, he signed off by saying; "I hope that I have shewn that India is obviously the place to come to"!

There was a similarly astute missive that year from OPM, Geoffrey Lane, on board HMS Encounter. Writing from his temporary base in Hobart he said;

"The point which has struck me most forcibly whilst I have been in Australia is that it seems ever so much more American than English, whilst in New Zealand the case is quite different. In Australia the general feeling seems to be "Australia for the Australians," whilst in New Zealand the people seem to be much more in sympathy with the Mother Country."

Crew of HMS Encounter, Russell, N. Island, New Zealand - 1912

Lane went on to describe how the great difficulty was the question of labour, which is "absolutely ruled by the Unions ... One perfectly true case of the ridiculousness of these Unions is the following:-

In New Zealand, a man who was getting married, was building a home for himself, and a friend of his, a plumber, offered to do the plumbing for him as a wedding present. Both men were run in by their respective Unions and fined, the builder because he had employed the plumber without payment, and the plumber for working without payment."

"My advice", he added, "to anyone thinking of coming out to this part of the world is to go to New Zealand in preference to Australia, and not to come until he is assured of a place he can go to at once, as living is 25 per cent dearer than at home, and it is very difficult to obtain a good "job" without plenty of experience".

Whatever young boys at Plymouth College might have thought on reading that, it is difficult for us now to imagine, however the after-school opportunities available at home were clearly on the increase. There can be little doubt that the letter sent back home from JA Butlin (one of the school's recent leavers and greatest all-rounders, an academic and captain of various sports teams he would have been a bit of hero to younger boys still at school), would have had some influence.

Signing himself BIRMINGHAM he wrote;

"Ever since its foundation, the Plymothian has published letters giving accounts of the doings of OPMs at Oxford and Cambridge; we believe we create a precedent by sending you a new University Letter, and we hope that such letters will appear again and again in your Magazine at time goes on." (nb There had been a similar letter from Manchester in June 1901 – see above).

"Birmingham University was founded scarcely ten years ago, in the midst of one of our largest manufacturing Cities, but it has grown rapidly, and the new buildings, which are some three miles outside the City, contain some

of the best and most up-to-date scientific equipment in the world. It is essentially an engineering University, although there are also faculties of Medicine, Arts and Commerce."

"The Students are almost entirely non-collegiate, but it is hoped that this drawback will be remedied as time goes on; there is already a hostel for women students."

"The new buildings are designed entirely for students of science and engineering: at present they comprise a chemistry block, a power station, a library and a large central block which contains, besides a great hall and refectory, all kinds of workshops and the apparatus necessary for the study of mining and metallurgy. The grounds also contain a tower 325 feet high, named after the Chancellor, Mr Joseph Chamberlain, on which wireless telegraphy apparatus is to be fixed shortly, and an experimental coal mine, from which mining engineers, including JA Butlin, may be seen emerging, looking extremely grotesque in Mine Rescue Apparatus."

Clearly the new student was impressed with his new surroundings, in what he termed "the second City of the Empire", and with his cosmopolitan collection of contemporaries, Plymouth never having been famous for its cross-cultural complexion;

"The University has Students from every part of the world; in order to be able to converse with everybody in his native tongue it is necessary to know twenty different languages, including Chinese, Japanese, Siamese, and that Spanish which is spoken in the States of South America."

Our correspondent also went on to outline the sporting side, or sides, of the University – three Rugby XVs, two Association XIs, three Hockey teams, tennis teams and a Golf Club ("chiefly confined to the Dons at present") … but no Cricket Club.

Butlin was one of two OPMs then at Birmingham, and it doubtless was a measure of the City's importance that in 1900 it had become only the seventh English city (after Oxford, Cambridge, Durham, London, Manchester and Newcastle) to offer such an institution. However Liverpool (1903), Leeds (1904), Sheffield (1905) and Bristol (1909), swiftly followed suit.

June 1910 Summer sunshine in the School Swimming Bath.

Clearly prospects for Nation's youth had never been rosier as University offered not only further education, but also further delays to that passage into a full-time working life. A much harsher prospect though was around the corner.

Ever since the question of compulsory military training had percolated through the pages of the Plymothian back in the early part of 1910 there had been a number of references to "war", implying that the Country generally and the School in particular were mentally gearing up for such an eventuality.

December 1910; the Debating Society vote unanimously in favour of being properly prepared for war.

"The preparation for such a danger could not be confined merely to men and ships: a reserve of material and of trained forces was also necessary," reasoned Mr Dodson.

Ist XV 1910-11. Back row; PG Fraser, CNJ Kennedy, J Dufton, EJ Eccles, HJ Simpson, BJ Gidley, H Snell. MIddle row; W Hosking, W Douglass-James, GRT Kennedy, WA Wroth, JC Bullock. Front row; PH Austin, R Coyte, RB Munday. Within a few years CNJ Kennedy (Captain), Douglass-James (Lieutenant), WA Wroth (Lieutenant) and HJ Simpson (Private) would all be killed serving King and Country. Austin and Gidley would both be wounded.

A similar theme ran through the OTC Report in the magazine the following July. In his account of the Royal Review at Windsor, attended by 38 school cadets our anonyomus reporter (Dodson again?) wrote:

"Many boys who had the good fortune to be present at Windsor, will no doubt look back to the event with pride. They should be proud in many senses; proud in that they represented a section of Englishmen who have realised their duty to their country: proud, too, in the fact that they were setting a fine example to those who have not yet realised this duty: and, indeed, proud in that they, by their performance, showed what it is possible for boys to attain in the sphere of military training."

Then came the a further twist of the patriotic scew;

"Such an event ought to make its impression upon those, who for some reason or other have not joined the Corps. Whatever their personal objection may be, they should always remember that there is an opportunity of learning a kind of work in which they might assist their country when in danger. It is the job of every patriotic Englishman to do this. Joining the Corps means a sacrifice in some small details. It certainly does to a small extent interfere with a boy's own personal arrangement, but this interference is too small to have any real influence except with the most selfish. Selfishness should be sacrificed to duty."

And then if that was not enough to persuade the reluctant to join the account continued;

"Another objection often raised is that the military training inculcates in the youthful mind the spirit of militarism, a desire to fight for fighting's sake. Now, on the contrary, those who have seen something of the trials of military life and training should realise that these trials alone are a safeguard against unwarranted military aggression. An untrained populace, ignorant of war, is far more likely to rush into it, than a trained people who realise its meaning."

Such a piece could have been written for almost any similar school magazine or even, in abbreviated form, for a newspaper editorial column and it is perhaps no surprise to find further exhortations for the boys to don uniform over the next few months.

In November 1911 the OTC report carried quotes from His Majesty's message published after the Windsor Review;

"I am to assure you that the development of this patriotic effort on the part of the Universities, the Public Schools, and other seats of learning to take their share of the responsibilities of National Defence, and to do their best to train the future leaders will be followed with much interest by His Majesty."

The following summer the boys read this in their School Magazine;

"You boys are about to take your places in a larger life than that which you have hitherto led, and your minds must be greatly exercised as to what the future may have in store for you. I would like to remind you that, while you are working for your own advancement, you must never forget that you owe a duty to the Country and the Empire of which you are members."

"You have had great advantages as British Public school-boys, and as British citizens you have even greater privileges. What do you mean to give your country in return? It is in the power of every one of you to give personal service, that is, deliberately to work for your nation as well as for yourself; but personal service means some sacrifice of self, the giving up of some leisure and of some amusement."

"At the present time your personal service is needed to persuade your fellow-countrymen of the great necessity there is for every able-bodied man being trained to defend his country in time of need. It is difficult to convince people ignorant of war of this necessity, or to make them realize that it is unpreparedness that leads to war, but the lessons of history will have taught you that disaster assuredly awaits the nation whose sons are unable to defend her, and I would earnestly beg of you that you do all in your power to bring home to people the fact that if we continue to shirk this, the first duty of citizenship, we cannot hope to retain our great heritage."

"As you know, some of our fellow countrymen across the seas have already adopted the principle that it is the duty of every man to be trained in the use of arms; believe me, boys, you can give no greater service to your country than by doing your utmost to procure the adoption of the same principal in the Motherland."

Yours etc.,
ROBERTS, F.M.

Not long after the distinguished Lord Roberts had penned this missive, which was doubtless published in all school magazines at the time, even the Headmaster nailed his colours to the mast voting against the Debating Society motion that *"the abolition of war would be beneficial to mankind"*.

The debate had been a lively one; SG Beare arguing that a war *"whatever the result was useless from an economic point of view, and disastrous from a moral and humane point of view."*

CJ Geldard on the other hand suggested that the *"value of war was not so much monetary as moral ... war brought out the best in man : the after effects of war were beneficial to both the victorious and the defeated Country, and the morals of every Country were improved and elevated by war."*

"Weeping widows, sorrowing mothers and starving orphans" were also cited by proponents of the motion, but the view that war *"was the producer of national and individual greatness"* prevailed and the motion was lost by two votes, the significance of the Head's vote certainly not going unnoticed.

As yet of course though the Country was not at war and apart from heavy clouds that clearly coloured the outlook for the future, life at School carried on, more or less, as normal.

The highlight of the summer of 1912 was the Garden Fete held in the School House grounds. Mrs Chaytor and a willing band of helpers served afternoon tea to some 400 of the 600 or so in attendance. The 5 o'clock drawing room concert attracted a large audience and there were plenty of takers for Mrs Palmer's home-made ice-cream. With the various stalls and the 7 o'clock Café Chantant over £45 net profit was made.

There were two new members of staff, Alfred Page and James King, the latter replacing Mr Gardiner who left to take up the post of Senior Science Master at Berkhamstead School. Mr Dodson married Miss Prynn, and the headmaster officiated, at Emmanuel Church, the Reverend Henry Chaytor being assisted by the Rev RH Ward.

The financial position of the school was somewhat improved with the receipt of the £500 grant from Plymouth Corporation and there were hopes of further funding from the Devon and Cornwall County authorities.

Meanwhile the rules for house membership were clarified;

1. To School House belong all Boarders and all who dine regularly in School House.
2. To North Town all Day boys, not included in (1), who live North of the railway line from Yealmpton Station to North Road Station and then North of the old Devonport Boundary which does not include St Budeaux: in Cornwall those who live North of the GWR main line.
3. To South Town all Day boys, not included in (1), who live South of the aforsaid line.

Speech Day was held in the expanded gymnasium, four days before the start of term, with the Mayor of Plymouth, Henry Hurrell, in attendance.

The gymnasium with its new extension.

1912

Summer fun in the Swimming Bath 1911. Several of these carefree young lads would not make it through to the end of the decade.

The Headmaster acknowledged the school's grant from the Corporation and said that *"no money could be used to better purpose – it would bear fruit a hundredfold"*. However, while advocating the advancement of the education of all classes and agreeing with the provision of a ladder by which boys could rise from the elementary school to the University, he said that *"the ladder ought not to be made too wide lest it should be used for the elevation of mere mediocrity to places beyond its capacity."*

"The great need of today," he continued, *"was education, and if the country was to hold its own in the world it must subsidize the means of education with no niggard hand. Germany, America and other nations with an intelligent outlook upon the future were doing it".*

Interestingly enough the Corporation announced a £50 Scholarship the following year, *"tenable at a University or other Institution approved by the Authority"* ... *"Candidates must be the sons of ratepayers in the Borough of Plymouth, must be over 16 years of age and be ready to declare their need of such assistance".*

While Chaytor continued to lead the School ever onward, numbers reaching an all time high in 1913 (over 215) with many being groomed for further education, so his predecessor continued to welcome past and present members of the school arriving in Cambridge with his, and Mrs Colson's, *"usual hospitality and kindness".*

At the athletic sports that summer UB Burke ran the first under five-minute mile and the last OPM column of the year was unusually brief but none the less interesting; *"The Royal Aero Club",* it read, *"has granted a Pilot's Certificate to Lieut. H Glanville, West India Regiment. We believe Lieut. Glanville is our first flyer, and we offer him our congratulations".* Later promoted to Captain, Glanville, then of the RAF, was accidentally killed six years later - in May 1918.

Burke, on the other hand, was later to join the Devonshire Regiment. Held as a prisoner for some time, he survived the war and was one of a number of OPMs to be awarded the Military Cross.

1913 saw the School with a new Chairman of Governors, Sir Alfred Croft, an old boy of Mannamead School, resigned and his seat was taken by a longstanding member of the board, Dr Albert Hingston. Hingston was clearly a happy choice, he had already spent a lot of time - and money - helping the School and *"it is not too much to say that but for him the School would not have surmounted its difficulties and been placed on a firm and permanent foundation".*

Likewise it was said of Sir Alfred Croft, that *"it is difficult to over-estimate how much of the School's present position and bright prospects are due to his wise council and assiduous care".*

Academically the School continued to thrive and we note that former Plymothian editor, AF Dufton, was awarded an Open Scholarship of £80 per annum at Trinity College, Cambridge for Mathematics and Natural Science. Meanwhile JJ Thill, son of the school's languages teacher John Thill (?), had gained a Prize Cadetship of £120 a year at Sandhurst (as a young Lieutenant he would be killed in France two years later).

The sporting life of the School rolled on as ever, although illness hampered the effectiveness of the Hockey teams. In the Sports, held on Easter Monday, 24 March, on a rain-soaked field, Burke failed to equal his time for the mile and only just finished ahead of DH Vittle, while PH Austin pipped them both for the Senior Ludorum. WR Brown won the sack race, for the third year running, and WE Prynn won the Prep's egg and spoon race.

Cricket was at times dissapointing; batting first against Corporate Officers the School were rattled out for 15, only three players troubling the scorers. In return the Officers scored 62 and indeed that seemed still to be the way of things, play continuing not until scores had been beaten, but until either both sides were out or time

ran out. Mr Chaytor had a top score of 48 that season and, coincidentally, he took 48 wickets as well, two less than SG Beare, who topped both batting and bowling averages that summer.

On the rugby pitch opposition from school sides continued to be thin on the ground and Arguam no longer appeared to be on the fixture list.

Fives limped on. Boxing, on the other hand, seemed to be gaining ground and there was renewed enthusiasm for gymnastic displays. Indeed Mr Blunt organized a particularly impressive one for the Garden fete that year, involving most of the members of the upper school.

Mr Blunt's 1913 Gymnastic Display at the School Garden fete, .

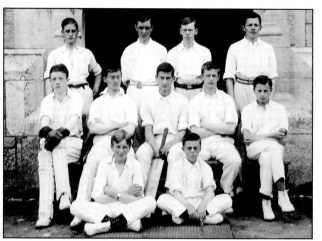

Plymouth College staff April 1912: Back row; CJ Kuhne, JL Powell MA, AH Page, BA, CW Dodson, BA. Front; H Sargent, J Thompson, MA, Rev HJ Chaytor, MA, FB Palmer, MA, EA Gardiner, MA. Movement this month saw Page arrive and Gardiner leaving.

Other images include; clockwise 1912 advertisement, cricket teams from 1910 and 1911, School Prize book-plate from 1911, Collier and Rendle ready to play, and two further pictures from 1911/12 both including Eric Corkery (front left below and middle row left, below left).

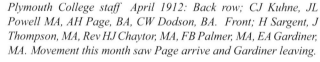

There was also a tennis tournament and a Cinderella dance on the same day. That dance was held in the expanded gymnasium, others were held in Big School. 120 attended the Annual Dance in January. Mr Chaytor was unwell and couldn't make it, but his wife arranged a very successful music programme and there was Bridge and Whist played in the neighbouring class rooms.

The following year it was agreed to also stage a "Juvenile Dance" on the night after the Annual Subscription Dance. Tickets for the junior event being 2/6d (12p), including refreshments – chaperone's tickets (non-dancing) were 1/- (5p).

Other notable events included two performances, in English, of the Greek play – the Frogs;

"The hearty laughter of those who came showed that they, at least, were agreeably disappointed to find the general spirit of burlesque more than 2,000 years ago was pretty much what it is today."

The Cast of Frogs; Mr Thompson second from the left in the middle row and Mr Chaytor standing on the right behind the "boat".

"Mr Thompson made an imposing and hieratic figure as Coryphaeus ... Some of the dresses were very pretty; Beare, Fairman and Snell are especially to be congratulated in this respect. Sir Hubert Parry's music lost nothing under the capable direction of Herr Kuhne. Mr Palmer and Mr Page were responsible for the scene painting and stage carpentry ... the Headmaster acted as stage-manager, prompter and scene shifter ..."

JK Michell, *"upon whose shoulders the brunt of the performance fell"*, played Dionysus and *"showed genius for gag and improvisation in cases of necessity"*. The giant Herakles was played by SK Beer, OPM, while AF Dufton was *"a corpse"*, a role he came close to duplicating in real life a few years later. He was one of the many OPMs wounded in the war.

The prospect of war loomed ever closer as 1913 drew to a close, but life at the College went on pretty much as normal. There were further staff changes with the departures of John Powell, who had been Chaytor's second appointment, and of Herr W Angermann *"whose stay with us has been all too short ... He carries with him the best wishes of all members of the School, and we shall be delighted to have a return visit from him"*.

We can only guess at the circumstances surrounding this particular departure, but certainly it was by no means uncommon for a Foreign Assistant to spend only a few terms at the School – he was almost immediately succeeded by Dr Ewald.

Curiously enough when Mr Gardiner came back in April of that year for his marriage to Miss NF Watt, again at Emmanuel, Herr Angermann was his best man.

Meanwhile the letters page of the Plymothian continued to reflect the sort of minor grievances that nevertheless mean so much to those concerned. One letter, however, told us more generally about the state of the uniform at the time than perhaps even he was aware;

"Dear Sirs,

May I call attention to the fact that School caps are being sold at shops other than the authorised one, namely, Adams & Baker, besides being sold at a cheaper rate. This introduces different shapes and poorer qualities. I understand that the change in design of the caps was made for the sole reason that the others were getting common, that is, the boys who did not belong to the College wore them, thus bringing down the "tone" of the College; so when the new caps were issued, Messrs. Adams & Baker received strict instructions

that they were not to sell school caps to any but College boys, but these other shops sell to anybody who ask for them. Cannot this be seen to? And cannot the school ties, blazers, etc., be sold at the above mentioned shop? Hoping this matter will receive due consideration, I am, Yours truly", *"A.S.P."*

What, perhaps was even more interesting was the reply from the *"Ed"* – *"We are informed that this matter has been under consideration. The design of the cap cannot be registered, and there is no means of preventing any shop from selling it"*.

Clearly this was a notable instance of the Editor/s dealing with genuine correspondence. An interesting missive from "Anxious OPM" suggests that this was by no means always the case; *"Dear Sirs,*

*The December number of the Plymothian reached me today (January 21st 1913). If I mistake not, this is the second consecutive number in which there has been no "Correspondence". I learn from your pages that most of the old grievances have been remedied, that the Pavilion is being taken in hand, and there is actually room in the Gymnasium on Speech Days for one's relatives. Surely, though, some grievances must be left? Is there **always** soap in the lavatory? Does not the School Crest need altering? Are the Fives-Courts all that they should be?*

Besides, if you will permit the question, what is a Junior Editor for? How can he justify his existence, nowadays? Does he reckon it enough to write his name beneath the able Editorial in your March number? Is it that he now no longer writes the "Letters to the Editors", or is it that he still honourably writes them, but the Senior Editor is all-powerful and refuses to publish them? I hate to ask these pointed questions, but I fear that there is something wrong somewhere."

Lack of space though was the simple explanation offered up by the - in this instance anonymous - editors as the reason why *"Editors do not write more often to themselves"*.

Plymouth College Rugby 1st XV, 1912-13: Back; ED Corkery, IT Drake, AF Dufton, ATS Byfield, W Hawk, KR Paton, UD Burke. Middle; CW Grant, HV Howarth, PH Austin, JHJ Simpson, CJ Brown. Front RG Carnall, ST Butlin and WE Stoneman.

Rugby Ist XV 1913-14. Back row; KB Bellamy, DH Vittle, JA Husey, PE Finnemore, , WV Aser, PL Ward, FD Hawkins. Middle; AG Bishop, ED Corkery, HV Howarth,, RG Carnall, WE Stoneman. Front; FH Greenslade, AG Hambly, WR Brown.

The 1913 Swimming Sports were staged on 21, 22 and 24 July, "in beautiful weather". "As a house competition they were a walk-over for North Town, which won the cup for the fifth successive time. Corkery was easily the Victor, Howarth partially knocking himself out in his attempt to win the 100 yards.

There was, of course, always space for the Cambridge Letter and it's amusing to note that the 1913 epistle contained these lines;

"JT Dufton from what we hear, takes life quite gaily, and we trust he is not leading his brother astray". AF Dufton was a new arrival that year and joined his brother at Trinity College. It is hindsight that makes this titbit interesting for, after his spell of war service, John Dufton was to return to Plymouth College and serve some thirty-seven years on the staff. Other young men of his generation were not so fortunate, however, as the next few years were to reveal.

Strangely enough the first OPM military casualty of 1914 was not a particularly fresh-faced victim of the whole sorry saga but rather a veteran of the South African War – Major JLJ Conry.

Lionel (Bob) Conry had joined Mannamead School back in 1886 and had gone into Sandhurst five years later. In the South African campaign he had distinguished himself under General Buller and was twice wounded. He took part in the relief of Ladysmith and in the actions at Spion Kop and Pieter's Hill. He won the DSO and Queen Victoria's medal with 4 clasps and King Edward's with 2 clasps and having been attached to the Egyptian Army in 1906 went on to gain two Egyptian medals and the Medjidieh.

Notice of his death came in a sympathetic message to Conry's mother from Lord Kitchener;

"I deeply regret that your son was killed in action on March 3rd, on the Atbara River, on the South East of Gadaret. In Major Conry's untimely death the British and Egyptian Services have lost a most efficient and gallant leader and officer and I beg you will accept the heartfelt sympathy of myself and his brother officers in this country."

"Your son was killed instantaneously gallantly leading his troops against outlaws; and was buried by his brother officers at a spot one hour south of the junction of the Atbara and Bahr-el-Galem rivers."

The outlaws, incidentally, were all killed or taken captive.

A fine footballer, he was the first to captain an OPM side (at the time of the amalgamation). He captained Devon in 1894 and played for both Argyle and Exeter in the 1890s. On one occasion he came down all the way from Sheffield just to play for the OPMs in the Amateur Cup.

Sadly his loss was to be the first of many in the following four years.

IN MEMORY OF
MAJOR JOHN CONRY D.S.O.
CONNAUGHT RANGERS,
COMMANDING GEDAREF ARAB BATTALION,
WHO FELL IN ACTION ON THE ATBARA RIVER
ON THE 5TH OF MARCH 1914.
MANNAMEAD SCHOOL 1886 1891.

On 4 August 1914 Britain declared war on Germany following the latter's rapid, aggressive assault on France through Belgium. War had broken out on the Continent a week earlier and although it was the assassination, by a Serbian nationalist, of Austria's Archduke Ferdinand, that had originally lit the touch paper back in June, the Great War itself was really a product of a number of elements at the time. Not least of these was the rising European spirit of nationalism and empire-building that had prompted the Franco-Prussian War some forty years earlier. All in turn fuelled by the heady mix of a general desire for capitalist expansion that followed in the wake of the industrial revolution, and the rise of popular government. Add to this a few traditional boundary disputes and the availability of a range of weaponry and lethal technology hitherto unknown in the field of battle and the scene was set for what, almost inevitably, was destined to be biggest and most brutal conflict the world had ever seen.

By the end of 1915 we had Austria-Hungary, Germany, Bulgaria and the Ottoman Empire - the Central Powers - locked in battle with Great Britain, France, Russia, Italy, Belgium, Serbia, Montenegro and Japan – the Allies. In April 1917, after the sinking of the Lusitania, the United States also joined the Allies.

In Britain, in the late summer of 1914 there was little notion of how bloody the next few years might be, or indeed that the conflict might last that long. The same gung-ho ethos that had seen the nation, on the whole, support the South African War, particularly through the remarkable first-hand coverage now available through the newspapers, was there as the first contingents of young men went off to meet their destinies. The Plymothian of November 1914 captured that attitude as well as any newspaper editorial of the day, exercising a degree of restraint at the same time;

"In a School, such as ours, Patriotism and Loyalty are naturally fostered, so it is not our aim to use exaggerated language in recording the manner in which all members, Past and Present, of the school are doing their duty in this terrible time."

"It is remarkable that the motto of Belgium, the country that has made such terrible sacrifices, is the same as that of the School – L'Union Fait la Force. The O.P.M.'s are proving that this is no mere coincidence of words, but of sentiment and action. Upon us now in the School is the duty of preparing to follow in their steps, so that each one of us may share in the glories which the School will win by splendid sacrifices, firm resolution in duty, and deep devotion to the King."

There was then a note on one or two examination successes and a few comments about various School clubs and societies;

"The Glee Club is postponing its efforts until the times seem more suitable for music. The Philatelic Society seems to have suffered a temporary depression, and the Natural History Society is not as energetic as it has been in the past. Interest in the Debating Society promises to be well-maintained."

"It is obvious, however, that the games and social life of the School must in some measure give way to the higher claims of Patriotism."

The editorial, credited to A.C.E. Snell and S.M.E. Fairman, was immediately followed by a poem from "O.P.M." – Up Plymouth!

"List the strain that stirs the strong in these troublous latter days,
'Tis our glorious College song "Quid, si fasti sunt breves?
Spes est grandiorum," now! Men to arms! Britannia calls,
Will you to a tyrant bow? Fight or be for ever thralls!
This, no petty civil broil fanned by passions soon to cool,
This, a fight for England's soil, Liberty and British Rule;
Hear you not the braggart toast honoured by relentless foes -
"To the Day!" – Shall bullies boast? Shall the British Lion doze?
Heed the fall of Greece and Rome, all sufficient in their power;
Cherish Country, King and Home, threatened in this anxious hour;
Headlong hurl the hostile hosts, shatter grasping German might;
Men of Plymouth, to your posts! Past and Present, arm and fight!"

1914 Plymouth men marching along Mutley Plain on their way to Millbay Docks and a ship that would take them to the Front.

For all this patriotic ferver, however, it's interesting to note that in a debate on the *"Demoralising influence of Newspapers"* earlier in the year one speaker, E.W. Horwill, had been moved to lament how *"10,000 spectators watched the Crystal Palace v Argyle Cup Tie, while only a handful assembled to hear Lord Roberts lecture on National Service on the same day ... The inference,"* said the speaker, *"was obvious."*

Interestingly enough in the course of the debate newspapers were roundly criticised because they *"Tarnished unimpeachable characters and embittered party strife"*, and because *"not only were newspapers often wrong in their views, they also made many grammatical mistakes."*

Moreover, *"little children, would read the papers in spite of their parents, and ignoring the edifying leaders would eagerly peruse accounts of suicides and murders."*

"Journalists provide what the public want, and not what they should have", argued R.W. Lethbridge.

It was not a one-sided debate by any means though and S.G. Beare spoke glowingly of the liberty of the Press *"for it enables it to tackle the biggest giants of wrong and oppression with impunity."*

North Town cricket team 1914 - next, North Town Athletics team.

An unamed athletics team from 1914

Beare and his supporters eventually won the day and the motion was lost by three votes. S.G. Beare was a bit of hero in school that year. He won the debating cup and he finished in the first three of all but one of the events entered at Sports Day, winning three outright and finishing comfortably ahead of D.H. Vittle to secure Victor Ludorum.

On the cricket field he ripped through a number of teams

1914 Ist XI: Back row HH Jago, EC Corkery, PE Finnemore, AG Bishop. Middle AG Hambly, SG Beare, HV Howarth, GV Swiggs. Front WR Brown, SM Williams.

taking six or more wickets on a number of occasionsand scored a fine 52 against Newton in a match the School won by one run. In his last three years at the School, Beare was also captain of the emerging Hockey team and in his last Plymothian end of season review he was able to report that; *"With the adoption of School colours and the institution of a photo, Hockey seems to have become recognised as one of the School games, and I feel confident that the Spring term will no longer be regarded as a slack time when some people play Fives and most people do nothing, but as one offering as many attractions, in games at least, as the football or cricket seasons."*

He concluded his remarks by noting that the *"game has been most enthusiastically taken up by the juniors, and if they can be coached, the next few years should see us as proficient in hockey as in any other game."*

During the summer Beare obtained a Junior Admiralty Appointment, he was wounded fighting for his country in March 1916 and was one of a dozen or so OPMs to be held as a prisoner of war.

The first official photograph of a School Hockey team - 1914. Back row; PA Harris, DH Vittle, HH Jago, SM Williams. Middle row; JA Drake, EC Corkery, SG Beare, JA Hussey, EA Jago. Front row; JC Reed, AG Hambly.

But to return to 1914, it wasn't just the social life of the school that was affected. Speech-Day was postponed and in the autumn term it was decided *"in consequence of the war, not to hold the usual Christmas Concert."*

Not surprisingly perhaps *"the serious condition of the European situation necessitated the hurried break-up of the OTC camp on bank holiday".*

We also learn from the OTC notes that November that *"immediately after the declaration of war practically every cadet and ex-cadet available came forward to do something."*

And at School there was certainly plenty to do for College became the *"mobilization centre of a Reserve Park".*

The School field, which months earlier had witnessed a Garden Fete gymnastic display "a most intricate piece of work, requiring 202 boys – the largest of its kind ever shown in the West of England", suddenly became a military base.

School Gymnastic Display 1914 and the boys spell out the year.

"For more than a fortnight (school) cadets provided the necessary guards both night and day in order to relieve the Regulars for their important tasks. Such work entails considerable discomfort, and our readers may form their own conclusions of those who cheerfully undertook this work, and sacrificed their own personal comfort, although such duties were not incumbent on them in any way whatever. The Officer commanding the A.S.C. mobilising here, on his departure for the front, said "Those cadets have been splendid and assisted us to a very great extent."

"After wishing our guests "Good-bye" and "Good luck," our energies were turned in another direction. From a mobilization centre the College became a training centre, where a large number of Territorial recruits were given instruction in drill and musketry by cadets. A Cadet-Sergeant taking in hand a body of fifty raw recruits and drilling them was a sight that made one feel the soundness of the O.T.C. movement, it was the realisation of the fact that whatever the O.T.C. movement had done – and it has many critics – it had produced the right spirit of being useful and knowing how to be so in a crisis."

Already, at this very early stage of the war we learn that "more than seventy O.P.M.'s are serving in His Majesty's Navy and more than a hundred in the Army, many of whom have been cadets in recent years and are now in the battle line."

"Fortunately", the account continued, "the casualty list is so far slight: - Capt. C.F.Burnard 2nd Batt. Royal Warwickshire Regt.; Lieut W.W.Jefferd, 1st Batt. Middlesex Regt.; and 2nd-Lieut. J.W.Ford, 2nd Batt. The Welch Regt. Have been wounded; the two former together with Lieut D.Paige, R.F.A., have been mentioned in despatches; 2nd Lieut. C.J.N.Kennedy, Royal Scots Fusiliers, is reported wounded and missing; 2nd Lieut. N.Prynn, D.C.L.I. has also been wounded, and is at present in Boulogne hospital."*

Spare a thought too for the languages teacher Harold Truelove who *"is at present a prisoner in Germany".*

A month later the situation had escalated dramatically, as the Headmaster was quick to acknowledge at Speech Day on Tuesday 15 December. *"Referring first to the* part the School is playing in the present crisis, he said that the roll of Old Boys on active service now contained over 250 names and the list was not yet complete."

He then added gravely; *"We have had some losses to deplore"* and he named S.W. Finch –a Naval Paymaster who had left School in 1898 and *"a particularly sad case, that of Assistant-Clerk C.G.Cook, who left School only last term to take up his appointment on the Good Hope, and who went down with the ship in the action in the South Pacific."*

On a brighter note he told a somewhat subdued Speech Day audience that the *"Old Boys who had been wounded were all progressing favourably and were hoping to be back again at the front as soon as possible."*

Mr Chaytor then went on to talk of the various uses that the School field had been put to by the Military and how NCO's of the School Cadet Corps had been used to drill recruits for the Royal Devon Engineers *"handling over 100 men in two or three weeks ... Col. Bastard was very appreciative of their services and, in a letter to Capt. Dodson, he wrote: "It seems clear proof of the usefulness of the Officer's Training Corps"."*

PLYMOUTH COLLEGE UNDER CONDITIONS OF WAR was the Western Morning News headline that accompanied this picture, with the caption "Army Service Corps encamped in the College Grounds. Excercising the horses the day prior to leaving for the Front.

1914 and the School field becomes a focus for the war effort. Farriers work in front of Main School, the Cricket Pavilion sits alongside the makeshift cook house and the field generally is deployed for the exercising of horses. Below, August 1915; Plymouth Voluntary Training Corps, Company Commander WA Sage, Adjutant.

1914

The situation also occasionally afforded the *"agreeable spectacle of sons drilling their own fathers "* (Chaytor 1927).

Since then, continued the Head, *"the ground has been used by the Royal Engineers and Royal Marines for training and we now have on our hands the Plymouth Defence Force."*

"Members of the Plymouth Defence Force at the College Grounds, Mutley. This force is formed of men who, though over the age at which they can enlist, still feel themselves capable of military duties, and are undertaking drill and training in order to place themselves at the disposal of the Plymouth Fortress authorities for local service." Doidges Annual.

With all this activity on the field and with a greatly felt need generally it is no surprise that the OTC numbers had doubled that term. They were about to grow yet further as Plymouth College, along with other public schools, continued to provide men to take commissions in the new army.

"In this matter", said Mr Chaytor, *"the country owed a great debt to the public schools"*, a fact that Lord Kitchener himself acknowledged in a letter to the Chairman of the Headmaster's Conference. Kitchener noted that it had been calculated that since the war had begun, just a few months earlier, some 10,000 ex-members of the Officer's Training Corps had been accepted for commissions – a figure which showed, he said, what valuable work the corps was doing.

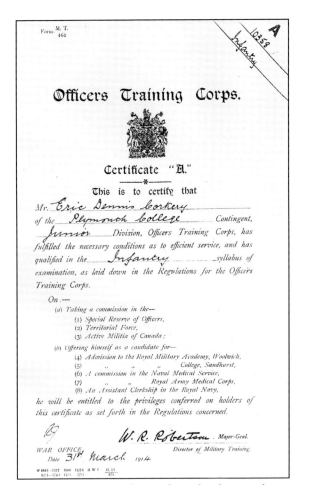

Eric Corkery's "Cert A" The certificate that for many boys was a passport to the front line of the frontline.

The war had a much wider impact, of course, on Plymouth generally; indeed on the Three Towns taken as a whole, which they were for the first time in October 1914. The question of amalgamating Plymouth, Stonehouse and Devonport had been first mooted back in 1835 and again in 1888. More recently, in 1902, Sir Joseph Bellamy had promoted a conference on the subject in Stonehouse Town Hall. However it wasn't until January 1914 that a full inquiry was opened on the matter.

Witnesses appeared for both sides of the debate, but perhaps the most telling testimony came from Major-General A.P. Penton, CVO, CB and Officer in Command South West Defences;

"In peacetime," said the Major-General, *"the organisation of the Three Towns into three distinct bodies does not affect us much ... In wartime it is an entirely different question. You would have the fortress commander having to go to three different bodies ... In fact if I was fortress commander here in wartime I should have to go to the three chief civil magistrates and say "One of you must represent the civil community ..."*

With the threat of war looming large it was no surprise to find that as of October 1914 there was only one authority to deal with – Plymouth.

As to what effect that would have on the newly grant-aided Plymouth College, Mr Chaytor was unsure, for, as of December 1914, a united Education Committee had yet to be constituted. However, it would appear that he thought there would be some reorganisation of secondary and higher education in the area. The Headmaster also made reference to the talk of a University for Plymouth, indicating that he thought it might now be a possibility, without commenting on the advisability of such a move. He did suggest, however, that there would perhaps be no longer a need for two separate Technical Schools.

Distributing the prizes at that Speech Day was Chaytor's predecessor, Francis Colson. No stranger to amalgamation issues himself, Colson said his satisfaction with the constitution of the School was increased *"by the fact that the Three Towns had become a United Borgough and,"* he continued, *"I am proud to think that Plymouth College is now the chief educational institution of the metropolis of the West."*

Colson also said that he was glad the temptation to raise money by selling the playground had been resisted;

"Other important schools are obliged to go a considerable distance from their work to their games, but to have the playground at the front door of the School is an advantage to the athletic and social life of the School that can hardly be over-estimated."

The former head also gave thanks to the efforts of Mr Thompson and made an oblique reference to the incomplete status of the School buildings, which, interestingly enough, earlier that year the OPM architect M Alton Bazely, then a School governor, still referred to as a *"dream for the future"*. Thirty-five years on and the original plans were still fresh in the minds of some! *"The school,"* said Bazley, at a complimentary dinner for Mr Thompson, *"had got the reputation and gradually it was getting the numbers"*.

Certainly the school reached its highest ever tally of pupils that summer and that it had reached such a point was due in no small measure to the man who was being toasted at that dinner.

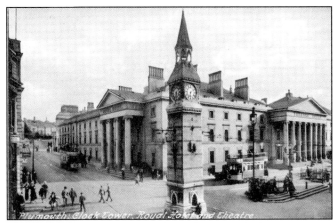

Royal Hotel and Theatre Royal, behind Derry's Clock.

Held in the Royal Hotel on Thursday 20 January 1914, the meal was well attended. Mr Colson was unable to be there, but sent a glowing tribute;

"While to the outside public the bath is the most striking monument of his liberality, I appreciate even more the munificence by which he enabled us to carry out in 1908 the great scheme of the incorporation of the school."

J.P. Brown, chairing the evening also spoke warmly of Joseph Thompson's substantial financial gifts, some of which he did not allow to be publicly talked of and …

"one condition of which had been that his salary – not a princely one – should be raised."

The reason for this was clearly not personal advancement - rather because Thompson wanted to raise the overall standard of salaries at the School and in the teaching profession generally.

"It is a fairly open secret," explained Brown, *"that Mr Thompson has devoted practically the whole of his salary to the benefit of the school."*

In reply Joseph Thompson informed those gathered in his honour that *"It so happens that I have no need to support myself through my work, but I feel that I ought to work, and I chose teaching because I like it and I feel that it is what I can do best. In order to do it well in the place in which I found myself though it was exceedingly desirable that the institution should be on a sound basis financially."*

"If I might give a reason for the help I have tried to give the school," he began to explain, after regretting that it wasn't more, *"it was that as Masters we are always preaching to the boys that the life of the school should be a reality to them, that they should revere its traditions and make traditions for those who come after; we teach boys to honour the school and it is a first necessity for being honoured that it should be a permanent, living institution."*

"The school," he added, *"was in a precarious position when I first came to it, and I want to claim credit for having first suggested to Mr Colson that they should change it from a Limited Liability Company to a Trust."*

In his concluding remarks at this dinner arranged to commemorate his 21 years at the school, he said;

"As long as I live the interests of the College will lie close to my heart. Personally I think very much less of the money I have given to the school than of the 20 years' work I have done there, conscious as I am of its many defects."

Here Mr Brown, the Vice-Chaiman of the Governors, interjected that he did not know of any defects in Mr Thompson's teaching.

"But you haven't been a pupil under me!" said Thompson amid much laughter.

The final word rested with the Headmaster who said that, *"although a list of the things we want would probably stagger the Governors, there is reasonable hope for the future. Numbers matter. Numbers mean money, without which we cannot get on. The school is a permanency, and, thanks to Mr Thompson, we have provided for the future."*

It is interesting to note that Mr Thompson himself must have seemed pretty much a permanency at the time. After all in the 38-year history of the school to date, only Herr Kuhne, who provided the musical programme for that evening, and Francis Palmer, also in attendance and who had come from Manamead School in 1896, had served the school longer than the 21 years notched up by 54 year-old Mr Thompson. Certainly it must have been heart-breaking for the three of them to get news of so many casualties among past pupils of theirs over the next few years.

"When the night wind shudders softly 'cross the empty playing grounds,
As it murmurs through the branches overhead,
There is mourning in the breeze,
- Deadened, muffled by the trees,
Half-sad and half-triumphant, mingled with the other sounds
For the dear old School is mourning for its dead.

When the humming bullet whistles through the fire-swept zone,
As the sharply-bursting shrapnel shrieks o'erhead,

Hid beneath the boiling surge
Of bloody battle, there's a dirge,
When the dead are laid unburied; in the homes whence
they have gone,
And the Mother Land is mourning for her dead.
We are sad at losing them, yet we rejoice that they have
died,
For every drop of blood that they have shed
Makes the victory come still faster
- Brings the enemy disaster -
And makes each Briton's heart beat true with fiercest
joy and pride,
For the Empire joins to praise the mighty dead."

So ran "M.E.'s" wistful and, as history would sadly show, somewhat naïve, verses – "Memento", which all but concluded the last School magazine of 1914. It was followed only by a report from the Debating Society ("*War correspondents do more harm than good?*" No by 4 votes … and "*Railways should be Nationalised*" again "No" by the same margin) and two letters, one bemoaning the "*deplorable state of what used to be the School path*", the other thanking those members of the School "*who have so generously contributed towards sending out cigarettes, etc., to the Suffolk Regiment*". The letter from the Suffolks came from J.J.Thill, who appears to have been the son of John Thill, another long-serving member of staff who'd joined as a languages teacher from Heidelberg School in 1896. His son J.J. had joined the School in 1901 and he left the School in 1912, he wrote;

"*I should like to give you some news, but unfortunately the Censor stands in the way. I can only say that we are nearly always in the trenches and that the weather is beastly!*
Wishing the School every success … Yours J.J.Thill."
Twelve months later, in the last Plymothian of 1915 we read that he was killed in France in action on the night of Sept. 30 – Oct. 1.

On the same page the deaths of six other OPMs were noted.

That December magazine was, for the first time, a two-in-one production and editors W Brown and S Fairman were presented with the unenviable task of providing the introductory text – they were suitably philosophical;

"*The war,*" they wrote, "*has drained away the best blood of the country, and for that reason the Public Schools have suffered heavily. We have not escaped, and with us as with the other Schools of England, all boys of military age and physique have joined the Colours.*"

Plymouth & Mannamead College Football XV., 1914-15. Back; PA Harris, WF Roper, SM Fairman, JA Drake, JC Reed, RW Lethbridge, HC Bracken. Middle; FD Hawkings, KS Bellamy, PE Finnemore, FH Greenslade, WR Brown. Front; GV Swiggs, HC Goodfellow, HR Selmon.

"*The younger fellows are left without the authority of such older boys as the seniors of previous years. It is their duty, therefore, to take care that the School, though young in years, maintains its former standard of efficiency.*"

"*The nation has at last realised that the situation is grave, that England and her Colonies are fighting for their very existence. Therefore the older Public School boys must go to serve and even to die if fate decrees it.*"

"*We have not been untouched by death and his grim hand has been laid in battle on many of those whose memory is still fresh in the minds of many of us. We can only offer our sincerest sympathy to their relatives, who must feel their loss far more than we do, and we remain sure that those who have died, and those who will die, sacrifice their lives willingly and gallantly at the altar of Patriotism.*"

Such words were not faintly written; before the end of the war Brown, Lieut. Brown of the RFA, as he was to become, would himself be a hospital casualty of the war on two occasions – in 1917 and again in 1918.

It was a year completely overshadowed by the conflict. Social events disappeared from the School calendar, as did most of the School matches, while the Debating Society did little else but examine the issues surrounding the war; 22 January 1915: HC Palmer proposed that "*the present European war is more of a blessing than a disaster to humanity*".

"*War is like medicine,*" he suggested, "*although not pleasant it benefits us, and it will instil a sense of honour in the nation.*"

HJWJ Westlake, opposing, remarked that "*the chief powers engaged in this terrible conflict have been preparing for war for several years ... It is a disaster to humanity that this preparation was allowed to continue to such an extent that war became inevitable. Lands and commerce have been destroyed, large sums of money wasted and there have been colossal losses of men just to satisfy the desire of the German Emperor. It is,*" he contended, "*a disaster to humanity to have such a being in its midst.*"

Westlake was outnumbered though as the motion was carried by six votes. The following month Westlake himself proposed that *"all neutral countries should combine to punish Germany for her breaches of the Hague Convention."*

SME Fairman, opposing asked *"are the Allies so uncomfortably situated that they desire help? Obviously not,"* he said, answering his own question. He then added *"America has always been an evil influence in councils and cannot be trusted. Besides which the increase in loss of life would be enormous and would not justify the intervention of neutrals".*

Several others addressed the floor and the motion was eventually lost by three votes.

As the year progressed the idea that the war might grind on relentlessly without any obvious inroads being made by either side was still far from people's minds and on Friday 15 March the members of the debating society voted against the notion that; *"further extension of the British Empire in consequence of the European War was undesirable".* The mood of the opposition, and to a certain extent of the warring nations themselves, being summed up by G LePrevost, who contended that *"in the interests of the welfare of the governed, it is the duty of Great Britain to extend her Empire".*

In October the question of conscription was raised in the School debating chamber; *"Necessary for the safety of the country"*, was how SME Fairman put it. He went on to show that there were 1,250,000 eligible young men in the country who would not join the Army. *"These men are urgently needed at the rate of 35,000 a week ... The man who has not joined voluntarily has put himself outside the Government and is therefore a slave and a coward and should be sent to the front".*

"Some people," he continued, *"suggest that conscription would cause civil war; if that is so, shoot them down with machine guns and give them a taste of war,"* Fairman proposed.

In the lively debate that followed the house was left divided and the motion was eventually carried by the casting vote of the Chairman – the Headmaster.

Kitchener's famous Army recruitment poster.

At the November meeting Captain Dodson was in the Chair. Discussing the motion *"Commercial enterprise has done more to promote Peace than War between Nations"* the house was once more divided and this time the Chair, not surprisingly perhaps, came out on the side of the opposition.

Clearly the war dominated most aspects of School life, the only other issues raised by the Debating Society that year apparently being the question of Vegetarianism and Competition. Of the former members clearly were reluctant to consider giving up their meat, despite HR

Selmon's contention that *"vegetarianism produced an increase of brain power"*. While of the latter, NW Trobridge's proposal that *"competition has a bad effect on character"* found few supporters. This despite his impassioned speech about *"worry, bankruptcy and ruin, dishonest lawyers, fraud, adulteration in trade, scamped work and starvation wages"*. E Aitken-Davies and FH Greenslade easily won the day with their talk of competition bringing out the best in man and survival of the fittest.

Out of doors competition was a little thin on the ground. Most team games were played against Service sides, Mr Chaytor and Mr Sargent both enjoying good seasons on the cricket pitch, the Head knocking up a fine 95 against the East Lancs Regt. Among the few school v school encounters were two clashes within three days against Kelly. In both, the Tavistock boys triumphed, Aspinal registering 151 not out for them in the first game at Kelly and scoring a brilliant 95 before falling LBW to Finnemore at Ford Park. Happily the juniors redressed the balance in their fixtures, only one player scoring more than six for Kelly in each of the games.

Sports day, Wednesday 5 May, was warm, calm and cloudy: WR Brown was Senior Victor Ludorum and HR Selmon Junior Victor. Selmon was unlucky at the end of the day though, for having already won the Junior Quarter of a mile, Long Jump and High Jump, he was competing in the Senior High Jump when he slipped and fell, suffering a serious compound fracture to his right arm in the process.

This was the second year in succession that there had been a serious injury in the High Jump, prompting "Bystander" to write to the Plymothian;

"One would have thought that after the unfortunate event of last year steps would have been taken to prevent such a thing from happening again. More than one Senior suggested the provision of a sand pit – as provided in nearly all big Public Schools - but little attention was paid by those of mightier wisdom to such suggestions ... Trusting that certain members of the Sports' Committee have at last learned a lesson, and that in future years either the event will be abolished or proper provision made."

What, no sand pit? How did they land? How did they jump? It is so easy to see an event listed all those years ago and assume that the same conditions applied then, as now, but consider the Editor's reply;

"The provision of sand-pits for a High Jump is quite unusual, and no such suggestion was ever brought before the Games' Committee."

The Sports Day that year was scheduled to have been held in the previous term, but according to the April magazine; *"the incessant rain of the last three months has continually made the ground unfit for any form of locomotion".*

Clearly the situation had not been helped by the Military occupation of the field.

"The war and weather alike have had a depressing influence upon School games. The A.S.C. removed a considerable quantity of turf from the playground during their occupation of the premises in the Summer holidays; it has been constantly used as a drill ground by the Devon R.E.Territorials, by the Royal Marine Light Infantry, and by the Plymouth Volunteer Training Corps, all of whom we have been very glad to see there."*

The Pavilion still under occupation in 1915.

But the upshot, of course, was chaos at times;

"Saturday 20 February 1915 – a House-match was played between North Town and South. The match was evenly contested, and at half-time the score stood at 1-1. Owing to the mud pond situated at the Devon Terrace end of the pitch, accurate passing in that vicinity was utterly useless; and, in fact, the ball became so confounded with the mud, as to be completely indistinguishable, with the result that all efforts to extricate it, only deposited vast quantities of virgin soil upon the limbs and faces of the players."

Despite this, however, the introduction of inter-House matches was one of the few bright spots in the Hockey calendar.

Generally it was not a good season – *"there were only school teams with which to arrange matches; and, unfortunately, owing to the prevalence of infectious diseases, all of these were scratched."*

"Like my predecessors," wrote EAH Jago, the Hockey Captain, *"I have found the position to be an unenviable one. Rarely have I been able to make up more than one game, which hardly seems creditable to a school of considerably over two hundred boys. Through the lack of enthusiasm displayed by the whole school, and especially by its senior members, small boys have had to play in the senior game, which incidentally they have neither enjoyed nor improved."*

But it wasn't just the Hockey enthusiasts who were struggling to make up the numbers as *"One of the XV"* was keen to point out;

"May I comment on the slackness of a few members of the School during the present Football season. They are not only invariably provided with some plausible reason for shirking voluntary games, but even when we have been playing a School match, they have been too unpatriotic to turn up and watch the game."

"During the War, we have lost and shall continue to lose most of the bigger fellows, so that if we are going to have a good XV in the future surely it is up to those Seniors who are left to be keener on the game and try to win matches for the good old School and not to spend their half-holidays in Picture Palaces or on motor bicycles."

Ah cycles … there was another tale of woe;

"The chaos which arises every day in the cycle shed at 12.30 or 4.45 is indescribable."

"Everyone is so eager to extract his own machine from the melee that no one cares what happens to the others. Pumps, etc., are often lying about in the dust, being knocked off, and thus lost in the general scrum."

"*Iron's*" suggestion was for dividers to be constructed in the shed, an idea the editors thought would be better off directed to the "*right quarter*", possibly meaning the IVth form during their woodworking hours.

One area where there was a little less jaundiced view on matters was in the newly formed Natural Science Society. Admittedly this was achieved through the passingf the Natural History Society, but by combining the remnants of that body with the what passed as the Science Library "*a new and more virile Society*" had emerged.

With subs of sixpence a term the new body was soon in receipt of its first collection of Curios. "*Coming from all quarters of the earth*", the donation came from Mrs Hogge, who also loaned the society a further collection. In addition to its material gains the NSS also heard a series of papers from its various members;

JC Reed – Torpedoes

HJWJ Westlake – Colour Photography

S Cuppa – Botanical Aspects

MM Carey - Wireless Telegraphy

HC Goodfellow – Photography

SME Fairman – Machine Guns

AT Phillips – Aquaria

PA Harris – Naval Guns and Shells

SGK Beer (OPM) – Collecting

Beer, a recent graduate of Selwyn College, Cambridge, had come back to the School that term as a member of the teaching staff.

For boys at School, though, there was little immediate prospect of taking a degree course at any University;

"*This year we have only one Scholarship to record – the profession of arms being that entered upon by the majority of those leaving the School.*"

Each magazine was full of names of new OPMs serving with Naval or Military Forces and accounts of Awards for those already in uniform, promotions, appointments and, inevitably casualties, as the Headmaster was duty bound to detail at Speech Day.

"*On the Roll of Honour, as it stands at present, and doubtless there are other names entitled to be there, there are just over 350 names,*" he said, to great applause, from the crowded platform in the Gymnasium.

"*Eighteen Old Boys have been mentioned in Despatches, five had gained the DSO, one the Legion of Honour, one the Russian Order of St Anne, and one the French Military Cross.*"

"*I am sorry to say though, that the losses are considerable, many of the names on the list being those of a comparatively recent generation, and some known to many of those among the present generation of boys.*"

That present generation, even in December 1915, included many who would become casualties themselves.

Recent School leaver Eric Corkery's parade day at the Royal Military Academy - 1915.

"*Since August 1914,*" the Head went on to say, "*84 commissions have been obtained by members of the College contingent – 9 in the Regular Army, 1 in the Royal Marines, 21 in the Special Reserve, 28 in the Territorial Force, 23 temporary commissions in the Army, and 2 temporary commissions in the Navy.*"

"*That,*" he added, "*is a considerable number for a comparatively small corps, like ours, the average*

numbers of which, during the seven years of my Head-mastership, have been between 60 and 70 ... They are rather higher now!*"

They might even have been higher earlier had it not been for the "*sloppy talk about the coming peace millennium, about universal brotherhood and the doctrine that the human race had grown too civilized for war*". Not the headmaster's words, but those of the guest speaker Lieut. Colonel WP Drury, the first Old Plymothian ever to join the Army.

Referring back to the "*beautiful but foolish and unpractical dream of peace*", Drury's version was that "*it had vanished as a breath faded off a window pane.*"

And then ..."*In the middle of all that talk, with the suddenness of a terrific earthquake, there burst upon us the greatest war the world had ever known, and all the nations were now fighting with the savagery of the prinitive man that we all had beneath our thin clothing of civilization. How much better it would have been,*" he added, "*if, instead of wasting time in talking about impossible things, we had listened to the wise counsels of that great and good soldier – Lord Roberts.*"

"*If we had, and if we had trained our great strength and prepared for this inevitable war, then probably the war would have been over by this time, and certainly tens of thousands of valuable young lives would have been saved.*"

This part of the speech had been prompted by the Colonel's third bit of advice to the younger members of his audience, namely "*Be Patriotic in the true sense of the word – Always be ready to sacrifice personal considerations of comfort and pleasure to the safety, honour and welfare of your country.*"

His other two maxims had been – "*Be ambitious; make up your mind to make a name for yourself in the world*" and firstly;

"*Put your back into the whole of your work, not only into those subjects you particularly like. Life,*" he mused:

"is such an extraordinary jig-saw puzzle that some day you will find that some scrap of knowledge that you have picked up in this school will be the very piece you want to fit into the puzzle and complete your work." Essentially however this was a speech designed to inspire unquestioning support for the war effort as indeed was the poem that in April 1916, in an unprecedented move, replaced the editorial and/or school notes which traditionally had always appeared on the first page of the Plymothian;

England

England, Oh! England
What is my blood but thine?
Hast thou no right then
To call on me and mine?

England, Oh! England
My fathers fell for thee;
Is there less love in
The blood that flows through me?

Take me and use me,
Dear England, as thou wilt;
Here is my hand, and
In my hand my Hilt.

England, my England,
Drain my blood to the last;
I will uphold thee
Until my life has passed.

I will uphold thee
Then, England, will I die,
Proud as my fathers,
And they as proud as I."

The poem was submitted to the magazine by Miss Dulcie Conry, presumably a sister of the late Bob Conry, and inevitably there was news contained within the following pages that told of more OPM casualties (Major E Colson, Captain AR Speirs Alexander and Lieut OC Maginness among them).

Despite all the Speech Day talk of honour and patriotism there were few real rewards to be reaped during the course of this wretched war. However, there can be little doubt that the position of the so-called fairer sex improved immeasurably at this time.

With so many men at the Front, more and more women were called into the workplace. In the twelve months leading up to January 1916 the number of working women in this country had risen by two million, as increasingly women were called in to do a man's work.

At the School it was no different and, it would appear, the first female, non-preparatory staff member – Miss Blagrave – was, to quote the simple wording in the School notes, welcomed *"as a Mistress this term"*. At some point in the next two terms a Miss Marks also appeared on the staff, only to be replaced in early 1917, by Miss Alice Trenchard, a London graduate, who appears to have become the first female member of senior school staff to stay more than one year.

Small wonder, therefore, when the traditional den of School sexism, the floor of the Debating Society, was called upon for a discussion on *"The fact that so many women are employed on men's work is to be deprecated"*, the motion was easily defeated.

The mood of the proponents of the motion appear to have been summed up by FJ Warne and HJWJ Westlake: the former arguing that working women would not be inclined to marry: the latter that *"the sudden release from restraint had to a certain extent carried the modern working girl off her feet, with the result that her attitude towards life was becoming frivolous, and she herself was becoming too independent"*.

EA Aitken-Davies on the other hand extolled the virtues of the fair sex and concluded his remarks by stating that *"the nation would not be rich enough after the war to allow the girls to stay at home unemployed"*.

Attitudes were certainly changing fast and it would not be long (December 1916) before the newly-installed Prime Minister, David Lloyd George, was announcing that the Government were, at long last, planning to give women the vote – as long as they were married and over thirty!

David Lloyd George PM

Wartime work for women in the construction industry.

It wasn't only attitudes to the fairer sex that were changing. Attitudes to sex itself were being changed as the prospect of a life cut short caused many to throw caution to the wind. By the end of the year more than 50,000 cases of syphilis had been reported among British servicemen, a statistic that provided a sobering accompaniment to an earlier report, published in Westminster, that estimated that 10 % of the urban population was infected with venereal diseases.

Prostitutes who *"haunt the camps of men in training"* were considered to be a part of the problem, but clearly the issues ran much deeper than that.

The government promised cash for diagnosis and for medical treatment. Meanwhile the increasing number of casualties at the front prompted the recently-arrived Classics and Divinity master, Geoffrey Gurnhill, to leave school for duty with the Red Cross in Italy.

Thoughts of War Service were clearly running through the minds of other staff members, among them Henry Chaytor himself.

The Headmaster had been Chaplain to the Devon Fortress R.E. (Royal Engineers) since 1912 and the outbreak of war changed what had been an almost honorary post to one of constant activity and thus the intervals of school work were filled with hospital visiting and other forms of garrison duty.

In 1916 though *"by way of reply to certain criticisms upon the amount of war service that the staff were rendering, I thought it was my duty to serve in France for a year"*, so wrote Chaytor in the Plymothian some years later (1927). Adding; *"This step was naturally not approved by some of the Governors and gained for me the permanent antagonism of the then Chairman"*, but he went *"I have never seen any reason to regret my action"*.

So it was that at the end of the summer of 1916 (and for him it was a summer crowned with a splendid 112 for the School against one of the many Service sides they played – RAMC) he headed off for France as a Chaplain to the Forces.

There was, according to PA Harris and HR Selmon, newly-appointed Plymothian editors, *"no general upheaval of School traditions and institutions, thanks to the able manner in which Mr Palmer has filled the vacancy"*.

Quite how much the Reverend Chaytor was able to anticipate what he was letting himself in for we cannot say, however, as soon as he arrived in France

he would have found himself in the thick of the most intense fighting the world had yet seen. Estimates put the number of British casualties on the Western Front, for August, September and October, 1916 in excess of 350,000.

The Head was also there to see a new weapon in action – the tank. It was in the middle of September that the moving, metal monsters first rolled across the muddy battlefield of the Somme, spitting bullets and spreading panic through the German lines and for a while it was thought that at last the deadlock might now be broken. But the Germans had tanks of their own, as the Head was to discover at close quarters. Returning on leave, in December 1916, he addressed the whole School about his experiences on the Somme, including a tale of a rude awakening.

"The new war weapon, tanks first went into action on the Somme in 1916, and are seen here filling up with petrol."

"It requires rather a stretch of imagination to picture our Reverend Headmaster retiring in haste from his sleeping quarters in the middle of the night before an advancing Tank", ran part of the account of his address in the Plymothian. It went on to say *"of the serious side he told us of scenes that impressed everyone present"*. One can but wonder what he said. Freshly-back from the Somme, he was doubtless there on the 15 November when thirteen divisions went over the top and 19,000 men were killed, with a further 57,000 wounded.

Despite his grizzly experiences the Head must have fired many of his pupils with desire to join him and certainly, thanks to the recently-passed revised regulations for

securing a commission, it had never been easier for young lads from the School to join up - higher up.

"To be eligible for a commission, a candidate must be either an efficient soldier or an efficient cadet in the OTC. The first stage is recommendation by his Commanding Officer, the second approval by the General Officer Commanding-in-Chief, and finally selection by the Army Council to join an Officer-Cadet unit. After a course in the Officer-Cadet unit, really a finishing branch of the OTC the candidate, if satisfactory in note and promise, is commissioned to a unit."

These new regulations meant that greater responsibility than ever was vested in the OTC and, not surprisingly, sport was frequently squeezed in to second place by extra OTC work – Wednesday afternoons were now given over to extra drill instruction.

Nevertheless attempts were made to keep up a reasonable number of fixtures across the year, although in each sport most of the opponents were service sides.

Having said that, the 1st XV had their two regular encounters with Kelly and won both handsomely. They also *"for the first time in the history of School Rugby, played a team consisting of Internationals and County players"* (The Barbarians – who won 5 – 35).

For the fledgling hockey players it was much the same story, and a fairly sorry one at that – the highlight of the season coming at the very beginning of the opening game;

"Harris, obtaining the ball from the bully-off, ran through and scored within a minute of the start."

The lead was not held for long and the game ended Plymouth College 1, 3rd East Lancashire Regt. 11. A hammering for sure and there were more to follow as the 4th East Surrey Regt., the 3rd Devons and the RN Barracks team all put nine goals past the College keeper, the School never scoring more than two in reply. The 6th Worcester Regt. and the RGA also inflicted defeats on the XI, the only successes for the School coming at the expense of the Royal Engineers and the London Electrical Engineers (who they beat twice 9-2 and 3-2).

Sports Day itself was held on Friday 5 May and, in the absence of many senior boys, Williams and Harris finished in the top three of most events, while, more impressively, LeMesurier won six of the seven main events and was second, to Harris's younger brother, in the seventh – the half-mile.

Williams picked up a second Victor Ludorum in the annual Swimming Sports and LeMesurier was again impressive among the Juniors. But there were few opportunities all round for athletic training and practice matches and sadly voluntary games were treated largely as *"a joke, as they usually are"*. There was a request made, via the Magazine that perhaps a senior boy or master should superintend such activities. But senior boys were thin on the ground and masters had plenty of other things to think about – with the Head in France and the School number high there was more for everyone to do.

Despite all his other activities, however, Captain Dodson still managed to chair the odd School Debate, including one in February that considered the notion *"modern methods of advertising are to be deprecated"*. JN Morris, proposing, argued that the object of advertisers is to outdo one another *"and to achieve this they often have to recourse to lying"*. What is more *"Magazines and newspapers are crammed with advertisements instead of interesting stories or news; tram-cars, theatres and railway stations are plastered with placards; hoardings disfigure the country-side and outrage the taste of the beauty lover."* This was a time when advertising was subject to far fewer regulations - the motion was, nevertheless, narrowly defeated.

A few weeks later Mr Thompson was in the chair for a debate on reprisals over the, as yet, undefeated Germany. *"Justifiable"* was AP Atwill's view, advocating, somewhat callously, *"the extermination of the German civilian population by organised air raids … the youths of Germany will one day cause another war"*, he insisted, *"if they are not nipped in the bud"*.

PJ Ahern, on the other hand, argued that reprisals *"would only call for fresh atrocities and lower the integrity of the country"*. *"Our object"*, he contended, *"is to win the war not to lose honour."*

For his part Mr Thompson criticised the *"vagueness of the motion"*, so Atwill spoke again and the House agreed that *"reprisals were justifiable"* by a margin of 7 votes to 4.

Curiously the next debate, staged a fortnight later was; *"That in the opinion of the House, all trade with Germany be stopped for a period of years"*. After hearing both sides Mr Thompson, from the chair, argued that *"it is a humiliated and not a destroyed Germany that we want"*. The motion was lost 8-3.

The cost of the war effort contunues to escalate. Friends and family turn out for another Army Officer cadet passing out parade.

Meanwhile the cost of the war continued to escalate. By the end of the year it was estimated that it was draining the country by as much as £5.7 million ***per day***; a fact that the Headmaster did not miss in his annual Speech Day report (Chaytor had hoped to be back in time to present it himself but was still in France on 27th November and Mr Palmer presented for him). *"Now that we have learnt how to spend six millions a day in the struggle for our national existence, we might hereafter be induced to spend six additional millions a year upon a department no less vital to our continuance as a nation. With such a sum at our disposal,"* he argued, *"it would be possible to provide staffs for our elementary schools in reasonable relation to the numbers in attendance, to provide a greater equality of opportunity for the children there taught, and gradually raise the whole status of the teaching profession."*

Chaytor concluded his report with a personal note of explanation, adding that *"there was neither pleasure nor profit in his present position at the front, except the pleasure of doing a little to advance the War and the profit of an experience which, like many unpleasant things, was highly instructive. He felt more than ever, after three months at the front, that they must not consider their convenience in preference to the national interests."*

"It was," he concluded, *"because they had an experienced and enthusiastic staff, devoted to the interests of the School, that he felt it possible to leave the School in their hands during his temporary absence. The parents of the boys need fear no diminution in the efficiency of the School."*

One wonders, however, how much they feared for the safe return of the Headmaster himself and despite the worthiness of his intentions there were those who felt he should not have gone. Furthermore it may just have been coincidence, but the December 1916 Plymothian, somewhat unusually, had four letters complaining about poor behaviour in various contexts within the School.

"One Living In Hope" thought that the Vth Form was in a *"decadent state"*, *"Songster"* wanted to draw attention to the *"very poor rendering of hymns at Morning Prayers"*, *"Pro Bono Publico"*, was concerned that too many boys considered attendance at

the Debating Society to be *"too much fag"*, while, more alarmingly, *"Nemo"* complained about the *"unruly behaviour of certain members of the Upper School."* *"As many of us know,"* he asserted, *"there are certain members of the School who band themselves together as Syndicates. These Syndicates have apparently no other aim in life than to make a nuisance of themselves and to disobey rules and hinder Prefects. The result is that a bad example is set to the Lower School and unecessary trouble is given to both Masters and Prefects. For the good of the School, may I ask those boys, who no doubt know who they are, to refrain from their unruly and childlike behaviour"*.

Was this all because the cat was away? And what if he didn't come back? In just those first three months that Chaytor was in France four OPMs were wounded at the Front and five were killed; three of them - Carnall, Williams and Snell - had been pupils under Chaytor and had been at the School the year war had broken out. The Plymothian then did not always make happy reading for past or present members of the School.

RG Carnall at School in 1914, killed in France 1916

Sadly too the deaths column was not only reserved for those in uniform. In December 1916 we also learnt of the passing of one of the Empire building OPMs, John H Greenaway, who died in Doom Dooma, Assam, of Black Water Fever. He was just 25.

It was around this time too that the School lost two of its early heads. Up until then it would theoretically have been possible for all former heads of Plymouth College to have convened and compared notes. However, just before 1916 came to a close the death was announced of George Bennett, the School's first Headmaster.

Bennett had gone to Sutton Valence School in 1883, was still there twenty years later and, presumably, retired from there as he was 70 when he died.

Less than twelve months later, on 15 October 1917, the School's third Head, John Batten, also passed away. Batten it had always seemed had School ink in his blood for when he was only nine he had started at the newly re-opened Haileybury School, a school that his grandfather had been a principal of when it had been the old East India College. In 1875, after four years at Cambridge, he became the first Old Haileyburyian to return as a master. Two years later he moved from Hertfordshire to Devon to take up a post at Kelly College – *"which had just been opened with very high expectations".* The next move came in 1882 when he was offered *"second Mastership and a house"* at Newton Abbott. Then came the invitation to become Headmaster at Plymouth College, which he obviously accepted.

"His career here was by no means unsuccessful," wrote another old Haileyburian, Francis Colson, who had been a small boy when Batten was *"head of the school".*

"He supplemented his splendid record as an athlete and a scholar by very fine social qualities, and was, I should say, very popular with the boys."

Colson continued; *"The numbers ran well, but in 1888, there was something of a slump. The financial position of the School, always exceedingly precarious, became at once worse, and it was evident that if a drop continued the existence of the School would be endangered."*

"Just at this time he had an offer through an influential friend of a good post in one of the greatest Insurance Companies in the world, and he determined to accept it."

Then, quite tellingly, the man who succeeded him at Plymouth College went on to comment;

"How far it answered his expectations I do not know, for though I received much kindness from him at the time of my appointment, and he visited the School two or three times after his resignation, I saw little and heard nothing of him in later years."

Like Colson you can't help but wonder how fate treated Batten in later years, certainly we know it was kind to Chaytor for by the Autumn term of 1917 he was back at the helm – his year of Service completed.

For the School it had been another year dominated by *"Military aims ... games and work have to give way to the requirements of the OTC".*

A view endorsed by the Head at Speech Day who said that University Scholarships must not be expected to appear in the programme until the war was over.

What destiny awaited the School leavers of 1917?

"The only career open to a boy over eighteen", he told the assembled parents, boys and dignitaries, *"is the Army or Navy. So after higher certificate examinations are reached only assistant-clerkships or entrances to Woolwich and Sandhurst must be looked for. No other distinction is desired,"* he said.

After praising the work of the OTC he went on to note that there were currently some 500 OPMs serving, *"of whom 140 have been casualties"*, but, he added, *"since last Speech Day the list of honours has somewhat increased and now includes 3 CB's, 4 CMG's, 15 DSO's, 1 DSC and 18 MC's, as well as some Foreign Decorations."*

DH Vittle, one of 500 OPM's in uniform between 1914-18

The Head also spoke of the valuable war work done by the boys of the School at the farm camp at Crediton. 30 boys had gone for six weeks and had worked a total of 5,200 hours between them, earning £91 for their labours (that's just under 1/- per hour, less than 5p). Unfortunately the camp itself had cost more than that but, thanks to a Government grant, the loss was minimal and the boys would have shown a profit had they not lost 3,100 hours through bad weather.

Mr Stansfield had organised the School's involvement and the contingent had left Ford Park on 6 August;

"Our quarters were in the gymnasium of Crediton Grammar School, where everything from food to bedding was extremely military."

"The first night was spent in joyous revel, but next morning we were ready for work. I do not think," wrote One of the Squad, *"that any of us fully understood what the work was to be. We had dreams of reaping in the golden harvest and living on milk and honey. Rain, I am sure, never entered into our calculations."*

"We arrived at our various farms about 9am, and were greatly surprised to find that instead of harvesting we had to weed thistles or hoe turnips. "The harvest

will soon come, we told ourselves optimistically, and returned to camp still and sore, not to say wet, for a rather heavy thunderstorm came on during the afternoon."

"The next day was a repeat of the first, and so was the next. Two weeks passed thus, and then a spell of fine weather enabled us to start harvesting. So we went through the six weeks, working hard and confident we were doing our best at National Service."

"Our experience," the writer continued, *"with the farmers was on the whole very pleasant, several were more than kind. They one and all confess that they never expected us to do the work we did."*

It was gratifying for all concerned to learn that *"The Public Schools Argricultural Camp at Crediton was acknowledged by the Devon Committee to be the most successful in the County."*

The scheme was only open to boys over sixteen – or exceptionally strong boys of fifteen – and so the number participating was respectably high.

Plymouth College already had good numbers staying beyond sixteen but thanks to a new initiative at the Board of Education it rather looked as though the number of boys continuing their schooling beyond that age was about to increase. That such a move was being proposed was due, according to Henry Chaytor, to the fact that the Board of Education had appointed a President who was qualified – *"not by the fact that he was politically acceptable, or because no other job could be found for him, but because he was really an expert in the work of the department he was to supervise."*

Mr Fisher was the man in question and not only did he immediately seek to make the teaching profession a more attractive and more rewarding one to work in, but he also oversaw the move towards the better provision of "advanced courses" within schools.

A grant of £400 per annum was allowed for these courses, courses which were intended to be the *"coping-stone of education at school"*.

"There is now," said Chaytor, *"a general consensus among educational authorities that a boy's career at school should last for general education until about 16 years of age; after that he should spend two years in specializing, and then proceed to a University."*

"Simultaneously," he said, *"there is an awakening interest in University education all over the country, and especially in this part."*

"A Committee," he added, *"has been formed to advance the cause of University education in the West, and it is hoped that their labours will soon pave the way to the foundation of a University College in Plymouth."*

Meanwhile Plymouth College had applied for grants for Science and Mathematics, and Modern Languages and so far had been granted the former with a promise that the latter would be recognised when the number of boys taking the subject was a little larger. By the way the School was growing, this looked like being sooner rather than later. Though the number of older boys was depleted on account of the war effort the Middle and Lower School were, that term, full, as indeed was the Preparatory Department, the total number at the School reaching a new peak – 250.

Such was the general level of optimism around that, despite the horrors of the War, there was even talk of reviving School Entertainments – albeit on a modest basis and with a view to raising money to pay for the slight deficit on the Agricultural Camp.

Another revival saw the dormant Photographic Society join with the reconstituted Natural Science Society, and, after three years completely in the dark, the old Dark Room was fitted out with *"a good stock of apparatus and chemicals"*.

Even the Debating Society seemed battle-weary and ready to discuss issues closer to home for the average adolescent:

"Rugby is cruel and should be abolished" – No – by 11 votes.

"Cinema more a source of education than of demoralization" – Yes - by 2 votes.

"The boy today is happier than the boy of 100 years ago" – No – by 2 votes.

"Tennis is much better than cricket" – Yes – by 6 votes.

"Duelling is an admirable way of settling disputes" - Yes – by one vote.

"A man's sense of honour is keener than a woman's" – Yes – by two votes.

And finally one that did have some bearing on the War Effort;

"The School Field should be dug up and seed potatoes planted," a proposal that was voted against by a healthy majority. In one way or another "food" was very much on the School psyche in 1917. A terse note in April magazine lay at the heart of problem;

"In the interests of National Economy," it ran, *"the Tuck Shop has been closed until further notice".*

A decision that was later challenged by *"Prefect"*;

"In your last issue you announced that the Tuck Shop had been closed in conjunction with Food Restricitions. How is it then," he wrote, *"that buns, very stale ones usually, are supplied every day?"*

He continued – *"Chocolate, on which no restrictions have as yet been laid, is not provided, but our precious wheaten articles are supplied in seemingly unlimited abundance."*

Then we learn that … *"By petition, it was the wish of the majority of boys that the shop should be closed, but,"* the writer went on, *"the rush for buns shows that they were not all sincere in their professed patriotism."*

The letter did not go unheeded, JT (Mr Thompson) replied; *"I would point out to "Prefect", firstly, that as to buns being stale, that is in accordance with the orders of the Food Control Department; secondly, that Chocolate uses up Sugar which is the scarcest of all commodities. Further, boys who come from a distance should be able to get food at school, especially if they have to stay late for games."*

Not that there were as many games as usual that year in what was an uninspiring time for most sides. The First XV lost all five school matches and all but two of their other games, recording their most impressive victory against OPMs, who were doubtless suffering from having a vastly-depleted pool of players to draw from.

With so few senior boys at school, opposing hockey teams, like the rugger teams, tended to be much heavier than the School's. They were beaten 9-0 by the Naval Barracks at Keyham and 7-2 by the Devon Regiment at Raglan Barracks, on the Barrack Square.

There was little more to shout about on the cricket square. Only two victories were recorded, one against the Army Service Corps, the other against the Somerset Light Infantry. The latter game saw Le Mesurier bag 7 wickets for 28 and score a fine 25 – which put him just eight runs short of the highest score for any member of the team that season. In the absence of Mr Chaytor and a professional he also ended up with most wickets that season – just ahead of Breeze. Mr Sargent topped the batting averages with a lowly 12.5.

Because of the OTC commitments, though, almost all cricket was played on Saturdays and there were few opportunities for practice.

Le Mesurier further distinguished himself in the Athletic Sports, finishing in the first three in most events and finishing behind Williams who won all the major events, apart from the hurdles, to take Victor Ludorum for the second time.

Young Le Mesurier had also been a star of the Concert organised by Mr Stansfield the previous Christmas, singing *"to the immense pleasure of the crowd, he need not have been so bashful"* was the official verdict. The concert incidentally was visited by a *"Dozen Assorted Charlie Chaplins"* who *"sang and acted appropriately in the chorus of Mr Stansfield's last song – The Chaplin Walk".*

If there was one figure that epitomised the popular culture of the day it was undoubtedly the funny, little, moustachioed man with the bowler hat and walking stick.

Back with sport, and of the two Fives fixtures against Kelly only one could be played – due to yet another outbreak of an infectious illness. Measles also led to the scratching of the first cricket match of the season with Kelly. It wasn't just the boys who were having

health problems either; Rolfe Martin, the recently appointed Science teacher, was off for some time, early in the year, with a "serious illness".

On a more upbeat note the Boxing Class was revived and there was even a suggestion that Water Polo might be played in the School pool – *"There are difficulties but they are probably not insurmountable"*, was the reply.

Exciting prospects for some and for the most part conceived and deemed to be practical largely because of the greater number of boys in the School. It was then, and still is now, a simple formula - the more pupils … the more options that become viable.

More boys also meant more teams and increasing emphasis was placed on the need for and indeed the desirability of more inter-house and voluntary games.

For Chaytor, teamwork was a core value and one that distinguished the English from the Germans. Reflecting, at Speech Day at the end of 1917, on his experiences in the base hospitals at the front he noted that;

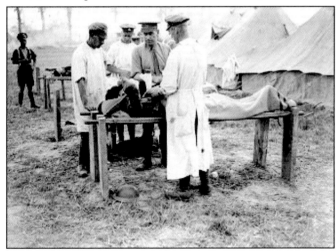

A typical field hospital.

"Wounded English officers invariably inquired if there were any men of their regiment there, and if they were and they were too badly wounded to get to one another,

an immediate interchange of sympathetic messages went on. German officers and German men came into the base hospitals together also, but he never heard a German officer inquire for any men of his regiment."

"That," felt the Headmaster, *"was the difference between the two armies, and it was the outcome of a different system of education. Our men, whether as a brigade or division, went into battle very much like a football team, everybody knowing that his job was to assist the others, and united by a spirit of self-sacrifice. The German division on the other hand, went into action as a soulless machine. That was largely,"* he said, *"the result of education. When that result was seen we need not be ashamed of our education, however much people might laud German education."*

He then concluded his thoughts on the matter by saying *"the German in the past might in some respects have been a more learned person, but he certainly never learnt the art of living."*

Small wonder, therefore, that the very next term he turned his attentions to re-organising the House system. School House became College House and was made up of *"boarders, dinner-boys and those resident outside the Borough boundaries";* a new house, East Town, which immediately became the largest numerically, was created; all of which left *"old North Town and South Town … much weaker than their newer rivals."*

For the boys themselves this was a momentous change and now with four teams it provided a much more balanced framework for inter-house team games. All houses could be involved at the same time, for the first time. Also, for the first time, all houses were required, via their house captains, to provide a report for the School magazine. The editors recording, under the heading *"House Reports"* that they proposed to devote *"some space in every issue to the discussion of affairs in the various Houses".*

The first essays in this department made interesting reading.

College House, under Le Mesurier and Slater (with the new English teacher, Arnold Lingley as their House Master), were quietly confident that despite their comparatively small numbers they should have *"a good chance of becoming Championship House".*

For the new East Town, Emerson and Phillips were keen to point out to their fellows that; *"Nothing can be achieved without practice. Cricketers and other sportsmen,"* they argued, *"are not **born** but **made,** and made by long and assiduous practice".*

North Town's rallying cry took a similar line through Captains Breeze and Ahern who noted that although they were now weaker in number, the re-organisation *"has taken a larger percentage of **duds** than of **stars** from our ranks".*

Finally Drake and Toop, for South Town, were of the opinion that they'd lost out in the Hockey thanks *"greatly to our lack of supporters".* But they later added, *"if only every possible boy will compete in the Athletic and Aquatic Sports and do his best all the term in Cricket, there is no reason why the other Houses should not have a rather big surprise when they find themselves up against South Town".*

Thirty-five-year-old Wilfred Stansfield (English/Maths and games master), another relative newcomer, was then South Town's House Master, but not for much longer for he soon went off, like Arthur Horrill (Gymnastics and Boxing), for War Service, just as Arthur Williams (Classics and English) had done the year before, after little more than twelve months at the School.

Clearly the War was still a highly disruptive influence on the School and particularly the staff and 1918 saw a number of short-term appointments made; only George Cairns staying for any great length of time.

Talking of short terms, summer term 1918 ended a little earlier than usual, but not because of any hostile activities abroad, rather because it was *"required by the Board of Trade",* who were anxious to *"avoid any congestion of traffic on the railways at certain periods of the year"*. *"Examining bodies"*, we learned, *"have fallen in with these requirements."*

Clearly more and more people were taking summer holidays and the train was the main mode of transport. Interestingly enough one of the early debates that year, with Mr Chaytor in the chair, was *"Is Devon better than Cornwall?"* A question that presumably was linked to its status as a holiday destination. For the record a somewhat depleted debating chamber found in favour of Cornwall.

Other less-than-burning issues this year included a proposal to adopt Phonetic Spelling, which was carried by one vote, the suggestion that *"Ignorance is Bliss"*, the Chairman deciding not on behalf of a divided house, and *"passage by air will become a more popular mode of locomotion than by either land or sea in the next 25 years."* Le Mesurier spoke in favour, Harris against. The motion was lost.

The War had not been entirely forgotten in the Debating Society though;

"Had Germany fought Great Britain alone in 1914 she would have been victorious" was a motion lost - the Chairman on that occasion, Captain Dodson, speaking against the motion.

Canadian Troops muster on Plymouth Hoe

"The Press during this War has shewn itself to be a great disappointment" was another voted against, albeit by a narrow margin.

Then there was another measure put forward by Le Mesurier, namely that – *"All Conscientious Objectors be disguised and made use of to farmers as scarecrows."* Happily this proposal was also lost, but doubtless young Le Mesurier would not have been too upset for 1918 was a glorious year for him. At the School Sports his principal opponent from the previous year, Williams, had now left School, leaving the field clear for him to win Victor Ludorum by a mile – actually he won every event but the mile (he was second to Harris). On the cricket pitch he was just as effective the undoubted highlight coming against the old enemy Kelly. He was chaired off the pitch after scoring a fine 108 and then, after the School had declared at 210 for 3, he proceeded to take seven wickets as Kelly were skittled out for 92. He and Breeze (who scored 75 with him against Kelly) finished at the top of the School batting averages and although Le Mesurier also took most wickets that season, Mr Chaytor, now back on the scene, topped the bowling averages with 34 wickets at ten apiece. Mr Sargent once more recorded the top batting average - this time a more impressive 29.83. Having earlier in the season scored a hatrick in the Hockey XI's lone victory against male opposition, Le Mesurier was clearly the stuff schoolboy heroes are made of. One sport that did not appear to hold any interest for him though was boxing. Twenty-five boys took part in the Tournament in April, indicating a larger appetite for the fight than in previous years. Bishop won the senior title, Pearn the intermediate and Brown class C (under 6½ stone).

As for the fighting on the Front though there were occasional signs that there were those at Home who no longer simply saw the War as an opportunity to display great levels of heroic patriotism.

Performing the Christmas concert in front of the wounded soldiers at Hyde Park Hospital (in the school building there) and again a few days later for the wounded at Wearde Camp must have been every bit as sobering as the news coming back from the Front of yet more OPM casualties.

At Speech Day on Friday 1 November 1918 the Head ran through the School Roll of Honour which revealed that 549 old boys had taken up arms for their country of which 99 had been killed, two were missing, another 90 had been wounded and 12 had been taken prisoner. More pertinently for the boys at school, particularly the older ones who would have known all the recent leavers, there were 200 cadets serving of whom 41 had been killed, 2 were missing, 51 were wounded and 7 had been taken prisoner.

In other words as a new recruit you had a 50/50 chance of being killed, wounded or captured – not very appetising odds at all to many young men, no matter how strong their patriotic fervour.

It was perhaps no surprise, therefore, when the annual War Office Inspection of the OTC had taken place that summer (June 26) that Lieut. Col. Truman, the visiting officer, urged cadets to study the lessons of war and *"laid great stress on a most important duty we could all perform, namely to do our utmost to counteract depression, wherever we met it, and that type of talk and influence in favour of making peace with an enemy in every way discredited and untrustworthy."*

"It was our duty", said the officer, *"to stick to it and then after victory to make a peace which would be lasting and worthy of the great sacrifices made."*

Mercifully, however, the Great War ended just ten days after Speech Day – on 11 November 1918. Nevertheless another four more OPMs had lost their lives that month and three more had been injured. Nationally, of course, the statistics were even more horrific.

All in all some 767,000 young Britons lost their lives in the four years of the War, plus a further 200,000 from the Empire, on top of that another 1,500,000 had been seriously injured – the total British war casualties topping three million (approximately 15% of the total male population of the country at the time – and therefore a significantly higher percentage of the 18-50 age group). On all sides the total was even more staggering with upwards of ten million men losing their lives.

A sad sight - a few of the ten million casualties of the Great War.

Tragically, quite a number of those that survived the fighting were struck down on their return by the raging Spanish flu that swept the world at the end of 1918. In the summer term Mr Thompson noted in his North Town report how *"most of our leading swimmers are or have been knocked down with influenza"*. The following term the death, *"from influenza"*, was recorded of RM Ball, a third former, as the outbreak took a further hold. It was not, according to the Headmaster, *"sufficiently bad to justify closing the School"*.

Bad as it was here, it was much worse in other places. In London 2,225 people died of the epidemic. In just one week in October, nationally, around 150,000 fell fatal victims to flu and globally it caused more deaths than the Great War. For the first time in modern society deaths outnumbered births in the last quarter of 1918 – unhappy times indeed.

The flu did not stop the Peace celebrations however, although at School, the end of the War appears not to have provoked much in the way of merrymaking.

"Although the Armistice has been signed, nothing extraordinary in our school life marked the event. However, it has been rumoured that the tuck shop will soon re-open with all its former enticements."

So ran the opening lines of the front page Plymothian editorial of December 1918. Thereafter it was pretty much business as usual. Efforts to raise £7,000 for a suitable School War Memorial rumbled on and in the early part of 1919;

"In recognition of the services of the contingent in connection with the War and of the number of cadets who have served in the commissioned ranks of HM's Forces", The Army Council sent the School a captured German field gun – as a trophy.

The School displays its Great War trophy.

At a special Memorial Service, held at the Garrison Church, Devonport, on Sunday 23 February 1919, the Head paid tribute to the 106 Old Boys who had fallen in the war.

He said that it was the case with Plymouth College, as with few other schools, *"that the losses represented almost a picture of the war in miniature. If we had the dates of the casualties before us we would see that they extended from the time the first shot was fired until the close of the hostilities."*

"When those who went to fight, returned home on short leave," he later added, *"the first thing they did was to see their home, and the next to visit their school. It was no mere animal attraction. The memory of their early school days was indelibly impressed, and passed into the blood until it became native to the memory."*

"The old boys had learned," he said, *"the greatest and noblest lesson of their corporate life – the lesson of citizenship, which means service for others and unselfishness. It is for the present generation to carry on the work of the past generation. The future of the country is in the hands of those who have to learn, and proportionately in the hands of those who have to teach."*

"A generation has been swept away by the ravages of war. One could say to the bereaved that the only explanation is the great Lord's sacrifice. There was, however, in the hearts of the bereaved not only great sorrow, but a sense of pride, and many of them would not have it otherwise. They felt," he continued, *"that those who had fallen had struck a blow for righteousness and truth, and done what they should."*

"It was my lot," the Reverend Henry Chaytor recalled, *"to sit at the bedside of wounded men who were dying, and never was a deathbed scene entirely unhappy."*

"There was grief, pain and regret, but there was also an immense satisfaction that the man had done his duty, done something to maintain truth, justice and honour in the world."

"For those who are living there is necessarily a certain sense of shame that those who have gone have given all and they who remain have given so little or nothing ... We can," concluded the Headmaster, *"only imitate them in the daily life of service and unselfishness"*.

For all the mental scars of the *"four years of nightmare"*, as Chaytor would later describe them, the Great War also brought many medals, among them the Companion of the Bath for OPM's Rear-Admiral GPW Hope, Major-Generals ORA Julian and AE Wardrop and Brigadier

General PCJ Scott. Wardrop was also honoured with the Commander of the Order of St Michael and St George, along with Brigadier General CL Lambe and Lieutenant Colonels AE Bewes, WG Simpson and GG Vawdrey.

For all those who had seen action in the Great War and witnessed the horrors and the carnage, life would never be the same again. Neither would it be for many of those who had been left at home.

"On the whole, the war period," Chaytor would later write, *"especially the latter part of it, was a dismal and harassing time for schoolmasters"*. Nevertheless the conflict crystallised a sense of national identity for the Country. The Government had extended its role through "Emergency Powers" and could intervene in industry and exercise control over food and licensing hours. At the same time Trade's Unions had gained ground by supporting the war effort, as undoubtedly had women's groups.

At Plymouth College the most obvious face of that change belonged to Alice Trenchard. Arriving at the School in 1917 to teach languages the twenty-six-year-old quickly became as involved as any other member of the senior staff in various aspects of the life at Ford Park.

Indeed she not only "refereed" a number of School hockey matches, but would appear to have been responsible for setting up two games with a Mannamead Ladies XI in the early part of 1918. On both occasions the School only fielded eight men, but they nevertheless won both encounters quite comfortably. It wasn't so much the scoreline that was important though – more the fixture itself. The times they were a-changing for sure and attitudes to all aspects of life were being subtly altered through the war years.

Even the work carried out by the boys at the Farm Camp helped to play its part in giving them a more balanced view of the world. The 1918 Camp was situated at Farford Farm in Hartland and ran from 2 August to 6 September. On average there were forty boys at the Camp, which was run in a Military way in place of the summer OTC camp.

"In all over 6,000 hours' work was done, and much valuable assistance given to farmers, who seemed to recognise the value of our assistance in helping to save the harvest."

The work continued into the following term as twenty-or-so boys clocked up nearly 750 hours work between them, lifting potatoes in St Budeaux.

This work, of course, did much to enhance the School's growing reputation generally, a reputation that the Mayor of Plymouth, Joseph Brown, was fully aware of as he gave out the prizes at Speech Day.

Not that you would expect anything less from someone who not only sent his five sons to the School, but also knew first hand all about the role of the vice-chairman of the School Governors. Nevertheless his comments are interesting as he stated that;

JP Brown Mayor of Plymouth

"The Education Authority of the Town had tried to do a great deal in the way of Secondary Education, but Plymouth College have a particular claim on their consideration, having been adjudicated by the Board of Education one of the three Schools West of Bristol for a special course of Higher Education."

"It set," he said, *"Plymouth prominently in the forefront of the district, the whole of Cornwall and a large part of Devon; and for those who like to make Plymouth a residential centre."*

"The School record," he concluded , *"in every respect is excellent"* … indeed *"he doubted, if measured by the part it had played in the war, that it could be excelled by any School in the country."*

He then begged the boys to be jealous of the honour of the School. He also presented a Challenge Cup to the School and immediately the Games Committee decided that it should be used as a House Championship Cup.

Education Authorities everywhere had their work cut out for them at this time as the Government's Education Act came into force, making school compulsory under the age of fourteen – previously it had been thirteen. The Act also encouraged the Local Authorities to develop a system stretching from nursery schools to evening classes.

At Plymouth College Joseph Thompson, once more, played a major part in the development of education here by offering the Governors £1,000 to found a leaving Scholarship, tenable at one of the Universities. Thompson was prompted to do this partly because there was no real agreement at this stage about how the School War Memorial fund should be spent. At that stage only £1,128 had been subscribed or promised - £100 of it by Thompson himself. Clearly it was some way short of the £7,000 that had been suggested and which it had been thought might be used to build a hall of some kind. Hence the dilemma: should the money be spent on buildings or scholarships (with particular emphasis on the sons of OPMs who had fallen in the war)? Thompson, no doubt favouring some sort of concrete memorial, obviated the immediate need for a scholarship fund by providing what was then a very substantial one himself.

Having taught the vast majority of OPMs who lost their lives during the War, the Memorial clearly meant a lot to Joseph Thompson and in the same magazine that noted the 1919 Treaty of Peace, he wrote an open letter urging those who had not yet contributed to the fund to do so;

"The Declaration of Peace seems a fitting time to

1919

appeal to all old boys who feel that they owe anything to their School to help perpetuate the memory of those belonging to it who have died to make such a peace possible."

"May I also suggest that present boys who are leaving might perhaps give a donation to such an object? My address is 44, Whiteford Road, Mannamead."

Over the next few months a dozen or more contributions came in, some from serving OPMs, one or two from mothers and widows, but none of the sums were as substantial as the early donations. Both the Mayor and the Chairman of Governors matched Thompson's £100 as did one or two others The Head and his predecessor also gave generously (£50 and £20 respectively), but a guinea or two (£1.1s.0d or £2.2s.0d) were more typical of the amounts proffered. The more time that passed the more difficult it became to raise money and enthusiasm for the project.

The account of the formal announcement of peace was quite telling;

"At last! At 3 o'clock on the afternoon of Saturday, June 28th 1919, the Treaty of Peace was signed, sealing the final overthrow of Prussian militarism. Exactly five years ago, the assassination of the Archduke Ferdinand provided the German Empire that excuse for which they were waiting in order to plunge the world into the fiercest struggle in the annals of history. That struggle, by the patience and heroism of the Allied peoples, has resulted in an overwhelming victory for Honour and Freedom."

But the partying had already been done, back when the Armistice had been signed, and so it is with little surprise that we read;

"The news in Plymouth was received with more philosophic calm and quiet assurance than that which greeted the announcement of the armistice. It spread only slowly, and the first intimation to many was when, as the clocks struck six, the guns of the ships in the harbour thundered forth and the salute of 101 guns

was fired from the Citadel. In the evening the streets were crowded, but the crowd was perfectly orderly and good-natured."

"What need for great excitement now that the war was over?" wrote Plymothian editors, FC Phillips and RA Bishop, adding;

"All honour to those that gave their all to make such a victorious peace possible".

All honour indeed. What must it have been like to be in the Upper School then, knowing that, had the War not ended when it did, it could well have been you on the next troopship over to France? How many of those younger boys, for all their keenness to join the fray, must have inwardly breathed a sigh of relief that they were just a year or two too young to answer the call?

Probably not RA Bishop though, he was a fighter, and a very good one at that. Two months earlier he had represented the School at the Public Schools Boxing Competition held, under the auspices of the Amateur Boxing Association, at the Polytechnic, Regent Street in London.

Reporting on the event the Western Morning News read thus;

"RA Bishop earned golden opinions. It is scarcely too much to say that no one during the whole day boxed in a neater or more businesslike style."

Entered as a lightweight, the feeling was that he probably could have won the welterweight title, which in the event Le Mesurier competed for but was knocked out by a boy from Eton in the first round of his first bout. Bishop on the other hand went all the way, disposing of three opponents on his way to the final, which he won with some ease.

The overall standard was not, we are led to believe, wonderful - *"very few of them knew how to hit ... a deal of energy was expended in punches that often landed without doing any appreciable damage"*. It was suggested that the School should do well in subsequent events, as long as some boys were prepared to train

hard enough and *"go through the necessary mill beforehand"*.

With numbers running at an all time high and the pressure on the OTC much relieved it is no surprise to find that it was not just boxing that witnessed new levels of enthusiasm in post-war Plymouth College. After struggling to achieve any serious interest in hockey suddenly we find that Mr Lingley was getting an average attendance of 90-100 boys and the School was able to field a 1st, 2nd and 3rd XI, each winning most, if not all, of their matches. Miss Trenchard was perhaps another attraction here – she even fielded a team for the 3rd XI to play (the School won 3-2).

The Rugby Football boys were not quite so fortunate, winning only two of their six games, but again most of their opponents were bigger, heavier service sides (the staff too were older and featured less in the sides – Chaytor played his last game of Rugger, aged 45, just before his year in France). Both games against Kelly had to be cancelled through illness; as indeed had the Fives matches - this sport also suffered from the growth in interest in hockey.

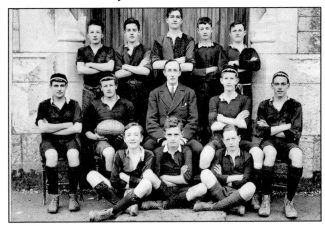

College House Senior Football Team, 1919, who "retained the House Championship in only its second year of existence".Back; EJ Pearn, BD Jones, GE Cummins, KE Budge, JH Pryce-Jones. Middle; FW Beer, RA Bishop, AG Lingley, Esq., RO Maddever, PH Penfold. Front; JHG Leatherdale, C Kingdon, JK Gosling.

1919

George Street, Plymouth 11 November 1918 - Armistice Day

No such conflict appeared for the Tennis Club though which was inaugurated this summer; *"For obvious reasons membership has been confined to the Upper School, but of these a fair percentage has joined. It is only intended as an alternative for those who cannot play cricket, so that the inauguration of the Club has had no prejudicial effect upon the latter."*

Also new on the sporting calendar was the imminent inter-house Cross Country challenge, which the Games Committee scheduled for the beginning of 1920.

On the swimming front there was a change too, as, after sixteen years, since the pool first opened in fact, Mr Searle finally resigned his post and was succeeded as Swimming Instructor by CPO Marker, RN.

Having won the previous year's Victor Ludorum, Le Mesurier was clear favourite to take it again, which he did, although without setting any new records, most of which had stood for more than ten years.

With Moore, the professional, back in the cricket team and with the Head too, the Ist XI won 12 of their 22 fixtures (3 games were drawn). Moore knocked up an unbeaten 180 against the RN Barracks, and topped the batting. Maddever was top boy with bat and ball, although Le Mesurier, in his last term, was just behind him. Notwithstanding an exciting two innings game with Kelly, which the School won, probably the most keenly contested game of the season was the School v the Masters – the boys won by one wicket. As with the hockey, so with the cricket as three elevens were fielded that summer; the 3rd's beating Devonport High School 2nd's and Corporation Grammar School 2nd's – against CGS, Kingdom took 8 wickets for 9, including 4 in 4 balls.

Division 2 of the Prep start to lighten their activities once more; Leigh, Holman, Westlake, Parry, Bond-Spear, Inskip, Lyddon, Pitts, Hodge, Ward, Coode, Serpell ii, Warren and Venning.

All in all it was a brighter year for the School, the Glee Club was revived, so too was the OPM Club – owing to the war and the fact that there had been very few Old Boys left in Plymouth there had been no meeting or social engagement for four years. And on the subject of Social Institutions, *"Fox Trot"* wrote to the Plymothian appealing for the revival of the Dancing Class, *"which ceased to exist because of the war"*. *"The ability to dance,"* said our correspondent, *"confers enormous social and other advantages on those possessing it."*

Another form of entertainment to visit the School that year was the Lantern Lecture. Lieutenant Commander Auten VC DSO, gave an account of the efforts and adventures of the anti-submarine branch of the Royal Navy during the war, to a large audience gathered in the Gymnasium. The lecture was illustrated by slides but, unfortunately, the light failed during the talk; *"We should like to state that this was in no way the fault of the operators, but resulted from a mistake by a Plymouth firm who supplied us with a discharged cylinder instead of a full one. Our reserve supply proved insufficient."*

Another interesting account of wartime experiences was provided by the former languages teacher Harold Truelove.

Arrested in Germany in August 1914 he spent a week in a Berlin gaol before, later, being held as an internee at Ruhleben Camp for four long years – *"few men, I suppose have had our opportunities for studying the art of killing time"*.

"We were aroused every morning at about 7.45 and expected to parade at once for roll-call." After that though it appears there were few demands made on their time. Inmates were allowed to buy papers, German newspapers, which they would compare with English, French and Italian periodicals smuggled from time to time into the camp. Food parcels came in regularly from friends and relatives at home;

"I kept an account of despatches and receipts, and I seem only to have lost two or three during the whole time; not a bad record considering that more than two hundred must have been sent to me in the four years."

Amateur actors banded together to provide good shows, *"a fresh piece being produced on average perhaps every fortnight. Athletics and agriculture flourished side by side, and the political aspirant found scope for his activities within the limits of the Camp Civil Administration."*

True love also found employment within the camp school ... *"but at the back of each activity was the sense of work created for work's sake, and merely as a means of passing time ... All were swept away when, on November 9th 1918, the Revolution broke out in Berlin, the red flag was hoisted in Ruhleben, and permits were issued to us to leave the camp from morning till evening pending our ultimate release."*

Truelove didn't return to teach at Plymouth College though, and his disappearance was just one of the many hiccups in the staffing of the School during the war years. Hiccups that made it all the more incumbent on the remaining staff to keep the boat steady. Thompson and Palmer were, undoubtedly, the two key figures in this and it's no great surprise to find both of them opting for retirement soon after the end of the war. One can only wonder if they would otherwise have retired any earlier.

Neither were they the only ones to bow out at this stage. The first post-war retirement party was for sixty-nine-year-old music teacher Carl Kuhne, who finally hung up his cap and gown after twenty-eight years on the staff. Clearly Plymouth College, like so many other similar schools, however far from the front, suffered great physical and emotional scars during the war, but for the young generation, who were to carry the school forward, the healing process was a swift one.

AM Stibbs secured the first *"after-the-War University Scholarship at Christ's College, Cambridge"* and a former graduate of that institution arrived in the first term of 1920 as the new head.

Francis Dale had gone to school at Oundle, near Peterborough, and had enjoyed a successful academic career at Cambridge. He was not long out of University when war had been declared. He served with distinction during the War and was awarded both the Military Cross and the DSO – *"for gallantry and good leadership whilst in command of a battalion of another regiment".* For the record, the specific event for which

Dale had been singled out had been when he had led his men across the River Selle, near Le Cateau, on 20 October 1918.

"The operation was extremely difficult, but after daring reconnaissance, his orders, combined with his spledid leadership and example, were responsible for the complete success of the operation" (from **Men of Harlech – The Regimental Journal of the Welch Regiment**).

On two occasions later, Dale led his battalion though heavy barrages and intricate country with the *"greatest courage, gaining the objective and capturing four '77 guns".*

Major Francis Richard Dale

Then a temporary captain, he left the service as Major Francis Richard Dale and came to Plymouth College from a top redbrick school in the north of England - Leeds Grammar.

At thirty-two he was also sixteen years younger than Henry Chaytor, a difference that the retiring head thought was both significant and important.

Describing how the early part of his time at Plymouth College had *"taken a good deal out of him"*, Chaytor, addressing his last School Speech Day, informed his audience that he had thought sometimes that the *"School would be better with a younger, fresher man."*

That said, however, he added that there was no need to fear that the new man *"would alter materially the character of the School"*, Mr Dale, he said, was a *"broad-minded man, fully alive to all modern developments in education".*

For his own part, Chaytor said that although he was exceedingly sorry to leave ... *"I have succumbed to the attractions of a University post (at St Catherine's, Cambridge), and the prospect of being among libraries and in the midst of the most cultivated society in Europe, perhaps in the second best place in the world – Oxford being the first".*

Chaytor was, of course, an Oxford graduate himself and as such the first to have been a head at the School. He was not the first Plymouth College head to be seduced by the prospect of a post at Cambridge though; his predecessor, Colson, had gone in the same way in 1908 and at a similar age (Colson was 51, Chaytor just a few weeks off 49 on leaving the School).

17 December 1919 was a major day of farewells though, and Chaytor, referring back to the leaving presentations that morning in Big School, said the School was losing, in addition to himself and Mr Thompson, Messrs Martin and Anstice as well. The Head, incidentally, was presented with a silver kettle and a spirit lamp, Mr Thompson with a silver loving cup and Mr Martin and Mr Anstice were each presented with a pipe.

Predictably, these moves would be followed by the biggest wholesale changes in the staff room since the School had been founded. Three new members of staff, House, Highatt and Dufton arrived before the end of 1919 and in the following twelve months another six new members of staff would come to Ford Park.

Of the nine, ten including Dale, only two would still be at the School by the end of the decade – interestingly enough though one of them John Dufton, himself an OPM, would go on to set a new record of years on the staff, eventually retiring in 1956. But we are leaping ahead of ourselves a little.

John Dufton joins the Staff

As Henry Chaytor left the School in 1919 he did so satisfied that he had, in just eleven years and with considerable help, taken Plymouth College from being a potentially ailing institution with just 130 boys to a situation that saw it very much at the forefront of education locally, with 300 boys on the roll.

"Under the present conditions," he said, *"it will soon be necessary to start a waiting list, and before long we may have to have an entrance examination, unless,"* he added, *"the accommodation can be extended, but I see no immediate possibility of that."*

Sentiments that he reiterated that evening at the Old Boys Dinner held in his, and Thompson's honour, at the Grand Hotel on the Hoe. He also again thanked Joseph Thompson and the OPM Club itself;

"The OPM Club has always attracted my deepest interests," he said, *"and I would like to be regarded as a permanent member."*

Thanking the Old Boys for their token of appreciation he added that he would do all in his power to further the interests of the Club.

In his speech, Mr Thompson said it had been a pleasure for him to devote a portion of what he called his *"little surplus"* to the College in an attempt to put it on a surer foundation than when he first knew it.

"When I first came the School was new and had but few traditions," he said, *"but if the School was going to collapse it was no good getting boys to make traditions and so I helped materially for that reason."*

He concluded his remarks though on a wistful note;

"Six years ago I was present at another Dinner attended by Governors and old boys and I cannot look back without being filled with the greatest sorrow in thinking of what has happened since then, and how many have passed away in the War. Many old boys figured in the casualty list and their familiar faces have been brought prominently into my memory tonight."

The final figures, also disclosed earlier that day at the Speech Day proceedings had been 106 OPMs who had lost their lives out of the 566 that had served, a further 93 having been wounded.

That same Plymothian also carried details of Roger Porter, who Thompson and Chaytor would have known well as he left the School in 1913. A former member of the 14th Battalion Royal Warwickshire Regiment, he had been gassed while serving in France and passed away at his home in Saltash on 3 February 1920 – he was just 21. The shadow cast by those horrific events had still not completely passed and for many never would entirely.

But life went on. Maddever and Bishop were the new stars of the (rugby) football team which, itself, was not especially successful. Happily, however, the newly-established 2nd and 3rd XV's both won all their matches; the ability to field so many teams a healthy reflection on the increased number of boys in the School.

The greater numbers helped all aspects of the School's sporting programme and boxing, which some people objected to, flourished.

"On what grounds they object I do not know, there is no more healthful exercise in the world," argued the retiring head, *"it teaches a man self-control too."*

The hockey teams also flourished and the 2nd XI found a new fixture against St Dunstan's Abbey School. The first game, curiously enough, was played on Valentine's Day 1920, the School winning 8-0 with Rooks scoring

4. In the second encounter the margin was even greater – 11-0 – Rooks (with 5 goals) again scoring freely.

One of the rising stars in the School, GP Rooks made an early impression on Francis Dale when the new head chaired his first meeting of the Debating Society on 30 January 1920.

The proposal before the House was that *"the Dartmoor Hydro-Electric Scheme should not be proceeded with".* Donnelly and Rooks led the opposition and the motion was defeated by a large majority. If the concerns of the Society were anything to go by, normal service appears to have been pretty well resumed by the time Dale arrived at Plymouth College. Not that the War was now completely off the agenda as debates on President Wilson's fourteen points for Peace – generally they were not thought to be drastic enough – and the German treatment of prisoners, had earlier shown. Furthermore, in only his second school debate, Mr Dale found himself in the chair for a discussion on The Covenant of the League of Nations – which as contained in the Peace Treaty was deemed, by a narrow majority, to be impracticable. Dale, himself, and Captain Dodson both spoke for the motion.

Essentially, however, the post-war world of Plymouth College was a very different one to that which Henry Chaytor had found in 1908 – the last vestiges of Victoriana had been swept away by tanks and technology and Britain was now fully in the grip of the Twentieth Century. For all the losses sustained on the battlefields of France and Flanders, the School was now bigger, in pupil numbers than it had ever been.

Furthermore the *"annual accounts showed a small balance and it might be said that the College was definitely accepted by the town as an integral part of the educational organisation of Plymouth ... upon which there had been no universal conviction in 1908"* (Chaytor 1927).

Mutley Plain and Ford Park in the early twenties.

MR DALE'S DIARY

"It was a long stride to Plymouth in 1920" wrote Freddie Dale 2nd Battalion Worcester on the occasion of his Diamond Wedding, many years after leaving the School. So it must have seemed as he uprooted his young family from their wartime home in Leeds and brought them down on the train to Plymouth.

The School, as he then found it, would have been much like many similar institutions There were eight classrooms, a prefects room and the Headmaster's study in the main block.

Big School laid out as a classroom.

Big School was where the southern part of the library is now and the science labs, such as they were, occupied a room and a half across from the old quad at the back of the School.

The Science Laboratory with readily accessible chemicals.

With school numbers rising, there was increasing pressure on space. An extra classroom had been created out of a small semi-basement room in the main building, but the room, which had in the very early days served as a science laboratory, was small, poorly-lit, had a concrete floor and did not make for a good teaching environment. Furthermore, the gymnasium was the same "temporary" affair that it had been for forty years – but there was little money available for improvements.

When Dale arrived at the School it was running at a loss each year – for the year ended 1920 the accounts showed a deficit of £479 and twelve months later £968, which doesn't seem too bad by current standards but in 1921 the School fees were only £21 per year, while the Prep fees were just £15 (having only recently been increased from £10). The Governors were looking to increase the senior fees to £24, but in the meantime money was very tight. The situation was not particularly helped by the fact that almost half of the boys staying on in the sixth form (9 out of 22) were Free Scholars through the local authority scheme. This scheme saw the admission of 10% of any year's intake as Free Scholars and as they were generally bright boys they were somewhat disproportionately represented in the academically selective sixth form. The Governors also awarded a few open scholarships each year, covering part, or the whole, of the fees.

Generally, though, an increase in pupil numbers meant an increase in revenue and to ease the space problem and the financial situation a large army hut was erected, in the autumn term of 1920, near the gym. Known quite simply as "the Hut", it provided three good-sized classrooms, each with a small cloakroom, and it was to serve for a number of years.

The main block, of course, remains today. It is worth remembering that in 1920 the classrooms would be lit only by gas and heated by a coke fire. Each classroom had its own open fire and it was, doubtless, the job of

Mr Lear, the school porter, to clean out and light each of the fires on cold mornings.

The "Hut" provides three extra classrooms.

The staff common room then was accessed by a wooden staircase and in it the 6'3" former Army Major would have found very few masters with any great experience of Plymouth College. With Chaytor and Thompson gone, only Francis Palmer, John Thill and Bert Sargent had been there more than more than ten years. Of the three, the languages master Thill went in 1922 while the veteran second master, Palmer, retired in July 1920; *"He finished his long term of fine service by one service more – he stayed with the new Headmaster long enough to see him fairly started,"* wrote Dale a few years later.

The new head could have asked for no better guide to surroundings he found himself in. Palmer had joined Mannamead School in 1877, the year Plymouth College had been established and so, for almost twenty years, prior to the Amalgamation, had watched it grow from his vantage point half a mile away.

Once the two schools had been combined his role was again invaluable and during Mr Chaytor's absence for a year in France it was he who acted as Headmaster: *"And kept the work going well, and during that time he continued to do his own work as usual, including even the job of managing the books and stationery department – a piece of heavy and very useful but thankless work which he carried on for many years to*

the great advantage of the School."

So ran an anonymous editorial piece on Palmer published in December 1920. The writer (could it have been Joseph Thompson?) also informed us that: *"As a Master many boys perhaps thought him a hard driver, but he never spared himself either in teaching or in any other matter which affected the welfare of the School."*

Palmer's 43 year career at Plymouth and Mannamead College, was indeed truly remarkable and has, to date, never been eclipsed - in terms of duration - and perhaps, with retirements coming ever earlier, never will be.

Following his departure the short, tubby, kindly, Bert Sargent became second master and he in turn would come to ease Dale's successor into his post. But that is to jump forward too far.

Bert Sargent, Dale's new No.2

Back to what was undoubtedly a smoke-filled staff room in 1920 (Dale, incidentally didn't mind if boys smoked so long as it wasn't either in School or on Mutley Plain). Apart from Bert Sargent there was a marked absence of older men.

Goerge Cairns and Arnold Lingley

George Cairns and Arnold Lingley were, like Sargent,

just about to turn fifty. The others, with the exception of the OPM, John Dufton (28 when Dale arrived), were all in their thirties – roughly contemporary with the new head himself. Indeed of the half a dozen or so teachers appointed in 1920 – House, Highatt, Osmund, Mayne, Dobson, Dodd and Beaumont all were aged within three or four years of the new head – he seemed very keen to build a team of men he could understand and relate to.

Having said that, though, there was no immediate period of staffing stability when Dale took charge. He didn't suffer fools gladly and there were a number of fairly prompt departures. Indeed three or four of the teachers who started with Dale in 1920 also left within a year or two (House 1920, Highatt '21, Dodd '22, Richardson '23, Mayne '24). *"It was said that if new staff didn't reach his standards they would be encouraged to look for another position"* commented John Spear, who was a pupil under Dale and who would later return to the School, after Second World War Service, as a teacher. At that time, incidentally teachers at Plymouth College were on a probationary period of just one term, a spell that the Inspectors felt could usefully have been increased to a year.

There had been a great number of comings and goings throughout the war years too, as Messrs Horrill, Stansfield and Williams all left in 1917/18 for War Service. All three men were in their late thirties/early forties and only Horrill had been on the staff before the war. Unlike Chaytor these men did not come back to Plymouth College. Of the teachers that joined the staff in 1919, fresh from War Service only John Dufton, the OPM, stayed for more than a few years under Dale. The only real survivor among the wartime appointments, then, was Arnold "Shanks" Lingley, English teacher and boarding house master.

As for the boys, there was an absence of older individuals in their ranks too. Dale was keen to build up his sixth form, but it was clearly going to be an uphill task.

At the end of his first full year there were only 22 sixth formers and a similar number of fifth formers, which made it difficult to field heavyweight rugby teams. Looking toward the future, though, the number of boys was rising at a healthy rate and he had 59 boys in the fourth form and 60 and 61 in the third and second forms respectively. The job in hand was to try and keep them at school longer. To do that, though, it was necessary to ensure that more boys passed their School Certificate, for this was a condition of promotion into the sixth form. In July 1921 only 11 boys passed. It is worth remembering, though, that not so many boys were being schooled for university then because there weren't nearly so many universities, or places at the existing establishments, to aim for.

It was a point made by the Chairman of the Local Education Committee, WL Munday at Speech Day in 1920, when seconding the vote of thanks to the guest speaker, Sir Isambard Owen, Vice-Chancellor of Bristol University.

"England," he said, "is badly off as regards University teaching and many people feel the need of a University for the extreme West of England."

The same sentiments had earlier been expressed by JP Brown (then Vice-Chairman of the Governors); "the establishment of a University in Plymouth or Exeter," he said, "would not entrench upon the province of Bristol, but would stimulate educational interest in the neighbourhood. Neither would it diminish the number of students who would go from this School to Oxford or Cambridge, but would rather increase that number. The Governors of Plymouth College", he added, "desire above all that the School should become more and more identified with Oxford and Cambridge."

As of October 1920 the latest boy to forge that link was FC Phillips who had just won a Science and Mathematics Scholarship at Corpus Christi, Cambridge. Phillips was an exceptional student and somewhat unusually had contributed a lengthy essay on the Theory of Relativity to the April 1920 Plymothian - possibly the first time such an academic piece had been published in the magazine.

At that time the School was thought to be sending what was termed a "fair number" of boys to the universities and "an even larger number" into the Army. The School Inspectors also noted that "boys from the School have been very successful year after year in the examination for Paymaster Cadetships in the Royal Navy." This is, perhaps, exactly what you would expect in a town that was then very much dominated by the Services. Indeed such was the influence of the Dockyard and the Services in Plymouth in the 1920s that when the Ford Motor Company wanted to establish a plant they were discouraged by the Government who didn't want competition for the workforce.

Most (85%) of the boys then in the School were local - from Plymouth - and out of the 366 on the roll (99 of them from the Prep) only two dozen or so were boarders. Nevertheless with the school growing in reputation all the time and with more emphasis in society at large being placed on education, there was much for the new head to build upon.

Valletort Villas - side view, south-facing aspect

Incidentally, the boarders then lived in College House, the present Headmaster's House (1 and 2 Valletort Villas – the head then living in 2 Dunkeld Villas, now part of Colson House). Mr Lingley was the boarding house master and the boys slept no more than five to a room, sharing just two inside toilets and five outside - plus four urinals. The younger boys were expected to be asleep by 8.45, the older ones 9.30 or 10pm and 7.30am was the time for everyone to get up.

"Plymouth College, The Boarding House" - Valletort Villas.

No.1 Shaftesbury Villas, Ford Park.

The Prep was based in No. 1 Shaftesbury Villas, which had been arranged to provide four classrooms on the first and second floors with a fifth class accommodated in the "new" hut some fifty yards away.

Incidentally, there were, also cloak rooms and lavatories in Shaftesbury Villas, plus living accommodation for the Mistress in charge (Miss Footner in 1921), and a caretaker and his family.

Miss Footner takes charge 1921

It's interesting to note that, while the Prep was a most valuable supply of pupils to the main school, and while its numbers had recently increased dramatically, from 27 to 99, the School Inspectors, in 1921, noted that the *"salaries paid to certain Mistresses are so low* (two of them were paid around £200 a year) *that the Governors can only expect to secure the services of women living at home in the town and their choice is thus restricted"*.

Not surprisingly, then, the Prep staff were not very highly-qualified, but they were, according to the Inspectors, *"efficient and bring much enthusiasm to their work."*

There were five mistresses in the Prep at that time, one for each class, the numbers in which ranged from 17-26. The impressive fourfold increase in numbers over the previous ten years had essentially been due to closure of other private prep schools in the town and *"a reduction of the age of admission to 5 years following the decision of the Girls High School to restrict its Kindergarten girls owing to a lack of accommodation"*.

These changes had been watched carefully by Florence Lethbridge, who, from 1909 until her untimely death in October 1920, had been Headmistress of the Prep. Miss Lethbridge had turned these circumstances to the School's advantage and made the Prep into a formidable and essential arm of the Main School.

A devoted teacher, *"who would stand no nonsense and had a remarkable power of getting good work done,"* Miss Lethbridge was also *"well known in Plymouth for her work in connection with St Andrew's Church,*

and on the Board of Guardians. Always unsparing of herself, she devoted many hours to the task of cheering and helping the Workhouse inmates ... But it was her work at the College she most loved."

Remarkably despite the ever-improving standing of the school locally, there was, as yet, no formalised school uniform although ... *"everyone wore a cap and school tie, plus a jacket or blazer and trousers ... The School cap was then black with a red ribbon around the edge."*

Schoolboys; Frank Blamey, Arthur Lyddon, Peter Hamley and Horace Lyddon on their way to Ford Park in 1921.

Morning school comprised four periods and ran from 9am though till 12.30, with a short break. Then there was a two-hour gap before afternoon school, – a three-period session which ran through to 4.45pm. The long break was there so that almost all boys, apart from the boarders, could get home for lunch. Small wonder, therefore, that Plymouth Tramways Committee's proposal to increase their fares was keenly enough felt to become a matter for the Debating Society. In practice, incidentally, about 250 boys went home for lunch, the other 70-odd paying 1/4d (7p) for lunch in the Boarding House.

School Dining Room

Boarding House lunch, or dinner as it was known, was as follows;

"Cold or Hot Meat, Hot Vegetables or Salad, varied by Cottage Pie or Minced Stew of fresh meat, Ox Heart or Liver (senior table), followed by Jam Tarts, Plain Suet Pudding and jam or syrup. Milk Puddings, generally with fruit, Baked Puddings, etc."

Curiously enough food came very high in the overall scheme of things in the School Prospectus, published at this time. The brochure began with a foreword featuring a picture of the boarding house (presently the Headmaster's House) and a few introductory comments;

"A strong feature of a House Master's work is the **personal** *element. The boy is studied. The boy is watched, weighed up, guided in motive and aspiration, relative to his opportunities."*

"Personal interest is the key to success with boys."

"You cannot beat it."

"But, Mother says, this is all very well. I want to know what will my boy have to eat!"

However, before providing prospective parents with a meal-by-meal account of what their sons were likely to eat, there followed a fascinating section on food generally;

"Diet is of chief importance, since good food means health, and the rest follows, though some fellows catch the last train (?!)."

"Yet no matter how wholesome the food, unless a boy knows how to eat (and a surprising number do not know) he will lay up trouble for himself."

"We do not profess to feed our boys like turkey cocks, as they must survive beyond the coming Christmas, but we do wish them to stow away so much as they can digest and a bit more. This quantity varies with each one."

"Some parents would be surprised at the whims existing among a group of boys. Who would guess immediately that a majority asserts often that, in a pudding, currants are preferable to sultanas?"

Neither did the writer's colourful culinary prose end there, for as with anything else there was always the possibility that any cooked up could end in disaster;

"Try as one will to prevent them, accidents will happen. The cook gets out of bed the wrong side, with the result that the porridge is burned and the pastry for dinner is no light-weight. **When** *these untoward catastrophies do engulf us, we know all about it (and of course the cook hears about it), for the house Master and his wife have their meals with the boys, and can remedy the culinary malady."*

Porridge, it should be mentioned, wasn't all that was on the menu for breakfast, there was also *"Fried Bacon on Toast, or Scrambled Eggs or Fish."* Plus, *"Marmalade. Bread and Butter. Tea."*

Tea itself was *"Bread and Butter, Cake or jam and fruit at intervals"*, while Supper comprised *"Bread and Butter and Cocoa."* However *"Boys can bring in sardines, jam, etc. Eggs can be boiled"* and *"Milk can be provided"*.

Through the medium of this particular prospectus the School was anxious to point out that its concern with diet didn't simply end there though;

"More often than not, each boy at meal time has

a mannerism which must be converted into "table manners". Either the food is sluiced down or a spud pouts the cheek to the better telling of how Phillips minor bluffed the Lower Fourth Beak, or, the bread, in spite of ready access to a knife, is gnawed. It may be considered bad taste to harass one's feelings by such references. Yet, it is necessary to take the liberty to show that our curriculum pays attention to details affecting health, etc."

Such was the concern for health and mental and physical fitness that even if a boy wasn't School team material there was always an opportunity for exercise.

House Team, 1920: Back row; K Westbrook, BD Jones, DG Sherwell, KE Budge, JK Gosling. Middle; GE Cummins, FW Beer, AG Lingley Esq., PH Penfold, WC Kingdon. Front; K Lear, TC Tredinnick, R Andrews.

Wednesdays and Saturdays were half days in the School week and for those not involved in School games there were always the "Vols" – voluntary games that everyone was expected to play at least once a week – unless there was a first team fixture with Kelly, in which case the whole School was expected to turn out and provide support. Something that Dale, in his gum boots, with umbrella in hand, was always ready to do – such was his level of dedication.

Indeed looking at his various commitments one wonders what time he ever had for his own life. Running the school then was as much an all-consuming occupation as it has ever been, and it's hard to imagine how he coped with no clerical support and 21 teaching periods per week. But he did and he found time to star in and produce plays on a regular basis. He even wrote the occasional piece himself, as he did for his first Garden Fete on Saturday 29 May 1920. Performed on the lawn of College House, *"for the first time on earth"*, Dale's dramatic piece was written in heroic couplets and cast him as Hermes alongside Miss Wilson as Pallas. Various other members of staff took part in what was to become a regular vehicle for Dale's theatrical leanings. However it is clear that for the new head these dramatic productions were more than just opportunities to entertain the pupils and parents, they were a key element of his team-building and it wasn't long before this natural leader of men had formed a Staff Dramatic Department.

Of course it was so much easier to find an audience for such entertainments in those days, there was little competition in the home – no videos, no televisions. Gramophone players were very much a novelty, there were no long-playing records and radio was in its earliest stages. Indeed the account of the arrival of the first "Wireless Installation" in the School, in the summer of 1922, is entertaining in itself:

"Thanks to the energy and perseverance of Mr J.T.Dufton, assisted by members of the Advanced Science Course, a wireless receiving set is now in full buzz in the Physics Laboratory. A visit to the roof on Whit-Monday resulted in the disturbance of the dust of ages on the rafters above Big School, and finally with much ingenuity and a long length of wire, an aerial was erected. Some wag has been heard to enquire whether the structure was intended to hasten the drying of the House laundry – what irreverence for the noble works of science! (In passing it might be mentioned that the

weird and wonderful apparatus by which the College is ventilated excited much comment)."

The account continued: *"Although the town is in an unfavourable position for the reception of signals from the East of England, the craggy heights of Dartmoor forming an impassable barrier to all but the strongest oscillations, we are able to hear time signals from the Eiffel Tower; and since we cannot see our way clear to remove Dartmoor for some time to come, we must perforce be satisfied with the converstation carried on by local shipping, and faint indications of messages from Cherbourg across the Channel. Rame Head, the local station, is always rushing in with loud and raucous voice and is nearly always rude enough to use code."*

A typical 1922 amateur wireless set.

"No doubt in the future, when the Government finally turns on the broadcasting mains, we shall be able to receive anything from a University lecture to a cheery message from an OPM in a distant quarter of the globe."

To put this in a national context it is worth pointing out that in November 1920 the pioneering wireless company Marconi had their licence withdrawn by the Post Office because they had broadcast a concert by Dame Nellie Melba. The Post Office were yielding to pressure from those who disapproved of wireless telegraphy being used for mere entertainment!

In February 1922, however, Marconi were broadcasting again, sending out weekly half-hour programmes from Chelmsford and a daily service from 2LO - their station based on the top of Marconi House in the Strand, London. These were broadcasts the School failed to receive. However, in October, a consortium of radio manufacturers formed themselves into the BBC – initially the British Broadcasting Company (as opposed to Corporation) – and on 14 November 1922 the new organisation, under their general manager, John Reith, took over 2LO. The next day, following a plan to turn it into a national service, they opened stations in Manchester and Birmingham. Broadcasting began in Plymouth itself, via station 5PY, in March 1924.

In the early days, the BBC, under John Reith, was famous for its high moral tone, and again this was mirrored in education generally. At Plymouth College all boys throughout the School had two periods of Religious Teaching each week and two lots of homework. The teaching was Christian, but undenominational, and pupils were expected to memorise selected portions of the Bible.

Rote learning was also a feature of the French department at that time and the Inspectors recommended that a blackboard, big enough for 8-10 pupils to write on at the same time, would save time when it came to testing grammar and correcting spelling.

Latin, Greek, Spanish and German were also taught at the time of the 1921 Inspection and found to be satisfactory. Spanish, however, had only been introduced during the war, at the suggestion of local shipping companies, but only fifteen boys in the whole school were studying it and out of the five that had just been examined not one of them gained a credit in the subject towards their School Certificate. The verdict of the Inspectors was that *"it seems doubtful whether it is worth continuing it in a school of this character and size"*.

Other areas that came in for criticism in an otherwise complimentary report were the Science facilities, which the Governors were looking to renew anyway, and the Art Department. The latter, in 1921, was virtually non-existent – there was no designated art room, the subject was taught by a visiting mistress, who came into school to give two lessons a week to the first and second forms and one to each of the third and fourth forms. *"There are,"* noted the Inspectors, *"few facilites for the work and little is attempted beyond object drawing with a pencil".*

There were few facilities for Manual Instruction too, but here, despite overcrowding, it was felt that good work was being done. The overcrowding of the non-OTC members for gymnastic training was not so kindly looked upon as it meant that 70 non-cadets were grouped into one large class for two 45-minute lessons per week; a situation that wasn't helped by the fact that the Gymnastic Instructor had little teaching experience – *"It would be much to his advantage to take at an early opportunity a holiday course in Physical Training ... which he himself desires."*

The Physical Training then, incidentally, included *"Swedish educational gymnastics, boxing, swimming, the usual field games and athletics".* Although Dale's time at the School wasn't particularly marked by a period of sporting excellence, the gradual filtering through of more sixth formers led to a certain improvement in results. And while bigger numbers in the School meant it was less likely that you would get a single athlete who would dominate Sports Day, a number of significant records were broken in the twenties.

Yet more might have been broken had games master Arnold Lingley's suggestion for a running track around the School field been taken up:

"A track which would break away from the path near the tennis lawn and skirting the railings up to the orchard pass through an opening in the top fence so as to join the main path near the hut." As for the School field itself; "the grass was kept under control by a horse-drawn cutter and in the summer holidays it was occupied by a flock of sheep", presumably to keep the grass down and fertilised.

The new pavilion.

As of August 1921, the School had a new pavilion. Built at a cost of £1,027 it was described by Dale as being *"by no means elaborate or extravagant, but an adequate and useful building"*.

The structure cost more than was available in the Pavilion Fund, but the aim was to clear the deficit (£177) at the next School Fete.

Freddie Dale, doubtless, sorely felt the lack of a decent Pavilion at his first Plymouth College sports day, Saturday 1 May 1920, for the rain fell almost continuously. Nevertheless, after a short meeting the Committee decided to *"hold all the events except the High Jump and the Hurdles"*, which were later scheduled for May 10th.

The old pavilion.

This year also saw the Cross Country Run included in the Athletic Sports Programme for the first time. Run on the last Saturday of the Easter Term, 27 March, it was won by AW Stafford in 1hr 2mins 40secs and in those days it was still truly a cross-country run:

"The course, measuring roughly 7¼ miles, ran from the top of Hartley Hill (where there were but a handful of houses), to Crownhill hutments; thence across nine fields to the road leading to Plym Bridge; from Plym Bridge along the truck lines to Marsh Mills, and home by road via Laira and Alexandra Road."

Life in this part of Plymouth was still pretty rural, but then life generally was that much more simple viz: the

"(UN)OFFICIAL GUIDE TO OTC CAMP":

"Camp – A collection of absorbent tents situated in the wettest part of Salisbury Plain.

How to get there *– Get up at 5.15 am, wash, dress, breakfast, fight your way into a kit. Then pile kit bag on to your shoulder and hike off for the station. A London and South Western train conveys you by easy stages to the place the Ah-me Council has decided is to be your resting (?) place for ten days."*

Bed *– A sack of straw (called a palliasse), three blankets and as many insects as the tent provides"*...(and that's if you were lucky – when the School's Corps arrived at Tidworth Park Camp in the summer of 1922 they were too late to get any palliasse straw and had to sleep on bare boards for the first night!).

Tidworth Camp.

A section of what would appear to be the first post-war photograph of the whole School and its front-of-house setting would be used for all subsequent shots.

Miss Heath and Miss Footner sit to Bert Sargent's right, then the Headmaster, Mr Dodson, ?, Mr Dufton, Mr Osmund, Cairns, Thill and Miss Ruby Robinson and Miss Loveless.

Colourful as those images of straw beds and insects were they were nothing to the pictures conveyed by a letter to the magazine from the recent school leaver Grenville (GA) Le Mesurier. Giving his address as Maskeliya, Ceylon, he wrote:

"Sitting here listening to the myriad sounds emerging from the Jungle close by, I find myself dreaming of the old School.

"The incessant barking of my two terriers reminds me that I am not as lonely as I feel. Even while I write, I can hear the screams of the jackals, the gruntings of wild pigs, and the hissing of snakes. I can recommend planting as a fine out-door life, very interesting and well paid. After 2½ months I was earning enough to live on, besides being given a bungalow and four servants free of charge."

"You will see from these details that the least clever amongst you can make a good start, but the work is essentially a man's work. The coolies, who consist of South Indian Tamils and Singalese, (the "Irish" of the East), are most unpleasant persons when annoyed. The life is at time lonely, but with some sort of conveyance, such as a motor-bicycle, it is more than tolerable ..."

The Empire was clearly still full of golden opportunities, even if life in them was a little primitive. Science and communications technology had yet to create the global village and the perception of the world and the people in it, was somewhat different to the way in which it would all soon come to be seen. Nevertheless it is a little surprising, perhaps, that one of the motions put before the Debating Society that November, concerned an issue over which there is little question these days, but clearly was felt to be sufficiently contentious in 1920. The proposition was that:

"In the opinion of this House, men and monkeys descended from the same common stock". Admittedly there was little opposition, and the Headmaster himself, chairing the meeting, spoke for the motion, but it suggested that a Biology Department was also

something that the School might consider before too long. Although it should be noted that once again interest in the Natural Science Society was on the wane.

Clearly certain Victorian values were still to be found in pockets of the School and in the annual visitors debate, in 1921, we find CR Serpell OPM (and clerk to the governors) *"in a carefully prepared speech"* outlining *"the evils of intoxicating liquors"* but rather ignoring *"the practical side of Prohibition and the causes underlying the excessive drinking that leads to poverty and crime".*

The headmaster was again in the chair and the opposition movement was led by another OPM J Woolland, who *"denied the justice, wisdom and expediency of Prohibition".* His remarks, it was noted *"seemed to meet with the approval of those members of the fairer sex who were present."*

After other members discussed the failure of Prohibition in America, CJK Coggle suggested that if excess was repressed, with regard to alcohol, it would, subsequently, appear in other forms and that anyway *"a little wine is good for the stomach".* Meanwhile Miss K Byfield, a visitor, expressing the woman's point of view, said, *"they were influenced by the desire for forbidden fruit".*

Miss Byfield was, undoubtedly, one of the School's more welcome female visitors that year. Judging by the letter from "Observer" in the April 1921 Plymothian, not all visitors were as favourably viewed.

"Dear Sirs, Having had occasion to pass the College Grounds some few times during my life, I have noticed a board of quite considerable dimensions, on which are inscribed the words: "Plymouth College. Private Grounds."

"I am sure that to the meanest intelligence these words do not convey the impression which is given by a doormat with the inscription "Welcome" ... and yet many times during the day one may observe ladies and

gentlemen, who, having nothing whatever to do with the College, perambulate along the strictly private path which traverses the gound behind our magnificent pavilion."

"Surely this could be remedied in some way or other ... for disregard for the privacy of the College grounds must inevitably lead to disrespect for the College and all its works."

It is interesting to note that no mention is made of any actual crime associated with this alien access and it should also be remembered that the School occupied much less of the surrounding area in those days.

There was, of course, always one day a year when any number of visitors was welcomed – College Fete Day. The 4th June 1921 was a particularly fine day, the weather was perfect and the organisation, which was left *"entirely in the hands of the Old Boys of the College,"* was admirable.

Twelfth Night revellers; Savage, Conybeane, Hill, the Headmaster, Budge, Morton and Hatch.

There were games, musical entertainments – most notably an Orchestral Concert staged by WP Weekes OPM - a Punch and Judy show and a Field Gun Display. In the grounds of College House the Headmaster and Miss Ruth Wilson, put on some "Plays" with the help of the senior boys, there was a Dance in the Gymnasium and a Boxing Competition. Boxing was very popular generally then around the Three Towns and at the "Cosmo," off Union Street, many of the top names of the day appeared. At the School Fete a number of boys fought out the final rounds of the competition and Corporal O'Shaugnessy and Private Kenifick, Ist Battalion RMF staged an exhibition bout. Four OPMs, Bawden, Bray, Tidboald and Lieutenant Breeze acted as judges, referee and timekeeper. A few days earlier 20 year-old Alfred Breeze had *"helped the School Ist XI out of a hole"* by turning out for them against St Germans.

Tragically, two weeks later he was killed, just outside Dublin, while serving with the 2nd Battalion Worcester Regiment. Breeze, a former Ist XI Captain had only left the School in the spring of 1919. He was one of over 500 British servicemen to lose their lives in the Irish conflict before a truce was called – less than three weeks after his death.

His loss was keenly felt at School; he had also captained the Football and Fives teams and won his Hockey colours - *"There were perhaps few boys as much respected ... both on account of his work in the games of the College and his never-failing good temper."*

There was to be more than just the one black cloud over the School that June, though, as the day after Breeze was buried, AGF Duff, a young boy in the second form, died from septic pneumonia. The same summer magazine also recorded the death of Dr Hingston.

Charles Hingston had become a Governor of the School under the new scheme in 1909 and four years later had succeeded Sir Alfred Croft as Chairman of the Board. His contribution over the next few years was significant and his approach is perhaps best summed up in an excerpt from his obituary;

"Although of course all School-boys learn and all School-masters teach, not all Governors govern. From the beginning, however, it was clear that Dr Hingston intended to give to the development of the School a governing attention."

The account continues; *"The financial strain of the war involved a constant watchfulness over its expenditure. The periodically recurrent difficulties of balancing expenditure against income were complicated by the need that recently arose for the extension of the Boarding-house and the Preparatory School. To both of these enterprises Dr Hingston contributed not only active and watchful interest, but ungrudging financial support."*

Following the death of Hingston, who *"was not himself a family man"*, JP Brown, whose five sons had all passed through the College, was elected Chairman of the Governors. His Vice-Chairman was another non-family man, and one who had not long been appointed to the board, although he had long been familiar to it – Joseph Thompson.

Sadly, it was a role that he was to enjoy for less than a year, for on the 29th April 1922, Joseph Thompson passed away. His death was marked by the longest obituary ever to appear in the Plymothian, written by the man who had appointed him – Francis Colson.

"I met him, I think, first in January, 1891 (it may have been 1892). The cause of his coming to Plymouth College was that one of the staff, JB Greenway, who died some years ago, had obtained a term's leave to go abroad to improve his German. Thompson therefore came originally for one term. Our numbers were at that time rising steadily, and though Mr Greenway was back in May, I asked his substitute to remain and give us help for some hours a week. He agreed, and as the numbers continued to rise, the relation developed into a permanent mastership."

"I had known from the first that Mr Thompson had no financial need to earn his living, and that his only reason for joining our staff was his wish to do some useful work."*

Colson then went on to outline the help, both financial and otherwise that Joseph Thompson rendered the School, noting amongst it all that, *"it was in 1901 that he offered to devote the absurdly inadequate salary which he had received, to what is perhaps his most permanent Memorial, the Bath."*

Thompson's "most permanent Memorial" - the Bath."

Other donations were chronicled, including the expenditure of over £1,000 to buy out the "shareholders" in order to achieve the conditions under which the School could plan for the future.

"When I resigned in 1908," Colson went on, *"there was a feeling in the Staff as well as elsewhere that he*

ought to be Headmaster. For a time I think, he considered the idea favourably, but ultimately he did not send in his name. I believed at the time and still believe that he was right. For one thing I doubted that his health and temperament would stand the worry, and in this I may have been wrong, but I am sure that by his refusal he rendered the teaching profession a real service. That profession has never quite come to be regarded as Orders are or were, as a work of high social service. But it ought to be. And the spectacle of a man of high ability working hard for nearly thirty years in a comparatively obscure position and refusing to receive either money or promotion for it, did more for the ennobling of educational work than any amount of eloquence could do. That he also greatly raised the School in the eyes of the people of Plymouth is indisputable."

Having described his fine academic qualifications (Latin, Greek, History and Philosophy at Oxford) Colson said that his former colleague was "a capital arguer ... a good musician ..." and "not exactly an athlete but could, at one time, I think, beat anyone in the School at Fives."

"It may be thought," he concluded, " that this says too much of Joseph Thompson's work and too little of him as a man. Yet with him perhaps more than with most people the work was the man. At any rate it reflected the transparent single mindedness which governed his whole life and joined to an essentially kind heart endeared him to the many generations of boys who came under him and will always remember his influence."

Joseph Thompson was, undoubtedly, a most remarkable man and it is quite possible that the whole history of the School and its ability to survive might have been quite a different one were it not for his contribution. But perhaps Colson was telling us more than he let on when he wrote of Thompson's "essentially" kind heart. Freddie Dale in his memorial address added little to Colson's appraisal but interestingly enough spoke of

Thompson's "disinterested" kindness.
"Like other Schoolmasters," he said, "it was possible to "draw" him; it was even possible to "rag" him: but the most thoughtless boy who ever tried to do these things never failed to realise and appreciate his disinterested kindness".

Roger Serpell, son of the then Clerk of the Governors, and a pupil at the School at the time, said that Thompson was not particularly liked, but everyone was happy with the money - and the swimming pool, adding; "he was probably a sadist – I think he rather enjoyed beating boys".

Form 1A (c 1921) Back row; Sanders, Ruse, Kelly, Jeffery, Serpell R, Hatch, Hilton, Harvey. Middle; Heard, Dale (son of the Headmaster), Whitburn, Gard, Mackintosh, Gerry, Davis. Front; Holditch, Jillard, Damerell, Shepherd, Pinhey, Grimshaw, Norris. Note the variety of tie styles.

Beatings, or "bummings" as the boys often called them, were a regular part of School life in those days and each teacher seemed to delight in devising their own style with regard to this form of corporal punishment. Although there were exceptions; Miss Hammond, the visiting art teacher, whose methods were criticised by the inspectors, and who Roger Serpell described as a "dead loss", invented her own punishment "of making

us kneel on wooden slats". This happened on a regular basis "when we behaved badly, which was frequently, as nobody was interested in drawing circles or squares". It should be remembered by all those who think that teaching is badly paid now that it was much worse then, and although Dale clearly didn't suffer fools gladly there were nevertheless one or two members of staff who were perhaps a little less than effective at that time. Indeed George Cairns who was only really entrusted with first form teaching was possibly a candidate for the exception to the rule expounded by Dr Hingston's obituarist that, "all teachers teach" and consequently his pupils did not always learn much – "harmless ... no use at all" is how one former student described him. His name is not particularly conspicuous among those involved in extra-curricular activities either. Many others were though – like Captain Charles Dodson who attended all 11 of the Debating Societies meetings in the 1920-21 session and who, until that summer, was commander of the School OTC.

"He assumed command when the Corps was somewhat in its infancy, and by sheer hard work and untiring energy brought it to its present state. A glance at the list of successes obtained by members of the Corps during Captain Dodson's period of command will prove what a deep debt of gratitude is owing to him by both present and past members of the Corps for the most efficient training they have received from him."

Captain Charles Dodson

Dodson left Plymouth College to take on the Headship of Salop; he had been at the School since 1910. He was just 22 when he arrived and he was, undoubtedly, very close to many of the young men who subsequently passed through his command and then served their country in the Great War. With a heavier heart than most he would have gone into Big School in the afternoon of Wednesday 6 October 1921 for the unveiling of the Plymouth College and Mannamead School War Memorial Tablet.

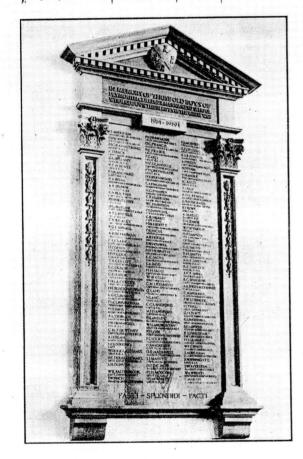

Plymouth College War Memorial.

"Because of the restricted accommodation the ceremony was witnessed by only a comparatively small company, consisting of the relatives of the fallen, several of the Governors, the staff and the Prefects of the School."

Mr Dale, who had of course served in France himself, said that there had been a little difficulty in deciding to what use the money subscribed for a war memorial should be put. *"It had been hoped something could be done towards adding to the building, but,"* he said, *"the only necessary and feasible addition was beyond our means ... and would be for some time."*

"It has therefore been decided that the best use to make of the money was founding a War Memorial Scholarship to enable a boy from the College to continue his education at a University. Personally," said the Head, *"I think it is a growing need of the College to provide more opportunity for University training."*

"It is also recognised that some visible memorial should be set up."

Sentiments echoed by Brigadier General Lord St Levan who removed the Union Jack covering the oak tablet, a tablet which had been designed by OPM Governor MA Bazeley and which featured the names of 111 Old Boys known to have lost their lives in the conflict.

"I do not think there can be too many memorials", he said. Adding later, *"It is the business of those who remain to see to it that they did not die in vain. They set an example, and memorials such as we see this afternoon are as signs pointing out the way of duty."*

"To the boys of the School it would form a very great help on their starting out on life, for it might come to them to take their part in defending their homes and their families. We hope and pray that such a war might never occur again, but it is no use blinding ourselves to the facts, and nobody, I think, can feel any assurance that the world might not be involved again."

Prophetic words indeed and little could Lord St Levan have realised how, in time, they would come to resound around the walls of Big School. At the time though there were other, more immediate, concerns and later that day both he and the Headmaster appeared before an expanded audience in the old gymnasium for the annual distribution of prizes. Here, it would seem, the item highest on Freddie Dale's agenda was the imminent visit (due the following week) of the Representatives of the Board of Education. *"I fear,"* he said, *"the experience for a headmaster of two years' standing of a visit of six emissaries direct from Olympus, wandering about the school for four days and asking questions at awkward moments. It will no doubt be a little alarming, but I hope that it will also be interesting and helpful."*

Then he made the observation that the Board of Governors was currently very much impressed with the need for economy – *"I don't think they* (the Inspectors) *will find Plymouth College extravagant. If anyone studies economy we do. Let Lord Rothermere or the Hon. Esmond Harmsworth come here and see if they can get an exercise book to which they are not entitled out of Mr Sargent,"* he said to a roar of laughter. Mr Dale also took the opportunity to thank the Plymouth Education Authority who, significantly for the School, had increased their annual grant from £1,000 to £2,000 and he mentioned that the Burnham scale had just been adopted for the salaries of the assistant masters.

It's interesting to note, incidentally, that the man leading the team of HMI inspectors was the father of one of the assistant masters, John Dufton and as Dufton junior was an OPM himself we can only assume that Dufton senior wouldn't have had an entirely dispassionate view of the School.

John Dufton was to be the longest-serving of all Chaytor's appointments and was generally seen to be *"a good soul"*. In 1921 he had been at the School just two years; before his retirement he would serve a further thirty-five years. Among his various responsibilities in that summer of 1921 he was a judge at the School Aquatic Sports and although that year's competition yielded no great surprises or achievements – HJ Dunn (of College House) was easily Victor Ludorum – it did produce one fascinating piece of information; a table of Percentage Distance Swimming. That is a record, right across the School, House by House, of just how far the boys of Plymouth College could swim.

PERCENTAGE WHO CAN SWIM

	50YDS:	200YDS:	500YDS
College Hse	83.14	69.2	54.32
East Town	83.33	50.0	36.66
SouthTown	90.48	38.1	33.33
North Town	48.56	34.3	24.26

The clear conclusion here was no great surprise – that the boarders could generally swim much further than the day boys. Doubtless they had more opportunities for practice, as they did in almost all sports. But swimming especially, as there were no public swimming baths in Plymouth at that time.

The improvements in bathing facilities at Tinside were less than a decade old as the twenties dawned and there was still no public pool, so there was great excitment when Devonport's new swimming bath (below) opened at Bullock's Dock in 1923.

The principal opportunities for public swimming in those days would have been off the Hoe and it is, perhaps, no great surprise either to find that of all the houses there was a greater percentage of boys from South Town (i.e. those nearest the sea) who could swim at least fifty yards.

These percentages represented a great leap forward from the pre-pool days, but, generally speaking, 1921 was not a vintage year on the School sports front. Commenting on the cricket the Games Master, Shanks Lingley, referred to suggestions that the fielding lacked unity, the backing up lacked alertness and the batting was characterised by *"cross-hitting"*.

"Next year the first two teams will be often in the field to practice as a team. I asked for this form of practice this year, but it was considered inconvenient owing to trains, distance from home, music lessons, tea, swimming bath and the usual excuse of the coal strike. These attractions, important as they are, must not be allowed during the next Season to interfere with the Unity of the team."

The problem, however, was apparently not confined to cricket. As the editors of the Plymothian observed *"some of our correspondents (people do really write to us occasionally) seem inclined to lament the absence of all sorts of societies. In a town with such attractions as Plymouth possesses, we cannot hope to maintain too many School Societies."*

The times they were a-changing, and electronic entertainments, particularly the then silent, silver screen was also starting to eat into time previously set aside for hobbies and sport.

Notwithstanding the cricketing criticisms, though, the season was not altogether bad, although the School did lose heavily to the first OPM side to have been fielded since the outbreak of war. Underhill's four catches *"one taken low in the slips"* helped the Old Boys enormously.

The rugby was similarly undistinguished - Kelly inflicted a notable defeat, there was success, and failure, against Newton and a notable draw with Seale-Hayne College. There was also an entertaining review of a book of Rugger Rhymes in the magazine;
"The whole of tackling is summed up in the three lines
"Low, low, go for him low,
Whether he's fast or whether he's slow,
Tight round the knees, man, don't let him go."
Boxing meanwhile, *"one of England's most manly sports"*, we must surmise from "Straight Left's" letter was *"sadly neglected"* that year.

The *"exceedingly hot"* School Sports Day was comfortably won by South Town, with LR Bryant (who won the under-16 220 yards), taking the Victor Ludorum title, scoring over half of North Town's tally in the process. He also finished second in both the Open 100 yards and the Cross Country Run.

Meanwhile the Hockey highlight seems to have been the charabanc trip to Exeter, the team played their only inter-school fixture of the season there – they lost 2-0.

The following season the hockey team managed three inter-school fixtures beating Exeter this time, in a memorable 5-4 encounter, and drawing 2-2 with the Royal Naval College and going down 7-2 to Seale-Hayne College. Of the six other fixtures four were lost. The 2nd XI fared better and were undefeated in seven outings, registering two 13-0 victories over Mannamead Ladies.

There was a similar picture for the Rugby (still referred to in the magazine under the heading Football). Of the sixteen matches played only six were against schoolboy sides and overall more were lost than won. There were also a couple of drawn matches, including a tight 3-3 tie with an OPM XV (the OPMs were still a year or two off constituting a regular team).

In the cricket Kelly won the home and away fixtures, thanks largely to the services of the two Kelly brothers. In the first match, played at Kelly on a *"bumpy wicket"*, Bryant, Morton and Steer were all dismissed – caught R Kelly bowled F Kelly.

The School team line-up for an away game charabanc trip - note the folding roof, the horn, the non-pneumatic tyres and the warning flag.

Only Lucas conducted himself with any real credit - in both innings he and *"extras"* scored more than the rest of the team put together, he also took four wickets, while Strachan turned in an impressive 6-31. In the return match, played on a *"sticky"* wicket at Ford Park, F Kelly was again in fine form for his school taking five wickets and top scoring with 61. Once again Lucas top scored for the School. However, if the School had a batting hero in the summer of 1922 it had to be 33 year-old Walter Gingell.

Gingell had arrived the previous year to teach Maths and English. In his first winter he had played the odd game of hockey for the Ist XI and, against non-school sides only, played several times for the Ist XI cricket team. His contribution was never less than impressive and the School won all the games he played in.

Walter Gingell

An unbeaten 102 helped the School declare at 191-4 against Plymstock. He struck 56 against Keyham, 40 against Tavistock and 68 against the RNE College. In that last game he enjoyed lengthy partnerships with Moore, the School professional, Freddie Dale and Bert Sargent. The School declared at 257-6, Mr Dodson, next man in, was denied a chance to wield the willow.

One suspects that Dale was just as keen to get his staff together on the playing field as he was to see them acting together on the stage and he played a number of Ist XI games himself.

Dale's team-building extended to partners too. At the 1922 School Fete, Mr and Mrs Dodson were in charge of transforming the gymnasium for the day. Mrs Lingley staged an operetta there in the evening and Mr and Mrs Gingell *"produced their comedies at 6pm., and a deservedly cordial reception"*.

Later still in the evening *"the supper stall was served by Mesdames Naish, Osmund, and Sargent, guarded by their worst halves"*.

In the dusk there was what then had become a bit of a Fete Day tradition - a torchlight tattoo on the School field. Incidentally, in addition to her Fete Day orchestral efforts, Mrs Lingley also assisted with the music teaching in the School and was said to be *"infinitely more terrifying than Dale"* (Roger Serpell).

Mrs Lingley played a major part in the Annual Christmas Concert too, she sang a *'Song of England'* and opened the show with Mr Dodd, the two of them playing Saint Saens's piano duet - *'Marche Heroique'*.

The Reverend Henry Dodd was another of Dale's recent appointments and, although he didn't stay long, he and his wife contributed to a number of musical evenings. So, indeed, did Mrs Naish who, with her husband Walter, was another of the short-stay staffers in the early twenties.

Dodd was succeeded in the Religious instruction department by the Reverend Bernard Benskin. Famous for his three-wheel, no-gears Morgan motor-car, Benskin was possibly a trifle over fond of caning, despite being a man of the cloth.

He would punish when he felt like it – *"Pour encourager les autres"*. *"Fetch me the weapon"* was the usual prelude to a punishment of his own invention – he would strike the tips of boys fingers with a two-foot cane. The smarter miscreants got used to pushing

Benskin an early Morgan man.

their hands forward to take the blow on the fleshier part of the hand.

The Reverend Benskin, who was thought to have been a bit of a coward in his own way, was fond of telling his boys that there was a lot to be said for wearing a dog collar when you find yourself in trouble.

Generally though the sort of trouble he meant was car trouble – he was evidently a lousy mechanic and the car often needed a push.

Joining the School with the Reverend Benskin at the end of 1922 was Lionel Lord, who curiously enough, was born on Christmas Day 1898 and thus, at 23 became the youngest member of Dale's expanding common room.

Lionel Lord

An enthusiastic young man, Lord had become North Town housemaster before the end of his first year and lost little time in firing up his new charges.

As House Captains Hatch and Bryant reported, Mr Lord, *"has given us a new "House Spirit" and enthusiasm. We now possess a Crest and a Motto, and House Records have now been started. A red star on a green flag now waves along the touchline during our house matches."*

It wasn't just House Spirit that Mr Lord seemed partial to however – *"Boys, never drink tawny port"*, he announced to the 6th, as he walked into one classroom, somewhat hungover, his hands and fingers held in an affected sort of way.

Despite his apparent delicate nature Lord was one of Dale's more enduring appointments, indeed after a year or two with him at the helm the Head's ship was starting to settle somewhat. It was doubtless a welcome period of stability following the turbulent years of the war.

Indeed as the war receded in memories of some so we find the OTC once more appealing for recruits. Having said that, though, there was a good number at the 1923 Camp, over fifty, *"which constitutes a record attendance in the history of the OTC as in previous years the numbers have never reached forty"*. Much of this was due to the efforts of Mr – Captain – Naish.

Fresh-faced OTC recruit - Arthur Lyddon cycling to School - 1921

"Our numbers are, I am glad to say, increasing, but we shall not be complete until every eligible boy in the College is in our ranks," he wrote in his December 1922 report, adding, *"I have been asked several times recently what it costs to belong to the Corps. The only expenses incurred are 30/- (£1.50p) entrance fee, and a subscription of 2/6d (12½p) per term. The subscription for those attending camp is 30/- inclusive."*

Interestingly enough at that time 6/- (30p) would have bought you a year's membership for the OPM Club, while a guinea (£1.05p) would have secured membership for four years and you could have had life membership for £3.13.6d (£3.67p).

Not everything had a price on it though, and at the beginning of the April term a new and subscription-free society was formed at School – the Classical Society.

Consisting of members of the Classical VIth (there were only five or six boys in it) and Classical Masters (even fewer), meetings were held weekly in the Headmaster's house and Mr Dale himself presided.

"We have alternately read and discussed portions of Greek and Roman authors and listened to papers given by members," wrote DR Stephens in his first report.

"It was decided," he added, *"at the first meeting that the minutes should be written in Latin; I have, however, abstained from using the same tongue in this report for reasons which I hope will commend themselves to the majority of readers."*

The writer then concluded his remarks *"by expressing the hope that the Society, though young (quid si fasti sunt breves?) will be a worthy supplement to the other School institutions and that these words of Cicero may justly be applied to it in the near future: "Splendet per sese ipsum semper"."*

DR Stephens was one of the first to read a paper to the group (The Greek Bucolic Poets), needless to say he provided no translation for his last remark and, equally unsurprisingly, the initial rush of enthusiasm soon peaked. Within a couple of terms the meetings

had become fortnightly, not weekly. Furthermore, two of the first three papers read in the Autumn term came from masters – Mr Dale himself and the newly-arrived Mr Lord. It would seem to have ever been the lot of new masters to get involved with new or ailing societies and, consequently, it is no real wonder to find the keen, young Science master, John Dufton, reviving the Photographic Society in the summer of 1923.

Once again the boys spell out the date (1923) in the gym display.

Science was one area where the School appeared to be in danger of falling behind some other institutions, but in reality it was an aspect of education that was still in its infancy, as was the wider issue of University education. University was not seen as a major stepping stone in those days and much to the Headmaster's dismay the Town Council of Plymouth (City status was still a few years away) had, as he put it, *"short-sightedly followed the lead of other towns"* in cutting down the number of educational scholarships. *"It is now possible to say,"* he contended in his Speech Day address, *"that a clever boy is cut off from his best hopes in life because he is a Plymouth boy."*

"Such a policy," he added, *"accentuates the reproach against secondary education in the South West – that so few boys stay at school between the ages of 16-18. The value of secondary education is largely lost if it ceases at 16."*

Distributing the annual prizes, Dr Farnell, the Vice Chancellor of Oxford University and a School Governor, agreed and dwelt upon the place of benefaction.

"The average cost of each student at our University is about £500 a year, but I only pay two-fifths of that sum. Without the liberal gifts of past benefactors University education today," he said, *"would be restricted to the rich."*

"Many of the older Public Schools are richly endowed," he went on, *"and so are able to carry out whatever improvements are thought necessary. Plymouth College,"* added Dr Farnell, *"is not so fortunate and it is to be hoped that some generous donor will give the School some real financial assistance. There is no form of philanthropy more charming,"* he ventured, *"than that of helping local institutions. Given freedom from financial distress, there is no reason why the College should not reach the highest rank among public schools."*

Neither was it just university education that was in danger of becoming more exclusive – the cost of course at Sandhurst had also been materially raised *"and this of necessity limited the number of boys who would naturally have entered Sandhurst from the School".*

Such considerations notwithstanding MA Thomson won two substantial (£80 and £100) Exhibitions for Classics at Exeter College, Oxford that year and Corkery and Jones won places at Sandhurst, Colenso likewise for Woolwich.

Among the other notable school leavers that year were WH Savage, off to Balliol College, Oxford and GP Rooks. Rooks was one of those rounded individuals who almost certainly would have gone to university in a more modern climate. He played rugby and hockey for the school, was Junior Victor Ludorum in 1919, equalled the school 100yds record in 1922, was swimming secretary, a Lance-Corporal in the OTC, secretary of the Debating Society (he won the cup in 1921) and a sub-editor of the Plymothian.

The record for the 100 yards then, incidentally, was 11 seconds, a creditable time by any standards. Interestingly enough, the record time for the mile was

beaten at the following years' Sports Day – just, by one-fifth of a second. IS Hodges clocked a time of 4 mins 58.6 secs. Hodges finished joint Victor with WG Bartholomew who, rather unusually, took the title for a second time.

School athletics seems to have been a fairly in-house affair in the twenties - there are no references to inter-school competitions, whereas there were for all the other sports. Although had it not been for Kelly one wonders if Fives would have managed to limp on from one year to the next.

Even then most encounters with the opposition were unsuccessful; the aforementioned Bartholomew, then reckoned to be the strongest player in the School, with team-mate Bowden, being the only pair to win even one game against the old firm in 1922. Even that was one game more than they won the following year.

"True we suffered defeat – and no uncertain defeat – in both our matches with Kelly: our conquerors were all at least a class better than we were; but while not detracting from the merits of their victories, for our own selfish purposes we should like to point out that they are fortunate in the possession of covered courts ... As our courts are not covered, on many days it has been impossible to play at all, while on many others proper Fives has been out of the question owing to the sodden condition of the courts: this gives justification for those interested in the game to put in a plea for covered courts in the near future."

The Fives enthusiasts were not the only ones complaining though. The Plymothian editors were *"once again voicing the age-old "grouse" that we have not had enough contributions."*

If anything though there were more contributions in that particular edition than had ever graced a School Magazine in the past: hunting reminiscences from a globe trotting OPM, a poem extolling the virtues of Whitsand Bay, a mock-classical skit set outside the Prefect's Room, a humorous piece – Bryan the Black,

or life in the Middle Ages, a philosophical treatise on a broken pane of glass, an academic item on Isotopes and the Structure of the Atom (from FC Phillips, who, two years earlier, had contributed serious essay on the Theory of Relativity) and an article on the "Desecration" of the tomb of Tutankhamen.

The discovery, on 26th November 1922, by Howard Carter and the Earl of Sandwich of the 3,000 year-old tomb of Tutankhamun had aroused great interest and amusement around the world. The following term's Plymothian reported, in its Cambridge letter, on the *"epoch-making discovery which has resulted from Cambridge undergraduate research in the realms of Egyptology ...*

Tutankhamun's burial mask

In the presence of Lord Cumanrun, the Sultan and Queen Cleopatra and other celebrities, the tomb of Toot-an-kum-in was opened, and we are able to announce that the much-discovered King Toot was none other than Phineas, of London medical fame."

Meanwhile, under a section marked "Rumours", we were told that *"the recent discoveries at Luxor have caused a mania for excavation on the Hockey pitches, as a result of which several spherical objects, thought to be balls, have been unearthed".*

Interestingly enough the most sensible piece on Luxor in the Plymothian had appeared three years earlier in July 1920. Covering an unprecedented seven pages it was credited to "Walud," who had served in the EEF towards the end of the Great War;

"Throughout the war the Authorities endeavoured to grant every man serving a short period of leave ... the favourite localities in which to spend leave were Cairo, Luxor, Aswan and, for those at base, Jerusalem. Luxor and Aswan are usually combined and nearly every officer in the force has spent one leave in this district."

A rare, and unusual, 1920s Plymothian photograph.

The piece went on to describe the area in some detail and did much to bring the exotic middle east to life for its schoolboy audience;

"Luxor, the name being derived from the ancient Arabic name El-Uksur, meaning "the temples," in reference to the temple over which part of the village was built..."

It is tempting to assume that Walud was Francis Dale, or at least a member of staff who had been serving abroad (Richardson or Dufton perhaps). It is hard to imagine that any OPM would have been afforded that amount of space. Somewhat unusually too, the magazine was prefaced with a photograph of the Statue of Ramases II – Luxor Temple.

Clearly someone on the staff had a good knowledge of the area now exciting such great interest.

Despite the protestations of the Plymothian editors it was clearly a productive time on the literary front at the School and in addition to the official organ of the College there were a few other "publications".

"Frequently one hears of the foundation of form magazines; as frequently one hears of their abandonment. The Editorial memory recollects such periodicals as the "Fourth Form Gazette" and the "Fourth Former" which appeared as deadly rivals and both lasted for two fortnightly issues. At last, however, we have in our midst a form magazine, which seems to have struck the right note and to deserve a permanent place amongst the School Institutions. We refer, of course, to Form IIIA's magazine "Chin-Wag". This periodical is run on sound, if rather novel lines. It appears only once a term, thus avoiding the hard labour inseparable from fortnightly productions. One copy is produced which is passed from hand to hand, thus avoiding expense and enabling photographs and drawings to be included. We have examined the first number and have found the reading matter to be both (sic) useful, interesting and varied. One is provoked to voice the thought that at once occurs. If such good literary fare can be produced in a form magazine, why is it not entered for the Plymothian?"

"We wish this magazine the popularity it deserves and hope it may continue its labours and so become as

established an institution as the Plymothian itself."

Sadly Form IIIA's magazine did not go on to become a school institution, but it did last more than two issues – just – and it did get into print – after a fashion.

The magazine was clearly the product of the fortuitous coming together of one newly arrived schoolmaster, Canon Benskin, and two young boys who would go on to carve out names for themselves as journalists - LR Hunt and JC Trewin.

In his autobiography (Up From The Lizard), Trewin speaks highly of his old history teacher - *"the most invigorating and original of schoolmasters ... Boys warmed to his crisp sense of the ridiculous – endearingly he would talk on occasion like a wandering voice from a Travers farce – and, at the same time, they found themselves infected by his obvious passion for the things he was talking about."*

"He had a way of welding his form: we were never bound so loyally as in Benskin's year, and I think he had for us a special regard as the first of his forms to meet in the splendid isolation of Room One (JC Trewin – Up From The Lizard)."

Trewin and Hunt unwittingly began their journalistic careers early *"by editing one of Benskin's children, a form magazine called The Chin-Wag ... I still have a thumbed copy of the third and final number, typed miraculously by Hunt, compact of articles on butterflies, slow-worms, railway engines (full credit, of course, to Trevithick), birds' eggs, the gum bichromate process, and even – for we were nothing if not topical – the new and fashionable broadcasting. There was also a cosmopolitan serial, with French dialogue,"* wrote Trewin, adding, with respect to his own contributions, *"I seem to have been alarmingly fertile".*

The magazine flourished for that one year. The next Form IIIA did not continue it and Trewin, on graduating to Form IVA, offered his literary pieces to the Plymothian, viz April 1924, his poem *The English Channel"* which ends thus:

*"Following in their traces
As Time's sickle swung,
Ships of every nation,
Men of every tongue,
Sailing, ever sailing,
From their native quays
Adown the English Channel,
The Highway of the Seas."*

That Benskin continued his idiosyncratic ways in Room One is in little doubt and if proof were needed it appeared right under Trewin's poem under another batch of "Rumours". This time however the Plymothian editors were less than complimentary about the junior class, as the rumour in question suggested that;

"Debates are held in IIIA. (Our readers need not be unduly perturbed by this intelligence since our Regent's Park correspondent assures us that similar functions frequently take place in the ape house there. We therefore assume it to be natural)."

However, to return to 1923, as Trewin notes, broadcasting was the *"new and fashionable"* medium that summer and at the School Fete among the usual attractions there was, in one of the huts, *"a wireless concert in progress ... Paris and Cardiff were heard and the air was full of many voices. The exhibition of wireless apparatus was the most complete we have ever seen."*

Meanwhile in the Pavilion *"the records of Melba and Caruso were heard"*.

It is hard not to over-emphasise the impact that the wireless and the gramophone record had on society at large, as well as the boys and staff of Plymouth College, but it is clearly no coincidence to discover that in that same term the first ever Music page appeared in the Plymothian. Previously (and not counting the earlier efforts to record sound) the only music that anyone had heard, without travelling, had been self-generated, local or from visiting musicians. Now, via the new sound equipment, the greatest talents in the world could be

heard in the home, or in school. It was a breakthrough that was almost as dramatic as that of the invention of the first printing press, a few hundred years earlier.

Consequently it was no great surprise to read that *"Thanks to the sympathetic attitude of the Headmaster and the Editors to the above Art, a page in the School Magazine is to be devoted henceforward to MUSIC NOTES."*

Nellie Melba sings

"Music," the writers continued, *"is at last coming in to it's own. The Consultative Committee to the Board of Education has recommended : -*

i.   *That Music and Art have equal parity with other subjects.*

ii.   *That music be made a principal subject for the Second Subject examinations.*

"This alters the whole status of Music in Schools and makes the subject one of personal urgency for heads, teachers, parents and boys – especially boys – musical or otherwise."

*"Public Schools:
The older Public Schools have already made Music an integral part of their School life and look on a new boy, knowing and caring nothing for Music, as a rank outsider and a heathen Chinee."*

"It is "up to" Plymothians to see that the College is capable of holding its own in this as in all other respects, and for the high gods (the Prefects and VI Form) to make it a point of honour to back up the musical activities of the School with all the powers at their command."

"Our progressive Headmaster, always ready to give new ideas a fair trial, has kindly consented to the following developments in the School Music."

1 – *A Music page in the Plymothian*
2 – *Special board for Music Notes*
3 – *Formation of a School Choir and Glee Club*
4 – *Appreciation classes*
5 – *Gramophone recitals*
6 – *Music classes for Upper School and if possible "Sing-songs"."*

Advertisement from a twenties School Fete programme

"On Friday, June 15th, an important meeting was held in the Prefects' Room, to discuss the formation of a School Choir and Glee Club. It was unanimously decided to do so. The Headmaster and Music Director have offered to entertain the Seniors annually, the Juniors to be rewarded with an extra "Half" each term; needless to say there will be no lack of Juniors."

Such, of course, is not to say that the School had hitherto neglected music altogether. Clearly there had been "Glee Clubs" in the past and the School, in Frederick Lohr and then Carl Kuhne, had had excellent music masters. But they were both visiting masters and the subject was not regarded as a major part of the curriculum. Having said that the School had not been

Important paper work - a selection from the archives of Marshall Ware. Clockwise; The Oxford and Cambridge Board Certificate A, the 1923 Prize Day programme, the envelope that contained Marshall's School Report in 1923 and below it the report itself. Marshall Ware with the cup he won that year. At home in St Budeaux with his School cap and full uniform and below the Sixth Form as they lined up in the summer term of 1923.

OXFORD & CAMBRIDGE SCHOOLS EXAMINATION BOARD

School Certificate A

I. Ware, Marshall L.

born 1 June 1906 attended the following Secondary School(s), viz.

Plymouth College from May 1919 to July 1923

and pursued a course of study in the subjects enumerated on the back of this Certificate.

F. R. Dale Head Master

II. After an examination in the following Groups of Subjects:

Group I, English Subjects; Group II, Languages; Group III, Mathematics and Science

he was awarded the School Certificate of the Oxford and Cambridge Schools Examination Board in July 1923, and passed with credit in the following subjects:

Scripture Knowledge, History, Spanish, Elementary Mathematics, Physics and Chemistry.

L. M. Farnell
Vice-Chancellor of Oxford

El Pearce
Vice-Chancellor of Cambridge

T. G. Bedford
Secretaries to the Board

III. THE BOARD OF EDUCATION have inspected the School and recognise it as an efficient Secondary School, and accept this Examination as reaching the approved standard, and as being suitable for the (last-named) School.

Signed on behalf of the Board of Education

Assistant Secretary

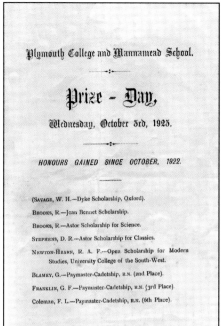

Plymouth College and Mannamead School.

Prize - Day,

Wednesday, October 3rd, 1923.

HONOURS GAINED SINCE OCTOBER, 1922.

(SAVAGE, W. H.—Dyke Scholarship, Oxford).

BROOKS, R.—Joan Bennet Scholarship.

BROOKS, R.—Astor Scholarship for Science.

STEPHENS, D. R.—Astor Scholarship for Classics.

NEWTON-HEARN, R. A. F.—Open Scholarship for Modern Studies, University College of the South-West.

BLAMEY, G.—Paymaster-Cadetship, R.N. (2nd Place).

FRANKLIN, G. F.—Paymaster-Cadetship, R.N. (3rd Place).

COLEMAN, F. L.—Paymaster-Cadetship, R.N. (6th Place).

Plymouth College.

F. Ware, Esq.,
The Kloof,
St. Budeaux,
Devonport.

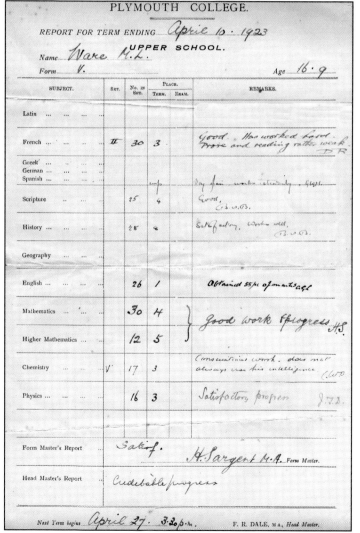

PLYMOUTH COLLEGE.

REPORT FOR TERM ENDING April 10. 1923

UPPER SCHOOL.

Name Ware M. L.

Form V.   Age 16.9

SUBJECT	SET	No. IN SET	TERM	EXAM	REMARKS
Latin					
French	II	30	3		Good. Has worked hard. Prose and reading rather weak. D R
Greek					
German					
Spanish			unp		Very fair, works steadily.
Scripture		25	4		Good. C.B.W.B.
History		28	4		Satisfactory. Works well. B.W.B.
Geography					
English		26	1		Obtained 55 p.c of marks age
Mathematics		30	4		} Good work & progress HS
Higher Mathematics		12	5		
Chemistry	V	17	3		Conscientious work. does not always use his intelligence.
Physics		16	3		Satisfactory progress
Form Master's Report					Satisf. H. Sargent M.A. Form Master.
Head Master's Report					Creditable progress

Next Term begins April 27. 3.30p.m.

F. R. DALE, M.A., Head Master.

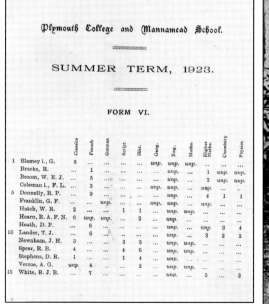

Plymouth College and Mannamead School.

SUMMER TERM, 1923.

FORM VI.

	Classics	French	German	Script.	Hist.	Geog.	Eng.	Maths.	Higher Maths.	Chemistry	Physics
1 Blamey i., G.	5				unp.	unp.	unp.				
Brooks, R.		1							1	unp.	unp.
Broom, W. E. J.		5							2	unp.	unp.
Coleman i., F. L.					unp.		unp.				
5 Donnelly, R. P.		9					unp.		4	1	1
Franklin, G. F.			unp.		unp.	unp.	unp.				
Hatch, W. R.	2			1	1		unp.				
Hearn, R. A. F. N.	6	unp.		2		unp.					
Heath, D. P.		8					unp.		3	4	
10 Lander, T. J.		6					unp.				
Newnham, J. H.	3			3	5		unp.		3	2	
Spear, R. B.	4			4	6		unp.				
Stephens, D. R.	1			1	4		unp.				
Vercoe, A. G.	unp.	4		2		unp.	unp.				
15 White, R. J. B.		7				unp.			5		

1923

161

without its musical successes and the same report that informed us of the subject's new status, also passed on congratulations to Serpell, Hancock, Holman, Toms and Treneer, who had all passed the last Royal Academy Examinations.

It was also noted that the British Music Society was due to hold a Festival in Plymouth, in the Guildhall, that coming October.

It is also significant that, after the initial problems surrounding the broadcasting of music by wireless operators, we should read in the following term's Plymothian that the British Broadcasting Company *"are trying a new experiment with music ... They are starting a series of lectures on Music given by some well-known musicians and with the illustrations played and sung by Competent Artistes."*

"It has," we were told, *"so far been most successful. The object is to bring music into all homes and raise the standard of the public by making them understand and appreciate real music. Boys who are thinking of buying a good Wireless Set may have an opportunity of hearing some really interesting lectures."*

It should be pointed out that even then there were wireless sets ... and there were wireless sets, and in the 1924 Plymothian "ARS" produced an amusing piece on *"Buying A Wireless Set".*

In it, the hapless would-be purchaser is offered all manner of elaborate contraptions, from *"a piece of equipage which resembled a cross between a grand piano and a profiteer's town carriage with a unique system of condensers, negolithic rheostats and meglomaniacal tuning"* to *"a seven-valve set with four-valve amplification, guaranteed to pick up Glasgow without you having to chink two half-crowns in front of the loud speaker ... for a mere 120 guineas".*

"Th-that is a lit-little above m-m-my p-price, I w-wanted s-s-something about f-f-five s-shillings," I said in a still, small voice.*

"Sir," said he (*"I call you "sir" because it is difficult*

to discard a habit of courtesy that I formed in my early childhood), here is a nice little set which can either be used as a Cheese dish or a Child's money box, cheap to run, easy on petrol, three forward speeds and one reverse, with balloon tyres, twenty two and sixpence."

"This last phrase was delivered with such force, and with such a ferocious gesture with the hammer, that I eagerly accepted this offer and departed, with a small square brown box, homewards; there to erect a suitable aerial, which would not interfere with either the clothes line, the chicken run, or the window boxes."

In addition to the increased availability of music through the new media there were also new music periodicals, including *"two excellent Music Magazines which should be in every house. Music and Youth for the Seniors – full of short, pithy articles – grave and gay, especially appealing to music lovers".* And the new Junior paper *"Panpipes"* which not only has *"delightful little stories, but some very short and very easy pieces for the piano by Abe Rowley, called "Adventures at the Piano"."*

Interest in music at the School had never been greater and boys were exhorted to join the new Gilbert and Sullivan Fellowship that had just started up in Plymouth, *"with the approval of R D'Oyley Carte Esq."* A few months later Forms IIA and IIB had a "Sullivan" afternoon ... *"a short talk, illustrated by gramophone records of selections from his various Operas, very kindly lent to the School by R Monk Esq., OPM."*

For whatever reason Forms IIA and IIB were clearly at the forefront of the new musical awareness and in the September 1924 magazine it emerged that: *"The privilege of choosing the new gramophone (for the School) fell to the lot of IIA and IIB, assisted by some of the Staff."*

The Columbia Granofola

Three machines were tested; a Cliftophone £13.13s, Columbia Grafonola £11.3s and His Master's Voice. *"After listening to several song and instrumental records, the Columbia was chosen as being the most suitable for the required purposes ... Messrs Parker and Smith (from whom the gramophone was bought) kindly gave six records to start the music library. We hope many others will do likewise. In some schools the singing classes subscribe regularly a small sum sufficient to buy as many records as are required during the term."*

At this stage there was no talk of the new music and the corrupting influence of the Jazz Age, there was concern though over the *"deleterious influence of the Cinema".* In a heated school debate both Mr Lord and Mr Gingell supported the notion that the cinema was having a bad effect and, in the end, the House agreed with them by a narrow majority, 21-18.

One of the year's top films.

Mr Lord, who also served as treasurer of the Debating Society, was a regular speaker at meetings and was among those who *"deplored professionalism in sport"* (they were outvoted 19-23) and *"deplored the action of Mussolini in the recent Graeco-Italian crisis"* (along with a healthy majority of others 28-9). There was, however, much less support for a motion proposed by Mr Lord himself – *"That people suffering from incurable diseases should be painlessly put away"* (Pro.3, Con.13, Neutral.19). On a more humanitarian note it was rather more encouraging to see that he led the opposition to NC Cornish's proposal that *"all Railway porters should be Black men"* a motion that was overwhelmingly defeated (5-31).

Walter Gingell was that year's Debating Society Chairman but it was, once again, on the cricket pitch, that he generated the greatest excitement and, one suspects, respect. In one game alone, against St Germans, he took 7 wickets for 51 runs, plus a catch, and was unbeaten on 63 - knocked up in just 40 minutes. Captain Lambert was St Germans' star player scoring 40 of their 91 runs. He was, however, one of Gingell's seven victims and when he came on to bowl, Gingell scored 22 off one of his overs. Once again the young teacher topped the batting and bowling records for the School that summer, and they appeared to win all the games he played in. Among the boys LE Williams was the most effective with the bat, an unbeaten 98 the best score of the season, and CG Creber topped the bowling, although LR Bryant took rather more wickets.

Circket hero Jack Hobbs

The cricket score sheets were a regular feature of the Plymothian and that summer in particular the game was enjoying enormous popularity, helped undoubtedly by the achievements of Jack Hobbs, every schoolboy's hero, who, on the 8 May 1923 scored his 100th first-class century.

Not everyone found the sporting records in the Plymothian that interesting though and in their regular appeal for contributions the new magazine editors urged their peers to consider how … *"A school magazine reflects the character of the school – or at least how a school can be judged from the character of its magazine. It can be a mere record of official events, couched either in bold unimaginative prose or utter journalese, while at the end are piled lists of cricket scores and averages or tedious accounts of football matches. On the other hand it can be a comic paper – childishly frivolous."*
"The ideal school magazine should be looked forward to not only by old boys who yearn to know how the old school is going on, not only by boys still at school who wish to see their names in print, but by everyone into whose hands it may come. This is an ideal we have tried to attain. That we have not reached it we admit, but the fault lies not wholly with ourselves – it lies with the school."
"Apart from supplying official and routine reports, practically no contributions are sent in."
Small wonder that Benskin's boys' *'Chin-Wag'* should have been so admired. Such is not to say that there were not a number of interesting pieces in that term's magazine and, for once, the Oxford letter was particularly informative. Talk of Oxford's streets being crowded with American tourists, debate from ex-president of the Union, Hilaire Beloc about *"the decay in modern youth of a knowledge of wine"* and, *"in the last week of term, Mr Pringle and Mr Lloyd George came to our Arena and battled for our delight".*
"In the end Radical Rancour succumbed before Welsh Wizardry … The victor departed from the hall between two upright and cheering rows of listeners. Considering that 90% of his audience distrust him, it was indeed annoying that the ex-premier won such applause." (There could be no doubt though that the former Liberal Prime Minister's powers were on the wane and in a debate at the School in December 1923 the House decided by 24-19 majority that *"the Liberal Party was now obsolete"*).
These were, of course, among the glory days of Oxbridge, when old boys from schools around the country ensured that they paraded themselves around their colleges in plenty of style. The increased presence of members of the fairer sex doubtless added an extra touch of flamboyance.

In that term's Cambridge letter we learnt that: -
"The streets of Cambridge will shortly be adorned by sights hitherto peculiar to our sister university. We refer to the granting of titular degrees by the Senate to the students of the women's colleges. It is rumoured that a leading London daily will offer a tempting prize for the most alluring design for the new academical dress."
Remember, though, that the men were possibly even more colourful than the ladies. In a letter to the Plymothian WJ Lang Cornelius OPM, noted *"that a large number of blazers are being worn this season with various badges of school, clubs, etc., several OPM's have asked, why does the OPM blazer lack a badge?"*

OPM cricketers in 1923 - note the variety of blazers. Side included DH Vittle (back row third from left), PA Harris (seated far right) and GC Willis (second from left back row).

Blazers then, of course, were generally exactly what their name suggests - a blaze of colour, not simply dull, blue/black affairs but gaudily-striped garments, that, rather like the *"old school tie"*, didn't always need a badge or crest to identify them.
Nevertheless the query was a timely one for the OPM Club was rapidly getting itself into much better shape than it had ever been before the war.

The cricket team had added a number of half-day and evening fixtures to its regular Cricket Week commitments and there was talk of forming a regular Rugby XV. The following season three fixtures were played, the School were heavily beaten by the much heavier OPM side, but against Argaum and Kingsbridge, the OPMs struggled a little, losing both narrowly (0-5 and 3-11 respectively). A hockey side was also fielded and they managed a 4-2 victory over the School and around the same time a number of OPMs got together to form an Automobile Club. Walter Gingell was elected President, Messrs Dobson, Dufton and Canon Benskin, with his three-wheeler, were Vice-Presidents and some two dozen OPMs became founder members. Social runs and hill climbs were favourite activities of the club and most members seemed to be motorbike owners. RR Harvey on his 490 Norton, GH Harris with his 348 Beardmore-Precision, Modley on his Royal Enfield and Walling with his great 969 Harley Davidson, were among the Club's leading lights.

It is worth remembering that, just as we take motoring for granted these days – very few homes are without a car – the car and the motorbike were, like the gramophone, the wireless and the cinema, still very much novelties in the twenties.

There were not many cars seen in Plymouth prior to the Great War. In 1920 there were fewer than 200,000 cars in Britain in total. Over the next five years that number trebled thanks, in no small measure, to the introduction, in 1922, of Herbert Austin's Austin Seven (below).

This was the first true *"people's car"* to be produced in this country and at £165 it was £20 cheaper than Henry Ford's Model T. There were hundreds of different models competing for the market in those early days and William Morris, whose famous *"bull nose"* Morris Minor was, with the Austin Seven, the home-grown market-leader in the late twenties, flew a Union Jack above his Cowley works and used the slogan *"Even if you don't buy a Morris, buy a car made in Britain"*.

1922 Morris produced at Cowley.

For the schoolboy in the twenties *"car spotting"* was a popular pastime, aided and abetted by cigarette-card collections, they looked out for Hillmans, Rileys, Triumphs, Swifts, Beans, Clynos, Jowetts, Trojans and Morgans. Small wonder that so many remember Benskin's Morgan - and the trouble he had with it. After all, up until 1920 there had been no petrol stations in Britain. Garages, themselves, were far from common, so most drivers carried petrol on board, in cans, and had to learn to do their own running repairs. Inflatable tyres didn't appear until 1925, the number of colours available was very limited in the early days and there was no driving test to pass – most people learnt from their fathers and friends. There was, however, a speed limit – throughout the Twenties it was just twenty miles

an hour. Few people stuck to it, though, and from time to time someone would fall foul of it. Matinee idol and screen-star Owen Nares was fined £1 for driving a car at 29 mph in 1921.

More affordable and more popular than the motor car, at first, was the motor bike. In 1920 there were 50% more bikes on the road than cars, but, by 1925, there were slightly more cars around – 579,901 as opposed to 571,552. Either form of transport, of course, offered something that neither the train or tram could – personal freedom. Freedom to travel, to go to new places as and when you wanted, and, more significantly for many young men, freedom from the watchful eye of the parent or partner. Many motorbikes were equipped with pillions for girl-friends – *"flapper brackets"* - and were a major contribution to the perceived sexual freedom of the era; a freedom that started to manifest itself in the divorce rate statistics.

From the pages of the Plymothian little of this comes through. We do, however, see that motor mania bit deep for a year or two.

At the general meeting of the OPM Automobile Section, held in the School Library on 31 March 1925, no less than ten fixtures were announced including four social runs, a paper chase, a couple of speed hill climbs, general competitions and a reliability trial.

Don't think it was just the young men involved in this exciting new passion for only a few months earlier, we had learnt that 68 year-old former Second Master Francis Palmer, *"has sustained a severe accident while motor-cycling"*.

Somewhat more bizarrely a motor-cycle race was included in the programme of the School Sports *"for the first time"*, in 1925. *"The event was thoroughly enjoyed by the eight competitors, and provided a few "thrills" for the spectators."* Arranged at short notice *"it is hoped,"* said the report, *"that this item will be a feature of the sports next year, when a much larger entry may be expected."*

As more cars start to appear on the road and Mutley Plain gets busier, so the motor-car and motor-cycle craze among OPMs, affluent toads and other wealthy young men, quickly subsides.

165

Just in case you're wondering the course was just a mile long, it was won by GH Harris on his 500cc N.U.T. and several of the eight competitors *"crashed"*, but *"no serious consequences resulted"*.

For the OPM Automobile Club, itself, more serious consequences were to arise as the result of ban put on speed trials by the "N.A.C. (National Automobile Club) and the police authorities." Because of this we read that *"club activities have been somewhat confined to social runs ... These runs have been very enjoyable, but have rather lacked support."*

This was unlike the American Hill Climb held that August in Kingsbridge. Around 500 turned out to watch the event which was open to any solo motor cycle. Twenty-two entries were received and OPM's figured prominently in all three races. Mortimer won the 350cc class, Dunstan and Harris came second and third in the 500cc and Dunstan third in the unlimited class. Interestingly enough a Miss Laurance finished third in the 350cc race.

At the end of the year, at the Automobile Club's AGM, it was decided to have an OPMAC dance after the Past v Present Cricket Match at School. However, no social runs or hill climbs were mentioned in the report and so it was no great surprise to find, at the AGM of the main club at the end of 1927, it was reported that there had been very little support for the Automobile Club for over a year – *"This was due to the fact that nearly all of its previous supporters had disposed of their motor cycles in preference for cars, and the latter were not suited for such events as this Club organised."*

The news was, of course, entirely consistent with the national picture which showed car sales ahead of motor cycle sales for the first time and, although in later years a different climate might prevail, for the time being it was resolved that: *"this branch of the Club be discontinued and that the assets be taken over by the main Club, with the exception of 8 silver cups and 9 silver medals, which were to be presented to the School*

Games Committee for disposal at their discretion".
Other OPM sections thrived, however, most notably the Cricket and Rugby. The Hockey section got off to a hesitant start in February 1924 as an OPM side beat the School 4-2, but two weeks later they were unable to raise a side to play Plymouth Hockey Club. If the School situation was anything to go by, though, the future for hockey was looking quite bright. It perhaps helped that the Staff were doing their bit to promote the game too. In January the 1st XI started their season with a game against the staff:

"The Staff defended well for the first twenty minutes, but before half time their defence was penetrated," is how the game was modestly recorded, for the boys were 5-0 ahead by half time and went on to add a further three goals before the final whistle. *"The Staff made several attacks on the School goal but failed to score".*

The result didn't really matter, though what was impressive was the fact that seven of Dale's small band of teachers turned out, plus Miss Kelk from the Prep, John Dufton's wife, and the amazingly-tall PB Huxham, (perhaps the tallest boy ever to pass through the School) who kept goal. The eleven was completed by the Head himself.

A few weeks after their performance on the hockey pitch, Miss Kelk and Mrs Dufton were seen again, in a different guise, as members of Dale's newly-formed Staff Dramatic Society. Sadly, the Head was not well enough to appear himself but the three-part entertainment went on as planned, with John Dufton taking Dale's part in *"The Shadow of the Glen"*. Mrs Gingell and Mrs Osmund each produced a part of the entertainment and Mr and Mrs Benskin (they had married the previous summer) were among the others to appear in this new Society's theatrical debut.

Also making their debuts this year were new staff members David Davies and Maurice Coggin; they replaced Gerald Mayne and Richard Rutherford. A languages master, Rutherford was one of Dale's

shorter-staying staff members. *"He never got on the same wave-length as the boys"*, said one former pupil. Coggin, who also taught French and German was to be another who didn't stay long – *"His heart was never in teaching, he was raggable, but he was a nice man so you felt guilty about it"*, recalled David Serpell. Happily his successor, William Woodcock, who arrived in the summer of 1925, would stay for twenty years.

For the most part, though, Dale's later appointments would outstay him at the School by some considerable distance; one notable exception perhaps being Walwyn Adams who arrived at the end of 1924 and left less than two years later. Adams came to take over the OTC from Walter Naish, who was a Latin and English specialist. It was in the OTC, though, that Naish really made his mark in the four years he spent at the School. Complemented for his *"patient kindness and cheery helpfulness"*, he did much to promote the national standing of School's OTC.

Plymouth College OTC Band

In his last OTC report Naish spoke highly of the OTC's performance on the Hoe when the Queen of Rumania visited Plymouth and added his endorsement to Colonel Fuller's compliments on the performance of the OTC band at the Annual Inspection in June 1924 ... *"I am sure they reflect great credit on Mr Wright, their instructor."*

1923/4 Scrapbook; East Town Rugby XV, North Town Athletics team, 1st XI Cricket Team and Gym Display on the School Field.

1924

The School Orchestra, on the other hand, was apparently *"growing much too slowly to suit the conductor, who wants at least six more violins, viola, 'cello, cornet, horns and a double-bass"*.

There were more boys than ever to look to now for music and for games. By the end of 1924 there were over 320 boys in the Main School and a further 76 in the Prep. Notwithstanding this healthy increase in numbers, though, the 1st XV lost all fifteen of their matches in the 1923/4 season and the team was described by the Head as *"being without talent"*.

The hockey team also lost all but two games, their memorable encounter with the staff, and 3-3 draw with Plympton Grammar – thanks to a late equaliser from Mr Holman, who, together with Walter Gingell played in most of the School's non inter-school fixtures.

It was perhaps no coincidence, therefore, to find that, at the start of the following season, 54 year-old "Shanks" Lingley had "retired" as Games Master and was succeeded by Walter Gingell. Significantly, too, we find that newcomer David I ("Di") Davies was given charge of the Rugger. The 26 year-old graduate from Wales *"not only knows the game well, but has the happy knack of getting others to play it in the right way"*, wrote the 1st XV Captain - RP Donnelly.

One of Gingell's first tasks as Games Master was to provide the Annual Sports Fund Accounts and it's interesting to note how much then was spent on; Railway Fares (around £10 for the year for Rugger, Hockey and Fives teams together), Char-a-banc hire (£1.10/-), Hire of Horse (£7) and "Scything Field" (£3). For some reason Cricket and "Wages" (for the groundsmen and the School professional?) ate the lion's share (around £120 or 75%) of Sports Expenditure.

In addition to the established sports a new activity appeared in the fixture lists in 1924 – Water Polo. Although the game had been played in the School for some years *"it has only been introduced as a School Game this season."*

"Unfortunately fixtures with other schools were made impossible, but it is hoped that the game will grow in popularity."

Clearly a major element in the decision to make the game more competitive was the fact that PB Huxham, goalkeeper for the Hockey team, also swam well and served as goalkeeper for the Water Polo team.

The fact that the lad was an incredible 7'4" tall and could stand, head out of water, in the deep end of the pool, undoubtedly prompted a few to think that a School Water Polo team may be a bit difficult to beat. As it transpired they lost to the Port of Plymouth (U18) side in their first fixture, but beat them in a return match and drew 2-2 with Plymouth Amateurs (U18).

HB Huxham - standing head and shoulders above his peers

The School was, of course, still relatively low in sixth form numbers. There weren't nearly as many boys of sixteen, seventeen and eighteen, as the Head would have liked and it was his ongoing objective to improve that situation.

Addressing his Speech-Day audience that October, he said that, *"the task before the boy who comes into the School at eleven is no light one. He comes with a knowledge of English subjects and arithmetic, studies which he continues. Then we expect him, in four years, to learn enough Latin, Greek or German, Physics and Chemistry etc., to face an examination of matriculation standard in nearly all those subjects. We are confident,"* he went on, *"that such a boy, when he enters the Sixth Form with a School Certificate and concentrates on*

Classics or Science will be able to go far."

"I believe that the same advantages and abilities for public service can be gained from either of the advanced courses."

Dale's passion for the Classics was clearly underlined in his next pronouncement; *"What boys need for citizenship is not a brain too soon imbued with facts that can be got from any handbook, but that enlightenment which is an intellectual and spiritual quality, learned by having thought hard and deeply. To study the Classics, to spend years of school life in the company of great minds studying great questions with the peculiar power and charm of the ancient masters, is a great adventure and a high privilege."*

The Head wasn't blind to the modern sciences though and continued; *"A knowledge of scientific subjects is absolutely necessary to conditions of modern life; and I urge the Governors to consider seriously, and as soon as possible the erection of a new Science block at the west corner of the building."*

This last plea was prompted by the need identified by the inspectors, to improve the School's science facilities and by the proposed road-widening scheme of the Council *"which might at any time bite off the gymnasium, fives courts, and the outer edge of their present laboratories."*

Another emotional lever that Dale was about to use, in this drive for new labs, was the fact that in just over two years time the School would be commemorating its fiftieth anniversary. What better way to celebrate survival and, at the same time point to an even healthier future?

New laboratories would also help to build a bigger and better sixth form.

"The English public school standard is very high," he said, winding up his speech, *"and to carry out this aim in all branches of school life is a very great task. I am sure that with an older and a larger Sixth this task will be fully discharged."*

Start of the Cross Country run - note the Tram ... and the crowd of spectators.

Interestingly enough, Lady Astor presented the prizes that year and she began her speech by stating her intention to keep politics out of education. *"I am confident,"* she said, somewhat confusingly from our present perspective, *"that I can keep politics out of things that really matter. There are,"* she added, *"certain minds who cannot keep politics out of anything, and they are the very ones who never really look at the things that really matter. Children should be taught to think clearly and justly – it is one of the country's greatest needs."*

The Plymouth MP then indirectly acknowledged the way the twentieth century had seen a move away from manual work. *"I believe that business is one of the finest ways of serving the country. Anyone would think it a crime the way some people talk; but no – England has been built up by business. I beg any boys going into business to realise that it is just as much a form of service as anything else in the country."*

It's hard to know whether boys agonised over their careers any more then than they do now – but in the absence of the late-twentieth century media bombarding all and sundry with images, both fictional and otherwise, of different occupations, the influence of family and friends would have been much greater. The subtle influence exerted by the reported exploits of old boys, through the School magazine, would also have been much greater then.

Consider the story of Leonard Rogers, published in the April magazine. Son of a naval Captain living in Hartley, he had gone to St Mary's Hospital, London, after leaving the School and had later become Professor of Pathology at the Medical College of Calcutta. *"Closely associated with researches into tropical diseases, Sir Leonard's greatest achievement is, undoubtedly, the discovery of the cure for leprosy."*

Another OPM in India was WHA Bishop. *"Captain Bishop,"* we read, in the September 1924 magazine, *"has been instrumental in quelling the recent Agency Rebellion. His plan of raising the price of the rebel leader's head to 10,000 rupees, and of dividing the country into small squares with its own little garrison was accepted by the Madras Government. As a result the rebel leader and his lieutenants were caught within a fortnight though he had been chased under the old scheme for over two years at the cost of £4,000 a month. Captain Bishop has been awarded the Indian General Service Medal. He hopes to leave for England on January 12th, and we look forward to a visit."*

In December we learnt that another serving OPM, Flying Officer John Franklin had been killed while flying in Iraq, while back at home, London, Eden Philpott's Play, *"The Farmer's Wife"*, at the Court Theatre, had just reached it's 300th performance.

A fine cross-section of achievements and one matched that year by the endeavours of JH Newnham and RP Donnelly, both of whom won Stapeldon Scholarships to Exeter College, Oxford, the former for Classics, the latter for Science.

Prizes await winners in the new Pavilion.

Donnelly, as well as being a gifted academic, was also a fine sportsman and for all his promotion of scholastic success Dale was, nevertheless, mindful of the importance of sport in creating well-rounded individuals. Speaking at the OPM Dinner, at the Royal Hotel in January 1925, he suggested that *"most of you present here remember your schooldays by what happened in the field, rather than in the classroom. It's true in my case, at any rate,"* he said.

Trophy time at Sports Day - the Headmaster looks on.

Later he added, *"I would prefer to have each fellow leave the school a good, straight chap, with his faculties developed to enable him to play his part as a citizen of his country than to have a long list of successes."*

Clearly in addition to the work in the classroom and on the field, the School stage continued to absorb the Head's interest. After illness ruled him out of appearing in the first Staff Dramatic Society production he stole the limelight in the second show – Lord Dunsany's *"The Gods of the Mountain"*.

Plymouth College from the air - mid-twenties, pre-science labs.

"Remarkable for its grim humour, its insight into human nature, and the literary quality of the dialogue; and it was exceedingly well rendered and staged. Though the character of Agmar, the master beggar, dominates the play, the performance owed much of its success to the way in which the minor characters were presented, the teamwork being so good that the action never dragged, as it might very easily have done."

"Mr Dale's playing of the part of Agmar was the outstanding feature of the performance. He looked well and moved with great dignity in his Eastern costume, and he delivered the fine lines which fell to him, both as false god and scheming rascal, with insight and distinction."

Clearly Dale enjoyed being centre stage, but the key word in all this is "teamwork" – at least half of the regular staff had parts.

Being part of the team was a core value in Dale's approach to work and play and if you didn't fit into that framework – forget it.

In the Easter Term of 1925 the Reverend Henry Beaumont left, after five years, to take up a parish in Yelverton. "Unfailing in patience and kindness, and a sportsman too, Mr Beaumont is a real friend who we lose with deep regret."

Beaumont's replacement was DT Newnham, of whom we know nothing save for the fact that within the year he too had gone and had been replaced by the more endearing and enduring Guy Hill.

Generally, though, 1925 was a quiet year for the School. There was some success for the sports teams, but overall the results were disappointing. There was a rare win for a Junior Fives pair against Kelly, the first win of any kind against them in some years. The Water Polo team, without the towering Huxham, only lost one game, their first, against Plymouth Amateurs.

Walter Gingell made a valuable contribution to most 1st XI matches, scoring an impressive 67 against Plymouth, in an opening stand of 90 with RB Spear.

FW Baskerville won the senior Ludorum at Sports Day, winning the mile just ahead of SHC Martin, and GH Broderick won the Junior version, having won most events in his age group.

1st XV 1925; Back row; FW Baskerville, JH Rowland, R Pierce, SH Martin, RA Rogers, EEB Algate, RV Hoare. Middle; GJ Palmer, RB Spear, AR Straw (Capt.), LE Everett, RD Williams. Front; JE Langdon, SK Wibberly.

Press picture from the same season; Back row; ME Ruse, SC Whitburn, RV Hoare, SK Wibberley, RG Pierce, SHC Martin. Front row; RA Rogers, RG Williams, RB Spear, AR Straw, LS Everett, JW Wiltshire, FW Baskerville.

The Rugby season was relatively uneventful, other than that the OPM's announced that they proposed to run a Regular XV next season, "providing that the necessary support is forthcoming from OPM's in "the district"." …. "At present "The Club" has a ground in view which is on the outskirts of Plymouth."

Undoubtedly the greatest success of the year fell to GEL Whitmarsh who "got further than any other boy at School in a Cross-word Puzzle Competition organised by "Skillwins"."

"The College," ran the notes in the Plymothian, "is much indebted to his patience and ingenuity for some useful amenities."

And how much indebted were they? £100 – a very substantial sum in those days, roughly equivalent to full main school fees for one year from five pupils (i.e. something well in excess of £20,000 today). A cheque was sent to the Headmaster and used to good effect in School, £13 being spent on chairs, and about £75 on furniture, flooring and decoration, with a further £15 going on pictures.

The whole episode generated great excitement and it should be remembered that crossword puzzles were very much a novelty in 1925. Indeed the first crossword to be published in an English newspaper had appeared in November 1924, in the *Sunday Express*, and the first cryptic crossword had come out in the *Saturday Westminster* in early 1925 (it would be another five years before *The Times* published their first puzzle).

The whole affair prompted AR Straw to produce a Shakespearian skit for the Plymothian;

Caesar: "O thrice accursed brain, that will not grasp,
The several secrets hid behind the clues,
Which are the salient features of these cross-words,
For hours last night I laboured with the squares,
Till black and white spots danced before mine eyes,
Just for a word – of letters seventeen,
That signified a village small in Wales."
But never would the word come to my brain!
Ha! A thought – perhaps it is – but shh!
I'll write it down and keep it right well safe

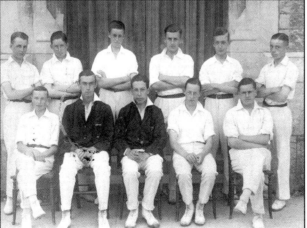

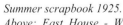

Summer scrapbook 1925.
Above: East House - Winners of the 1925 Athletics Sports; standing DG Spear, RP Donnelly, FW Blamey, GF Snell, HR Hunt, LB Spear, PW Rundle, JLP Weekes, RJ Pierce, GEL Whitmarsh, RM Barraball. Middle row; RB Spear, JH Curtis, FW Baskerville, RV Hoare, BTH Hendy. Front row (holding cups) HC Lyddon, BA Blight, RD Smith, CC Hill WR Westlake.

Top picture: Everett wins the 100 yards ahead of Hoare in the middle and Straw on the right. Right; Curtis pips Hoare and Straw in the 440 yards – Bert Sargent holds the tape, SHC Martin's certificate for coming second in the mile. Swimming pool group is Newnham, Hoare and CJ Palmer. Above; Cricket team - unnamed - from 1925, with SHC Martin standing on the far right.

From prying eyes of others, who are out
To win the prize of gold which is at stake.
('Tis offered by the well known Daily Wail.)
Enter Brutus ...."

Curiously there appears to be no indication that Whitmarsh benefited directly from his efforts. The unspent balance of the £100 -£1.9.1d – went into School Funds.

AR Straw with his feet up with Hendy, Whitmarsh & Hoare (on the mantelpiece) – "This was in the old library, we were 'outcasts'- in the sixth form but not going on the Army, University or Church. We were left to our own devices, plenty of free periods" Ralph Hoare.

Straw's piece for the Plymothian, meanwhile, was one of many he submitted around this time. College House Captain, he was made School Rugger Captain that year too, and gained his colours for the Water Polo team and just missed out on winning the 100-yard sprint at Sports Day – clearly another of Dale's great all-rounders. His literary efforts, though, were another indication that the bigger the sixth form, the better the overall standards of every aspect of School life.

The Plymothian, by now, had edged its circulation up to around 600 and the magazines were more-substantial and better packaged than ever before.

Interestingly enough, the March 1926 magazine opened with a lengthy review of the records of Mannamead

School – most of which were gleaned from the pages of the old school's magazine, a rare and informative instance of looking back. However, with the fiftieth anniversary of Plymouth College itself just around the corner, there would be plenty more of that in the next twelve months.

Illustrations start to appear on the cover of the Plymothian - Christmas edition images from 1923 and 1926.

As the School geared up for its Jubilee so the Headmaster and the Governors were pressing on with their ambitious plans for the new Science Wing; this in spite of the fact that the Council's plans to enlarge the borders of Hyde Park Road had yet to be carried out.

Building work progressed throughout 1926 and by the end of the autumn term work on the new Laboratories was *"fast approaching completion, except for internal fittings and new apparatus."*

To link in with the new development, a concrete staircase was built in place of the old wooden stairs; a welcome move as it was noted that the *"new steps are wider and seem to support the tides that pass up and down between periods with a more assured durability"*.

The contractors used for this work, incidentally, were Pearn Brothers of Pennycomequick. The Governors

had obtained half a dozen quotations for the job and had gone for the lowest. Pearns had pitched in with £5,245 for the building work and £1,269 for the fittings, which made them some £500 (almost 10%) cheaper than the next lowest, from Elliott and Tallemy and £1,285 (some 20%) less than the top price, from Spencers. Curiously, though, Spencer priced the fittings at £1,007, which was less than all but one of the six tenders – Solomon and Rennic quoted £868.

The final figure, including architects fees and an escape staircase and a new water supply, *"as directed by the town"*, came to £7,073.10.0d - the largest capital outlay the School had taken on since phase one had been completed back in 1880.

It wasn't the only improvement the School witnessed leading up to the Jubilee Celebrations though; *"Electric light is also being fitted throughout the College and should be ready to dissipate the gloom of any dark days which may occur next term"*, we read in the Christmas 1926 edition of the Plymothian.

Hendy, Straw, CW McDougall, Arthu Goldberg and SHC "Bob" Martin hard at work - note the old light fitting.

Earlier in the year the apparatus in the Gymnasium *"was augmented by the addition of new double beams, wall bars, square ladders, a vaulting box and climbing ropes"*. And then there was the *"new annexe to the pavilion containing baths"*.

These were all changes that boys of all ages could appreciate, and benefit from, and that made the School that much more marketable. Not that the School spent a lot on advertising itself in those days - £19 in 1927, less the annual fees of one pupil. The general improvements, though, and the conspicuous new Science Block would have done a lot to draw attention to the place.

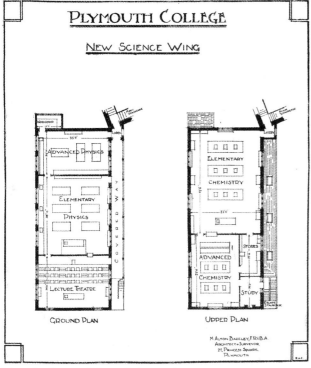

Plans for the new Science Laboratories

Not surprisingly all this activity seemed to create a healthy, buoyant, atmosphere around Ford Park. Indeed one wonders just how literally uplifting BT Hendy found it for, on 1st May 1926, he set a new High Jump record at the Sports Day. MF Morris's jump of 5'2½" had stood since 1894 and was the oldest of all the School's sporting records, that May day though Hendy added another 2½" – he also equalled the 100yd sprint record, finishing just ahead of LS Everett.

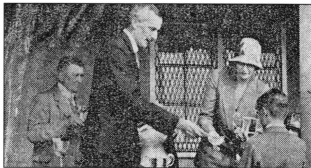

1926 Sports Day press cuttings; John Dale jumping, McDonald winning the Hurdles, juniors three-legged k race, Snells striding out, the junior sack race and the Headmaster presenting prizes with Mrs Priest.

Everett, however, pipped him in the Long Jump and Hurdles, but narrowly lost out to his rival, who was that year's Victor Ludorum.

Frustratingly for Everett it was the third year running he had been Proxime Accessit - but as someone who had represented the School at Rugby, Hockey and Cricket and who was about to head off to St John's, Cambridge with an Open Exhibition for Science, it is unlikely that he was particularly worried.

RB Spear, that year's shot-putting champion, was someone else who had played all three major games for the School first teams. Another gifted academic, he was bound that summer for Exeter College, Oxford.

Spear and Everett were among the top performers that year, but clearly it was a good year all round;

"Particulars of the Summer Examinations results, which give us eight Higher Certificates and 23 School Certificates will appear in our next number ... The number of Higher Certificates is, we believe, a record for the College."

Certainly the number of School Certificates, itself, was something to crow about; the last three years had shown an average of 26 as compared with 11 in the first three years of Dale's headship.

Everywhere you looked improvements could be found, even the Fives team managed to win all their matches – against Kelly and Wellington - and the Staff. Perhaps it was the somewhat unusual fixture with the Staff, the week before the Kelly encounter, that had sharpened their skills or, perhaps, it was the enthusiasm, and coaching, of Messrs Goodridge and Lord that brought an end to a long run of defeats. Either way, the fact that so many of the Staff turned out to play (Goodridge, Lord, Holman, Savage, Hill and Dale) must have been a great advertisement for the game within the School.

There was, of course, a heavy staff presence at the Fete that summer too, *"Flapper's Delight"* and *"OPM Mixture"* were popular among the consumables on offer. The OPM's appear to have been particularly good value that year; EH Babb, *"the ventriloquist"* giving two shows with "Dinah" and "Dick", and the Automobile Club providing thrills and spills in their second Ford Park appearance (they appear not to have been a feature of the Sports Day earlier that month though). LW Modley excited all with his *"unrehearsed"* contribution to the OPM Motorcycle Gymkhana; *"steering his machine by pieces of string, he lost one string and, after careering madly about the field, crashed into the railings. Very little harm was done – except to the railings".*

The OTC also gave a display; *"this was a great success – "tin" hats and blank ammunition lending to the excitement."*

This, incidentally, was Mr Adams', second and last Fete Day in command of the OTC as he left the School that autumn. In his comparatively brief stay - he arrived in January the previous year - the OTC numbers had risen to 160 and the Corps had been organised into four platoons, each commanded by a cadet. Also, the uniform had been altered – *"by discarding the old breeches and wearing instead trousers, as is done in the Regular Army".*

Adams was, perhaps, not one who failed to fit into Dale's "team" or measure up to his standards, as we read in the notes that *"his fine work in command of OTC makes the School much indebted to him, as well as his work in the class-room and on the field. His departure is a very heavy loss to the Staff Dramatic Society – his performance in "Gods of the Mountain" will not easily be forgotten. We wish him all good luck in his new work."*

Such accolades were not generally handed out to staff who had spent so little time at the School so, perhaps, the sentiment was quite genuine. Strangely, his successor stayed for an even shorter period of time. Mr Vipan, who had commanded the OTC at Rochester School and was *"well qualified to maintain the high traditions of the Plymouth contingent"*, left after just

two terms. *"He was one that the boys tried it on with – and failed,"* recalled one old boy. However despite this success over the boys, his stay was brief..

As a former serving officer himself, was Dale a difficult man to please in that department or was it circumstantial? Whatever the answer Rudolph Dawes, who had, like Dale, served in France, lasted considerably longer than the Head's three previous appointments in that post.

A date with a Fete in the early twenties.

To return to the Fete of 1926, it was during the afternoon of that day that the foundation stone was laid for the new Science Block.

"I'm rather afraid that the building will not be a very beautiful one, compared with the front of the school," said the Headmaster in an opening speech. *"But not being in the same style is not to say that it will not be a very fine building,"* he added, presumably so as not to offend the architect Alton Bazeley, OPM, who at that point presented the Chairman of the Governors, JP Brown, with a silver trowel.

This act was complemented by another presentation to the Chairman, this time of a handsome, inscribed mallet, from the building contractor Mr Pearn.

"I declare the stone well and truly laid," said the bearded Mr Brown. *"It has been impossible to do*

satisfactory work in the old premises, especially as the school has recently grown considerably. Because we now have advanced courses in classics science and mathematics, a distinction we share with only two other schools south-west of Bristol, we needed to find extra accommodation."*

"Science," continued the Chairman, *"is being more and more recognised as an essential part of education. Fifty years ago science masters were thought to be in a domain of their own and science and religion were thought to be opposed to each other. Scientific teaching was looked upon with suspicion. All that has changed today."*

"Plymouth College," he concluded, *"is going to provide equipment which will be second to none in any school in the West of England."*

The Mayor of Plymouth, Richard Mitchell, then thanked Mr Brown. *"A good school is a wonderful asset to a town and I'm glad to know that Plymouth College is going forward in leaps and bounds."*

Thereafter, the work on the new labs also went ahead in leaps and bounds. It was fast approaching completion by the year-end and a new concrete staircase was built in place of the old wooden stairs at the western end of main school. *"Wider they seem to support the tides that pass up and down between periods with a more assured durability."* We can only wonder at how rickety the old ones were.

So another year came to an end. A good one it was for the school too, with expansion at the top and the bottom. Not only were more boys staying on in the sixth form, but there were more than ever arriving at the Prep.

Forty-six young lads entered at that level during the last year, an increase of 50% over the previous year. Among the many new boys was one, CJ (Jim) Woodrow, who, though little did he know it, was about to embark on a seventy-three year association with the school, retiring as a governor after many years service in 1999.

1926, JP Brown lays the foundation stone of the new Science Block

Other notable events at the end of that year included the game between Devon and the Maoris, which forced an early kick-off at Ford Park in the game with Kelly. Once again, though, the school team struggled. Tackling, although improved, was still weak, as there was *"still a marked disinclination to bring a man down by the legs."*

The School v Kelly – Ford Park

But while schoolboy rugby was still trying to get up steam, old boy rugby was progressing apace. Nine games were played by the newly-constituted OPM RFC and although only four were won, the team finished with a positive points tally and the games had all been very convivial.

"After a pleasant mud scramble we entertained the cadets (of HMS Erebus) to tea at the Mikado Café." And later in the season after the home tie with St Luke's College, *"we were invited by the Exeter men to a Smoker at the Duke of Cornwall Hotel, at which the secretary and the captain were made very welcome."* At the OPM AGM, held in the school library, the age-old question of discrimination between Club Members (i.e. paid up OPMs) and Old Boys (non subscribers) came up and it was announced that arrangements had

been made to prevent the sale of colours to the latter. On the subject of school colours, writing in the jubilee edition of the Plymothian, the following autumn, the Headmaster said, as an aside; *"By the way OPM's our cap is now in circles of black, thin red, and green."*

With hindsight it seems a little strange that it had taken so long for the green of Mannamead School to insinuate itself upon the school colours, particularly as the OP's and the OM's had determined their combination of magenta, chocolate and light blue, soon after the amalgamation. One can only wonder at what did eventually prompt the move. Perhaps this too was tied in with the desire to create an impact during the jubilee year of 1927.

Certainly the year began well. On the February 18 the new Science Block was opened and the whole school turned out at 3.15 pm to witness the occasion. The honour of officiating was accorded to Dr Cyril Norwood, the Headmaster of Harrow School.

The New Science Block is opened 18 February 1927.

Francis Dale opened the proceedings with a few words of thanks to the architect, builder and the workmen, and then introduced the honoured guest, telling his audience that here was a man who had devoted his endeavours to improving the standard of education in the country.

Dr Norwood, in a speech *"which impressed even the smallest junior"*, was quick to point out his unfitness

for the task; *"I am not a scientist and indeed I've never wanted to be one but I understand the necessity of providing recruits for the armies of research."* Dr Norwood then went on to almost underline why he was unfit to perform the task in hand.

"Personally I neither overrate nor underrate the study," he continued, *"but I feel it my duty to mention that the teaching of Science costs more than all the rest of a boy's education. I'm impressed by its use to humanity and agree that it is a necessary part of a general education, but it is not all."*

We can only guess at what the assembled scientists made of his speech, but we do know the Lord Bishop of Plymouth, a new school governor, felt *"sure that the Headmaster had been wise in not asking a Scientist to open the laboratories"*.

Meanwhile the Chairman of Governors, JP Brown said that he hoped that the effort and amount expended would *"be rewarded by the advent of many pupils from this and neighbouring counties."*

Doubtless the new facilities were an attraction to potential new members of staff too; complete as they were with a master's study, library, and a communicating lift to the lecture room and physics department.

Interestingly, the colour scheme for the new development had a green-tiled dado, a zinc-white ceiling (what better colour shade of white could you want in a science lab?) and red *"Marbolith"* floor.

Clearly the school science masters - Charles Osmund, Chemistry, and John Dufton, Physics - were delighted with the new development. As the Head was quick to point out in his piece for the jubilee edition of the Plymothian later that year, however, the new Science Wing has proved *"no more than adequate in use."*

He added, *"We are rightly proud of it; but everything about it is demonstrably necessary. It has taken off the Science Staff a most unfair handicap. They now have room to work in, reasonably adequate apparatus, and a laboratory attendant at their disposal."*

Elementary Physical Laboratory.

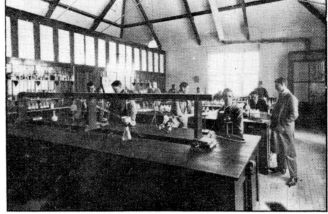

Advanced Chemical Laboratory.

Elementary Chemical Laboratory.

Lecture Room.

PLYMOUTH COLLEGE.

The Chairman and Governors and the Headmaster request the pleasure of the Company of

at the Opening of the New Science Building at Plymouth College, on Friday, 18th February, 1927, by Dr. Cyril Norwood, Headmaster of Harrow.

Speeches in the Gymnasium - 3.30 p.m.
Reception in Big School - 4.30 p.m.
(Please present this Card).

R.S.V.P. to Mr. Serpell (Clerk to Governors), 1, Sussex Street, Plymouth.

Bottom left; Dr Norwood gets the keys to the new Science Labs. Above; Invitation to the official opening. Various; the New Labs.

Advanced Physical Laboratory

Above FH Dale, Dr Norwood and JP Brown lead the party out of School. Right; John Dufton on the left, Rev Benskin alongside him with Bert Sargent far right and Mr Osmund in the front three without a hat or mortar board. Above left a picture postcard of the new Science Block.

1927

Several pages later he concluded his review by musing on the future. *"Our hopes are strong,"* he wrote. *"This is not the place to enlarge on educational ideals. But to us schoolmasters it is always a comfort to reflect that we have them, and that in some measure ... We are the music-makers: we are the dreamers of dreams".*"

Curiously, music was another area where there was, an albeit minor, development that year. As the Music Director, Mrs Lingley, noted in her magazine report; *"the Headmaster has kindly agreed to raise the status of Music in the School by allowing a Singing Prize to be given to each of the singing forms annually, thus putting the singing class work more on a level with other subjects."*

A good part of the Head's optimism for the future, of course, was the growing contribution made by the ever-important Prep School Department. This had, itself, developed well during his term of office to date and he gave a potted account of it in his Jubilee report.

"The Preparatory was fortunate in replacing Miss Noble by Miss EA Crick, who had been serving as a "Wren". It has never looked back. The age of admission was lowered from six to five – it seemed absurd to admit boys only at six when the law chased them to school at five. So the new fifth division was started under Miss RE Robinson, who has now given a large number of Plymouth College boys their first acquaintance with p's and q's. A blow fell when Miss Lethbridge died – she was entirely devoted to her work and loved to study the progress of her pupils through the Main School. Miss Crick left to take a Bishop brother to Australia, and Miss Footner has now been some years in charge, with Miss AB Heath, Miss MA Kelk, Miss Robinson, and as second-in-command Miss KG Loveless. The numbers of the Preparatory, which uses the West room of the Hut as well as the house in Ford Park, have been for some years about 100, and a contingent of some 35 boys moves up annually into Main School. This contingent is the core of the College in tone and standard, and

the loss of the Preparatory – a loss which has through misguided democratic zeal befallen other Secondary Schools – would have been a grievous blow. The board insists that it shall be financially self-supporting: it insists (rightly) that all boys must qualify intellectually for Main School – just a few fall by the way: but it did not insist on the absurd suggestion that Preparatory fees must be raised to the same level as in Main School."

Absurd indeed, particularly as at that time the female staff at the Prep were on very much small salaries compared to their Main School counterparts. Important as the Prep was seen, the teaching staff there were not perceived as being in quite the same professional league – besides which … they were women and women did not have the same earning potential as men in any career, no matter how valuable the work they did.

As far as a substantial number of Plymouth College boys were concerned, however, the Prep remained their first point of contact with school, where, as the Head said, they first became acquainted with their p's and q's. All the more tragic then the news on 1st November 1927 that the teacher who was in charge for that first year entry at five, Miss Robinson, had passed away.

Miss Robinson had arrived at the school in April 1920 and at the time of her death most of the boys at Plymouth College-Prep and Main School - would have passed through her hands. A patient, enthusiastic and sympathetic young woman she *"had a thorough understanding of the best modern methods of dealing with little boys."*

Miss Ruby Robinson

In her first few years she had played a major part in the games at the Prep, but had taken more of a back seat when found to have a serious heart condition. She

nevertheless continued her teaching until just a few days before her death. Miss Robinson was only 29.

The school also lost another valued servant that year – Mr JC Pryor. Founder of the long-remembered Pryor's Academy, Mr Pryor had been the visiting Shorthand teacher at the school since 1901. *"Many College boys owe a great debt to the quiet effectiveness of Mr Pryor's teaching."*

In the absence of electronic typewriters, lap-tops and e-mail, shorthand teaching continued at the school under the guidance of Mr Pryor's daughter.

1926 The General Strike - workers protest in Plymouth.

The spoken word also continued to thrive under the auspices of the Debating Society. Among the resolutions passed in the House that year we had broad agreement on the suggestion that *"The Activities of the Trades' Unions of to-day are Inimical to the Interests of the Working Classes"* (memories of the 1926 General Strike were still fresh); there was repudiation of the proposal that *"This country should adopt Fascism"* (Oswald Mosley was starting to make his mark on British Politics); a majority decision felt that *"Railways as a means of transport will not be superseded in this country"* and finally *"The House"* shook its august head at the proposition of GR Lavers *"That the Study of Classics is of no value in Modern Life".*

Mr & Mrs Lingley and Co. Back row; Todd, Brown, Rhys-Jones, Axworthy RG, Harvey R, Serpell DR, Gillingham W, Periton R. Middle; Pitts JG, Threthowen, Haigh RM, Toms, Anon, McGlasham, Anon, West DAP, Treneer. Front; Smith AF, Everett LS, AG Lingley, Mrs Lingley, Rowlands, Lingley LG. On ground; Anon & Periton W.

181

Later in the year DR Serpell proposed *"That the Government should put a ban on attempts to fly the Atlantic"*. The motion was lost 16 to 5 and curiously the debate was held barely five months after the 25 year-old Charles Lindbergh had won, for his backers, the $25,000 prize for completing the first solo flight of the Atlantic. The flight captured the public imagination and made Lindbergh a hero.

Charles Lindbergh and the Spirit of St Louis.

It took him just under 34 hours to complete the 3,600 mile journey; a journey which had seen him soar as high as 10,000 feet above the water to as low as 10 feet at times. There had been a shaky start as his plane, the Spirit of St Louis struggled *"drunkenly"* into the sky

laden with petrol. To put the value of the prize money into some sort of context, petrol at that time cost, over here at least, 1s4½d (7p!) - a gallon.

Other issues raised in the debating chamber that winter included *"This Society views with great apprehension the outlook for the future of Plymouth"* (carried 18-9) and then in an impromptu session, and for reasons best known to himself, Mr Gingell proposed that *"School Porters should wear spats, frock coats, and should powder their hair"*. The motion was carried, but it is not clear whether there was any attempt at implementation.

Walter Gingell was Chairman of the Debating Society, and fellow staff member, Lionel Lord, was the Treasurer. In the games department the roles were reversed, Gingell was Hon. Treas., and Lord the Games Master. They had much to celebrate that year. For the first time since Dale had been at the School the 1st XI won all their school matches – although they were skittled out for just 26 by Plymouth.

1927 School 1st XI: Back row; RG Parker, NE Ellis, PW Rundle, GA McGlashan, PE Roberts, CD McDonald. Front; JLP Weekes, LG Lingley, SC Whitburn, RM Haigh, NM Palmer.

Haigh, Whitburn and Weekes were the main heroes, together scoring almost twice as many runs as the rest of the team put together, and taking the lion's share

of the wickets. The whole team contributed, though, and *"well earned the half holiday granted in honour of the occasion"* (winning all the school fixtures). The 2nd XI performed similarly well and there was a 3rd XI *"which has been very useful in bringing to light the more promising of the younger players."*

One welcome addition to the Cricketing trophy cabinet was the Challenge Cup for Fielding, presented by CH Watt, OPM. Whether it was coincidence or not the fielding that season was a marked improvement on the previous few seasons – *"and there has not been so much in evidence of that lamentable dropping of catches, which was so disastrous a feature of the previous two seasons."*

School Athletics also received a boost this year with the awarding of colours for the first time; Broderick, Snell, Rundle, McDonald and Baskerville were the lucky recipients. Broderick (Open Quarter) and McDonald (100 yards) both equalled the school records that summer and Rundle and Baskerville finished first and second in the Open Mile – and what a climax that was.

For in order for East Town to win the sports championship, for the fourth successive year, they had to win the first two places in the last event. That event was the Open Mile and Rundle and Baskerville were both East Town boys!

In addition to the cricket and athletics there was also the Tennis Club; *"The School court seems to have been well patronised during the season. There is no doubt that people are keen enough to play provided that the court is ready for them.*

1927

North Town Snr Cricket Championsihp. Back row; RE Baker, CC Sitters, JV Ackland, NC Cornish, EJ Voss, PE Roberts. Sitting; JE Langdon , JF Lloyd, SC Whitburn, SC Martin.

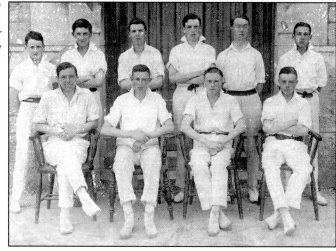

1926 Senior Rugger: Back row; GH Broderick, AG Robins, C Graham, DT Annear, AC Dingle, J Fleming. Front row; NE Elliott, CG Sims, SCD MacDonald, ME Ruse and RW Gard.

1926 School 1st XV. Back row; ME Ruse, CCJ Sitters, RW Gard, C Graham, RW Rundle, EG Downing, NF George, DG Giles. Seated; SC Whitburn, FW Baskerville, EEB Algate (Capt.), CCB Sims, RJ Pierce. Front; FK Carter, GFN Snell.

Junior Cricket XI 1926: Anon, GW Bendle, FK Carter, PG Davis, H Coleman. Centre; AFC Kitchen, DG Spear, E Terrel, KDC Bowden,. Front; W Gillingham and FW Bowden. Below a 1920s Prep School Play.

1926

183

It is not exactly clear though what *"ready"* meant, clearly it was hardly Wimbledon standard as we were told that *"the condition of the court itself is not so bad as it might be, considering that the ground is used for Rugger and Hockey during the winter terms. But if the ground is to be made even it must be rolled during the Easter holidays when the ground is soft."*

It was no easy task though and C Graham in his report made it quite clear that a lot of hard work was done by Messr Gingell and Lingley and Pro Heywood and *"all those who helped to pull the very heavy roller over the very soft and rough ground during the holidays"*.

1927 1st XV. Back row; NE Ellis, JCW Remfry, WD Bazley, CCJ Sitters, JM Fleming, GFN Snell. Seated; FK Carter, PW Rundle, SC Whitburn (Capt.), NF George, NE Elliot. Front row; CD McDonald, WHJ Frost, EN Richardson, LN Trethowan.

On the rugger pitch the main stories came from the OPMs who finished their first full season having won only only 13 of their 36 matches, but, having scored 346 points and conceded only 354, a number of the defeats had been by one or two points only. The 2nd XV played seven games and 68 players, *"all of whom were Old Boys"*, partook in the season's fixtures. On an individual level, founder member GL Wakeham was selected for the Plymouth and District XV to play against Albion Reserves and was heartily congratulated.

Clearly the Club was back on its feet in some style and the Head was not slow to acknowledge the fact;

"The OPM Club, broken through the war, was in great difficulties when I first came; but now, through the work of a devoted few – I must mention JC Bowering, PA Harris, DF Gibbs, NF Crawshaw – the Club has recovered a very effective vigour; the Cricket, the strong new Rugby Football Club, the Dinner, the Dance, all flourish now: and one may feel as one sees the OPM tie about the street that College in Plymouth is in the midst of friends."

Timely comments as the newly-elected Mayor of Plymouth, William Priest, was not only an OPM, but was also the youngest Mayor in the history of the Borough. On a more modest level, but also demonstrating a certain amount of civic concern was OPM President, Lieut-Col. WP Drury, who, at the Annual Dinner, appealed to members of the Club, *"as Plymothians born and bred, to aid the preservation of the Tudor Buildings of Plymouth, on the Barbican, which,"* he said, *"are threatened with demolition by the Town Authorities"*.

One such threatened building was 32 New Street and it was around this time that the newly-formed Old Plymouth Society acquired the premises - then in a ruinous state. Three years later, having restored the property, the Society gave it back to the City, it has ever since been known as the Elizabethan House.

32 New Street is reprieved.

In later years yet more threatened buildings would be saved by the Plymouth Barbican Associaton which grew out of the Old Plymouth Society. It was chaired for many years by Jim Woodrow OPM, just a young schoolboy when Drury gave his speech. Doubtless the Lieut-Col would have be pleased.

The OPM Club then was at last coming in to its own.

Numbers had risen substantially in the last two years, from 150 to over 200 and all sections appeared to be healthy. The only negative note came from a discussion on Club Colours where it was revealed that *"London Members had designed a tie of their own, incorporating the Club Colours, which they were wearing instead of the true Club tie."*

The cover of the Jubilee edition of the Plymothian.

However, as Mr Colson observed in his Jubilee Plymothian contribution;

"Nothing does more to promote a keen sense of unity in an institution than a keen sense of rivalry between its parts."

Certainly there were just those ingredients present at the School Fete that year as two teams of OPMs played each other with the Daily Mail Push-Ball;

A section of the 1927 School photograph. Staff, from Dale (far left), Arnold Lingley (English), Charles Osmund (Chemistry), John Dufton (Maths/Physics), Rev Bernard Benskin (History/Geography), Guy Hill (Greek/Scripture), Walter Gingell (Maths/English), Lionel Lord (Classics), William Woodcock (German/French), Eric Holman (Chemistry/Physics), Herbert Dobson (PT/Swimming).

1927

"Much amusement was caused by the match between OP "Men" and OP "Maidens" ... His Worship the Mayor of Plymouth "pushed off" at this game, and retired to a place of safety."

1927 Jubilee Garden Fete programme.

The maidens were in the guise of ancient and modern "flappers" and small wonder they gave the crowd fun. Yet again the Fete was a great success; other notable features included an exhibition of model yachts in the School Pool, crowded houses for the Cinema Shows in Big School and, in addition to all the usual side shows and attractions, there was also a *"livestock exhibition."*

So much, though, for the extra curricular life of the school, what about the rest of it – the teaching side of things?

"The work of the School is organised with an eye to the two "Advance Course" Sixth Form divisions. Boys specialise in the Sixth, and to some degree in the Fifth. Below the Sixth, all Main School Forms have an A and a B division – the work is kept parallel as far as possible, but the "B" side does not carry so many subjects. A boy in IVa "does" Latin, French, Greek or German, Chemistry, Physics, Mathematics with the beginning of "Trig", Scripture, History, and English. "Non omnia possumus omnes", of course, and not everyone "makes" an Advanced Course. But they all work with that aim before them, and the School and Higher Certificates of the Oxford and Cambridge Joint Board, which are taken by Rugby, Oundle and other such schools, set the highest standard possible – it pays, in the end, not to lower the fences." So said the Head, adding by way of a post-script on the subject – *"If we have a few Old Boys, as at present, taking First Class Honours at Oxford, we shall have probably managed to give those who aim lower the qualifications for their job."*

Having read that and then the following term read the Oxford Letter of February 1928, we can but wonder what impression schoolboys gained of the academic life at University: the writer waxing lyrical about a Debating Society production at the New Theatre; the forthcoming Presidential Debate *"when Mr Winston Churchill is on the Paper to defend HM Government"*, a little bit of Rugger and Soccer; RP Donnelly's craze for riding a *"borrowed"* bicycle – which had to undergo extensive repairs - and JH Newnham, who *"divides his time between Rugger and a motor car – not his own".* Our Oxford correspondent also wrote; *"we are pleased to note that our Women's Colleges are being put in their proper place. Only today we noticed that official Ministry of Transport warning notices bearing the letters SCHOOL have been placed in the road on either side of one of them."*

Women's Lib still had a long way to go – although, significantly, three months later an act went through Parliament putting women on equal footing with men, in ballot box terms at least, as the age at which women were able to vote was brought down from 30 to 21 (the voting age then for men too). The new measure, brought in by the Tory administration, was expected to benefit the Labour party at the next election with five million *"flappers"* able to vote for the first time. Among these was Miss KA Rowe, a former Plymouth High School girl, who arrived at Plymouth College in January 1928 to take Miss Robinson's place at the Prep.

Miss Rowe was clearly one of the new generation of young ladies and was one of the first graduates of the newly-founded (1926) Reading University. As such she was a far cry from the older spinsters traditionally associated with primary education.

The times they were a-changing and Plymouth College was very much looking towards the future. Indeed, in a rather literal flight of fancy at the Jubilee Luncheon held in the Royal Hotel, Lieut Col Drury CBE and OPM President, endeavoured to paint a picture of the school in fifty years time – 1977;

"At the sound of the school bell the air would become thick with clusters of boys flying towards the now-completed College by the aid of detachable wings, which on alighting they would park in the aviary. In class-rooms, masters clad in dungarees and hidden in fire-proof iron boxes would control the modern forces of education, transmitted by the kinema, the loud speaker, the dictaphone, television and other mechanical inventions."

1927 Scrapbook: Hockey 1st XI; DFS Giles, NE Ellis, NC Cornish, CCJ Sitter, GA McGlashan. Middle; NM Palmer, LG Lingley, CD Mc-Donald, GFN Snell, SC Whitburn. On ground; WER Treloar. Election Song. Beales and Carter at the finish of the Junior Quarter Mile, Carter's certificate. OPM Dinner ticket - Plymouth. OPM Dinner menu - London. OPM Seven-a-Side tournament held at Ford Park. The Plymouth College playing fields, now under the care of Pro Heywood, who would appear to have been the School's first full-time groundsman.

The Song that Won the Election !

Melody - "The Animals went in two by two."

Candidate.		Chorus.

Old Candidate. It's true you went to school to learn . . . Ugh-Ugh. Ugh-Ugh.
To sew, to sing, to spell, to swim . . . . . Perhaps. Perhaps.
You ar'n't so very young you know . . . . O, don't be jealous,
dear old Beau.
But can't spell Parli'ment . . Can you? Can you? Can you?
Now take your turn to push a "pram". Not much! Not much!
Without such flimsy fickle fibs . . . . Bah! Bah! Bah! Bah!
Don't stick the job on your old man . . . He should be proud to
take a turn.
And "loaf" down Old Town Street . . For shame! For shame!
For shame!

Chorus. That's the way to rule the roost and *get* our way.
That's the only thing to do if *we're* to stay.
And drive old fogies from our steps, with, "*Thanks* for nothing,
not to-day."
And show our own turn's come; at last, to-day, to-day.

SEVEN-A-SIDE RUGBY COMPETITION,

SATURDAY, 26th NOVEMBER, 1927,

Organised by The Old Plymothian and Mannameadian Rugby Football Club,

under Rugby Union Rules, and with the permission of the English Rugby Union.

President :—H. SARGENT, Esq.

Captain :—P. A. HARRIS. Hon. Treasurer—G. L. WAKEHAM. Joint Hon. Secs.—L. E. WILLIAMS, C. E. BRACKEN.

COMPETING TEAMS.

Royal Naval Engineering College, Keyham, I.

1st Batt. Duke of Wellington's Regiment.		Old Public Schools VII.	
Forwards ...	L.-Corp. Townend.	Forwards ...	B. C. C. Pratt.
	L.-Corp. Jones.		J. H. Rowe.
	Private Downs.		H. R. Cornish.
Half-Back ...	Lieu. W. R. Browne.	Half-Back ...	S. P. Job.
Three-quarter	Lieu. Dalrymple.	Three-quarter	W. T. Burgess.
	Lieu. Orr.		H. S. Endean.
Back ...	L.-Corp. Goodwin.	Back ...	E. T. Jago.
Reserve ...		Reserve ...	W. J. Greening.
	Colours Maroon.		*Colours—Black and Yellow Hoops.*

Royal Naval Engineering College, Keyham, II.

Plymouth College.		O.P.M.'s.	
Forwards ...	N. F. George.	Forwards ...	P. A. Harris.
	K. Carter.		G. L. Wakeham.
	N. E. Ellis.		R. V. Hoare.
Half-Back ...	C. C. Sitters.	Half-Back ...	E. C. Holmes.
Three-quarter	G. F. N. Snell.	Three-quarter	M. D. Steer.
	N. E. Elliott.		L. E. Williams.
Back ...	W. Lyst.	Back ...	C. E. Bracken.
Reserve ...	E. N. Richardson.	Reserve ...	G. H. Harris.
Colours—Black and White Quarters.		*Colours—Red, Blue and Green Hoops.*	*Colours—Chocolate, Light Blue and Red.*

SILVER TROPHY PRESENTED BY H. SARGENT, Esq.

Old Plymothian and Mannameadian Club.

LONDON DINNER

MENU.

Caviare d'Astrakan
ou
Hors d'Oeuvre Parisienne

Consommé Sarah Bernhardt
Crème de l'omate

Turbot in Braisé Forestière

Noisette d'Agneau Grand Veneur
Petits Pois à la Française

Sorbet au Kummel

Poularde en Casserole à l'Estragon
Pommes Noisette

Brioche de Foie Gras de Strasbourg aux Truffes
Salade de Saison

Biscuit Glacé Yvette
Friandises

Café

Criterion Restaurant. October 15, 1927.

O.P.M. CLUB.

ANNUAL DINNER

AT THE

"DUKE OF CORNWALL HOTEL,"

PLYMOUTH.

On FRIDAY, 28th JANUARY, 1927,
at 7-30 p.m.

TICKETS 7/6.

Plymouth College and Mannamead School.

Annual Athletic Sports,

This is to Certify that *F. K. Carter*

obtained *1st* place in *Long Jump (under 18)*

Dist. 15 ft. 11 in.

Sargent
C. W. Osmond
L. F. Lord } *Judges.*

◆◆◆ 1927 ◆◆◆

187

An interesting vision and to put it in perspective we need to remind ourselves; that the kinema was still silent when Drury made his speech; that the first-ever sound recordings had been made the same year that Plymouth College started, fifty years earlier, and that, in 1927, television was very much in its infancy having been demonstrated, by John Logie Baird, in London, for the first time, in January 1926.

One further vision projected by Drury that was, happily, also well-wide of the mark was his notion that *"Idlers would be caned by an electric switch operated by an omniscient headmaster seated in another room."*

What was fascinating, however, was to see that even fifty years on there was still talk of completing the school building - by implication – in line with the original plans.

On a more down-to-earth, and yet at the same time even more idealistic level, the Bishop of Plymouth, at the Jubilee Service of Thanksgiving, spoke of the school's soul. This, he said, was more important than the staff, the Headmaster, or the buildings;

"At school we learnt to lose our lives that we may find them and the self we found was a noble self than that which we lost, for it was one which had learnt to give and find its joy in giving."

In the short term the gift the boys were doubtless most grateful for, though, was at the annual prize-giving, held *"for the first time in the history of the school in the Guildhall"*. There the Rev GA Weekes, Vice-Chancellor of Cambridge University, distributed the prizes and at the conclusion of the proceedings asked the Headmaster for a whole holiday for the School in honour of the occasion ... *"He was much applauded"*. Happily for Francis Dale his Jubilee pronouncements were all made against a backdrop of success for the school. Both the rugby team and the fives team won all their inter-school fixtures during 1927, an unusual feat at the best of times. However, *"such a standard can only be maintained,"* he said, *"by giving every possible encouragement to those who were growing up. Let all boys play their part: for a boy to be driving a car in term-time was a very bad thing."*

1927 Jubilee Year and for the very first time in the School's history Speech Day is held in the Plymouth Guildhall.

The head also used the sporting successes to pitch a rise in the school fees. *"A year or two ago the fee was raised by 2/- (10p) a term; the result was that a permanent groundsman is now at work. Now unfortunately it appears that the main school fees will have to be raised next term by £1 a term. It is mainly the result of having provided the present very fine Science accommodation. Here again a satisfactory arrangement has taken the place of an unsatisfactory expedient. It is the better value given that justifies the change."*

Determined to add value in his own way was new master Rudolph Dawes. Dawes had just turned thirty when he arrived in 1927. A serving officer during the war, one of the first things he did at Plymouth College was to introduce another uniform – that of the Boy Scouts.

In his first report we find that *"the Troop numbers fifteen and meets on Monday evenings and occasional Saturday afternoons."*

A small and committed band they were expected to be; *"Boys who become scouts are asked to do so with the intention of remaining in the Troop throughout their school career, as it is in this way that the best interests of scouting can be served."*

It would appear that this new organisation had some impact on the OTC, for in the last magazine of 1928 we find the Scout notes taking up more space than the OTC notes, with the author of the latter complaining that; *"we have only had 13 recruits this term, a disappointing number in view of the considerable number of cadets leaving before the end of the school year."*

Whatever the feeling between the two bodies there was little to separate their HQs as the now redundant, old Physics Lab and the Carpentry shed were pressed into service for the OTC and the Scouts. Meanwhile the prospect of the Local Authorities claiming that north-western corner of the school site for road widening appeared to be receding, perhaps prompting the Chairman of the Governors, JP Brown, to offer the School a new North Gate.

Plymouth College OTC - 1927 - assembled at the back of the Main School building.

Speaking at the 1928 Prize Giving (Speech Day), the Headmaster said this gift was a great one – *"but not so valuable as Mr Brown's unending service to the School."* Furthermore he suggested that no inscription for the new gate-way would be more in accordance with Mr Brown's views than *"Let no one go out from here without an education,"* which meant *"without a sound foundation for life."*

Mr Brown, for his part, after he had presented the prizes, congratulated the Headmaster and the boys on the School's brilliant record for the past year. In truth, however, it wasn't an especially remarkable year, although RTR Clark and RCF Serpell had both gained places at Oxford and EJ Voss, School Hockey Captain, was on his way to Cambridge.

Bad weather and measles had adversely affected both Hockey and Fives fixtures, and the Cricket had been a slight disappointment on the previous year. Not nearly such a disappointment as the Water Polo turned out to be however. In a rare piece of personal criticism the Games Master wrote; *"It is a matter for regret that the destinies of the School Water Polo teams were not entrusted to a more enthusiastic and energetic Captain than NM Palmer proved to be."*

Palmer was runner up to GR Bailey in the Aquatic Sports that summer (JR Spear, destined to become a famous name in the history of the School, won three junior events), but it was on the Cricket pitch that Palmer displayed his greater talents, hauling 34 wickets at an average of 9.9. HC Lyddon also performed well with the ball and NE Ellis topped the batting averages thanks, in no small measure, to a fine unbeaten century against Newton College.

Interestingly enough, Norman and Ellis partnered each other in the new School Double Tennis Tournament. They won their first round encounter, played like all the other first round ties, over just one set, but either through that same lack of enthusiasm – or some other factor – they failed to take a part in the second round. Overall winners of the Championship were LB Spear and GFN Snell, who beat FE Williams and CD McDonald in the only three-set match of the tournament: 6-8, 10-8, 6-3. Williams, writing the notes for the Plymothian, described the playing surface as *"fairly good"* ... *"But it could have been made very much better if only some of the tennis enthusiasts had been sufficiently enthusiastic to turn up and roll the court during the Easter holidays, when the ground was soft."*

Certainly it wasn't too soft in May for the School Athletic Sports, held on the Thursday 3rd and Saturday 5th. *"On both days the weather was favourable, and this fact was reflected in the performances, especially in the longer distances."*

1928 Hockey 1st XI: Back row; EJ Voss, JLP Weekes, LN Trethowan, HW Beales. Middle; NM Palmer, LG Lingley, CD McDonald, GFN SNell, NE Ellis. Seated WER Treloar and RW Periton.

1928 Cricket 1st XI: Back row; AFC Kitchen, PW Rundle, LB Spear, EI Terrell. Front; NE Ellis, HC Lyddon, NM Palmer, LG Lingley, AG Robins, CD McDonald.

The Open Mile was particularly exciting; JM Fleming beat the school record but nevertheless came home six yards behind his East Town rival PW Rundle who lopped nearly five seconds off the School Record, with his time of 4min 54sec. The win put Rundle one point ahead of Snell to give him the Victor Ludorum and helped secure, for East Town, the House Championship for the fifth year running.

"Plymouth College boys giving a Gymnastic Display"

Whether it was this result or a general concern over fitness – *"the last twenty minutes strain of a "rugger" or hockey match which a degree of developed fitness can respond to often leads to a successful result"* – Lingley was prompted to write to the Plymothian suggesting a running track around the field.

"A training run from our North Gate is not a cheerful proposition because it necessitates immediate hill-climbing, dodging from the curb-stone to the road and back again, as well as manoeuvring to avoid puddles or slippery spots."

Lingley therefore proposed a track *"which would break away from the path near the tennis lawn and skirting the railings up to the orchard pass through an opening in the top fence so as to join the main path near the hut. Such a track would not be in the way of any game and that portion of it on the lower side of the "rugger" pitch would be acceptable to spectators."*

Aware that there were unlikely to be any significant funds available for this work, Lingley suggested the *"possibility of voluntary spade work or disciplinary pick and shovel work, as has been justified in some schools. Voluntary labour,"* he said, *"could overcome the first job of making a trench"*.

It would appear however that the first real job was getting anybody to support the idea. On the 15th November the notion was brought before the Debating Society and thrown out, along with the suggestion of *"Compulsory Conscription in the OTC and Scout Troup"*.

Other issues up for debate that winter included; *"Conservatives and Liberals should unite to oppose Socialism"* (rejected); *"The House welcomes the move by Lord Buckmaster for the abolition of Capital Punishment"* (but only just 12-10); and that recent favourite Cinema (note no longer Kinema) *"has a deleterious effect upon the community"*. The motion was lost 12-23 and it's interesting to note that NM Palmer made his maiden speech on this occasion, needless to say, supporting Cinema.

The twenties boy was finding more and more tantalising attractions to occupy his mind and his time; the cinema, the wireless and the comic. Back in February the debating chamber had already decided that *"Comic Cuts is the leading periodical of the day"*. Another debate looked at the proposition the *"Greyhound Racing will supersede all other forms of National Sport"*. Greyhound tracks were springing up all over the country and the sport was fast becoming a favoured alternative to horse racing among the gambling fraternity.

However, with Surrey's Jack Hobbs recently eclipsing WG Grace tally of 126 first class centuries and with Dixie Dean (pictured right) netting 60 goals in 39 games to help give Everton the First Division Championship, schoolboys were not short of sporting heroes.

There were one or two heroic figures among the ranks of the OPMs too. Sir Leonard Rogers was making great headway in the fight to cure leprosy, one contemporary describing his work as *"one of the greatest feats of medical science for very many years"*.

Meanwhile, Flying Officer Coggle OPM managed to earn himself the Spanish Cross of Military Merit for his part in saving the lives of a Spanish airman and his mechanic, who had been forced to come down in the Egyptian Desert.

Perhaps even more heroic had been the action of William Dixon in July 1928 in Brindisi. *"Mr Dixon was returning from a visit to Tasmania and shortly to be married. He was standing outside the Hotel Opporto with a party, when Mr Dixon noticed a baby girl in danger of being run over by a motor car. He promptly sprang into the roadway and rescued the child."* Tragically however Dixon himself was killed in the incident and was buried in Brindisi the next day. William Dixon wasn't the only young OPM to lose his life that year, as former secretary of the club, twenty-two year-old Douglas Gibbs, also died, in Bedford, after a short illness.

On a brighter note another OPM returned to the school in a teaching capacity, when Walter Weekes came in to replace Mrs Lingley, who was forced to give up music tuition under medical advice. Doubtless this was secretly a relief to many boys, who found her to be *"infinitely more terrifying than Dale"*.

Mr and Mrs Lingley were among just a handful of staff members not to take part in the end-of-year Staff Dramatic Society's production of Arnold Bennett's *"What the Public Wants"*. Mr Woodcock took the lead in this *"satire on modern cheap sensational journalism"*, and Messrs Dale and Lord were his brothers. Mrs Woodcock played Mr Lord's wife and Mrs Osmund was the mother of the three sons. John Dufton, Eric Holman and Di Davies (who produced the show) also appeared as did the Gingells and the Misses Rowe and Kelk from the Prep.

"WHAT THE PUBLIC WANTS" Arnold Bennett's satire on the journalistic magnate, received sympathetic treatment from the Plymouth College Staff Dramatic Society at the College, Plymouth, last night" Western Morning News.

The appraisal in the Plymothian makes fascinating *"between the lines"* reading. *"The College staff must certainly be most heartily congratulated on their efforts, as the performance was most interesting and showed little tendency to drag, notwithstanding its length and the fact that the action, owing to there being few incidents of a dramatic nature, has to be conveyed almost entirely by dialogue."*

It was the second staff production of the year with HC Lyddon the only pupil to appear in both. The Literary and Debating Society were also very active, reading, early in the year, a number of one-act plays, including Lieut-Col WP Drury OPM's *"A King's Hard Bargain"*. Later in the year their Annual Entertainment was made up of two short plays; John Brandane's *"Rory Aforesaid"* with the Serpell brothers, Roger and David, and others taking on a variety of Scottish parts, and *"Thread O'Scarlet"*, with, amongst others, GHO Mills and HC Lyddon who *"by his aplomb and cigarettes, heightened the dramatic effectiveness of the criminal and lunatic"*.

Programme.

13TH AND 14TH NOVEMBER, 1928.

The Plymouth College Staff Dramatic Society

PRESENTS :

'What the Public Wants'

A PLAY IN FOUR ACTS,

by Arnold Bennett.

Sir Charles Worgan, Newspaper Proprietor ⎫	*Mr. Woodcock*
Francis Worgan, Wanderer ⎬ Brothers	... *Mr. Dale*
John Worgan, Provincial Doctor ⎭	... *Mr. Lord*
Saul Kendrick, Manager of Worgans, Ltd.	... *Mr. Holman*
Holt St. John, Theatrical Manager	... *Mr. Davies*
Samuel Cleland, his Stage Manager	... *Mr. Dufton*
Simon Macquoid, Dramatic Critic	... *H. C. Lyddon*
James Brindley, Earthenware Manufacturer	... *Mr. Gingell*
Edward Brindley, his Son ...	... *G. H. O. Mills*
Page Boy	... *W. P. Cundy*
Emily Vernon, Widow ...	... *Miss Rowe*
Mrs. Cleland (Henrietta Blackwood)	... *Mrs. Gingell*
Annie Worgan, Wife of John Worgan	... *Mrs. Woodcock*
Mrs. Worgan, Mother of the Worgans	... *Mrs. Osmund*
Mrs. Downes	... *Miss Kelk*

The Play produced by Mr. Davies.

Acts I. II. and IV. IN LONDON.

Act III. IN BURSLEY.

Price 2d.

Boys smoking on stage in a school play? How times change! But this was 1928 the year that it was officially announced that the British were the world's leading smokers – burning up an average of 3.4 pounds of tobacco per year, per head! And most of it was due to the increases in cigarette smoking (cigars and pipes were actually on the decline) thanks in no small measure to the craze of cigarette card collecting.

John Player's Hints on Association Football cards.

Despite the rival attractions of the Cinema the straight theatre was still very much holding its own and it's interesting to see an early Plymothian contribution from one schoolboy who would go on to be a great theatre critic – JC Trewin. Trewin had various pieces published in the school magazine but the closest to his heart was clearly the piece inspired by watching one of Old Mannameadian Eden Phillpotts' plays at the Haymarket Theatre in London. It was the stage set that prompted Trewin to launch into a reverie. The set supposedly represented a part of Devon's coastline but was taken by the young Trewin to be more reminiscent of his beloved Lizard Peninsula.

"The people of the Lizard," he wrote towards the end of his piece, *"many descended from the crew of a Spanish galleon wrecked in the days of the Armada, gain their*

The O.T.C. Camp. Tidworth Pennings 1928. + P.M.C 'Lines' No 7 Tent.

1928 Tidworth Pennings OTC Camp. Above; "A photo of our lines before "Sunday Inspection", our tent No.5 L Cpl Dingle, Cadets AG Robins, HW Beales, Baxter, AP Collings. Three general views. Right; "Mess Orderlies" - Beales, Carter, Revington, Treloar and Robins. Standing in uniform - "Taken after Brigade Field Day - Beales, Carter, Treloar and Robins. Below No.7 tent; H Revington, WER Treloar, Beales, Robins, FK Carter. Right; "Just after reveille - Robins, packing kit for inspection, Beales, standing and Carter with towels.

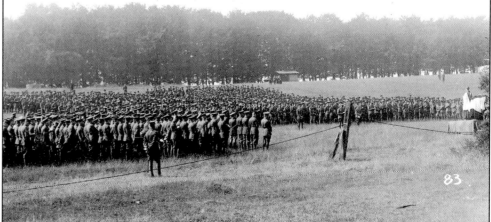

1928

livelihood from the sea and from the serpentine rocks of Kynance. They know little of the outside world, and an excursion to the market-town – ten miles distant – is an adventure talked of for months afterwards ... And such is the spell of the Lizard that those who have left it always wish to return."

Then he added; *"Nowadays the Lizard is becoming "known". In the Summer months lumbering motor-coaches roll across the moor from Helston. Tourists crowd to Landewednack, the tiny parish church where the last sermon in the Cornish language was preached; they load themselves with serpentine ornaments, and they tramp in their scores through Pistol Meadow to stand on England's most southerly headland. At nightfall they trail back over the downs whilst owls hoot mournfully in the valley of Bochym. Then a great peace falls on Goonhilly – and the Lizard gives itself up to the night."*

With the advent of the car, the cinema and the radio, the world was opening up. There were few forgotten corners and as people saw and heard more about the rest of the world than any generation before them, so, new means of transport became available to take them to these hitherto unheard of places.

Neither was the traffic all one-way. On Tuesday 28 February 1928 twelve members of the School Choir were asked to broadcast again from the Plymouth Studio, for the Children's Hour. *"They sang some old English songs – "The Carmen's Whistle," with a whistling accompaniment by Starling being especially popular – some Sailor Shanties, and a solo by W Spencer. They have been invited to go again."*

Television was still very much in its conceptual infancy – *"Friday 7 December 1929 NSE Pugsley read a paper on "Television". Although a difficult and rather involved subject he contrived to make it interesting and understandable."*

Radio audiences meanwhile were growing at fantastic rate. Sales of wireless sets were booming – the BBC were selling crystal sets for £2-£4 and many people were making their own receivers. John Reith of the BBC claimed that 40 million people could now pick up their broadcasts. By the end of 1925 some 1,654,000 wireless licences had been issued and by the end of 1927 it was estimated that double that number of homes now had sets.

Complete with a Royal Charter, the new British Broadcasting Corporation (not Company) expanded their operations and in 1927 started live sporting commentaries; the Grand National, the Boat Race, Rugby, Football and Tennis were all brought to life in people's living rooms for the first time.

Captain HBT Wakelam (above left) Christopher Stone (right).-

Capt HBT Wakelam was the Corporation's first regular sports commentator and the whole experience was rather novel for all parties. Wakelam's only official instruction was a little poster mounted at eye-level in front of him, on it the simple legend – *"Don't Swear"*. He didn't, but the excitement was tangible. A wife of one former Welsh international wrote to Wakelam saying he was a *"plague and a menace"*. Evidently her husband had been so caught up in the commentary that he imagined himself back on the field and had smashed up most of the living room furniture.

Music too played an increasing part of the output and Christopher Stone – editor of the Gramophone magazine - became the first radio "disc jockey", although he never liked the term. Neither was all their music of the classical variety, Carroll Gibbons, Bert Ambrose and Jack Payne were among those dance bands regularly heard on the airwaves while locally The Waldorf Versatile Five and Grant Arnold's Quintette were the typically-twenties combos that entertained the OPMs at their annual dance – held both in 1928 and 1929 at Boots Café. Popular as these events were, there was an even greater turn out for the OPM Rugby Club Dance at the Mikado Café.

BBC Dance Band leaders Jack Payne and Henry Hall

The dance craze, incidentally, had started here just as the Great War ended; the first Palais de Danse had opened in London in 1919 and before long the lively young things of the twenties were foxtrotting and tangoing their way around the smarter restaurants and hotels across the country.

Francis Dale and other staff members were regular attendants at many OPM functions, and both Dale and his colleague Bert Sargent could be relied upon for a song at the annual dinner.

The Club itself was going from strength to strength with membership nudging the 300 mark. There was even a suggestion at the 1929 AGM that the possibility of a Club Room might be looked into, but others thought the expense might be too great and that instead *"meetings might be arranged at one of the public restaurants in the city, perhaps once a fortnight"*.

Already the newly-constituted London Section were holding meetings, on the second Monday of the month, at the Bedford Head Hotel, in Tottenham Court Road.

The sartorially elegant 1929 OPM Cricket XI, well turned-out in an interesting array of shirts, scarves and blazers.

Clearly the rejuvenated, post-war OPM organisation was thriving and for those interested "*ties, blazers, silk squares, wool scarves, sweaters, bathing costumes, rugger jerseys, rugger stockings, plus-four flashes and cuff links"* were all available in Club Colours … and hockey shirts were on their way. However while the Rugby section continued to field two fifteens on a regular basis, the Hockey section were having a long-familiar struggle *"as all the OPMs seem to attach themselves to other clubs"*.

Meanwhile the school hockey players, notably Lingley jnr (team captain), the Periton boys, GFN Snell, LB Spear and HC Lyddon, were frustrated by the weather. In his 1929 Easter report Mr Lingley noted that *"only six matches have actually been played at the time of writing, while an equal number have been cancelled."* Weather, not measles, was the only culprit this time around.

1929 1st XI Hockey: Back row; KW Wickett, H Coleman, HC Lyddon, TW Hockaday. Middle; RJ Gould, LB Spear, LG Lingley, GFN Snell, RW Periton. Front; WJ Gillingham, W Periton.

1929 1st XI Cricket: Back row; JG Rhys-Jones, PW Rundle, H Coleman, RG Parker, KW Wickett. Front; AFC Kitchen, HC Lyddon, LG Lingley, EI Terrell, LB Spear.

On the cricket pitch Lingley and Lyddon again were prominent, but the season's hero was undoubtedly EI Terrell, whose bowling gave the school the edge in a number of games; 6-25 against the 2nd Devonshire Regiment who only scored 54 to the PMC's 97; 7-24 against Yelverton who were skittled out for 36 chasing the School's total of 112 and 8-72 against Plymouth Cricket Club giving the School a well-earned draw.

On the athletics field there were no new records but there were new *"standards"*;

"This year standards have been introduced into the Sports Training. Trials have been held on two mornings a week during the holidays, and points awarded to Houses when boys have passed the standard required of their age. The scoring has been calculated on a percentage basis to balance the uneven numbers in the Houses. The aim of the scheme is to give an opportunity to all who are keen on athletics and of helping their House in the Sports Championship."

Training Scheme.

This year standards have been introduced into the Sports Training. Trials have been held on two mornings a week during the holidays, and points awarded to Houses when boys have passed the standard required of their age. The scoring has been calculated on a percentage basis to balance the uneven numbers in Houses.

The aim of the scheme is to give an opportunity to all who are keen on athletics of helping their House in the Sports Championship.

Details of standards and scoring are as follows:—

STANDARDS.

	SENIOR.		JUNIOR.	
	Over 16 yrs.	16—15 yrs.	15—13 yrs.	Under 13 yrs.
100 yds. …	$12\frac{2}{5}$ sec.	13 sec.	$13\frac{3}{5}$ sec.	$14\frac{4}{5}$ sec.
220 yds. …	28 sec.	$29\frac{3}{5}$ sec.	$30\frac{4}{5}$ sec.	$33\frac{3}{5}$ sec.
440 yds. …	65 sec.	69 sec.	73 sec.	—
880 yds. …	2 m. 35 sec.	2 m. 45 sec.	—	—
High Jump …	4-ft. 6-in.	4-ft. 3-in.	4-ft.	3-ft. 6-in.
Long Jump …	16-ft.	15-ft. 1-in.	14-ft. 3-in.	12-ft. 9-in.
Cricket Ball …	70 yds.	65 yds.	60 yds.	50 yds.
Weight …	23-ft.	20-ft.	—	—
100 yds. H'dles	17 sec.	18 sec.	—	—

Certainly if the scheme was introduced to kerb the dominance of East Town on Sports Day it didn't work. East Town boys Snell and Lyddon were Victor Ludorum and proxime accessit respectively and Junior Victor was housemate HJ Bartholomew. Fellow East Town runner, PW Rundle, won the Open Mile for the third year in a row but didn't match his previous record winning time.

A close finish in the quarter-mile for boys under 15 years: Bartholomew winning from Butchers and U'ren.

North Town Snr Cricket: Back; BG Skelton, DJA Brown, FK Carter, KD Bowden, W Periton, AJ Giles. Middle; DR Serpell, FRL Heath, H Coleman, FR Price, HR Voss. Front; RW Periton, RJ Gould.

One of the greater successes of the year came in the relatively new sport to the school – tennis. WM Spencer not only won the Junior Tennis Championship of Devon, but also managed to get through to the last sixteen in the Junior Championships at Wimbledon.

Overall though while it was a comparatively uneventful year on the Sports Fields it was not so in the academic stakes.

The summer of 1929 saw a record number of Higher Certificates awarded to the School – 16. The VIth form was growing and PW Rundle, BR Jillard and LG Lingley all won Cambridge Scholarships. Curiously enough we also had the first ever Plymothian to feature three University letters in one issue.

The regular Oxford and Cambridge missives both made reference to the weather;

"Of course, like the rest of England, we have been frozen and thawed and snowed on ... the whole University from the Chancellor down to the Under-dogsbody has learnt to skate (Oxford) ... "The Cam was frozen and it seemed probable that the Lent races would be interfered with – luckily the thaw set in just in time" (Cambridge)".

The thaw was not without its own problems though – notably in London where 14 were killed and millions of pounds worth of damage caused after the Thames burst it banks.

Curiously, though it was not from London that the third letter came, rather *"from the heart of a great manufacturing city"* – Bristol;

"We are five in number, and we hope that those to whom the classics of Oxford and the mathematics of Cambridge alike call in vain may find something in Bristol to ease their troubled minds, and to satisfy that thirst for knowledge for which OPMs are so widely and so justly famed."

Most boys (80%), however, didn't go to any of the universities, for them *"the Services, the Professions and business"* beckoned.

Dale inspects his troops.

"Members of Plymouth College Officers' Training Corps being served with ammunition for their field day on Dartmoor." WMN

"We must not neglect the average boy," said the new Head later that year at Speech-Day (note Speech Day not Prize Giving) - *"he is our chief concern."*

"If we can make of that average boy an upright and honourable man, able to think and act for himself, we have accomplished no mean thing."

The Head was speaking in the Guildhall as, again, this venue was chosen in preference to the old gymnasium. It was only Ralph's third week in the School.

Francis Dale had left Plymouth College at the end of the summer term after ten years at the helm;

"Ten years is very little in the life of a School, so little that I leave behind me some boys who were here when I came. But in a man's life the years between 36 and 46 are no small matter. Perhaps my best years, I would not have spent them elsewhere than at Plymouth College."

Dale left to take up the post of Headmaster at the City of London School and he was succeeded by another Cambridge Classics man, a man of a similar age, who like Dale had served in France, his name Herbert W Ralph.

1929' - Herbert Ralph arrives and Francis Dale moves on.

Ralph came to Plymouth College from Chester, where he had been Headmaster of King's School for five years. There he had fewer than 300 boys; *"and I knew every boy by name and by sight, and a great deal about him personally. Here I have a School whose numbers have reached 400. It will take me several years to get to know these boys in the same intimate way."*

So said Ralph at his first Speech Day. He followed it by setting out some of his hopes and his expectations;

"There are bound to be enormous differences of home conditions and environment, physical ability and temperament of the boys."

"On the one hand I have a boy who lives a few minutes' walk from the School, who is probably provided with a room in which to work by himself undisturbed. On the other hand there is the train boy, who probably does not get home until six, and has not the same privacy. One boy may be a glutton for work, and able to do all that the master set him or his parents allow him. And again there is the boy who will make heavy weather of even the barest minimum."

"Now a word in time from the parent to the form-master, subject master or headmaster will save endless difficulty and misunderstanding. In the same way we ought to be told of any case where a boy spends noticeably more or less time on his homework than is laid down in our School Rules."

"Lastly, I want to say a word about the idle boy. I suppose the idle boy does not exist at Plymouth College! I said, at my first assembly, to the School, that I had come to Plymouth expecting to work very hard myself – an expectation realised to the full – but I expect everybody else in the School to do the same. I have no possible use for the idler. I confess to a sneaking regard for the mischievous boy, and I will make allowances for the boy who is not clever: but idleness is really an unpardonable sin. In these days of competition every boy ought to learn from the very beginning that in his own efforts chiefly depend his future. No boy in the main school is too young to realise his responsibility in that direction."

In this way the new head set out his stall after just two weeks of holding the reins. The boys, and the parents, could be under no illusions as to what lay ahead of them. Ralph himself was under no illusions, either, as to what had gone before him. The twenties had been a good decade for the school; numbers had grown steadily, there had been enormous social change as the country tried to put the Great War behind it and the OPM Club

had flourished. Ralph arrived to find an increasingly impressive list of successful past pupils, among them two who were mentioned in the first Plymothian under the new head – Lieut Col Drury, who had just become Mayor of Saltash and F Seymour Cocks who had left school in 1899 and had just been elected MP for the Braxtowe Division of Nottingham.

Among the newest generation of old boys were now Dale and Lingley junior and one wonders if Dale had deliberately postponed his departure until his son, John, had completed his schooling here. Lingley, on the other hand, was not about to leave; now approaching sixty and, with the notable exception of Bert Sargent, his junior by one year, the oldest member of staff by some twelve or more years, he was clearly resigned to seeing out his days here – indeed he apparently applied for Head's job when Dale left, but his name was fairly quickly crossed off the list of hopefuls. Lingley, the tallest man on the staff apart from Dale, was very much an "old style" teacher, he was a bad man to cross – he reputedly once tore the leg off a chair and thrashed a boy with it, drawing blood in the process, although he did, evidently bring some ointment in for the lad the following day! As too his classroom technique itself, to quote one former pupil; *"he taught English without any sense of literature".*

Lionel C ("Elsie") Lord (pictured right) was also on the list of candidates for Dale's job and at one point appeared to be quite sure he'd get it – but he was to be disappointed.

Meanwhile Lingley's son, Loris, was following his father's footsteps and heading off to Cambridge.

PT teacher Hubert Dobson, was also leaving, his replacement – twenty-eight year-old Ian Edwards whose responsibilities upon arrival included that of looking after the hitherto neglected subject of Art in the School. Few could have anticipated the number of years he would put into the School and many are they who perhaps would have sought for a reduction in that term. However such is to look too far into the future, let us return to 1929 Dobson is departing after the best part of ten years, having arrived at the same time as Francis Dale.

The last picture of Dale to appear in the Plymothian while he was still headmaster.

Dale's biographical note in his last Plymothian noted how, during his time here, the Headmaster had been President of the Association for the Reform of Latin Teaching in 1922 and 1923, and how he had been a member of the Headmasters' Conference and of the Burnham Committee. He was also, from 1920-28, a member of the Plymouth Education Committee.

More importantly for the man himself, Dale was keen to reflect on the personal side of his time in the South West; *"We could row or swim in Plymouth Sound And there was Dartmoor, where we had a family camp At Hartford by the River Erme; we monopolised the Erme valley,*

Five miles of rich heather and plenty of whortleberries, Worts.
There dear friends, May Moor and Lucy Broad, stayed with us."

So ran a few lines of Dale's Diamond Jubilee "address" to his family, clearly indicating his love of the Moor. Tall, imposing, with an almost theatrical nature and a dramatic delivery - *"and sometimes known as Satan"* - Dale was a team player, a respected academic and teacher, who had taken the School number from under three hundred to almost four hundred. He left behind sizeable shoes to fill.

How would his successor measure up?

1928/9 1st XV: JG Rhys-Jones, FR Spearman, DG Spear, TD Parker, NM Palmer, HW Beales, FG Westlake. Middle; RG Parker, LB Spear, GFN Snell, PW Rundle, FK Carter, HC Lyddon. Front AJ Northcott.

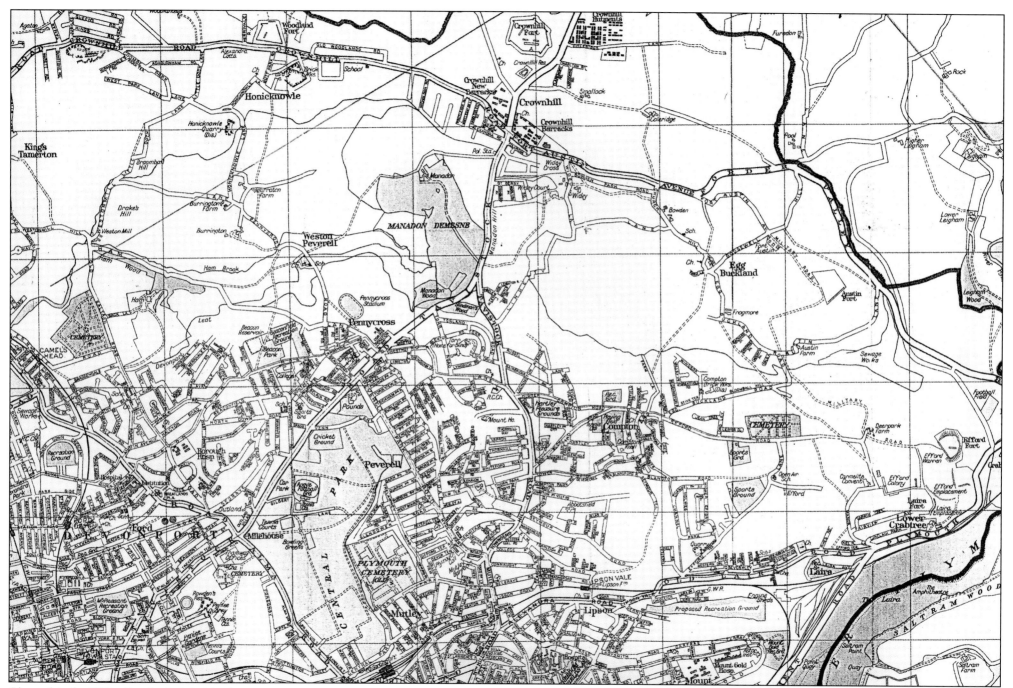

Plymouth in the 1930s - the city starts to take shape.

INTO THE THIRTIES

HW Ralph

While we can only speculate on the reasons for Francis Dale choosing to move on in 1929 there can be no doubt that the timing was, all things considered, quite good His son John had just completed his studies at the school and the school itself was relatively settled.

1928 had been the first year since the Great War that there had been no changes in the common room. After the initial hiccups in the early 1920s with various comings and goings - six of Dale's first nine appointments left after less than five years – there was now a marked stability among the staff. From the very beginning Dale's game-plan to recruit "team players" had been very obvious and of the nineteen or so full-time, main-school appointments made in Dale's time all but two were made before the end of 1925.

Not that there were that many staff members. When Ralph arrived in the summer of 1929 there were just fourteen full-time assistant masters and two part-timers – just as there had been in 1921. This, despite the fact that there were now 322 boys in the school, as opposed to 267 back then.

This gave a somewhat uncomfortable average number of 22 boys per Master and in a school that was generally regarded as having a *"substantial Sixth Form"* (Interim Inspectors Report, Oct 1930), this was three or four more than would normally be expected.

This *"substantial sixth form"*, incidentally numbered 38 out of 322 and it was on account of it's success with Advanced Courses that the School was in receipt of grants worth several hundred pounds from the authorities. There were three groups in the sixth form; Science and Mathematics, Classics and Modern Studies. The rest of the school was in five year-groups each with roughly sixty boys, divided into an "A" and a "B" form.

Apart from the heavy teaching loads and the high pupil-teacher ratios, the staff seemed happy enough though and other than the departure of Dobson and the arrival of Edwards there was to be only one further change in the staff line-up before 1933. While this settled squad clearly had a steadying influence over the school as a whole, there were certain financial implications for the new head. Dale's initial wave of appointments had all been men of a similar age to himself. Consequently,

when Ralph arrived ten years later, there was only one man in the common room under thirty - William Woodcock, and he reached that particular milestone just a week or so into Ralph's first term. Of the others, four out of the fourteen were already on maximum salaries and a further four were approaching it.

One of the inevitable consequences of this was that the school's running costs were increasing all the time. There was also a sizeable debt in respect of the new science block, which had seen the school's mortgage increase by £7,000, taking it up to an all-time high of £22,000. Additionally there had, more recently, been a *"special expenditure"* of £778 on repairs and renewals incurred in converting half of the former boarding house in Valletort Villas into a suitable residence for Mr Ralph and for the transference of the Prep into the other half of the house.

So it was, that notwithstanding the rise in numbers since Dale had taken over, the school was running at a loss. The good news, however, was that this loss was diminishing and with a further healthy increase in numbers in Ralph's first term there was even the prospect of a small surplus in the not too distant future. The worry was that unless younger, and hence cheaper, staff members were recruited, that surplus would soon be lost to a steadily-increasing wages bill.

That bill, during Ralph's first year, was £7,271. A paltry sum by today's standards, giving each member of staff somewhere around £500 per annum, but remember the school fees then were only £27 a year and brought in just under £5,500 annually. The shortfall was met by grants, largely in respect of the 73 "Free Place" pupils; £3,045 from the Board of Education, £1,832 from the Plymouth Education Authority and a further £100 from the Devon Authority.

Incidentally, it's perhaps worth noting here that not all members of the City Council thought the money was that well spent referring to the School as an *"academy for snobs"* and comparing it unfavourably with certain

"socialized" Secondary Schools in the City.

This view the editor of the Plymothian was keen to refute; *"such an assertion should perhaps be ignored, we do, however, wish most vigorously to deprecate the inference, so easily conveyed that Plymouth College is a "home for snobs"; that is, a school where ill-formed taste and manners take the place of natural good breeding. The School's aim is to turn out boys with some sense of scholarship, an education unaffected by political feeling, and, above all, the character of a gentleman. If the School were to depart from these principals, it would fail to fulfil the purpose of its foundation. It is our belief that the School has not failed."*

Clearly staff wages weren't the only outgoings, but apart from maintenance and loan charges there were few other demands on income – the annual administration bill amounted to just £218 – less than half the wages of any member of staff.

Who then did the bulk of the paper work, the letter writing and set up all the interviews with prospective parents? It was the Headmaster.

"The Governors provide me with no clerical assistance of any kind," he wrote, in a later letter to the Board of Education. Given that he also taught 26 periods a week and was spending *"on an average, nearly two hours a night in preparation and correction of written work,"* the head's load was a particularly heavy one.

So too, incidentally, was that of the newly appointed PT and Art master, Ian Edwards, who was *"poorly treated"* in respect of *"free periods"*, however his lot was somewhat compensated by an extra payment of £25 per annum. Most teachers had a *"reasonable allocation"* of *"free periods"*.

Ian Edwards PT & Art

There were three other masters though who received extra payments; the two responsible for the Advanced Courses (£50 each) and the second master, Bert Sargent, *"who receives £50, as such and £60 for his duties in connection with the purchases and sale of Text Books."*

To put these figures in some sort of context, the latest Morris motor car, the Morris Major, was currently available for £215, a gallon of petrol was 1/7d (under 7p) and you could buy an 8lb turkey for 2/- (10p).

Another new Morris Major rolls off the production line.

The idea of recruiting extra staff was clearly an early one on Ralph's agenda, so too was the question of addressing the temporary teaching huts, the inadequate assembly hall and a gymnasium that was well past its sell-by date.

Thus despite concerns over his colleagues' and his own workload - *"I am aware,"* he was to note a year or two later, *"that for the headmaster of a Secondary School such a teaching timetable is probably without parallel"* - the new head seemed content, at first, in getting to grips with the new challenge before him.

It would appear that from the very beginning he was happy enough with the school curriculum as it was then constituted. Ralph himself, like everyone of his predecessors at the helm at Ford Park, was a Classicist and while the number of Classical students at the school was not particularly high it was an important part of the school's identity.

In fact, only a handful of boys benefited from this particular branch of sixth-form study, but that wasn't all that surprising given that there were only around six boys taking Greek in IIIA, IVA and VA, the other lads opting for German as their second language. These small classes however did not bother the head, they doubtless formed the bulk of his teaching load, and neither did they bother the inspectors. *"The provision for Greek in these forms is an essential preliminary to a strong advanced course in the Sixth Form, for which it must be remembered the School receives a special grant of £400* (Interim Inspection Report 1930)*."*

Curiously, the only real curriculum problem identified by the Inspectors in their report that year was in terms of the provision of "non-academic" teaching, *"particularly (but not solely) for the "B" Forms."*

"Art is carried up to Form IVB, but receives only one period a week in that Form and in the two Third Forms. Music receives only one period a week in the first two years and is not continued thereafter. Two periods are properly given to Physical Training through the five years of the main course, but most of these periods are of only thirty minutes. Manual Instruction is confined to a single period in the first year and two periods in the second year. Some development of the "non-academic" side of the curriculum, probably involving some increase of total teaching-time, would in fact appear to be reasonable and indeed desirable."

It wasn't just a question of time, though, there was also the problem of premises – there was no Art room, no room for metal work, indeed, in their summing-up, the inspectors generally felt that the School buildings were, despite the recent redecoration, *"below standard in several respects"*. Furthermore - *"the playground is rough and most of the desking is obsolete"* and … *"there is no provision for drying clothes."*

Clearly the report would have been a great help to the new head as he made his appeals to the Board of Governors, for the inspectors affirmed that: *"the school was being run economically"* but that *"some addition to the staff would be justified and indeed desirable"* and, furthermore, that as far as buildings were concerned, *"considerable expenditure spread over a period of years will be necessary."*

For his part, the Chairman of Governors, JP Brown, was doing what he could out of his own pocket and on Monday 6th October, 1930, somewhat significantly just a week before the Inspectors arrived, he formally presented the School with new wrought-iron gates for the North Entrance.

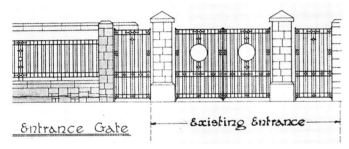

1930 - new gates and crest (note the crown on the cross and the position of top two elements).

"Planned by Mr Bazeley, with bronze plaques bearing the new arms of the School designed by Mr Edwards, the gates present a dignified appearance and provide a more worthy entrance."

DAT DEVS INCREMENTVM

Architect Alton Bazeley, OPM, thereby added yet another of his deft touches to the evolving appearance of his old School. Meanwhile, in this simple statement we find the only clue to what, in the longer term, has probably been Ian Edwards' most enduring contribution to the traditions of a school he was to spend so many years at - the design of the College Arms.

Impressive, even now, the new gates doubtless were great morale boosters in their day and couldn't have failed to impress the Inspectors when they arrived. Remember the school site was that much smaller then and this was the principal entrance. One wonders, however, what the Inspectors made of the "Old Lab".

This humble structure had *"as its name implies, started its career as the School Laboratory, with Dark Room attached; it gave way to larger buildings, and became a store-room for choir apparatus – thus at least maintaining an association with the Muses; in more recent years it was raised to the dignity of a form-room; and now it has been forced down to the depths and become nothing more or less than a home for the Scouts' trek-cart – a garage."*

So wrote the editor of the summer term Plymothian (DR Serpell?), who was moved to action following the establishment of a Vegetable Garden on an erstwhile *"pleasant piece of wasteland"*. This he felt had a *"deleterious effect on the character of the school"*. *"The Vegetable Garden,"* however, he added, was *"but a single innovation amongst many. Of them all, none, not even a ban on Free Periods, not even the convict system in the Gym., has caused us more sorrow than the degradation of the Old Lab."*

It is, perhaps, surprising that no-one then considered using the Old Lab for metal work. The piece is further revealing though in its view on Free Periods – part of Ralph's *"no time for the idle boy"* philosophy? And the *"convict system"* in the gym – was this a very early and thinly- veiled reference to Ian Edwards and his heavy-handed intolerance?

Whatever the inference, David Serpell was in his last term at school. He was head prefect and doubtless more than happy to take a couple of pot-shots at the old school before heading off for Oxford. It had been a good year for the young man who was one of those Dale had referred to in his leaving address as having been at the school before he arrived and was still there to see him go. WJ Gillingham was another distinguished leaver that summer, along with RG Parker, KW Wickett and RHH Morley, who, like Serpell was off to Oxford.

Other visitors to the land of wide-bottomed trousers that year, according to the Easter Plymothian's "Oxford Letter", included bandleader Jack Hylton, Winston Churchill, John Drinkwater, Walter De La Mare, Sir Nigel Playfair, Austen Chamberlain, Nancy Astor and, of course, David Serpell's older brother Roger who had *"at last succeeded in going round the North Oxford Golf Course in 130"*. Meanwhile, over at the other place, Cambridge, Shanks Lingley's son and recent leaver, Loris, *"distinguished himself by gaining his Golf Colours at Downing College"*.

Golf was becoming increasingly popular at the time and there was even a suggestion that an OPM Golf Section should be formed. NK Ralph, WG Haydon, LR Bryant, LE Williams, CD McDonald and J Woolland were to be the inaugural golfing committee. Among those to raise the profile of the game nationally were the Prince of Wales (later King Edward VIII) and the Duke of York (later King George VI) both of whom served as Captains of the Royal and Ancient Golf Club – in 1922 and 1930 respectively.

Golf grips the nation.

The twenties also witnessed the first international matches between Britain and America and in the following year, 1927, Samuel Ryder presented a new transatlantic trophy. On an individual level the Grand Slam man, Bobby Jones, did much to popularise the sport, winning the British and American Open and Amateur championships in 1930. This was also the year that steel-shafted clubs were legalised over here, so it was small wonder that there was greater interest than ever before among the nation's youth.

With an ever-increasing sixth form there was, not surprisingly, greater interest than ever before in most sports at Plymouth College.

Fives was flourishing under HW Beales, the School captain, thanks in no small measure to the weather; *"the courts have been available more than usual, owing to the remarkable weather conditions."* It wasn't just the older boys taking advantage either, – *"It is pleasing to record that the juniors have displayed a more satisfactory interest in the game."*

On the rugger front, HC Lyddon led the team through a good year; school sides were beaten and there was a hard fought draw against the OPMs to end the season. A film, "Rugger", was shown to raise money for the games fund and netted a profit of £1.1.3d (£1.06p). Meanwhile, HWK Kelly wrote a disdainful piece for the Plymothian entitled *"Mainly about Rugby Football".*

"Despite all this peace propaganda," he wrote, *"we tolerate, even encourage this game of Rugby Football. This so-called sport – I shudder to think that such a boorish, bloody, bestial, barbaric battle should be dignified by being classed with such noble pastimes as ping-pong, mah jong, tiddly-winks, minature golf and push penny (known to the vulgar as shove ha'penny) – is a relic, unfortunately one of the best preserved, of the Stone Age."*

Although couched in humourous terms the boy was surely speaking from the heart. Already a member of the School Fives Team and the Water Polo team, and a future captain of both, the clearly quite capable Kelly never got his rugger colours and his thoughts on the game have been shared quietly by more than a few of those who have followed him over the years through the gates of the College.

East Town Jnr Hockey Champs 1930: J Woolley, TK Butland, RFJ Smeardon, RR Eslick, KG Platt. Seated; GE Smith, JW Ford, JR Spear, HG U'ren, MT Parker. Front; JM Luscombe, HJ Hur-

On the hockey pitch the Periton brothers starred in attack, while Gould (who was also a fine tennis player – he won the Men's Singles in the P&D League Tournament at Hartley that summer) and Gillingham rallied the defence. Overall a disappointing season perhaps but one which saw the greatest number of games played for many years.

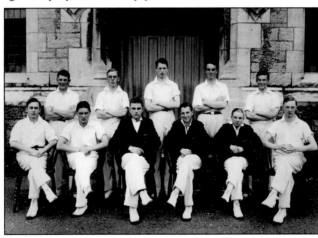

1st XI Cricket, 1930. Back; AJ Giles, DR Serpell, CL Bright, DG Spear, DJA Brown. Front; KW Wickett, JG Rhys-Jones, RG Parker, H Coleman (Capt.) HG U'ren, FR Price.

The cricket results were similarly unremarkable, again the most notable feature being that not one of the sixteen fixtures was scratched on account of the weather – *"surely a record".* HG U'ren was the leading all-rounder and was just pipped in the batting averages by RG Parker, who scored sixties in two of the six games that the School actually managed to win. Rhys-Jones bagged the most wickets and DR Serpell picked up the fielding prize.

On the water polo front there were five fixtures. The first three were won comfortably by the School, Skelton scoring a hat-trick in each game and JR Spear also getting onto the score sheet in each game. Gillingham and Kelly were the latest team members to be awarded colours, and for the first time since the introduction of Water Polo Team Colours, the Games Committee authorised an outward display of the distinction – a *"small black and red School badge on the costume"* and *"the addition of the letters PMC WPC on the blazer pocket above the School badge".*

JRS wins his colours

The Games Committee also made *"a departure of considerable importance from the old method of awarding Colours. There are to be in future 2nd xi or 2nd xv Colours for those who are included in the Final Order 1st xi or 2nd xv as distinct from those who get their 2nd Colours but remain in the 2nd xi or 2nd xv. There is little alteration in the details of the Colours themselves, but a chart explaining them all is now hung in the lower corridor. The main addition is a Scarf for all winning 1st Colours in any game."*

Incidentally, JR Spear ended up Victor Ludorum in the Aquatic Sports, ahead of Skelton and Pointon.

The annual athletic sports were held, a little earlier than usual, on Wednesday 9th April, and *"owing to the weather being wet the High Jump and the Preparatory Sports were postponed until the Summer Term"*.

DWB Carnaghan was the Victor Ludorum and he also won the Senior Cross Country run where he finished just ahead of RL Bowden. GE Smith was Junior Victor although HG U'ren won more events.

There was one other "sporting" arena that the School competed in this year, and that was in the OTC *"Country Life"* Shooting Competition. It was the School's first attempt in the event and although *"We were well up to the average in the grouping and landscape target shooting, but our rapid firing and snapshooting requires more practice,"* was Guy Hill's verdict after the School came 46th out of 49 teams competing.

The OTC Camp that year was at Tidworth Pennings, between 29 July and 6 August - three officers and 33 cadets went from School. *"For the second year in succession we were very unfortunate in the weather, but fortunately most of the rain fell when we were off parade, so though the programme of training was curtailed, we never got wet through, and the sole casualty was one case of jaundice."*

1930 also saw the departure from Devonport of the 2nd Battalion Devonshire Regiment, whose officers and NCOs had help the School Contingent with their training. *"We are to receive instruction and supervision from the Norfolk Regiment instead, who have taken their place at Raglan Barracks."*

The School was, of course, still placing many of its leavers in the Services and among the most recent batch was Lieut. PB Huxham, the swimming giant who, we read in the Christmas term magazine, was now swimming for the Army, the Services, and Hampshire. Another old boy of similar rank, Lieut AP Revington (RAF), *"has been doing a lot of flying in Iraq"*. Flying was still a very newsworthy activity, the R101 had recently passed over Plymouth,

The R101 makes its flight over Plymouth and the Guildhall.

Amy Johnson was making the headlines with her flight to Australia (CR Finken even occupied three pages of the Plymothian with a poem about her escapade), and Major Cartwright came to the School and gave a "Cinematograph" lecture on the history of Aviation.

April 1930 - Amy Johnson prepares to start her epic journey

On a sad note, however, Pay Commander Hugh Littleton was reported as having drowned at Hong Kong.

Other OPM news included reports of HJ Stevens and GA Le Mesurier, both of whom were tea-planting, the former in Assam, the latter in India; *"he does not hesitate to give his very decisive views on coolies and coolie labour. He writes very eloquently on the Indian trouble and describes Ghandi as an outsider in dangerous political fanatics"*.

Interestingly the School Debating Society, in their Annual Visitors Debate found, by a majority of 65 to 19, that *"the time has not yet come to grant Dominion Status to India."*

Meanwhile we read that WR Hatch, *"who is Empire-building in S Nigeria"*, was also having problems with the natives; *"he has been interviewing local Chiefs to try to arouse some enthusiasm to combat the plague of locusts, but he finds it difficult to stir the average man from his inertia. The latter is too lethargic to do anything, and will probably sit still and let his corn be eaten up."*

And the Rev AM Stibbs, *"who went out to the China Inland Mission 18 months ago, writes that he has had a tough job learning the language. He has however, begun to preach to the natives in their own tongue. At his station, Shunking, transport is rather primitive, and motor cars are still sufficient of a novelty to attract a crowd of people."*

On the younger OPM front it was announced that there were currently seven old boys studying at Cambourne School of Mines and one or two at Bristol University, from whence George Hutchins sent home a piece *"On A Modern University"*.

In it he described the main differences with Oxford and Cambridge as being a lack of tradition and with its constitution being purely a secular one.

"Probably visitors and freshmen alike in Bristol are struck by the obvious newness of our buildings; the University obtained its charter twenty-one years ago. There are other peculiarities which freshmen notice; first the absence of colleges, for the majority of students live in their own homes and the remainder in hostels or halls varying in size from a hundred and fifty to twenty-five students. There is no pride of sex among us, men are not sufficiently foolish to assume that they have a monopoly of learning."

And neither was our "modern" correspondent attempting to say that learning was all-important.

"There are some on the other hand who urge that if their degree be but a poor third it may be compensated by a few sound friends against the view that the first class specialist is of greater value to society than the cheerfully inefficient – the trial is the only satisfactory answer to this question. It is of course unnecessary to say that the University is a collection of individuals learning how to get the best out of life by putting the best into it – it is useless unless the best is put in. It is during the process that a man discovers what his best is and if he is a man he gives it without more ado."

Life in 1930, although in many respects very different to that of the present day, clearly presented the nation's youth and, more specifically, the young boys of Plymouth College with much the same dilemmas as today. At Cambridge new technology then, as now, had its place distracting students as "Cantabrigiensis" reported that *"a portable wireless set beguiles many a weary hour for the inhabitants of Warkworth Street."* Was this Lingley's portable, the same one that was wafting *"Jack Payne's soothing, if mechanised, solace"* across the waters of the Cam before the revision plans kicked in?

Jack Hylton and his Orchestra - Happy Days Are Here Again

More than ever before the music of the thirties was aimed at the younger generation. Young people after all were those who bought the records, who danced at the balls and who were quick to tune in to the technology and seek out the stars made by the new medium. Hence Jack Hylton's visit to Oxford - he'd sold millions of records in the twenties - and the reference to Jack Payne, who in 1928 had been invited to form the BBC Dance Orchestra.

Jack Payne's Orchestra

Meanwhile back in the world of Oxbridge there was also news of the School's former Headmasters; *"the degree of D.Litt. of Cambridge University has been awarded **honoris causa** upon the Rev HJ Chaytor, MA, now Senior Tutor at St Catherine's"*; his predecessor, 73 year-old Francis Colson had just been appointed a member of the School Board of Governors and Francis Dale had recently met up with the son of the Clerk to the Governors, Roger Serpell in Oxford.

Curiously, a third Francis, also destined to be a Plymouth College head, was in the School news this year. *"Mr FW Lockwood of St Catherine's College, Cambridge, has been at School for the practical part of his training year. He has given valued help in the Class room, on the football field and in the OTC."*

Little could he have guessed at what the future was to have in store at Plymouth College.

Also on the staff side, Messrs Harris and Major were two temporary visitors that year, from the University College of the South-West, completing their teacher training. Meanwhile among the regular teaching staff

there were nuptial celebrations for both Eric Holman and Di Davies.

There was no movement in the staff room that year, though, and it wasn't until following summer that there was any alteration to the full time squad, when the quiet and unobtrusive George Cairns retired, shortly after his 60th birthday, in April.

His replacement was to be one of only a very small group of appointments made by Ralph who did not stay until retirement – John Price. 24 year-old Price had been to school in Paramatta, Australia and had come to England to study at Keble College, Oxford. There may well have been some concern at the outset as to whether he would stay for long, but there was no doubting his commitment as the young Australian, the youngest staff member by some distance - he was even a good six years younger than Ian Edwards - threw himself into his work.

On the face of it 1931 was, for the most part, a fairly ordinary year; following the success of Classicists HR Voss, FJ Bowden and RB Nicholls, who were off to read Classics at Magdelene and Jesus Colleges, Cambridge and Keble College, Oxford, respectively, AM Woodley was awarded an Open Exhibition in Natural Science at Exeter College, Oxford and E Butchers won a Natural Science Open Scholarship to Keble. There were no great sporting triumphs to report and it was very much business as usual across the various groups and societies.

The Debating Society's Annual Entertainment took the form of two plays Allan Monkhouse's *"Grand Cham's Diamond"* and Lord Dunsany's *"A Night at an Inn"*. Lord Edward Plunkett Dunsany was clearly a bit of a favourite with Mr Woodcock for the 1929 Christmas Concert had seen the staging of his *"Lost Silk Hat"* and the 1930 Christmas extravaganza featured his *"Jest of Hahalaba"*. Probably the Irish story-teller's most celebrated work, however, *"Travel Tales of Mr Joseph Jenkins"*, was published in 1931.

Christmas 1930.

As an interesting aside, the 1930 Christmas Concert *"witnessed a departure from the usual custom, a charge being made for the admission. The proceeds went far towards paying for the stove that had recently been installed; and the people who came armed with fur coats and foot-muffs, prepared for the worst, were doubtless happy"*. Meanwhile the *"Grand Cham's Diamond"* was no ground-breaking piece either as the staff had presented a version of it just a few years earlier.

Outside of the School, JC Trewin's adaptation of *"Alice in Wonderland"*, had been well received at the Repertory Theatre in Princess Square (Plymouth), while that now quite-distinguished old boy, Eden Philpotts, had just produced "another successful West-country Play, *"Devonshire Cream"*, at the Playhouse, London. The 1931 League of Pity Entertainment, again featuring a William Woodcock production, took the form of three plays; *Suppressed Desires* by Susan Glaspell, in which Mrs Dufton's voice *"got the worst of a tussle with the City of Plymouth Tramways"* – as they rattled along Hyde Park Road; *The Shadow of the Glen,* by John M Synge (with almost the same cast as it had had eight years earlier) and AA Milne's *Wurzel Flummery*. The last of them, the second Milne production in recent years, starred Mr and Mrs Woodcock, Mr Davies, Mrs Dawes and the young Australian, John Price, whose acting was *"manifestly acceptable to the Lower School, but whether his was the right interpretation of Milne's whimsical creation is more than doubtful."*

Staff presentations, of course, had a major advantage over the boys' shows in that there was a ready pool of female acting talent to draw upon. The boys, on the other hand, had to improvise. In the 1930 Mock Parliament WJ Gillingham had been the female MP for Sutton, and in the *Grand Cham's Diamond* PJ Osmund whose *"wig looked like a wig"* was mother to HN Clemas as Miss Perkins.

Happily, the Literary and Debating Society's Mock Trial did not require the same kind of wig. Interestingly, though, we read that the part of Ronald Outcast, *"a disreputable and somewhat unclean specimen"*, who was accused of murdering a Mannamead man, was *"ably sustained by JR Spear."*

The trial was *"greatly appreciated by an audience of about a hundred visitors"* who were treated to *"excellent renderings of residents in districts as far apart as Mannamead and Laira ... and much amusement was caused by the appearance, complete in uniform, of a worthy Cinema Attendant, admirably performed by FJ Bowden".*

Cinema was then gaining an ever-increasing hold over popular culture but not without a certain amount of resistance and, one winter debate, there was much heated argument over the proposition that *"the Stage is fighting a losing battle with the Screen"*. With the *"followers of the theatre"* on one side and *"the more depraved cinema enthusiasts"* on the other one detects a certain bias in the report. Nevertheless the day was carried, just, by the House *"showing faith in legitimate drama"*.

Behind all this was the long-familiar Luddite-inspired theme that *"The Tendency of Modern Life is to the Destruction of Character"* and also that *"A further advance in Science is undesirable"*, both of which were motions put before the House in 1931. As was the proposition that *"All Education should be under State Control"*. Not surprisingly this debate was attended by the President of the Debating Society and Mr Osmund. *"Mr CW Osmund gave support to PJ Osmund who proposed the motion, whilst the Headmaster sided with WC Gingell, the Opposer. The motion was narrowly defeated."*

Curiously enough, later in the year there was overwhelming support for the Impromptu Debate on the proposal that *"Masters should wear mortar-boards and carry canes as in all the best school stories"*

The best school stories doubtless including those about the Fat Owl of the Remove, Billy Bunter, who had made his first appearance as minor character in Frank Richards Greyfriars School yarns in 1908.  By 1930 William George Bunter had become quite the star of that most popular of all boys literature around at that time – "The Magnet".

The tuppeny Magnet, the termly Plymothian and the 1930 £1 note.

Throughout the twenties comic books had become increasingly popular and it was no great surprise to find another suggestion that there should be cartoons in the Plymothian. Among the other more serious issues considered that year in the School Debating Society were the proposals that *"The British Empire is threatened with Disintegration"* which found little support, and *"This House views with alarm the incompetence of all Political Parties and would welcome a Coalition Government in the present emergency."*

The latter debate was an Inter-School affair and it was a pupil from the Corporation Grammar School who opened the discussion. It was 20th February 1931 and in Westminster there were ongoing difficulties with the Lib-Lab pact that was currently keeping Ramsay MacDonald's Labour Government in power. Problems with Lloyd George's Liberal proposals for Proportional Representation were about to scupper the alliance that had already been defeated on a handful of occasions in the Commons.

Before the year was out the former Labour hero, MacDonald, was to lead a coalition government that

would have the backing of just 13 self-styled National Labour MPs, together with 473 Tories and 68 Liberals. The remaining 52 regular Labour MPs condemned their leader as a traitor. Macdonald, meanwhile, accused his former Cabinet colleagues of running away from the economic crisis; a crisis that was exacerbated by a huge hike in the unemployment figures – up to 2.71 million in a population of 44.8 million, prompting a call for a drop in the dole from 17/- to 15/- a week (85p to 75p). The King voluntarily took a £50,000-a-year cut, while sailors were presented with a pay cut that took their basic down to 25/- (£.1.25p) a week, prompting the Invergordon Mutiny.

Plymouth College teachers, on almost £10 a week, seemed very well-off by comparison.

They did give of their time quite freely, however, and on 6th May *"an experiment was made in inviting parents of boys in the Main School to spend an evening at the School to meet the Staff and see examples of work, in particular Woodwork, Mapwork and Art. In addition, portions of two gymnastic lessons were illustrated by the members of Forms VB and 1A, whose keenness and agility made a very great impression on the visitors. The OTC represented by a Lewis Gun Section under the command of Captain Hill and by a demonstration platoon commanded by CSM E Butchers carried out exercises on the field; and members of the Science Sixth conducted experiments in the Physics and Chemistry Laboratories for the instruction and entertainment of parents."*

The evening was clearly a great success and it is hard to imagine that this was a first;

"There is no doubt that the function, besides being an extremely pleasant one (fine weather contributing much to its success), served a useful purpose. Parents had the opportunity of meeting individual members of the Staff and discussing the work and prospects of their boys with the masters actually concerned with teaching them."

"It will be possible, we hope, to hold a similar "At Home" in future at the beginning of each Summer term: this year some 250 parents were present: we shall be prepared to entertain many more next Summer."

If the weather was kind that night, it certainly wasn't a general feature for the year. Ten OPM rugby matches had to be scratched *"owing very largely to the bad weather conditions – our ground at Chelson Meadow has often been underwater."*

At least four School hockey matches were scratched, again, *"owing to the ground being unfit",* and eight out of twenty-one 1st XI cricket matches were lost to the elements. As the Scout Troop Leader noted *"we were fortunate in having the **Summer** during camp" (that was July 25th to August 5th).*

Notwithstanding the vagaries of the weather, the season wasn't all bad for the School's sporting sides. The Hockey boys won their only inter-school match against Newton College, and they beat the OPMs *"for the first time in many years";* a single goal from Captain RJ Gould was all that separated the two teams.

1st Xi Hockey 1931. Back; HR Butchers, AM Woodley, HJ Bartholomew, E Butchers, HG U'ren. Front; AJ Giles, TW Hockaday, RL Bowden, RJ Gould (Capt.) R Periton, DG Spear.

On the rugger front, sticky conditions and pitch changes marred what few fixtures were played. JG Rhys-Jones in his Captain's report found little to highlight although the 2nd XV won five out of six of their games. The two Spears, the two Peritons and three Butchers all played for the Firsts.

1st XV Rugby, 1931. Back; HR Butchers, HC Reid, FR Price, KB Langdon, ER Freathy, KL Ashfold. Seated; HR Lawry, JR Spear, GHS Giddings, HJ Bartholomew (Capt.), JS Phillips, AJ Giles, AE Butchers, Front; HG U'ren and R Periton.

Soggy wickets spoilt the chances of any big scores in the cricket, only FJ Williams and R Periton hit fifties. They also topped the bowling averages, though Giles and U'ren both picked up a number of wickets. So too did Terrell for the OPMs in their first encounter with the School that season, he finished with 8-12 as the School collapsed for 27, Mr Gingell's 11 being the only score over 5 – Mr Lord was not out 2.

The majority of the five Water Polo matches were played in heavy rain, and *"while not necessitating the cancellation of any games – the dampness of the "ground" being immaterial – it has made playing conditions difficult."* That said, however, the School won all five matches, they scored 23 goals, JR Spear netting 15 of them, and only one goal was conceded *"while we were blinded by the only two minutes of sunshine during the season".*

Spear was also the star of the aquatic sports once more, finishing Victor Ludorum again, with 36 points, almost half the total scored by his East Town house.

In the main Athletic Sports no new records were broken and HJ Bartholomew and HJ Jones were the stars of what was, for the first time, a three-day event. DWS Pettett was Junior Victor, while RL Bowden and HG U'ren were conspicuous in the open events.

School Fives carried on although the home game with Kelly was scratched because of an epidemic of 'flu at the Tavistock school. There was a Doubles Handicap Competition held at School, however. Mr CR Serpell put up a prize of 21s (£1.05) worth of sports gear to each pair of boys, of the same House, who should win a handicapped Fives Tournament. Despite the attractive prize only eight pairs took part and the competition was aptly won by Fives Captain HW Kelly and R Periton.

Meanwhile, in the Inter-Troop Scout Sports at Mount Edgcumbe, the School were *"fortunate enough to win nearly all the events in which we competed"* and won the competition outright.

And while they were fortunate with the weather for their Summer Camp, the Half-Term and the Whitsun Camps were virtual wash-outs. Like the Scouts, the OTC also managed to have their camp during what was universally agreed to be *"one of the best of the Summer".*

"The afternoons were spent in bathing, sun-bathing or playing games and in the evening we repaired to the "Duke of York's Theatre," where rich and varied entertainment awaited our pleasure – songs, poems, plays, music, jazz, news items on slides and even real audible "talkies"."

This was the Duke of York's Camp and it was the first time that Plymouth College OTC had sent representatives. The party were conveyed to Southwold from London, *"after a luncheon at, and inspection of, the Royal Mews of Buckingham Palace".*

On the Wednesday of the Camp *"we received a visit from our Royal host, the Duke of York, who partook of the camp routine until the Thursday evening when the whole Camp turned out to cheer as the aeroplane in which the Duke left flew low over our heads".*

The camp was clearly a great success; *"There is but one outstanding regret; that it did not last longer. No-one seeing the cheerful faces of the boys in the Camp or the sympathetic farewells as the all-too-short friendships were severed, for a time only we hope, could doubt the success achieved by his Royal Highness in eliminating the feeling of "class distinction", that horrible anachronism, among the youth of today."*

One other great trip that year saw twelve members of the Upper School spending Easter in Paris with Di Davies. Crossing from Plymouth to Le Havre on the *"Mexique"* they made their way to Paris where, in just over a week, Mr Davies managed to show *"them so much of the beauty of Paris architecturally and historically in a way that could not fail to excite interest."*

Notre Dame, the Louvre, with the Mona Lisa and the Venus de Milo, Versailles, Montmatre and the Boulevards *"at their best in a blaze of electric light"*, clearly delighted the boys, as did the Paris Underground and Radio Paris, which was broadcast *"on the wireless with which some of the carriages are equipped."*

There can be little doubt that the full accounts of these various camps and expeditions must have had an inspiring effect on the rest of the School. The Plymothian then was almost certainly better read than it is today, there being that much less competition in either the reading or entertainment stakes.

Certainly 1931 was a good year for the School Magazine. The number and standard of the contributions was up, significantly, and noticeably there were a number of items from Shanks Lingley, JC Trewin, and a host of others, particularly in the Christmas edition.

"I am waiting gloomily for the First Robin."

"The miserable bird will arrive in a large envelope. It will be standing in the snow with a church spire and some holly behind it. It will be accompanied by this sort of couplet:

Listen to the silv'ry chime:
Mirth and joy at Christmas-time

And the whole creation – complete with a bow of green ribbon – will call itself a Christmas-card."

Trewin then launched into an attack on the whole Christmas card phenomenon – *"red-faced men with sacks, stage coaches, interiors of old inns, Christmas trees, holly"* ... *"and the same jingling rhymes that were heard at the court of Edward the Confessor".*

"Presently, a postman will ring the overworked bell – Dickensian double-knocks have gone out of fashion – and I shall realise that all the people who have omitted to write for many months, are sending Christmas cards in the hope of wiping off their debts."

Lingley's festive offering was a four-page story piece on an incident involving a plum pudding in Africa, while another contribution, from Wol (an AA Milne reference?) reflected on the proposal from Professor RE Zachrisson, of Uppsala University to adopt a simplified phonetic English spelling called "Anglic".

"Enough, sez Proefesser Zachrisson, enough
Of ploughing and rough troughs of tough sloughy dough,
That set wun a-coughing – enough of although.
Your spelling is obsoleet, hard and abserd.
Ie'd maek yu lern Anglic, where every werd
Is alwaes proenounsed just ekzaktly as spelt.
Ie, from Uppsala, deesiededly felt
Yor spelling unfitted for modern comers:
No spelling is mor idiotik of wers
For yues az a world-wied biznes tung.
But Anglic wil shortly be ritn and sung
By Englishmen evrywhere. Simpl to reed
The prezentdae speech wil it quikly sukseed.
Thus quoeth the proefesser, and doutless all thae
Hooz weekness in spelling is noetabl mae
All eagerly long for that duebius day."

That particular Plymothian (Christmas 1931), incidentally was also the first one to include a list of School Officials;

The Head of School, Prefects, Captain of Rugby, Hon. Sec., Captain of Hockey and all the other sporting sections, plus Hon. Sec. Of the Literary and Debating Society, the Senior NCO of the OTC and the Editor of the Plymothian.

HWK Kelly was the first Head Boy thus honoured, he was also Captain of Fives, Water Polo and Hon. Sec. Lit. & Deb.

Perhaps this was another of Ralph's little innovations, all of which added a touch of dignity to the everyday life of the School. As the Head, himself, was to report at Speech Day, it had been quite a satisfactory year overall. The present number at the School, 432, constituted a record and the honours secured during the year included *"First place in the Special Entry in to the Navy, five open awards at Oxford and Cambridge, two State Scholarships and two other Scholarships tenable at a University, Eleven Higher Certificates and twenty-eight School Certificates."*

After the Headmaster's report, which was delivered to *"a much larger audience than of recent years"* ... *"the whole School sang the sea-shanty "Shenandoah". The rollicking boisterous spirit which usually permeates such songs was conspicuously absent. Only about half the School sang, and of that half, very few gave full vent to their powers. These faults cannot be excused by the favourite plea that the School lacked practice, for Mr Weekes had rehearsed the musical items many times before Speech Day. The faults probably lay in the sobering effect of the occasion, and in the School's habitual apathy in such matters."*

The prizes were then distributed by the Commander-in-Chief of Plymouth, Admiral the Hon. Sir Hubert Brand, who spoke of patriotism, the Westcountry and success. *"Success always comes to the cans, and failure to the can'ts,"* he said, adding, *"there is no electric elevator to success, step up the stairs and don't stare up the steps."*

Undoubtedly, the Headmaster was a "can". Curiously, however, there was one area where the word "can't" came into play in 1931 and that was with respect to the Plymothian and the OPMs.

"In view of the serious position of the Club's finances it was decided at the Extraordinary General Meeting to discontinue the practice of sending 3 copies of the magazine to members each year. In future only the Easter issue will be forwarded, and this will contain the Xmas Club notes for the year together with a brief account of the School events."

The EGM, held at the School, also decided to *"limit the yearly grants to the Rugby Football, Cricket and Fives Branch Clubs, to £5 each in the case of the Football and Cricket Clubs and £2 in the case of the Fives Club."*

Clearly the mid-twenties boom time for the OPM Club was receding in the face of problems that, doubtless, had their origins in the national financial crisis and that winter it proved impossible to raise an OPM 2nd XV. By the time the Easter Plymothian had gone to press in 1932, however, there was a cheerier note;

"The Club is progressing. The corner has been turned, but only just. Our sporting activities could be widened, our social functions should be larger. See to it, ye Plymothians."

OPM RFC, season 1932-33. Back row: LE Williams, CE Bracken, TA Pearn, AWC Lyddon, AR Northcott. 2nd row: FR Curtis, RT Wiltshire, AF Butchers, DG Spear, JR Spear, AJ Giles. Sitting: NE Elliott, CJ Phillips, GL Wakeham, WHJ Priest, FGP Westlake, RD Smith, RG Parker. Front row: HR Lawry, AFC Kitchen, AJ Northcott, FJB Briggs.

Section of the School photograph, July 1931. Note that the gun is still in place. Left; Cecil Atkey with his mother and brother, the boys both in their 'best' school uniform. Right; 1931 South Town Rugby Juniors; Standing, BA Morgan, EC Carson, REV Johns, SL Heal, JG Wescott. Middle, EA Perkins, MJ Chandler, LH Clemas, A Edmunds, GAS Rattray. Front, PGM Collins, FW Buet, JR Ife. Far right; 1931 South Town Rugby Seniors; Standing, HC Reid, RJS Rattray, FE Williams, LH Clemas. Middle, HG U'ren, ER Freathy, GHS Giddins, JS Phillips, AF Butchers. Front, NA Burt, KL Ashfold.

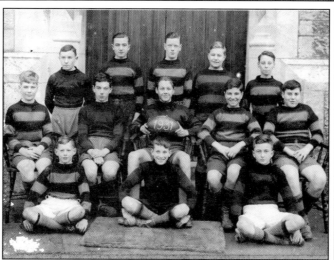

This was part of the first-ever magazine-within-a magazine editorial for the OPM section of the journal. The section ran to over ten pages and included an outline review of the School's year. One part of the School it didn't mention, however, was the Preparatory Department. Generally overlooked in the magazine, it certainly wasn't overlooked by the Inspectors who paid a visit to the junior section in November and sent out their report early in 1932.

The Prep had, of course, moved into the other half of Valletort when that building was converted into accommodation for the arrival of the new Headmaster. This clear link was seen as a good thing by the Inspectors, who also spoke favourably of the *"general supervision and control exercised by the Head Master"*. The report did, however, suggest that the Prep was a little too isolated, not from the Main School, but *"from other Junior Schools and Junior School teachers"*.

Miss Footner, described by one past pupil as *"a gorgon"*, had been Head of the Prep since 1921 and half of her small staff of four (Miss Loveless and Miss Heath) had also been there ten years or more, while Mrs Ellis had arrived here as a supply teacher in 1922. This physical and philosophical isolation from other Junior Schools and their teaching practices tends, said the report, *"to make a staff lose touch with modern developments and to lower, unconsciously, the standard of what can be achieved with, and expected of, young boys"*.

While not overly-critical of the premises – *"There are five classrooms of which four are very fair rooms, but the fifth, used for the youngest Division and at present entered only through another classroom, is too small"* – the Inspector was clearly not overly impressed with the staff;

"Loyal and hardworking, but not unnaturally in view of the salaries paid, it is not highly-qualified and as a whole it cannot be regarded as more than moderate."

The standards of English and arithmetic were singled out as the main area for concern, in the lowest division – *"The teacher should go and see how arithmetic is treated in a good infants' school that works on individual lines, particularly with a view to learning something about modern apparatus"*.

The standard of drawing and handwriting was also thought to be rather poor, but History, Geography, Nature Study and French (*"now taught only in the top two divisions"*) fared better.

Nevertheless it was felt that *"one or two wall-maps, and some additional pictures for French teaching are required ... Some of the blackboards need renewing ... A gramophone for the teaching of French and Music, and a few suitable illustrated reference books for History and Geography would be useful"*. There was also a similar note to that found in the report on the Main School – *"the replacement of desks by light chairs and tables would enable the most to be made of the cramped space"*.

Overall then the impression conveyed is one of a fairly dated and formal approach in fairly dated and sterile surroundings and one can but wonder what impact this had on prospective parents. While the Main School numbers had been growing at quite a satisfactory rate, numbers at the Prep were the same as they had been ten years earlier – 94. There had been a slight moving of the goalposts in as much as boys now came at age six rather than five as had been the case until fairly recently, nevertheless most lads were aged eight plus and nearly all went on into the Main School.

The message to the Headmaster was plain enough; if the School as a whole was to grow then it was important that the Prep should grow too. It was no great surprise therefore to find one or two changes following in the wake of the report. Mrs Ellis, after just five terms of full-time work in the School, took the retirement option – *"we record our appreciation of much hard and unobtrusive work"* was how her career here was summed up that summer.

Miss Loveless, happily belying her name - at last - was also on her way;

"We have to congratulate Miss Loveless on her approaching marriage to Mr J White, which is to take place this Summer in South Africa. Many generations of boys who have passed through the Preparatory School will acknowledge the debt they owe to her untiring help and sympathy and her intense devotion to the School which she has served since January, 1913."

Miss Loveless leaves - 1932

One former pupil, fondly recalls the little couplet her peer Miss Lethbridge had them all learn in the wake of the troubles in Northern Ireland;

"The green, white and yellow for the dirty Irish fellow and the red, white and blue for the jolly English crew". Remember the School lost one or two old boys in those troubles and their tragic ends were not lost on the ladies of the Prep who shared their suffering.

Like the Prep, the Main School had also been criticised for the standard of its reading matter and, significantly, in the Easter 1932 Plymothian we find a list of more than seventy new books which had been added to the School Library. The list included Robert Louis Stevenson's great novels, Conan Doyle's Sherlock Holmes stories, Kipling's *Kim*, *Jungle Book* and *Just So Stories*, Rider Haggard's *King Solomon's Mines*, plus works by Scott, Sheridan, Priestley. Thackeray, Buchan, Dickens, Marryat and the technical tomes of Gibbard Jackson. There was also the newly-published History of Plymouth by Charles Bracken (who was then Headmaster of Corporation Grammar School) and ten titles, including *Beric the Briton* - bringing history to life - from GA Henty.

The supply was privately-supplemented, later in the year, by P Smerdon, who contributed Darwin's *The English Public School*, Burke's *The English Inn* and Priestley's *English Humour.*

It was a good year for humour. The Christmas Entertainment had been full of it, even though the actors in both JJ Melhuish's *The Old Geyser* and Temple-Thurstan's *Snobs*, were *"inclined to under-estimate the mirth-provoking power of the dialogue ... there was a tendency to carry on talking throughout the numerous laughs that occurred".*

Once again the lack of ladies had little bearing, *"AJ Biscombe as Dorothy wore a very complete disguise"*, in the former and *"HW Broad as the tradesman's wife, gave and excellent and well-sustained performance"* in the latter.

The Christmas Concert, like its predecessors, was held in the Gymnasium and it's interesting to note that the tired old premises was itself subject of a witty piece in the following term's magazine.

Purporting to be from an unpublished work by Dr AJ Cronin, it ran thus; *"The Gymnasium floor was already ankle-deep in rain water and long icicles hung glistening from the wall-bars, when fourteen large men in bathing costumes and calico bonnets plunged through the splintering ice which lay in the inky water of the swimming bath ... Rain became hail and jagged lumps of ice .. rattled and jumped on the tin roof and the swimmers heads."*

"Meanwhile the polo-match proceeded ... the leather ball was swollen to twice its normal size with hard wrappings of ice. Overhead some frenzied demon was playing havoc with the elements. Blue flames flickered round the tram-standards and drain pipes: iron gutters crumpled up and slobbered molten streams on to the pavement: the concrete swimming bath crumbled and split: trams were tipped over into private gardens and the fronts of houses were sliced away like pats of butter ...It was now half-time."

The piece was signed *"Rocco"* and may well have been the current magazine editor C R (Rocco?) Fincken, who gave a paper that year to the Literary and Debating Society, entitled *"Satire as a means of moral reform"*. However exaggerated Rocco's fiction was, the old Gym was clearly past its sell-by date, unlike the Water Polo team, which was probably enjoying its finest-ever moments – thanks in no small measure to that powerhouse figure – John Spear.

Their season could hardly have been more successful; Port of Plymouth, Plymouth Amateurs, Devonport RSA and the OPMs all comprehensively beaten as the end of season statistics ran, played six, won six, goals for 26, goals against 3. Of those 26 goals 22 of them were scored by JR Spear; *"The power behind his shots has increased considerably since last year and he is untiring in his efforts,"* said the Captain, HWK Kelly, who also noted that most of the team had completed their last season. There was one hope for the future though;

"Mention must be made of FBW Blight, a newcomer to the side, who has led the attack throughout the season, and despite his immaturity, has shown himself to be a powerful swimmer who should prove to be a force to be reckoned with in three or four years time."

FW Blight star swimmer

For John Spear, however, the summer term water sports had provided a fitting conclusion to an excellent sporting year. Described as a *"heavy second rank forward who has used his weight to advantage"*, he won his 1st XV rugby colours, he also picked up 1st XI hockey colours and featured in 1st XI cricket – *"one of the best fielders in the side"* ... *"scored a few runs in rustic fashion"*. He was also the only East Town boy to win a field event, putting the weight, in the School

Athletics and, along with FW Blight he set two new records in the School Aquatic Sports – he also finished up Victor Ludorum for the third year running. Platoon leader Spear also captained a Scout's Water Polo team at the Summer Camp at Salcombe, and needless to say they won both matches.

It was, however, thought to be his last School event; *"JR Spear has now left us and we wish him every success in his new sphere"*, ran East Town's closing note. JRS's valedictory appeared in the same magazine and that October he scored an unconverted try for the OPMs playing against the School at Ford Park.

But, come the summer term of 1933 he was back, a newly-appointed School Prefect and holder of *"a warrant for the position of Assistant Scout Master to the School Troop"*. It was the first time that a pupil had obtained such a position.

But we're jumping ahead. John Spear wasn't the only sporting hero of his day - there were others, among them Henry U'ren. Like JRS, U'ren was a member of the School Rugby, Hockey and Cricket teams.

"Although small of physique has tackled and fallen well. Is fast and has a useful cut through," was how he was described in the 1st XV review.

Fast he certainly was; he won the Cross Country run, overtaking Ashfold who had led for the first three miles, in the last half-mile; he won the mile, half-mile and quarter-mile in the School Athletics and finished a close second to FR Price in the 100 yards - Price incidentally set a new time for the 100 yards hurdles. But as U'ren picked up more than double the points of Price, his nearest rival, he was comfortably Victor Ludorum.

Henry U'ren

Interestingly enough, this year was also the first that the School had a direct opportunity to measure its athletic prowess against that of another educational establishment as on 30 March the School welcomed the boys from Newton College in an inter-school competition. Events were held as team challenges and although individually three events (out of eight) were won by the School, their aggregate scores only gave them a winning margin in two: the Long Jump, thanks to HJJ Bartholomew and DWS Pettett, and the Half-mile, courtesy of K Stagg, KL Ashfold and HG U'ren, who finished 5th, 4th and 1st respectively.

U'ren's speed also made him a key player on the wing for the hockey team, with Price behind him on the right, nevertheless it was R Periton who was the main light for the firsts. Scoring in most matches, with centre forward and team captain HJ Bartholomew, also netting a few, it was still a frustrating season for the prolific Periton with the School suffering five of its six defeats by a single goal, including a thrilling 5-4 setback at Paignton.

1st XI Hockey, 1932: Back; HG U'ren, HJ Bartholomew, ER Freathy, KB Langdon, HR Lawry. Front; AF Butchers, JR Spear, AJ Giles, R Periton (Capt.) HR Butchers, FR Price.

On the hockey front, incidentally, it was interesting to note that in this season there were a dozen old boys of the School playing for the Belair Hockey Club in Plymouth – was it a coincidence too that there was no OPM Hockey report that season? Well that's not strictly true, there was one hockey reference, to an evening game with the School which OPMs won 2-1.

There was also a game between the School and Belair. At half time the School were losing 1-4 but in a thrilling second half the School pulled back with goals from Periton, HR Lawry, G Noakes and the Captain Bartholomew. It finished up 6-6.

Somewhat less frustrating was the Cricket Season – *"one of the most successful that the School has ever enjoyed"* and on the face of it, thanks mainly to the bowlers rather than the batsmen. U'ren took 35 wickets at an average of ten runs apiece, and Periton a further 31 for 11.8. DJS Stevens and K Stagg were also among the wickets and Periton, U'ren and Stagg all hit scores of 60 plus, Periton averaging 24.

Most matches were won, two of only five defeats (out of sixteen) were at the hands of the OPMs, two others came courtesy of Plymouth Cricket Club and Devon Barbarians. Four Plymouth College boys, including U'ren, were selected to play for Devon Colts, with AJ Giles topping the batting and EI Terrell the bowling.

School Fives was as much a struggle as ever – *"although interest in the game is as great as, if not greater than ever"*. Nineteen pairs entered the Doubles Handicap which was won by FJ Bowden and GHS Giddings, who beat Collins and Lawrey 15-11, 18-14.

Games with the OPMs, the Staff and Kelly (away) were all lost, but somewhat remarkably the home tie with Kelly was won. AF Butcher with JR Spear, and R Periton with HWK Kelly, being the most successful pairs.

It was HWK Kelly's last season, he was off to Christ's College, Cambridge. His valedictory note appeared in the same magazine as that of CR Finken, who was also off to Cambridge, A Burt, off to Oxford, KB Langdon, already at Sandhurst and HR Lawry and JR Spear - whose destinations were not given.

The new Oxbridge undergraduates were welcome additions to the OPM ranks of the old universities – *"our numbers are rapidly decreasing"*, "Cantabrigiensis" had written earlier that year. The Oxford letter meanwhile was a little more upbeat;

"LB Spear is working hard, but finds time to play Hockey for his college", ER Broad was rowing, E Butchers, *"working hard and playing hard, and has earned his Hockey Colours"*, RHH Morley, *"plays Soccer for the 1st XI, but broke his arm early in the term in a league match"*, RB Nicholls was playing rugger and DR Serpell was *"peeved with his Tutor"*.

The main reason the numbers at Cambridge were going down that summer, incidentally, was because most of the existing OPM contingent graduated then;

"Tuesday 21 June, was a red-letter day in the annals of this ancient University, for on that date no less than four OPMs – LG Lingley, BR Jillard, EJ Voss, PW Rundle – were admitted to their degrees in the Senate House ... Our only regrets were, first the inadequacy of the public recognition of the OPM contribution to the dignity of the occasion, and, secondly, the official "black and white" regulations, which even our notorious independence of mind had not the hardihood to flaunt by wearing that latest outrage in club colours, the OPM University tie."

After getting a 1st in Classical "Mays", Voss, we learnt, was *"hinting vaguely at a rest cure in Germany"* and was apparently *"undeterred by the report that an Englishman the other day was roughly handled by a crowd in the streets of Berlin"*.

That summer, however, the situation in Germany showed signs of further escalation and the government there threatened to impose stiff measures to counter street rioting in Berlin. Meanwhile, a group of Hitler's Nazis rioted in a Berlin court after five of their colleagues were convicted of murdering a Communist. Hitler, himself, was under pressure to mount a second putsch (his first in 1923 had landed him in prison) following

Below right 1932 Plymothian cover, note the light coming into the lower corridor from the right. Below Sports Programme.

Above left; South Town Swimming Team 1932: Top row, ML Bartlett, FW Blight, LH Clemas. Third row, RA Williams, SL Heal, TB Penhall. Second row, DT Johnson, HN Clemas, GA Rattray. Front: L Evel, DS Ormsby, AJ Gillman. Above; Comedy cricket; Geoff Spear, Pearn, Leslie Clemas, Mike Chandler and McCaffery.

Above: 1st XV, 1932; Back; DWS Pettett, FE Williams, ED Price, RHM Heriot-Hill, GE Smith, HC Reid. Seated; KL Ashford, R Periton, JS Phillips, HJ Bartholomew (Capt.), HG U'ren, ER Freathy. Front; MLP Bartlett, RJS Rattray. Below: 1st XI Cricket 1932; HR Butchers, HR Lawry, EJ Kelley, JR Spear, SV Collins, RE Lawry. Front; DJS Stevens, HG U'ren, FR Price (Capt.), R Periton, K Stagg.

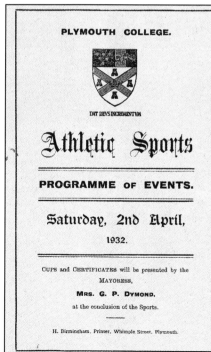

his failure to become Chancellor. The Nazis had just become the biggest party in the Reichstag, but although their 230 seats doubled their previous number, they were still short of a majority in the 608-seat chamber.

Voss, however, opted not to visit the country and that autumn term found him back in Cambridge … *"he knows as much about the Pepys library as most Magdalene (or Cambridge) men".*

Also making national news that year, incidentally, was the new Shakespeare Memorial Theatre, Stratford, which opened on 23 April 1932. Replacing its famous Victorian Gothic predecessor, which was destroyed by fire in 1926, the controversial, new building was designed by *"an unknown woman architect"* - Elizabeth Scott. The whole saga was the subject of a full history of the Shakespeare Memorial Theatre and was part-written by a young OPM fast making a name for himself in literary and theatrical circles – JC Trewin.

Curiously enough, Trewin was responsible for a second reference to Pepys in the Plymothian that year – in *"The Pepys Tradition"*;

"Someone will present me with a diary this Christmas" … *"a Certain Relation regards me as a confirmed keeper of diaries, as a man who cannot sleep peacefully without first making record of the misspent hours. A few diary-addicts, I am aware, go to lengths. Nightly at eleven o'clock, with fountain pens poised, they open crown quarto volumes and set fiendishly to work…"*

"In twelve months' time I shall look at my diary and see a series of blank pages speckled here and there with entries revealing a great depth of character: entries that, when my diary is exhibited in the British Museum in years to come, will thrill readers as much as the journals of Evelyn. This sort of thing: "Jan 10th Wet. Saw B., 5-30. Toast." "Oct 29th. Wet. Gave X.Y. bks".".

"Terse, you notice. Strong and Silent. No verbiage. That is the way to write a diary, but I confess that I grudge the effort. Still while an Aum of Hock remains at thirty gallons, my diary must continue."

Another OPM doing well in the world of words was Wilson Harris, *"until recently Editor of **Headway**, has become Editor of the **Spectator**".*

Wilson Harris was a former editor of the Plymothian and one can but wonder what he thought of its present incarnation, particularly the Christmas edition which always seemed to be the biggest of the year.

Hollywood hearthrobs Clark Gable and Joan Crawford

Trewin supplied a second amusing piece about the correspondence columns of newspapers and magazines. There were various poems, including an ode to the stars of the silver screen, notably Clark Gable and Joan Crawford, and advice on how to write successfully. This latter piece recommended not including your address when you sent off a speculative manuscript, that way you will never suffer that disheartening experience of having your article returned!

On a more informative note, an earlier Plymothian piece that year, by GHS Giddings, explained how *"the pylons are approaching Plymouth".*

Giddings continued; *"Tentacles of wires and towers will soon link up the City with the English Grid System. A Government Committee in 1925 recommended the*

erection of these high voltage transmission lines in order to inter-connect the large power stations of the country; it also suggested the formation of an Electricity Board to supervise the whole scheme."

The article then became rather technical but it was fascinating to learn that the *"shape of the steel towers or pylons was designed with the assistance of Sir Reginald Bloomfield, RA., and they are about 66-ft high."*

However, it was the last paragraph that doubtless generated the most excitement; *"The grid will not give us electricity for nothing, neither will it create a universal utopia. But it will ensure the universal availability of electric power at a reasonable charge."*

A local electric tram promotes domestic electricity.

The City's Electricity Showroom shows off its latest product range

Plymouth College Cricket Festival. Hambledon Club Cricket pays homage to batsman laid up by 'body-line' at Ford Park.

It is difficult now to appreciate the impact that this had back in 1932, but it is interesting to note that one of the School debates that winter was on the proposal that *"Mankind must throw off the bondage of the machine or perish"*. The vote, incidentally, was split and it was left to the new Chairman, Mr Osmund, to give the casting vote. Charles Osmund succeeded Walter Gingell who was retiring after ten years in the chair.

Among other debates the new man chaired was the well-supported notion, or rather motion, *"That the Press exercises a pernicious influence over the people"* and a varied range of Impromptu topics, including;

"Boxing as a sport is not brutal" – agreed, but perhaps not surprisingly as Messrs Price, Lingley and Edwards were partly instrumental in setting up a School Boxing Club that term;

"That crossing the Atlantic in an aeroplane is at present dangerous and unnecessary" – agreed, again not surprisingly, as statistics showed that over 40 RAF airman had been killed in the early part of 1931, nine of them in Plymouth when a flying boat had sunk. The first transatlantic flight by a seaplane however had arrived in Plymouth back in 1919.

"That modern-day dance music was highly spiritual" – agreed.

And finally there was general support for the proposal *"that Armistice Day poppies should be of uniform design and indefinite price"*.

The last motion was also a timely one. Earlier that year the School Scouts had been on a trip to France during which time they had *"walked about 30 kilometres around the Somme Battlefields"*. Then, for the first time since the Great War, there was a piece in the Plymothian written by someone outside of Plymouth College – PHB Lyon, the recently appointed Headmaster of Rugby School - and its subject was Armistice Day 1932;

"Thirteen years ago men and women stood silent on the first anniversary of Armistice Day, their hearts filled with deep personal emotions of pride and sorrow.

It is thus that you, who knew them not in your lives, can honour the memory of those who died for you. The finest tribute you can pay them is to fill that silence, not with vague and formal sentiment, but with a determination with God's help to carry on their work."

"They died for freedom, for justice, for their country's good; for these ideals you must live. They were forced to strive for them in war, though many knew what all men know today, that war can never bring them. For war tramples on freedom and ignores justice; and war is fatal to the good of all countries alike, combatant and non-combatant, victor and vanquished. War is futile and destructive; whereas peace is full of vigour and purpose, the essential condition of human progress."

"But if you would preserve peace and make it a secure and certain thing, then you must show the same courage and constancy, with which your fathers withstood the assaults of the foe, in the longer and yet more desperate struggle against the common enemies of mankind."

"For peace is not secure: everywhere fear, suspicion, selfishness and misunderstanding lead men and nations astray."

Lyon then went on to discuss the importance of the League of Nations; *"If the League is to be powerful enough to save civilisation in the coming years it needs the strength and vigorous support of every nation like our own, with her noble traditions of leadership and high principal."*

"... In the two minutes of silence, look not backward only to those who made that noble sacrifice, but forward to their ultimate reward, to a world where their descendants enjoy all that they died to secure. And then determine to unite all your qualities of mind and will in that noblest patriotism, which seeks for our country a glory based not on world-domination, but on world-service, and the enduring gratitude and affection of those she has helped to lead out of darkness into light."

It is a timeless text, but one that was undoubtedly prompted by Hitler's drive towards National Socialism and the more frightening targets he had in his sights beyond those domestic goals. Small wonder that an earlier Impromptu Debate had decided in favour of making OTC membership compulsory, or that the Duke of York's 1932 "Camp" was also such a great success. *"Certainly a "Camp" in the accepted sense, being housed under canvas, but apart from this, camp-life was non-existent. Every luxury and convenience was provided, such as electric light, water laid on, etc., and staff of servants to supply every want."*

The 1932 War Office Camp at Tidworth Park was also enjoyed by those who attended, although, *"unluckily the period of the camp coincided with a spell of bad weather"*. Small comfort for the seven cadets who were debarred from attending because they *"had been in contact with a case of chicken pox"*.

HJ Bartholomew was then Company Sergeant Major, the senior boy in the OTC, he was also Head of School and House Captain of East Town.

1932 had been a bad year for East Town – they lost the Athletic Sports Shield, having held it for the last nine years - but it was no great surprise as there were only fifty boys in the House. They had also had to scratch from the Rugger as there were only half-a-dozen seniors in the House who could play the game.

South Town Athletics Champs - 1932 - H U'ren, Captain.

"South Town Cock House 1933. Taken on Saturday January 14 1933" is the handwritten legend on the back of this historic photograph. South Town were winners of the Cock House Cup (left) the Athletics Shield (centre) and the Swimming Cup (right). Eric Holman (seated behind the shield, was the South Town Housemaster, however, within a few months the old house system would be scrapped and a new system put in its place. Furthermore, within a year or two this view would cease to feature in such photographs as this door on the north side of main school would become, instead, the door to the new school gymnasium.
Front row in seats: Williams, Bridge, Guest, Reid, Clemas (Captain of Swimming), Phillips (School Secretary of Rugger and House Captain), Mr Holman (Housemaster), U'ren (School Captain of Cricket, Athletics and Rugger), anon, Freathy, Burt, Noakes, Chandler

College House was, then, in a similar position and North Town was not much better off. On this basis the inter-house competitions had little real credibility and although the proposal was out-voted the idea of an inter-house Yo-Yo competition was doubtless, in part, symptomatic of the rather silly state of affairs. It was a situation that prompted all the House Captains to give their support to an open letter to the Plymothian calling for a reform of the School house-system.

"If new boys were allotted to Houses in numbers proportionate to their respective numerical inferiorities and without regard to residential qualifications, comparative equality would be gained, because in addition to the influx of new boys, a certain number of seniors leave at the end of each term. It may be pointed out that the scheme does not interfere in any way with the present constitution of the Houses."

There followed an interesting final paragraph;

"Before this letter is read it may be that such a scheme will have been put into force; in that case our letter will serve as a witness of the unanimous support which we, as representatives of every House, wish to accord it."

South Town Inter-House Rugby Champs: Back; NA Burt, J Guest, LH Clemas, ML Bartlett, FE Williams. Seated; K Ashfold, ER Freathy, HG U'ren, JS Phillips, HC Reid. Front; G Irish, R Rattray.

But as of December 1932, no such scheme had been put into force. However, with some 350 boys in the main school the idea of having only 50 or so lads in each of two of the four houses was clearly not sensible and thus it was that with effect from the beginning of the Summer term an alteration was made to the House system.

Palmer's House (formerly South Town) Swimming Team - Summer 1933. Standing; D Braddon, R Hutchinson, LH Clemas, PS Anderson, AW Street, RA Williams, IR Ife, SL Heal. Seated; FW Blight, HN Clemas (Captain), GA Rattray and DT Johnston.

Henceforth, House membership would no longer depend on residential qualifications and new boys would be distributed evenly between the Houses. To mark the change it was decided to move away from the old names, with the notable exception of College House. Thus North Town became Thompson's (after the original master of that House), South Town became Palmer's (again after the long-serving second master, who had come down the hill from Mannamead School) and East Town was named after the master who had been running it successfully for so many years – Bert Sargent.

Recently-elected (December 1932) President of the OPM Club, sixty-two year-old Herbert Sargent had been at the School for thirty years and was an enormous influence on generations of Plymouth College boys, perhaps none more so than the first ever Captain of the newly-constituted Sargent's House – John Spear.

The announcement of his successful matriculation was in the Easter Magazine and he was back for the Summer term, newly appointed Prefect and Assistant Scout Master to the School Troop – it was the first time a member of the Troop had attained a commissioned rank.

It was to be a good year for the young Spear, scoring a fine unbeaten 51 in his first cricket match of the season, against Plymstock, and once again starring in the Water Polo team and aquatic sports. But we are leaping forwards again, there was the Easter term to negotiate first and it got off to an ominously bad start.

On 30 January 1933, just a few weeks after his fiftieth birthday and after a very short illness, the Senior Science Master, Charles Osmund, died from an acute attack of pneumonia. Osmund had joined the School back in 1920 and was one of only two of Dale's first generation of appointments still on the staff.

"As a Schoolmaster he insisted on the value of the primary virtues of thoroughness, method and accuracy, and in his relations with boys and staff he displayed a corresponding sincerity of purpose and contempt – which he never hesitated to express – for anything that savoured of affectation and superficiality. He was a man of strong and clearly defined opinions and, if he did not always suffer fools gladly, he had a very generous tolerance of the mistakes of youth and inexperience and was as just in his award of praise as of blame. His fairness and candour earned him the respect of pupils and colleagues alike."

Osmund, a churchwarden of All Saint's Church (Sparkwell?), was buried on the edge of his beloved Dartmoor;

"He knew it and loved it as perhaps few have done who have known it longer."

His loss was a great blow to the School, but there was an even greater shock to follow as, just a few months later, the only other surviving Dale appointment, Walter Gingell, also took early leave of this mortal coil.

Though he hadn't been in the best of health the previous term *"it was little thought that there was anything radically wrong"* and his death, on 2 May, came after only two days illness.

Walter Gingell was only forty-four and *"in his passing the School has lost a keen and capable Games Master. Able to play most games himself – he had played for the Cambridge Seniors in Association and won his College Colours for Cricket and Tennis – he possessed a genius for the financial and administrative side of School Games. He was ever anxious to improve the conditions under which games were played and it is largely due to his thought and effort that the School is so efficiently equipped in this respect".*

"A member of the Devon County Cricket Club, he worked hard for Schools Cricket, and the Junior Cricket of Plymouth and District has much for which to thank him."

"His teaching work dealt with Junior Forms and Middle School Mathematics and there are many who will always remember the quiet hours spent in Hut B."

One of the closest buildings to the back of the relatively newly built Barton Building (1930), Cecil Atkey recalls being flogged by Gingell *"for putting my watch right by the Barton midday hooter"*. By one of those strange quirks of fate Hut B, itself, wasn't much longer for this world either. The site for a new building which was to replace the old huts had already been cleared and, just three weeks after Gingell's sad demise, the Foundation Stone for the new extension was laid.

The ceremony was performed by the Bishop of Plymouth on Friday 26 May, *"which was also this term's Parent's Evening"*.

The ceremony began a little earlier, at 3.30pm, when the Bishop, the Right Rev. John Masterman, *"accompanied by the Mayor and Mayoress of Plymouth and the Governors of the College, was received by a guard of honour formed by the OTC. The architect, Mr M Alton Bazeley, presented the Bishop with a silver trowel, and the Bishop's Chaplain conducted a brief dedicatory service. In his address the Bishop maintained that the School Buildings represent the continuity of the life of the School, and that the Foundation Stone is a symbol of that continuity"*.

Set in stone - a start to the new gym 26 May 1933. M Alton Bazeley presents the Right Reverend John Masterman with a silver trowel.

"Pupils and staff change", he said, *"and even Governors have not been given immortality: the Building, however is our legacy to the generations that follow."*

He then added, *"It is true that we may not be able to boast a very long past, but that need not forbid the anticipation of a great and glorious future."*

Replying, Chairman of the Governors, JP Brown, noted that *"there are some who regret that architectural difficulties prevent the completion of the original design – but the new extension will be more convenient and practicable."*

Maybe fifty-three years was not considered to be a very long time, but it is, perhaps, nevertheless remarkable that there were those still harbouring hopes of fulfilling the original 1880 plans, although clearly the new-erected Science Labs made the prospect of a Chapel on that western site, a complete non-starter. There was also the question of finance; the School Architect had been charged with the task of providing at least three new classrooms, a gymnasium, large enough to include dressing rooms and a permanent stage, plus a larger assembly hall. Bazeley's solution to the problem made the most of the existing structure - after all why construct new classrooms **and** new corridors when you could simply adapt the downstairs doors and create new openings off the existing corridor upstairs? By constructing the new classrooms, off the northern wall of the school, considerable savings could be made and Big School could also be enlarged.

The eastern wall had, up until now, never been finished and pending future developments there had, so far, been no staircase at the eastern end of the main school building. Now there was a chance to redesign that end internally and externally thanks to *"the fiat lux of Bishop Masterman who induced the architect to break with windows a stretch of otherwise blank wall"*.

Sadly, however, the Bishop's own light was to go out before the building work was completed, for, after battling many weeks with pleurisy and pneumonia, the man who had been Vice-Chairman of the Governing Body, died, on 25 November 1933.

Prior to his suggested improvements the School's eastern wall had been left a rough, slate-hung, ragged-edged affair, and one that was conspicuously avoided in picture postcards of the place. Henceforth it would present an altogether more pleasing aspect, far more satisfactory for the new head who made no bones about his own feelings at the ceremony.

"When I first visited the School, some four years ago there were three things that made a vivid impression on me; the first was the beauty of the playing field (and at this point he thanked the School Groundsman – Heywood – for his efforts); *the second was the*

handsome and imposing front of the School Building and the third, unfortunately, was a less favourable impression."

The infamous old huts and the gymnasium

"The "Huts" and the Gymnasium," he said "stood in painful contrast to the rest of the School and I felt that there was always the danger that this would be reflected in the work of those that occupied them. I am therefore sure that I am justified in predicting that a nobler building will prove a setting for nobler ideas."

"You can now see," he concluded, "the promise of that very thing on which I had set my heart when I first became Headmaster, namely the substitution for a virtual eyesore of permanent quarters that will possess both dignity and capacity."

The School's east end prior to 1934

The ceremony over, boys and visitors began to disperse. Some headed for tea in the Marquee, others went for a look around the School Buildings and all the while the Band of the Royal Marines played a selection of pieces on the field. Later in the afternoon IVa performed in the old Gymnasium and the OTC "gave a plausible exhibition of field tactics".

And so began the building work, work that was intriguingly, and anonymously, described later in that term's Plymothian, in a Pepys-style piece headed "Journal".

"This day on certaine businesses of work to Plymouth, which I had great mind to see, having never been there, and found it very pretty and people of good fashion in it, albeit seeming slow of wit against a Londoner."

Our writer then went on to complain about the "devilish noise of the trolley-cars" and to praise the pleasing streets and great public buildings;

"The people I hear, do have a pretty new conceit on their water-front, and do grow mightily proud of the place, with frolics in the waters by torch-light" – this was a reference to the Hoe Lido which the Corporation had just built to help the City in its bid to become the tourism capital of the South West. Our scribe then turned his attention to Ford Park.

The City's newest attraction - Tinside Lido

"Took coach, by and by, to the north of the town where I do presently spy a handsome building, and at pains to discover its use, which I did at first foolishly misinterpret, by reason of a fearsome great cannon at the entering thereof, but later did plainly perceive to be a school. And so did wonder at the purpose of the labour being carried on, and was long in dispute with myself whether it was to destroy the old building or raise a new one, and so fell a-talking with a scholar, that pleased me exceedingly, being strangely grave and manly, albeit with a curious affectation in his neckerchief. He in no wise loath to inform a stranger, and do tell me that this process be indeed a new building to succeed less comely accommodation, part of which I avow to have already conceived to be a barn or some such storage."

"Thereupon I did remark a kind of great engine for the lifting of the stones within the very walls that were being builded about it, and all of a sudden felt to be wondering how this engine was to be removed outside, when the building done, and for diversion did put it to the boy to test him, and he returned that it was purposed to retain it within, that it might do much to bring out the natural climbing ability inherent in certaine of their persons ..."

Clearly this building work on the old quad excited plenty of interest among the boys and the staff, so too did that "fearsome great cannon".

"As the quadrangle buds and blossoms beneath our eyes, we begin to have hopes that the new building will not disgrace the old. It is early yet to comment, so let us look elsewhere for the subject of the Editorial. We need not look far – just around the corner."

Thus began the Summer Term Plymothian editorial. It continued;

"Imagine our friend the Iglug of Bathoo being shown over the school premises; his English is almost perfect, and as he approaches the front door, the following exchange takes place."

"Ig of Bath.: "This edifice is not beseiged?"

222

We: "That is our howitzer. We won it in the war you know."
I.o.B. : "But the war – is it not over?"
We : "Why yes. Yes, of course."
I.o.B. : "I think I guess. It is a piece by Upstein – perhaps an old boy?"
We : "Upstein? Oh, Epstein! No, it's just the Gun."
I.o.B. : "It is not Epstein? Then you keep it as being beautiful?"
We (doing our best): "Well, it's set in a concrete base whose strength and simplicity is fully in keeping with the spirit of modern art."
I.o.B. : "Oh."

Then came the "but-seriously-though" bit; "Surely the gun need squat no longer before the School. Admitted, it symbolizes fittingly the ugliness and stupidity of war, but we think the Spirit of Peace disdains such propaganda. Besides, its presence is liable to misinterpretation, for one might well think that the proud spirit of militant nationalism was still abroad."

And indeed of course it was, with Sir Oswald Mosley stirring his followers and fellow-Fascist sympathisers into action - despite being stoned by crowds at meetings.

Meanwhile the Plymothian editors were respectfully suggesting that "this relic of the Great Holocaust should be replaced by something more representative of a time which aims at reconstruction."

In this they were echoing the highly-publicised sentiments of Oxford students as expressed in the previous term's Oxford Letter; "The one thing your readers will scarcely wish to be told more about is surely Oxford's attitude towards Pacifism. But the Pacifist debate at the Union, and the subsequent leaders and letters in the imperial-minded press, the delivery of parcels of white feathers, the invasion of the Union by patriotic Life Members – all these have provided the only excitement of the term: unless, that is, the Great Frost and the Great Thaw count as excitements."

The annual Inter-schools Visitor's Debate that term also confronted the peace problem; the proposal here though was that "Disarmament is not the path to Peace." Representatives from seven local schools were present – Plymouth High School, Devonport Secondary, Stoke Damerel, St Dunstan's Abbey, Corporation Grammar, Sutton Secondary and Devonport High – and while both sides were alike in considering World Peace desirable, the majority felt that peace would only be obtained by means of an international police force and further that disarmament "useless by itself, must be the outcome of a change of heart which had not yet taken place".

However, although not everyone shared the leanings of the Oxford students, the Plymothian editors did - so too, to a certain extent, did the Headmaster.

The howitzer was removed soon after the Plymothian plea appeared. "There is no question," said Mr Ralph, "that the terrace is better graced by a flagstaff".

The Big Gun moves on.

The Head was speaking at the OPM Annual Dinner in the Royal Hotel in February 1934. There he informed the assembled party of around 40 Old Boys that the gun had been sold for 30s (£1.50p) and that the money had gone to Earl Haig's Fund.

"There are people," he said, "who feel that its removal is a slight to the memory of those men in whose honour the War Office gave it to us. Nothing, of course, is further from the truth. The School War Memorial is in Big School, and we honour it every year."

Addressing the peace issue Mr Ralph then asserted that "membership of the League of Nations is quite compatible with membership of the OTC".

"Peace is one of Britain's greatest interests. We have been fighting for it for centuries and now we must struggle to maintain it. The League of Nations, " he said, "must at all costs be preserved as a barrier against war." However, he then added, "Until the League is more active in enforcing the principals of collective responsibility, it will continue to lose prestige and fail to discharge its function."

"Britain must struggle to preserve peace. Unless we maintain our Navy, our Army, and Air Force at a sufficient standard we will no longer be in a position to discharge our obligations." To which he added, "Where then are we to find Officers but in the training corps of the Public Schools?"

While the pacifist line was manifestly popular with the nation's young idealists, anxious to avoid the horrors of another holocaust, the reality of the international situation was an increasingly gloomy one. Just four months before that Annual Dinner, Hitler had effectively pulled the plug on the Geneva Disarmament Conference, saying that Germany would take no further part in the talks because of the "humiliating and dishonouring demands of the other powers."

"The German people", he said, "and their government are deeply humiliated by the deliberate refusal of a real, moral and actual equality to Germany."

Clearly all the pacifist talk was being carried out against a backdrop of intense activity in Germany. Jews were being persecuted, opposition parties banned and plans were announced by Hitler's Cabinet to have all "imperfect" Germans sterilised. Neither was it only in Germany that the Militarist spirit prevailed.

In the summer of 1934, in Italy, Mussolini watched the Italian football team give the Fascist salute before beating Czechoslovakia 2-1 in Rome in what was only the second-ever World Cup Final. There was a military-backed Dictator in Austria - a country that was about to sign a co-operation pact with Hungary and Italy. By this time, too, Mussolini was urging German rearmament.

Small wonder, therefore, that there was talk of peace on the one hand at School and reports of the *"greatest number of recruits for several years"* joining the OTC on the other.

OTC Cadets set off for Tidworth

Twenty-eight boys joined the OTC at the start of the 1933-34 academic year and a similar number of cadets, at 30/- (£1.50p) a head, attended the Annual Camp at Tidworth Park in the summer of 1933;

"Our only complaint – a most unusual one – was the excessive heat. Much valuable training was carried out, while nearly all the Cadets paid a visit to the Southern Command Tattoo."

There were two other camps of note that summer for the School. The first Duke of York's at Southwold was another unqualified success;

"The Duke himself spent an informal twenty-four hours in Camp, taking part in all the bathing activities of the Camp and even sharing our biscuits, after bathing, on the beach. Among our visitors were Lord Clydesdale, who lectured on the aerial conquest of Mt Everest, showing some very interesting lantern slides and films, and Lord Burghley."

The Scouts, meanwhile, had their Camp at Saunton, North Devon;

"The efficiency of the camp was of a high standard, in spite of the fact that the SM was absent for the last few days through illness."

Happily, however, illness itself appears to have been less of an issue in the School in the thirties than in previous decades although Eric Holman missed some teaching time in the early part of 1933. More dramatic, though, were the sudden and unexpected deaths of Osmund and Gingell, which, in turn, precipitated a series of appointments that were to have an enormous long-term impact on the School - although no-one could possibly have anticipated just how significant that impact was to be.

With two new appointments already required, Ralph was forced into looking for a third, following John Price's early return to his native country. Although the newest and the youngest staff member, Price had made an indelible impression on the boys and on his colleagues;

"Whatever he has touched he has infused with new energy, and this has been as true of his class teaching as of his work on the field. He has thrown himself with characteristic enthusiasm into every department of our corporate life, and the School will not quickly forget his vigorous and unselfish service."

Thus the scale of Ralph's problem was raised another notch. The first new master to arrive that summer was twenty-five-year-old Bill Batrick, with a Phd from London newly-tucked into the athletic waistband of his trousers.

Batrick arrived to take charge of Osmund's Science students. Meantime Alfred Blatchford was temporarily appointed to take care of Mr Gingell's classes. However, Ralph had in mind making not two new appointments to cover Osmund and Gingell's classes, but a minimum of three, on the grounds that the School was now intolerably short-staffed.

Battrck joins the staff

In a letter to the Education Board in October 1933, Ralph spelt out his case, freely quoting the Inspection Report produced soon after his arrival in 1930.

This included the boys-per-master ratio which was then the *"unusually high figure of 22"*. Three years on *"the proportion is exactly 26 boys to one Master, there being 364 boys in the Main School as compared with 322 in October 1930, and 54 boys in the Sixth Form, as against 38 in that year."* All this meant that masters had fewer free periods than ever and that they were working at full stretch. Three years earlier the Inspectors had said, *"Some addition to the staff would be justified and indeed desirable"*, now, argued Ralph, *"the need for another assistant master cannot be disputed."*

Ralph had put his feelings about the staffing on the back burner for three years simply because of the *"equally urgent need of new buildings"*. Now that *"perhaps more pressing needs had been met,"* he wanted to tackle his other primary concern.

Indeed, given that *"the Assistant Staff numbered, as today, 14, when in 1921 the last General Inspection was held, and there were only 267 boys in the School"*, then Ralph's case, that there were now almost 100 more boys in the School was virtually impossible to contest. One can only wonder at his patience in not pressing his case sooner.

THE ANNUAL DINNER

WILL BE HELD AT

THE ROYAL HOTEL, PLYMOUTH,

ON

Saturday, 18th March, 1933, at 7-30 p.m.

The President (H. Sargent, Esq.) in the Chair.

TICKETS 6/-

R.S.V.P. to:
A. GOLDBERG,
Westwell Park Chambers, Westwell Street,
Plymouth.

The photograph of the "Plymouth Supper-Dance appeared in the Evening Herald with the caption - Some of the 200 dancers who attended the OPM's dance at the Royal Hotel Assembly Rooms." The picture was taken from the Gallery.

Below right part of the Tidworth contingent - that same summer, and right, the camp itself.

Above: South Town Snr Hockey, 1933; Back; RJS Rattray, LH Clemas, G Budge, SL Heal, IR Ife. Front; NA Burt, HG U'ren, ER Freathy (Capt) EG Noakes and FE Williams. Below: South Town Rugby XV captained by Henry U'ren.

Clearly the task of getting the new building work under way with no clerical assistance, had taken most of his, almost non-existent, free time.

By October 1933 the new buildings were well under way, but the task of appointing three new members of staff had also been a time consuming process and it all meant that Ralph had found it, *"impossible to see any of the work of my staff – either in the Main School or in the Prep"*.

"I should like therefore to engage, at the earliest opportunity, the full-time services of an additional assistant master, to take over the teaching of English in the Sixth Form and two of the junior forms, together with some Elementary Latin and History. For English and French the Modern Sixth would be taken apart from the members of the two Advanced Course, and by a recasting of the present time-table I should be able to give some relief to three of my present staff as well as to myself."

He then concluded his missive with;

"It is perhaps not irrelevant to point out that two of the present staff (both of whom are at their maximum salary) are due to retire, one in 1934, the other in 1935, and that their retirement will result in a very considerable reduction of the salary bill."

Of course, Osmund and Gingell would have been on higher salaries than their young replacements and consequently some saving would already have been made. Ralph's request was not, therefore, likely to go unheeded.

In the event there were to be a number of changes. Following Bill Batrick that summer Cyril (Charlie) Barnes and Ted Mercer arrived to replace Price and Gingell respectively. Both men were just 23 years old and not long out of College. Then came the welcome additional English master, WGM Jones – Meyricke "Jumbo" Jones - in the first term of 1934. Jones was just a few months older than Mercer and was six months younger than George Bonser, who arrived later

that year to replace the retiring Bert Sargent. Lingley's retirement in 1935 prompted another new face in the English department – another fresh face too, in the form of 23 year-old Hugh Dent. There was to be one other change that year too as William McDonald Porter, an old hand of 28 arrived to take the place of Ralph Dawes.

New faces - young faces Cyril Barnes, Edward Mercer, Meyricke Jones and George Bonser arrive at Ford Park

Thus it was that in just over two years the entire character of the Common Room was changed. When

Ralph arrived as Headmaster the average age of the assistant master was over 41, by the end of 1935 there was only one member of staff over 42; the Reverend Benskin and he was to be the next to move on, in 1937. But for him the average age of the staff in 1935 was just 32, with 42 year-old John Dufton the most senior member of staff, the only one who had served under anyone other than Dale and Ralph.

For all the sudden changes, between 1933 and 1935, only those with a very powerful crystal ball would have been able to predict that the seven young men appointed in that time would go on to spend the best part of forty years together as teachers at the School. Notwithstanding the Second World War it would not be until ill-health forced Hugh Dent to retire in 1966 that this particular seven-a-side team would lose a player, the others all retiring in the 1970s.

Back in 1935, however, the new ideas, the enthusiasm and the energy they brought with them was invaluable to Herbert Ralph and to the School. With the official opening of the new buildings in January 1934 there was an air of a new era dawning for Plymouth College.

It was, doubtless, a sensation that 75 year-old former-head Francis Colson was more than familiar with – the main school building was still relatively new when he arrived back in 1889 and the merger with Mannamead was still some years off. What were his thoughts that Friday in January when the Lord Mayor, E Stanley Leatherby, deputised for Colson's old acquaintance, Sir Arthur Quiller-Couch, to perform the opening ceremony? We can but wonder what they all thought as the smell of new wood of the gymnasium floor, the stage, the wall-bars and the desks in the new rooms - nine, ten and eleven - greeted the investigative noses of the visiting dignitaries. Conspicuous among the absentees that day, along with the *"suddenly indisposed"* "Q", was the Chairman of Governors, MR JP Brown, who had so recently contributed the handsome new gates for the School.

1933

It would be hard to overestimate the impact of the changes that took place at Ford Park around 1934. Death, departure and expansion brought a host of new, fresh faces into the erstwhile ageing staffroom, meanwhile just six years after the creation of the new science labs, the second biggest building programme since the School's foundation not only brought new light into old corridors and classrooms, it also created new classrooms, an expanded Big School and a state of the art gymnasium with a bonus theatre facility.

PLYMOTHIAN   EASTER, 1934

Mr WL Munday deputised for him that day while the longstanding Clerk to the Governors, Charles Serpell read the address that Sir Arthur *"long a friend to and a Governor of the School"* was to have delivered.

Among those already with an eye on the new facilities were the members of the newly constituted School Boxing Club – for some of course it would come too late and before the old gym was finished it was to stage a competition open to the whole School across eight "weights". Messrs. Lingley and Price put up medals for the competition and judged the fights. RHM Heriot-Hill was the Open Champ while the other titles were awarded as follows;

Heavy Weight - HJ Bartholomew, Middle Weight – NA Burt, Welter Weight CE Otway, Light Weight – HR Butchers, Bantam Weight – BA Morgan, Feather Weight – D Culliford and Fly Weight – J Butland.

Teacher John Price was also active on the Rugby field. His coaching and general help, along with that of Ian Edwards, was much appreciated by the boys, notably the Heavy Weight Champ, HJ Bartholomew, who was also Captain of the 1st XV. The rugger season was a comparatively happy one for the firsts as they won nine and only lost five. Among those five defeats came two at the hands of an invigorated OPM side and one to the Erebus, *"which is now unfortunately gone, terminating many enjoyable games there"*.

Newton, Kelly and Dartmouth were all well beaten, the biggest disappointment perhaps being the 6-11 setback against Wellington. Heriot-Hill and HR Butchers, *"although handicapped by his size"* played full back rather well, as did U'ren, Phillips, Ashfold, Freathy and Periton. Conspicuous by his absence that term was JR Spear, but he was back in the Easter Term to play for the Hockey team. Happily their two encounters with the OPMs resulted in wins for the School. In a season where the team scored freely only one game saw them score less than three goals (a 1-1 draw with Dartmouth College), nevertheless they only won five

of their ten games. Their most crushing success came at the expense of Newton College, who went down 8-1, team captain Periton finding the back of the net five times. Spear, U'ren and Noakes were all awarded their colours.

Periton also scored quite freely in the cricket that summer too, knocking up over 300 runs and hauling in some 30 wickets, HG U'ren was the true star, though with over 500 runs at an average of 30 and bagging over 50 wickets at an average of 9.9. Small wonder that both were selected to play for Devon Colts that season.

RE Lawry got as far as the trials, and along with K Stagg, SV Collins and DJS Stevens, picked up his School Colours for the season. With a larger sixth form than in previous years there was seldom any call for staff members to play in the side, although Pro Heywood made a number of appearances. The School was also able to field not just a Second XI but also a Third team, who managed six fixtures including one notable contest away to Sutton 2nd XI. Thanks to Hurcomb's splendid return of 8 wickets for 8 runs, Sutton were dismissed for 18. Sadly, however, the School only managed 17 in reply. It was one of only two games the 3rds lost, the other being at the hands of St Boniface firsts who won by two runs, Hurcomb this time taking 5 for 16. Among the other notable scorelines was the dismissal of the entire Plympton Grammar 2nd XI for just 12 runs.

In the Water Polo, that summer, the team played six games and won all but one; 2-1 against *"the heavier and older"* Devonport RSA 'A' Team at Mount Wise. It was the first time the School had lost at this sport since 1930 – however, it was also the first time they had had a match with a swimming club's A team. Once again JR Spear scored in every game, but this time he was out-scored by team-mate FS Blight.

At the School Aquatic Sports both boys set new records; JR Spear in the 440 yards open and the 100 yards open, FS Blight in the 50 yards open. JRS once again

finished Victor Ludorum, just ahead of Blight. It was a good year for the School swimmers, though, as Blight, Spear and Rattray all played for Plymouth Amateurs' winning team in the final of the Devon County Junior Water Polo Championships.

Plymouth and Maanamead College Water Polo Team 1933. Standing; TB Penhall, LH Clemas, RF Tuckett. Seated; FW Blight, DWS Pettett (Capt.), JR Spear and GAS Rattray.

"Blight has also brought distinction to the School in outside events by gaining second place in two "long distance" swims. The Breakwater – Plymouth Pier and the Saltash – Plymouth Pier, the latter being open to Devon and Cornwall."

Despite John Spear's impressive points tally, the School Aquatic Sports were won by Palmers. His house, Sargents, finishing a clear, but not close, second. The Athletic Sports held a few months earlier, were, curiously enough, still run under the old house names and South Town were clear winners, HG U'ren's impressive haul of 80 points, helping his house enormously and giving him Victor Ludorum by a massive margin.

1933 Rugby, Cricket and Hockey Teams:
Above 1st XV; A Edmunds, K Stagg, JM Tyrrell, NA Burt, MLP Bartlett, FW Blight, G Irish. Front; RJS Rattray, ER Freathy, R Periton, HG U'ren (Captain), JR Spear, HC Reid, ED Price.

Left:Hockey 1st XI; Back; GE Smith, NA Burt, ED Price, DW Gay, FE Williams, SV Collins. Front; HG U'ren, ER Freathy, R Periton (Captain), JR Spear, EG Noakes.

Right: Cricket 1st XI; NT Jenkins, MT Parker, JM Tyrell, RE Lawry, JR Spear, D Castle. Front; DJ Stevens, R Periton, HG U'ren (Capt.), K Stagg, SV Collins.

U'ren won five events; the mile, in which he was just ten seconds off the School record; the half-mile where he was less than a second off the record; the quarter mile, where he set a new record; the one hundred yards, in a time equalling the record and the long jump, where he posted the best distance for twelve years. DW Pettett won the high jump and hurdles and was second to JR Spear in putting the weight.

South Town Athletics Champs 1933: Back; W Petherick, IR Ife, REV Johns, M Laver, G Trethewy, PH Hawke. Front; G Budge, ER Freathy, HG U'ren (Victor Ludorum), HLP Bartlett (Junior. Victor), JS Phillips.

The summer of 1933 also witnessed the staging of a major in-School tennis competition. Twenty-six couples took part and the final was won in straight sets (8-6, 6-3) by RE Lawry and K Platt. BN Nelson and CJ Woodrow, were the beaten finalists and HN Clemas, in his end of season notes, commented that *"a permanent court would be welcomed"*.

On the subject of courts, there was no news of any great Fives activity that summer but there was an interesting passage in the Games Master's report for the year;

"From information received it appears that the civic authorities have not made up their minds about the widening of Hyde Park Road so that a thorough restoration of the Fives Courts is unwise, but air-pockets will be re-cast and the walls re-dressed." He also noted, incidentally that *"the cricket square has*

been nourished with chemicals" and that the *"buttercups and plantain roots"* were about to be attacked on the traditionally much-maligned School Field.

"There was an old iron railing across the top of the Field", recalled *"the General"*, in a tongue-in-cheek piece in the Christmas Plymothian. It was written by old boy, and former magazine editor, David Serpell, and the *"reminiscences"* make interesting reading;

"Only prefects were allowed to jump over it (the railing) ... the rest had to go round by the path at the side. I'll wager that it'll still be there, and small boys will still be creepin' through it, on the pretence that they hadn't jumped over it."

"Being a prefect really meant something, and I remember as a small boy wonderin' what it felt like to march up and get my cap from the Head."

"Then there were the school occasions, like Speech Day, though I'm not sure that the best fun wasn't at the smaller ones, like the Concert or the Staff Dramatic Society's show. A small boy only begins to understand his form-master when he has seen him missin' his cue as an Irish beggar or a Scottish I-don't-know-what. Now I come to think of it, bless my soul, it was almost a tradition that the Staff should act in some outlandish dialect or other, I don't know why. Maybe they thought they wouldn't be recognised."

Certainly the Staff Dramatic Society seems to have faded with Dale's departure, which is not to say that the Staff didn't still appear on stage from time to time, but that those appearances were by no means as regular as they had been in the twenties.

Another tradition seemingly lost to time was also recalled by the *"General"*;

"I remember too how on Speech Days the distinguished visitor would ask for a holiday, though we used to have an anxious time waiting for him to stand up and ask for it ... An' we used to have a holiday too if we won all our school matches: now that was a tradition worth havin'."

Clearly the Ralph era was marked by a number of changes, some more subtle than others, but they were only to be expected as the proverbial new broom brought sweeping changes to both fabric and the personnel of the School.

That they were changes for the better could hardly be doubted; *"A military hut, Is an ugly cocoon, For the boy butterflies, Who start a mental life, Therein"*

Wrote "Boy B" at the end of a piece, *"Even So"* in the Christmas 1933 Plymothian, a fitting epitaph perhaps for the three old huts that had, at long last, been rendered redundant.

There were a number of fine pieces in that edition of the magazine; among them a poignant piece on Princetown – *"Granite Fair"* by AGG and N's *"News Item"* on hypnotism helping patients cut down their weight.

We also learnt that the Sports Pavilion was to be given an overhaul – *"the addition will consist of two features – a top room for team teas and lunches faced with a balcony and some architectural embellishments to render the front attractive ... a clock has been promised"*.

Loans and donations were being sought – *"the estimated cost is £400" ... "Because there are days of financial stress, though those competent to judge say there's plenty of money about, it is suggested to extend subscriptions during the period of next year. Quite a number will be willing to offer 6d., 1/-, or 1/6d (2p-7p) a month, some others may be willing to offer a fiver in instalments."*

Certainly, with an ever-increasing sixth-form, the potential for games at the School was looking better all the time and it was no great surprise to find a 4th XV being fielded that winter; something that would have been inconceivable just a few years earlier.

Something else that will, perhaps, seem almost inconceivable for anyone familiar with certain members of staff in their later years was the 1st XV match that winter against the Worcester Regiment.

The Big Gun appears for the last time on a School photo and daylight is still clearly visible on the other side of the Main School entrance foyer as staff and pupils line up for the 1933 panorama.

The School won the game 35 – 3 and among those who got themselves on the score-sheet that afternoon in November 1933, were Bill Battrick (2 tries), Ted Mercer (one conversion) and John Spear (2 tries), who was then playing as a schoolboy. A future Chairman of Governors and Lord Mayor of Plymouth, George Creber and another master, Charlie Barnes, were also members of the team.

It wasn't just the Main School that was enjoying an influx of young blood, the Prep was too, Miss V Dinsmore joining that same term as Messrs. Barnes and Mercer. The following term the three of them appeared, with various other members of staff, in the first-ever production, on the new stage, in the New Gymnasium. The play chosen for this auspicious production was Oscar Wilde's *"The Importance of Being Earnest"*. Mr Woodcock produced and Messrs, Davies, Dufton and Lord completed the list of male players, while Mrs Dawes and Woodcock and the Misses Lawrey and Dinsmore provided the female interest.

"Whether it was the effect of the new lighting and stage-equipment, or the knowledge that what they were doing they were doing in the cause of art and charity, it is hard to say, but each of them helped to make the first play in the New Gymnasium a memorable one."

"... Mr Mercer – who seemed perfectly at home holding an oval tray – and Mr Dufton – who supplied an unbelievable amount of pleasure by the way he creaked on and off in the second act – represented faithfully two types of servant .."

This was not the first time the New Gym had been requisitioned for extra-curricular activities, for just eight days after it was officially declared open, it played host to a School Dance, the proceeds of which were devoted to the League of Pity, who also benefited from the Staff Play. A subsequent dance was held to raise monies for the Pavilion Extension Fund.

The previous year's League of Pity effort, staged in the old gym, which included a *"very creditable dramatic representation of the story of Christopher Columbus"*, was not quite so sophisticated, but every bit as enjoyable *"on both sides of the curtain"*.

The Literary and Debating Society were also active on the dramatic front, the *"Doubtful Tragedy by Euripides"* and *"The Invisible Duke"* being their 1933 offerings. On the debating floor itself, those assembled for the inter-school evening considered whether or not *"the principal evils from which the present age is suffering"* were due *"to man's invention of the machine, and its developments"*. Later in the year HC Reid and RE Lawry proposed that *"Germany is destined to cause the destruction of Europe"*. In the event the motion was successfully defeated 24-11; RCD Jasper and JE Butland leading the opposition. However it's interesting to note that military activity in Germany was, directly or indirectly, not without its impact on Plymouth College leavers – *"there is a marked trend to the Services,"* said the Head at Speech Day, *"while University Scholarships are less numerous"*.

That Easter, for example, HR Butchers had won a Paymaster Cadetship in the Royal Navy and former Head Boy, HJ Bartholomew, had won a King's Cadetship at Sandhurst.

Despite this there were an increasingly-healthy number of old boys at University, as the 1933 London Letter bore witness; *"We now muster eleven, but London is so vast that individual encounters are rare. Nevertheless, the OPM dinner, which will have taken place when this letter reaches you, will once again have reunited us."*

Included in the eleven were WJ Gillingham and BG Skelton at Imperial College and J Dale at University College. Added to this the 1933 Easter and Summer term Head Boy, PJ Osmund, had just won an Open Scholarship in Classics, to Keble College, Oxford, while PO Wickens was off to New College, Oxford, and K Stagg, to Emmanuel College, Cambridge.

Meanwhile among the older OPMs; Alexander Maxwell, had just been appointed Permanent Deputy Under-Secretary in the Home Office; F Seymour Cocks, MP, had just been appointed member of the Joint Select Committee on Indian Constitutional Reform and Major-General Sir Leonard Rogers KCSI, CIE, had just retired after a long and distinguished medical career, which included a spell as President of the Medical Board at the India Office.

On a sad note, Arthur (AM) Woodley, who had left School the previous year for Oxford, died suddenly, as did Cicely Thompson (nee Colson), the daughter of the former Headmaster. *"A kind of unofficial secretary to Mr Colson, her interest in the School began when she was very young"* and she had, *"at infinite labour"* compiled the only record of old boys of the College (the former High School) and of Mannamead School."

Miss Colson was certainly still a young woman when her father had appointed 32 year-old Bert Sargent to teach at the School.

That had been back in 1903 and since then the genial mathematician had served under three other headmasters and taught hundreds of boys; *"No member of the Staff has ever been able to claim acquaintance with so many genereations of Old Boys; and it was in recognition of his services to them that in December, 1932, he was elected President of the OPM Club."*

Bert Sargent

So ran part of the page-long tribute to him in the July 1934 Plymothian acknowledging his retirement; retirement, that was, from the School, not from Plymouth; *"We hope we shall continue to see him with Mrs Sargent on the touch-line and in their old seats in the front row of the Gymnasium."*

Bert had clearly been a very popular figure and *"had built for himself so secure a place in the life of the School that it is difficult to envisage it without him."*

"No man can have so thoroughly absorbed into his being the traditions of the School or had such opportunities of helping to turn out the type of boy for which the School stands. Of his success as a teacher of Mathematics a prodigiously long record of successes in Certificate, Service, and Scholarship examinations is adequate evidence: as a schoolmaster of the old pattern (we use the phrase as a deliberate compliment), he insisted on the value of those virtues that are indispensible for success in all subjects – accuracy, thoroughness, and hard work."

Little could anyone have guessed that his twenty-five year-old successor, who like Sargent was a Cambridge graduate, would come to clock up an even longer spell on the staff. George Bonser, had distinguished himself at Queens' College and was the seventh inductee into that group appointed by Ralph, who would go on to serve a minimum of thirty-one years on the staff. No-one could have foretold that in 1934, however, and Bert Sargent's thirty-one year record was the longest the School had known up until that point (unless you add together Palmer's time at Plymouth College to the years he had already spent at Mannamead School).

Two of those other young appointments had extra-curricular engagements that year as both Ian Edwards and Charlie Barnes were married; the former at Whitchurch and the latter at Truro.

As it transpired, news of his marriage was one of the few occasions that the young PE and art teacher, Edwards, would be mentioned in the Plymothian for his work outside the classroom. This was unlike Charlie Barnes who, in addition to his efforts in the dramatic world of the School and on the sports field, was soon to take over the OTC from Guy Hill.

Ted Mercer, with whom Barnes appeared that year in both the *"Importance of Being Earnest"* and the Literary and Debating Society's production of *"The Monkey's Paw"* was another great allrounder. He, CLB and Bill Battrick were rugby regulars too and although

it was by no means a vintage season for the 1st XV, they did manage to win their first three games, all of which they had been losing at the half-way stage.

The Rugby team had, as it so often does, lost a number of its leading lights that summer, including the Captain, Edmunds, Stagg and John Spear. JRS was perhaps the biggest loss. Described at the end of his last season as *"undoubtedly the best all-round forward, both in attack and defence"*, *"combining speed and weight to great advantage"* it was predicted that he *"should go far in the game."*

He certainly went as far as he could in England, without leaving the country, for that autumn he registered as an undergraduate at Durham University and quickly made it into the County side up there. But he wasn't looking to sever his links with the School that quickly and together with RM Prideaux, who had taken his place at Keble College, Oxford, had agreed to act as ASM of the Scout Troup; *"They will be able to render valuable service during the vacation,"* noted Troup Leader, BD Pearn.

Plymouth and Mannamead College Water Polo VII - 1934.
Standing; DT Johnston, LH Clemas, RF Tuckett, W Cranfield.
Front; SAS Rattray, JR Spear (Capt.) FW Blight.

John Spear, in his last year at the School, was also *"quite a mainstay"* of the Hockey team and a valuable member of the cricket team, both with the bat and as a *"good reserve wicket keeper"*, he was Victor Ludorum of the Aquatic Sports, for the fourth year running, and finished second in the Athletic Sports having won the high jump and putting the weight, an event in which broke the School record, which he had set the previous summer. He also finished second in the hurdles.

The star of that year's athletics event, though, was undoubtedly another quality, all-round sportsman Henry U'ren, who won all four running events – from 100 yards to the mile – and was just three inches off Blackwell's long-standing long-jump record of 20 feet 8 inches (set in 1900).

U'ren also bagged the most wickets and most runs that season for the 1st XI, which included a record first wicket stand of 174, with K Stagg, against the Royal Sussex Regiment, *"U'ren compiling a brilliant century"*.

Captain of the firsts, Periton, also had a good season hitting several fifties, including an unbeaten 75 against Exeter, who were comprehensively beaten, thanks in no small measure, to Tyrrell's haul of 5 for 11.

Periton and U'ren both scored freely for the Hockey XI; the former hitting six in the School's 12-1 mauling of Newton College. He also scored the first goal in the rain-affected game against Torbay Hockey Club. Both sides fielded players who had already played earlier that day and the School tired first, going down 5-3. The game against Plymouth was tighter, though, and the School won thanks to a lone score from U'ren.

OPM hockey was also thriving, in that there were plenty of fixtures. Sadly, though, they only won two of their seventeen matches and just scraped a draw with the School. Curiously enough the OPM cricket team played the same number of matches that season and were notably more successful, losing only one. Hon. Sec. Giles was the star turn, with Palmer and Bryant useful, too.

The rugby section continued to progress and the Fives and the Swimming sections were *"just keeping their activities going"*.

Total membership of the OPM club at this time was 405, although *"of this total a disquieting number now owe their subscriptions"*.

Which is not to say that the pot was empty as various financial grants were made;

"To Rugby Club £5 and a gift of £5 for pavilion expenditure at Honicknowle; to Cricket Club, £5; to Fives Club, £2; a grant of £5 being voted to the Hockey Club conditionally on its acquiring a ground."

On the social front over 170 attended the Annual OPM Dance at the Royal Hotel, just 40 went to the Annual Dinner at the same venue and a similar number made it to the London Dinner at the Coventry Restaurant in Wardour Street. All three events, for some reason, took place in February.

Messrs, Colson, Chaytor and Dale were among those attending the London bash. All three former heads expressing their continued interest in School affairs.

The current head, incidentally, spoke at the Club AGM and appealed to all OPMs, who had not already given a chair to the newly-expanded Big School to do so as soon as possible – the cost ... 10/- (50p). The head took the opportunity of explaining the new buildings to the meeting – the meeting itself being held in the School.

One of the lesser-publicised, new developments around the School at that time was the Tennis Court. The sport had had a somewhat chequered history at the School since the earliest days. Indeed, curiously enough, the first-ever Wimbledon Championship was held the year the School was opened in 1877. Cohu, the School's second head, had won an in-school tournament while he was briefly here and, had he stayed longer, tennis might have developed a greater profile. However, when a site was chosen for the swimming baths, the School court became an unhappy casualty of the new

development. After that attitudes towards the activity blew hot and cold. On the one hand it was deemed not to be a fit sport for Public Schools, then on the other there was a majority in the Debating Chamber who, in 1917, thought it better than cricket. Interest revived somewhat in the 1920s and at the end of that decade the School had two particularly fine players; Spencer, who won the Devon Junior Championship and Gould, who won the P&D mens singles tournament.

The biggest influence on the sport around this time, locally and nationally, however, was undoubtedly Fred Perry. Perry made his first appearance for Britain in the Davis Cup at Carhullen Tennis Club, at the top of Hartley, in Plymouth, in April 1931. Later that summer, the twenty-one year-old Perry made it through to the semi-finals of Wimbledon, losing out to Sydney Wood, who eventually took the singles crown without playing another match. His opponent, Frank Shields, withdrew before the final. Two years later, though, Perry helped Britain take the Davis Cup after seven years of French supremacy. Two months later he won his first major singles title when he became the first Briton to win the US Open since HL Doherty in 1903. Suddenly everyone was talking about Fred Perry and in 1934 he consolidated his role as a world champion by becoming the first Briton for twenty-five years to win the men's title at Wimbledon. Like the US Open he would go on to win it on another two occasions and, although no-one could have guessed it at the time, it would be a lot more than twenty-five years before another British tennis player would make such a mark.

Back in 1933-34 though Perry-induced tennis fever was high - in certain quarters - and following the appointment of Edward Freathy as "Secretary of Tennis" in the autumn term of 1933, his successor, RA Williams, opened his first report with the words;

"The Tennis Club at School is a comparatively new institution; but it is, nevertheless, beginning to take a prominent place in the School's summer activities.

We have now no less than sixty members from the Vth and VI forms and many applications for membership have been received from the IVth. These we have had, unfortunately, to refuse, as there is only one court available and it is only with great difficulty that we can meet the needs of our present members."

"A "doubles" tournament is in progress at the time of writing and in the near future we contemplate holding a series of House Matches. These latter will, of course, be unofficial, but it is hoped that next year the importance of the Tennis Club will be more fully realised by the authorities."

The ill-fated ER Freathy

On a sad note, we learned that the 19 year-old tennis-loving Freathy, a recently appointed School prefect, had fallen victim to a sudden and severe attack of bronchitis and pneumonia in Janaury 1934 and after a few weeks' treatment at home had been taken to Didworthy Sanatorium. In July he was moved again, this time to Plymouth Central Hospital (in Lockyer Street) and then, in October, the unfortunate young man, an only son, died at his home.

Less than three weeks later, however, Freathy's death was overshadowed at School by the loss of Miss Footner – Headmistress of the Prep.

Miss Footner had been ill for some time, had not been in School since June and had been *"obliged to submit to what proved to be a most dangerous operation; her courage and strength of will helped her to survive this, and after a few weeks in a nursing home she was able to return to her rooms, and in August undertook the trying journey to Bath."* Sadly, that is where she died, after many weeks of sleeplessness and constant pain.

Above Plymouth College Fives Team, 1934.

Below: Cricket 1st XI, 1934: Back; D Castle, JM Tyrrell, NA Burt, NT Jenkins, GW Irish. Front; JR Spear, RE Lawry, R Periton (Capt.), K Stagg, HG U'ren, SV Collins.

Above: 1934 Hockey 1st XI: Back; RE lawry, JK Hoare, JM Tyrrell, K Stagg, GW Irish. Front; PR Turner, HG U'ren, R Periton (capt.), JR Spear, DW Gay, SV Collins.

Below: 1934 Rugby 1st XV: Back; CW Pearce, JL Ronson, D Castle, DW Gay, CJ Hallett, RF Tuckett, DE Ballentine. Front; RF Hoar, GAS Rattray, RE Lawry, AKD Edmunds (Capt.), GW Irish, REV Johns, AW Street.

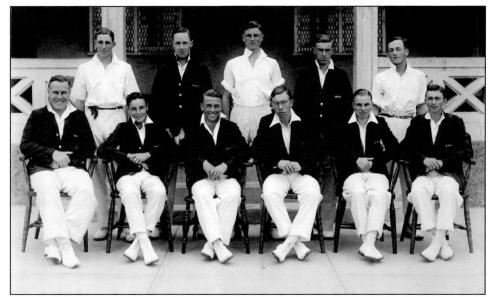

Her obituary in the Plymothian ran; *"It is scarcely an exaggeration to say that since her arrival in January 1921 her whole life had been centred upon the Preparatory School; it was, at all times, her first interest and its success and development almost her only care."*

Miss Footner - Prep Headmistress

The piece concluded with the words; *"The School loses in her another loyal and devoted servant."*

By a strange coincidence Miss Footner's arrival at the School had been occasioned by the death of her predecessor, Florence Lethbridge, and this had provided Francis Dale with an early and unexpected problem. However it is likely that privately his successor, Herbert Ralph, viewed Miss Footner's death as a mixed blessing. The rather damning Prep Inspection of 1932 was doubtless still fresh in his mind and this unanticipated turn of events gave Ralph a welcome opportunity to revolutionise the running of the Preparatory department of the School.

This he did in a most dramatic way by appointing the first-ever male head of the Prep. More than that even, ECA Firman was the first-ever full-time male member of staff at the Prep.

Like the newly-appointed Main School English master, Meryick Jones, Charles Firman had freshly graduated from Keble College, Oxford, and this too marked him out as an altogether better qualified member of staff than previous Prep appointments.

Charles Firman

There could be no doubt that having tackled his primary objectives with regard to the buildings and staff of the Main School, and indeed the location of the Prep, Ralph now had the ideal chance to change the Prep in other ways.

It was, therefore, no coincidence to find that in his very first term at Plymouth College Mr Firman introduced the House system into the "Junior School", with Ralph himself presenting a Shield *"to be awarded to the leading House in the Sports each year".*

Ralph presents the new Prep House Shield.

That first summer, 1935 – *"excitement ran high in the Prep. as Sports Day, Tuesday, June 4th, approached. Events, altogether new in the Prep. were to take place, three championships had to be set up, the School would be competing in Houses, with the House Trophy to be won."*

As it transpired, Sargents were the first-ever winners of the Shield thanks, in no small measure, to young PM Winn, who won the under-12 220 yards, 100 yards and the long jump. Similar events were held at under-10 and under 8-level. Never had the boys been so pressured into competition.

"A further innovation was that the distribution of certificates took place in the pleasant, shady grounds of the Prep, itself, the Headmaster (Mr Ralph) presenting them, as usual, after Mr Firman had had an opportunity to speak to the parents about the place of games and lessons in school life, and the value of team spirit."

Should there have been any doubters, even then, that this marked the beginning of a new era for the Prep, then by March of 1936 they would surely have been convinced.

Speaking at the Prep's first "At Home", Mr Firman, welcoming the visitors said there was a two-fold purpose to the occasion; *"To enable you to meet the Staff and discuss any problems in connection with your boys and be able to see some of the boys at work."*

"The work done in the Preparatory," he explained, *"is progressive and leads straight up to that done in Forms 1A and 1B",* adding that *"promotion into the College depends upon the ability shown in Division I and on the results of the July examination."* He further remarked on the enthusiasm shown for games, both last term and this.

Plymouth College Prep House Rugby Champions - College House: Standing Murray, Tolputt, Butters, Vittle, Hancock. Sitting; Hopwood, Brown, Stafford, Hussell and King.

The Preparatory School pose for their first photocall independent of the Main School.

At that point Mr Ralph began to address the parents. He spoke appreciatively of the changes and improvements that Mr Firman had made in the Prep during his first year as Head Master … *"and I hope it will be the first of many such years."*

Mr Ralph then announced that another new master had been appointed as Form Master of Division II. He was to take up his appointment in the Summer term, in place of Miss Lawrey, who, rather conveniently for Ralph, *"is leaving us after four years valuable work to be married".*

Miss Lawrey's replacement was another well-qualified young man - twenty-five year-old Cambridge graduate James Westhead. Westhead's appointment, though no-one could have known it then, was, amazingly enough, the tenth to be made during a six-year spell under Ralph, that would result in a period of over thirty years service to the School.

Westhead - another fresh face.

The Prep was rapidly becoming a scaled-down version of the Main School – with the boys working in a way that prepared them for the syllabus of the secondary school. They were also now part of a house system that mirrored that of the Main School and there was a newly-instigated Prefectorial distinction whereby the new Prep prefects, appointed in the autumn term of 1936, became the first to wear the Prep School Prefect's Cap – *"made up of the College Colours, running from back to peak-tip, as distinct from the cap with circles of College Colours".*

Plymouth College had undoubtedly had heads before who had played a major part in shaping the destiny of the School - Colson, Chaytor and Dale among them - but not since the site had been first developed had there been quite so much structural change at Ford Park and not since the first batch of teachers appointed here had there been such wholesale changes in the staff room.

Lingley's departure, in the summer of 1935, meant that the last of the real old guard had gone. Turning 65 at the end of July, it had been ten years or so since he had retired as games master and therefore none of the boys then at the School would have known him in that role.

Lingley takes his leave.

For the current generation he would have been best remembered as the Master of College House – the boarding house;

"A word of farewell to all College House boys, past and present, from Mrs Lingley and myself," he wrote in his last address to the lads. *"With the majority of our Members living in other counties and outside the City boundary, it has been impossible to maintain anything more than a superficial contact. Our small House has numbered over one hundred and forty since 1917. One has enjoyed having had a hand in your varied interests at School and afterwards. Some forty or so I have prepared for "Confirmation". Mrs Lingley, on behalf of the Governors, has enjoyed studying each boy's personal needs and, not least, catering for that ever-ready-vacuum of a boy's life by providing a balanced and varied diet."*

He then added, somewhat enigmatically, *"a word of appreciation to all who have helped to maintain the* **esprit-de-corps** *of the House towards the School and towards itself. As regards the School's generous tradition that offers a link of rememberance on retirement I would like to say that at my definite wish the promoters consented to refrain from further considering it in my case."*

Quite why he didn't want to be remembered, in whatever way it was, is not clear - one wonders, too, just how clearly his boys understood his last pronouncement to them; *"May each of you, past and present, continue to face the issues of life with a harmonizing incentive and a nurturing preparation, respectively, as befits the dominating asset of your character."*

With Shanks gone and the visiting handwriting master, William Meech, about to follow him, there was, remarkably, only OPM John Dufton, still on the staff from Chaytor's time at the School and he was still in his early forties. This left only the Reverend Benskin to represent the over-fifties in the Common Room. Thus it was that when he left to take up the parish post at Antony in 1937 the staff room truly had a youthful countenance.

But we've moved on too far – to return to 1934 and while Ralph is rather rapidly achieving his aims at Plymouth College, partly through determination, partly through circumstance, so we find that worldwide, the Depression has created conditions where single-minded men of vision have pushed through to the fore in many countries in the world. While one hesitates to draw any obvious conclusion from the situation it is, nevertheless, noteworthy that by 1934 half the governments of Europe were run by dictators and by 1936 seventeen out of the thirty would be.

And who were these, generally-fascist, figures? Men like Hitler, Stalin, Mussolini, Franco and the Austrian, Dolfuss, all of whom were born between 1879 and 1892, making them the product of the same generation as Herbert Ralph, who was born right in the middle of that period, in 1885. Certainly there can be no denying that as part of his visionary approach, building for the future of the School, that all of Ralph's appointments, after Ian Edwards, were, comfortably, more than twenty years younger than their headmaster. Significantly this applied to the Prep as well, where, not only was there a massive change in the age profile, but for the first time ever there was a move away from the single, somewhat-matronly "miss", towards a younger and highly-qualified "sir".

Such is not to say that Ralph necessarily espoused any extreme, right-wing views himself, merely that his approach was not without contemporary parallels. However, while most of the new European heads-of-state achieved their status inevitably in the wake of much internal bloodshed, Ralph was "fortunate" in that the older guard at Plymouth College, those who didn't move or retire, simply died in harness – Messrs Osmund and Gingell and Miss Footner. All of them between 1933 and 1934 and curiously all of them were a similar age to Ralph himself.

Interestingly enough, the inter-school debate that winter, held in Big School, considered the motion *"that this House would welcome a dictatorship in Great Britain"*. Representatives from Devonport High School, Corporation Grammar School, Stoke Damerel Secondary, Sutton Secondary, Plymouth High and Devonport Secondary for Girls, met with College boys and resolutely found against the motion - 97 to 26.

By this stage, Sir Oswald Mosley was doing his best to establish what he called a "modern dictatorship" in Britain. His British Union of Fascists (BUF) Party had now been going two years and his party's rally in Birmingham, early in 1934, had attracted an estimated 10,000 people, 3,000 of them fanatical supporters. Fiercely anti-Semetic and pro-German, the BUF were rapidly alienating more Britons than they were attracting, particularly with their increasingly-violent tactics and the tendancy of the Party officials to wear black shirts and leather belts, a la Mussolini.

The Plymothian Oxford Letter of July 1934 noted that *"even the Daily Mail informs us that those beset by Sir Oswald's bodyguard will only be summoned and found guilty if they hit back".* While the Autumn epistle recorded that *"Sir Oswald ("Mussolini") Mosley intends to take his life in his hands and visit us".*

Remaking the World - Fascist meeting in the Drill Hall, Plymouth

While Mosley, a former Tory, Independent and Labour MP, was doing his best to exploit the largely-unsatisfactory situation that had brought the largely-Tory National Government into existence in 1931 under the Labour leader Ramsay Macdonald, Britain was nevertheless largely wary of Mosley's neo-Nazi extremism and not impressed by Hitler's various outrages against other countries and, indeed, his own countrymen.

Consequently it was no great surprise to find that when the newly-revived, OPM Debate was held six weeks later, it took for its subject, *"That this House affirms its unqualified support of the League of Nations"*

The fact that the House found decisively in favour of the motion was little help, however, to the League itself, who were being roundly abused by member-states Germany and Italy.

In the face of such apparent impotence another of that season's School debates had addressed the motion that *"Europe does not consider peace worth fighting for."*

PR Turner, a future head boy, and GWRS Johnson,

proposed, T Deacon and JG Wescott opposed and were successful as the motion was lost 17 votes to 11.

As we have already seen, the *"quiet and unobtrusive"* Herbert Ralph was very clearly a pacifist and a keen supporter of the League of Nations. However, he also firmly believed that Britain needed to be able to defend itself and, like many other Public School headmasters in the 1930s, did his best to promote the OTC.

Their 1934 Camp was at Twesledown - it was the first time the School contingent had been there. It was unseasonally cool for early August and the 31 cadets, who Guy Hill took to Aldershot, were sent home a day early because of a violent wet spell, although curiously the main complaint was of sore throats - brought on by the dryness of the summer.

That other uniformed section of the School, the Scouts, was also being encouraged from all quarters and during the Easter Holidays, earlier that year, a meeting was held to inaugurate the OPM section of the Troup. The meeting took the form of a Supper and *"was attended by several old members and present senior members of Troop".* It was decided that the OPM contingent should be called the Bulldog section and that Mr Willis, a good friend of the Troop be its SM. Willis suggested that they have about four meetings a year, *"the first to take the form of a Weekend Camp ... this was held at Shaugh at Half-Term and proved to be most enjoyable."*

Despite the ominous shape of the war clouds gathering over Europe they were yet a little too distant to darken the thoughts of most younger members of the School and it's interesting to note that the Headmaster, who had steered Plymouth College through the Great War, Dr Chaytor, spoke mainly of *"character"* and *"leisure"*, when he presented the Prizes at Speech Day that October.

"In view of the great changes which are coming over the world," he said, *"many classes of society will have more leisure than in the past. Education will have to show how leisure should rightly be employed."*

Dr Chaytor said he deplored the importance laid by employers on "Matriculation".

"The Headmaster," he continued, *"has already given admirable reasons why boys should be kept at School. In later years begins the development of character, and success in life depends as much on character as ability. Mere cleverness without character will not get a boy very far. Only in the later years at school will a boy discover character."*

Alderman Monday, the acting Chairman of Governors (who was to be knighted in forthcoming Birthday Honours list) gave the vote of thanks and, responding, Dr Chaytor, mindful of an oft-lapsed popular tradition asked for holiday for the School. In the event, Saturday 13 October was made a *"whole holiday".*

Clearly holidays and leisure time were increasingly becoming an issue. Indeed, Plymouth Corporation were doing their best to promote the City as a holiday destination, and in October 1935 they would open the New Sea Water Bathing Pool (the Hoe Lido) at Tinside.

A typical thirties railway poster for Plymouth - the tourist resort.

Shock waves resounded around Torquay, Paignton and other south-coast resorts in Devon, but not everyone in Plymouth was convinced the move would succeed;

"The attempt to turn Plymouth into a holiday resort is doomed to failure", was the motion RA Williams and LH Clemas put to the School Debating Society in December 1934. DL High and JK Hoare opposed *"and just carried the day by one vote".*

Doubtless all the School's keen swimmers were delighted though, especially the aforementioned LH Clemas, who won his Water Polo colours that season and his team-mate FS Blight, who also improved on his previous year's second place position by winning the open annual Breakwater to the Pier swim.

Increases in leisure time were also making an impact in other areas. Nationally Joe Davis made news when he became the first UK Professional Billiards Champion. Closer to home, *"Anonymous"* contributed a lengthy (over two pages) piece *"For Those Who Attempt To Play Billiards",* to the School Magazine.

The first term of 1935, meanwhile, witnessed the formation of yet another "new" (there had been an earlier incarnation of the society before the Great War) leisure-time, hobby-linked, club in the School – the Philatelic Society;

"At a general meeting on January 28th, the Headmaster kindly consented to act as President, and the following officers were elected:- Chairman RF Tuckett, Hon Sec., SB Jackson and Hon Treas., FRS Pearce."

Three days later, at the first ordinary meeting of the Society, Tuckett and Jackson *"gave a display of recent Empire issues"* and a fortnight later Hallett gave a paper and display on *"Italy's Commemoratives".*

Although Britain had led the field in the stamp world, the Country had been relatively slow to realise the commercial potential of *"Commemoratives".* and although there had been a set commissioned for the Empire Exhibition of 1924, other countries were already far more productive in the philatelic terms.

However, although stamp collecting was already a long-established hobby - several OPMs expressed early offers of displays to the fledgling society - interest was really intensified when domestic stamp production, itself, became more interesting, as it did in the 1930s.

Stamp design becomes more fashionable and so does collecting.

Curiously enough, the renowned cataloguer and stamp dealer, Stanley Gibbons, had started out in Plymouth in the mid-nineteenth century, although little has ever been made of the fact; there is, however, a discreet plaque in Lockyer Street.

However notwithstanding stamps, science, meccano and more physical pursuits, one of the prime leisure activities of the mid-thirties was the cinema and nowhere, in pages of the Plymothian, was its influence more clearly demonstrated that in MJC's page-long, gangster-style skit on Caesar;

"Caesar was the big noise round here once, wasn't he? Why have you gone back on him, you dirty yeller rats, huh?"

It wasn't just the street slang of the Hollywood

gangster and Jimmy Cagney that appealed to the schoolboy of the thirties – Jan Stewer clearly exerted a similar influence on some; *"Us 'ev got a rare villij kriket tame, 'ev us. Us calls ourselfs "Olewel hunbeatables. 'Twas lass August Benk 'ollerday wen us fixed up a metch agin' Nooton Farohs."*

So began the next-but-one Plymothian piece to MJC's in the Easter '34 Magazine. The Reverend Benskin doubtless revelled in the amount of "original" material that gave the School's literary organ its thickest issue for some time.

One of the most entertaining contributions around this time, however, was the piece from *Hypselus*, in the April 1935 edition. Entitled *"Reminiscence: A Kaleidoscopic Nightmare"* it captured something of the schoolboy experience of the thirties - and a long way either side of it.

"First day at School: timetables, lockers, preps., vols., exams.; Latin: bam-bas-bat; History: one on the paw, Caesar, Ben Hur; Gym, Physics, Manners makyth man, Form matches, Cricket, Swimming, Exams.; 3A: Chinwag, Latin boiled owls, duplex, triplex, multiplex, assinus es, abi Romam ... Romam abeo, Caesar (Invasion of Britain), Hann-I-bal; English: debates, funniest experiences, Poems, Stories; Greek: paradigms, declensions; Chemistry: Oxides, Air, Acids, Salts, Litmus; Cricket; Form matches, how (as in all best school stories) we won a glorious victory over 4A by one wicket, with our captain injured and our best bat ill; 4A: Gym., thank you boys, thank you sir; Greek, Bootlaces, Moke, Towhead, Soap, Nicknames, Xenophon; Latin: Gallia in tres partes .... Ovid (selections Shuckburgh); Physics, Boyle's Law, Cricket, Swimming, Exams.; 5A: work: years of discretion, House Matches; Maths.; Cos A + Sin B = X, "bomb", Greek: Alcestis; Latin: Cicero, Ovid, Tristia (very, since it brought me my first taste of detention); "School Certificate," Sixth Form: more work, sense of duty, "you're in the Sixth Form now," Thucydides, Euripides, etc., etc., ad nauseam,

Swimming, with discussions on Co-ops, Combines and Modern Dancing, more work, Verse, Latin (" ... not even if scanned"), Plays, Mock Trials, the world's problems discussed and "solved" by half-a-dozen schoolboys in a small upper-room, Atheism v Christianity, Exams., Exams., Exams., Prefectship, "stop talking", "get off that bike", more Exams., Lines, Meetings, more swotting for yet more Exams., O.P.M.'s "old So-and-so at ....," "remember old So-and-so? A great fellow ...."

One suspects here again the hand of the long-left JC Trewin - one of Benskin's earliest converts to the joys of creative writing, and former co-editor of Chinwag. It was by no means his only contribution to that edition.

Another piece that had all the hallmarks of coming from an OPM concerned the London – Exeter motor trial of 1934. This *"consists of a night run to Exeter, at a speed of 26 m.p.h., a stop for breakfast and then five test hills to be climbed."*

"We had a 9-hp Singer Le Mans and outside Exeter we had a brief halt to put the hood down and change the rear wheels to competition tyres. The first hill was Fingle Bridge, steep, loose-surfaced and twisty, but with screen flat the Singer climbed easily, at times touching 6,000 revs. Per minute, with the writer sitting on the floor holding first gear in case the jolting sould knock it out of gear."

The 1935, 9-hp Singer Le Mans

"After Fingle came what the papers call the "piece de resistance", Simms Hill, with muddy surface and 1 in 2.5 gradient; only 17 climbed out of 364 entrants."

"There was a long delay here and despite all our efforts of "ouncing" to make the wheels bite we spun to a standstill half-way up. At once a rope was attached to the front axle and we were hauled to the top by means of a steam engine."

There were three more hills after this, and what the effect of hundreds of cars scrambling up them in the darkness was, we can only now imagine. But this was state-of-the-art motoring in 1935 and if it seems exciting now, consider how it must have struck the spellbound schoolboy.

There was more in the next Plymothian as JA Brunyee recounted details of *"the most famous speed trials in England"* at Shelsley Walsh.

"Shelsley is visited largely by the enthusiasts who work for weeks before the event on a car of their own creation. Most of the specials are sprint cars – spidery contraptions – nearly all chain driven, with sketchy bodies."

Then, *"in a class by themselves are the real racing cars – Alfa Romeo, Bugatti, ERA and Maserati."* Most of which, including Raymond Mays' ERA, cross the finishing line in a burst of around 100 mph.

How times have changed. There were at the time just over 35 million motor vehicles in the world and in Britain, under the terms of the recent Road Traffic Act, a speed limit of 30 mph had just been introduced for built-up areas. Police Cars with gongs were brought in to halt offenders. *"Why 30, why not 10? Why go at all?"* asked one student lobby.

The Transport Minister responsible for introducing all of these new measures was Devonport MP Leslie Hore-Belisha and in September 1934 the country saw the first of a new type of pedestrian road crossing, marked out with studs on the road and yellow beacons on the pavement.

Twelve months on and there was an impromptu proposal put in the School Debating Chamber *"That pedestrian crossings be placed outside the entrance to a class-room, and that prefects be disguised as Belisha Beacons."* Needless to say, it was unanimously rejected by the boys attending. It is interesting to note, however, that early Belisha Beacons fell prey to many a naughty school boy as the glass globes proved all too tempting for the mischevious catapult- wielding miscreant and it wasn't long before the golden globes were recast in alumunium (it wasn't until the early 1950s that the winking globe was introduced).

Another of Hore-Belisha's measures was the introduction of the compulsory Driving Test and, a few months later, compulsory "L" plates for learner drivers.

These were watershed years in the motoring world. Sir Malcolm Campbell was regularly making front page news with his Bluebird. In March 1935 he set a new land-speed record of 276 mph and then, just six months later, at Bonneville Salt Flats, he became the first to break the 300-mph barrier. Boys who were fortunate enough to attend the Duke of York's Camp the following summer would be lucky enough to have an *"entertaining and illustrated lecture on High Speed Motoring"* by Sir Malolm himself.

Malcolm Campbell prepares to "fly" in his Bluebird

This was a time for a great number of major improvements and refinements in motor-car design, many of them quite simple. For example, it was in 1934/5 that the first one-piece windscreen, the first flashing indicator lights, the first headlamps mounted in the wings, recessed door handles and windscreen washers appeared. On the roads themselves Percy Shaw's Cat's Eyes made their first appearance, although it would be sometime before they spread around the country. Catching on much quicker and capturing the hearts of a generation of schoolboys was the latest product from Frank Hornby's Meccano Company – the Dinky Toy – the world's first die-cast metal motor model.

If the motorbike had been the key to an affluent young man's freedom in the twenties, the motor car was what he sought in the thirties. Films were full of them and tobacco companies seemed to release endless series of cigarette cards with all the latest models, including the celebrated, two-seater Austin Seven, now available for just £102.

St Andrew Street - Beware the learner driver in the new car!

Cigarette cards also covered other interests of course; film stars, footballers, sportsmen, ships and even stamps, and the boys (mainly) who collected them,

swapped them, sold them and made up various games to play with them. You didn't have to smoke yourself to collect them, there would always be someone in the family that had the tobacco habit, mother, father, big sister, brother. Smoking was, after all, a cool thing to do, viz., this remarkable Plymothian piece from 1935 – *"On Pipes"*.

"Not Bagpipes. Certainly not. Nor Drainpipes: not even Gas pipes. I mean – just pipes. After years of contented cigarette smoking I have at last been decoyed into buying a pipe."

So began this two-page eulogy to the tobacco industry's second-greatest accomplice, prompted by the humble scribe's persistent friends; *"There is something about a pipe, the feel of the bowl in your hand, the pleasure of filling it from a pouch of fragrant tobacco, of puffing out clouds of smoke, and watching the pipe gradually mature, until it becomes an old friend – you miss these things with cigarette smoking."*

And so our anonymous author consults his tobacconist who *"mourned over Empire tobaccos, he regretted to say – and especially in Jubilee Week, - that whilst we might be great at building battleships, with tobacco – no."*

'Tobaccnist', Ford Park corner

The selection nonetheless made ... *"I watched the tobacco being shovelled into the pouch (of fine smelling pig-skin, rubber lined) and felt the pipe in my pocket, a feeling of mystic exaltation swept over me. I had joined the brotherhood of the pipe: the incense of tobacco was in my nostril. I left the shop treading on air."*

And so it went on, eventually concluding with the line; *"Of course, there is something **satisfying** about a pipe."*

Of course these were the days when there was an almost constant weed-generated fug emanating from the staffroom and it was not unusual for masters to smoke as they taught, so perhaps we shouldn't be too surprised to see the piece in the School Magazine. It was interesting that no name, fictional or otherwise, was there to identify its author though. Doubtless it came from an OPM and one wonders how many other OPMs contributed either anonymously or under strange pseudonyms.

Certainly, for many boys, OPM epistles must have still been a fascinating source of information about the world at large. The April '35 issue positively bristled with interesting pieces from the *"far-flung Empah"* and the hope was that other *"former Smiths iv and Joneses iii will straighten their evening bow, bite furiously on pipe, sip gently the glass of milk, clap hands for the punkah business, and dictate immediate Plymouth-bound letters to adjacent dusky belle, who, clad only in Birmingham beads and a smile, pounds briskly a typewriter. (Forgive us prithee, if the local colour is wrong, but Hollywood assures us it is accurate). As we were saying, even though you live in Saltash or Bloomsbury, don't forget that your vapourings, marriage, murder or mistakes will interest the boy who sat behind in Room I."*

And so to M.C.C. in South America; *"Buenos Aires. The largest city of the Southern Hemisphere, the largest city of night life, cabarets, blazing electric signs, narrow crowded streets with a continuous din of hooting traffic, controlled by police whistles, jabbering humanity from all parts of the world, shouting all languages, gesticulating wildly. This is the City where a native football match becomes a bottle-shy between the spectators and the referee, where the losing team and supporters play havoc with the railway coaches on the return journey in order to relieve their feelings."*

"This is the City of beautiful women and less attractive men, all of whom take their pleasures very sadly, where a mild flirtation may become at any moment a "drama passionale"."

"A City of beautiful plazas, magnificent clubs, polo grounds, rose gardens, and picturesque monuments, where life has very little value, and everything is possible if the tip is sufficiently large."

Meanwhile, from AM Stibbs (who was at School during the Great War), in West China, came a further, fascinating account of his life in Shunking, 1,700 miles from the sea.

Here still *"motor cars and bicycles are rare enough to be taken notice of as something out of the ordinary. The local people saw their first aeroplane in 1933, but since then the military have built an aerodrome outside the city, and for the last year an aeroplane on the move has been a commoner sight than a motor-car. Overland travelling is ordinarily done on foot or in a chair carried by two coolies. There are no express trains, and thirty miles a day is good going."*

"Everything is carried by man power, and amazing are the powers of a good Chinese coolie. With the two halves slung at each end of his shoulder pole he can carry over 100lb. Twenty-five miles a day."

"We are," wrote the Reverend Stibbs, *"well cut off from the outside world, but cannot call ourselves remote. Wireless news sent on from Chungking sometimes reaches us within four or five days. But ordinarily Shanghai newspapers are two to three weeks old before we read them. Home letters have taken six or seven weeks."*

"Possibly," added our OPM missionary, *"some who read this will not think this sounds like "life" at all. Nor should we were we not here to proclaim Him who is the source of Life which is Life indeed."*

Stibbs was by no means the only OPM missionary working in the field. Earlier in the year RB Spear and his colleagues had baptized 112 people in Devanampalayam in India. *"But this was followed by a boycott, and the only work that could be done by the missionaries had to be carried on at night in the houses of the people. When the boycott ended the villagers gave "RB" a tumultuous welcome. The people surged around him*

with drums and other less musical instruments and danced in the Eastern style. Shortly afterwards trouble broke out again and the cottage occupied by "RB" was burned down and one of his converts was beaten mercilessly, on which "RB" modestly said, "We went again"."*

Foreign Correspondents - doubtless there were boys at School eager to collect the stamps on OPM missives.

A little more appealing to most boys, in lifestyle terms at least, was RW Macklin's further account of life as a Commissioner in the British West Africa;

"A Commissioner is very much a maid-of-all-work. In addition to purely administrative duties he often combines the functions of a police magistrate, revenue officer, and police officer. He is expected to render first aid to sick natives and do anything else needed."

"Many Commissioners," he wrote, *"are now accompanied by their wives, so the standard of comfort has improved considerably. Pay is quite good; commencing at £470 and rising by £30 increments to £720, then by £40 to £960. Living, however, is more expensive than in England."*

"It is essential that one should be able to sympathise with and to take a genuine interest in the natives. Obtain their confidence and they will do anything for you."

"Shooting is the normal recreation, partridge being everywhere. Pigeons are numerous and take some hitting. Geese, duck and teal are in the swamps, while the lesser bustard, or "bush turkey", is rare but excellent eating. You may raise antelope, wart hog, and various beasts of prey, or, rarely, lion."

"In the Gambia where I am, the country is open and parklike. A few miles, however and the scene changes to scrub, but there is practically no luxurient tropical vegetation anywhere in this province. Creeks and riverbanks are clothed with a dense belt of mangroves, harbouring a host of obscene creatures, such as land crabs, jumping fish, and hordes of biting flies, including the tse-tse, the carrier of sleeping sickness. This disease is almost unknown among Europeans, though common enough among natives. Europeans are frequently bitten, especially if their duties necessitate much travelling by launch. I have known only two cases in fourteen years. I have myself been bitten hundreds of time. It is not therefore to be regarded as a deterrent to anyone thinking of coming to Africa."

"Malaria is the disease that everyone gets sooner or later, but if one takes quinine regularly, preferably in liquid form, malaria seldom troubles anyone leading a sane life."

"Helmets," he added, *"are necessary from about 7.30 to 4.30. The sun must be regarded seriously ... "If these rules are carried out – and they present no difficulty – there is no need to contemplate ill-health."*

"Tours are now of 18 months, followed by 18 weeks vacation in Britain. Time spent on the voyage does not count as leave. Full pay is drawn at all times."

HJ Stevens, in Assam, had his own entertaining tales of Empire life. He'd been hunting in the Himalayas, on the back of an elephant, all had gone according to plan until the creature, for some reason, panicked *"and made off into the jungle as hard as he could go ... small trees being broken down by his huge weight. A branch swept away my topi, creepers ripped the shirts off our backs. I think it took me six months to work all the thorns out of my back."*

Curiously enough the letter that followed the second part of Commissioner Macklin's communique was from an OPM in Italy, where there was a certain amount of resentment regarding our success at Empire building. Mussolini was looking to increase his popularity with the Italian populous by avenging an earlier humiliation when the Italians had suffered at the hands of the Abyssinians almost forty years earlier. For some time Mussolini had been building up his forces and the Abyssinian Emperor, Haile Selassie, had appealed for support from the League of Nations, but to date had received little concrete assistance.

Haile Selassie - the Abyssinian Emporer - on horseback.

When our OPM had wandered around Messini the previous September, he had found that some of his party were booed on the street and *"two men were spat upon from the pavement ... Englishmen were not popular."* Our correspondent was in no doubt about the mood of the Italians; *"they point to Britain's colonization and ask why they cannot do likewise. Italians love a scrap and are quite eager to push ahead against the Abyssinians. This was of course before the sanctions bloc (approved of by the School Debating Chamber in October 1935 and actually imposed by the League of Nations a few weeks later) was initiated."*

"Italians love fighting ... while they are winning."

"Mussolini," wrote CJP, *"stands or falls by his enormous venture. Is Italy behind him? I cannot forget a remark an Italian told me over the coffee cup. "There are in Italy, signor, thirteen million men of military age. Of them one and three-quarter million are Fascists. The rest are cowards." Adio."*

As it was to turn out Mussolini's far-from-efficient fascist machine was ultimately successful in Abyssinia, just as Hitler was successful in reclaiming the Rhineland. In Spain, meanwhile, Fascist rebels kick-started a civil war and back at Plymouth College yet more old boys aired their views on fascism in the OPM debate.

The motion on the table, proposed by OPMs Rogers and Clemas, was that *"In the Opinion of this House the Policy of the British Union of Fascists is both necessary and desirable."*

Two of the other ten OPMs attending, Prideaux and Reid, opposed, and in so doing managed to carry the day, with the motion being rejected 20 votes to 11.

The debate itself, however, was an indication that Moseley's party was still picking up support and there were several well-attended and rather volatile party meetings and rallies in Plymouth itself.

If there was any doubt about the increasingly-gloomy outlook over Europe one only had to read between the lines of the Headmaster's Address to the School on 11th November 1935.

Clearly this was intended as a reminder of the sacrifice made by an earlier generation in the Great War – but equally there was more than just the one message for the present generation.

"There are some who are tempted by their horror of war to forget what we owe to those million men who died for England and made peace possible in this country; and in their condemnation of war they are led to belittle the profession of the soldier. But it is still the

Top left, "Plymouth and Mannamead College Fives Team 1935. Back; PS Anderson, MLP Bartlett, CKJ Hallett. Front; AHM Smyth, DD Mears (Captain), RE Lawry.
Above: OPM RFC 1934/35.
Left: "Plymouth and Mannamead College 1st XI Hockey Team, 1935; Back PECMB Kelly, WL Collins, VJE Boatright, RF Tuckett, DE Ballantine, HL Palmer. Front; RE Lary, PR Turner, DW Gay (Captain), HG U'ren, GW Irish.

military virtues that to-day are, deservedly, the most admired – courage, endurance, loyalty, generosity, unselfishness. In the last resort it is the soldier who takes upon himself the burden of others and gives his all for them. If the absence of war meant the absence of the military virtues, the world would be the poorer for it. Happily, war is not the only sphere in which these virtues can be exercised. There is plenty of scope in peace for courage, loyalty, unselfishness. That they are more difficult to maintain in peace makes them the more precious. It cannot be denied that for most boys and, for that matter, most men, peace has a feeble attraction: this is because it is too often regarded simply as the absence of war. It is not surprising that so negative an idea is so little attractive, for it implies a conception of life from which danger and struggle are absent. This passive idea must be replaced by a positive idea which implies energy, struggle, courage. There is plenty of scope in the world for adventure and effort; there is plenty of danger and suffering to be faced. The good citizen of peace, like the good soldier, must be on the watch for the enemies of peace, whether those enemies are the stagnation and dry rot that threaten to come with peace, or the destruction and ruin that come with war. No boy in the School today is old enough to have known or seen anything of the struggles and agonies of the Great War; no boy is too young to understand something of the responsibilities he must face when he leaves School. It will be the duty of each to contribute something to the work of a constructive peace – and not least by shouldering without complaint his own burdens and sharing those of others."

Stirring stuff and it's worth remembering those words when we read the following summer's OTC Notes in which the officer in command, Charlie Barnes, was able to report that "the list of those wishing to attend Camp at Rushmoor this summer has exceeded the allotted establishment. Our hopes that this improvement in enthusiasm, due in no small degree to our present NCOs,

is a prelude to a claim for a larger establishment."

One of those freshly enthusiastic NCOs was, doubtless, the Officer-in-Command himself, CLB, and it's interesting to note that one of the first innovations under his leadership was a new piece of silverwear for the School prize cabinet – the Inter-House Shooting Competition Trophy.

College House became the first holders of the new trophy and shooting was clearly on the up – "In the Empire Test we have a higher percentage of 1st class shots than usual – there are tentative arrangements for School fixtures again."

Tidworth, venue for Plymouth College OTC Camp - 1935

It is significant, too, that there was at this time a new, two-term system of training … "recruits will be particularly welcome and will find it easier for themselves to join at the beginning of next term" – the summer term – he wrote. Curiously enough, CLB's first Field Day, the previous summer term, had been a truly inclement affair. Arranged for the 17 May … "soon after our arrival at the scene of operations, rain followed by a snow-storm drove us back home." Back home where the "nets" showed up "like gaunt black skeletons on the snow covered field."

Notwithstanding the unseasonal weather at home it was Hitler's storm troopers abroad that were giving greater cause for concern. Having styled himself Der Fuhrer (the leader) after Hindenberg's death in 1934, Hitler had stepped up his programme by several gears

and at Nuremberg in September '35 he announced that all of Germany's Jews were no longer to be counted as German citizens, they were now merely "subjects" without rights.

The Vice-Consul for Germany in Plymouth, S Carlisle Davis OPM, who had recently been re-elected Chairman of the Plymouth branch of the English Church Union, and had recently been president of the National Chamber of Trade, was clearly perturbed, as were a good many people around the world. This had led to a discussion in the Church Assembly, on the persecution of Jews in Germany the previous November. The Nazi's outrages continued unabated, however.

On the other side of the coin we read in the Cambridge Letter that Aneurin Bevan was among those attending the Peace Rally held in the university city. The Oxford Letter, meanwhile, was more concerned that "the innermost sanctuary of bachelordom has been profaned and women have spoken at the Union."

The termly missive also informed us that "C Prior, of Keble, plays Rugger when the days are fine and a gramophone when they are wet", while DJS Stevens, of Exeter, "wears a 1st xi blazer and carries a tennis racket wet or fine."

Manifestly there was no shortage of OPM news, one way or another in the pages of the Plymothian and it was encouraging to read that the OPM Club now "undoubtedly has the highest membership of any old boys' club west of Bristol – 453." Membership had, we read, increased during Bert Sargent's Presidency and the new occupant of that office, Walter Weekes, was able to report that a number of old "boys" were rejoining the club. All of which meant that in addition to being able to revive the School OPM Debate there was "progress in all branches of the Club's sporting sections, especially in Hockey, which now has its own ground at Peverell Park." There was also talk of "a cross country run or athletic sports between (the more immediate) Past v Present."

Another innovation was the OPM weekly luncheon, held at the Royal Hotel every Thursday at 1pm. *"You have only to drop in any Thursday. Ask for the OPM table. It will cost you only a modest half-crown (unless of course you are very thirsty)."* There was even talk, for the first time in many years, of the Club possibly hiring a room at a hotel, for certain days during the week.

OPM RFC 1935/6 "Among the most popular Junior Rugby teams in Plymouth" read the Evening Herald caption. Standing; David Spear, Ron Lawry, Leslie Clemas, Colin Bright (Captain), Venning, 'Arry Edmunds, FB Briggs. Kneeling; Arthur Lyddon, GFN Snell, Bell, Michael Parker, Huncombe and George Creber.

Below: George Creber's completed fixture card.

DATE.	OPPONENTS.	Gd.	POINTS. FOR.	POINTS. AGT.	Result.	DATE.	OPPONENTS.	Gd.	POINTS. FOR.	POINTS. AGT.	Result.
1935.						1936.					
Sept. 21st	Devon't Services 'A'	H	6	19	L P	Jan. 4th	H.M.S. *Drake*	A	0	14	L P
,, 28th	Plymouth Argaum	H	0	11	L P	,, 11th	Old Suttonians	A	–	–	S
Oct. 5th	St. Austell Hornets	H	0	6	L	,, 18th	St. Luke's College	A	0	21	L P
,, 12th	TECHNICAL COLLEGE	H	58	0	W P S	,, 25th	Devon't Services 'A'	A	–	–	S
,, 19th	R.N. Coll. Dartmouth	A	0	11	L P	Feb. 1st	Royal Marines	A	3	7	L P
,, 26th	St. Luke's College	A	6	8	L P	,, 8th	St. Austell Hornets	A	0	34	L P
Nov. 2nd	DEVPT. H.S.O.P.	H	14	3	W P	,, 15th	Rover Scouts	H	8	5	W P
	Old Suttonians					,, 22nd	O.P.O.	H	6	L	L P
,, 9th	H.M.S. *Drake*	H	0	14	L P	,, 29th	Civil Service	H	0	6	L P
,, 16th	Plymouth College	A			L P						
,, 23rd	Kingsbridge	A	0	15	L P	Mar. 7th	Liskeard	A	3	12	L
,, 30th	Okehampton	A	0	16	L P	,, 14th	Camborne Sch. Mines	H	14	3	W P
						,, 21st	Prince of Wales Vols.	A			S
Dec. 7th	Camborne Sch. Mines	A	3	21	L P S	,, 28th	Kingsbridge	A	6	9	L P S
,, 14th	Devonport Y.M.C.A.	H	3	8	L P	April 4th	Okehampton	H	10	0	W P
,, 21st	Plymouth College	A	–	–	S	,, 11th	Totnes	A	6	3	W P
Thrs. 26th	Plymouth Argaum	H	0	6	L P	,, 18th	Devonport Y.M.C.A.	A	0	9	L P
Dec. 28th	Rover Scouts	H	11	0	W P	,, 25th	PLYMOUTH ARGAUM	A	0	6	L P
			101	145					156	282	55 131

APPEARANCES 24
POINTS SCORED 15   PLAYED 28 WON 7 LOST 21 SCRATCHED 5

Clearly the Club was flourishing; the Rugger side played over 20 fixtures, the cricket team had nineteen matches (Whitburn bagged a couple of centuries) and the hockey sides had thirty 1st xi and twenty-four 2nd xi games respectively. OPMs also had use of the School Fives Courts on Sundays and *"the College bath"* for swimming, every evening 6.30-8 (except Sundays).

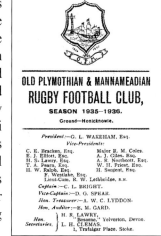

Despite the evidence of a happy liason between the School and Club, particularly in the sporting arena, the Headmaster was keen to point out to the old boys at their annual dinner that year that there was more to life than sport.

"Public schools, had been regarded as homes of the worship of the successful athlete. Games," said Ralph, *"were still over-valued in England, and by no means only in the schools, and over-valued in the sense that pre-eminence in games gave a boy undue rank and importance. It might be that the public schools had taught England to play games, and this country had taught Europe, but it was a very large chicken that came home to roost. Schoolmasters must definitely and firmly counteract that dream of influence; they must pay less lip service and give much more weight to intellect and knowledge."*

"There is urgent and immediate need in this country and elsewhere for efficient leadership. More than ever before the country calls for men of resource, initiative, and a high sense of responsibility."

Possibly as a follow-on from this, Jackson and Loosemore proposed *"That the prominence given to Sport is out of all proportion to its value,"* that October, only to find it heavily rejected by a vote of 26-11.

We should, of course, remember that this was the time that competitive games were introduced into the Prep and teachers were still very heavily involved in bolstering up the School side whenever they played non-school sides. Mr Mercer had another good season with the bat, scoring 62 for the Staff against the School. Mr Bonser took five wickets in the same game. Jenkins and Lawry bowled well for the School, but it was HG U'ren who again starred with bat and ball, hitting a handful of half-centuries and taking a number of useful catches in the field. Indeed he won the School Fielding Cup and was unlucky not to be selected for his county, as he hit five centuries playing club cricket during the summer, including two in consecutive innings for the Somerset Stragglers against the United Services.

U'ren also won all three sprint events at the School Athletics but, despite adding the long jump title to his haul, finished behind both Carder and Ronson, who were Victor Ludorum and Proxime Accessit respectively. Nevertheless he acquitted himself well in London where he represented the School in the Public Schools Athletic Meeting and later he won the Devon County half-mile Championship.

Thompson's House Athletic Group, 1935: Standing; DN Baker, DC Prideaux, KE Kevern, DO'C Mahoney, GJ Wycisk, J Pitts, RW Whiting, TW Sargent. Sitting; DW Gay, VJE Boatright, DL High, JL Rounson, DE Carder, MD Solomon, LN Muddeman.

1935

Kitchen and Wycisk were the junior stars, while U'ren distinguished himself once more on the Hockey pitch. One of three players that season to collect their colours, (GW Irish and RE Lawry were the other two), U'ren was also selected to play for Devon against Cornwall. In the swimming bath RF Tuckett reigned supreme winning all five main events and setting two new records in the process (in the 50 yards – 30 seconds; and the 100 yards – 69.6 seconds). Fellow water-polo player K North was runner-up and together the two of them helped the School team win four of their eight water-polo matches. Not the School's best season but not a bad record when you consider none of the eight fixtures were against other schools and one set of opponents, the Plymouth Amateurs, included three of last year's School team in their line-up.

DL High was another of the current water-polo players that season, although it was to be his last; he had just been awarded a State Scholarship as a result of his Higher Certificate Examination performance. Other leavers that year included RCD Jasper, the *"School Pianist"* since 1932 and HG U'ren, who was bound for Glasgow and the West of Scotland Rugby Club.

Other major Rugby news at this time included JR Spear's performances for Durham County and his international trials and Meyricke Jones' selection in the Autumn of 1935 to play for Devon.

Like "Jumbo" Jones, fellow English teacher, Hugh Dent, who came to Plymouth College that same term, was a Keble College graduate. However, whereas the one held sway on the rugger pitch, the other very quickly made his mark in that place he would long be associated with – the Library.

Dent is appointed

Up until now there had been different libraries for different sections of the School. However, in his first report, after less than a year at the School, Mr Dent noted that the Library in Mr Davies' room, *"founded on the remnants of the old Middle School Library, is rapidly developing into a general School Library, whose books are being borrowed by members of all forms except the Firsts' and Sixths' (and they will be welcome)."*

He then added; *"It is at present a free library with no system of punishments or fines except for loss or damage. A library can only be run on these lines if everyone who uses it will remember that in fairness to the other users he must bring his books back after a week, either to return or renew. We trust you to keep this privilege: it is in your hands. And in your hands, the books will either remain clean or become dirty, either keep their appearance of newness or become dog-eared and backless."*

If Hugh Dent was quick to make his unassuming presence felt in the Library, he also found himself fairly swiftly on the other side of the debating chamber from that other new member of the English department, Meyricke Jones. The occasion was a rare, but welcome, Staff Debate, the issue was *"That no good purpose can be served by further support for the League of Nations"*. Jones and Westhead proposed, the Head and Hugh Dent opposed, and successfully defeated, the motion by a narrow majority – 23-20.

If the Staff were, once again, acting more as a team, both on and off the pitch, the credit must surely go to the man who put the team together – Herbert Ralph. With the arrival of Dent and MacDonald Porter in the autumn of '35, although he couldn't have known it, Ralph had assembled a remarkable collection of young men.

Mac Porter joins the line-up

The youngest of them appeared together in the Staff Dramatic Society's March 1936 adaptation of George Bernard Shaw's *"Arms and the Man"* - and very popular it was too.

"For the first time for a number of years the performance was not confined to one night, and a crowded and appreciative audience attested the success of the experiment. The "stars" of the previous production were content to dim their glories at the rise of a new galaxy of constellations."

Produced by Charlie Barnes it starred five of the six most recent appointments at Plymouth College, Ted Mercer, Meyricke Jones, MacDonald Porter, Hugh Dent and Charles Firman, all of them, including the producer, still in their twenties.

The female parts were taken by Miss Pryor, Miss Tudball, Mrs Porter and Mr Dent, whose *"quiet role"* as Nicola, *"contrasted effectively with those of the more vigorous studies."*

Miss Tudball and Mr Mercer were particularly well received and during the intervals the *"enthusiastic audience greatly appreciated the delightful music of Mrs Firman, Mrs Davies and Mr Porter... the whole production reflects the utmost credit upon Mr CL Barnes."*

The School end of term concert had featured two short dramatic presentations, *"The Jest of Hahalaba"*, by Lord Dunsany and F Sladen Smith's *"The Poison Party"*. Mr Jones produced the former, Mr Woodcock the latter. RF Fowles was Hahalaba, the Spirit of Laughter, in the one, while SB Jackson was the King and RE Crosby, the Queen Mother, in the other.

The musical part of the evening was conducted by the newly appointed OPM President, Walter Weekes and the class singing was accompanied by Dr Harold Lake. *"In Praise of Neptune"*, *"The Lass with the Delicate Air"*, and *"Where the Bee Sucks"*, were among the songs heard and *"although there were signs of nervousness"* ... *"the programme went off as well as ever"*.

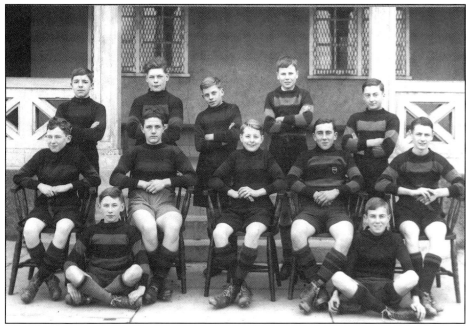

Above: Junior Rugby; Standing DJ Algate, RG Bennett, J Bishop, AB Woodrow, E Richards. Seated; FC Ballantine, GJ Wycisk, HG Sparks (Capt.), DO'CMahoney, WH Moon. Front; D Prideaux, J Pitts. Below; College House Rugby; RL Isaac, DF Rickard, JR Ede, JDT Griffiths, FW Bolton. Seated; G Luxton, KJ McIntyre, RE Lawry (Capt.) MLP Bartlett, D Castle. Front; SK Lawry.

Thompson's House Aquatic Group, 1935. Standing; CJ Atkey, HB Tickle, GJ Wycisk, R Vinton, AJM Down. Seated; DL High, DW Gay, RF Tuckett, DE Ballantine. In front; RG Atkey. Below: Junior Hockey; Standing; D Prideaux, DJ Algate, GJ Wycisk, EC Corre. Seated; J Bishop, RW Whiting, FC Ballantine (Vice-Capt.), KE Kevern, J Pitts. Front; TW Sargent, RG Atkey. Absent; MS Hallett.

This was quite a happy term for the School. At the first Inter-School Sports Competition, held at the County Ground in Exeter, on 21 March, the Plymouth College team, under JL Ronson, had finished a creditable second to Blundells, well ahead of the rest of the field, including West Buckland, Hele's (Exeter), Plympton Grammar, and Kingsbridge, Torquay, Tavistock and Ashburton Grammar Schools.

Ronson, himself, won the javelin, while Castle *"ran a good 100 yards, Kitchen showed great promise with a well-run mile and GL Spear did well in the Hop, Step and Jump."*

In the Hockey, the School put eight past Newton College at home and three away, without conceding any, and beat Kelly 4-1. Soggy surfaces and cancelled fixtures damped the team spirit at times. However on an individual level, Ted Mercer played the odd game for the School and Castle, Irish and Lawry were among those who turned in consistently good performances for the side. Indeed Lawry was chosen to play for the Devon "A" team against Cornwall "A". Turner, Collins and Boatright were among the others who won their colours that season, while Lawry, Castle and Irish were equally distinguished on the rugger field. Lawry was the team captain and although a number of games were lost, when you consider some of the teams the boys were playing they acquitted themselves rather well. This season they played their first game against Dartmouth RNC 1st XV against whom they put up a brave fight, as they did against Plymouth Albion, who only just beat them 9-3.

Altogether the School was ticking along very nicely; it had a thoroughly-rejuvenated and expanded staffroom, several new classrooms, a new gymnasium, a newly-invigorated Preparatory Department and there was the immanent prospect of a new pavilion. And yet still the head wasn't ready to rest on his laurels; at least *"not until the unsightly group of huts to the left of the School have been demolished."*

The body of King George V lies in state in Westminster

Whatever Ralph's agenda for the first term of 1936, however, it was overshadowed by the death of the King. In the first Plymothian of the New Year (April 1936) there was no editorial – just this:

"All other events of the term sink into insignificance beside a loss which has gone to the hearts of millions of men and women in every part of the world. The whole nation and Empire mourn a King who was truly a friend and a father to his people. It is no exaggeration to say that King George V knew and understood his people as none of his predecessors ever did. Devoting all his powers to the common good, never seeking his own glorification, never sparing himself, by his personal contacts, he made us a more united nation than at any time in our history. He was a personality whose influence for sanity and stability in the troubles that have shaken the world was felt as well abroad as in this country. In an age when monarchies have fallen on every side, the British Throne has been solidly established. Beneath this personality was set a foundation of religion – a simple religion based on the conviction of his responsibility and duty to God. He was a King who made service and duty the ideal of his life, and not only of his official life, but in his private life as well. His ideal of responsibility, of self-sacrificing work, and of self-identification with the life and sorrows of others, has given us a new idea of what a kingly life ought to be."

There was no name at the end of the tribute, but there was no mystery surrounding the authorship, two pages on, the School Notes opened thus;

"We are grateful to the Headmaster for kindly writing the foreword to this term's number of the Plymothian."

It certainly was a remarkable in memoriam; most effusive and one that would have left all who read it in little doubt about Ralph's views on the monarchy, or at least King George V, for this was not your typical *"The King is dead, long live the King"* piece. There was no mention of Edward VIII who, after all, had been proclaimed King several months earlier, on 21 January, the day after the late George's demise.

Curiously enough, just as the *"conspiracy of silence"* promoted by Lord Beaverbrook, a friend of Edward VIII, contrived to keep details of the King's love affair with Mrs Simpson out of the British press until December, just a few days before he announced his abdication, so there was absolutely no significant mention of Edward in the Plymothian.

Edward and Mrs Simpson

(There was just a one line entry in the Preparatory School Notes – *"On January 22, the School was able to listen in to the broadcast of the Proclamation of Edward VIII"*.)

Indeed it would not be until July 1937 that we would find mention of the monarchy within the pages of the School Magazine once more. If we were in any doubt that the Head was employing the maxim – *"If you can't think of anything nice to say about someone then say nothing"*, then we only had to read between the lines of the seemingly-anonymous piece that was, undoubtedly, written in the Headmaster's study.

"When we review the crisis of last December (1936), *one conclusion is inevitable – that in a difficult and unhappy situation one figure stands out above reproach and above the accusation of anything like self-interest. In those anxious days the King whose Coronation we celebrated in May showed a resolution and dignity that are beyond all praise and spared no effort to move his brother by appeals to his chivalry and his sense of duty to the Throne."*

"It is no exaggeration to say that we owe directly to the qualities of the present King – and his Queen – the recovery of the country from the shock of the Abdication. What was needed was the immediate restoration of confidence at home and throughout the Empire: that confidence was recovered then, and it has grown since then: and it was founded absolutely upon the country's knowledge of his sense of duty. Like his father in many respects, he resembles him most closely in finding that same strict sense of duty the guiding rule of his life."

Here, then, we had the perfect insight into Ralph's own philosophy, his own version of the values that were required to get the best from life generally and specifically to prepare Britain for whatever troubles loomed ahead.

He continued; *"It is not often realised today that a hundred years ago, when the greater part of Europe was ruled by Kings and Emperors, the shakiest throne in Europe was to all appearances the throne of Britain. King George III and his sons George IV and William IV, by their misfortunes and weaknesses had left their subjects little inclined to respect their successors and far from convinced that they desired a long continued succession. But Queen Victoria and Edward VII and George V have proved to the world that a monarch can be the first servant of a nation; and though six months ago people were openly saying that the crisis might be the end of monarchy, today, established more firmly than ever upon the affection and loyalty of an Empire, the British throne will stand when more pretentious structures have fallen."*

Queen Elizabeth and King George VI on the balcony of Buckingham Palace with the Princesses Elizabeth and Margaret.

The circumstances of His Majesty's accession confront him with special difficulties such as none of his predecessors ever had to face: and he is entitled to a special sympathy from all of us. King George and Queen Elizabeth have said that they are sure of their people: their people are equally sure of them."

"May their reign be long and prosperous."

If these then were the qualities that Ralph looked for in his King and Queen they were equally what he looked for in his boys, his staff and indeed in his own behaviour. This was the Head who had arrived at Plymouth College mindful that his own workload was likely to be almost untenable, that his staff were already overburdened and yet that there were other more pressing aims. So it was that he gave of himself and expected his staff to do likewise until the new buildings were completed, and then and only then, looked towards improving the lot of his men in the staffroom.

Ralph clearly looked for loyalty and commitment from those around him and certainly, if we are to judge him on the loyalty and commitment displayed by those he appointed, there can be little doubt that he was good at spotting these attributes.

Undoubtedly he would have recognised them in two earlier servants of the School, both of whom passed away in 1936. Apart from Bert Sargent, there was no other master in the annals of Plymouth College, up to that point in time, who knew as many old boys as Francis Palmer. Indeed, if you add in his years at Mannamead, his 43-year-stint, from 1879 to 1920, puts him in a league of his own. Thanks largely to Palmer the amalgamation of 1896 had been far smoother than it might otherwise have been and it was quite fitting that he lived to see his name employed as one of the four main School houses.

Unlike Palmer, Joseph Pearce Brown had never taught at the School, in fact he left school (in Bury) when he was just 14, however his influence and assistance here extended over just as many years. His association began in the 1880s when the first of his five sons who went through Plymouth College, Kenneth and Harold joined the School. Ralph, James and Charles Brown later followed in their wake.

Around the time of the amalgamation Brown became a Governor *"and from that date till my departure in 1908, was in my eyes the one Governor of high value".*

So wrote Francis Colson, in what was the longest obituary yet to be printed in the Plymothian. *"I do not say that I always saw eye to eye with him, and I think that he sometimes disapproved of the course I took, but at any rate he was there to give advice."*

Having played a major part in converting the School from a company to a public trust, Brown was elected Vice-Chairman of Governors in 1909 and became Chairman in 1921. *"His time in office will be remembered by the erection of the new laboratory and the enlargement of the School buildings, as well as by his personal liberality shewn in the gift of the fine gates."*

Joseph Pearce Brown

"A Magistrate, Councillor and Mayor for two successive and momentous years (1917-19)," Mr Brown was closely involved with many other civic and church activities, but even during his last, long illness *"he shewed no abatement of interest and insisted on being fully informed of all that was done or happened"* at Plymouth College.

At the time of his death, Brown's son Ralph, was serving as Vice-Chairman of the Governors and among the new appointments the Governors had to consider that year were the replacements for Miss Lawrey, in the Preparatory Department, and for Mr Lord, in the Main School.

Lionel Lord was leaving to take up the Headship of Bury Grammar School; *"We have for some years hoped and feared that we should lose him thus – hoped for his sake that a long overdue promotion of this sort would come his way, feared that the school would be deprived of one who had contributed so much to its highest interest."*

Lord had indeed been the perfect schoolmaster while at Plymouth College, *"his life bound up with everything to do with the School"*. Having long lived with his mother, he married after she died, and was in one respect at least an object of some interest to the boys *"when he walked he clanked in a mysterious way"*.

A stalwart of the Literary and Debating Society, one of Lord's last roles at the School was the production of *"The Spartan Girl"*, in the new gym; one of three plays put on during the Society's Annual Entertainment. AW Miller was Neptune, TS Fookes was Phoebe and WM Winn, a *"delightful"* Eustace. *"The players did it full justice, and had a magnificent set of pillars, on which Mr Lord is to be congratulated."*

"In Port" and *"Tails Up"*, produced by Messrs Dent and Woodcock, respectively, were the two other theatrical diversions that night and provided every evidence that the Society was prospering.

It was a good year, too, for the the School Science Society, *"which has been lying dormant since 1930 and was successfully rejuvenated this Term"* (summer 1936). John Dufton agreed to look after the finance, the Headmaster was elected President and AG Hesling was secretary to a five-strong committee. Two early visits were arranged – one to the City's Automatic Telephone Exchange, the other to the Marine Biological Association's Laboratories on the Hoe.

One of the principal extra-curricular excursions this year though was the trip to Belgium with Di Davies. Nineteen members of the Upper School went, spending three days in Bruges, visiting Ypres, Seebrugge and Sluys (in Holland), and several more in Brussels; *"Our stay here seemed to consist of innumerable tram-rides, and we visited amongst other places, the Palace of Justice, the King's Palace, the Unknown Soldier's Tomb and the Musee des Beaux-Arts. On the last day we went to the field of Waterloo."*

Of greater interest to the main body of the School however were the battles fought out on the field at Ford

Park and few sporting moments that summer were more talked about than George Bonser's hatrick, three wickets in three deliveries, all clean bowled, for the Staff versus the School on 16 May. However, despite returning figures of 6 for 32, Mr Bonser's feat was not enough to sway the game in the staff's favour, the boys skittling the masters all out for 93, twenty runs behind. Pro Heywood with 15 was the only one on the staff side to join Charlie Barnes in double figures.

It was Castle, though, who had promised so much the season before, who was the star of that match and of the summer. To the 46 he got in that game he added an unbeaten 122 at Dartmouth against their seconds and several sixties, yielding a massive 884 runs for the season. Lawry bagged a fine 100 not out in the Past v Present fixture; the recently-departed U'ren hitting 60 for the old boys, before being bowled by Lawry.

Thanks to Castle's success with the bat, and Lawry's with the bat and ball, the School had a fairly successful summer, even putting up a good show against a touring side, from Wolverhampton, who came down with Partridge, *"the Warwickshire county bowler,"* who finished up with 4-21.

In the School Athletic Sports, JL Ronson, who had done so well in the Inter-School event, won Victor Ludorum by a comparatively-narrow margin from MLP Bartlett,

Fives Team, 1936; PS Anderson, CJ Hallett, DE Ballatine. Front; RE Lawry, AHM Smyth (Captain), MLP Bartlett.

1936

equalling the 24-year-old School record for the half-mile in the process - and, had the ground been not so soft, he probably would have beaten it.

JD Bishop was the Junior Victor, while dropping yet another age group, the Preparatory Athletic Sports were notable for the introduction of Standard Times (first advocated for the Main School years earlier by Mr Gwyther and first used in the Summer of 1929) and Standard Certificates.

"Boys not actually competing on the day were able to obtain Standard Certificates for results in Heats."

Among the Standards in question was any time under 16 seconds for the Under 12 boys, 17 seconds for the U-10s and 20 seconds U-8s. The Long Jump Standard was around the ten-foot (3 metre) mark and the High Jump around three-feet (one metre). Twenty-five boys gained Standard Points.

More and more the Prep was coming to mirror the Main School. Competition was being introduced in all aspects of the Prep day, in the classroom, on the sports field and in the gym;

"The boxing class meets as usual on Wednesday afternoons in the Gymnasium, under the instruction of Qtr.-Mast. Serg. Featherstone, RM. All the boys are making good progress and not a few look like being good boxers."

It was Rugby though that made the biggest impact in terms of providing a scaled-down version of the Main School for the younger boys; *"The whole school is now playing Rugby Football (December 1936), and it has been fortunate that the weather has been good, so that there could be plenty of practice. Maximus play quite a good game and are now tackling well and learning to run straight and pass out to the wings. Major and Minor are very keen and although there are many newcomers in these games, they seem to be picking up the fundamentals very well. Minimus like nothing better than to have to run after the ball and then to fall on it in a heap. But they have learned to tackle, to*

take a pass and "jump for it" in the line out ... House matches should be played next week."

Curiously enough, at the same time as we had this new situation where there were more younger boys than ever sporting the School Colours on the rugby pitch, came a proposal from J Leighton Fouracre OPM that *"like members of other Old Boys' clubs, the OPMs should incorporate in their colours those of the "old school"."*

The proposal was made at a special general meeting of the Club held at the School that summer, and held it was following a request signed by 22 members. The suggestion was that the magenta, blue and brown of the OPMs be changed to green red and silver, making them more in line with the School colours.

Quite where the impetus for this proposal came from is unclear, but special general meetings were, and still are, very rare and it's interesting to note that the proposal was actually seconded by the Headmaster, Herbert Ralph himself.

Samples of the new colours were shown and there were amendments suggested for the crest as well.

OLD PLYMOTHIAN & MANNAMEADIAN
RUGBY FOOTBALL CLUB,
SEASON 1936–1937.
Ground—Honicknowle.

The meeting was informed that the price of the new colours and crest would be about 4s6d (22p). OPMs Nelson and Breeze opposed the changes and H Elliott said that if new rugby and hockey shirts were purchased it would involve a lot of expense. Fouracre, however, said he could see no reason why the two colours should not run concurrently for a while.

Nevertheless when the proposition was eventually put to the vote it was defeated by a large majority. Although a subsequent refinement, whereby the Club adopt the School Crest with the letters OPM, underneath was carried. Again Ralph supported the motion and nor was he finished there, for the final proposition of the day came from the Headmaster himself.

Essentially this concerned the tidying up of OPM subscriptions, there being an ongoing problem of people either missing payments or moving on and not providing forwarding addresses. The proposal therefore was that *"as an alternative to the annual subscription of 6 shillings (30p) members could make a prepayment of one guinea (£1.05) for four years, two guineas for ten years, or five guineas for life membership"*. For those who had already been longstanding members the suggestion was that *"an abatement of one guinea should be made for every ten years subscription previously paid"*.

From an administrative point of view the proposition made a lot of sense, but it wasn't simply a suggestion from the floor and in supporting the motion Mr Ralph read a report from a sub-committee which had been appointed to consider the matter.

Clearly, having made considerable progress with improvements to the fabric of the Main School and its staffing, and to the Prep School and its staffing, the energetic and capable Headmaster was now doing his best to sort out the OPM Club and, at the same time, certainly as far as the club colours were concerned, make it more obviously an extension of the Plymouth College experience.

As you might imagine his speech at the Prize Giving that September in the Guildhall, although overshadowed by the death of the Chairman of the Governors, was a still upbeat affair and he spoke of *"changes made at the School since the last Speech-day which no-one regretted."*

"A house in Shaftesbury Villas has been acquired which would be used as Scout Headquarters and additional changing rooms and the old, unsightly blocks of huts have been demolished..."

"Changes which no-one regretted ..." Really? Please sir, then what about AHM Smyth's Plymothian editorial that Christmas; *"The Huts have vanished: a simple expression, yet one that symbolises the piercing of the defences of tradition by the siege-engines of utility. No longer shall we speed through the rain to burst panting but triumphant through those aged portals. No longer will the sweet savour of chestnuts roasting upon miniature furnaces, lighten the tedium of other less technical portions of the curriculum. Even the Scouts, last defenders of the ancient citadel, have retreated and established themselves in a drawing room complete with gas-fire, electric light and other modern conveniences. Violent hands have rent the vitals of these ancient relics. Grass now shall flourish over their last resting place; the grave of tradition has no other monument. Their soul has fled in terror from the grasping hands of the navvy."*

Smyth spoke for a generation who developed an emotional attachment to these inanimate structures which had, despite their shortcomings, nevertheless, helped to shape their schoolboy experience, and the loss of them was like having part of your life prematurely consigned just to the memory bank.

"Still, they were rather ugly," concluded Smyth, who was also head boy that term. A bright boy he can have been in no doubt that the days of the huts had been numbered throughout his time at the School, as the Headmaster had been plotting their removal since the

day he accepted his post at Plymouth College.

However much pleasure Ralph derived from imparting this news and however much the parents enjoyed hearing it, there can be little doubt that for most of the boys, sitting patiently in the Guildhall, it was, then as it is now, largely a test of endurance, as one particular Plymothian piece, just a few pages on from the Speech Day report, bore witness.

The Guildhall and Westwell Street from Princess Square - 1937

"Without the airless chamber the sun shines clear and bright. But within, the ghosts of departed heroes flit to and fro amid the gloom. Obedient to the orders of the High Priest, the garb of those attending on this ceremony is sombre and dull." And if the clothing was thought to be dull, so too were the orators;

"None save the initiated comprehend this mystic speech. The profane throng gazes on in wonder, awed by the profoundness and solemnity..."

Another typical Speech Day and yet another gently-mocking Plymothian contribution undoubtedly vetted and checked by the Reverend Benskin in whose overall charge the magazine had been for some fifteen years. But not for much longer, as over Christmas '37 the Headmaster noted, with much regret *"that we find ourselves obliged to drop the pilot of this periodical".*

Benskin made a big impression on many of his pupils, particularly those who had a base for a year in Room 1, and in some instances that impression was quite a physical as well as mental one;

"No other form so left its mark upon my mind, although in all, the College had me in its charge ten years, and I can only attribute this phenomenon to the felicity of my sojourn in Room 1, or alternatively to the increased mental liveliness provoked by the occasional exercise of certain weapons kept by the form master in an "armoury" there against emergency."

So wrote *"Anon"* who almost certainly was regular, post-school contributor and former-editor of IIIA's short lived journal Chin Wag – JC Trewin. He continued, *"despite the fact that some eight years have passed since the College passed me on to the Greater Outside World with a rather too audible sigh of relief, I realised that I was able to recite the complete alphabetical form list for the year during which I adorned IIIA."*

"Being of an idle disposition I wrote this list down and tried to think what had become of us all. To some extent my efforts were successful, and because it occurs to me that a successor usually feels a certain morbid

curiosity as to what awful fate befell his predecessor I append my results for the former's information – or (if he so prefers it) - as a warning."

"Altogether there were twenty-nine of us, but I do not know what happened to five of that number. Three of these left the School soon after and naturally disappeared out of my ken. Of the remaining twenty-four, four became doctors; two went into the Church, and two to balance matters into the Law, one into each branch. Two more – the bravest – became school-masters. Then two went into banks and two (who were appropriately joint editors of the form magazine) became journalists. One of them, who is now on the Morning Post, contributes not infrequently to this magazine. Engineering and Science claimed three of us, and of these one at any rate is already very properly distinguished for the work he had done."

"Of the others one is, or was, a chartered accountant in Ireland and another eventually became a commercial traveller. Four, so far as my information is trustworthy, went respectively into real estate, the insurance world, a shipping company, the employ of Imperial Airways. The last one knew the rest of us for sinners, so became himself a publican."

"I think that is the lot. It is odd that no-one went into the Services and I should hate Mr Duff Cooper to hear about it; but the chances are that the forms preceding or following us made up for our defection."

Before laying his pen to rest our scribe added;

"Of the twenty-nine, nine went to one or other university (including that of Saskatchewan): and seven remained in Plymouth. One has died, and four to my knowledge have married – a doctor, a clergyman, a school-master and a barrister."

A fascinating insight to the early fate of the Reverend Benskin's first ever form in Room 1, assembled originally in the late summer of 1922, and no doubt their former form-master enjoyed reading the piece as much as anyone.

Certainly the combination of information and light humour was a welcome one and contrasted somewhat starkly in that particular issue with a lack of OPM notes; "Apathy seems rampant among OPMs. The weekly luncheon collapsed though lack of support. The originator of the scheme attended in hope, until three solitary luncheons at the big table convinced him that his was the only interest."

Another gloomy day in Plymouth - 1937

Whether it was apathy or just simply the weather, it's not clear, but the winter of 1936/37 was a fairly dismal one; "Rain and occasionally snow have not only provided the chief topic for conversation this term," wrote Smyth in his second Plymothian editorial, "they have driven us to abandon our usual athletic pursuits. True some of the more reckless went running but they were very few indeed. Other more august members have spent their leisure hours, of which they seem to have an abundance, in preparation for the Great Event." At which, on the night of 18 March, they "revealed to admiring members of the neater sex how profitably they had spent their term. They had forgotten how to side-step but their quick step was above reproach."

There was a reasonable amount of Rugby played before Christmas, but there was little in the results to "enthuse over".

"In the "tight" the School forwards certainly met no superiors, at long last they were persuaded to heel quickly from the loose, and in the loose rushes magnificently led by Ballantine (almost a GS Conway with the ball at his feet), they gave many defenders a harassing time."

"Our best performances were against Dartmouth RNC 1st XV, RNEC 2nd XV, the OPMs, the City Police XV and the Redruth Wanderers, all of whom we managed to defeat once."

Strong winds and muddy pitches, after days of continuous rain, made playing conditions difficult but inter-school matches went well and both Ballantine ("probably the finest all-round forward produced by the School since JR Spear") and GL Spear had "the distinction of playing for the Devon Public Schools XV."

Castle, Ife and McIntyre were among the other School rugby stars, with Castle, Ife, Ballantine, Hallett and Bishop all acquitting themselves well on the hockey pitch too – when weather permitted. Results were patchy but Newton were well beaten in a game played in a continuous downpour the School, "flicking" and "pushing" in the mud, rather than trying to hit as Newton did. In non inter-school matches Mr Mercer proved once more to be a prolific scorer; netting a hat-trick in the 5-3 defeat of the University of the South West in Exeter, scoring the lone goal against OPMs and bagging two of the ten put past the Royal Marines at Mount Wise.

On the Fives front, Smyth, who in addition to being head-boy, Plymothian editor and troop leader of the scouts, was also Captain of Fives, was able to report "a marked increase in the number of players – in spite of the handicap of open courts and frequent rain."

Much of the credit for the revival of interest in this, the most erratically-supported of the school games, was "due to Mr Dent, who has spent many hours in playing and coaching."

"*The junior members of the School are most enthusiastic,*" he noted, "*a fact which was attested by the unprecedented demand to play over the half-term ... Unfortunately it rained.*"

Attesting to the awful conditions and affirming to the oft-heard plea for improvements to the fives courts there was yet another pithy piece in Plymothian;

"*PLATO, REPUBLIC XI*

Socrates. *Tell me, Callicrates, do the authorities of this Academy pursue the system of joint mental and physical education?*

Callicrates. *They do. But although the scholars, of necessity, are compelled to imbibe learning to cultivate their minds, if such a course is possible, the system of games is voluntary.*

Socrates. *I understand. Are all the scholars willing to cultivate their bodies?*

Callicrates. *Pray Socrates, do not be misled by the word "voluntary." The scholars only exercise volition in choosing whether to play on Wednesday or Saturday.*

Socrates. *Then do the scholars play games only in deference to the demands of Authority?*

Callicrates. *The majority do: others do so, in order to clothe themselves in coats of many colours; others, in order to appear heroic in the eyes of those members of the neater sex who adorn the field of play.*

Socrates. *How excellent a system. Am I to understand that the authorities wish to improve the physical well-being of the youth by regular exercise?*

Callicrates. *You are, Socrates. Unfortunately few scholars have been able to benefit from exercise during this past term, owing to the almost incessant rain.*

Socrates. *Consequently, the mimic battle, called hockey has been rarely played. Yet tell me; are not the structures known as Fives Courts commonly roofed in; and is it not possible to play in such covered courts in all weathers?*

Callicrates. *It is.*

Socrates. *Then is it not illogical that the authorities who profess to be eager physically to educate the scholars, should thus withhold such an opportunity for bodily exercise?*

Callicrates. *True, Socrates. But this is Plymouth not Athens.*

This is Plymouth ... in the thirties, St Andrew's Cross & Basket St.

The foul weather also affected the Cross Country run, for although the weather was fine on the appointed day – Wednesday 10 March – "*the course was very heavy owing to the previous rain and snow storms*".

Nevertheless RRC Kitchen completed the 3.5 miles course at Marsh Mills in just over 26 minutes and GG Crocker and GF Mutton were not too far behind. Trevaskis won the junior event, run over 1.75 miles, finishing ahead of Heather and Naylor.

Ten days later, at the Devon Public and Secondary School's Athletic Association Inter-Schools Sports held at Blundell's School, Kitchen again ran a good race under still-heavy conditions, beating all-comers in the one mile. Blundell's won the event, for the second time, with Plymouth College finishing fourth. Castle, Sherriff, Spear and Guppy were among the School athletes at the event and Guppy ran a particularly good hurdles race. Not surprisingly, the following week he won the School hurdles event, and the 100 yards. His 72 points

were not enough to give him the Victor Ludorum title though. That went to GL Spear, who rather remarkably won the high jump, long jump, shot putt, javelin and discus. The last event was won with a throw of 98ft 9 ins which, had he thrown it at Blundell's, would have won him the event there too. Not surprisingly Kitchen won the mile quite comfortably, again under "*adverse conditions*", nevertheless his time of just under 5 minutes was not far off the School record.

VG Bolam was the Junior Victor, with KE Kevern as his nearest rival and it's interesting to note that among the extra events held across the 22, 23 and 24 March, JR Spear was back in town to win the Old Boys 120-yard race in a time of 15 seconds.

JR would have enjoyed watching his brother winning the title that eluded him at School, but there was little doubt about history repeating itself in June when GL Spear won the Aquatic Sports Victor Ludorum title for the second year running. He finished ahead of RP Vinton in all but two events, although the latter's acheivements ultimately helped steer Thompson's to a narrow victory over Sargent's in the House points tally.

There were further points at stake in another aquatic event that Summer Term as the School staged a Swimming Match with RN College, Dartmouth. Described as "*an innovation for both Colleges*" and one which "*proved a very interesting and useful addition*" to the sporting calendar, there were five events contested;

"*Viz:- Diving, Plunging, 100 yds Free Style Race, Medley Team Race and a Free Style Relay Race.*"

"*Dartmouth were very fast and won three races; points were halved in the Diving whereas the Plunging was easily won by the College.*"

Vinton, in "*a magnificent plunge of 56ft 11in*" won the event individually with Garratt about 18 inches behind him. Also, on a purely individual level, Mahoney won the diving. Spear, Atkey, Anderson, Baker and St Clair Johnson were among the others who represented the School.

If there was a predictability about the Spear involvement in the Swimming Pool, there was a similar déjà vu moment in the Scout Troop too, when, following Smyth's departure from the School in the summer GL Spear took over as Troop Leader, a position JR had long held. Interestingly enough both Smyth and JR and a number of other old boys were at the Scout Summer Camp in Portlemouth which was a record breaker *"in the number of Scouts attending and the fact that there was no rain."*

Scouting Spears - JR and GL - Summer Camp 1937

Although not a first team cricketer, there was one other sport that GL Spear acquitted himself particularly well in – boxing. In the 1937 Price Open Challenge Cup final, he only just lost out to D O'C Mahoney, the School Boxing Captain, in the final round – on points. School boxing appeared to be on the up and forty boys joined the Boxing Club in the Summer of '37.

There were two meetings a week, Tuesdays for Juniors, Thursdays for Seniors and F Ash, a former contender for the World Fly Weight title was there to give instruction and *"under his skilled guidance the standard of boxing improved considerably"*.

If Mr Ash was an inspiration in the Gym, there could be little doubt that Pro Heywood was on the field;

"Hail, honest H-yw—d, in thy Juggernaut
Thou sunburnt Keeper of the College field
Before whose arts both weeds and worms must yield
On wickets, pitches and the Prefects' court!
That toilest daily, till the red sun sets
To catch the fish that flounder in thy nets.
Anon in Winter, to the whistle's toot
Teachest the young idea how to boot;
Riding in rattling state o'er thy domain,
How like that Greek of old thou seemest now
That yoked the fiery bulls beneath his plough
And sowed the dragon's teeth upon the plain!
Continue long to flatten out the bumps
And sow the College field with cricket stumps."

"Pro's Poem" was simply signed "D", but many were they that shared its sentiments. In the summer of 1937 Pro bagged 31 wickets for the School in various matches (including 6 for 5 against Plymstock) and scored nearly 250 runs at a very useful average of 35. Only George Bonser managed to take more wickets, and only Castle and Ted Mercer scored more runs. Mr Mercer had a particularly good season; having achieved notable success on the Hockey pitch, he opened his

batting account with three half-centuries and finished the season, after 12 innings, with an average of 42.5. One boy, however, managed an all-round performance that he'd only hinted at the previous season.
"On Wednesday 2 June, batting for the School against the Royal Naval Engineering College, Keyham, D Castle scored 125 runs in 90 minutes."
The knock included 22 fours and was complemented by a series of fine half centuries giving him an average of just over 48 in the 12 games he played for the 1st XI. Indeed the only inter-school game that the School lost that season was when Castle, the team captain, was away at the Oval playing for Devon.

Douglas Castle's cricketing prowess was by no means limited to his batting as he also took a couple of dozen wickets at an average of just ten runs that season – *"a more than useful spin bowler and all in all a sportsman in the best sense of the word"*.

Ballantine also played well and picked up the Fielding Cup, while Atkey and Nicholls showed a lot of promise. Collister was another batsman who *"sees the ball well"* and who enjoyed a good partnership with Mr Bonser – scorer of 54 - against the OPMs.

As for the OPMs themselves they had a reasonable season, winning or drawing more than half their 21 games. There was, however, already a familiar gripe emerging as player loyalty was increasingly difficult to hold;
"Congratulations must be awarded to HG U'ren, who once again represented the OPMs in the Devon side. Gratifying is it indeed to realise that there are still OPMs who stick to the Old Boys, even after they have been chosen to play for the County."
Generally though there was no obvious shortage of loyalty to the "old school" and in 1937 we had the unusual situation whereby Charles Serpell, OPM, gave an address to the Upper and Middle Forms of the School and a few months later, his son, David, also an OPM was back at the School teaching for a term.

Serpell senior, whose address was on "*The Law As a Profession*", was of course the Clerk to the Governing Body, while David, who was offered an appointment on the staff, was en route to a post in the Government and so declined the offer. Curiously enough, however, that same term saw a young Harry Trevena follow his brother into the School, joining IVA, blissfully unaware that he was to spend most of the rest of his life at Ford Park.

Ernest Dundas (right) a new face in the staff room.

The staffroom did see one new, full-time member that summer, though, as twenty-seven year-old, Ernest Dundas came to fill the gap left by Lionel Lord's departure from the Classics department. Like Lord, Dundas was a Cambridge graduate, and the young Merseysider already had three years teaching experience under his belt, at Oulton High School. His appointment levelled up Ralph's Oxbridge choices. He had now brought in three graduates from each University, and curiously enough the next teacher to join the team would be an Oxford man, Charles Hill, replacing another Oxford man, Rev Benskin.

Herbert Ralph had known the Reverend Benskin longer than any other member of the staff;

"*I met him first when he was a youngster of fifteen at Llandovery College; and looking back I can recall, not indeed any promise of the dignified presence of today, but unmistakable signs of that gift of humour and* high spirits which in those days called for a watchful magisterial eye and today does much to relieve the gloom of the Winter term."

Ralph continued; "*We both left Llandovery just before the War, and it was a happy surprise to find in 1929 that one who had been a pupil so many years before was now to be a colleague.*"

He then added; "*There are some aspects of a man's work the value of which it is impossible to assess. Although, on the academic side, Mr Benskin's work has been chiefly associated with History, I believe his most valuable contribution to the life of the School to have been the teaching of Scripture; especially has this been true of the Monday morning periods in which he has given the Sixth Form an opportunity, denied to many of us of an earlier generation, for the exchange of views and the frank discussion not only of the problems of the Bible, but of the problems and difficulties of life itself. I remember with extreme distaste the long double period of Greek Testament with which every Monday of my own Sixth Form days commenced, the relentless dissection of the text of the Pauline Epistles, and the utter failure of our distinguished headmaster to infuse his subject with any human or spiritual interest: and I have not ceased to be grateful to Mr Benskin for undertaking at my request the sort of work he has been doing with our Sixth Forms.*"

The phrase "*at my request*" is the interesting one here, as once again we see the Headmaster looking at an aspect of School life and seeking to improve upon it. Provoking thought was an important aspect of the School experience for Ralph, who wanted to look beyond the confines of the examination system. As he observed at Speech Day that year – quoting a former Headmaster of Rugby School in the process;

"*Examinations have a way of finding out that kind of sloth that likes to learn by heart and won't take the trouble to learn by understanding.*"

"*There is a good deal of intellectual laziness about* today that will not take anyone far, not even through a School Certificate examination. Every boy must realise that his chance in life depends upon what use he makes, not of his memory, but of his mind.*"

Sir Alexander Maxwell, CBE, OPM and Deputy Under-Secretary of State in the Home Office, made a similar point, after presenting the Prizes at the same event. Stating first that those seeking an adventurous life should not despise the Civil Service as a career - – "*I myself have had many queer jobs.*" He said that the sort of boys the Service was looking for were those who "*learned to tackle a job and get to the bottom of things, not merely content with surface value, or putting up a good show.*"

Stirred, himself, by the literature of Ancient Greece and Rome, Sir Alexander quoted liberally from another Civil Servant, Horace, and noted how his verses "*would send him into a concentration camp in some of the great Countries of Europe today.*"

Here, then, was another of the occasional, and slight, references in the Plymothian to the events in the world outside of Plymouth College. Not that there was a lack of awareness in the School itself. As you might expect the Headmaster was most keen that the boys be fully aware of what was happening elsewhere and it's interesting to note that, just a week or so before Speech Day, the School had adopted the Government line on Spain.

AG Helsing's proposal that "*Great Britain should give active military support to the Government of Spain*" was narrowly defeated (14-11). Already tens of thousands of young men from France, Belgium and Britain (including George Orwell), and indeed young anti-fascists from Italy and Germany had joined the International Brigade in Spain. Meanwhile Franco's army had tens of thousands of "volunteers" from fellow-Fascist states, Italy and Germany. The British Government had decreed that anyone enlisting for either side would be liable to a two-year prison sentence.

Scout Summer Camp Scrapbook 1937: clockwise from the left; on the coach, Millbay and the site from Salcombe, Herzogin Cecilie at Anchor, Bathers, Cooks DLT and HD, Troop Leader attempts pipe-lighting on Bolt Head, nursery bathers Jordan and Mills, and right -the Intruders. Four tent goups clockwise; the Owls (pictures 1 & 2 (Trobridge, MIller, Jordan, Mills, Lake and Glen, Badcock, Brown and Gilbert (in front) , the Curlews and the Seals.

At the same time Britain had just completed a two-year plan to treble its air force when CH Pezey proposed to the House that *"the construction of and use of Aircraft should be universally opposed."* Needless to say this one was rather more heavily defeated 31-8, nevertheless with a further six abstentions it suggested that the Literary and Debating Society was itself quite bouyant. Mr Woodcock, recently recovered from a bout of appendicitis, was still Chairman of the Society but Hugh Dent now succeeded Mr Lord as Treasurer. The recently-revived Science Society was also thriving with membership reaching the *"record total of fifty"*.

1937, the Western Morning News Offices, Frankfort Street, with the Co-operative building just to the right.

Members this session enjoyed a Lantern Lecture on the Western Morning News, there was a visit to the Plymouth Electricity Works and GG Gray gave an interesting lecture on *"Colour in relation to photography"* – during which several colour photographs were shown to the audience. At a later meeting Gray and Hesling spoke on *"Elements of Photography"* and *"took, developed and printed a photograph during the course of the lecture, explaining each process as they went along."*
Another newly-constituted association around this time was the Musical Society, chaired by Mr McDonald Porter. JA Brown played Greig's *"To The Spring"* at the inaugural meeting and later an outing was organised to Hele & Co's Organ Works. On 2 March, Walter Weekes gave an *"enjoyable talk on the Life and Works of Beethoven."*

The quality of music performed in the School certainly seems to have taken an upward turn since "McD P" arrived, although clearly one or two with longer memories felt that there had been plenty of fine musical moments in the past too; *"Sir, If you had said in your last number that the Concert of October the 23rd was the most artistic one given at Plymouth College since the war, you might have been correct; but I am afraid you are not aware of the performances that were given years ago, from the time of the late Mr FN Lohr, when he and the late John Pardew, with Dr Moreton and other giants of the past appeared and gave us of their best. Spencer Dyke too, an OPM, has often adorned them, and the late Miss F Woolland, probably the most brilliant violinist in Plymouth for the last 50 years. Then again CG Pike played, also RV Ball, and on one occasion a professional orchestra of about 40 performers gathered from all the best local professionals, was conducted by Mr Walter Weekes. Give the present its fair share of praise, but do not forget others,"* wrote J Leighton Fouracre OPM, to whom the Plymothian editor pointed out that the article in question was actually written by Mr Walter Weekes ARAM, FTCL, OPM, Music Master himself.
Mr Weekes however left Plymouth at the end of 1937 and retired from the position at School that he had taken on from Mrs Lingley almost ten years earlier. However, he vowed to continue some kind of association and agreed to come back to lecture on orchestral concerts.
Although a somewhat senior OPM Walter Weekes was by no means the oldest in 1937 and interestingly enough a little bit of correspondence started up in the pages of the Western Morning News as to who actually was the oldest old boy then. The question was posed by 76 year-old James Hodson of Bideford, who was a former border at Mannamead in the mid-1870s. However, FR Stephens of Crownhill had a few years on him – born in 1851, in St Budeaux, when there were only fifty houses there, he used to walk to school in the summer and was

a weekly boarder in the winter. *"I was one of the Rev Dr Holmes' pupils for about two years, 1864-5,"* he wrote, *"Dr Holmes sometimes preached at Pennycross Church and would dine at my father's house."*
A contemporary of Stephens was 82 year-old Ben Pethick, then was living in Ivybridge and had recently attended a local hunt meet. Thomas Adams, of Hope Cove, was another 1870s boarder; *"I remember rice-puddings on Tuesdays and "figgy duff" on Fridays."*
Dr HW Webber, meanwhile, a contemporary of Eden Phillpotts, was, like Phillpotts, an ardent fly-fisherman and claimed to know every pool in Dartmoor rivers. A great nephew of Dr Holmes, Webber was retired in Oxford after 45 years and had begun motoring in 1910. Phillpotts himself had just added a collection of poems on Dartmoor to his *"long list of books"*.
Other gems to emerge from the correspondence was the story of the classical master in 1875, the Rev F Osborne, who *"stayed only six weeks after a "tiff" with the head. Osborne wore a black beard and was genial and kind. The mathematics master was Mr Bennett, but those lessons were not so popular."*
"In the '70s bullying went on wholesale, unknown to the head, who was well-liked, being dubbed "Dear old Who's-He". Contemporaries were the three sons of Rev Hall-Parlby, the three sons of Col Douall, the sons of Admiral Pope, and General Coode."
The old boys weren't only looking back though, they were also looking to the future and in July 1937 an appeal was circulated to members pointing out that the Club had decided to give the School, out of accumulated Club funds, a leaving Scholarship of £25 per annum to cover the next three academic years, with a hope of making a more permanent grant … *"The idea at which we aim is a capital sum of at least £1000 to ensure the permanency of the proposed Scholarship."*
The Headmaster too had an eye on the future and to that end there were yet further developments at the Prep; *"The great event this term (Easter 1937) has been*

Scout Summer Camp 1937: above; the Troop after Parade. Below from the left; Smyth, Tuckett, Smerdon - labour saving, KEK, JRS, AHMS, GLS and DLT, AHMS helps Geoff to build an oven.

the extending of Division 5 classroom into a large classroom in which the whole school can meet in comfort for Prayers, Lectures, etc. The boys in the Preparatory School now have their own "Big School" which is a most valuable asset."

The official opening, which took place on Parents Day (March 12) was fully reported, under the headline *The New Wing*, in the Western Morning News, thereby giving the School valuable publicity.

Plymouth College Preparatory School - 1937

"Importance of the preparatory school and the mutual advantage derived when it was attached to a public school was emphasised at Plymouth yesterday."

"Before a large assembly of parents and friends of the scholars, Mr R Brown, vice-chairman of the College Governors, declared open the extension to the Preparatory School of Plymouth and Mannamead College."

For his part the Prep Headmaster said, "he was grateful that the extension had been possible. Now it was possible to move the small boys to the sunny side of the house. In addition, accommodation was provided in which the whole School could assemble for daily prayers and the room served the third purpose in that it

could be used for lectures."

Mr Firman then spoke about homework – "preparation" – and said that in September he had "arranged that boys should do preparation on three days of the week in school and at home on two days. His object was to train the boys to get a maximum done in a set time without interruption. On the whole the experiment was proving a success."

As to the work of the school generally Mr Firman said that there had been recent agreement in a conference in London that all preparatory schools, "whether private concerns or attached to public schools, should mould their curricula to a revised plan. The plan suggested was such as had been in operation at the Preparatory School for some years."

"We are preparing the boys along lines approved and sponsored by the College," he said. "I am inclined to the view that public schools which have preparatory schools on their foundation are at an advantage."

"They can follow the progress of their boys from an early age, and the boys themselves are brought along gradually and not "pitch forked" into a form half-way up the school."

"At the same time the preparatory department of these schools has the advantage of contact with the parent school, which means that the boys have at an earlier age a clearer view of esprit de corps and service."

Had there been any doubt about the success of the changes to the structure of the Prep, brought in by Ralph, then they only needed to look at the figures;

"In the past two years the number of boys in the department showed an increase of 30 per cent."

"There is an essential link between the Preparatory and the Main School," said Ralph, after the others had spoken, "for the parent body can see its boys gradually developing, and I am pleased to say that since I have been at the College no fewer than four captains of schools have served their apprenticeship in the Preparatory department."

Clearly it was a happy day all round and great Public Relations for the School. The report concluded with the information that Ivan S Hodgess, an OPM architect based in Plymouth, was responsible for the structural work and that Walter Weekes was there to conduct the School Choir at the conclusion of the formal ceremony.

Clearly the Prep was going from strength to strength across all aspects of school life – well almost all. The Hobbies Club reported that numbers were slightly down this year;

"Stamps, Meccano, and Ship Building and Fretwork are the choices this year, and although there are fewer members than last year, plenty of keenness is evident by those who attend. HMS Nelson is very nearly complete and HMS Queen Mary is rapidly taking good shape."

SS Queen Mary

Hailed as "Britain's masterpiece", the original Queen Mary - the Cunard White Star liner - launched at Clydebank in September 1934, and crossing the Atlantic for the first time in 1936 - had captured the imagination of many boys, old and young. At over 75,000 tones she was undoubtedly bigger than anything the world had so far seen. With the Government embarking on a massive defence spending programme there were occasionally opportunities, locally, for boys to see ships being launched. In December 1936 the Prep's "prefects and sub-prefects" had been present at the launching, by Lady St Levan, of the Sloop HMS Sharpshooter. Eng.-Commander Cooke, RN, supplied the tickets for this event and six months later the boys were back in the Dockyard again, this time for the launching of the new Minesweeper, HM Sloop Seda ... *"again the thoughtfulness of a parent in sending us a number of tickets made it possible."*

Parental help has regularly been a useful resource for the School, and seldom is that service more happily rendered than when the parent is a past pupil himself. Douglas Vittle, who had left the School some twenty years earlier, regularly helped with Prep sports by taking *"a game on games' afternoons."* He also presented a *"very fine Trophy for the Cock House of the Preparatory School"*. Meanwhile his son, Peter, was to be found opening the batting for the Prep in their *"eagerly anticipated"* Paters v Preparatory cricket match. Vittle senior didn't play and, as is customary for such fixtures, the Prep won rather comfortably, DCH McDonald taking six of the Paters' wickets, including that of Mr Firman, but not that of McDonald senior who was dispatched by PO Williams who clean bowled all three of his victims.

Among the new additions to the Prep Library this term, incidentally, were *The Picture Book of Trains, Saracen Junior* and *The Secret of the Lab* both by Major Gurdon, and of *Wolfskin,* by another man from the military, Major Charles Gilson.

As for the military wing of the Main School, the Summer term saw Mr Jones (Lieutenant WGM Jones, RA (TA)) arrange a visit to shoot six-pounders at Renny and a party of NCOs were taken to RAF Mount Batten. On 12 May, three days after yet another damp field day, Sergeants VJE Boatright, AE Harvey and IR Ife represented the School OTC Contingent at the Coronation Procession in London. Boatright and Ife also attended the Youth Empire Rally at the Albert Hall on the 18th and the special service in Westminster Abbey the day after that.

Meanwhile Headboy, AJM Smyth, in his capacity as Troop Leader of the Scouts, represented the School as a member of 50 Scouts representing Britain at the American Jamboree in Washington DC. He sailed out of Southampton on the Aquitania in June.

Scout Leader AHM Smyth

"While we were actually in camp at Washington, we were the centre of attention for Americans who had originally emigrated from this country. We received far more invitations than we could accept to visit American Homes and give our hosts some idea of the conditions of life in this country. But as the Chief Scout said, the object was not to attempt to prove British methods of scouting superior to American; but to try to appreciate something at least of the American's view point as distinct from that of Hollywood."

"On the more strictly scouting side we were not inactive. The British camp attracted innumerable American Scouts, anxious to see these British Scouts who actually slept on the ground. We signed autographs as fast as we could write. But the Scots in their Kilts were in most demand; no film star could have had a more enthusiastic following than these scouts in Kilts, whenever they moved through the encampments."

There were but fifty British Scouts, organised in eight patrols and *"we were fortunate in having with us Ralph Reader, the Holborn Rover, who is the author of the annual "Gang Show". Under his direction we learnt the songs from his shows which ensured us an enthusiastic reception whenever we joined in a Camp-Fire."*

"The chief official function was the review by the President of the United States. The whole body of

scouts, 25,000 strong, lined Constitution Avenue while he drove along. The temperature in the shade was 98F, but we had no casualties."*

That same Summer the Duke of York's Camp at Southwold was once again hailed as a great success by all fortunate enough to attend;

"We made friends with schoolboys from Scotland, Wales and Ireland, with boys who helped to build the Queen Mary, and with boys who made razor blades, sweets, motor cars and tooth brushes. The fact that such firm friendships were made in such a varied community proves beyond doubt the absurdity of the words "class barriers" which is just what our Royal Host wishes to demonstrate." So wrote Miller and Lockwood, two of the Schools leading prefects, both of them destined to leave School for University places the following summer and both, sadly, kllled in the forthcoming war.

In 1937 Smyth and Ede were the two greatest academic successes, the former heading off for New College, Oxford, the latter for King's Cambridge. The news from Oxford itself that year was that PR Turner had *"recently become very popular by acquiring a wireless set"*. Not surprisingly mention was also made of boat race, as Oxford won for the first time in fourteen years. John Gielgud, Robertson Hare, George Bernard Shaw and Eden Philpotts were among the visitors to the University town that year, but more was made of Lord Nuffield's enormous contribution to the University and the Proctor's decision to restrain the *"former splendours of November 5th."*

"The only diversion was caused by a number of misguided (?) individuals who decided to throw a bottle party on the King's Highway. Not content, however, with throwing the party, they threw the bottles as well. This literal interpretation of a well-known social formula caused incredible destruction to some of Messrs. Dunlop's most excellent products."

The Cambridge contingent reported similar restraint:

"The Police defeated the University on the night of

November 5th, for the first time for several years, after a rather tame game which was spoilt by the proctor's refereeing. With the contempt that victory breeds, the Police allowed the University a free hand on Poppy Day."

On the popular culture front in Cambridge we learnt that – *"Richard Tauber, Myra Hess, Sir T Beecham and the London Philharmonic Orchestra and Paul Robeson have also contributed in a somewhat expensive manner to our enjoyment."*

Back at School the main musical entertainment at the annual concert came courtesy of the Staff Trio – Mrs Di Davies, Mrs Firman and WDMcDP. *"Unfortunately the trio which provided, with the exception of Mr Frederick Harvey OPM (who sang Devon for Me and the Gay Highway), the best entertainment of the evening, was forced to compete against the noise of general conversation."*

Sladen-Smith's *Sunset at Bagdad,* produced by Charlie Barnes, and JM Barrie's *"Seven Women",* a Meyricke Jones special, were the two theatrical diversions that night. On 1st May Hugh Dent produced his own Mark Twain-style play, *Corpse Follow Cat,* with IIA taking all the parts. Notwithstanding the fact that *"make up and clothes cannot disguise unbroken voices",* the entertainment was well-received.

Meyricke Jones - not acting this time!

As was the Prep's League of Pity evening, which featured the boys in *"Sir Roy",* by Constance Sturmey, *"The Pied Piper"* and scenes from *"As You Like It".*

At the Main School around this time it's interesting to note that gradually more and more original contributions were creeping in to the entertainment on offer. The School was not short on literary heroes; John Rowland was well-known for his crime novels about Dartmoor, JC Trewin was emerging as a young writer and, from 1934 onwards, as a national theatre critic, while Eden Phillpotts was at the time one of the biggest names in English literature. His play, *"Carrier Pigeon"* was one of three read at the February 4th 1938 meeting of the Literary and Debating Society and clearly he was a great source of inspiration to the School's young English teacher and librarian, Hugh Dent. At the previous L&D meeting, Dent had read *"Greyfriars"* his study of School Stories and while undoubtedly the antics of the Fat Owl of the Remove, Billy Bunter, and his chums, were the inspiration for the title (the Magnet comic for boys had started serialising Frank Richard's stories in 1909), Dent would have been well aware of Phillpott's *"Human Boy"* stories centred around Merrivale (Mannamead?) School. Dent had already written and produced his own dramatic piece for School based on Mark Twain's Huckleberry Finn characters and so perhaps we should not have been unduly surprised to see, what appears to have been the first School Play to have been written by a schoolboy at Plymouth College, *"The Grecian Low Down"* being staged in the Gymnasium 1st April 1938.

It was the first of three plays performed by the Literary and Debating Society that night and it was also produced by the author concerned - RE Crosby. Crosby, a school prefect, was a sub-editor of the Plymothian and Hon Sec of the L&D Society, and his play, which featured a lot of *"humorous blank verse"* was described as an *"amusing frolic, on the whole, which probably succeeded in its purpose".*

"DJ Viner looked quite villainous at times, but JW Trobridge presented a surprisingly good-natured aspect. The police-force were miraculously well-assorted, from J Webber's mountainous and bucolic sergeant to the minute and admirably cast DAT Farrar."

The two other productions that night, incidentally, were Robert Victor's *"The Pen Is Mightier ..."* which CL Barnes produced and Hugh Dent's adaptation of Sheridan's *"St Patrick's Day* or *The Scheming Lieutenant".*

The former was deemed to be the *"most generally successful of the evening",* while the later, *"a gem",* was remembered for the contribution of the *"red-coats and the rustics (especially the rustics)"* – namely GB Guinn and TJ Mutton.

The previous theatrical experience to this evening in the School had been the staging of the Staff production of "Laburnum Grove"; *"Not an easy play to produce or act ... a dangerous choice ... static to a degree. The plot is feeble and the moral indecisive."* Such was the pre-match judgement of the invited critic, who on this occasion was the newly-arrived history master, Charles Hill.

Twenty-three years old and a *"sometime scholar of Pembroke College, Oxford",* Hill had taken over Mr Benskin's work in History and Divinity, and to be invited to comment on the performance of his new-found peers in the Common Room, within such a short time of arriving, must have been a fairly daunting task for the young man.

Mr Firman was the play's producer and Messrs Mercer, Davies, Dundas, Dufton, Woodcock and Westhead were all cast, along with Mrs Dufton, Mrs McD Porter and Mrs Guy Hill.

Of them all our critic informs us that Mr Davies *"played with great success a part which cannot be called easy or pleasant to act",* "Mrs Hill and Mr Westhead, as Elsie and Harold, made clear the deadening effect of the suburbs upon romance" and Mr Mercer, *"in spite* of the serious handicap of the bananas, made us laugh in a role where the wit is scarce and the humour forced. Throughout he was Mr Mercer."

For those not fortunate enough to have witnessed the performance themselves there was an interesting Epilogue that immediately followed Hill's two and a half page review.

"A master, (we won't mention names)
Proficient both at maths, and games,
Was once prevailed on to portray
A character in someone's play
They said "It's just the part for you!
Just think of what you have to do.
Between the lines you have to eat
Bananas; it should be a treat!"
He liked to get beneath the skin
Of any part he featured in,
So read up books on Singapore
And ate bananas by galore.
When the day came, he missed his lunch
To leave room for an extra bunch,
Removing skins with fingers deft,
Ingurgitating what was left.
Scores he consumed with nonchalance,
Yet never missed his cue-line once.
And after that, he was still able
To teach Ib their Fyffe times table,
For, like a Rugger man, he knew
That he could BUNCH and TAKE IT too!"

The poem was credited to Delta and was one of a number of amusing Plymothian pieces from around this time – like this delightful play on the English language;

"Tough a Prefect or Why I Am Not Wearing A Cap"
"The wind was rough
And coughld and blough,
I kept each hand within each cough.

It chilled me through,
My noughse grough blough,
And still the squall the faster flough;
And yet although
There was nough snough
The weather was a croughel fough.
It made me cough
Pray dough nought scough –
I coughed until my cap blough ough."

TSF was responsible for that piece and generally most contributions were initialled – apart from the Foot Notes.
"We hear that a member of IIb has been brightening his bedroom by writing mottoes of his own devising on the covers of old Plymothians. His first effort "Jazz is Life" seems to deserve greater publicity."
****
"In higher circles, we have admired the suggestion that no boys should be allowed on the Fives' Courts till they are proficient at the game."
****
"Kruger's Whiskers (in case they crop up in the General Knowledge Paper) are a confection to be obtained near the College at 2 oz a 1d. We believe the tuck-shop are contemplating a nice line in Hitler's Moustaches, done in liquorice."

While they may not have made much impact on the pages of the Plymothian, Hitler's antics were still dominating the pages of the British press and, recognising the increasing inevitability of another war, Britain had been rapidly building up defensive capabilities. The Government's two-year plan to treble the strength of the air force was completed three months ahead of schedule, in the early part of 1937. Prime Minister Stanley Baldwin had asked for an extra 2,500 pilots and most had now been trained, but it wasn't all plain sailing;

on March 18th 1938 Pilot-Officer FE Williams, who left the school less than three years earlier, was killed *"when the aeroplane that he was piloting – a Swordfish Bomber – crashed near Corfe Castle, Dorset ... We offer to his parents our sincere sympathy in this tragic end to a promising career in the Royal Air Force."*

Williams - killed near Corfe

Sadly Williams' early death wasn't the only one reported in the Plymothian that term as there was a notice too of the death, on New Year's Eve 1937, of Gordon Sparks. The sixteen year-old, who had just passed the School Certificate, had been all set to join the Sixth Form when he was laid low with appendicitis, which developed into a bout of peritonitis.

Young Gordon Sparks

Tragic though it was, the death of the young OPM pilot had little effect on the youthful enthusiasm for flying machines, and it was no great surprise to find that within months of the launch of Britain's great aircraft-carrier, the Ark Royal, there was a change of heart for the Prep School modellers.
"Aeroplanes are being constructed in place of ships. At present three planes are being constructed, two stationary models and one flying model. The plan is to form a Model Aeroplane Flying Club for the Summer, and it is a good preliminary to learn something of construction. It is hoped that not a few boys will get flying models by next term, so that some interesting time may be spent in the field during the Summer."

Without a doubt the popularity of Captain WE Johns' creation, James Bigglesworth – Biggles – helped to foment interest among young boys. The famous fictional pilot made his first appearance in 1932 and along with his pals, Ginger Hebblethwaite, Algy Lacey, and Lord Bertie Lissie, was an instant success.

It wasn't greatly surprising to find *"Biggles and Co"* mentioned as the only new purchase for the Prep Library that same term.

RAF Mount Batten with four flying boats moored in the Cattewater.

The Prep trip across to RAF Mount Batten later in the year would also have done much to stimulate youthful interest in flying machines;

"The chief interest was the Sea-planes four of which we had the luck to go aboard. The place was very interesting. While we were there a report came in code from London about a German Ship which had caught

fire in the Atlantic. We also had the luck to be fitted with parachutes. The aircraftsman who showed us round made the trip most interesting."

Further up the School we find the older boys increasingly drawn into the OTC;

"All cadets between 14 and 15 years of age have been issued with uniform this term," ran the notice in the July magazine. *"We admire the boy who was seen walking along the Plain in Corps Uniform and a boater,"* ran an earlier, "Odd Note" in the same issue, adding by way of an explanation *"... It was Ascot week; and the boy, of course, was in IIb."*

The School contingent was inspected that Summer by Captain FS Reid of the War Office; *"The Headmaster entertained him to lunch and in the afternoon a party of Certificate "A" holders and candidates carried out a T.E.W.T. on Roborough Down as part of the Inspection."*

Five members of the School contingent had passed into various branches of the Services earlier that year – Sgt. Mahoney – RM., Cpl. Duff and L-Cpls. Crouch and Sheriff – Sandhurst, and L-Cpl. Nash – RN. Meanwhile CJH Wright from form IVa *"gained second place in a field of 1,000 candidates in the competitive examination for enlistment into the Army as an apprentice tradesman. He will go to Woolwich to be trained as an artificer and hopes to qualify eventually for a commission in the Royal Artillery."*

Plymouth College OTC had plenty to be proud of and even the shooting team were improving, rising fourteen places in the County Rifle Competition. *"We hope to compete with Kelly before the term ends."*

Competition in various areas with Kelly was nothing new, however, curiously enough, we find the young CSM IR Ife stating; *"Our first Field Day in conjunction with Kelly College took place in brilliant sunshine on March 3rd (1938)."* Was there no-one around who could remember the old Field Days with Kelly? Certainly the description of activity around the River Walkham on

the slopes of Cox Tor had a very familiar ring to it, as did the account of the joint tea at Yelverton.

Not only then were the OTC numbers healthy but the level of commitment appeared also to be on the way up. *"Camp this year will be at Strensall, near York – new ground for us. It is encouraging to find that nearly all eligible cadets wish to attend this the most effective part of the year's training. After camp, a considerable body of cadets will go on to France with a Warwickshire Cadet Battalion."*

Fifteen boys from School had already been to France that April, with Mr Davies and Mr Dundas. They set out on Monday 11th April and reached Le Havre from Southampton at 6.30am Tuesday morning. The sightseeing began immediately;

"Having slept in a proper bed for a change, on Wednesday we visited the Louvre to see, amongst many other wonderful works of art, the famous Venus de Milo and Leonardo da Vinci's Mona Lisa. After a journey by Metro. (underground travel no longer unnerves us!) we visited the Invalides where Napoleon is buried."

The whole trip went smoothly thanks to the efforts of the two masters, who could easily be forgiven for the one, self-inflicted casualty, a boy *"who had decided to develop a rash, due, beyond any shadow of doubt, to an excessive consumption of hors d'oeuvre and cider."*

No serious harm seems to have come of it and the visit *"called forth some quite impressive French from the members of the party. Even the most diffident soon learned to be thankful in small "mercis"."*

The second school group to visit France that year were nine members of the OTC contingent that had gone on camp to Strensall. That trip itself was an enjoyable enough experience; *"all ranks agreed on returning to Plymouth, after a long yet comfortable train-journey, that this was the best Camp the Corps had had for many years ... We are grateful to those military authorities who did so much to ensure our comfort and to give us up-to-date training."*

Supermarine Southampton IIs flying over the City in the late '30s

This training included demonstrations of anti-tank guns, camouflage, and the firepower of the Bren gun. The timetable left space for a little exploration of York, where, according to CSM Symons; *"interests were divided between the Cathedral and precincts and the attractive cafes with which the ancient city abounds."* For the nine who didn't come straight back home from Yorkshire there were yet more sights to see.

"Our small party left Wellington Barracks, joined its Company, caught its train, and finally embarked at Dover." Arriving in France they were treated for the first, but by no means last, time during their visit, to a rousing rendition of the Marseillaise. Curious crowds at Callais were matched by an appreciative, welcoming throng at the station at Soissons where a short bus journey led the party to the Barracks, and their billets … *"with the flags of the two nations over the door."*

The Battlefields of Aisne, the Pont des Anglais, the rebuilt cathedral of Reims and then the French capital were visited in turn;

"Paris, despite the slight drizzle impresses us greatly," wrote the future OTC CSM, RE Crosby, who was also the current editor of the Plymothian. He continued; *"The ceremony at the Arc de Triomphe proves in every respect worthy of the occasion. Then Les Invalides and Notre Dame mingle their tributes to earthly genius and heavenly power before our wondering eyes … On leaving Les Invalides, we notice an OPM blazer being photographed with a girl on each sleeve. We would give much to know the name of the occupant."*

"Armistice Glade, the famous railway coach in which the Peace was signed, the spot where "The unfounded and presumptuous pride of the German Empire received its deathblow at the hands of the free peoples," did not then strike us as an anachronism."

One wonders what went through the minds of those nine schoolboys as they left *"this country of sincere hospitality"* with their minds full of warm memories, particularly of Reims and the new cathedral:

"It is undoubtedly a noble monument to the tenacity of the nation that rebuilt it from the ashes the German gunners made. Though all other memories should fade, the cool lingering drink (of "limonade") outside the café in Reims will remain with us."

Clearly the entente was truly cordiale and this piece makes interesting reading alongside other items in that autumn term Plymothian of 1938.

"Michaelmas usually conjures up visions of wind, rain and snow, and a roaring fire; but this cannot be a Michaelmas term in which the tennis racket and river have been more favoured than the football field. The last two months have really been just another beautiful English Autumn – but things have changed. Although nothing has impaired the magnificence which Nature can offer, although the beauty of glorious architecture still stands unaffected by the lapse of years, yet the spirit of Cambridge is not what we knew it to be. Gone are those carefree Autumn parties, and gone the spirit of revolt which made a proctor's duties interesting. The change has been gradually taking shape during the last few years, but it was crystallized two months ago, when the European crisis showed us the first red light ahead. Even to the majority of us who are uninterested in Japan's doubtful progress, who are not directly moved by German brutality, who regard the Spanish War as a purely local incident, even to them it has become apparent that we have now outlived civilization's Golden Age."

"It is true that recent events have provided good food for the digestion of dilettante politicians, but the distinguished speakers who have addressed the Union and political societies, have failed to arouse general enthusiasm, and have merely succeeded in depressing us. Mr Atlee, it is true, fresh from his triumphant reception at Oxford, visited the Socialist Club after the much heralded advertisement, but he unfortunately found that members of the Pitt Club, - equine gentlemen with yellow waistcoats – and certain other individuals, who have far too much money and too little brains, can evince a rowdy and unintelligent sort of political animosity when they have dined well. He will visit Oxford again but not Cambridge."

To date Plymothian editors had rarely offered much of an insight into the social climate of the day, but through the long-established varsity letters the unease of the nation that autumn was clearly discernable.

"The reason for this," wrote our Oxford correspondent, *"is, I think, that the "Crisis" which now seems so very long ago, so profoundly affected everyone that for nearly a month everything seemed unreal, and we all wondered whether we had really evaded the disaster that had been so close upon us, or whether it had all been some horrible dream. But now life here has once more become what we are accustomed to, although there appears to exist a certain apathy which has affected every pursuit. The dons forgave us our bad collection papers at the beginning of term, and even asked us to forgive them their bad lectures for, they said, they had found it impossible to concentrate whilst writing them."*

"… Peace in our time," announces Prime Minister Chamberlain.

The "Crisis" in question centred around Chamberlain's "Peace" negotiations. On his return from the celebrated conference in Munich with Daladier of France, Hitler and Mussolini, Chamberlain, with a signed agreement in hand, announced to a cheering crowd: *"There has come back from Germany to Downing Street peace with honour. I believe it is peace for our time."*

The School lines up once again for the camera.

By this time, 1937, Headmaster Herbert Ralph has made most of the changes he wants to make to the staff. Of the thirteen teachers he has appointmented since arriving eight years ago, only two have moved on, the rest will still be here in ten years time, and most of them will still be here in thirty years time!

1937

Not everyone, however, shared that belief and many MPs, including many of his own party, saw it as a sell-out to Hitler. Under the terms of the agreement German troops were to enter ceded Czechoslovakia territory – the Sudenten region, inhabited by a German speaking minority – and the rest of the world would do nothing, leaving the hapless Czechs with nothing more than an agreement that the rest of the country would be protected against aggression.

Germany was already gearing up for war and Britain had mobilised the fleet four days before the summit. It looked like a very uncertain peace, but the Prime Minister was adamant.

"I am a man of peace to the depths of my soul. Armed conflict between nations is a nightmare to me, but if I were convinced that any nation had made its mind up to dominate the world by fear of its force I should feel it should be resisted. Under such a domination the life of people who believe in liberty would not be worth living."

Chamberlain flew out to meet Hitler three times, his last trip, to Munich saw him with Von Ribbentrop and Hitler. Behind the British Prime Minister is Sir Neville Henderson.

In Oxford the Union were quick to express their views;

the motion before the floor was *"That this House disapproves of the policy of Peace **without** Honour".* 320 agreed, 266 did not and the motion was carried, as was the notion that *"War between nations is sometimes justifiable."* This prompted our OPM correspondent to note that; *"once again Oxford is a University for men, by Gad sir!"*

Back in Ford Park, there was a close call for the earlier and similarly-themed debate *"That the maintenance of peace should be the supreme aim of the Government."* Summers and White argued for peace but Crosby and Miller managed to persuade the house otherwise by a 25-20 margin. The debate was the first of the term and was held before the Munich agreement. In a later post-*"Peace for our time"*-debate White again found himself on the losing side when he and RCS Pointon failed to convince the house that *"Security is the greatest aim of life."* The motion was opposed by two school prefects, SG Ward and RW Harris, who were Hon. Sec. and Hon. Assistant Sec. of the Literary Debating Society, respectively. Ward was also a sub-editor of the Plymothian, along with Jinman and Bradshaw, providing one of the fullest editorial teams to date. It was also quite a full magazine and included a further, lengthy contribution, from "JLW" that gave us a somewhat unusual and unexpected insight into the spirit of time: *"It was Wednesday the 24th August when my German friend and I walked along the crowded and swastika-beflagged streets of Hamburg, anxious to get a view of the German Fuhrer. It seemed that all the two millions of this great city were out with the same aim as ourselves. As we were waiting under the towering statue of Bismark, uniforms of all sizes, kinds and colours, seemed to pass us by."*

"The Fuhrer was due here at 11 am. After we had waited for 2½ hours, that time had arrived. Even though we were hemmed in by Brown Shirts, we were in an excellent position. All of a sudden everybody seemed to go mad, thrusting their right hands forward

and screaming "Heil"."

"A car passed slowly at only a few feet distance – it was Hitler. He was dressed in a light brown uniform and, strange to say, he was smiling. By his side sat Admiral Horthy, the Hungarian Regent, who was paying him a courtesy visit. The glimpse only lasted a few seconds, but it was one of the most exciting experiences I have known."

"After that we pushed ourselves through the crowded metropolis until we reached the Town Hall. After waiting for a considerable time in a Hitler-mad crowd, we were again honoured with his presence. Despite the fact that the rifle of a black steel-helmeted S.S. man interfered with my view, we were again able to see that medium-sized and apparently ordinary man."

"In a quite casual way he saluted his worshippers, as did also the Hungarian Potentate. Again I was surprised, he looked quite agreeable and something like a smile creased his tired and worn looking features. He then jumped into a black limousine and drove down the well-guarded streets to the station, from which he was going to make his departure."

"Determined to see him again, we fought our way through the seething crowd of Nazis and exasperated, green-uniformed police. After a space of ten minutes, we arrived by the beautiful Alster, a lake in the heart of the city, which was crossed by the railway track. Scarcely were we there two minutes before the green and red beflagged train of the Hungarian Regent rushed by."

"Then came the Silver Giant, the train which carried the cause, as many consider, of most of our troubles. As he passed, that astonishing and indeed remarkable man came to the window. In true German fashion he returned the crowd's salute. It was only a few seconds but I was satisfied."

"I had seen the German Fuhrer who, though beloved in his own land, is looked upon with mixed feelings by the rest of the civilised world."

It is difficult now to imagine just how schoolboys and OPM's reading their Christmas Plymothian would have felt about this piece and about Hitler himself. In between JLW's sighting of "the Fuhrer" and the publication of the magazine the Germans had marched into Czechoslovakia and Hungary and following Hitler's "arbitration" had annexed for themselves the southern parts of Slovakia and Ruthenia. Less than two years later, however, the Hungarian premier, Count Paul Teleki, would take his own life, rather than join the war as a German ally. But again we are jumping ahead too far.

Let us return to the autumn of 1938 and the tension that was almost tangible at home and abroad, and which cast a gloom over so many events, including Speech Day.

"October 11th was a day of charged atmosphere and conflicting feelings, with the undertones of the recent crisis vaguely jarring upon our pleaure in welcoming two friends of the College in the pulpit at St Andrews, and on the Guildhall platform."

The two friends were both formerly familiar figures at Ford Park, the Rev Benskin and FR Dale. Benskin in his sermon in St Andrews spoke of various popular *"School Stories"* and the need for a School Chapel, while Dale mentioned the remarkably good results in the School Certificate Examination and also paid a tribute to that *"wonderful man Heywood"*.

In a speech that had *"a personal quality that softened the usual austerities of Speech Day"*, Dale also informed his audience that the New Pavilion *"may become a reality in the coming year"* - welcome news to all of the school's sporting enthusiasts.

Not that the old pavilion had particularly stifled any sporting achievements. The 1937/38 teams had all acquitted themselves as well as they could. The rugger team had lost *"many of their old stalwarts"* and had to build a new team around their Captain FL Axworthy, fly-half IR Ife, scrum-half BH Hyland and

the remarkable 14 year-old WAH Trask. He *"should go far in the game"* was the verdict on this boy who was *"amazingly well-built"* for his age. In terms of schoolboy rugby he would do, sadly, however, the war was all too soon to cut short his promising career, as it would that of another of the year's sporting heroes REG Oxenham.

School Cricket team photographed for the 'Herald': Standing; Turner, Atkey, Oxenham, Kevern, Trask, Muddiford, Bishop. Kneeling; Gilbert, Sargent, Ewens and Nicholls.

"There was a young bowler called –x-nham
Whose deliveries had plenty of shoxenham.
He had the Staff sighing
As he sent their bails flying,
And succeeded completely in foxenham."

All six of Oxenham's victims, three of whom failed to score, including Mr Battrick and Mr Dundas, in the School v Staff fixture were clean bowled *"after a heavy shower of rain had made the wicket treacherous"*.

Along with Atkey, with whom he scored almost as many runs as the rest of the team put together, and Hicks, with whom he took many more wickets than the rest of the boys in the team put together, Oxenham found himself in the Devon Colts side that summer. A genuine all-

rounder he still had another season of school cricket to look forward to, although he was unlikely to surpass his unbeaten century against Kelly, particularly when the old rivals were dismissed for just 99.

CJ Atkey and N Maddaford were among the stars of the seconds. A 3rd. XI was also fielded and, somewhat remarkably, Gilbert took eight Tamar Central School wickets for just two runs. Messrs Mercer, Bonser, Hill and Heywood were among the older hands to help in those 1st XI fixtures against non-school sides and, with the exception of Pro Heywood, the same gentlemen also helped to add a little substance to the 1st XI hockey team that season.

It wasn't a vintage year for hockey, though. None of the inter-school fixtures were won, although teams from the RAF and Royal Marines were beaten convincingly.

1st XI Hockey, 1938. Standing; JG Hicks, RW Whiting, JE Collister, J Pitts, BH Hyland. Seated; JD Bishop, KE Kevern (Hon Sec.), PS Anderson (Captain), FL Axworthy and RG Atkey.

Two other masters closely involved in the sporting arena were Messrs Jones and Barnes who looked after the Senior and Junior Boxing respectively. However the fine weather kept many boys out of doors and interest in pugilistic pursuits was said by the School boxing captain, J Ivory to be *"at a low ebb"*.

Interest in the sport was being encouraged at a much lower level, however, in the Prep where Sergeant Muir RM had replaced Quarter-Master-Sergeant Featherston (who had gone to be PT Instructor at Eton) as Boxing Coach.

On the athletic front, the School were placed an uninspiring fifth at the Devon School's Meeting at Blundells but there were records broken at Ford Park in the School Sports.

J Pitts, the fastest boy in the school that summer emerged as Victor Ludorum, with Kevern, who finished second in the hurdles, putting the weight, discus and javelin, ending up Proxime Accesit. The last two events, were both won with new school records, by Collister in the discus with a throw of 92'10" and CJ Atkey in the javelin, with a throw of 124'10".

Pitts - Victor Ludorum

Among the juniors the speedy Kent and the stronger Trask tied for Victor Ludorum, while in the sub-juniors PF Hopwood won the high jump, long jump, 100 and 220 yards, with CF Lyon and AWJ Phillips close behind.

At the Prep Sports, DN Kelsey was the odds on favourite for the title of Victor Ludorum which he took for the third year in succession, although PD Vittle was not far behind him and indeed pipped him in the 440, for which he received the Challenge Cup.

The young Vittle and his brother both played in the Prep House Cricket which was instituted for the first time this year, Wynton, Willcock and Heywood were among the other future stars. In the Boys v Paters match, incidentally, P Vittle took five wickets, including that of Pro Heywood and Mr Bonser, he also top scored with 29, while Wynton claimed the wicket of his father.

In the swimming pool R Vinton, the School's swimming captain, was comfortably ahead of the field in five events, while L Smerdon was among the promising juniors. Four Water Polo fixtures were played and only one won, but all the opposing sides were non-school teams and none of the defeats were unduly heavy.

One School sport with no fixtures at all was the much-maligned tennis. However there was good news on that front as RET Saunderson, Hon Sec., was able to report that, thanks to the help from Mr and Mrs Ralph, there was a new surround to the Court. The Headmaster and his wife had also assisted in other ways and, although no tournament had yet been held, the attendance at "Vols." had been encouraging, and even though subs had been raised to 2/- (10p) the prospects looked good.

Although tennis, fives and other school sports facilities were not without their critics, at least boys of Plymouth College had a variety of sporting options open to them, unlike the estimated *"five million children in England and Wales who have no playing fields regularly available"*. So wrote Mr Hill, in the summer Plymothian, adding, *"the National Playing Fields Association is trying to remove this injustice by buying land for conversion into permanent playing fields. Its members are boys and girls of public and secondary schools who pay a subscription of 6d each per term – it is hoped that all those in whose lives the playing field is a normal and everyday feature will make some small but steady effort to help provide for those others to whom it is a luxury, or to whom it is unknown."*

Mr Hill was ill for much of the following term and Mr TJ Cooney, from Trinity College, Dublin and London University, was in school for several weeks to teach in his absence, and that of Mr Jones too. At the same time Mr AJM Painter, of St Luke's College, Exeter, and an old boy of Blundells, arrived at the Prep to replace Miss Dinsmore.

Miss Dinsmore had been the last female to have been appointed to the Prep staff back in 1933, and had during her time been in charge of Division IV *"and has, as well, done a considerable amount of very valuable work for the Art and Manual work in the School."*

"One is bound to say how quietly and yet how effectively any work she has taken on has been done, and how very responsive to her all boys have been. She will be missed in the School."

Miss Dinsmore's departure meant that the only post-Dale Prep appointments still on the staff were male – Messrs. Firman (1935), Westhead (1936) and now Painter. In three swift years the previous exclusively-female dominance of the Preparatory Department had changed once and for all - with Miss Heath's retirement imminent that balance would soon swing yet further.

1939, and then there were two - the lone ladies left (Miss Heath right)

Excluding wartime, however, there had still been no full-time, female presence in the Main School Staff Room. Female presence generally at Ford Park was a rarity and dramatic productions frequently pressed boys into feminine roles, as evidenced that term with the production of *"Knock"*, the Jules Romaine play that cast RW Harris as Doctor Knock and Pezey and the newly-appointed headboy Crosby as the Lady in Black and the Lady in Violet respectively. *"Pezey's countrywoman caught the audience's fancy and Crosby gave us the contrasting dame with typical balance ... while Tonkin and Webber played the village idiots with gusto."*

Crosby's predecessor as Headboy, AW Miller, had left at the end of the Summer Term, having won an Open Scholarship for Classics. At the same time his contemporary and fellow classicist, AE Lockwood was bound for Cambridge, with an Open Exhibition. Two further colleagues, Anderson and Duff, also took their leave of Ford Park - the former for the Custom and Excise Service, the latter for Sandhurst. The future must have looked so bright for these four young men. Little could they have imagined then that all of them, not just Duff, would end up in uniform and that not one of them would live to celebrate their 25th birthday.

Unlike veteran OPM James Hodson who was again writing to the magazine with memories of his chums at Mannamead School in the mid-1870s, among them Cuthbert Fitzgerald, a boarder, who went to New Zealand for sheep farming and died in Cape Town, where *"he left his friend and OPM Batchelor £500."* There was also *"Charles Hope (son of Admiral Hope) who was first in England in the Indian Civil Service examination, and later obtained a judgeship in India and who remembers Dr Holmes's three Chinese boarders, nicknamed Ching I, Ching II and Ching III? Very nice fellows too. Ching I was a champion organist.."* SB Williams was an old Mannameadian who was at the School in the late 1880s; *"we had a very old carpenter who was over 80. He was, in his younger days, on the old wooden battleships."*

It was in this issue of the Plymothian that we find the first ever OPM notes in the style that John Spear would later make his own in the OPM Magazine. Curiously enough, in this first batch of notes, which appeared under the heading *"We Have Been Informed That"* … we read that *"JR Spear is on the staff of St John's School, Leatherhead and has been playing Rugger for Blackheath".*

We also learned, amongst other things, that *"A Goldbery was elected for Valletort Ward to Plymouth City Council … HG Hurrell is chairman of Plymouth Chamber of Commerce … Dr C Lindsay is president of the BMA and presided over their annual meetings held in Plymouth last summer"* … and that CP Brown had been created a JP.

Another member of a family with long and deep links with the school, Roger Serpell, was best man at two OPM weddings this year, those of JC (John Courtney) Trewin and his brother David. At the latter, in Torpoint, the Rev Benskin officiated.

It was a relatively buoyant time for the OPM Club, particularly *"in the realm of sport, where the Club most effectively justifies its existence".* The cricket (under PJF Shepherd), rugby (under NE Elliott), and hockey (H Coleman) were all producing well-regarded teams and even *"in the Fives' Court and the Swimming Bath, the club, in a quiet way – has kept up its end."*

The OPM side that lined up to play the RNEC in 1938. Man in coat anon, Westcott, RV Hoare, Rowles, LH Clemas, HB Tickle, D Spear, FW BLight, Rattray, Snell, HR Lawry, I Briggs. Kneeling; D Culliford, FW Bolton, N Elliot, KD Eke, REF Johns.

There were however a couple of gloomier items, most notably concerning the early death of Canon John Haldane, aged 57. Haldane, together with Walter Stoneman *"was practically wholly responsible for the foundation of the London branch of the OPM Club".* There were a number of other OPM obituaries recorded at the end of that December magazine and curiously enough the first Plymothian of 1939 opened with a few more obits. One, reported in the School Notes, concerned the death, *"in an air crash in Palestine, of Squadron-Leader GHO Mills, who left the School in December 1929. He had had a brilliant career in the RAF and is believed to have been the youngest Officer holding the rank of Squadron-Leader."* Promoted just two days before his demise, Geoffrey Mills *"was piloting a plane with two passengers when the engine failed. He ordered his passengers to jump with their parachutes. They escaped, but the plane lost height in the meantime and crashed while the pilot was trying to land it."*

The other two obits concerned the *"passing of two old landmarks from the field. The barren plum-tree in the "Orchard" and the squat ugly block of concrete that has for some score of years done duty as a Pavilion."* *"The new Pavilion is on the high-road to completion, growing daily into a building really worthy of the School."* *"The Pav. is dead, long live the new Pavilion."* In the event the new Pavilion was opened on Saturday 20 May 1939. Dr John Murray, Principal of the University of the South West, performed the official ceremony, the band of the Royal Marines were in attendance. The afternoon was combined with an *"At Home"*, held by the staff for parents, and a cricket match between the School and the OPMs. And there were plenty of OPMs around that day, indeed as the Head said, the Pavilion was a *"family affair"* – *"designed by one OPM, Mr JL Fouracre, erected by another, Mr GL Wakeham, and paid for by the College."* There was also a rumour that the new scoring board *"which had mysteriously descended upon the field, was rumoured to be the joint -gift of Lieut. NJP Revington, Mr GL Wakeham, Mr DI Davies and the OPMs".*

The Plymothian account, précising the Head's words, continued; *"After the erection of the iron gates, and the replacing of the huts by the new buildings, the pavilion represented a new stage in the process of adding to the amenities of the College. Future territorial ambitions were not denied, but would be settled by peaceful negotiations: there was a hint that covered Fives courts would be the next objective, after the completion of the hard tennis court near the Physics Lab."*

The new pavilion - designed by one OPM and built by another.

Clearly Herbert Ralph was a bit of a tennis enthusiast and later in the same magazine we find the writers of the tennis section report thanking *"the Headmaster for kindly allowing us the use of his court ... We have found this considerably better than the old court, and the standard of play had shown a corresponding improvement."*

"The upper forms," we read, *"have shown considerable enthusiasm for this game; it is to be regretted that the authorities do not find it possible to give it official recognition. We hope that it will be placed on a firmer footing when the hard court is available for use."*

Reading between the lines of Dr Murray's speech, at the opening of the new Pavilion, one suspects he would have heartily approved the moves towards establishing tennis as a part of the school's sporting curriculum. The opening of the new building, he said, *"was a symbolic*

and almost sacramental rite in the English cult of the game. The Pavilion meant, the better recognition of the imagination of muscle and eye working together and whipping up the intelligence."

The fitter and better coordinated the body the more active and imaginative the mind was the message here and certainly, although the results may have been patchy, there were plenty of fine performances in the sporting arena that year.

"We recorded our first "rugger" win over Kelly since 1933 and playing grand open football completely outpointed Newton College. Kings', Taunton, paid us their first visit and maintained their unbeaten record (which had then stood for two years) but only by a narrow margin ... And in club games the side played hard to defeat a strong and much heavier Devon Barbarians XV."

Ted Mercer opened the scoring in the game against the Barbarians, played at the OPM's ground at Elburton, but otherwise the sides were all made up of schoolboys, few fitter and faster than Trask. Atkey, Axworthy and the Bishop boys were among the other stars and Hyland looked a good prospect for the following season.

In the Hockey stakes Atkey again was outstanding and Hyland was rated the most improved player in the XI, however only one game – against Kelly – was won, despite the fact that in several games *"we were demonstrably the better side".* Part of the problem rested with the forwards who, in front of goal, *"were never good and sometimes unbelievably bad",* according to the harsh critic in the annual report. Mr SF Florey was a part time coach and occasional player (thanks to the weather incidentally some practices were held in the (empty) swimming bath, *"in itself not an unsuccessful experiment"*) while KE Kevern was the *"energetic and industrious captain."*

Kevern, twice a former proxime accessit in the School Sports, at junior and senior level, also again came within an ace of taking the senior title in the summer

of '39. Having won the hurdles, weight and discus, he finished second in the javelin and level on points with RW Tonkin who finished second in five events, three of them just behind JD Bishop, the eventual Victor Ludorum, by a margin of just three points. New school records were set in both the discus, courtesy of Kevern, and the javelin, through Baker, while Bellingham, Murch and Trask were among the others who acquitted themselves well on the day. Sadly, however, all five of these young athletes would have their names on a board together in the school within five years or so thanks to an even greater contest where they truly would give all they had to give.

Back in the summer of '39, however, the impending clouds of war did little to dampen the sporting spirit. Among the younger boys Harland was the Junior Victor, while DH Kent won all three of the U16 events.

In the inter-school sports at Tiverton the School improved their showing on the previous year – just. While in the swimming pool the School Water Polo team lost most of their fixtures, although once again none of their seven fixtures were against schoolboy opposition and they did record victories against both Plymouth Amateurs and Plymouth City Transport. WR Douglas, who was also that year's Aquatic Victor Ludorum, was the team captain and every time the team registered at least one goal RG Bradshaw's name was on the scoresheet. Paull was another of the team's stalwarts while among the junior swimmers P Johnstone won five pool events - Squire finishing second four times.

On the cricket pitch, the previous season's hero, REG Oxenham, *"a grand cricketer who simply lives for the game,"* took a remarkable 50 wickets (more than the rest of the team put together) at an average of just 6.8. He also scored quite freely with the bat, although his biggest score at school that summer came in a Senior House match when he scored an unbeaten fifty after taking all ten wickets in an impressive demolition of the other side.

Oxenham, Kevern and Trask - the future looked so bright.

Sadly all three of the School's leading batsmen that summer – Oxenham, Kevern and Trask - were destined for an early departure from this world, Trask's character assessment in the Plymothian had a decidedly eerie quality given the benefit of hindsight;

"A reliable opening bat, content to watch and wait. Unfortunately, he consistently lifts his bat in the direction of point or third man. Players like Ponsford and McCabe do this, but they are no ordinary mortals."

Of the other sports that year there was little to say about Fives, save that the courts were in an *"appalling condition"* and that of the two matches played, against Kelly and the Staff, both were lost. SCAN Bishop was the senior Cross Country champion, and RW Pepperell, was the junior. The races were run at Marsh Mills. The course was a particularly soggy one and the times were correspondingly slow.

The individual performances that perhaps made the most impression though were those of WAH Trask and TJ Mutton in the final of the School Open Boxing contest; Mutton, *"at a considerable disadvantage in weight"*, lost after a *"fight that will be long remembered"*. Ivory, Hirons and Mahoney were the Welterweight, Featherweight and Flyweight winners, while Pengelly R, Vittle P and Woodcock J, were the 6-stone, 5½-stone and 5-stone champs respectively.

Clearly the fighting spirit went a long way through the School, perhaps not surprisingly given the social climate that year. Certainly, given the circumstances, it was no surprise to find that another sporting side had been revived at Ford Park;

"This term (Easter 1939) the School Shooting Team was re-formed for the first time after a long period. We have had postal fixtures with many teams on the miniature range, and others, on the open range have been arranged for next term. The team has experienced considerable success against strong opponents and we hope that Shooting will take its place among the other School activities.

As if to emphasise just how well the activity had already infiltrated the Ford Park Calendar, there was even a House Championship within the School – it was won by Thompsons.

With militarism rampant across the whole of Western Europe it was only to be expected that an upsurge of interest in shooting should be a by-product of the increased interest in the OTC:

"The Company is now at home in the new formation, nor are the platoons as unwieldy as their unusual size would suggest. Over strength as they are, they will become still larger when the present vast squad of recruits goes into uniform."

While on the subject of uniform the newly-promoted CSM Crosby, in his report noted that: *"Not every Tuesday is fine, and it is a pity the uniform appearance of the Corps does not extend to raincoats. A buff macintosh is just as weatherproof as a blue for every day purposes, and looks far better with uniform. If parents insist upon the buff we shall no longer witness a smart body of well turned out Cadets turned into a motley mob of mingled macintoshes by a shower of rain."*

By the Summer Term we learn from Cpl. R Garratt (Shooting Captain) that *"every member of the OTC who has attained the age of 15 years has shot on the open range at Tavistock at least once."*

"It can hardly be said that every member has fired with great success, but it is hoped that with practice the OTC will attain such a state of efficiency that it will reach the standard of Bisley."

Garratt junior then thanked *"WA Garratt, Esq., for kindly volunteering to train an inexperienced Butts party, who have shown in their marking that Mr Garratt's efforts have not been in vain."*

It was then interesting to read that *"As the range is at Tavistock, transport has been the chief difficulty, but several members of the team have procured their parent's cars and the CO has always put his car at the team's disposal."*

"Thanks are also due to the Headmaster who has given the necessary permission for the cadets who are required for shooting to have leave of the last two periods on Friday afternoons."

Bellingham, Garratt, Brady and Scott all won their shooting colours that term. For both young Cpl. Bellingham and Sgt. Scott it was an honour they would never live to tell another generation about, but again we're looking ahead too quickly.

Corporal KE Bellingham

Back in the summer of '39 the enthusiastic and bigger-than-ever Plymouth College OTC contingent was a little dismayed to learn that *"owing to the requirements of the Militia"*, there was to be no camp. *"This is particularly disappointing in view of the keen spirit of the Company and the excellent training afforded in camp. Instruction administered in bi-weekly doses cannot compare with even a period of one week spent in continuous practical training in competition with other contingents."*

While CSM Crosby was undoubtedly disappointed to miss out on another camp, as senior NCO in the OTC, Head of School, and editor of the Plymothian, he could not fail to have a better understanding than many of his peers of the situation at large.

The Magazine itself was full of references that gave an indication of the situation in Europe, some more oblique than others. The previous winter the annual OPM Debate of the Literary and Debating Society had considered that *"This House does not approve of intervention in the internal policy of Foreign Powers."*

Captain WGM Jones

Whitmarsh proposed and SB Jackson seconded. The motion was opposed by Goldberg and Fookes, who carried the day with a majority of 23 to 5, with 3 remaining neutral. There was no doubting the inference after Christmas behind the lecture given by Mr Jones - or rather Captain WGM Jones - to the Upper School, on 22 February 1939 on Air Raid Precautions.

Meanwhile in the summer term Cantabrigiensis informed us that; *"apart from the inevitable examination fever, the burning question in Cambridge has been Conscription. It is difficult to estimate the reaction of 4,000 undergraduates most of whom take no active part in political activities, but it would probably be nearer the truth to say that the greater part is resigned to the policy, though unenthusiastic, and that a strong minority opposes it on political and ethical grounds."*

"The Union, of course, voted against conscription, but Mr Winston Churchill came up at the invitation of the Conservative Club and by his militant oratory reversed the Union's decision by a large majority."

This term's Cambridge letter also informed us that JR Ede (then at King's College) *"was in Italy and Greece at the time of the Czechoslovakian and Albanian coups d'etat, and gave us a graphic account of what really happened."*

If you wanted to know what life was like as an undergraduate at Cambridge at that time it is interesting to note that the same report asked readers *"not to believe Picture Post's typical popular misconception of a day in the life"* ... *"We heartily endorse the Oxford retort: "If that's a day in the life of a Cambridge undergraduate, thank Heaven I'm at Oxford"."*

Immediately below this disclaimer incidentally was a quirky piece *"Fly In The Ointment"*:

"It was the Summer of 1959. The Dictator sat back, looking happily through His atlas and sucking the last bit of birthday-cake off His thumb. Dr Boebbels (Master of the Birthday) also sucked his thumb, but he sucked it nervously, chewing the nail from time to time: he was waiting for a cable, an important cable."

"Not come yet?" he asked anxiously as World-Marshall Poering looked in, the corners of his mouth reaching to his fourth chin. Through the window could be seen the twenty-ton lorry that accompanied him everywhere with his medals."*

"No news, I'm afraid." Nervously they glanced up at their Master, for they knew well that as soon as all the icing was gone he might put the awkward question. "No news, except of a minor revolt in the Youth Movement at Ford Park, England."

"The Septuagenarian Dictator leapt to his feet, raising a furious treble shout: "How many times have I told you that that department is never to be called by any name but Adolfland? Would you insult Your Master to His face?"

"Adolfland, Adolfland, Sire!" gabbled the other two, licking His toe alternately and fervently. "A minor revolt in Adolfland, Sire, but the rest of the world is quiet."

"Oh, a mere nothing indeed, Sire, only some three hundred boys involved; they shall be liquidated tomorrow."

"If only they could keep up the conversation He might forget the cable from Borneo. But it was not to be. A "yet-more-worlds-to-conquer" light gleaned in the pale eyes: "Ha, ha!" he laughed. "By this time tomorrow we shall have it running down the Hitlerstrasse in Berlin." Both bowed seven times at the mention of the Name."

"Just then a messenger flew in through the window, folded his swastika wings and bowed seventy times as he presented a cable. Eagerly the hands clutched it; one glance, and the Lord of the World, Giver of Peace to all true Aryans, had fallen dead – dead of disappointment."

"By the side of the body lay the message that had killed Him."

"Grappling-irons broken. Impossible to transfer the Equator to Berlin till next high tide."

The author of this mirthsome piece of fantasy projecting some twenty years into the future, signed himself - *"Homo Insipiens"*, and one can but wonder how the boys reading it perceived it at the time. Schoolboys have always been quick to find humour in the sad and the serious, and in this instance there's little doubt that the humour was decidedly influenced by the Tommy Handley *"It's That Man Again"* BBC radio series that was first broadcast from *"Radio Fakenburg"* that summer. The title of the programme came from a newspaper catchphrase used to describe Hitler's latest outburst and the series prominently featured the Plymouth-born, and raised, Jack Train in a variety of guises (Col. Chinstrap would become the most famous).

This was undoubtedly the dawning of the golden age of radio, the medium that would inform and entertain the nation through the troubled times ahead. Consequently it was no great surprise to see an earlier Plymothian piece that year dedicated to the radio vehicle that was responsible for immortalising the careers of "Big Hearted" Arthur Askey and Richard "Stinker" Murdoch – Band Waggon. In March 1939, when this piece appeared, the second series of the programme (which started the year before) had just ended … and the third, and final, series would start in October:

Radio giants Askey and Murdoch and ITMA's Tommy Handley.

Of all the programmes on the air
There's none to beat Band Waggon
And any that think otherwise
Deserve a good Sand-Baggin'.

When it is on, I hurry home
From Vols. with eager step
A perfect evening lies ahead
But for that awful prep.

"Band Waggon, Come on and take a trip
Upon the Band Waggon, it's a wow boys
It's a grand Waggon …" but don't forget the prep.
If you don't do it, there's a row, boys.

You settle down to do the Maths
But the efforts soon relax
The neatest problem stands no chance
Against Big Hearted's cracks.

And nobody can do the prep.
With proper concentration.
When they are thinking all the time
Of Stinker's operation.

On Thursday, everyone feels tired
The Prep. Are all disgraces
And Askitoff would not take off
The frowns on master's faces.

"The Flat is locked, the Waggon's parked
(They've stopped it for some reason)
But there's a problem to be solved
Before it starts next season.

Should there be prep. On Wednesday night?
That's what I want to know!
Drop us a post-card, will you, chums
Just write "Prep.": "Yes" or "No".

Although doubtless tongue in cheek, the idea of appealing for support from fellow pupils to banish homework on a certain night, so that they could all tune in to their favourite programme, was a novel one, but the notion was almost bound to recur. As indeed was Arthur Askey's "catchphrase", an early example of the genre, Aye Thank Yoo, abrieviated to *"Aythnkyo"* to give us the name that the writer of the above used as his pen-name.

Comedy was destined to play a crucial role over the next few years and certainly the pages of the Plymothian revealed long-familiar bids for escapism, and not just from the political situation at large: *"Have a peanut."*
"No thanks, I've got too much prep. to do. Wish they wouldn't talk so loud on that confounded platform. Never give a fellow a rest here."
"Never want one – the amount of work you do."
"Just as much as you do, stinker."
"Terrible phug in here. Who's eating humbugs?"
"Who do you think?"
"Oh! Him!"
"Hello, what's the clapping for?"
"Somebody's cracked a joke – didn't hear it; can't hear anything here: never mind – let's clap."

"Where are those peanut shells?"
"Under your chair. Don't step on 'em you fool! They'll crackle!"
"Let 'em. 'Bout time we had a holiday."
"Yes it is. But it can't be helped, and even if we do get a holiday, you bet they'll fix it so that we get it at half-term or something. Never give it to us at a sensible time."
"Ah, he's finished. Let's have a jujube: Thanks."
"'Bout time it finished, isn't it?"
"Yes; what flicks are you going to to-night?"
"Dunno, Regent's not bad – bit soppy, but still I could stick anything after listening to speeches all day."
"Same here. Leave your shells and toffee papers under that chair. Don't be a litter lout."
"Come on, Hooray …. Hoo-o-o-ray!"

The piece was titled *"Speech Day From Below"* and signed *"S.ii"* and despite its implicit, and certainly timeless, attitude, it is peppered with references that tie it into the culture of that period.

Peanuts in shells, jujubes, humbugs and toffees – tuck shop treats that were very much the domain of the long-serving Marsh.

"Ev'ry day just past ten-thirty,
Quitting jars and pots of dirty
Chemicals, he makes his road
To his little green abode.
There he stands within his shelter –
Then the charge comes, helter-skelter –
But he's braved it many summers,
Ready there to serve all comers.
Fortified behind his Mars's
Chocolate creams and licorice bars's
Handing this one toffee strips,
Giving that one Derby tips.
Advice from us who've been here years,
    -   "Abandon hope of buying beers;
Abandon hope, too, that you will
Pass off dud coins into his till."

He ne'er saw Xerxes lash the sea,
But oft, in cup provided free,
He's witnessed from his green chateau,
Jone slap the College H2 O .
The piece de resistance, though,
Is watching how he starts the flow
Of lemonade, and deftly woos his
Frothy "heads" on penny boozes.
Though now he sell us Milky Ways
The Army claimed his early days
"Quick March" the order used to sound,
"Quick, Marsh," today, when break comes round."

"Marsh Militaire" was the title of that tuck shop ballad, "Orion" its author and, as we were to assume that Orion was one of the older boys, the chances were that for him a military march was just around the corner.

Someone for whom there were no more corners, or pages, to turn however was Mr H Birmingham. Based in Whimple Street, Harry Birmingham, for many years, had been the man who had seen to the printing of the Plymothian; *"A genuine interest in the affairs of the College, no less than professional pride, went to secure such accuracy. Spelling and punctuation were, of course, his province; he had strong views on the hyphen, the diphthong and the diaeresis. He would check each cricket score, and ensure, if need be that the runs really did add up to the total indicated; he never flinched before the polyglot erudition of a University Letter. He contrived to convert each business interview into an act of hospitality, and to meet such a character was one of the privileges of editing the Plymothian."*

Birmingham's obituary appeared in that summer's edition of the Plymothian, the same edition that carried a University Letter that was remarkable, not for its multi-lingual scholarship, but rather for the fact that it referred to Undergraduates by their Christian names. The first OPMs to be thus honoured were Roy Prideaux, Peter Smyth, Alan Woodrow and Stafford Jackson, the

self same Stafford Jackson who within the year would find himself back at Plymouth College on the other side of the desk as one of the wartime replacements for those young members of staff called up to serve their King and Country.

It is one of the ironies of Ralph's success in drastically reducing the average age in the common room that come the declaration of war, on 3 September 1939, it would only be a matter of time before most of his new appointments had had the call to arms, but for those much younger there was another perspective;

"In the summer of 1939, things began to change in England. Air raid shelters were being dug and important office doors sandbagged. We had practice air raid alarms and found out what the sirens sounded like, hoo-whooing up and down for the warning. blowing level for the All Clear."

This is how KE Southwood, who joined had joined the School three years earlier, later recalled events. In a beautifully written account of his wartime experiences in and around Ford Park, he captured the typical schoolboy take on that fateful day in September;

"Three weeks before my 14th birthday Germany invaded Poland. When Britain declared was I was excited. I wanted to ride through the streets with a sign saying "War!". At thirteen that was the total of my thoughts about it. There was no way we could lose and it might be over by Christmas. We had the greatest empire ever, on which the sun never set, and we were the greatest nation in Europe."

The Plymothian editor was a little more obtuse but still quite informative;

"After a Saturated Summer, a Muddlesome Michaelmas. It has been been a term of innovations and surprises, attended even by portents. The College has made Territorial Concessions (from its Staff), has submitted to the rationing of foolscap, endured the curtailing of afternoon School, and bravely denied itself detentions. Ersatz ink, of course, is no novelty to us. We have seen

the evacuation of Pro., and the introduction of the feminine touch in our education. May we say that we found the gowns rather disappointing?"

"Rugby has been made more interesting, and more dangerous, by having a Beecher's Brook excavated in a corner of the field, and by further distractions on the touch-line. Hence the fractured skull and collar bone. We have had victory over Dartmouth, an unmaterialised Balloon Barrage, and a completely practical Cert. "A" squad; there is marsh in the trenches, and more in the tuck shop."

Soon to be a familiar sight.

There was no Mercer in the classroom though, and no Jones either, both were already serving as Captains in the Army. Meanwhile both Porter and Painter entered the services as 2nd Lieutenants. For Mr Painter, a member of the Territorial Army, who had entered the Prep less than twelve months earlier, the call up must have been a bitter-sweet one, his short time here had been blighted by the five-month illness of his wife, whose death was announced in the Easter term.

Painter's wartime experience too was to end tragically - in Burma five years later – he was to be the only wartime casualty among the staff. There would, however, be more than sixty old boys who would not survive the next six years including four of the ten school prefects that autumn term, among them JSJ Scott, the newly-promoted senior NCO of the OTC – but, once again, we're ahead of ourselves.

Among the new arrivals at Plymouth College that term were Mrs Worley, Horace Meek, Mr Dufton senior (for the first few weeks of the term), and two ladies who were no strangers to Ford Park - Mrs Ralph and the recently retired Miss Dinsmore.

"The biggest thing that year was undeniably and literally the barrage balloon. One day we arrived at school to find some airmen with a winch mounted on a cage topped trailer, spreading the silver fabric out on the grass. The cage was to protect the winch operator from the whipping of a snapped cable. By break time the giant balloon like a huge plump Mickey Mouse cartoon of an airship was up in the air and the airmen were holding court around the winch which was out of bounds to us. Sometimes it would be impressively close to the ground, swaying like a circus elephant a hundred feet up. At other times it would be equally imressively high, a miniature wild beast, two thousand feet up in the sky, with the rest of its herd, all breasting the wind and heading in the same direction. Every break there would be an admiring group of boys around the winch joking with the airmen, the boys in their worsted trousers and striped blazers, and the airmen in their coarse blue uniforms and leather jerkins. Being on man-to-man terms with these men, especially the corporal, became the in thing." KE Southwood.

The balloon at Mount Batten.

"We were all issued thin floppy black rubber gasmasks with heavy pig snouts, and celluloid windows. They got hot and steamy inside within five minutes so that we couldn't see anything and it was like being inside a bicycle inner tube. We had to carry them everywhere with us, and various tin cans and boxes to hold them became the latest fashion."
KE Southwood.

Above; the gasmask cometh to Mutley. Top; The School lines up in 1939.

Amid all the upheaval there was, not surprisingly, an even greater take-up for the OTC than there had been the previous term;

"The Contingent is now larger than it has ever been before, for it consists of 190 N.C.O.'s and Cadets." - a very impressive tally indeed considering that the School then numbered less than 350 - *"Owing to a large body of recruits, a Sixth Form Squad has been formed ... This squad has since been congratulated on its progress and has been formed into a fourth platoon."*

KE Southwood was one of the new recruits;

"This meant I got a midget Great-War-style khaki uniform, the colour of cow-dung, buttoned up to the neck, with a large flat round cap of the same colour, black boots, and khaki puttees. I suppose, against a background of cow-dung, we would have been invisible. Puttees were strips of rough cloth which we had to learn to wind around our shins, from the boots up nearly to the knees. We tucked the bottoms of our trousers inside them and the rest pouched out over them like skinny plus-fours. Perhaps they were to keep the leeches out of our underpants. Tiny aeroplanes could have landed and taken off on the top of my cap, like a little round aircraft carrier."

Plymouth College OTC NCOs and Senior Cadets: Summer 1940. Back row, l-r; Frogaty, Caren, Pugh, Hutchens, Day, Middle, Pearn, Harker, Lawry, Symes, Ede, Bellingham. U'ren, Tranter. Front; Robins, Chapman, Summers, Bence, Masters, Atkey and Reynolds.

"Mr D.I.Davies has rendered valuable assistance this term in training Stage 2." The forty-one year-old Di Davies would not quite see the academic year out at Ford Park however, as, during the summer term, the talented languages master would resign so that he might *"undertake specialist work in the Army"*.

There was another version of events however. It suggested that the abrupt departure of the popular Welsh French master *"whose broad humour and confidence kept us attentive and entertained"*, did the indescribable with another woman and was divorced by his wife. Either way, before coming to Ford Park, Davies had worked as an expert on Poison Gasses and that's the field he was evidently going back into. *"He used to terrify the boys with stories of what happened when you bayoneted someone ... "you could smell what they had for breakfast" he would say"*, recalled Cecil Atkey. After John Dufton and Eric Holman, Davies was the third longest serving member of staff when he left with a fine record of *"preparing boys for both School and Higher Certificate examinations."*

Davies replacement was *"a little man who seemed to know nothing at all about boys. His weak jokes were greeted by loud, raucous laughter lasting minutes at a time, while he feebly and foolishly tried to persuade us that the joke was over. I think he really didn't know what was happening,"* recalled Southwood.

"A fish was nailed under his desk drawer causing a stink we happily put up with for some days. The top was taken off his desk, the legs upended and the top placed on the bottom, as it were. He didn't seem to be sure whether all this meant he was popular or not. Great fun, even if cruel, but with a crueller side. His son was in our class."

Davies departure also left a gap in the games department for, since the outbreak of war, he had acted as Games Master, with the unenviable task of preparing boys for matches with service sides as schoolboy opposition became increasingly thin on the ground; even the pitch

itself was thinner – *"narrowed by ARP construction work."* However, despite *"an almost moribund fixture card" and "doubts as to whether each game played would be the last, the 1939 season proved to be one of interest and achievement."*

"Before the term started officially we had adopted the plan of giving any Service Unit in the district a game, and as a result, in spite of adversity, we carried on to achieve fuller results than ever before."

And while teams from the Royal Naval Engineering College, the 6th Devons and HMS Vindictive all registered victories over the 1st XV., against Devon Yeomanry, RNC Dartmouth, the Royal Artillery, and the Devon Barbarians the boys were more successful, as they were in their only home fixture against a school side – Sutton High. Away trips against Sutton, Kelly and Newton (where they lost in the last minute) were less fruitful and yet *"from each game we learnt much that we were able to apply immediately by defeating sides apparently more experienced."*

HMS Impregnable, for example, failed to live up to their name and the School walloped them 56-3. They also beat OPMs and OPOs, but lost a later keenly-fought return fixture against the OPMs 11-0 with John Spear scoring two tries and converting one of them.

Ted Mercer also scored against and indeed for the School in separate fixtures, on one occasion fielding his own side. The latter game was unfortunately clouded by *"a severe head injury"* sustained by RG Atkey, but otherwise the season appears to have been interesting, but relatively trouble-free.

Atkey, Axworthy, Oxenham and Trask were among the stars with Mutton superb at full-back where he *"had such brilliant moments that we forget those few lapses that left us with our hearts in our throats."*

For OPM rugby the war could not have come at a more inopportune time. The 1938/9 season had been the most successful in the history of the Club – *"Not only were more matches won than ever before, but the*

season was marked by all-round keenness, playing ability and team spirit."

1938/39 OPM Rugby XV; Back row, WH Trask, AWC Lyddon, RRC Kitchen. Middle, KH Ife, GL Spear, KD Eke, FW Blight, WA Culliford, N Trahair. Front, RV Hoare, HR Lawry, NE Elliott (Capt.), GL Wakeham (Pres.), DG Spear, GFN Snell, RF Fowles.

Clearly the club intended to carry on during the war but a number of players were soon lost to the Services, including; Spear, Lawry, Trahair, Carter, Clemas, Kitchen, Rattray, Blight, Ife, Culliford, Johns, Tickle and North … *"We wish them well, and a safe return."* Happily they would all return, but it is likely that none of them imagined they would be away quite so long.

It wasn't to be so long, however, before boys were reading of the first reported casualty among OPMs serving in His Majesty's Forces – RHM Heriot-Hill, Lieut RN (Air Arm), a former School boxing champ, who had left Ford Park in 1933.

It was a difficult time for OPM news, *"as so many OPMs are serving with the Colours, several biographical snippets have had to be withheld. Please excuse us."*

Meanwhile, among those titbits that posed no threat to national security was the news of HC Lyddon's marriage in Kent and two OPM nuptial ceremonies at Emmanuel Church - for Messrs Condy and Periton.

We also learned that JHS Gillingham was now West of England Inspector of Electrical Installations in Government Ships, the Rev JR Walkey was Chaplain in Chief to the RAF and Honorary Chaplain to HM the King and that SB Jackson was treasurer of the Oxford University Dramatic Society.

Drama at School was still very much the domain of Hugh Dent – *"if all the plays produced this term by Mr Dent were placed end to end, they would fill the Gymnasium, although not all of them were staged in the Gym; "the Dent Players" also produced "The Dear Departed" at Virginia House."* The latter venue was also visited by the *"Jazz Band"* which had been rumoured to exist at the College. It is a six-bit band, but whether swing or hot we would rather not say. The accordian (sic) player does without music – he can't see it through his hair anyway."*

Whether such ensembles had existed before or not, this certainly appears to be our first reference to a School band of any kind that played anything other than straight, classical or folk music. It's also the first reference to pupil's hair length, interestingly enough, at a time when short back and sides was about to be de rigeur for a large section of that generation.

Incidentally, with Mr Porter now in uniform full-time, there was a post to be filled in the Scout Troop and while Mr Dundas had helped with duties at the 1939 camp at Werrington, it was Hugh Dent who took over as Hon. ASM. Here too numbers were up – *"from 29 to 40, necessitating the formation of a new patrol - the "Swifts"."*

Among the new activities pursued by the Troop that summer was an elementary Signalling Class in Morse and *"Messanger Duties for the A.R.P. Organisation"* … *"and they have carried on either as full-time messengers or as casualties, etc., during exercises."*

JW Trobridge was the new Troop Leader and an intensive waste-paper collecting campaign was being planned for the winter.

Everyone was being encouraged to do their bit for the country at home and abroad. At the annual Prize Giving, held this year in Big School, Sir William Munday reminded his audience of the famous lines;
"Here and here did England help me
How can I help England?"
He added that the chosen motto of the Prince of Wales was in the same tradition: - *"I serve."*

Having been forced out of the Guildhall for the Prize Giving, the annual Commemoration Service was held some three weeks earlier, at St Andrew's. The Bishop of Plymouth gave the main address, his central text being that the *"only salvation for Europe is to follow Jesus Christ."*

The Christian perspective was also central to a page in the Plymothian devoted to the Plymouth Crusaders, based, since 1906, in Mutley Baptist Church. Keen not to neglect the ever-present struggles to be faced on home soil, JEV, in his piece on the group, drew attention to one of their main activities; *"At Christmas time, presents are taken round to hundreds of poor families in the Plymouth slums."*

Christmas 1939 was destined to be an odd one for many children, far removed from the traditional picture of cosy domesticity conjured up in Clement Moore's early-nineteenth-century and perennially-popular poem *The Night Before Christmas* which, curiously enough, was one of the new titles presented to the Prep Library that term, along with *Biggles and Co.* and *The House At Pooh Corner.* Judging by another poignant Plymothian piece that term - *"Us 'aves 'vacuees"*, one suspects that the works of Jan Stewer were popular in the Senior Library;
"You young fellers must be a' wonderin' what us be doin' 'bout this yere tiff we be 'avin' wey 'itler; well, oi'll tell 'ee."

"As oi be too ole fer all this milisher stuff, and missuz, 'er widen be much cop ine the "Whats," us thought as 'ow us wude 'ave zum of they 'vacuees what um be

zending down from Lunnen; now thihs were 'bout a month agone, an' of course us diden 'spec but to 'ave a couple o' little maidens, what wude help missuz 'round the 'ouse like an' zort o' look purty – you naw what oi means. Well last Monday evenin', Jack Edwards – 'e what keeps the carrier van – 'rived back wey the 'vacuees for the village 'an they parked us off wey two."

"Come to look at um ine the marnin' us found they wuz boyes – two of the durtiest, sassy-faced boyes as oi've zeed ine all me born days, waden us vexed! Well when missuz 'ad washed their faces to make zure they waden niggers an' they 'ad eat all the bread an' jam us 'ad ine the 'ouse, they zed they wuz gwaine out "to zee if there wuz anythin' worth zeein' in this yere dump."

"'bout dinner-time us smelled a hoffal smell, aze 'twuz they boyes, and a reg'lar fine pickle they wuz ine too, zed as 'ow they 'ad fallen in the pig-sty; one oi fergot to clean out last month."

Taxing the Christian and humanitarian ethics on the part of surrogate parents and the evacuees alike, this was an increasingly-common and very real experience, with 1.5 million children being moved out of London and various other English cities and large towns, and into the countryside, at the end of August 1939. Doubtless quite a few boys at the School, living in large houses outside Plymouth, found street-wise children from up the line, being billeted in their family homes.

As well as rural Devon and Cornwall, Oxford and Cambridge too were filling up with (undergraduate) evacuees from London but as yet there was no concerted movement out of Plymouth generally or Plymouth College specifically;

"At a meeting of the Full Board held in the School on July 15th, the Governors reaffirmed their decision not to move the School until Plymouth is declared an Evacuation Area."

Parents may have been worried, but when Ralph announced to the School that there were no plans to

evacuate, *"there were cheers from the ranks of the OTC ready for anything the Jerries could throw at us".*

While some went off to fight for King and Country many left behind did their bit. A Park, OPM (second from right) is with town clerk Colin Campbell and six local Gas Information Officers.

"Every now and then the siren would hoo-whoo during the day and we would all troop out of our classrooms into the small cloakrooms just across the hall. This was supposed to be safer. All it seemed to do was to cram us into a smaller target. We'd all go together or not go at all." Southwood.

Meanwhile the formal notice, posted at the beginning of the July 1940 Plymothian, continued;

"Negotiations however are proceeding with a number of Hotels in Devon to which, in case of emergency, the School may be moved. It is not at present possible to give full details of the scheme, but parents are assured that, in the event of a compulsory evacuation, these new School Houses would be conducted at the lowest possible cost. Meanwhile any parents who wish their boys to be included in the School Scheme, but have not yet notified the Headmaster, are asked to do so without delay. Details and instructions will be circulated at the appropriate time."

The first bombs on Plymouth had fallen on 6 July 1940 and, as of 14 July, there had been five raids and

6 July 1940 Plymouth's first bomb hits demolishing four houses.

many more alerts. To date ten civilians had been killed and many more injured. On the 15th July bombs were dropped on RAF Mount Batten, as well as in open country in Plympton and Ivybridge. As the Western Morning News Correspondent, Pat Twyford noted;

"There was now no longer any question in anyone's mind as to the vulnerability or remoteness of Plymouth as far as air attack was concerned. Plymouth was bang in the front line."

The grim reality of war hits home.

At least that was the perception down here. The Government, however, had yet to see the situation in quite the same light and the South East was still seen as the most likely target area. It was no surprise therefore to find that The King's Camp that year was not held at the usual venue, almost on the eastern most extremity of England, at Southwold in Suffolk, but rather at Abergeldie Castle, on the Royal Estate at Balmoral; *"The change was made to enable His Majesty to spend more time in Camp."*

Indeed although only *"one representative was selected from each public school and factory, instead of the usual two".* There was undoubtedly a greater Royal commitment than was usual. *"On the Sunday afternoon the King and Queen extended an invitation to all of us to go to Balmoral Castle for tea. After shaking hands all round, their Majesties joined us at tea. Each day during the week that followed we went for walks in the mountain country around us. The King accompanied us on these walks, which were actually planned by him. We received several visits from the Queen and the Princesses at our entertainments each evening. The climax was reached when on the last night we were taken to the hill that overlooked the Castle. There a huge bonfire was lit; it was said that the flames could be seen for thirty miles around. There again the King joined us and joined in the singing of "Auld Lang Syne". The sight of the King's Pipers marching around the fire to the tune of "Over the Sea to Skye" is one which will not readily be forgotten."*

So wrote the School's representative, SG Ward, who was also then Head Boy and Editor of the Plymothian. In terms of Public Relations the piece could hardly have been more effective; *in coal mines and silk factories, people who were going to Oxford, people who made aeroplanes: almost every walk of life was represented. We left the camp with the feeling that the aim of his Majesty had been achieved: we had "got to know the other man's point of view"."*

If the King's Camp served as a great leveller, so too did the war and the privations that went with it.

King George VI had founded an annual camp for 400 boys, half from public schools, half from industrial areas, in 1921, when Duke of York. Here the King and Queen, and the princesses, sing at that last pre-war camp at Abergeldie, near Balmoral.

"When rationing runs rampant and coupons are the rage, When butter is not thought of, and shopping takes an age;
When food controlling factions begin to fill the House – Just think of Marshall Goering, as thin as Mickey Mouse!"
"The U.S.A. is making its stockings out of coal, A special kind of paper is turned out by the roll, Synthetic rubber also is met with everywhere, But you should see the Germans, the things they use out there!"
"Where suits are made of woodpulp and all the moths are starved, Where buttons all are sculptured and button-holes are carved,
And fibre belts and braces are welded extra tight, And hammer and cold chisel are needed every night."

"When leaflet raids were in the vogue and pamphlets a la mode, And countless bits of paper were littering up the sod,
When Churchill quite unaided was sinking untold ships, A lot of exhortations cloaked ersatz fish and chips."
"Now his belief in safety has surely been exploded, The dice of Fate against him are now quite fully loaded; The chance of his surviving is daily growing littler, It's not surprising that there's an ersatz Hitler!"

DJA Koln, signed the piece, and it was written for the Christmas Plymothian not long after the excited signal "Winnie's back" had circulated around the British Fleet as Winston Churchill had been reinstated as the First Lord Of the Admiralty, a post he had held 25 years earlier at the outbreak of the First World War. It was also very soon after a bomb had exploded in a hall in Munich where Hitler had been speaking only moments before. Seven were killed and over sixty were injured in the incident, but having left the proceedings earlier than anticipated, the Fuhrer himself, the undoubted target of the explosive device, had emerged unscathed. For all that the boys at School may have fictonalised and trivialised the antics of Hitler and his henchmen there can be no doubt that as they progressed through the School and the OTC and reached their final year, the realities of war would have appeared very real indeed.

"The popularity of the OTC continued, but masters kept disappearing. Captain Hill (Guy Hill) was too weatherworn and old, so he continued to command us. The rumour went around that Mr Edwards was really a Nazi but that the call of King and Country and the awful thought of being thought a shirker drove him to volunteer. Hugh Dent and Charles Hill turned out to be conscientious objectors, to the disgust of the old soldiers in the OTC, though I don't remember feeling any disdain myself," recalled Southwood.

"Dent decided to join the Army as a noncombatant, eventually joining the Intelligence Corps. Clearly Hill had to go Plymouth College was very patriotic."

In December 1939 there were at least two Old Boys, TCS Pointon and PH Panter, who took part in the action off the River Plate, Uruguay - the former on HMS Exeter, the latter on the Ajax.

HMS Exeter above, damaged below

Below 1939 - The Graf Spee is scuttled in Montivideo harbour.

It was the combined efforts of these two ships, together with the Achilles, that led to the scuttling of the Graf Spee, the pride of the German fleet. It was one of the first great British successes of the War and in the March Plymothian, Pointon and Panter's connection appeared alongside news that Wing-Commander AP Revington had been *"mentioned in despatches"*. It was all very glorious and somewhat glamorous, however, that same month as the magazine was being read for the first time, Capt.RE Dennys, who had been at School throughout the First World War, died in France and, a few weeks

later, Pilot Officer P Ramsay, who had left School less than eighteen months earlier and would have been known to most Ford Park pupils, was killed in France. Putting a brave face on the Continental situation, Mr Chamberlain told Parliament that *"Hitler had missed the bus"* and that Allied strategy was strangling Germany's economic life. But that didn't stop Holland and Belgium falling to the German blitzkrieg four weeks later, leading to their surrender at the end of May. By that time though the discredited Chamberlain, not helped by the Allies efforts in Norway, had handed over the leadership of the Country to Churchill, Labour refusing to serve under Lord Halifax, Chamberlain's original suggestion. The new Coalition Government had Labour leader, Clement Atlee, as deputy Prime Minister, with Halifax staying on as Foreign Secretary and with powerful outsiders like Lord Beaverbrook, the newspaper magnate, and trade union leader Ernest Bevin being recruited into the War Cabinet, in moves reminiscent of the Great War.

By the end of the month the process of evacuating the encircled British troops from Dunkirk on the French/Belgium border had begun. By the 4th of June the evacuation, code-named Operation Dynamo, was complete. Many lives, and many ships, were lost, but a third of a million men were rescued and in the Plymothian that July we were informed that there had been news *"at first hand or indirectly, of many OPM's who were successfully withdrawn from Dunkirk and Normandy"*.

Among them were RJS Rattray, GW Irish and KJ McIntyre. News filtered through too that *"AHM Smyth, who interrupted his classical studies at Oxford to join the Army, at the outbreak of war, has been mentioned in despatches for distinguished work in the actions that preceded the withdrawal from Dunkirk."*

It also emerged that BAS Sherriff (of the East Yorkshire Regiment), who had left School less than three years earlier, was being held prisoner and his contemporary,

June 1940 the evacuation of Dunkirk.

French troops in Plymouth after Dunkirk.

AG Duff (now serving with the Loyal – East Lancs – Regt.), who left School for Sandhurst at the same time, had, *"after successfully making his way across France to Marseilles, managed, at a third attempt, to board a ship for, presumably, Gibraltar."* Sadly however Duff would be reported *"lost at sea"* later that year.

In Germany meanwhile, troops were issued with English phrase books in readiness for an invasion of Britain and at Ford Park CSM JSJ Scott used the OTC Notes to explain the advantages of joining the Corps to those boys who had yet to sign up.

"The primary object of the training is to produce a ready reserve of leaders for H.M. forces. The introduction of militia training has in no way affected this object, a

statement supported by the War Office; for there still must be leaders; indeed the numbers required have risen rapidly. The advantage gained by three or four years of preliminary training in a contingent of the OTC must increase for any individual the possibility of being selected as a leader in the relatively short period of militia training. Experience is proving this premise, and it is hard to understand how in the present position anyone can ignore the opportunity presented by our privileged position; the possession of an OTC contingent is a privilege granted to few schools."

"For boys intending to enter any of H.M. Forces as officers, early membership of the OTC is essential. It cannot of course help the candidate in face of a low educational standard, but it is of real value in interview and record to the normal entrant. More basically, it tends to produce the right type of candidate, self-reliant and ready to take the initiative."

"In conclusion, this growth of initiative, self-reliance and readiness to accept responsibility is as important to the boy as it is the country as a whole. The dictates of both self-interest and patriotism point the same way."

CSM Scott left Plymouth College that summer. Three years later, in the summer of 1943, his parents received a letter containing these lines; "It may be of some consolation to you to know that your son was a very gallant officer. I spoke to him a moment before he led his platoon into attack. The Germans were holding a high rock. He was a fine leader of men. He took his platoon to the top, with very few casualties, and turned the Germans out. He was killed by a burst of machine-gun fire and died immediately. His men told me it was entirely due to him that the position was captured. It was a most important feature affecting the whole operation in our part of Sicily. I always had the very highest opinion of him. He was exceptionally cheerful whatever the conditions. It was like a tonic to meet him ... His feat, which will be recorded in the history of the regiment, has been an inspiration to all of us here."

In recognition of his bravery, on the 19th July, in Sicily, Scott was posthumously awarded the Military Cross.

Back in Ford Park and back to 1940, two other deaths occurred which cast their own clouds over the School. In the early part of the year Bert Sargent's wife, "for twenty years a familiar figure at School functions of every kind", sadly died, followed just a little while later by the wife of a former head, Mrs Colson. "The steady growth and success of the Boarding House, when it was removed to Valletort Villas in 1894 had largely to be credited to her supervision and unremitting care and to her power of getting on well with subordinates and maintaining discipline and efficiency of service in the house," ran the notice in the Magazine.

"Mrs Colson, by her care for the diet and health of Boarders, contributed in a great degree to the success of the House and the School. Those who remember the long years of Mr Colson's headmastership will know how much he himself and the Governors depended on the services which Mrs Colson from her position and influence was able to render to the tone of the Boarding House and of the School as a whole."

Two other deaths were noted in the same editorial that summer; those of Alderman WL Bastard, "For many years a Governor of this School"and Dr FE Price, "who for some years has acted as the school's medical adviser.

The good doctor also had put both of his boys, one of them a fine athlete, through the school. Another departure, announced in the following edition of the Plymothian, was that of TD Leavey, who had left school just three years earlier and who lost his life serving with the Merchant Navy. Leavey was First Radio Officer on board the ill-fated SS Arandora Star, erstwhile flagship of the Blue Star Line which set sail from Liverpool on 30 June 1940 having been boarded up, armed and painted battleship grey, with a cargo of prisoners of war and a large number of German and Italian interns - "aliens" living in Britain at the outbreak of war, who had been taken from their families and detained by British Authorities as representing possible danger to the safety of the country.

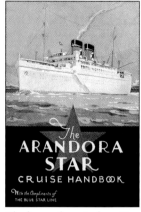

The Arandora and her passengers were bound for Canada (most of the families of the interns having been relocated to the Isle of Mann) however at 7.05am on 2nd July the ship was torpedoed and in just over half an hour had sunk with the loss of 682 out of the 1,571 lives on board. Some two-thirds (474) of the Italians, a third of the Germans (156) and a quarter of the British on board (96) were lost, including Leavey.

The luxury liner Andora Star

The War was increasingly impacting on all aspects of school life and at the beginning of the year another two temporary members of staff – Mr WE Gaskin and 37 year-old mathematician, Herbert Gould - were welcomed into the Ford Park fold and, before the year

Stafford Jackson OPM..

was out, Stafford Jackson, a young OPM, 50 year-old Richard Rigby, from Brentwood, and Kathleen Goad, a 40 year-old teacher from the girl's school Headland College, had all joined the main school staff. Headland College, incidentally, in Headland Park, opposite Plymouth High School for Girls, evacuated to Gunnislake during the war, never to return.

There were staff changes at the Prep too; as Mr Morley arrived to teach Set A in the Lower School and Mr Parkyn came in to deputise as Master of the 2nd Division for Mr Westhead, who joined the Royal Signals Corps in November 1940.

Plymouth High loses roof tiles as the Blind Instutute, opposite Headland College, takes a direct hit.

Damage but not devastation in Wilderness Road.

December 1940 a bomb hits Lisson Grove.

The previous few months had seen a gradual increase in the number of air raids over the City and slowly the tally of death and destruction was mounting.

"Most nights that winter the raid would last half an hour or so. Perhaps there would be two or three warnings. The plane would fly across the city, engines throbbing, and the beams of ten or twenty searchlights would wave like the antennae of giant cockroaches and, every now and then catch a small point of light in the dark sky. Then they would all converge and the little white light, perhaps just discernable as an aeroplane, would slowly pass across at the apices of the great white triangles, all moving together and changing shape to keep the plane brightly lit."

"At the same time the guns would go off, hurling shells up the searchlight beams, and we would see pinpoints of light around the white spot. Sometimes we would see the spot flash red and everybody would say, "Got that one alright!" with glee and enthusiasm, before retreating inside. But that was rare. If the plane was overhead we'd get showered by lumps of hot splintered metal, zipping down from the dark sky and smacking into the ground. It was no time to be looking out for successful hits," (KE Southwood).

Most alarms were false ones though and people fell into little routines of their own;

"Coming home from school that winter, I would finish my homework, play at war with Harold Bassett for a bit or make model aeroplanes, eat supper, and then sit with mum plyaing cards or doing a jigsaw puzzle until the sirens sounded," recalls the Southwood, who at fourteen was quick to don his helmet and *"go to the post"* as a messenger.

"I would walk out of the back door of the house and down the garden path in my tin hat to the back door of the year with the searchlights probing and the airborne engines drumming and my heart full. Looking, in the 1980s and 90s, at news film of boys riding in jeeps, waving automatic weapons in civil-wartorn Beirut or Somalia, or Palestine, and grinning at the cameraman, I can understand, at least a little, I wasn't bloodthirsty, and I might have jibed at shooting somebody, but the action and the excitement made me breathe deeply with sheer joy. Two nations were putting on a giant firework display and I was free to walk though it without an adult to interfere."

"A bomber might fly over Devonport and I might hear distant bombs falling, leaving me free to gaze up at the lights in the dark sky over the black roofs. Sometimes a bomber would come over our end of the city and the action would be all around and right overhead. I would hear whizzing noises and jump back into a doorway while the jagged lumps of steel whacked over the cobblestones or the pavement. Then, when it was over, I'd go out and see if I could find any, still hot, and put it in my trouser pockets. By the end of the winter I had a boxful of what we called shrapnel."

Given a ratio of around ten alarms to every actual raid and, compared with what was to come in a few months time, the damage was slight, prompting the writing and then publication in that December 1940 Plymothian of a piece – *"Alarms and Excursions"* – the appearance of which would have been almost unimaginable a few months later:

"With the sirens loudly sobbing, and with distant pom-poms throbbing
The appetite for air raids quickly falls
And with whistling H.E.'s falling and the wardens sweetly calling,
The funny thing is that it quickly palls.
You get used to visitations – even thrills have limitations
And regard the raids as merely passing squalls
As I write I hear a Jerry, flying above my terri – Tory,
greeted with great vigour by our eager shot and shell
And the crack-of-doom and whistle of the earthward-fallen missile
Goes unheeded by the citizens, excepting where it fell."

Police Incident 25: 28 December 1940, Wilton Street. Plymouth gears up to deal with the destruction caused by enemy bombers. As whole houses are reduced to rubble so that rubble is carried away as swiftly as possible, leaving great gaps in long-standing local terraces.

Certainly the School itself was remarkably fortunate during the war. The staff and senior boys took fire-watching duties on the school's relatively-flat roof during raids and a number of incendiary bombs were extinguished. Across the road, Hyde Park Junior School was less fortunate and the whole of the top floor was devasted by fire.

For schoolboys these could be fairly exciting times; *"I had the weird experience of travelling home from the cinema, in the blackout, on the open top deck of a tramcar when an air raid started. As we swung off Mutley Plain a small shower of incendiary bombs fell in Hyde Park Road ahead of us (the School had a lucky escape). The tramdriver kept his cool, running quickly over the starting fires, dropping off and picking up passengers (rapidly decreasing), at the regular stops!"*

December 1940 bomb damage in Belgrave Lane.

So recalled William Beattie who was coming to the end of his second year at the School in the summer of 1940;

"There was little panic during these air attacks and with familiarity everyone became fairly blasé. During one early day raid we had a Latin lesson in a school basement, taken, unusually by the headmaster, Dr

Ralph, who attempted to acquaint us with the use of the gerund and the gerundive. In the ongoing war situation I found it difficult to concentrate on Caesar's Gallic Wars and wasted most of the lesson illustrating my exercise book with Spitfires and Messerschmidts. Inevitably I fell into the set trap in the evening's preparation. Although, even now, I have not grasped this obscure point of Latin grammar, I still, after sixty years, have not forgotten the lines I had to write out as a punishment ... "Cum nuntiatum esset Helvetios ad provinciam nostram iter facere conare, maturat (Caesar) ad urbe profisci"."

It wasn't just William who was fascinated by fighter planes as the RAF geared up for the aerial Battle of Britain with Goering's pre-invasion Lufftwaffe raiders. This was a time for flights of fancy, war heroes and collecting slivers of shrapnel on the way to school.

Back then School finished each day at 4.15, although, in the winter, *"as a concession to the blackout, we were allowed out from the last lesson about 15 minutes early"*, says Leonard Lean, one of the boys who owed this special privilege to the fact that he lived across the river in Saltash and therefore needed to catch an earlier train – *"but we were not allowed to go into our form room and leave the afternoon's work books. As a result, we had to carry them home as well as carry the prep books round during the afternoon: a very full and heavy satchel."*

You jump on board from either side here at North Road Station.

Under normal circumstances if the *"4.25 twin-auto unit was a minute or two late from the sidings (which it often was, being delayed by a late-running train of any variety), we could just get that, otherwise we generally got the special tender train, with its five ordinary non-corridor carriages (so rather more "posh"), leaving at 4.35."*

The Blackout didn't just affect the day to day schoolboy experience, it also had a knock-on effect for the old boys. The OPM's Annual General Meeting was held in the School Science Lecture Theatre on 3rd December at 5.15 and only nine members attended; *"The Black-out and Active Service accounted mainly for so sparse an attendance, nevertheless there was a member of the Press there, as the meeting decided that "this meeting was looked upon as a private affair of the club." The Representative of the Press withdrew – as a consequence of this there was no report of the meeting in the local paper."*

There was a brief discussion about the OPM Scholarship, officers were elected en-bloc and it was decided not to hold an Annual Dinner or a Dance. Ralph Brown, OPM and School Governor and son of the previous Chairman of Governors, was in the chair and after a few words of sympathy for Mr Colson, on the loss of his wife, and a few moments silence for the Old Boys who had lost their lives in the previous twelve months, the meeting was closed after just twenty five minutes.

Meanwhile the Old Boys of the School at Oxford were wistfully contemplating the possible loss of their own lives; *"The lights have gone out over Europe. In the gardens of the Colleges at Oxford the roses are blooming. Another term is over. We bid farewell to our tutors and "scouts", book our tickets for home, and depart. The trains that carry us away may not bring us back, at least not in civilian clothes, for many months. We have been called upon to make the great sacrifice that our fathers made before us, and we do not shrink from the task."*

"National pride and love of Liberty and Justice will triumph, but the agony will be great, and the men who were well-known at Oxford, and those who were lesser-known but who might have been famous in afterlife, will lie side by side, limp and unrecognised amid ruin and desolation. But now, as we take a last look at the things we have loved, the gardens, the quadrangles, and the towering spires, we realise that certain things will never perish."

Some things, perhaps, but not necessarily those made by man, as London was about to find out, followed weeks later by Coventry, and then before the year was out - Birmingham, Liverpool and Southampton. Plymouth's turn too would come - but we are jumping too far ahead.

Although the world was at war in 1940, some things about life at school were fairly normal, as the Plymothian editorial that summer was at pains to point out;

"They used to study the globe in our Schools and Colleges in days when the earth revolved sedately enough to make study possible. Now it whizzes round so crazily that it makes you dizzy to look at it; there is even a fear that it may fly off the handle altogether. The peoples are scattered, the countries lose their shapes: Petsamo gets mixed up with Mayale, and Nicaragua merges into Bessarabia. Amid all this we have tried to fix on paper some of the quieter aspects of recent life in Plymouth College"

Unfortunately among the quietest of these was record of the Hockey team;

"It would be injudicious to attempt anything like a detailed examination of last term's hockey, for the season was abnormal in many ways. War deprived us of our pitch, and of some of our best fixtures; and the new fixtures we had were not particularly well balanced. The term was unusually short. The weather, even for Plymouth, was unusually vile. Indeed, perhaps my own most lasting impression of the hockey season of 1940 is that of the constant session of seagulls upon Ford Park;

these melancholy fowl gathered almost daily until the end of term to gloat upon the discomfiture of hockey enthusiasts. Rain stopped us playing at Newton; and the most unkindest cut of all was the outbreak of spotted fever which isolated Tavistock and so prevented our visit to Kelly. In the end not a single match with another school xi took place, a fact which in itself shews up the unreality of the season."

"All matches, except a handful at the end of term (and these were evening games), were played upon rain-soaked pitches; some on quagmires hardly fit for soccer."

Nevertheless Lawry, Hyland, Heathcote and Atkey all managed to get themselves into the Devon Schools XI that played, and defeated, a County XI at Newton.

The winter weather wasn't just bad for Plymouth, incidentally, as January witnessed the worst storms in Britain in the century to date. The Thames froze over for the first time since 1888 in a cold wave that caused chaos across Europe.

Happily the summer saw an improvement. College *"comfortably"* won the Athletics championsip, with help from Senior and Junior Victor Ludorum Cup winners RJ Reddecliffe (who ran a 10.5 sec, 100 yards in the Devon School sports at Kelly) and ED King, respectively. Sargents fared less well, provoking the House Captains to comment;

"Unless every member of the House takes an active interest in the House's sporting activities, it will be impossible to wish Sargent's every success in the future. So we urge everyone, in the words of a former House-master, to "Give it some wood, laddie!""

Happily that was something one or two of the cricketers were able to do, Nicholls and Atkey in particular, with both of them bagging a ton – the former against the officers of the Royal Naval Barracks, setting up a comfortable victory for the School, the latter against OPMs in the last game of the season. The newly-appointed maths teacher, Horace Meek, twice hit more

than 90, while his younger departmental colleague, George Bonser, clean bowled six of the first XI in the Staff v School match, nailing Gilbert LBW to give him figures of 7-23, with pro Heywood mopping up the other three wickets for 13, giving the Staff what seemed like an unlikely victory after they themselves had been dismissed for 84.

THE STAFF.		THE SCHOOL.	
G. H. Bonser, Esq., b. Ewens	16	R. G. Atkey, b. Bonser	0
C. L. Barnes, Esq., b. Miller	11	H. S. Rendle, b. Heywood	0
H. L. Meek, Esq., b. A. J. Gilbert	23	S. K. Lawry, b. Bonser	28
I. S. Edwards, Esq., b. A. J. Gilbert	7	G. B. Kerswill, b. Bonser	3
W. H. Heywood, l.b.w., Miller	3	K. G. Gilbert, l.b.w., Bonser	5
W. E. Battrick, Esq., b. Lyon	4	G. W. Sargent, st. Hill, b. Heywood	11
W. E. Gaskin, Esq., b. Miller	0	D. E. Ridpath, l.b.w., Heywood	3
H. W. Gould, Esq., b. Lyon	1	R. H. Ewens, not out	4
C. P. Hill, Esq., b. A. J. Gilbert	16	C. F. Lyon, b. Bonser	0
H. Dent, Esq., not out	3	J. D. Miller, b. Bonser	0
E. G. Dundas, Esq., did not bat			
Extras	0	Extras	2
Total	84	Total	56

A. J. Gilbert 3 for 11; Miller 3 for 22; Lyon 2 for 6.　　Bonser 7 for 20; Heywood 3 for 13.

Staff v School scorecard from the summer of 1940.

Ewens and Gilbert were the two main bowlers for the firsts with Cuss and Brokenshire impressive for the seconds. Most games were clear-cut, but a couple were notably close; needing two runs with two wickets remaining, the School lost away to Truro by one run. The next match, also away, a week later, on 25 May, against 303 ITC was tied; the School declaring at 125 for 3, a score the opposition managed to equal with their last man at the wicket. The School, incidentally, had the OPM Cricket Club and NJ Revington and GL Wakeham, to thank for their smart new score board.

On the swimming front, Robin, Mutch and Johnstone dominated the School Aquatic Sports, while Robin, Squire and Kelly all gained colours for the Water Polo team, who had a fairly unremarkable season. Sutton High School was well beaten, twice, and a few heavy losses were sustained at the hands of non-school sides, but *"there was some difficulty in arranging matches, because of hostilities, and sides withdrawing for the duration"*.

It wasn't just the war that was causing problems. After the difficulties experienced by the hockey players in their efforts to find suitable non-soggy surfaces to play on, *"the summer spell of unusually dry weather"* which *"outlasted the holidays"* saw the rugby players, that autumn, faced with *"sun-baked grounds and hard pitches, which for three weeks precluded any attempt at serious football."*

The delay in starting the season was, however, *"profitably spent in practice games, conducted under revised rules"* producing a team that *"bears comparison with some of the best xv's of recent years. FL Axworthy has brought a wealth of experience, gained over three seasons as Captain, to assist in handling the team and extracting the utmost from its members."*

Back row; Ron Atkey, An Other, AN Oother, Wally Hirons, Unknown, GB Kerswill. Seated; Yeates, AN Other, ditto, Len Axworthy, Ken Nicholls, Caben, Anon. Front; Anon, Jack Brokenshire

Coeval fixtures were becoming more limited through the exigencies of war, but the *"experience derived in playing heavy local sides, and fast, clever Service xv's was put to profitable use in the important matches against Schools. Away we lost to Devonport, Dartmouth and Sutton: at home, we beat Devonport and Sutton, and drew with Kelly."*

The report then ran through the 2nd XV's *"chequered"*

career and the *"enterprising and successful"* one of the junior sides, *"marshalled under the generic term of Colts".*

Then came the age-old soap-box moment;

"There yet remains a word to be said about the Voluntary Games, which this season have been played on Saturday mornings, in addition to Wednesday afternoons. These organised games form the nursery from which we recruit likely players: official sides absorb at most fifty boys: the Vols. cater for the remainder of the School. Until boys realise that attendance at these games is a duty incumbent on them as attendance at School, our playing standards are likely to remain stationary. Something has to be done in these games over a long term, to give a fillip to the rugger throughout the School. Punctuality and the wearing of prescribed kit have been insisted on: talking while the game is in progress has been surpressed, pitches have been provided and everyone of the 180 or so games has been competently refereed: moreover, there has always been a master or two in constant supervision. Too frequently, however, the organization behind the games has been rendered nugatory by the absence of players. A belated excuse the following morning is no remedy for the confusion caused the previous afternoon. Probably this evil will adjust itself, but it can only do so through the good sense of the individual, who by taking less thought for himself will thereby contribute more to the happiness of others. Of such is the essence of esprit de corps."

Tribute was then paid to *"the whole Staff for their loyal co-operation in assisting with the Vols: in particular to Mr GM Hill for handling the House matches: to Mr CL Barnes for his care of the inter-school games: to Mr H Dent for carrying the Colts, and all their troubles, on his shoulders: to Mr WE Battrick for his active crusade in the pursuit of physical fitness, and to those senior boys, Prefects and members of the xv's who have taken a whistle and done their job. Captain E Mercer has played and refereed occasionally: his*

constructive criticism and trenchant comment have been both stimulating and helpful. Our thanks to Pro completes the list: his ubiquity still ranks second to the ungrudging measure of his labour."

In the same edition Captain and Mrs Mercer were congratulated on the birth of a daughter. "Ted" was one of eight staff now on active service *"and the departure of others was imminent,"* said the Headmaster at Speech Day that November, adding; *"The elder boys had before them the duty and privilege of military service."*

The general call-up had come on the first day of January that year as two million 19-27 year-olds had received their marching orders. While in May, as the Germans were moving into France, Anthony Eden, the War Minister called for all men *"not presently engaged in military service between the ages of 17 and 65 to come forward and offer their services".* Within a week 250,000 men had enrolled as Local Defence Volunteers;

"The LDV, the LDV,
We'll have Batts. in our Belfry:
If they come with plane and tank,
Hitler's troops will draw a blank.

The ARP, the ARP,
George is guarding you and me
He may not like our attitude
Still we're full of gratitude.

The AFS, the AFS
Nothing damps their fearlessness
Someday Lear may save the School
With a Stirrup-Pump and the Swimming Pool.

QED, QED,
We'll win, as clear as ABC,
Someday we will see, DV,
Adolf Hitler, RIP."

Who do you think you are kidding Mr Hitler? Various units of Dad's Army set up base at Ford Park.

So wrote *"A Man of Letters"* in the July 1940 Plymothian. That same month Winston Churchill, who had taken over from Chamberlain as Prime Minister in May, suggested that the name be changed from the Local Defence Volunteers to the Home Guard. Made up of men young and old, many of them veterans of the Great War, keen to *"do their bit"*, this was Britain's first citizen's army since Napoleon had threatened invasion almost 140 years earlier.

From the very beginning NCOs of the School OTC had been involved in the training of these Volunteers. *"The corps has also formed a platoon of volunteers who have already done much useful work."*

The following term the OTC notes recorded that; *"important changes have been made in the routine of the Corps. There is now only one parade a week of one-and-a-half hours, instead of two shorter parades, and the Company now parades by stages instead of by platoons. Both of these alterations have resulted in a great saving in time, so that now a longer period each week can be given to training."*

After the usual Corps promotion, field day and Cert "A" notes had been dealt with, we also learnt that the present Company Commander, Captain CL Barnes, was about to start on active service; *"We are extremely sorry to lose the services of an officer of such efficiency and tactical knowledge. It only remains to wish him "good hunting"."*

The Scouts, too, faced changes in their routine – *"a scout has to be prepared to do unusual things in wartime: to go from door to door collecting wastepaper or Spitfire money, to give up his clubroom or his camp."*

Happily, however, camp was not given up; *"robbed of our favourite site, we found another at Lewannick."* This camp, near Launceston, according to Troop Leader-to-be PL Bayly, was shorter than usual but *"was amply compensated by the perfect weather."* Mr Dent was the Scout Master and several *"wide games were organised by Mr RW Pile; one game was planned in which the troop was to detect two member of the staff who were to act as escaped convicts – or possibly inmates of Bodmin Asylum. They were to smoke cigarettes to assist us, but, much to our regret, the game did not take place, as the Home Guard might have joined in with more vigour than was intended."*

All in all, though, the camp was a great success. Mr and Mrs Ralph paid a mid-week visit and *"as we piled into the country bus that warm Saturday morning to return to Launceston and home, all were sorry to leave such a well-conducted camp. We all hope to have another such next year; if not, well, we have had one most successful war-time camp. Indeed, considering the difficulties involved in rationing and transport, we must congratulate Mr Dent and the Troop-Leader on their excellent effort. May they live forever, as the Arabs say!"*

As it transpired there would be more camps. Mr Dent, though, was called up and 36 year-old Wilfred Savage, an Oxford graduate who had been a pupil at the School during the First World War, came back to teach and serve as Scoutmaster.

Wilfred Savage the second OPM to come back during wartime.

Savage came from the King Edward VII School, in Sheffield and was already an ADC in the Scouting world and he would certainly have remembered Carl Kuhne from his school days (Herr Kuhne had retired at the end of the Great War.) A great favourite in his day, the old music master was now ninety and he, and his wife, were about to celebrate their Golden Wedding. To commemorate the event a number of OPMs collected subscriptions which they presented to the couple at their home in Bigbury. Sadly Mrs Kuhne died a few months later.

William Brown and chums, Henry, Ginger and Douglas, stars of many well-thumbed Richmal Crompton yarns from 1922 onwards.

Also collecting money were the young boys of the Preparatory School, 83 members of the NSG (National Savings Group) had managed to save 5,243 sixpences and during War Weapons Week alone had taken £71.9s.0d. Pinocchio, released that year as an animated feature for the first time by Disney, was a new addition to the Prep Library, along with Richmal Crompton's William the Dictator. Faced with the same hard pitches as the senior Rugby boys, Rounders was played for the first three weeks of the autumn term at the Prep.

On the rugger front the Main School also lost the services of a true stalwart of the side, whose departure was commemorated with the Plymothian's first rhyming Valedictory;

"Farewell to FL Axworthy, who joined the School in '33; Upon the field, he was in heaven; Thrice Captain of the Third Eleven; At Hockey too this valiant soul would risk a limb to save a goal. But Rugby was his chief obsession; Captain for three years in succession; A mind of steel, a frame of granite; The Team did well when LENNY ran it."

"School Pianist", VJ Summer, was the subject of the only other valedictory that term and both young men were bound to serve their King and Country. Both, happily, would survive the War, unlike the Easter '41 edition of the Plymothian which was a casualty of it;

*"The moving finger writes, and, having writ
Moves on: not all your piety and wit
Can call it back to cancel half a line."*

"Omar Khayham is appropriate for most occasions, but we must not expect him to forsee a Blitz which could cancel, not half a line, but a complete issue of the Plymothian. Worse things have happened in history, and worse things have happened in Plymouth, than the destruction of our humble efforts to record and comment upon your activities. We consoled ourselves by thinking of Carlyle, who had the mortification of learning that the manuscript of his masterpiece, lent to John Stuart Mill, had been used by a careless housemaid to light a domestic fire; and we applied ourselves to the task of literary salvage with the hope that what was retrieved could be made better than what was lost. Our habit of writing half of the articles ourselves, and largely re-writing others from the conceit that our own style of grammar and calligraphy is better than that of our contributors, made the task comparatively easy."

"But it is hard to know in what key to compose an Editorial for an issue that will reach you at the beginning of the Summer Term. We must therefore try to forecast the mood and the circumstances in which you will then find yourselves, and seek to accord therewith. It is our hope that fury and despair will then be replaced by energy and determination; that perhaps even cheerfulness will break in. If such is not the case, we would prefer that this issue too should be consigned to the flames."

20-21 March 1941 Plymouth is subjected to relentless aerial bombardment and after months of comparatively minor damage, suddenly the heart is ripped out of the City.

Curiously enough, apart from this somewhat quirky editorial, doubtless the work of Mr Dundas, from May 1941, references to the Blitz of Plymouth were few and far between. Yet, as the Editorial team implied, the four nights of heavy aerial bombardment of Plymouth, on 20 and 21 March, and Devonport, on 22 and 24 April, left deep physical and emotional scars across the City. Nor was the Plymothian the only publication with problems; *"The Western Morning News for April 22 1941 was produced, six pages of up-to-date news, in a building encircled by fire, with bombs crashing down all around."*

Old Town Street is burnt out and the Pier is left skeletal.

So wrote journalist Pat Twyford in his war diary, published after the War, with additional commentary, as *It Came To Our Door.*

he April 24 he wrote; *"Last night it became no longer possible to make the night publication of the Western Morning News at the Frankfort Street offices. Every effort was made to do so until round about midnight, and then the position was so hopeless that it was decided to once more make an emergency publication at the Exeter offices of the Express and Echo. That meant another night dash by car to Exeter with key editorial and mechanical staff."*

"The fearful picture of Plymouth as we left the inferno behind us, was one I shall never forget. I was driving all the way to Exeter, especially when we got to the top of Haldon, colleagues sitting in the car with me were looking back, watching the terrible glow in the sky which marked the burning city."

It was indeed a terrible time. Over those two nights in March the death toll was *"no fewer than 336 men, women and children of the civil population. These included 14 babies and 3 nurses at the City Hospital."* Among the casualties was a boy from Va - TR Watts; *"He had entered the School with a scholarship in 1937, and made rapid progress in all his studies. He was an able boy of a lively and cheerful disposition, and his death is a tragic end to a life of much promise."*

That same month Lieutenant LJ Ball, who had left the School back in 1923, lost his life in an incident near the Hoe *"when assisting in the removal of a time bomb".* In the April raids, two other serving OPMs, both of them former Head Boys, PS Anderson and AW Miller, were killed. Sad times indeed at Ford Park, as the list of past pupils, who had given their lives for King and Country, was further swollen by the news of three young OPMs who had all left the School in 1933 – two of them, JA Guest and EA Perkins, had died in action in the Mediterranean on January 10, on HMS Southampton and HMS Illustrious respectively.

HMS Southampton sunk by a Stuka attack in the Mediterranean in January 1941 with young OPM, JA Guest, serving on board.

A cruiser, Southampton had been crippled by German bombers in the Sicilian Channel, while Illustrious had also been hit by Lufftwaffe dive-bombers but had managed to limp into Grand Harbour, Malta.

HMS Illustrious; the ship survived the Lufftwaffe attack, but EA Perkins, OPM, did not.

The third member of the class of '33 to be lost that year was KL Ashfold, a fine athlete, who was a Pilot Officer with the RAFVR. The deaths of Paymaster Lieutenant Commander HJ Reeder - who had left ten years earlier and served on the ill-fated HMS Kelly, sunk during the Battle of Crete on 23 May 1941 and seaman KJ Stone, who was on HMS Dido in the same action and who died six days later - were also reported in the catch-up August edition of the Plymothian. On a happier note, SGB Spriddle, who'd left School in '39, witnessed the sinking of Germany's newest, fastest and supposedly unsinkable Bismark around the same time – 27 May - from the deck of HMS Dorsetshire. Just three days earlier the Bismark had sunk HMS Hood with all but a handful of the 1,421 men on board going down with her.

By December, when the Magazine had settled back into its normal publication routine, the OPM death toll had reached double figures, with Paymaster Rear-Admiral TR Waterhouse the latest casualty; *"He had served*

under the White Ensign all over the world and returned to the Navy from retirement at the outbreak of the present war." A tribute to him appeared in the Times that September; it spoke of his tact, consideration and patience and of his *"fine work as Naval Secretary to Vice-Admiral Sir James Fergusson".* Waterhouse had left Plymouth College before even the Boer War.

By this stage a total of over 225 old boys and members of staff were listed as being on active service. More than a third of them had left since 1937 and, in theory, could all have just been completing, or continuing, a degree course.

As it was the OPM university numbers were greatly depleted – with just one student at Oxford; *"It has been observed that "Oxford never changes", but that was yesterday. This term has seen revolutions that appall. Impression of the town is composed of expanses of those monotonous colours affected in time of war ... we have seen Heinkels in the Giles, and the dons going to it in the Parks, complete with ARP rompers and helmets."*

"In view of these mortal blows and imminent conscription, I would address to you, my reader, the old 3a Grammar tag: Nos morituri te salutamus." The situation at Cambridge wasn't quite as bad; *"We left hastily after our exams, last June, sped by the Government, and with some foreboding that we might be the last resident members of the University for years to come. The noise of Army lorries then blended with the strains of College choirs, and gown and square gave place to the forage cap."*

"But the varsity has not closed down: we have put in two terms since then ... our numbers are down by half, but this deficiency is hardly noticed." In the capital there was a slightly different picture again; *"The only OPMs now left in the University of London are those reading medicine. At the outbreak of war, London and Home Counties were divided into sections*

for Hospital Service, with a Teaching Centre in each section. Lunatic asylums, Schools and Country houses have been taken over, and many of us are at work in such places. Others, who remained at the base hospitals in London, had an exciting time during the Blitz, fire watching on the roof, or treating casualties in the basement."

That London letter had appeared in the overdue issue, No.270, of the Plymothian, in May 1941. The capital had known nine months of bombing by that stage. However, few Londoners, our scribe among them, could have been prepared for the events of the eleventh of that month, when, in brilliant moonlight, 550 German planes dropped hundreds and hundreds of high explosive bombs and more than one hundred thousand incendiaries on the city. There were 1,400 civilian deaths, the highest toll to date for a single raid, and it brought the London tally to over 20,000. The British Museum, St Paul's and the House of Commons were among the major buildings hit, the last being reduced to rubble. The indomitable spirit was being severely tested and for the first time people were seen weeping in the streets.

Nor was it just London and Plymouth, as Portsmouth, Belfast, Clydebank, and Hull were added to the list of bombed cities that already included Coventry, Birmingham, Southampton and Liverpool.

At the other end of the County, Exeter *"has proved a peaceful backwater after the turbid maelstrom of Plymouth"*, however, that situation too would change. For the time being, though, there were some half a dozen OPM undergraduates mentioned, including RG Hutchings *"who began the term as "Nobody's Baby" seemed likely to end it as "Everybody's Sweetheart"."*

It was noticeable that, as the war progressed, more and more references to popular music, most of them somewhat oblique, crept into the pages of the Plymothian. The May edition had a section entitled *"Answers to Correspondents"* in which we read;

"HUTCH – So glad to hear that you and your friends did so well on your little dance. It was very good of you to give all that money to the Lord Mayor's Fund. We had heard that it was to go to the poor – the poor prefects."

"BOOGIE-WOOGIE – It is odd that you can't catch any of the music from the Staff-Room during the break. Do they still take their morning tea?"

"JOE-EGG – Thanks for the joke about Fire Watching and Old Flames. Yes, it would be a good idea to pass it on to their Scouts as a Good Deed for the Day: but what do they think about it?"

The Scouts indeed were busy in all sorts of ways; three of the senior boys had *"the privilege of visiting Mount Batten aerodrome, where they inspected a Sunderland flying-boat. The troop also took part in a procession to encourage people to take an interest in their gas-masks."*

An ad-hoc fire-bucket, as part of the fire-prevention endeavours water tanks were erected all over the City.

"To our other war-time activities has now been added salvaging furniture from bombed houses, and acting as guides to the military in devastated parts of the City, while there is a possibility that in the near future we many be able to help in the erection of the new indoor air-raid shelters."

Before the year was out the Troop had undertaken *"further war service, in checking occupied premises in the city for the Fire Prevention Officer."* While *"individual Scouts have also done good service, both during raids and after; Lawrence, Oliver and Leatherby have been awarded National Service Badges."*

The contribution made by the boys of Plymouth College during the war was gaining a greater profile with each passing month and the fact that the School did not evacuate must, in itself, have had a good effect on local morale, even if there were certain practical and financial considerations behind the decision. It was clearly a close call, however, and on 16 May 1941 the Headmaster sent out his second letter on the subject that week;

"I am now able to state definitely that the Governors of the School have decided not to undertake any form of total evacuation. But they unanimously approved, at their meeting yesterday, my suggestion of nightly evacuation, the main features of which are as follows. As many boys as possible should be provided for in areas outside the city and, for the most part, in homes of other boys attending Plymouth College, with supper, bed and breakfast, for which a reasonable payment would be made to their hosts. The boys would spend the day in Plymouth, at school and with their parents, but would leave for their billets each evening and return to school every morning immediately after breakfast. The object of this arrangement is to make it possible for boys to secure a sound night's sleep."

"The scheme has already been launched in the Main School and a number of boys placed. If you care to include your son in the scheme, I shall be glad to see you, without appointment, at the school, on any day and at any time in school hours."

Clearly some parents had made their own decisions much earlier than that, however, and at the beginning of the autumn term there were 26 pupils named who had been admitted to, or had *'rejoined'*, the School. Of those 26, only 10 were entering the first form.

But in the context of what was happening all around Ford Park; *"That we are still functioning as a school in our own premises is perhaps the most significant fact in the record of the past year."*

That at least was how the Plymothian led into the Headmasters report in the account of the November 1941 "Prize Distribution".

It was held in Big School and the assembled body heard Mr Ralph recall that;

"Since last March the effects of the War have told with increasing severity upon the City and the College. Of seventeen members of the Staff, eleven had already been enlisted for Active Service. Plymouth College," he said, *"could not evacuate, as other schools had done, without a severe strain on resources, an inevitable loss of numbers and a break in the continuity of the School which might have proved disastrous, besides forfeiting the use of its buildings, equipment and playing fields. If further dangers awaited us, there was the scheme of nightly evacuation available for all, which already had functioned happily and usefully. The scholastic record of the past year compared well with any previous year,"* he added, *"and the playing fields have been used as never before, not only by the School teams but by every possible combination of Service Units."*

Referring to his present Staff, Ralph said they had combined their ordinary work *"with various forms of National Service and the prefects and senior boys cheerfully discharged the extra duties required of them."*

He thanked them all and added, *"any one who is not helping to win this War is helping to lose it."*

There was not a boy in the School who could not somehow make a contribution, although that did not stop regular pleas from certain quarters, *"there are still several boys in the school who have not yet joined the Group"*, wrote OPM, now staff member, Stafford Jackson that summer. *"Since the School National Savings Group was started in April 1940, a total of £2,175 has been subscribed. This,"* he said, *"is a magnificent effort, and one of which we should all feel proud."*

At the same time we learned that the Prep School NSG now numbered 56 members and *"the average weekly amount collected is £7, while since the beginning of the Campaign the Group has been responsible for collecting the sum of £472.3s."*

During weapons week the hope was to collect enough money for a mortar – or two.

To put these sums in some sort of context the average British working-class family was then living on a budget of less than £5 per week, spending £1.14s.1d (£1.70p) on food, 10s.10d (54p) on rent, 9s.4d. (46p) on clothes, 6s.5d. (32p) on heating and lighting with little more than £1.5s.7d (£1.27) for everything else. Against these figures the War itself was costing the country a mind-boggling £11 million – per day!

These were strange days indeed particularly when even if you did have money it didn't mean that you could necessarily buy what you wanted, as certain food, fuel and clothing all became subject to rationing. When would it all end?

"I remember, I remember, the days before the war.

"The customs and occasions whose departure we deplore.

When cheese and onions – common things – one tended to ignore,

And roofs and cellars were held attractive to explore.

How pleasant on Detention Day, to sit within Room Four

And listen to Albion or Argyle's supporters' roar.

There were quite a few Fifth Formers then who hadn't joined the Corps,

And bones weren't given to the Scouts, but thrown for dogs to knaw.

The Tuck Shop opened every day with quite a decent store,

And teams had two lumps in each cup, while Captains could take more.

If worm casts showed upon the pitch, poor Heywood nearly swore,

But now the field is pitted with incendiaries galore.

Then Meyrick, Eddy, Mac and Bill would grace each corridor,

And voices that cry "Squad" or "Fire" then shouted "Play" or "Fore".

There'd be complaints if sandbags were found parked upon the floor,

And Breaks could not be brightened by the strains of Artie Shaw.

Then no-one knew what life was like behind the Staffroom door,

But now it's even known what masters sound like when they snore.

Ah well! Perhaps in years to come I'll say, till I'm a bore.

I remember, I remember, the great days of the war!"

There was no name or initials identifying the author, leaving SK Lawry, the then editor, as the most likely candidate. However there was no doubting the authorship of this next patriotic piece – *The Leader* - reproduced very soon after its appearance in the Daily Telegraph, and written by Frederick Seymour Cocks, notable OPM and Nottingham MP who had left Plymouth College, at seventeen, in 1899;

Winston Churchill

"John Churchill fought for England,
Brought Louis to his knees,
He broke the line at Blenheim
And struck at Ramillies;
Amidst divided counsels
He took the clear-out way,
He hit dooms hard at Oudernarde
And charged at Mapllaquet.

The Sun King was defeated
Two hundred years ago,
Now comes another Churchill
To fight a grislier foe;
When Hitler spawned o'er Europe
There dawned a dolorous day,
But Churchill stood for England
When England stood at bay.

He saw the Nazi menace
Clouding earth and sky,
He told the State and Senate
To build their bastions high;
His warnings were unheeded
(And O, the price we've paid!)
But when the Wrath descended
We called him to our aid.

He faced the scowling dangers
With steady eyes and keen,
With Courage high as honour
And Confidence serene;
He spoke for King and People,
He showed the conflict whole,
In speeches charged with wisdom,
In words that steeled the soul.

'Midst weakness and confusion
His voice rang clear and high,
He launched the word that thrilled us

And taught us how to die:
"This was their finest hour"
(To that our hearts we give),
He spoke of Britain's birth-right
And showed us how to live.

The valley lies before us,
Pain marches at our side,
Death hovers o'er our cities,
But higher mounts our pride;
Though storms blow ever fiercer,
We press on to our end,
With Freedom as our watchword
And Courage as our friend.

We cannot breathe in bondage,
We children of the sea,
We live to crush Hell's vanguard
Or die to set men free;
In air, on land and ocean
And 'neath the guardant wave,
We seek and slay the foeman
Or perish whilst we save.

Beyond the circling perils
Rises the aureate height
Where Evil shall be broken
And Tyrants slain in flight;
Though nights be bright with terror
We shall be "Grim and gay,"
When Britain's arms sweep forward
Where Churchill points the way.

Through him the soul of Britain
At last has found its voice,
And Freedom sounds her clarion
For brave hearts to rejoice:
Before our marching legions
The shadows fade and flee,

As dawns from West to Eastward
The day of Liberty.

O Judge of Right! For whom we fight,
Speed on our Victory!"

Victory was certainly the watch word that autumn. The BBC was already promoting the "V" for Victory Campaign, with the opening notes of Beethoven's Fifth Symphony – which are the same as the Morse code for V – being heard repeatedly on all overseas broadcasts. Said Churchill himself; *"The V sign is the symbol of the unconquerable will of the occupied territories and a portent of the fate awaiting the Nazi tyranny".*

Seymour Cock's timely ode would have struck a resounding chord across the nation and the boys of Plymouth College could not fail to have been impressed that a current MP, in regular contact with Churchill, was also an OPM and a bit of a poet. Interestingly enough, Seymour Cocks was one of just a handful of persons present at the opening of Lord Byron's tomb, in Hucknall in Nottinghamshire, just before the war (June 1938) when the Home Office granted permission for the investigation – there had been some concern that the great bard's remains weren't actually in the tomb. But to return to Ford Park. Apart from the impact on local morale, there were other consequences of Plymouth College staying put, not least of which were the difficulties in finding fixtures and fulfilling them; *"It is doubtful if during any season in the School's history there can have been a term when so many varied obstacles have appeared tending to interfere with the smooth running of the games. Curiously enough for these parts, and quite contrary to accepted practice,* weather vagaries cannot be held strictly accountable for overmuch hindrance. Our problems in Cricket, Swimming and Shooting have extended far beyond the weather, and since it is neither politic nor within the scope of these notes to dwell unduly on their intrinsic nature, it must suffice here to note that by hard work, enthusiasm and good will, they have been resolved, and Cricket has flourished for its second wartime season. We hope, too, convincing evidence has been afforded the interested onlooker, that throughout a time of stress a mission has been fulfilled, and that players have performed a minor form of service in providing the only regular cricket in the locality."

There was no official fixture card produced, however, and many matches that had been arranged had to be scratched, but "a gratifying feature was the readiness with which both boys and local sides got together", although "we did not always meet the opposition we expected ... it has been a privilege and a tonic to welcome Army sides to the School and see the "square" peopled with khaki-clad figures."

In the event the first XI mustered fourteen fixtures and the seconds managed another ten. Atkey was undoubtedly the star performer, averaging almost 40 and scoring 65 plus on four occasions, including 88 against Gresham School, in a record first-wicket partnership of 125. The School were chasing a score of 212 and managed it, the combined scores were in themselves a new Ford Park record for an inter-school match.

Lawry also batted well as did Mr Meek who demonstrated how runs "should be made and made quickly" when he posted an unbeaten ton against a Royal Engineer's XI in July; "there is something reminiscent of GL Jessop in his lightning crack on raised toes past cover point."

In that same game Mr Bonser took 5 for 17 adding to his impressive tally that season – he finished with 31 wickets, going for just 220 runs off 100 overs; "Bowling from the top end of the square he has been almost unplayable: his rhythmic action, perfect length

and unerring accuracy have been a joy to watch."

Glibert, Lawry and Ridpath also bowled well, and there were new nets – "matting on concrete – to the north of the pavilion", in which to hone their skills. However, it was the wicket-keeping captain Atkey who garnered the highest praise – "one of the outstanding players turned out by the School over the last twenty years ... and has made a notable contribution to all School games."

School 1st XI, 1941: Standing; CF Lyon, JR Trevaskis, AE Wilton, GR Heather. Seated; DE Ridpath, KG Gilbert, RG Atkey, SK Lawry, GW Sargent. Sitting in front; KL Palk and BEF Andrew

1941 School Hockey XI; Back row; RM White, MC Tonkin, H Trevena, DJ Harland. Seated; SK Lawry, KG Gilbert, RG Atkey, HS Rendle, AN Other. On ground PMW Winn and CF Lyon.

This notable contribution also included winning the Cross Country run from Marsh Mills and being Captain of the Hockey (the first XI lost only to Gresham School and six of the team – Rendle, Lawry, Gilbert, Sargent, Lyon and Atkey – were selected for the Devon Public Schools XI, with Atkey again as captain).

Victor Ludorum of the School Sports, however, was sprint and long jump star DJ Harland with the hurdling DW Hamlyn as Proxime Accessit. Trevaskis won the mile and middle distance races, while Dennis threw well and Larkworthy won most of the junior races.

AL Strachan, a member of the Plymouth Education Committee and a newly-elected School Governor, presented the cups and certificates and congratulated the winners on their performances;

"If one of Hitler's aeroplanes had come over during the Sports," he said, "the crew would have noticed a defiance that Hitler could do his worst, a confidence that there would always be a Plymouth College, and that there would always be an England."

Employing similar rhetoric Thompson's house captains, led by Atkey "the mainstay of nearly all our house teams", concluded their notes with; "We urge all members of the House to keep fit, and go all out in games and work. England and Thompson's House have no room for shirkers."

Certainly there were no worries in that department in the School pool as another athlete to gain his colours that summer, EH Robin, also of Thompsons, was senior swimming victor while DP Johnstone won the junior title for a remarkable second time. Unfortunately for some this competition was held during Examinations Week, but nevertheless results were up on the previous year and Thompsons finished ahead of the field.

They also performed well in the Inter-house Shooting competition thanks in no small measure to the top-scoring Atkey and Mahoney. The competiton was held on a local range but before the year was out a new, miniature range had been built on the School premises;

"Shooting has not yet begun ... but it can be expected that the shooting of the Corps will improve immensely through it."

The OTC, incidentally, had now been renamed the JTC and JR Trevaskis was the Senior NCO.

One activity that all houses were being exhorted *"to maintain as a live centre of interest"*, was Chess. The newly-arrived maths master Herbert Gould was a County player *"of mark"* and under his Presidency a new Club was formed;

"Chess is excellent relaxation and a game for thinkers: it should therefore take a permanent place among School societies. Mr Dent has already heard of the Club and has written to ask if he may try conclusions with his friends."

Certainly those responsible were right to be concerned about an *"enthusiasm which only too soon evaporates"*, after all this was not the first attempt to establish such a club, but one of the last times the Chess Club was mentioned in the Plymothian, it was reported as *"struggling"*, and that was in 1910, two years before Mr Dent was born.

Hugh Dent of course was one of the eleven masters on active service, but while they were gone, they were certainly not forgotten;

"Scoutmaster Dent used to camp in a Tent,
But now he's in khaki he must have a Marquee."

"Mac and Bill went up the Hill,
(The Messrs. Barnes and Porter).
Mac went down to serve the Crown,
And Bill joined up soon after."

Although they were serving wherever, the common room was never too far from their thoughts. *"Mr Barnes, Mr Porter and Mr Dent have written inquiring of our success, Mr Batrick was on leave to see the Kelly match and Mr Mercer and Mr Jones have both*

descended on us this term and talked football 'til the small hours."

Also in uniform, but back at School, was KE Kevern, *"whom we welcome back to the Troop as Assistant Scoutmaster"*. Kevern, who'd only left two summers before, marked his return with a fine century for the OPMs playing against the School.

One departure from the staff not occasioned by the hostilities was that of Miss Heath, who was retiring *"after twenty-one years service with the Preparatory School.*

She has tackled her work with patience and untiring enthusiasm in one of the most exacting posts that any scoolmaster or schoolmistress could be called upon to fill, and has secured for many generations of boys of Plymouth College the foundations on which they were afterwards to build."

Miss Heath

Mr Ralph presented Miss Heath with a silver inkstand and a silver bowl and spoon and wished her many happy years of retirement, while Miss Heath presented a copy of *"Out with Romany by the Sea"* by George Bramwell Evens (Bramwell was a Methodist minister of gypsy descent and was a popular Children's Hour broadcaster with the BBC, often accompanied by two young girls, Muriel and Doris, and Raq the dog).

On the same day that Miss Heath took her leave of the Prep, Mr Firman left on war service and he was presented with a silver pencil and a set of brushes.

Meanwhile, back on the subject of Libraries there was an ode to the Main School Library in that same edition of the magazine;

"No flowers, no curtains or such finery,
But a photographed gem of a Greek Statuary
Hangs above Captain H or Perhaps Mr D
In our tolerant School Libraree.

We do not play marbles or shove-halfpenny,
But sometimes indulge in a Greek Spelling-Bee,
And the big words are looked up by little Bayly
In our decorous School Libraree."

Little Bayly, incidentally, was a regular contributor to the Plymothian and was also Troop Leader of the Scouts that autumn. After a summer camp at Lewannick, again, Mr Kevern led senior members of the Troop to the Brynback rest-camp for two weeks.

The autumn term had a late start, 16 September, and a short half-term, which was just a long weekend – Saturday Ist and Monday 3rd of November. Once again the war created havoc with the fixtures;

"Transport restrictions have led to the abandonment of many fixtures which in years past have proved among the most attractive, in other cases clubs have temporarily suspended activities, while the "black-out" requirements have sadly interfered with daily practice after School and ruled out useful work in the Gym."

But games there were, all but one of them played at Ford Park and most of them lost to bigger service sides. However the Kelly match was close at 9-14, as was the first encounter with OPMs which was lost 14-18. Two victories were recorded over the Home Guard though, and a third, against a scratch side organised by Major Mackie, who together with George Wakeham was thanked for their *"energy and resource bringing XV's regularly to Ford Park."*

JR Trevaskis was the new rugger captain, he was also Head Boy, Senior JTC officer and editor of the Plymothian. However, he left at the end of that term, having bagged the Gwyther History prize, the Benskin Divinity award, and a place at Queen's College Cambridge.

But Trevaskis's wasn't the only departure that December, as the military service call up came for 32 year-old Ernest Dundas;

Ernest Dundas gets his call up.

"Mr Dundas' departure came as a severe shock to us; not only did he occupy the Editorial chair since Mr Benskin vacated it, but one might almost say he was the "Plymothian" in that the Editorial and the great majority of the more tasteful contributions invariably flowed from his pen."

In his place came fifty-two year-old Douglas Drew *"a distinguished classical scholar of St John's College, Oxford, who has held important posts at British and American Universities."*

Interestingly enough, it was just at this time that America entered the War. The Japanese attack on Pearl Harbour, on Sunday 7 December, had been what it took to end the efforts of the isolationists to keep the United States out of the war. Britain declared war on Japan the following day and then, on the 11th, in Berlin and Rome respectively, Hitler and Mussolini declared war on America. On 22nd Churchill arrived in Washington to talk with Roosevelt.

Back at Ford Park, we learnt of more OPM war casualties; MLP Bartlett, a fine athlete who'd passed into Sandhurst in 1936, later transferring to the RAF, was killed piloting a bomber in the Middle East; RG Trethewy, who'd joined the Royal Engineers and had moved across to the Royal Artillery, was killed in Malaya; and Captain GS Pitts, who entered the Services from School in 1931, was the senior Marine casualty among more than 800 men lost on HMS Barham after she was sunk off Soloum in the Mediterranean, by the German U-boat, U-331, in November 1941.

November 1941 - HMS Barham keels over having been hit by a German U-Boat in the Mediterranean.

HMS Barham explodes prior to sinking with twenty-six year-old OPM, Captain GS Pitts, RM, among the 800 men that were lost.

The challenge was there for every schoolboy and over the Christmas holidays a few NCO's in the JTC went on a course in Weapon Training. The new shooting range at School also came into use and *"almost every member of the JTC has had an opportunity of practice."*

Significantly, the School also had visits from *"Lieutenant Going DSO, RN, an Observer in the Fleet Air Arm who gave an illustrated lecture to the Sixth Form"* and Major JE Clowes who came to speak on the work of the Royal Armoured Corps.

Nor was the appeal to the Schoolboy psyche restricted to these efforts as the Chairman of the Governors, Sir William Munday, writing simply as "WL Munday", produced a piece for the Plymothian on German Labour Camps;

"We have, I suggest, something to learn even from Nazi Labour Camps. Though the ulterior motive of their founders is obviously militarist efficiency, yet their professed objective is wholly sound, namely that every citizen, whatever his social position or means, should devote six months of his time between his eighteenth and twentieth birthdays to unpaid manual labour for his country."

Sir William had been given a tour of just such a camp in the summer of 1938, through the British Embassy, and so was speaking with first hand knowledge;

"Every Labour Camp is in the country, well away from the pleasures and distractions of town life. There are 2,000 such Camps in Germany. No holidays and no visits of friends are permitted, but some time is allowed off on Sundays. Each Camp has a complement of 200 from April to October, and of 150 from October to April when winter reduces the extent of outdoor work. Jews are rigidly excluded."

"In these camps work varies – in some districts drainage works, in others irrigation, road-making, forestry or general agricultural work is the main feature of the curriculum."

The British party was treated well and after luncheon there were songs, God Save the King was sung in their honour, sports and exercise, and nothing was apparently kept back from them; *"Seeing that we were looking curiously at one corner which was curtained off, the Leader drew the curtain when, with something of a shock we saw an altar furnished at either end with candlesticks in church fashion, but in the centre, in place of the Cross, was a bust of Hitler! We were told that on festive occasions the altar was taken out from its corner and patriotic songs were sung before it.*

Needless to add, this object of Nazi veneration was vividly suggestive, not to say thoroughly sinister, in its implications."

Sir William clearly wasn't over-enamoured with all aspects of the Camp;

"Excess of regimentation, and of supervision, and worse still racial and religious intolerance are demoralising specialities of the German Labour Camps. But, out of Germany, none of such blemishes is an essential feature of the labour camp. And, on the other hand, the wholesome country life, the regular hours, the nationally serviceable outdoor work, the social contacts, have a high educational value. In these respects we in England may well learn much from our present enemies."

And it wasn't just a male preserve; *"We were told that the "Fuhrer" had ordained corresponding camps for girls in which all kinds of house-work would take the place of the labour performed by the lads."*

In Britain too women were getting the call. Back in March Ernest Bevin, the Minister of Labour, had announced the first steps in a massive mobilisation plan for young women, with the aim of getting 100,000 recruits for factory work; *"I cannot offer them a delightful life. I want them to come forward in the spirit that they are going to suffer some inconvenience but determination to help us through."*

Few anticipated the long-term effects of women being called to work during the war.

Nor was the work expected to be done voluntarily; female trainees were being offered £1.18s (£1.90) per week, mature men, in their early forties £3.0s.6d (£3.02p).

Before the year was out, however, the goalposts had been moved as Churchill announced that all single women between the ages of 20 and 30 were to be called up; some to work in anti-aircraft crews, others to do desk jobs currently being done by medically-fit men. Meanwhile, men could now expect to be called up, up to the age of fifty and, at the other end of the scale, the call-up age was lowered to eighteen-and-a-half, and all boys and girls between sixteen and eighteen were expected to register; *"We must be careful particularly that our boys do not run loose,"* said Churchill.

Here the idea was that youngsters should be encouraged to take up appropriate pre-military training. However, there was to be deferment of call up for university students and others who had approved places in higher education.

Plymouth College thus fitted the profile well and although university numbers were down there was still the usual missive from Cambridge – bemoaning the cost of a postage stamp, then 2½ d (1p) – and Exeter, where the fresh young undergraduate H Trevena was *"providing some of the harmonic nourishment we need in these times"* with his distinguished piano playing.

Music, particularly American music, received a number of references in the School periodical around this time – some of them quite tenuous;

"Pardon me, pueri, est hic the Chatanuga Choo Choo" was one - another appeared in a piece, *Corporals All*, which mentioned a meeting of the Brains Trust (another idea borrowed from the BBC) where one of the questions tabled was *"Which is Bing's best record? ... Even the Colonel realises the vital importance of Swing."*

And then there was a lively L&D discussion on *"the comparative merits of Swing and Classical Music"* where *"DW Hamlyn and RW Russell led the discussion and gramophone records were played to illustrate various points raised."*

The Society, which had been dormant for a while after

the *"severe air raids of last year,"* also had a Brains Trust meeting of its own with Stafford Jackson in the Donald McCullough Chairman's role. The Headmaster, Mr Savage and Miss Goad were among the panellists. Mr Jackson and Miss Goad both contributed pieces to Plymothian that year too. The former's a well-constructed, short story across two pages, set in Paris, the latter's a full page, patriotic eulogy to England at Eastertime;

"The very names of the flowers in the hedges in Spring seem to bring back a fragrant glimpse of an older England: cuckoo-pint, or lords-and-ladies, or parson-in-the-pulpit, if you prefer it, milkmaids, lady smocks, birds' eyes. Shakespeare knew them well; they were growing in English lanes when the news of the coming of the Armada was flashed from beacon to beacon along the coast, and the children were gathering them while Nelson kept guard with his fleet off Cape Trafalgar. They are a part of those English things which do not change, and we believe that Englishmen of generations to come will still love them when Hitler has become just a foolish name in a history book."

And so it continued; seeking out the red, white and blue of the campion, stitchwort and speedwell and the *"lovliest of all blue flowers, the bluebell, appropriately dedicated, in days gone by, to St George, England's patron saint."*

If there had been any doubt about the impact of the feminine touch at Ford Park, here was proof in prose. The influence was evidenced on stage too, with Mr Jackson's production of Denis Johnston's *"The Moon the Yellow River"*, starring Jackson himself and Miss Goad. Quite the longest piece in the Plymothian that year was Mr Holman's critique of the production, which also featured Barbara Butcher and Mollie Cornelius.

It would appear that Mr Savage impressed the most though, *"with his flawless rendering of the humourously cynical George"*.

Honourable mention was also made of the incidental

music, which was *"in keeping with the play's high quality"* and *"was given by Mrs Queenie Spooner, with Mr and Mrs HWC Gould."*

Mr Gould, along with Messrs Savage, Rigby, Drew and Meek were vital to the running of the hockey that winter, especially the latter who *"efficiently refereed most of the School matches"*.

It wasn't the easiest of seasons though; *"The first team has not had a large measure of luck this season. Taking into account the average age, which is only 16 years 9 months, this must be one of the youngest sides ever fielded by the College for very many seasons."* The report continued, *"until boys can be persuaded of the value of remaining at School much longer, there appears to be no remedy; nor may they hope to achieve that balance of mind and body, the importance of which in their years of adolescence, has recently been so forcefully stressed by the President of the Board of Education."*

Underlining this lack of luck, the firsts drew with Kelly, but lost, twice, to Gresham's School - in Newquay and at Ford Park - and once to King's School, Canterbury, again at Ford Park.

Gresham's School had evacuated down here during the war and the celebrated sixteenth century school (WH Auden and Benjamin Britten were pre-war pupils) provided a number of welcome fixtures prior to their return to Holt in Norfolk. King's School, from Canterbury, incidentally, was another evacuated institution to provide a sporting fixture or two. While from the remnants of the Plymouth Schools that were left behind, there were senior boy inter-school matches against the Emergency High School. In the hockey stakes this unlikely amalgamation fielded an *"inexperienced but plucky"* eleven who were easy meat for the School 3rd XI who beat them 17-3 – *"Our centre forward took full advantage of his opportunities and scored eleven goals."*

Another Spring Term sport was that with the most

chequered history of them all – Fives. Once again Kelly provided the only fixtures - both were lost - and once again complaints were logged about the *"extremely poor condition of the School courts, which appear to be both parade grounds for the JTC and bombing sites for the Home Guard. Two of them are still without doors."*

Plymouth's temporary shopping facility - 'Tin Pan Alley.'

The Cross Country run was, once more, at Marsh Mills, *"courtesy of Mr R Cundy"*, and was won *"in commendable style by DJ Harland. RL Turner was the first man home among the juniors and the Price Cup, open only to first formers, went to PW Skinnard."*

"There were nine entrants for the Senior race and all but RA Pengelly finished: he unfortunately developed a strain and finished somewhat ingloriously on the back of RJ Lyon's bicycle somewhat late in the afternoon."

Marsh Mills, for so long a green and pleasant idyll, was, by 1942, starting to reflect changes; *"the surroundings are beginning to lose their rural touch and the presence of a prosaic soccer pitch, fully grown since a year ago, if not adding directly to the hazards, caused a start and finish on the road."*

Four days after the Cross County, on the last Saturday of the Easter term, 29 March, the School took part in Inter-school Sports held at Kelly; *"the afternoon was cold and sunless with a biting easterly nip in the wind that called for mufflers and thick coats."*

"We entered for all the events and took a team of fourteen boys, accompanied by Mr OH Sykes, who acted as timekeeper, and EJL Holman, who judged."

This year, the competing schools agreed to drop Junior events and the meeting was hailed as a great success.

Having said that, the School finished sixth out of seven, finishing half-a-point behind Plympton Grammar. Kelly were convincing winners and presenting the trophy, Mr HW Hale, himself an Olympic-trial runner, stressed the value of these meetings and said *"that so memorable a meeting has been possible under war-time conditions is a tribute to the way in which the represented schools have faced the difficulties."*

Dartmouth, Blundell's, Devonport High and Tavistock Grammar were the other schools in question and JW Faulkner was the only College Schoolboy to win an event – the javelin. However CF Lyon, who came second in the pole-vault, *"may have increased his height had he used a longer pole."*

Faulkner, Lyon, Dennis and Harland all won their Athletics Colours and Harland added 100 yards, the 220, 440 and half-mile to his Cross Country success, setting two new records in the process. While Athletics Captain NG Dennis, with a throw of 102ft10in, added another 7ft onto the School Discus record. Tonkin pipped Lyon and Hamlyn as Proxime Accessit, while Turner and Brazier were the two Junior front runners.

In a short speech the Headmaster referred to the wisdom of the Governors in not evacuating; *"Thus has been retained full use of our laboratories, classrooms and playing fields."*

Dangerous structures are removed as the City prepares to rebuild.

Senior victor in the Swimming Sports was AJ Squire, while, for the Juniors, RL Turner proved he was just as quick in the water as he was on the track. Squire was also an *"indefatigable"* captain of the Water Polo team during a season *"noteworthy for sterling effort if not spectacular achievement."* All but one of the eight fixtures were held in the School Pool (between 9th June and 6th July), all but two were lost and none was against another schoolboy side.

The Prep boys were also making use of the pool, *"several boys have gained certificates for swimming twenty-five yards, one boy – fifty – and yet another – Luckes – two hundred yards."*

Twelve older boys, incidentally, succeeded *"in passing a new "test" introduced this term – the half mile".* Meanwhile, the School narrowly lost a swimming match against the RNE College.

Like the Swimming, the Cricket season was not spectacular in the achievement stakes, and gear was increasingly difficult to get hold of. Nevertheless six boys succeeded in bringing off a hat-trick; one of them in an inter-school match, when leg-break specialist GW Sargent took 7-27 to give the School a fifteen run win over Plympton Grammar. Club Captain Lyon took

the most wickets, and scored the most runs, including an unbeaten 56 in a tied game against Gresham - his 4-20 helping along the way. In a later game against Gresham's, Woolf bagged another 7-27. The reliable Mr Bonser had four five-wicket hauls, while top score of the season went to K Nicholls with an unbeaten 92, playing for OPM's against the School. Nicholls, the OPM Captain also scored 71 against a "Club XI" made up of schoolboys and masters.

Meanwhile a later item in the OPM notes read;

"Cricket enthusiasts will be interested to hear that AJ Biscombe, now serving in the Middle East, met "Fanny" Aulton, of the Somerset Stragglers, and Capt Myberg, the Worcester Regt fast bowler out there. Both sent their good wishes. Whilst in Cairo, Biscombe saw a report in a local paper of the concluding match of the OPM Cricket Week against the Ulster Regt."

Interesting to imagine OPM's serving abroad picking up news of the old School, rather than just information passing the other way.

Among the losses suffered by the OPM Club around that time was the Club Register, a victim of the April '41 blitz. A new one was duly started and placed in the School Common Room and *"any Old Boy visiting the School is asked to to see that his name is entered therein and to add such private information as private address, and if serving in the Forces, rank, unit etc."*

Staff member Stafford Jackson was then serving as OPM Secretary and, despite the circumstances, was warmly thanked for arranging an OPM Dance in St Gabriel's Church Hall on May 8th, which *"brought a welcome addition to the funds of the Club."*

Inevitably, however, the main OPM news was of a very sad nature as the August Plymothian reported the deaths of VG Bolam, AE Lockwood, EK Saul and JH Hibbert, while two more, LF Guppy and SCAN Bishop, were reported missing, all of them had left the School in the previous ten years.

Bolam, a pilot officer with the RAF and a Sports

Junior Victor from the mid-thirties, was killed in a flying accident; Lockwood, another pilot officer, who'd left School bound for Cambridge in 1938, was killed in action as were Saul, a sergeant-gunner, and Hibbert, a sergeant, both of them also with the RAF, Hibbert breathing his last in Libya, in the North Africa campaign.

Guppy, another strong athlete (he won the Navy Gold Medal for the 440 yds at Keyham where he had been a cadet before the war), was a lieutenant serving with Royal Navy and it later transpired that he had been killed in action. More happily Bishop was found – alive – *"a prisoner of war in Japanese hands".*

The December magazine had more gloomy news as former School welter-weight boxing champion Lieutenant CE Otway, who'd left School to join the Army in 1934, was reported killed in action. So were GAG Hopping of the RNVR and REG Oxenham, a great sporting all-rounder, who had been the star of many a sporting side, prior to leaving School in 1939. Oxenham had joined the Western Morning News on leaving. A Sergeant-Pilot with the RAFVR, he was on an operational flight when he lost his life. His funeral service was held in St Gabriel's and the School was well represented..

The famous RAF roundel on the side of a Lancaster bomber. Schoolboys the length and breadth of Britain were fascinated by exciting flying war machines - on both sides of the Channel.

These deaths brought the known total of OPM fatalities to 25 and the Headmaster read out all the names during an Armistice Day service in Big School on 11 November 1942. It was also reported that HP Lowman, a sergeant, flight engineer, who took part in the "Thousand Bomber" raid on Cologne, had been taken a prisoner of war. Sadly he, too, would not survive the war.

May 1942, in answer to the Lufftwaffe's attacks on British cities and more than twelve months after the Plymouth Blitz the RAF mount their first massive bombing campaign over Germany with 1,000 bombers creating chaos over Cologne.

Other OPM prisoners of war at this time included HS Trembath, CJ Hallett and AK Street, while the number of serving old boys was growing all the time.

Many of those doing their duty for King and Country were occasionally in touch with the School and there was one telling remark in the College House notes that August;

"We have recently heard from Mr McD Porter, whom many boys still in the House will remember as one of our pre-war Housemasters ..." It was almost as if he belonged to another age, but then for any Schoolboy three years is a long time and within in a week or two of publication it would be three years since war had been declared – and still no sign of a conclusion.

Active servicemen were not just recruited from the Main School staff; with Messrs Painter, Westhead and more recently Firman, all on duty. It meant, of course, that the Prep was without its Head. CG Richards it was who had come late in '41 to first assist Mr Firman and then deputise for him and at the Prep Sports in the Summer of '42 Mr Ralph expressed appreciation of Mr Richards' work and advised parents *"when in any difficulty with their boys to consult Mr Richards, as he had had many years' experience and he knew practically everything there was to be known about boys".*

Mr Ralph also praised Mr Sykes' good work with games and sports. OH Sykes had arrived in December '41 and along with Mrs Hill and Miss Beare, was keeping the Prep on a steady course. Sykes had served in the Royal Flying Corps during the First World War and he came to Plymouth College with his wife Marjorie who would, later in the war, help on the Main School staff.

Meanwhile the next generation of soldiers, sailors and airmen - the School JTC - were improving their shooting skills in the new range and had even entered a team in the Country Life shooting competition, although their standard *"did not appear to have been exceptionally high".* But the standard was improving, as indeed was the general appearance of the Corps;

"A number of cadets have been issued with battledress, and we look forward to the time when the smartness of the Corps is further increased by equipping all cadets in this uniform."

That November schools across Britain were also sent a direct appeal from Sir Stafford Cripps, who had joined the War Cabinet earlier in the year:

"My generation," he wrote in a piece that was edited and reprinted in the Plymothian, *"were young men and women after the last war and I think we failed to rid the world of the tragedy of war, because we took too lightly the difficulties of winning the peace. We succeeded in winning the war, but then we allowed ourselves to*

relax because we never realised how great our effort must be to put things right in the world if we wanted the peace to endure. You must do better than we did. You must learn from our mistakes as I hope we have done. All of you are doing your best today ... but you will be helping, too, by keener study and by fitting your body and mind for the hard tasks that lie ahead ... You must cultivate intelligence now, while you have the opportunity and physical energy and fitness, which will make you worthy citizens to face the adventures and dangers of a full life of service to the country."

The Plymothian editor then cited the couplet from the Carmen – *"Praebeamus fortiter - Studium virtutem"* and went on to quote the Lord Privy Seal further;

"You must learn to know and understand other peoples in the world – our brave Allies in America, Russia and China, our brothers in the Dominions, the Colonies and India, our friends in the persecuted and suffering countries of Europe. With these people you will have to work and build after the war, as world citizens looking far beyond the narrow boundaries of your own locality and even of your own country."

Back then to the Carmen; *"Exultamus omine, Urbis et locorum."*

"This then is our task," continued the editorial. *"Let us go forward with confidence knowing that, with God's help, we shall not fail."*

Sir Stafford had already left the War Cabinet by the time the December '42 Plymothian was published. He left on 22 November, one week after church bells had rung out across Britain to mark Montgomery's victory at El Alamein. It had been the first time that bells had been rung since the threat of invasion back in 1940 and there was a feeling that at last the tide was turning, but there was a note of caution from the Prime Minister;

"It is not the end," said Churchill, *"it is not even the beginning of the end. But it is perhaps the end of the beginning."*

Certainly an air of optimism was to be detected in

the beginning of that December '42 editorial as it, somewhat uncharacteristically, cast an eye back over the previous year;

"A year that will go down as a memorable one in the annals of all freedom loving people. Time will not dim the remembrance of those who defended Stalingrad, who marched with the 8th Army, who flew with the RAF, who brought the convoys through the Mediterranean or to Murmansk, or who won for Malta its George Cross. In years to come it will be our right to look back on the events of 1942 with some measure of personal satisfaction. Now it is our duty to look forward to the future with a sense of grave responsibility."

After Churchill's trips to America and Russia, most notably his twenty-year agreement with Stalin and the formation of the United Nations (which Foreign Secretary, Anthony Eden, claimed was the key to the post-war world), the future was starting to look more hopeful. Sure there were hardships, as sweets joined the ever-increasing number of items on the rationing lists, but there were discernable signs of strength and even the School Literary and Debating Society supported PT Perkins motion that *"This house advocates the immediate invasion of Europe."* It was close though; 12-10. Other discussions resulted in a vote of confidence for the Home Guard – Woodcock and Watt had tried to persuade the house that it was inefficient – and a thumbs-down for the suggestion that there should be a compulsory national youth organistion.

Incidentally Mr and Mrs Woodcock, together with Mr Savage, had been instrumental in organising the Harvest Camp at Buckfastleigh that summer as some twenty-five boys spent three weeks *"corn-harvesting (stooking, re-stooking and carting), silage making, thistle-cutting and potato-digging".*

For the record, the previous September the Government had ordered that potatoes should be sold at one penny so that people would be encouraged to eat more of them. Among the party of twenty-five in Buckfastleigh were

the vast majority of the School's troop of senior Scouts and it was healthy to note that the Troop itself was up in numbers so much so that a fifth patrol, the Foxes, had been added. Of the other four – the Curlews, Seals, Swifts and Owls – it was the latter who won the patrol competition, thanks in no small measure to JD Berryman who added ten new badges to his sleeve gaining two Gold Cords and a Bushman's Throng in the process. Berryman's badges included explorer, reader, missioner, cook, camper and carpenter, while WH Joce and Williams ii were among those to win gardener, rabbit keeper and firemen badges.

There were fewer wins for the first fifteen however, as they managed only two victories from their sixteen fixtures – but they were lucky to have any fixtures at all, as Mr Savage was to observe:

"This season the Ministers have been at it with a vengeance – he of Home Security shattered ours by planting a water-tank upon the ground hallowed by many a scrum and try, while his colleague of Transport threatens to rob us of our few remaining matches with other schools. Nevertheless, by a miracle of the surveyor's art, Pro managed to lay out a rugger pitch, and by taking on all comers of any age or size, the Secretary conjured up a remarkably full programme of matches."

Of the sixteen fixtures, though, only four were inter-school affairs - home and away against both Kelly and Gresham's (at Newquay) - and the best result there was a 6-6 draw with the evacuated Norfolk boys at Ford Park. The only victories came against the *"less experienced"* Dockyard Apprentices and RNC Dartmouth when *"undoubtedly we played much better than in any previous game"*.

The problem was a simple one though; *"to challenge the giants was easy: to play them and beat them was a task almost beyond our powers."* For the most part the oppositions faced were older, heavier and stronger.

"It is greatly to their credit that they showed so much

of what we like to think is the peculiarly English quality of not knowing when they were beaten; the oftener they lost, and the more points were scored against them, the harder they seemed to play."

Over and above all that, an unfortunate accident in the first practice accounted for the Captain, Tonkin, *"who we hoped would prove a match-winning wing three-quarter."*

The 2nds were even less successful, drawing just one of their five fixtures and losing the rest, while the Colts, led by Turner and Berryman, happily fared better, winning five and drawing one of their seven encounters.

R Turner, AN Other and DF Pring

Dennis, Johnson and Lyon were among the School stars on the pitch that season, while DF Pring was thanked for his *"efficient work as a touch judge"*.

His brother, Keith, meanwhile, was among the thirty new first formers to start at the College that autumn, along with TEJ Savery, one of forty new boys in the Prep, and BAL Johnson, one of fifteen or so boys joining further up the School. Miss Prankerd, too, was a newcomer, on the Prep staff that term.

Clearly the decision not to evacuate was proving prudent and at the *"informal distribution of prizes"* in Big School that November, the Bishop of Plymouth congratulated the School on *"sticking it"*.

"It is," he said, *"a privilege and an honour to have "stayed put" and the School is a symbol of what the City stands for."*

"Our national characteristics are brought out by the war, and what is true of nations is also true of schools."

There was a feeling, however, in the first Plymothian of 1943, that the School maybe wasn't doing quite as well as it should be, not in some areas at least;

"In academic achievement and in sport we can more than hold our own with our contemporaries but the many opportunities for cultural activity are greviously neglected. The attendances at the meetings of the Literary and Debating Society have been lamentable and the standard of speaking poor. Little inclination has been shown to take part in discussions, to attend concerts, to produce a play, or to write an article for this magazine. These are vital parts of a school's activities. The opportunities and facilities are not lacking, and if a few of us can avail ourselves of them as well as meet the demands made upon us by National Service, why cannot others? To put it bluntly the majority are content to see the few "carrying the baby". The time spent in developing our ideas and talent in these spheres will be time well spent. Let us show, therefore, more keenness on the one hand, and more encouragement on the other."

The stimulus for this piece was the new, Government-financed Council for the Encouragement of Music and Arts, which had been set up with one eye on the post-war world. Mention was also made of the recently published Beveridge Report and the *"campaign against ignorance, want and disease, and the planning of post-war housing and education."*

Sir William Beveridge's radical report, published at the end of 1942, had recommended the creation of a Ministry of National Security and sought to create a world in which the entire adult population of Britain was covered by a compulsory insurance scheme that would give protection against sickness, unemployment, and old age and would provide support for families. Means-tested dole payments were to be largely abolished. It proposed full and free medical treatment for all and retirement pensions for everyone – up to £2 a week for couples.

The term Welfare State was quickly coined and the media gave it full backing. The BBC broadcast the news to Nazi-occupied Europe, stating that here was proof that even in the middle of war this country was dealing with its internal problems.

Field Marshall Montgomery leading from the front at El Alamein

Clearly there was more than just the victory at El Alamein that was beginning to lift the clouds of war;

"Although the struggle is not yet over, it seems the daylight has come and that the sun mounts slowly. The immensity of the struggle that has been waged and is yet to be waged, in the theatres of war, will never be fully realised by those of us who have not taken part in it. Our debt to our fighting men can never be repaid. But we who have been left to "carry on" at home have had our struggle too, for the task of training ourselves and others to play their part as good and useful citizens in the New World to which we look forward, has by no means been easy during the past three years. Now is the time to take stock and start putting our house in order."

Patrick Abercrombie and Lord Astor plan the future of the City..

In Plymouth at large, Lord Astor had helped secure the services of Patrick Abercrombie to assist the City Engineer, James Paton Watson, in the production of an equally-radical *"Plan for Plymouth"* and this would be published later in the year. Meanwhile, at Plymouth College itself, here was the editor appealing to the boys and staff to apply themselves to these new challenges. Not all were impressed however. Indeed, after a *"heated debate"* on the merits of the Beveridge Report, its adoption by the Literary and Debating Society was only recommended thanks to the casting vote of the Chairman. The House was similarly split on the question of State control of Education; the case, proposed by PL Bayly, eventually being approved by nine votes to eight.

Above, visionary plans that were substantially made real over the next ten to fifteen years. Below - what might have been. Right; the old street plan makes way for a layout that is remarkably familiar today.

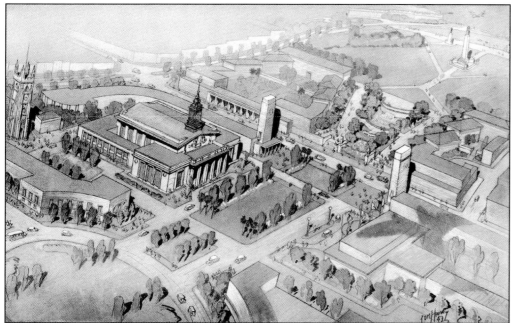

PROPOSED CENTRAL LAYOUT
SHEWING PROPERTIES EXISTING   1943

REFERENCE

EXISTING PROPERTIES

SITES AVAILABLE FOR RECONSTRUCTION

PREVIOUSLY CLEARED SITES

PROPOSED CENTRAL LAYOUT SHOWN THUS

SCALE OF FEET

Happily WR Fielden's motion that *"Britain has degenerated since the beginning of the century"* was argued out by RA Pengelly and a majority of those attending, however that number was disappointingly low.

The number of Old Boys reported as missing or killed that Easter was depressingly high. Former Headmaster, and First World War hero in his own right, Freddie Dale, had cause to grieve over the loss of his son, MD Dale - killed in action on the Indian Front.

GR Bayley, who came to the School a year before Dale snr., in 1919, was reported missing *"after an operational flight over enemy territory"* – he was later said to have been killed in action. As was DW Bryant who had left School in 1938, the same year as KR James, who was also serving in the RAF, and who was reported as missing, at sea, as it transpired - but he was never found.

Neither was AJM "Sandy" Down, another airforce man, who had joined School the same time as James and two years before AH Day, the fifth RAF OPM to be listed as dead or missing that Easter.

A Down at school

Day's death we read was *"accidental"*. Down had been a lively lad at School, it had not been unknown for him to foil Percy Battrick's chemistry experiments by blowing down the gas pipes from the back of the class, supplying the Bunsen burner that sir was about to use at the front. He was also favourite to volunteer to put *"a couple in the bank"* when the Reverend Benskin was closing an uneventful lesson and looking to give his favourite cane, "Sunnyside Up" an airing. The two strokes administered then would be offset against a future misdemeanour!

Completing the role call of misery that Easter was the news of WAH Trask, a very promising athlete and sportsman, who had only left the School in 1940. Commissioned in May 1942, Trask had recently joined the Royal Marine Commandos and was on HMS Fidelity, a disguised, former-French, merchant vessel, which was reputedly conveying a party of 51 Marines to Indo-China in December 1942.

HMS Fidelity a disguised French merchant vessel sunk by a U-boat in December 1942 with a promising young OPM WAH Trask.

Barely twenty, Lieutenant Trask was second in command of that Marine complement, there were also another 280 crewmen on board, plus at least four others, including one woman.

Armed with four 4-inch guns, four torpedo tubes, two Kingfisher seaplanes and a motor torpedo boat, Fidelity had not long rescued two boatloads of survivors from the Empire Shackleton when she herself was torpedoed, by a U-boat (U-615), four days after Christmas 1942. The ship limped on however and wasn't sunk until a second strike the following day, when she was finished off by U-435 at half-past four that Wednesday afternoon. The German U-boat commander, Strelow, reported seeing over 300 survivors on rafts later that afternoon and again the following morning, but none of them lived to tell the tale. Two managed to make their escape in one of the seaplanes, however, and seemingly another eight managed to get away in the MTB. The others all appear to have met a watery grave in the Atlantic, somewhere off the Azores.

The known OPM death toll had now gone above thirty, with a further six old boys being held prisoner of war. Back at Ford Park the death was also noted of Mr Lear *"for over twenty years the Senior Porter at the School."*

Mr Lear had lost his wife the previous summer and had suffered a severe breakdown as a result. *"Although muscularly strong"* Lear had not been in the best of health for a number of years, *"but in spite of this he met the increasing demands upon his strength and time without complaint. During the heavy air attacks of 1941 he was constantly on duty at night, at the School or his Warden's Post, never sparing himself, and always in action where the need was greatest."*

On an altogether happier note there was the news that Wing Commander JW Bayley (who joined the School three years after his OPM RAF colleague and presumably, brother, GR Bayley, in 1922), had been awarded the MBE, while two Naval OPMs, Commander WH Roberts and Pay-Commander Hussey, had both been awarded OBEs. *"Roberts left for Dartmouth in 1914, where he was awarded the King's Dirk, Hussey will be remembered as an outstanding cricketer."*

Success stories at School that Easter included two more young lads bound for the Navy, RW Russell and MA Spencer, with Russell gaining first place Special Entry into an Engineering Cadetship.

Headboy, NG Dennis was one of four Oxbridge Scholarship winners (two of the awards Dennis's and Youngs were worth £60 a year, while Hamlyn and Hilson both secured Scholarships worth £100 per annum). Hamlyn, incidentally, was bound for Exeter College, Oxford, and there was further sadness that Easter as news came down that Dr RR Marett, the Rector of Exeter College, had just died.

Marett, a philosopher and anthropologist, was a Governor of the School and had taken a keen interest in the many Old Boys who had passed from the College into Exeter College. He had also presented the prizes at the Prize Distribution some fourteen years earlier.

The Oxford Letter, back in the magazine after a brief absence, lamented not only Marett's demise but also the fact that *"the University has received its condemnation until after the war, for after July the undergraduates who read the "more humane studies", as they are called, will no longer be here".*

The *"days of leisure and abundance"* had also slipped from Cambridge, as numbers there too were down.

The Exeter Letter was not quite so gloomy; *"Despite the exigencies of wartime and the imperious demands of the STC, we, of Exeter, have nevertheless managed to find time for work and a modicum of pleasure as well".*

Among them, H Trevena, who *"can almost invariably be found in the telephone room, where he is phoning "purely on business, of course". We feel he misconstrues the GPO slogan "Telephone time is precious"."*

The hockey playing Harry T

Among the other undergraduates mentioned that term was GW Sargent, at Christ's Cambridge, who was, evidently *"conspicuous on the hockey field if only for his red socks".*

In those difficult days of rationing, new kit was not particularly easy to get hold of and Sargent's socks were doubtless a measure of expediency rather than pure nostalgia for the old school where the current first XI *"looks far smarter in their white shirts, dark pants and red stockings than it ever did in dingy coloured checks ..."* Which was just as well as *"coloured shirts are becoming a memory".*

Indeed earlier in the year the Government had said that only standard grey or blue school uniforms would be allowed - to save on dye.

Nor was it just clothing that was becoming increasingly hard to come by as *"goal posts and sticks are only issued under special licence. We had to face a season with only a dozen new sticks at our command."*

The stick shortage created problems outside the main

teams too, for, combined with one or two other little problems, it meant the virtual disappearance of hockey "vols", which in turn had a knock on effect for the standard of playing in the School generally. The First XI were further hampered by a lack of experience. The average age of the team was just 16 years 2 months, nevertheless they did manage to win a number of matches, notably against Plympton Grammar, twice, the RAF from Mountbatten, twice, and Kelly, at Ford Park. They lost resoundingly to Kelly away however and similarly struggled against King's Canterbury and Gresham's, despite having the home advantage on both occasions.

One other victory that must have been particularly sweet to one of the newer members of the side - BAL Johnson – *"very young and very promising"* – came against an OPM side that included his older brother – the School won 5-1. CF Lyon was another star; *"one of the best players we have turned out"* - a worthy captain *"acting as the school's ambassador"* on and off the field.

It was an important role to be sure for increasingly all sports played at Ford Park were drawing hitherto unprecedented crowds, thanks not just to the removal and evacuation of other Schools, but also the closure, voluntary or otherwise, of other clubs;

"Home Park had been one of the targets when the Nazis wreaked their fury on the city in 1941. It so happened that the grandstands were packed with furniture salvaged from the houses damaged in the earlier raids. What an appalling bonfire it all made as the raiders' incendiary bombs got their hold and the high explosives dropped into the furnace to blast what was not burnt!" (HP Twyford – It Came To Our Door – first published in 1945).

The Home Park blaze would have been visible from many parts of the City and the firewatchers on the roof of the main school could have almost felt the heat.

"The Argyle headquarters were a sorry mess after that onslaught. The great grandstand, stretching the length

of one side of the ground, with its offices, dressing-rooms, and training rooms underneath, was reduced to a shambles."

"For a while the grass grew long and rank on that once well-kept pitch where we had watched twinkling feet and quick brains match their skill in the national game."

Argyle's grandstand and the offices and dressing rooms (below) are burnt out, the fire being part fueled by furniture store there.

"Then the game got a small measure of revival through the formation of the Plymouth City Club and the Plymouth United Club. Some good games were seen against Service teams, which often included players from the greatest professional clubs in the country. But the old keen competitive spirit of Plymouth Argyle in League football was dead, at least for the war."

"The well-known Rugby clubs, Plymouth Albion at Beacon Park, and Devonport Services at The Rectory also put up the shutters when war broke out. They, too, became silent memorials to happier days."

"Another club which immediately closed down for the war was the Plymouth Cricket Club at Peverell Park. This, I think, was rather a pity, because there were more cricketers than ever in the district through the Services, and quite a number of the local players were still about. A cricket match on a pleasant Saturday afternoon was a welcome diversion, and we were grateful for the fact that a good programme of fixtures was available at the Ford Park ground of Plymouth College ..." It was, he added, *"quite a sportsman's "oasis" during the summer months, (Twyford)."*

But it clearly wasn't just the summer months, it was all year round, for all sports; *"As civilian Rugger has almost disappeared from Plymouth, our games attract quite a number of Rugger enthusiasts, and we are pleased to see them, though a few of them seem apt at times to imagine themselves back at pre-war Beacon Park, with their pristine liberty to instruct the players and bait the referee. Schoolboys,"* carried on the report that winter, *"can dispense with the over-vociferous spectator, however necessary an evil he may be to clubs who have heavy expenses to meet."*

However unpopular these spectators were with the staff, though, the crowds were clearly glad to have something to shout about. But it was difficult, at times, for the boys. All the main sides were younger than in peacetime and most of the opposition older, bigger and at times, particularly among the service sides, a great deal more skillful. Of necessity, too, the Ford Park pitches were drawn smaller to accommodate the instruments of war in attack and defence.

"I can see two guns "sitting" in the outfield of the Plymouth College cricket ground, quite adjacent to the Ford Park Road boundary. These were but two of many places where the United States Army set their anti-aircraft guns in and about the city" (Twyford).

With Charles Church in the background this was one of the many US Army Anti-Aircraft posts dotted around the city.

Whatever the logistics of the situation, there was no denying that many Plymothians, hitherto sceptical about the School, must have developed a fair fondness for the place during those difficult times. They must have been impressed too that the School *"stayed put"*, for that great limestone pile, set high behind a flat swathe of green made it a fairly obvious target.

As if to reflect the outside interest in the sporting activities of the School, more space than ever seemed to be afforded the various sections in the Magazine. There were fourteen pages of cricket in the Plymothian that summer and although *"no boy has scored a century, there have been wickets to gladden any batsman's heart"*.

It was the same for the OPMs too, who staged some sixteen (of their twenty-one) cricket fixtures at Ford Park that summer.

Skipper KJ Nicholls had a great time with the bat scoring over 700 runs, including a 96 and an 88 not out, while Pro Heywood and George Bonser each bagged over 50 wickets, the Maths man taking 5 for 5 and Pro 5-19 as they skittled the RAAF out for 25 at Ford Park that August.

To get back to the boys though, once again there was a lack of experience among the XI – but not always among the opposition;

The Kent and England all-rounder, Frank Woolley, who retired from the first class game in 1938, visited with the side from King's School in June, while *"a West Indies Test Player, CS Taylor, made a 50 n.o. against us for the Royal Engineers."*

For the School, for the second season running, team Captain, CF Lyon scored the most runs and took the most wickets, although GL Heywood was just behind him with a better average. IM Clarke, with a 76 against OPMs posted the highest individual score of the season, but didn't do much after that, while RL Turner *"kept wicket well"*.

Turner and Lyon also represented the School in the Inter-School Sports, held, once again, at Kelly. This time, though, there were only four schools competing, including, for the first time Clifton. *"Weather conditions were wretched: rain fell almost incessantly from a leaden sky, and competitors found it difficult to keep warm between events."* The young School side finished a clear fourth.

"For the Past v Present games there must have been over a thousand people watching at Ford Park" recalled Bob Pratt, who took part in a great many matches played there during the war years. With so many of the other schools de-camping to Cornwall or other parts of the South West and with other sporting clubs unable to raise sides or stage fixtures, Ford Park became a magnet for sports hungry Plymothians of all ages.

Right: A rugby match against one of the evacuated school from up-country - King's School - attracts a large crowd.

Bottom left: back row; IM Clarke, P Chislett, John Kellaway, Jackieohn Berryman, PN Lobb. Front; Pete Heath, Geoffrey Heywood, Bryan Johnson, Ron Turner and Bob Pratt.

The Past V Present teams line up (below right) for their game on 24 July 1943. Back row; Pro Heywood, George Wolfe, Ken Wilcox, Nobby Clarke, Alan Scott, Basil Andrew, Brian Williams, Ken Clarke, Ron Turner, Geoff Johnson, John Kellaway, John Reid, John Wynton, Eric Gould, John Hamley and Godfrey Heywood. Front row, John Dufton, Wilf Savage, George Wakeham, PT Kevern, RR Brown (Governor), Herbert Ralph (Headmaster), Cyril Lyon, Stafford Jackson and Eric Holman.- all players and staff apart from the Head, Eric Holman and Pro. Heywood were OPMs).

1943

311

Seven weeks later the School Sports were held in perfect weather. *"A new event – the Hop, Step and Jump – appeared in the programme; the Discus record was broken and satisfactory times were returned in the sprints."*

NG Dennis established a new – 104 ft – Discus distance. He also won the 100, 200-yards and Weight, but despite doing well in a number of other events he shared the Victor Ludorum with OWA Daw, the quarter, half and mile specialist. CF Lyon, meanwhile, gave them a good run winning the high jump, long jump and hurdles, while in the juniors JL Beamish finished just ahead of AC Rogers.

In between the two major athletics events were the senior and juniors cross country races. Marsh Mills, which had been in use for over twenty years was not available and so there was a new, rather longer, course; *"through somewhat urban surroundings, it is mainly confined to a beaten track. The start is at the College, then along Oxford Avenue to Linketty Lane, over the fields at Eggbuckland to Hender's Corner, along the main road, down Oxford Avenue and finishes by the water-tank at the bottom of the school field."*

RL Turner won the senior event, BAL Johnson, the junior, with the Price cup, open to boys under twelve, going to DL McCullum.

In other sporting arenas, there were the usual moans about Fives as, once again, Kelly won the only two fixtures by decisive margins. Kelly also beat the School, by a closer margin, in one of only two Shooting competitions. The other was against the Home Guard and was won quite easily. OND Selwood was Captain of the Shooting Team as well as being CSM of the JTC. Interestingly enough there were two innovations in the JTC that year; a course of Battle Drill and a Scheme of Physical Training – *"introduced because the new Certificate "A" regulations require candidates to attain certain standards of physical fitness."*

The reasoning behind this was fully endorsed on Field Day which, *"took the form of flanking attack from the north by the company on an enemy rearguard holding Wigford Down and under the command of Acting CQMS IE Badcock. The operation was well planned and highly instructive in the modern methods of attack. It showed clearly the necessity for synchronisation of movement, accurate timing, speed and physical fitness."*

JTC training that year was carried out almost entirely *"by our own officers"*, although later Major Mackie

British successes fuel the fertile minds of the nations youth via The Champion and Triumph during the autumn of 1943.

and Lieut Heywood, of the 16th Bn Devonshire HG, were thanked for *"enabling us to send corps members for many excellent shoots on the open range and for allowing us to use their training facilities."*

Who now knows what went through the minds of those young cadets as they went through their training.

"Whatever lies in store for us this much is certain," read the Plymothian editorial that summer, *"that by the time the next issue of this magazine appears some six months hence, great and terrible battles will have been fought on land, on sea and in the air so that 1943 may well be one of the finest, if not the finest year in our history."*

The German defeats in Russia, the relentless bombing of the Ruhr, the success of the Dambusters mission, the unconditional surrender of the Italians, after the resignation of Mussolini, and the triumphs of the Allies in North Africa, were all indications that the tide had truly turned against Hitler and Churchill, confident that all likelihood of an invasion had long passed, decreed that church bells could ring out again.

"Dare we hope that by the end of the summer term next year peace will have been declared?" continued the cheery prose.

"We have been at war now for four full school years. We have tried in these pages, to put on record a full account of our activities and achievements during that time. Schoolboys are apt to be cynical when their parents say, "Your schooldays are the best days in your life." For those who have spent the best part of their school career under war conditions, this must seem a paradox in addition to being of doubtful veracity."

"But let them not regret the loss of experiences which those of us who cherish memories of our peace-time schooldays had. The youth of to-day will have a tremendous part to play in the world of to-morrow, and it is our earnest hope, and indeed our steadfast belief, that when that new era dawns, as dawn it will and that right soon, they will not be found wanting."

The exigencies of war caused the School to start and end its annual cross-country run at Ford Park, rather than the usual rural route around Marsh Mills. Among the runners Clifford Quick, Geoffrey Fielden, Jackie Berryman, Ron Turner, John Wunton and Derek Pring. RA Pengelly as way secretary selected the route; "As I recall, I took us up to Hartley and round Linketty Lane".

1943

"For that great opportunity the past four years have been a preparation."

For all the talk of the war nearing an end there were still more than a dozen school leavers that summer destined for war service - Selwood, Sluman, Stedman, Brown, Lyon, Thomas and Tidboald among them – happily all would see out the war safely.

Others to get a late call-up included several OPMs who were well into their thirties, including FR Curtis, HM Gorrie, SF Hodge and R Hawken, who entered the service as a Naval Chaplain.

Meanwhile among the growing list of casualties there was news of Captain GAS Rattray who was killed accidentally in Wales.

Another who lost his life in this way was KE Kevern, whom many boys still at the School would have remembered. A fine athlete, all-round sportsman and former Scout Leader, he was accidentally killed in a battle exercise in September 1943.

KEK and JRS Scout Camp 1937

Three days earlier, on 16 September, Flight Lieut LC Murch RAF, died on active service in Benghazi, having earlier taken part in the Battle of Britain and been wounded over London in September 1940

Another war hero was Lieutenant JSJ Scott of the Devonshire Regiment, who had left School three years earlier and had been an inspirational leader of the OTC. Scott lost his life in Sicily, in July 1943, in a daring feat of bravery for which he was posthumously awarded the Military Cross.

The death toll was inexorably rising, and yet in Editorial that December there was hope; *"Rarely if ever before can the message of Christmas have had so deep a significance as it does this year. The thought of Victory and the Peace that will ensue is uppermost in all our minds. The triumphant home-coming, already experienced by a few, the welcoming back of relations and friends, the renewal of old aquaintances, the return to our former habits and haunts, these are our confident hopes for the coming year."*

"But some will not share these joys. Already thirty-seven Old Boys of the School have made the supreme sacrifice. Their names will be honoured and remembered with pride and gratitude. Their deeds, loyalty and courage have been and always will be an inspiration to us all, especially to their contemporaries and to those who serve in distant lands, on the sea and in the air."

Among the more notable living, serving, OPMs were Sgt Pilot GP Langdon and Sub-Lieutenant JG Wilson, who were awarded the Distinguished Flying Medal and the Distinguished Service Cross respectively; the former for his *"participation in attacks on heavily defended targets in Germany and elsewhere"*, the latter for his *"outstanding service in the face of the enemy"*.

Incidentally it wasn't just the boys at School who were looking to the future. Writing from a Regional Air Operations Centre Depot *"somewhere in England"*, Hugh Dent wrote – incidentally using his full name – this intriguing piece; *"The old Farmer speaks:-*

"I cannot remember now what they were building;
I think it was something for one of their wars.
The gentlemen-soldiers came strutting with canes,
And then came the boys with their tents and their stores.
Their huts like blue grubs stood and browsed on the hillside;
They shunted their engines and rattled their trains
Through meadow and ploughland, and what did they care?
On Harrison's Fallow they put up their sheds
With great irons roofs that seemed floating on air,
While over the hedge tall cranes pushed their heads,
Their stupid mouths cropping the tops of the trees.
I cannot remember now what they were making

It must have been something to do with the war."

Giving us a different perspective on the war, Dent's poem, one of the few fictional items to grace the pages of the Plymothian during the war, was entitled *"1963"*. Who could possibly have imagined then that come 1963, with the war long behind him, Hugh Dent would still be teaching at Plymouth College?

Turning the clocks back thirty five years, July 1908 was when Francis Colson left Plymouth College, and June 1943 was when the revered former headmaster died, at the age of eighty six. Clerk to the Governors, Charles Serpell produced a three-page obituary for the Plymothian; *"Even the smallest boy,"* wrote Serpell, *"could hardly have failed to feel the fire of his personality."*

Colson had joined the Governing Body some years after retiring from his post in Cambridge, *"and remained a Governor to the end, attending meetings regularly and always had something fresh and discriminating to contribute to the discussion of affairs."*

"Mr Colson has left us, but not unremembered. His works live after him," concluded the obituary. Indeed they do, as many of Colson's classical translations and articles are still available today, including *"The Week: An Essay on the Origin and Development of the Seven-day Cycle"*.

Curiously enough the current Classics master at Plymouth College in 1943 hadn't even been born when Colson left the School, however, strictly speaking, neither was Ernest Dundas exactly in School in 1943. Writing from North Africa, *"in good time to see the victorious conclusion to the Tunisian campaign,"* the 33 year-old Cambridge graduate was quoted as saying he had *"never seen so many oranges and eggs in his life"*.

Meanwhile, writing from the other side of the continent, Mr Battrick reported that his war work *"continues to be full of interest, though the sights of Cairo and the desert have long since begun to pall."*

Not in the imagination of schoolboys, however, as one of the hot new titles in the School library that term was Captain WE John's latest tome – *"Biggles Sweeps the Desert"*. Nor was it just Biggles, Algy and Ginger and Bill Battrick that were out in the dunes. Captain CJ Woodrow, who had left School in '36 wrote to inform the Plymothian readers that the African desert was *"swarming with OPMs."*

Captain WE Johns' latest action packed Biggles adventure hits the school library.

"First I met Jerry Hallett, in Alexandria the night before we both embarked for Tobruk in September 41. During the siege we often met and his capture was a great loss. Next I contacted George Sanders, just before El Alamein. Soon afterwards my younger brother was posted out here. He has been with us right through Tunis. Frank Bolton I found doing Coast Defence round Tripoli. We spent a pretty late night in his mess with endless reminiscences."

Another OPM correspondent to the magazine was FHA Crouch; a prisoner of war in Germany, Crouch sent *"a cryptically worded message from which we understand that BAS Sherriff made an unsuccessful attempt to escape."*

With the War still raging and Hitler having mobilised everyone from 16-65, one of the major debates that winter in School was whether *"Responsibility for the war rests upon the German nation as a whole"*. RJE Abraham proposed and WR Fielden opposed and a heated exchange ensued with the motion being defeated by a margin of one.

A similar margin saw the house support JR Brazier's motion that *"Communism cannot work"*. Meanwhile, in a joint debate with Plymouth High School for

Girls, there was a 51-18 vote supporting *"the general introduction of co-education"*.

The Literary and Debating Society seemed to be picking up again and in addition to the debates there were a number of readings and plans were announced to stage a play, jointly with the Tamaritans, in the New Year.

Literary contributions to the Magazine were thin on the ground, though, and at the annual Prize Distribution, new governor Dr John Murray announced his intention to mark his appointment *"by offering prizes for the best original poems submitted from the School."*

"If there are four hundred boys in the School I hope to have four hundred poems on which to adjudicate".

Forty of those four hundred boys, incidentally, took part in that year's Harvest Camp, which was held at Longclose Farm, Kingsbridge. The weather wasn't wonderful though and *"an unduly large number abandoned ship without good reason"*.

Getting even wetter, a month earlier, CD Fowler's exertions in the School pool won him Victor Ludorum, ahead of RL Turner, while P Chislett pipped JL Beamish overall in the juniors. Turner performed well in all sports that year, and earned the longest appraisal of all the First XV squad in the end of season Rugger notes and was one of five to win his colours - JE Easton, JF Spear, AR Cox and AH Lawrence were the others.

Once again it was a young side – *"surely the youngest that has ever represented the School"* and not surprisingly it *"suffered from the defects of its youth"*.

"Moments of brilliance alternated with moments of blundering" but again many of the opposing sides were much older and much bigger. Five games were won, two against service sides, two against school sides and one against an OPM XV. A couple of the defeats were quite crushing though, with over 40 points being conceded to King's School and RNEC Manadon, on away jaunts, without posting any reply. A game against the Home Guard was only just decided with the last incident in the game and on many occasions the side

played better than the scoreline suggested.

Half of the first team fixtures were played away, a higher percentage than of late, and significantly the away game to St Boniface's College was played at Buckfast. There were reasons to be cheerful however;

"Next season our youngsters may need to train only for victories no more serious than those of the playing field."

Plymouth and Mannamead College 1st XV - 1943: Back row JR Brazier, DCH McDonald, JDW Kellaway, CCA Quick, RK Warne, IM Clarke, R Pratt. Seated; AH Lawrence, RL Turner, JE Easton, JF Spear, ACT Scott. On ground; BAL Johnson and JD Berryman

Or even the coalfield, as that December, Ernest Bevin, Minister of Labour announced that one out of every ten men called up between the ages of 18 and 25 would be ordered to work in the mines, instead of going into the forces.

Either way it was starting to look as if the end of the war was in sight. In the meantime the list of those past pupils who would not live to see that day was still growing.

In March 1944 WB Gill, who had left School in 1933, and was serving as a Captain with the Devonshire Regiment, was killed during the a secret and spectacular Allied operation, 200 miles behind Japanese lines in Burma. In that same operation, AJM Painter, the young man who had arrived to teach at the Prep the year before the war started, was also lost.

"He was killed in action, gallantly leading his men of the Gold Coast Regiment in an attack on a village in the Kaladan Valley, Burma, on February 29th, 1944. He had previously been mentioned in despatches, and his death was a great loss to his Regiment."

Like Gill, Painter was a Captain with the Devonshires and although their time at PMC didn't overlap there can be little doubt that they were aware of the connection.

Two months later JC Chapman, who left the School the year Painter had arrived, was also killed in action in Burma. Chapman had been in India for some eighteen months before the start of that particular Burmese campaign and he had a younger brother, CG. The younger Chapman had left after the outbreak of war and, in the summer of '44, was serving with the Dorsets as part of the Expeditionary Force in Normandy - he would see out the war. KE Bellingham, a contemporary of the younger Chapman, was not so fortunate however. Bellingham had passed the Special Army Entrance Examination in 1940 and had been posted to the North of England where he underwent the greater part of his training, sadly he was killed in action in June 1944, as was PE Clark, another Captain with the Devonshires.

Clark had joined the School in 1924 and on leaving in 1930 had gone onto the staff of the Western Morning News. At the outbreak of war he was working as a sub-editor on the Daily Mail.

Tragically T Deacon's death came about as a result of injuries sustained while training. Deacon, a Lieutenant with the Oxford and Buckinghamshire Light Infantry, Airborne Division, had joined the Royal Army Medical Corps through the Territorial Army at the time of the Munich crisis and while still a member of the Corps managed to train and qualify as a solicitor. He then applied for a commission in the paratroops and, having passed through the Officer Cadet Training Unit was transferred to the airborne division in early 1943. For

such a bright young man to die in training rather than action, was particularly sad; it hadn't been all that many years previously that Deacon had been the principal voice of opposition during the debate in School over the question that *"Europe does not consider peace worth fighting for."* Partly through Deacon's powers of persuasion the motion was lost as the House decided that Peace was indeed worth fighting for. Not surprisingly perhaps, neither of those proposing the motion joined the Services.

One Old Boy who was in no doubt about that particular issue, was SME Fairman. In a School debate on conscription, some twenty years earlier, at the beginning of the First World War, Fairman had suggested that;

"The man who has not joined voluntarily has put himself outside the Government and is therefore a slave and a coward and should be sent to the front".

"Some people," he continued, *"suggest that conscription would cause civil war; if that is so, shoot them down with machine guns and give them a taste of war."*

Fairman, who on another occasion gave a talk to the Natural History Society on the subject of "Machine Guns", was a former editor of the Plymothian and it fell to him and co-editor, W Brown, to produce the first Magazine editorial during the Great War;

"The war," they wrote, *"has drained away the best blood of the country, and for that reason the Public Schools have suffered heavily. We have not escaped, and with us as with the other Schools of England, all boys of military age and physique have joined the Colours."*

Fairman in the 1st XV - 1915

"The younger fellows are left without the authority of such older boys as the seniors of previous years. It is their duty, therefore, to take care that the School,

though young in years, maintains its former standard of efficiency. The nation has at last realised that the situation is grave, that England and her Colonies are fighting for their very existence. Therefore the older Public School boys must go to serve and even to die if fate decrees it."

As fate would have it both boys were to serve in that war, Brown twice being hospitalised. Fairman, however, survived without mishap, and after the war he went on to serve in the Foreign Office and then the Metropolitan Police, eventually becoming Chief Constable of Hertfordshire. Indeed famously, in that capacity, in November 1940, concerned that the blackout was not being well enough observed in the area, Fairman went up in an aeroplane to survey the scene. He was not impressed and lost little time in letting his feelings be known.

Still only in his forties it wasn't that long before Fairman was back in military uniform and those earlier words of his unwittingly made a fitting epitaph when news of his own death, on Active Service in Italy, in May 1944, was reported in the Plymothian that summer.

Clearly however, even with the end of this second devastating conflict now in sight, students still had mixed views about the war.

In a major inter-school debate, held at Plymouth High School for Girls, DP Tidboald and Miss Molly Jones proposed that;

"The debasing influences of War are greater than those which enoble mankind."

More than 100 pupils attended and the house was fairly divided. However, in the end, the opposition, led by Miss Mary Prior and JR Brazier, successfully overturned the motion (56-50).

These were still uncertain times and while the prospect of a return to Situation Normal was looking decidedly more likely – it wasn't in place yet. Young people leaving school still had their thoughts dominated by the war.

Business as Usual - The School that refused to move - life goes on at Plymouth College, despite the intrusion of barrage balloons and, as seen here, a couple of American anti-aircraft guns.

Oxford, Cambridge, Edingburgh, Glasgow, Liverpool and Cardiff were all offering Naval Short Courses.

"One and a half days a week are devoted to the naval side of the course, and for the remainder of the week we were considered as ordinary undergraduates," wrote DFS Hick and GJ Thomas from Oxford.

"Nowadays the percentage of service cadets among the freshmen is high, and University and College teams are almost entirely dependent upon them. The RN and RAF cadets are permitted to read the subjects of their choice, so long as there is a course available, but the Army cadets all have to take Mathematics and Science. The RAF cadets pay much more attention to their service work in which they are tested almost every week. The RN cadets suffering from neither of these restrictions, are thus able to benefit more from their academic instruction."

"As Admiral-of-the-Fleet Sir John Tovey said at the final passing out parade, the Royal Navy has always missed much by not accepting men from the Universities, and now that this scheme has started, and its value in war-time recognised, it should prove a valuable source of supply for officers in the future."

A more subtle form of recruitment was the inclusion in that term's Plymothian of a book review. Under the heading "Book Received" there was no indication as to where the book had come from, or who was responsible for the review. Such reviews, however, were almost unknown in the School Magazine. Nevertheless the book in question here was *"Stand by to Ram"* – by Lanyard and published by Crosby Lockwood and Son at 6/- (30p), and it told *"of some of the exploits of the Navy's "little ships", the corvettes and the destroyers, in the Battle of the Atlantic."*

"The author is a Fleet Street man on active service, who writes vividly of the challenge to the U-boat menace."
And what a menace it was. Throughout 1942 when they were operating at their deadliest German U-boats were accounting for over 600,000-tons of allied shipping

every month, by late in 1943 it was estimated that over 700 German U-boats had been destroyed. But, thanks to improvements in detection, the tide was turning and German morale was ebbing away, hence this timely publication full of …*"real life dramas of hardship, endurance and undaunted courage which will appeal to especially to all who love the sea and the spirit of adventure."*

In addition to this somewhat unprecedented review, the May magazine also included the three winning poems in the competition instigated by Dr John Murray at the previous Speech Day. Dr Murray also judged the poems. The Secretary of the Literary and Debating Society, RC Trounson, won the senior prize, J Goatley the under-15 and MM Allen the junior.

There was also an account of the visit to Plymouth of the International Ballet – *"a party from the School witnessed a performance of Swan Lake and Twelfth Night"*. The trip was organised by Miss Goad and Mr Jackson. While still in a vaguely cultural mode, another member of staff, Mr Meek, oversaw the revival, *"after a lapse of about eight years",* of the Philatelic Society. FJT Harris was its Secretary and around thirty members met regularly for the *"exchange of stamps"*.

On the sporting front the Hockey benefited from having seven of the previous year's first eleven, although the average age of the side was still only 16 years and 10 months *"which is still very young for a 1st XI in inter-school and local club hockey."*

Nevertheless it was a strong side, losing only to King's School, Canterbury and RNEC Keyham, who fielded a much older side. Among the undoubted highlights was the game against another evacuated school – Gresham's;

"A superb game in which we had the support of practically the whole school. The standard of play was exceptionally high; probably nothing better has been seen at Ford Park. The game was fought out skilfully and cleanly to the last minute. One recalls the cheer

that greeted our first goal, and the perfect timing and execution of a penalty corner against us from which our opponents scored".

Unusually eleven players won their colours as the team – Willcock, Clarke, Wright, Brazier, Berryman, Hill, Cox, Johnson, Webb, Turner and Heywood - all merited distinction.

The happiest days of your life; Bryan Johnson, Ron Turner, Derek Pring, Bob Pratt and Peter Chislett smiling in the sunshine.

All three School teams however found opposition hard to come by and the first three of the 1st XI's fixtures were against Plympton, who were convincingly beaten each time, for the 2nd's two out of eight fixtures were against Plympton, again resounding victories for the School, while the Colts turned out against Plympton no less than four times in eight fixtures, losing three and winning just one.

But for *"difficulties inseperable from war-time"* and *"five weeks of wet weather which brought school games to a standstill"* there would have been yet more fixtures to test *"probably the best **team** we have ever had"* - Mr Holman's emphasis here being quite clearly on the word "team".

Somewhat unusually the Spring Term of 1944 also saw a Rugby Football team fielded;

"Though its activities were obstructed by bad weather, Enough was done to suggest that any match play is better than none to boys not finding a place in the representative Hockey sides."

AH Lawrence led the side and of the six matches (all away) three were lost and three won. *"All were well contested and well enjoyed. In some ways the most interesting was that against Totnes Grammar School, a Soccer school now seeing the light during the second of two football terms and meeting a PMC XV for the first time."*

The inter-school Sports, held again at Kelly attracted six schools and again PMC's performance left a lot to be desired.

Finishing fifth overall, one of the best individual performances was that of BAL Johnson, who finished third in the Hop, Step and Jump.

Johnson was also the star of the School Sports held the following week in perfect weather. Johnson won the 220, quarter and half-mile but finished second to Brazier in the Hop, Step and Jump.

Brazier also won the 100 yards and was Proxime Accessit, to Johnson, while JCS Roach won both the

high jump and discus. Clarke, IM, won the mile and along with Read, Trounson, Mitchell and Kellaway, his athletic colours.

Later that week Clarke, on the penultimate day of term, reasserted his prowess as a distance runner finishing ahead of Turner, and thirty-two others, in the Senior Cross Country. GA Rogers won the juniors event, ahead of a forty-seven strong field. JL Beamish, incidentally, was the junior Victor at the School Sports.

Another Sport contested that term was Boxing, which was enjoying a revival under its newly appointed Captain – JR Brazier.

"Thirty-eight boys took part and showed that the school welcomed the return of this particular form of exercise. Every bout was fought to a game finish and exceptional skill was displayed by most competitors, but in BAL Johnson and RH Church, the school has two most accomplished and polished boxers. Their opponents found them most elusive and aggressive, and O Plant, in waging battle with the former, supplied us with the boxing treat of the competition."

JR Brazier Handy with his fists!

On Tuesday 2 May at 10am the summer term started, but that was not the day destined to make it memorable;

"If for no other reason the Summer Term of 1944 will be memorable for the date June 6th. One's mind goes back to that Summer Term four years ago as we followed, on the wireless and in the newspapers, the advance of the German Wehrmacht though Belgium

and France. Anxiety and foreboding, coupled with the determination to preserve our heritage at whatever cost or perish, dominated all our actions. In contrast, the great events of this term have passed, not unnoticed, but without causing us to deviate from the steady course we have set ourselves during the years between. It was on June 4th, 1940, that Mr Churchill, in a speech that will surely be read with admiration by generations to come, said: "We shall fight on the beaches." The news of the landings, not on our own beaches but on the enemy's, was received with quiet satisfaction and calm confidence in the final issue, no more."

As the Allied Forces stormed ashore in Normandy, a wave of relief swept across the nation and when, before the end of the month, the Tricolour fluttered once more over Cherbourg, the light at the end of the tunnel really did start to shine brightly.

"It is in no spirit of undue optimism that our thoughts are already turning to the future," continued the Plymothian Editorial. *"The plan for the New Plymouth has been made known. What part will Plymouth College play in the building of the new city? With few exceptions, some noteworthy, the School, through its members and former members, has not figured largely in the civic life in the past.*

It is our hope that those who remained in the city during the days of its trials and tribulations will wish to take a full measure of responsibility for its future welfare, and that they will regard their schooldays, especially when hostilities cease and added opportunities occur, as a preparation for this service. Let us face the new school year with these thoughts in mind."

As if to endorse that exhortation, the long-serving Clerk to the Governors, CR Serpell, himself an old boy, offered a prize of two guineas for the best essay on *"The Functions and Future Development of Plymouth College in the Post-War Plymouth and District."* Coincidentally there was news in the School Notes of Serpell's second son, another OPM, David Serpell, who had briefly taught at the School; and who had just been awarded the OBE. David was Private Secretary to Major Gwillym Lloyd George, the Minister of Fuel and Power, who had had major problems that spring when 87,000 striking Welsh miners had closed 156 of the 200 pits in South Wales. A four-hour meeting with the miners leaders in Westminster was needed to help sort out the differences. Each day of the strike meant the loss of 70,000 tons of much-needed coal.

Denis Ewing Ballantine - "Tiny" - won the Military Cross for his heroics on 3rd June 1944, two days before his 25th birthday,. Later he would be promoted to Brigadier and appointed Chief of Staff Western Command. Left; in Thompson's swimming team 1935.

Among the other honours going to OPMs that year was a Military Cross to Major DE Ballantine, *"for his leadership and gallantry on the Italian Front".*

"At the end of May 1944, the Allies started their drive from the Anzio beach-head towards the Tiber. After attack and counter attack, the 2nd Battalion Wiltshire Regiment passed through Ardea, negotiating several minefields before being held up by powerful German opposition from a high ridge north-west of the town."

"In the early afternoon of June 3, the battalion attacked with three depleted rifle companies. The German forces were protected by minefields and barbed wire, and the only possible line of advance was up a valley leading to their objective, a spur, designated Point 51, in the centre of their position."

"Ballantine, a major with C Company moved up the valley, but his men suffered many casualties as they emerged into the open, undulating country. As they approached the spur, the enemy, dug in on the reverse slope, opened up with machinegun, mortar and shellfire from both flanks."

"Ballantine personally directed his company attack - running across open ground, from one platoon to the next, giving his orders. On two ocassions bullets glanced off his steel helmet; a third grazed his hand."

"No sooner had his compnay captured its objective than the enemy counter-attacked; but Ballantine had anticipated the move, and a platoon was in position and ready to deal with it. The citation for his MC stated thiat his skill, coolness and courage were largely responsible for the success of the operation."

Another OPM to receive the MC around that time was JB Faulkner for his part in the Kohima assault against the Japanese, in India, in April. There were also DFCs for Flight Lietuenant JH Corre *"for keenness and determination in operational flying. He had destroyed three enemy aircraft"*, and Flying Officer RH Ewens *"for high skill, fortitude and devotion to duty in various capacities in operations against the enemy."*

Closer to home there were Scholarship successes for the Head of School, Bayly (Classics), Berryman (English) and Lawrence (Natural Science) all at University College, Exeter, although, later in the year, Lawrence won a State Scholarship at Trinity College, Cambridge.

Increasingly schoolboys were able to think in terms of further education again, and focus on their study and sport. The 1944 cricket season saw the School play out the fullest fixture list in years; 22 matches, more than half of them won, only a couple lost convincingly and several won very convincingly.

A "School" XI at Plymouth Cricket Club; Back row, Godfrey Heywood, Ken Wilcocks, Steve Roach, Bryan Johnson, John Hamley, John Wynton, IM Clarke and DCH McDonald. Wicket-keeper Ron Turner in front with Derek Pring.

Plympton Grammar and an RAF side were both dismissed twice without reaching the total first posted by the School. Gresham's were beaten twice, D Pring taking 8-48 in the first match, while Hamley and Miles ended up with most wickets overall. The Captain, IM Clarke dominated the batting, scoring one unbeaten century, while Heywood, Wynton and Turner were also among the runs, each scoring at least one fifty. Nevertheless most of the matches were still against non-school sides, and yet despite this a *"boys' XI was played throughout the term".*

A long time in the planning the D Day Operation is a huge success, a wave of relief that end of the War may at last be in sight, sweeps over the country. Spirits are lifted and a lightening of mood is clearly visible.

Clockwise, top left: American troops stationed in Plymouth prepare for the cross channel assault. On the beaches a high price is paid but the rewards are much greater.

Below cadets R Turner and DF Pring enjoy a break. Right; The Gang's all here! Fun and frolics in Hartley Park. Boys and girls, the knees are out, verdict from the bench and goons in gowns, in front of School.

For the 2nds Brazier was the main danger to opposing teams and he also took eight Gresham scalps in one innings, while Webb scored double the runs of any of his fellow 2nd XI team-mates.

The number of Swimming matches entered into by the School team also showed a marked increase that summer as RNEC, Plymouth Transport and an RAF side were all challenged at Ford Park. Success was logged against the Transport boys, who nevertheless twice beat the School at Water Polo.

P Chislett was the star of the rain-soaked School Swimming Sports, with Fowler not far behind him. PJM Vaughan was junior victor with Martin in hot pursuit; Pring ii, was junior plunge winner - a star for the future - while Ratty set a new School plunge record of 47'2".

A summer term boxing competition was mooted but not staged although tuition was given *"as usual by the APTC Instructors, and, the enthusiasm amongst those interested in Boxing has been fully maintained."*

There was no outside help for the School JTC, however, although they appeared in an official parade and march-past *"for the first time in many years"*. DCH McDonald was the senior Schoolboy officer of the Corps and oversaw the Summer Field Day on Whitchurch Down on 3 June, the day after the Scouts had their Field Day at Bickleigh – *"This event which was introduced experimentally last term, is proving successful."*

Also proving successful was the revived Photographic Society, the object of which was to *"develop and print films, which together with Gaslight Papers, Negative Wallets, and Folders, can be obtained from the Society."*

The revival here, too. said much about the progress of the war. A year or so earlier, the taking of pictures outside of School would have been pretty much taboo, as would the idea of going off on a jolly in a motor for the day, as described, somewhat dreamily, in the piece 'Holiday' in that summer's Plymothian; *"We're off, and the countryside is lovely except for the stream of private cars all headed for the sea at top speed and the chara-bancs loaded with the boisterous trippers enveloping us in dust. We must be nearing our destination, for the ice-cream vendors with their gaily painted carts are much in evidence and we have just passed the fairground, with its rows of cocoa-nut shies and the music blaring from the roundabouts."*

It was a dream born of rationing that included other references to petrol, fruit, meat and cream, and despite being removed from wartime reality it was another indication that people were starting to picture a world without war again.

Mutley, little troubled by the Blitz.

Doubtless a similar spirit prompted a fresh burst of activity on the amateur dramatic front as the Literary and Debating Society staged three one-act plays, JJBell's *"Thread o' Scarlet"*, George Bernard Shaw's *"Village Wooing"* and AA Milne's *"The Boy Comes Home"*. Messrs Jackson, Savage and Miss Goad were the respective producers and CA Reeves, as Uncle James, in the latter play, was singled out for his *"malicious appreciation"* of the part.

It was, as it happened, one of Miss Goad's last extracurricular contributions to life at School as she was to leave at the end of the Autumn term, although not before playing the part of a *"dour but sympathetic landlady"* in the L&D Soc's 'The Wind and The Rain' the following term; *"She came to us in the autumn of 1940, and in four years has proved herself a most valuable and indeed almost indispensible member of the Staff. Her patience and good humour have been unfailing, and she has been willing to help in every direction and every emergency. These personal qualities, combined with a rare gift of teaching, have commanded our admiration and respect, and we gratefully acknowledge our debt to her. We wish her all success in her new appointment."*

Miss Goad wasn't the only one moving from Ford Park however, as the news gradually filtered through the School that the Headmaster was going to retire at the end of the school year.

Herbert Ralph had seen the School through the difficult years of the war and now that conflict looked to be nearing an end, the Head, who would be 60 in May, decided that it was time to go. The falling leaves weren't the only sign of the passing time that autumn. He still had many difficult duties to perform however and at the Commemoration Service that October, in St Gabriel's Church, the Head read a list of 48 former members of the School who had already laid down their lives over the last five years.

Among the new additions to that growing list was 2/Lieut RA Smith who had drowned while on active service, in July 1944, just three summers after leaving the School. In September, his namesake RD Smith, a lieutenant with Oxford Bucks Light Infantry was killed in Burma, while that same month VJ Harvey, NCO with REME Airborne Division, was killed in action at Arnhem. This was the action that it was hoped would bring forward the end of the war by several months. Tragically, however, the plan to sieze the bridge which would give the Allies control of the lower Rhine, was a bloody failure and of the 10,000 British paratroopers sent in, including Smith, only 2,400 returned. The following month, Cpl DN Baker, of the Royal Enniskillen Dragoons, was killed in Holland.

Four weeks after the Commemoration Service, the School held its annual Prize Distribution. Fittingly, the Head's last such occasion was also the first public prizegiving since the war had begun. It was staged, not at Ford Park, but in the building that, following the Destruction of the Guildhall and Council Chambers, the City Council itself was using for its business – Central Methodist Hall. Appropriately enough the Lord Mayor, Alderman HG Mason, was the guest of honour and Mr Ralph took the opportunity to make reference to the services rendered by the School to the City during the war.

"Since people had begun to return to the City the School has accepted entries up to the limit of its capacity," he said, adding, *"All manner of service units have been entertained on the field and offered the use of the premises."*

"I do not know what the City would have done without Plymouth College," he said with a measure of pride.

He then went on to tell the assembly that he lost fourteen of his peace-time staff to the war effort and yet the record for the year was as good as any previously. Noting and somewhat lamenting that the *"urgent needs of war were excluding students from university courses other than scientific subjects"*, he said *"subjects coming under the heading of Arts, might not help directly in winning the war, but could do much to help win the peace."*

Mr Ralph then extended his speech on education to include *"the greatest measure of education reform ever placed before the country"* – the Education Act. The Act, passed three months earlier, promised free secondary education for all in this country and the Head was keen to point out that *"the public schools have certain traditions, liberties and freedoms which are not incompatible with co-operation with the Ministry of Education and the local authority ... but, there are clauses in the Act which, owing to what the Headmaster of Winchester has called "the irresistible logic of*

Westminster, might tend to depress the standards we wish to preserve. We have fought hard for the retention of school fees," he said, *"as we fear without them it might be hard to safeguard the special character of these schools, and the right of parents to choose their boy's own schools".*

The Lord Mayor, speaking next, congratulated the Head on his report, on the School's success and referred with regret to the fact that it was Ralph's last Speech Day. *"The School and the City will miss his leadership,"* said Alderman Mason, before going on to address the subject of the Education Act himself;

"The conception of education as a training for some particular function in society has led people to believe that the purpose of education is merely to "get on". But I believe there is growing a higher sense of values. Every person should be taught to the limit of his capacity, to think for himself, to fit himself for leadership and to accept responsibility for service."

Quite what boys of 1A made of it all is not recorded, but one suspects that the novelty of the surroundings would have occupied most of their attention.

Central Methodist Hall on the right, at the back with the Blitz surviving Corn Exchange in the foreground of the picture.

Central Methodist Hall been rebuilt in 1940, partly through the money and influence of Lord Rank (of

the Rank Organisation), and consequently it looked not unlike a 1930s cinema inside. Indeed Lord Rank had intended to make religious films and show them in halls like this - a projection room was incorporated in the design. However it has never been used as such and during the war, this, then state-of-the-art building, housed not only the relocated City Council but its canteen, suppling up to 1,000 meals a day. Central Hall, therefore, would have been a source of some interest that Tuesday in November, on that first public, wartime Speech Day.

Certainly the occasion prompted a literary contribution to the Magazine, from Foculus – *"with apologies to Mr Pepys"*. The piece described the events in mock-seventeenth century speak and yet the references to shuffling, giggling, hands in pockets and adoring parents have a timeless ring to them as indeed does the passage describing the prize winners collecting their book from the guest of honour; *"Ye Lorde Mayor rising in his Dignitie of Office, with gold Chains ajangle, from behind the Pile of Books. Much ado; the stentorian Voice of Ye Heade bringing small Boys to their tottering Feet with Blushes mantling snow Brows. Murmurs from Ye Gallery and more Tittering from Back of Hall. Good Lack! How they do hastily grasp the Books to their Bosoms, lightly touch Ye Mayor's Hand and scurry back to the Haven of their Seat. Now come the bigger Boys; no mere Touch of Hands from them but grips that do make Ye Mayor wince. Methinks the Back of Hall now suffers from Convulsions."*

"Ye Lorde Mayor gives a Speeche well suited to the Occasion. His Jokes, which I did think passable amusing, did evoke much Laughter; but a small Joke do go a great Way at such Ceremonies."

While some older boys may have had a slightly mischievious agenda of their own at Speech Day it should not be forgotten that some of the more responsible big boys had the power to ensure that reasonable behavioural standards were adhered to;

"At last the School can really boast,
Its prefects are a noble host:
It gives a boy great joy to be
Their guest up in the library.

The genial Clarke will smile on him,
And ask in dulcet tones –
"Is it in very truth a fact
That you, dear lad, are Jones?
Against your name is written here
A really dreadful sin:
'Tis said that you have brought to School
Some carbide, in a tin,
With this said chemical, I think,
Intending to produce a stink.
Now is it true or is it not,
That you were author of this plot
To wreck the School's tranquility,
And fill the air with odours free?"

The boy peers oe'r the Lexicon,
And answers with a muffled sniff –
"I didn't think it would be wrong
To manufacture just a whiff"

"Now, this particular offence
I cannot overlook," says Clarke,
"So, Tiger, will you give him two,
To keep him from a further lark?"

Oh yes, it really is the aim
Of every boy to have his name
Inscribed upon the list of those
Required to come and "touch their toes"."

The piece was signed "C" - IM Clarke was then Head of School, while C Reeves and J Brazier, both prefects, were the two senior boys on the editorial staff of the Plymothian.

Brazier was also a gifted linguist, winning both the French and German prizes that year - he was also Captain of Boxing and Hon Sec of the Rugby team.
Once again the lack of senior boys in the School created problems for the rugger players, prompting games master Wilf Savage to write;

"OPMs nowadays are apt to make rather gloomy comments on the School games, not perhaps realising the implications of war-time conditions. It may surprise them to learn that nine-tenths of the School are Juniors, under fifteen, and that there are only a dozen boys over seventeen. The disparity in age and size between ourselves and many of our opponents is bound to be reflected in the results of the games, especially in the Rugger season. What is not always apparent to readers of the Plymothian is the spirit with which losing battles have been fought."

1st XV, 1944. Back row; R Pratt, GA Heywood, JDW Kellaway, MA Oliver, IM Clarke, JL Beamish, RC Trounson, P Chislett. Seated; JD Berryman, JR Brazier, RL Turner, JF Spear, BAL Johnson. On ground, B Webb and CD Heath.

Having said that there were a number of good wins, notably at home over Kelly, St Boniface College and Gresham's. The win over Kelly was the first since 1938, Pratt, Spear and Brazier all scored tries, while Kellaway and Johnson (twice) were the try scorers

against Gresham's; *"This was our last game with Gresham's before their return to Norfolk, and we were very pleased to end with a win a series of war-time fixtures which we have thoroughly enjoyed."*
King's Canterbury were too strong however, as were most of the Service sides. In House rugger, Sargents won the Senior Cup for the first time in fourteen years, beating favorites College in the final, much to the delight of House Captain, DF Pring. He was also Captain of the School Shooting team who won three and narrowly lost a fourth fixture against a mixed array of teams on the miniature range. There was also shooting at Tregantle Fort.
Field Day was held at Meavy that term, but again there was no camp for the JTC - there was for the Scouts however. They spent nine days at Lewannick, near Launceston. The Scouts, incidentally, were also granted access to the miniature shooting range. There was also another Harvest Camp, this time at Week, near Totnes. Twenty-eight boys were accommodated in the Youth Hostel there and enjoyed what was reckonned to be the most enjoyable of the three wartime camps;
"It might be said that the senior members of the Camp spent too much time on the Totnes-Week high-road, but surely that judgement is a little harsh considering the back-ache and boredom occasioned by pea-picking."
For the second term since its revival the Inter-School boxing tournament failed to happen. The revived interest in the Literary and Debating Society held firm though, and a number of play-readings, discussions, talks and debate were held, including a motion, proposed by WR Fielden, that *"This House supports the Plymouth Plan"*. JR Brazier opposed but the motion was carried 15-11. Happily there was no such majority for a later motion proposed by AR Martin and HKS Rundle, that *"The study of History should have no place in the modern school curriculum."* CA Reeves and JDW Kellaway led the successful opposition.
The hand of history was undoubtedly weighing heavy

on the hearts of that generation, as the compiler of the OPM notes that winter was to write to his fellow club members, *"perhaps many of you had hoped to have been again in Plymouth before this number was published."* Then, more optimistically the notes continued, *"In any case this will almost certainly be the last war-time Christmas number."*

An up-date of the OPM war records followed, headed by a list of those who had gained wartime decorations. Among them was GA McGlashan, who had left School in 1927 and was awarded the Military Cross. There was talk of funding an OPM War Memorial and of *"the desirability of having our own Club premises."*

Long a recurring theme of the OPMs, the attraction of having a clubhouse, where old boys could reminisce, socialise and where stories could be exchanged, was particularly obvious at this time. Clearly there were many fascinating tales to be told; like that of WB Trout, of the Durham Light Infantry, who had been captured at Tobruk in June 1942, then taken to Italy as a Prisoner of War six months later. After the Armistice with Italy he had managed to escape and was repatriated in June 1944. Squadron Leader FR Curtis had previously been reported missing but was another being held as a POW. In the May 1945 Plymothian there was a yet further extension to the Record of War Service; one that sadly brought the total number of Old Boys to have served during the War to over five hundred and pushed the list of those who had lost their lives beyond the fifty mark. Published in May the magazine, however, bore glad tidings; *"The victory in arms has been achieved and, who knows, by the time this appears in print the turmoil of battle may be stilled and peace be with us once more. It will, justly, be a time of thankfulness and happiness; but after the rejoicing and elation, after the preparations for the home-coming of those we love, let us pause to think of those who will not return and let us sorrow with those who wait in vain."*

"We of this City remember the nights of terror and destruction, fire and explosion, and the feeling of helplessness as we crouched beneath that rain of death, or struggled against overwhelming odds. We remember, too, that true spirit of brotherhood that arose in those difficult times. Erstwhile strangers toiled side by side amidst the fire and the debris without thought of personal safety, and shared cups of tea in the chilly hours of darkness and apprehension."

"We learned how to love our neighbour as ourselves, and were the better for it, but with the passing of danger and with the petty things of life once more occupying our minds, the bonds of true friendship have become strained. Selfishness is replacing altruism and the warm handshake now becomes a curt nod."

"To merit the peace that has been so long delayed, that love we found in times of trial must be recaptured at all costs, so that we may prove ourselves worthy of those who made the supreme sacrifice, and so that those returning may know that the hardships they have suffered and the long years of separation they have endured have not been in vain."

Plymouth Hoe - VE Day. Among the boys and girls celebrating there are College schoolboys Peter Chislett, Bryan Johnson, Peter Llewellyn, Bob Pratt, Julian Spear, John Hamley & John Beamish.

At Ford Park itself there was another quite quirky side effect of the war and one that proved that the trials endured by the comparatively youthful school sides had not been in vain. As 1944 ticked away the nation slowly cut back its demands on its youthful manhood for war work at home or abroad, and with the prospect of servicemen being demobilised and returning to work, schoolboys could once again consider a sensible spell in the sixth form and the prospect of further education. Consequently the average age of the boys in the School started to rise back up towards pre-war levels.

Teams, like the Hockey eleven, were able to capitalise on what they had learnt in previous seasons when they had been well below peace-time average ages. As it happened, the Hockey team had already shown much promise the previous season but when the heavy snowfalls of January 1945 eventually cleared and the season got under way the team immediately showed signs of being the most successful the School had ever seen. Not surprisingly, perhaps, as the Captain, IM Clarke was playing his fourth season for the firsts and had already represented the School on thirty-two occasions before the season started. Alongside him RL Turner, JR Brazier, BAL Johnson and GA Heywood were all playing in their third season, while AEF Hill, JR Berryman, and B Webb were veterans of the previous season.

In singing the praises of his team Mr Holman congratulated both Mr Savage, who had worked with the team from their days in the Colts and Mr Meek who *"presided over the destinies of the 2nd XI ... No faults or departures from a high standard of play have escaped his vigilant eye"*.

Clearly it was a very successful season, the 1sts winning thirteen of their fifteen fixtures and the 2nds losing only one – and that in the last minute.

"Far and away the season's finest match, and one that will live long in memory" was that against RNEC at Ford Park. This side had beaten the School 3-0 on

Valentine's Day at Keyham, and come the return match in March, this was still their only defeat in eight outings.

On the day, *"We gave an almost faultless display of schoolboy hockey at its best, and the eleven richly earned the Headmaster's concise encomium at prayers the following morning."*

Hockey 2nd XI, 1945. Standing; CD Heath, GA Rogers, KWF Clarke, RH Palk. Sitting; RH CHurch, R Pratt, JA Wynton, JF Spear, JCS Roach. On ground; PR Lyon and P Berryman.

The cold snap that delayed the start of the season was a widespread one, as the Cambridge Letter testified;

"Cambridge, so it is reported, was one of the coldest places in England recently – we believe it!!"

"A snowman appeared here recently and, on thawing, proved to be Mr Reddecliffe, who gave us some lectures on Tank Tactics. Other OPMs we have been glad to see are DE Ridpath and RJ Piper, both of whom are stationed near here in the RAF."

There were currently four old boys at Cambridge at that time and the news was that RC Trounson and IM Clarke were both about to join them, the latter reading Mathematics, the former Classics – further proof that the western world was returning to normal.

Sadly it was already back to what had become normal for Plymouth College in the Inter-School sports at Kelly – they finished a lowly fourth in a field of five.

School athletes achieved a number of thirds, but not a single first and only one second – JDW Kellaway in the discus.

BAL Johnson was Captain of Athletics and he won the half-mile at the School Sports in the last week of March. Strong finishes in other events earned him Proxime Accessit, shared with B Webb, but both were a little way behind JCS Roach and AG Rogers who in turn, somewhat unusually, shared the title of Victor Ludorum. GA Rogers was the junior Victor, with AR Newcombe not far behind him. Once again the Lord Mayor, Alderman HG Mason, and the Lady Mayoress, were in attendance at the prize-giving although on this occasion it was Miss Muriel Brown, whose five brothers had all been at the School, and whose late-father had been Chairman of the Governors for over twenty years, who handed out the prizes.

Thanks perhaps to the charisma of the Head of School, IM Clarke, who was also Captain of Fives, that much-maligned game thrived that season. Twenty-four pairs entered a Doubles Competition, which was won by Wynton and Roach, who triumphed over Clarke and Trounson in the final, and a close game was played with Kelly at Tavistock. Not for the first time two other fixtures - both with Kelly - were cancelled by the Tavistock boys.

An inter-school boxing tournament was also cancelled, through no fault of the School's but at least this term a House Boxing tournament was staged (and won by College). The number of entrants was down on the previous year but *"the standard of boxing was considerably higher, and evoked well-merited applause from the many spectators – nearly two hundred members of the School watched the Finals."*

"All the Senior bouts provided thrills and skill, but interest largely centred on the Featherweight group. Mention must be made of the winner of this weight, O Plant, who showed himself to be an extremely competent and aggressive boxer. With his successive opponents,

B Webb, RH Church and DF Pring i, he supplied the three outstanding bouts of the whole competition."

Clarke, Brazier and Johnson, incidentally, won the Middle, Welter and Lightweight titles respectively.

Proving that he was as good with words as he was with his fists, Brazier also won the Literary and Debating Society's Challenge Cup that term. Curiously enough early that term Brazier, with Trounson, had put forward the motion that *"The world would be a better place without personal ambition"*...and had been defeated!

Thorpe-Tracey and RJE Abraham's proposal that *"Capital Punishment should be abolished"* was also over-turned, largely through the eloquence of JD Berryman and CA Reeves. However, when WR Fielden and RC Trounson proposed that; *"This house will support the Tories at the next General Election"* the motion was carried by a single vote, although there were four abstentions.

Trounson was also Hon Sec of the Society and was keen to thank Mr Drew and Miss Coulthard for their help during the term. 21 year-old Pamela Coulthard had come in to replace Kathleen Goad, and the following term we found her *"sweeping aside all difficulties"* to produce Julius Caesar, with Brazier in the title tole, Tounson as Brutus and the *"outstanding"* Dodd, as Casius. This capable young woman was not here long, however, and before the end of the year she left for a post at Heathfield School. Someone who had been at Ford Park much longer and who had long been a great supporter of that particular Society, was Mr Woodcock.

One of only three of Freddie Dale's appointments left on the staff, 45 year-old William Woodcock had been at Plymouth College twenty years and his sudden departure at the end of the spring term 1945 was so that this French and German teacher could take up an important post with the Post-War, Allied Control Commission in Vienna. Known as the Avalon Project it started work on 4 July 1945.

"Palmers will miss his tall figure on the touchline at all the House Matches; but it is in the Common Room where his going is most keenly felt. Here his urbanity, genial good humour and pointed wit made him a respected and popular member, and his many friends can but wish that his visits in the future will be as frequent as his leave permits."

After 20 years linguist Woodcock takes on a European assignment.

Dr Ernest Ellingher

Making the journey in the other direction, albeit indirectly was 37 year-old Dr Ernest Ellingher, who came, via London, as Woodcock's replacement, *"from the Universities of Vienna and Prague - where he holds the degree of Doctor Juris".*

With the clouds of war lifting other revived societies continued to meet regularly, with both the Philatelic Society and the Photographic Society having talks and general meetings. In his end of term notes the Secretary of the latter, JP Woodcock, reported that *"an efficient film service was maintained by BWJ Ratty; AP Hesling again distributed gaslight paper, folders and negative wallets."*

The JTC had their Annual Inspection on February 14 and Field Day a few weeks later at Yelverton, with RH Church the senior NCO. JD Berryman was Troop Leader of the Scouts and they had their Field Day at Gratton Bridge;

"Leaving the train at Yelverton, the Troop had dinner and then proceeded to construct a "monkey bridge".

Impressed by its neat design and undismayed by the lack of equipment which was essential to the firm structure of any such bridge, the Troop Leader crossed first, and the rope over which his feet passed, and which should have been about four inches above the water, sagged six inches. He got wet."

Scout Summer Camp 1945. Photograph taken by DL Farmer - it appeared in the first edition of IVa's Forum Magazine, which was put together for "publication" in June 1946.

A similarly deflating experience was the lot of RM White, who had left School after the war had started, in the summer of '41. White, a lieutenant in the Devonshire Regiment, was a member of the Allied contingent that recaptured the Burmese capital, Rangoon, effectively marking the end of the main campaign in Burma, at the end of May 1945. The War was not truly over yet. Victory in Europe had been celebrated, but halfway around the world there was still the Japanese problem; Full of boyhood dreams of derring-do and gung-ho glory, White describes how the assault landing on Ramree Island *"was to have been something between a Roman triumph and an Elizabethan progress, with a touch of Cecil B de Mille for good measure – the while by courtesy of Gaumont British News. Sic – we thought, being loyal Thompsonians – itur ad astra."*

1945 and half-way round the world, the war is still not over for many British soldiers and several OPMs, including the JB Faulkner, pictured here in Burma. In April 1944 Faulkner won the Military Cross for his part in the Kohima assault on the Japanese in India.

But *"Reality in Rangoon"* was somewhat different and White's wonderful, dewy-eyed description of the events that followed were full of home thoughts from abroad; *"The sea voyage by LSI was uneventful, and as reserve*

1945

327

brigade we anchored outside Rangoon according to schedule. It was at this point that the action began to depart disastrously from the script. The entry into the town, far from being an all-conquering do-or-die effort, was humiliatingly reminiscent of a trip up the Tamar. The vast amound of kit that we were carrying imparted an unromantic end of the term flavour to the whole affair. Together with some four hundred perspiring soldiery in a craft designed to accommoate two hundred and fifty, we chugged sedately up the river and docked in Rangoon with no more ceremony than that accorded to the Turnchapel Ferry.

Rangoon in 1945. When the Allies arrived it was in a state of inde-scribable filth, with open road-side drains full of sewage.

Nor was our triumphal march any less ignominious a failure. We shambled furtively off the dock, bowed beneath our elephantine packs, and crawled wearily through the empty streets. The odd citizen whom, at rare intervals we did chance to meet, bestowed upon us a dispassionate and fairly disapproving stare and ejected an expressive stream of betel nut into a convenient gutter. After an endless march we collapsed in a side street and laid our weary heads to rest."

"From beginning to end of the entire dismal operation one shred of consolation was vouchsafed to us. At last we had discovered the origin of the grotesque railway engines that Emmett portrays in Punch. We had thought that they sprang from the artist's own fertile imagination, but now we know better."

"Nothing less than an intoxicated Heath Robinson in conjunction with a mad surrealist working under the influence of opium, could have produced such a diabolical contrivance as that train on which we travelled north from Rangoon. Puffing and wheezing like an asthmatic sea lion it wound its way, in the manner of the Laira china clay trucks, with fine impartiality, through all the side, and most of the main, streets of the City, leaving us at times with the disturbing suspicion that it had taken to the tram lines by mistake!"

"At every station, both of them in fact, we expected to see Will Hay pop out from the Office, or Horace Kenny tending his vegetables, and a brisk tote was run on the forecast time of the boiler blowing up. At some ungodly hour of the night the puffing beast gave up the ghost completely and stood shimmering gently in a markedly thirsty manner."

"Finally, amid scenes of unparalleled enthusiasm, we reached our destination, having covered thirty miles in the record time of twelve hours."

With such end-of-war tales of damp squibs from the Far East appearing in the Plymothian, it was doubtless a relief to the members of the JTC that they were unlikely to be involved this time around. Nevertheless, Field Day at Meavy that May was *"more realistic than of late, owing to the ample supply of blanks and thunder flashes."* There was also an equally lively and quite separate fieldcraft exercise for the JTC recruits. Meanwhile the Scouts too were increasing their range of activities, with weekend camps at Bickleigh and Field Days at Clearbrook. The Troop also took part in an Inter-Troop Athletic Sports at Collings Park – they finished fifth.

There was also talk of a Scout Troop Aquatic event in the *"School Bath"*. It was a busy year for that particular facility;

"A record number of boys have used the bath this term, no fewer than 180 have enrolled as members". Five water polo matches were played. Three of them were co-ordinated with Swimming Galas, but none of them were against School sides, although there was a further gala staged with Kelly that the School won. Of the other galas, all were lost against stronger opposition, but the water polo sides beat their Army and RAF opponents at the Royal Citadel and Mount Batten respectively.

Thompson's, with three of the School Water Polo side in their team (Kellaway, Reeves and Chislett), not surprisingly won an Inter-House competition while Chislett pipped Turner in the bath to take the Victor Ludorum of the Aquatic Sports on 2 July.

There was a Shooting House Championship as well, which was narrowly won by Sargents, while the House Cricket was comfortably won by College, who fielded six of the school's first XI in the side, including Nobby, Roy and Ken Clarke.

In a court *"rented outside the School"* there were ten full weeks of playing time found for a revived tennis competition - Palmer's winning the *"unofficial"* house challenge … *"Another year … it is hoped that the game **will** be officially recognised by the school"* There were also a couple of Shooting matches, two against Ford Park Rifle Club, one won, one lost, and another against Ivybridge ATC, which the School also won.

Inter-School matches of any kind tended to be a little thin on the ground, the 1st XI had cricket matches against Kelly cancelled due to bad weather. Of the other fifteen or so sides they played only one was a school XI.

PMC lost the away game, played at St Austell, *"but we took our revenge when they came to Ford Park. A record crowd witnessed the game. It was our last match with King's before they return to Canterbury: we shall miss our encounters with them as we have appreciated* their sportsmanship in never failing to give and keep a fixture."

The significance of these remarks should not be underestimated and later in his report Eric Holman gave us a more detailed context than wartime censorship had earlier allowed:

"Future cricketers who ransack records would do well to bear in mind certain facts which may now be told. Over the past five years cricket gear has been severely rationed and has only been obtainable on a Government permit. Clothes have required valuable coupons. Travel restrictions have imposed a bar on our accepting "away" fixtures and this, and a curious reluctance to come near Plymouth, have curtailed visits from certain outside teams. Net pitches have been flanked by a bomb dump on one side and a barrage balloon, with housing accommodation and dug-out for the crew, on the other. At the lower end of the field a static water tank has cut off cricket and hockey ground, and air-raid shelters runs the length of the southern side. Last year two A.A. (anti-aircraft) guns, complete with ammunition stores, were posted at short notice on the running track: Old Glory (an old nickname for the American flag) floated over the Pav. And the changing rooms echoed the accents of Tennessee. Neither the enemy, nor our Allies, nor the local authorities thought fit to drop bombs, pitch tents or sink tanks on the square. For this small relief we have indeed been truly thankful, and Cricket has gone on."

Cricket had indeed *"gone on"*. That summer season of 1945 the first XI were scoring around a thousand runs a month, foremost amongst the stars was Nobby (IM) Clarke, the eldest of the three brothers who all played for the firsts that year. He scored several half-centuries, and a marvellous ton - against Seale-Hayne College in the middle of June.

Like the Hockey XI, Eric Holman rated this one of the best sides the School had produced; *"Diligent search among statistics of previous years has failed to reveal*

any comparable figures. As is now the custom, an XI compsed entirely of boys, was played throughout the season. The XI was certainly the finest we have produced in the field and the most experienced."

"It is not without interest that the crowds at Ford Park who came to enjoy the cricket were larger than ever before."

D Pring did most of the bowling *"and harvested a tidy reap of wickets"*, including 7-5 against the City Police. He also played *"one very neat innings"* against the Australian Air Force at Mount Batten, who fielded a very accomplished side, including the first class cricketer Keith Millar, the Victoria player that Nobby Clarke hit for four off his first delivery.

The School 2nd XI, 1945. Standing; M Lunn, GE Coyte, FN Lyon, CD Heath, GA Rogers, SF Liddicoat. Seated RH Palk, JL Beaemish, R Pratt, JD Berryman and PM Dunkley.

Again, like the Hockey XI, this was an experienced team as the lads were able to eke out their school days to the full, consequently it was the eldest Clarke's fourth season in the firsts, his second season as skipper and meant that he played over 80 innings for the School. Wynton, Turner, Hamley and Heywood (Pro's son) had all played around fifty games or more. *"Every boy in*

the XI has been in the School during the war years and has experienced the peculiar trials by which we were beset,"* wrote the games master.

Of course no-one was more acutely aware of those *"peculiar trials"* than the man who led the School through those years, Herbert Ralph;

"Despite all difficulties he kept the traditions and standards of the School undiminished. He grappled with the manifold problems that have presented themselves with great determination and cheerfulness, never sparing himself although at times his health had not been good. One remembers the numerous occasions on "Fire Guard" duty, when the "Alert" sounded, not once did he fail to look in to see that everything was all right. A small matter perhaps, but one that illustrates his high sense of duty and responsibility."

"A person of great sympathy and understanding, in cases of illness or accident he has been the first to offer consolation, and in all cases of difficulty, most ready to offer his assistance."

"Nor," continued his anonymous biographer, *"has he relinquished his charge when a boy left the School. The writer has personal knowledge of the time he has devoted since the war to corresponding with Old Boys on active service and of the usefulness of his association with the OPM Club."*

A veteran of the First World War himself, he was all too well aware of the mental turmoils suffered by soldiers. He'd been Senior Classics master at Stoneyhurst for three years when he'd gone off to France in 1916 and had been wounded in March 1918. He was invalided out, back into his teaching post at Stoneyhurst.

Had it not been for the Second World War one suspects that Ralph would have gone much earlier. He was already older than any previous headmaster of Plymouth College had been in harness when the war started and now, at 60, he was a good nine years older than Colson had been when he left back in 1908.

Furthermore Ralph had achieved a great deal in the

first decade he'd been at Ford Park and richly deserved to rest on his laurels a good deal earlier than he did. However it was most fortunate that he did stay, for the School and for the boys;

"He soon knew every boy in the School by name and sight and a great deal about them personally ..."There can be few whom, when they left the School, he did not know intimately or who did not at some time benefit from his influence and advice."

"Idleness, on the other hand, he has always abhorred. One of the most striking characteristics of the Headmaster has been his almost amazing capacity for work. Whether as a teacher or an administrator, no pains have been too great for him, no detail too trivial to be overlooked. One has sometimes heard the complaint that here in Plymouth we have seen too little of Mr Ralph outside the precincts of the School. If this is so it has been because his whole time, his undivided interest and energy, have been devoted to the School itself."

Who knows what might have happened had he not stayed at School thoughout the war, indeed what might have happened to Plymouth College had the School not stayed in the City. Happily, any questions concerning the status and the survival of the School, had the decision been taken to evacuate, will forever remain in the realms of speculation. There can be no doubt, however, that the School's position in the City, having stayed put, and its status prior to, and throughout the war years, owed a huge amount to Herbert Ralph. When he left with his wife in the summer of '45, he too, in his heart of hearts, must have known that he had certainly done his bit for Plymouth College.

Above and opposite - A new era beckons at Ford Park as post-war Mutley Plain enjoys a spell as Plymouth's premier shopping area.

POST WAR WITH GARNONS WILLIAMS

"Plus ca change, plus c'est la meme chose"
(The opening line of Plymothian editorial Autumn Term 1945)

Inevitably the autumn term of 1945 was going to be anything but ordinary;

"This term, the first in the post-war period, has seen important changes in the School. A new headmaster, despite extravagant rumours, has acted with moderation towards all traditions. Changes there have been, but only where necessity demanded. On the staff, many who endured the war years give place to those who left on active service in 1939. While we regret the disappearance of familiar faces, we welcome back those familiar only to seniors. Meanwhile, the advent of peace, and the Labour Government have, strangely, failed to release the school field from military requirements."

"The world has not yet reached the promised era of peace and goodwill for all men. The Atom Bomb has created suspicion and discord. But, as yet, the tenor of life at Plymouth College pursues its even course and, we hope, always will, though the Atom itself shake it."

Clearly some of those changes were more a product of circumstance than of any new measures taken by the incoming Headmaster, Basil Hugh Garnons Williams. The decision to purchase *"the houses and grounds formerly used by the Mount House School, which is now at Tavistock"*, had doubtless been in the pipeline for sometime.

Mount House School, Plymouth   South Front School Group of Boy Scouts

Mount House had evacuated during the war and clearly the new location suited them. Meanwhile the Governors of Plymouth College could see potential in a growing Preparatory School in Plymouth, particularly with Mount House now out of the city. Consequently, despite the fact that the new premises at Hartley Road were not yet available – they were in the hands of the Admiralty – there was a larger-than-usual entry into the Prep, with 41 boys joining, pushing the junior school numbers up to 140. Meanwhile, with another 34 boys arriving in the first form of the Main School the total number of pupils went up to 460. However as the Headmaster noted in his Speech Day address, only 200 were over the age of thirteen *"and therefore, in comparison with other similar schools where thirteen was the normal age of entry, we should be counted as a school of 200"*. Two-thirds of the pupils, moreover, were under fifteen, which presented problems for the School when competing at senior games levels. That said, however, the new Head acknowledged that the School's record of University Scholarships and of Higher School Certificate successes was *"satisfactory"*.

*"**Very** satisfactory"* was the impression gathered by the new Head in his first few weeks in relation to another aspect of School-life;

"This is not," he proudly announced at Speech Day, *"a school consisting on the one hand of weedy intellectuals and on the other of athletic Philistines, it is a school of the all-rounder."*

More than that however, Garnons Williams wasn't really ready to say;

"Many far-reaching decisions will have to be taken which will affect the whole future of the School; but I do not wish to make declarations of policy before I have learnt more about the School."

Basil Garnons Williams was then 39. He had been born at New Radnor, Wales, in 1906 and was an old boy of Winchester College, leaving there to become a Scholar of Hertford College, Oxford, in the fall of

1945

1925. Another Classics Scholar, Garnons Williams appointment gave Plymouth College its sixth successive, classically-trained headmaster in sixty years. He came to Ford Park via Sedburgh School, where he had been appointed Classical Sixth Form Master in 1930, then Marlborough College, where he had been appointed Head of Classics in 1935. Significantly, perhaps, it was just two years before leaving Marlborough, to come to Plymouth College, that Garnons Williams, at the age of 37, married Margaret Shearme, daughter of an OPM, Commander Francis Shearme RN. The couple had a daughter soon afterwards and there was doubtless a desire on his wife's part to be even closer to her family roots.

The Headmaster, Rev Canon Spencer (Headmaster of Winchester) and Mrs Garnons Williams arriving at Speech Day 1945

Clearly Garnons Williams was looking to his own roots that Autumn too, for the Guest Speaker at his first speech day was the then current head of his Alma Mater - Winchester - the Rev Canon Spencer Leeson. Introduced by Garnons Williams as *"the most distinguished schoolmaster of his generation,"* Canon Leeson was clearly an impressive figure. He had been at Merchant Taylors School before moving to Winchester and while at MTS had overseen one of the most significant events in that School's history – the

relocation from a crowded, congested inner city site with no adjacent playing fields, in London, to the leafy reaches of Rickmansworth and Watford.

A deeply religious man (who would leave Winchester the following year to look after St Mary's Church, Southampton, and then accept the Bishopric of Peterborough in 1949), Leeson's lesson for the boys of Plymouth College that October, was that *"Knowledge is not an end in itself; it is the practical application of knowledge to everyday needs and to the needs of the future that is important."*

In conclusion, he stressed the need for religious education; *"Experience as a teacher has given me the firm conviction that without the guidance of the Almighty knowledge is dangerous and completely unavailing."*

The Lord Bishop of Exeter pursued a similar theme at the Annual Commemoration Service held. somewhat unusually, four weeks after Speech Day;

"In every school lesson, whether in the classroom, in the laboratory, or on the playing field, there is a treasure to be found. That treasure is Truth. The boy who learns to love Truth has learned a lesson that he will always remember. God is Truth and He will use men who love Truth, for the world needs them."

He then added that; *"School is not only the boys who are in it at a particular time. A school is a continuous, living society. Its past is as important as its present."*

The Bishop went on to say that he hoped that everyone present had felt a reverence for a great tradition when the Headmaster had read out the names of those past members of the School who had fallen in the war.

Of the fifty-four names now on that list it was sobering indeed to reflect on the fact that half of those men to have paid the ultimate price had left the School in the last ten years and more than a third of them had left in the three years prior to the outbreak of war. They would all have been known to those teachers now returning to Ford Park after their own active service duties.

It must indeed have been with very mixed feelings that Meyrick Jones and Hugh Dent rejoined Plymouth College that term under Garnons Williams. Glad to be back in one piece, sad that the price paid for peace was so tragically high. Clearly the reappearance of some familiar staff-room faces – they would have been new faces to most boys – meant the disappearance of others, among them the most recently arrived Pamela Coulthard who left that term to take up an appointment in Chiswick.

Clearly the idea of female teachers was purely a wartime stop-gap notion and significantly a debate was proposed, with Plympton Grammar, at the end of that term around the motion; *"That the woman's place is in the home".*

Like most of the debates that Autumn the theme was topical. On 5 October, Thorpe-Tracey successfully proposed that; *"the present Government is incapable of dealing with immediate post-war problems"* – the Government in question of course being the one elected in the first general election to be held in ten years – many had expected the Tories to be returned. In the event, however, Labour won their first ever clear majority in a landslide victory. Clement Atlee was the new Prime Minister, with Herbert Morrison, the principal architect of the Let Us Face the Future manifesto of social reform, as his No.2. One week later RE Benns was unsuccessful in his proposal that; *"the discovery of Atomic Energy was a calamity for mankind"* – the Atomic bomb had 2,000 times the blast power of Britain's Grand Slam bomb, and the Japanese claimed that 70,000 lost their lives at the Japanese shipbuilding centre of Nagasaki. Stalin immediately wanted his scientists to produce his own – over 100,000 workers had been involved on the development of the bomb *"the Manhattan Project"* in New Mexico.

The following week, on a lighter note, WWG Tompkins was similarly unsuccesful with his contention that; *"the Radio and Cinema do more harm than good".* The

results of the last two debates were probably not all that surprising given that, on the one hand, most schoolboys then derived hours of enjoyment from the Wireless and Cinema and on the other hand the Atomic bomb had precipitated the end of the war against Japan.

Interestingly enough, trawling through the College House notes, we learn that GC Lloyd *"was present on USS Missouri at the Tokio (sic) surrender"* on Sunday 2 September 1945.

USS Missouri anchored in Tokyo Bay, Japan, 2 September 1945, the day that Japanese surrender ceremonies were held on board.

Victory over Japan had actually come a couple of weeks earlier after Atomic bombs had been dropped on first Hiroshima and then Nagasaki on the 6th and 9th of August, finally forcing the Japanese to accept the terms of the Potsdam Treaty put forward at the end of July. As such the formal surrender by the Japanese Foreign Minister, in full morning dress, to the Supreme Allied Commander, General Macarthur, on Missouri, officially marked the end of the Second World War, a war that for Great Britain, had lasted only a few weeks short of six years.

Although, of course, those who had lost their lives in the war were those whose sacrifice was most in need of recording, there were some twenty or so OPMs who had won major honours during the war and while one or two of those awards were made posthumously, most were not. The OPM notes that term also included a resume of all those known to have been decorated during the previous six years.

Interestingly enough the OPM section of the Plymothian also included a piece from N.E.E. (NE Elliot or Ellis? – both were at School in the late 1920s) on another, albeit quasi-service experience, that had involved a good number of past pupils - the Home Guard. It was an organisation that the new Headmaster had himself served with – he was a 2nd Lieutenant in the 6th Battalion of the Wiltshire Home Guard. NEE's piece, however, was based on the author's experience as CSM of the Devon Home Guard, and as a chronicle of the six years of the war it read a little like a scene-setter for Dad's Army;

"The Home Guard has passed on. The number of Old Boys who have been in its ranks have been many. None of the honour and glory of the Regular Services, but just a sense of duty done. We stood down with a feeling of thankfulness and just a tinge of regret."

"We remember those early days and the anxious nights of 1940. "The Home Guard was ready" we read. I was lucky. I had a rifle and three rounds, and a forage cap,

what matter if someone else had the bayonet and the ammo did not fit, we were ready."

"Croft's pikemen were no legend. My platoon had a whole section. "They will make a nasty hole in a man" said our Major. "Take no prisoners!"

"Quite early on our shoulders became hunched and our arms bent with the wearing of pips and stripes. Our discipline was superb, and the lowest conscript was "Private". By 1941 stripes ceased to be issued to friends only of the Platoon Commander, but had to be earned, as per ACI. We no longer stood beer to the Company Quartermaster for a new tunic, for our new Regular Captain Quartermaster was strictly regular, and preferred whisky or gin."

"As time went on in the Home Guard we learned to suffer fools gladly where lethal weapons were concerned, and we thought precisely of our officers as they thought of us."

"By 1943 people had ceased to laugh at us – much. The Rocket Batteries had formed, and praise must be given to those who manned them on many a rough night. Beer was cheap at the NAAFI and a happy evening was often spent by us all."

"By 1944 most of us had become overtrained, and the Authorities decided to dispense with us and so save our wages. The Finals came in December and the Home Guard wore its uniform legally for the last Parade."

"As we marched through Hyde Park on that Grand Parade, my thoughts went back to 1940, and what might have been but for the grace of God. "Eyes left" and we saw the King – God bless him! – saluting us. His salute, fellow Home Guards, I pass on to you, and with it the salutes of high officers of the Allies and the cheers of a vast London crowd. The Guards band played us by to the tune "Old Soldiers Never Die". Yes, we were worth something, after all, and I leave you with your own happy memories, as I had mine when we marched away to the strains of "Auld Lang Syne"."

Who said satire was a sixties thing? This was 1945, the

war was over and the wave of relief that swept over the nation took on a variety of forms.

Meanwhile members of the JTC continued to train and the Corps entered a team in the Plymouth HG Rifle Club Small Bore League;

"We were placed in Division "A" and to date we have shot four matches, and although we have kept well up to our normal standard, we have lost every one," wrote the Captain of Shooting, DF Pring.

Bright young things - Dec 45. Back row; PSP Wills, FJT Harris (Major to Emmanuel), AEF Hill, AD Mortimore (Minor to Christ's), front; JD Berryman and DF Pring (Exhibition to Queens)

Pring was Captain of Boxing and was the successful candidate in the School's Mock Municipal Election held on 1st November. Standing as a "Patriot" he finished ahead of JE Abraham, Independent; RE Benns, Liberal; RAC Hender, Communist; HRS Rundle, Labour and SF Thorpe-Tracey, Conservative.

A few months earlier, in the General Election, three past pupils of the School were elected as MPs; F Seymour Cocks, held his Socialist seat for the Broxstowe Division of Nottingham; Commander Douglas Marshall, RN,

was elected Conservative Member for the Bodmin Division of Cornwall and Wilson Harris, editor of the Spectator, was elected Independent Member for Cambridge University.

There was a good Plymouth College representation at Cambridge that year; *"Thanks to the return of three of our number from war service, we claim that we now have the record number of nine OPMs resident at the University"*, with Clarke, Dodd and Trounson among the newest recruits.

The Oxford letter, meanwhile, expressed the hope that *"Dat Deus Incrementum"* may *"be true in the very near future"*. The missive also informed those schoolboys reading it that; *"the first fortnight of a "fresher's" life is still occupied in throwing into the fire all the pamphlets of Oxford's countless societies and rebuffing their College representatives"*.

The usual contributions aside, however, perhaps the most distinguishing feature of the Christmas 1945 Plymothian was the unprecedented number of pages – seven – given over to that season's rugby report.

"In the little world of the School Rugger, as in the world at large, this has been a season of reconstruction, and though the work has advanced, much yet remains to be done. The field is still straitened and disfigured by the remnants of its defences against raids; officialdom is ready with brave words about the needs of youth, but surprisingly dilatory in action. Kit of all kinds is still rationed and very difficult to obtain; it is probable, too, that the present diet of the average growing boy is insufficient to give him the vigour and robustness that Rugger demands. Travel is still difficult, but we have been able to arrange more games against schools, and look forward to the resumption of other pre-war rivalries."

However, notwithstanding all that, the small, but keen, squad produced some fine performances; *"At home we are so far unbeaten; had we been able to field our best XV throughout the season, we might well have also*

avoided defeat away."

The scalps of Sutton, St Boniface, Kelly, Launceston, and Truro School were all claimed at Ford Park, while there was a draw with Devonport High School, in which both sides failed to score. Happily PMC won the return at the Rectory 17-3. Service sides, RNATE and RNEC, and Old Public Oaks were also beaten at Ford park while Kingsbridge were given a close run, which was impressive considering that they were *"not a boys' team as we had expected, but their town side"*.

JF Spear was the Captain for most of the season and led by example, while the whole team generally acquitted themselves well;

"Much of the success has been due to the patient coaching of Mr Stanley Hurrell, the former Devonport Albion and Devon player." The Headmaster however was keen to point out that *"natural modesty has presented the author of the above account, Mr WH Savage, from saying how much of the success of the First XV has been a well-merited reward for his unfailing enthusiasm and skill in coaching"*.

Juicy (as in *"Do You See"* - a pet expression) Jones was also back to help with the Rugby and gradually the world was starting to return to normal.

In the Prep, Messrs Firman and Westhead had returned and so, slowly, Plymouth College settled back into a less disrupted routine, although such is not to say that there was no disruption involved in an environment where old faces were returning and more recent ones leaving, most notably the entire wartime female contingent.

"Had I not ...

Four or five women once that tended me?"

Was the intriguing quote that opened the Editorial of the first Plymothian of 1946. The quote was from Shakespeare's The Tempest and was significant on more than one count;

Firstly, it was the second stab at Shakespeare the School had had in recent years, as Mr Jackson *"followed Miss Coulthard's brave lead"* in tackling the bard.

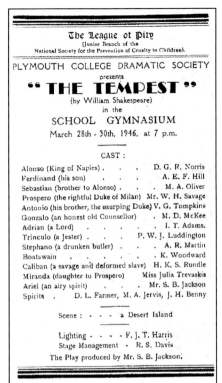

Plymouth College Dramatic Society take on Shakespeare with a bit of encouragement from the young OPM English master Scratch Jackson

Oriel (Nelly) Butcher, a Great War graduate from Cardiff University, with her husband Edward. Mrs Butcher taught English and Latin, and Edward, a former Barbarian and a founder of Plymouth Cricket Club, coached voluntarily at Ford park during the war.

OPM John Spear and Kelly College old boy Nigel Radford come together on the staff at Ford Park.

Spear, plus 31 year old history and Latin master Nigel Radford – both of them also fresh from serving their King and Country.

Secondly it was noteworthy that the master in question did not follow either Miss Coulthard's lead or that of Shakespeare himself, by casting only men – or rather boys – in the female parts. And thirdly, and perhaps most pointedly of all, the quote was pertinent because *"by the time this issue appears in print we shall have said farewell to the ladies who have filled the breach in the absence of the regular staff, all but two of whom will have returned from war service."*

All of the ladies *"have done most noble and useful work and have earned the respect and admiration of their pupils and colleagues alike,"* continued the editorial, adding; *"It will not be invidious to single out Mrs Butcher for special mention. She has given the School loyal service for over five years, and there are very few boys in the school now who have not at some time received instruction from her."*

Nelly Butcher, Marjorie Sykes and Mrs Hudson were then the last three to leave, following the earlier departures of Kathleen Goad and Pamela Coulthard. Who could have guessed that it would be another twenty years before there would, again, be regular classes taught by a female staff member and thirty years before there would be a full-time, female appointment?

Clearly, however, a clue to the male psyche of the time was implicit in the motion put before the House by the Literary and Debating Society, later that year, long after the ladies had gone. That motion? *"That Genius and Women have never been allied."*

As it happened there were markedly more comings than goings that year. In the Spring, MacDonald Porter, *"back from the Army"*, and Ian Edwards *"from the RAF"* joined Jones and Dent in the growing ranks of returning servicemen in the staff room. The summer saw the return of Barnes, Battrick and Dundas *"from Active Service"* and alongside them a very familiar *"old face"* at Ford Park – that of 30 year-old John

On leaving Plymouth College John Spear had obtained a degree from Durham and then secured a teaching post in Leatherhead School in Surrey before being called up. His contemporary, Nigel Radford, was another local lad and had been educated at Kelly College, indeed he and JRS could feasibly have met on the sports field as schoolboys. Radford had completed his education at Exeter College, Oxford, before taking a teaching appointment at Mount House School.

Another new appointee, destined to divide his time between the old Mount House site and Ford Park, was Leslie F Wills. Wills was originally appointed to the Prep staff in the first term of 1946, but come the winter of '46 it was announced that he had *"extended his activities to the Main School."*

New art master - Leslie Wills

"To many he needs no introductions. His pictures and photography have done more than introduce him to the School. His name is known far and wide."
Clearly his appointment did much to enhance the standing of the art department at the School, both at Junior, then Senior level, and doubtless Wills' essay on *"The Place of Art in Education"* had helped sway Garnons Williams in his decision to secure the services of the experienced 45 year-old for the older boys, as well as the younger ones.

In an expanding School, the wider the range of alternatives Plymouth College could offer Post-War Plymouth the better, and Wills' philosophy seemed ideally suited to the situation;

"In the general development of the mind the study of Art and the appreciation of Art must take a very definite place in a liberal education," was how he opened the first of several regular contributions to the Plymothian.

"It must be more than the display of a skill in the ability to draw and paint in imitation of nature and design; it must be used to see and understand the beauties and purposes of everything which surround us in our daily lives."

Historically "Art" had not played a very great part in the syllabus of Plymouth College and judging from his opening gambit that first term, and his subsequent rants in the Magazine, Wills was on a one-man mission to change that situation;

"The ability to draw lies not with the hand but with the mind which controls the hand. Dexterity in the handling of a pencil or brush can soon be acquired with practice. The Art Master does not teach a student to draw so much as how to see and think. Everyone can draw after a fashion, but some can produce only a meaningless scribble; from a mental vacuum nothing worthwhile can be expected. An artist has acquired a technique by practice, and is usually able to demonstrate this to others. Each person desiring to paint will develop his or her own technique and means of expression."

It was most unusual, if not altogether unheard of, for any master, apart from those involved in sport, to so actively campaign on behalf of their subject within the pages of the Plymothian and so it was little wonder that his words, and actions, had an impact on the Headmaster.

In his first full term of joint-school duties Wills had brought in both the Principal of the Plymouth School of Art, Lewis Duckett, and the Curator of the Museum and Municipal Art Gallery, AA Cummings, to speak to the boys ... *"both kindly gave a lecture on the value of Art in daily life as seen from their own perspective."*

John Bill

Another master brought in that year, whose duties were divided between the upper and lower sections of the School was another newly-demobbed man, 35 year-old John Bill. A former pupil of Bishop's Stortford School in Hertfordshire, Bill had studied Classics and Music at Braesnose College, Oxford, just four years before the arrival there of an Australian undergraduate, Alaistair Davies.

Davies had gone to Geelong Grammar School in Victoria, before coming halfway around the world to study Modern History at Oxford. Like John Bill, he too was fresh from the Services which meant that by the end of 1946 a dozen members of the Common Room had a war record.

Whatever common bond that gave them, doubtless, had little obvious impact on the pupils. The arrival of the last two staff members however, coincided with the departures of Horace Meek, who had been appointed the year the war had begun and was now moving to Brentwood School, and RPG Chesshire, who started at Plymouth College at the beginning of 1946 and who

left, bound for Dean Close School, Cheltenham, before the year had ended.

Someone who'd left the School nine years earlier was Lionel Lord. Clearly none of the boys at School in 1946 would have remembered him, however he'd been at Plymouth College some fifteen years and doubtless many OPMs would have been saddened that Spring to learn of his early death, at the age of forty-seven. LC (Elsie) Lord had left to take up the Headship of Bury Grammar School and had died in harness, leaving a wife and two children.

Lord's wasn't the only death reported in the pages of the Plymothian that year; additionally there was Lady Munday, the wife of Sir William Munday, Chairman of the Governors, and Admiral Sir William Eric Campbell Tait, the Governor of Southern Rhodesia. Campbell Tait had left Plymouth College at the age of fifteen in 1901 and had joined the Navy the following year.

"During the 1914-18 war he served in the battleships Collingwood and Malaya, where he was shipmates with HM King George VI. He was promoted Commander in 1921, Captain in 1926, Rear-Admiral in 1938, Vice Admiral in 1941 and Admiral in 1945. From 1942-44 he was Commander-in-Chief, African Station."

Of the younger OPMs there were also reported the deaths of a further eight Old Boys *"who have been killed or who have died on active service"* as the names of Bearne, Floyd, Eslick, Hutchings, Martin, Parker, Sweet and Waterhouse were added to the list of fallen. This brought the tragic total to sixty-two, some forty of whom had left School since 1933 and who would have been known to those staff returning from War Service. Throughout 1946 donations continued to come in for the Plymouth College Memorial to commemorate the all-too brief lives of these young men, most of whom would still have been under thirty in 1946. To put the figures in the global context, they look small overall -fifty-five million people around the world were killed during the course of the war between 1939 and 1945 -

but in the context of one small school in the South West of England, the losses were heavy.

But it wasn't all doom and gloom, there were more honours to celebrate, including a GCB *"a very high honour rarely attained by a member of the Civil Service"* for Sir Alexander Maxwell, a contemporary of Campbell Tait, who was also a Governor of the School.

For Old Boys of all ages though, 1946 saw a revival in many social and sporting activities;

A reunion dinner was held at Goodbody's Café early in the year, on 23 January, and forty members paid their 6/- for a ticket. Two months later the school gymnasium, *"gaily bedecked with flags, echoed with the sounds of revelry by night, when the Club revived its annual dance"*.

"The Rugby side has been restarted and is carrying out a full fixture list. The Chairman (AWC Lyddon) and Committee surmounted the untold difficulties of obtaining a suitable pitch, together with the necessary changing accommodation" – this new ground belonged to the National Playing Fields Assocation and was at Elburton.

"The Hockey enthusiasts, in their turn, have reformed", they too were looking for a pitch to call home,

"The question of playing pitches again brings to mind the suggestion that it would be ideal if a suitable ground could be obtained and shared by the many outdoor sport sections. It is hoped that this important acquisition may take place in the not too distant future, and afford the amenities of club premises for all interests."

Although nobody was necessarily hoping that such a facility might include a golf course a Golf Section was also started, with T Arthur Pearn its point of contact. Among the other items on the wish list were hopes that OPM tennis, swimming and rifle-shooting teams might be formed soon. Meanwhile, off the sports field, there was news of the newly-established OPM Masonic Lodge, with WHJ Priest, a School Governor and current Deputy Lord Mayor, as its first Master.

There was *"gratifying"* news too of the revival of the London Branch of the Old Boys Association, while some fifteen members turned up for the *"terminal gathering of OPMs in Cambridge"*.

There was also a comparatively healthy number of Old Boys at Exeter with *"no less than five of our number playing in the College, Rugby and Hockey teams. We sometimes hear of Godfrey Heywood (who is in our enemy's camp at St Luke's College), and were quite relieved when we found he was not playing against us in the Rugger match."*

The OPM Cricket team, of course, were fortunate enough to have the use of the School Field. The side managed an impressive twenty-six matches in their first post-war season, winning fifteen and only losing five, *"mainly due to the good bowling of GH Bonser and WH Heywood"*. The latter's son, the aforementioned Godfrey, turned out regularly towards the end of the season, *"and keeping wicket consistently well"*.

For all the successes enjoyed by Old Boy sides that year however, it was anything but a vintage year for the School.

The Rugby and Hockey early that academic year hadn't been too bad but as the year progressed and certain senior boys left, either for Oxbridge or National Service so we found the average age of the School first teams dropping back down to wartime levels and below. In 1945 the average age of that star side had been 17.2, in 1946 it dropped down to 16.7 the second lowest it had been since 1940 and the results started to show it. Twice the XI were beaten by older sides 6-0, all six goals conceded against RNEC at Keyham being conceded in one ten minute spell. Results against school sides were more encouraging with Exeter School beaten, Kelly drawn and Plympton Grammar – one won, one lost. It didn't help AEF Hill's captaincy however that he didn't have a consistent line-up. The problems for the 2nd's were even greater and the regular pinching of players by the firsts meant that *"it was impossible to keep eleven boys together"*. It was no great surprise therefore that the 2nd XI lost all eight of their fixtures.

Most successful of all was the Colts U15 side which won five of its seven games, but *"with five of the 1st XI and nine of the 2nd XI under 16 there was no point in running an under 16 Colts team."*

When it came to the time to get out the flannels and wield the willow, the situation hadn't improved any.

Back; S Liddicoat, D Berry, W Coyte, M Lunn. Middle; C Heath, FN Lyon, RH Palk, PD Smith, WJS. Front; PMD and Anon.

The 1946 1st XI cricket team recorded the least wins, the most defeats and the least runs of any of the School sides of the 1940s to date, even though they played more games than three of their equivalents. Not one player managed a double figure batting average, not one scored forty, let alone fifty or a ton and on one occasion the School were skittled out for 25 by Exeter. Although even less impressively the 2nd's were dismissed by Sutton for just 15 and Truro School dispatched the Colts XI for just 10. A vintage year it wasn't, although Lunn, Liddicoat, Dunkley and Sumner all bowled well, with the first two both taking eight wickets in a match, Lunn for just 13 against RNB and Liddicoat for 35 against Plympton.

"The call-up robbed us of DF Pring and only seven of last year's 2nd XI remained to form the nucleus of a side," wrote a resigned but not dispirited Eric Holman, who concluded his Cricket report for the year with a random review of the previous six years;

"From Dunkirk to Bread Points is a pretty solid chunk out of all our lives, yet that stretch represents the period during which the writer has watched over the School games. Daylight alerts – bombs and Yanks and A.A. guns – Gresham's and King's and Frank Woolley – the Australians "'aving a gow at it" – services sides in khaki – HMS Glasgow back from the beaches with JSG Hicks – the 1945 XI's and the crowds – IM Clarke and JR Brazier – it's all been very good fun, and infinitely worth while ... Curtain."

Things could only get better, but not quite yet. Clearly the signs were not good for the athletics season, and neither, for the Inter-School Sports, was the weather;

"Conditions could not have been much worse, a heavy drenching rain fell throughout the afternoon, making matters uncomfortable for competitors, officials and spectators alike. On a sodden track times were slow – the Hurdles was scratched, and the winner of the 880 yards completed the course with no shoes!"

Needless to say he wasn't a Plymouth College boy, as the School finished a familiar fourth out of five;

"Any assessment of our performance must take into account age and the highly individual effort called for in Athletics; it would seem that the top places in this contest invariably go either to the natural athlete or to a competitor so practised as to be almost professional in his showing. We are temporarily short on the former, and it is a moot point having regard to our circumstances, as to whether we are justified in going to extreme lengths of specialisation with a single individual. We think not."

Such considerations were irrelevant, of course, when it came to the School Sports at Ford Park, where, in terms of training at least, all boys were competing on a relatively level playing field.

Although just one week after the disappointing events and weather at Kelly, the conditions for the School sports were *"perfect"* and few could have enjoyed the day more than AEF Hill who won the discus and all three of the sprints, earning the title of Victor Ludorum along the way. DG Sheeres ran him close, but it was WJ Sumner who finished Proxime Accessit winning the hurdles and the hop, step and jump. The Captain of Athletics, CD Heath, won the long jump, while MA Oliver set a new record (5'1") in the high jump. TW Storey was the Junior champion while OWA Daw finished at the front of a field of 21 to win the newly-revived Old Boys Race. The one-mile winner, GA Rogers, finished ahead of a similar number the following day – Thursday 28 March - to take the Cross Country title, an event which, it was hoped, *"will be the last one to take place over roads ... it is up to the people in charge in 1947 to make the requisite efforts to organise a country race".*

Of the other sports staged that Spring, DF Pring, in his last term, led Sargents to success in the House Fives Championship. *"We made many attempts to arrange an inter-school match,"* he wrote, as Captain of Fives, *"but the arrangements always fell through."*

Described as a *"good all round player who has so many interests in games that he has scarcely time to improve his Fives."* The anonymous eulogist went on to add, *"As it is, he is in a different class from all his contemporaries."*

Among his other duties the aforementioned Pring was also Captain of Boxing and here again attempts to arrange an inter-school contest came to nothing *"but this will surely come if only we persist in our endeavours to maintain boxing as an active part of our Games' organization."* DFP continued, *"Every one will wish to congratuate JR Brazier, the School's first Colour, on his distinguished award of a Panther Colour at Oxford."*

Plymouth College Boxing Team: Back; J Palmer, P Berryman, P Vaughan, C Lean, P Flanders, A Harvey Front; C Arscott, P Spriddell, D Pring J Stone, J Goatley.

As it transpired three School boxers won their colours that year; JD Stone (Bantamweight Champ), PH Spriddell (Welterweight) and DF Pring himself, who won the Lightweight title by beating P Chislett.

Chislett's specialist area though was in the School Bath, where he finshed first in the 50 and 500 yard races. He also won the backstroke and came second to the boy who finished Proxime Accessit to him, NK Bennett, in the 100 yards.

With John Spear back at Ford Park it was inevitable perhaps that activity in the pool would increase and in his notes that summer JRS commented that *"for the first time possibly in its history, the Bath has been open to the whole School",* although he then added that *"a cold May and a sunless June have, to date, prevented overcrowding".*

The undoubted star of the Water Polo team in his own day, it was also no surprise to see JRS steering the School team to reasonable success. They won four of their five galas and half of their water polo matches (all of them against non-School sides) with five of the School VII (Chislett, Berryman, Bennett, Sumner and Luddington) all playing for the Plymouth Amateur Junior team that went on to win the Devon County Junior Shield.

It was also no great wonder that the School Scout Troop won the Local Association Swimming Sports at Mount Wise, for this was another area of School activity that JRS had much enjoyed and contributed to whilst he was a pupil in the School. WD McD Porter was back in charge of the troop as Scoutmaster, but John Spear's influence was obvious and in the Autumn term he was made Assistant Scoutmaster and Troop numbers grew to eighty-seven, necessitating the creation of three new patrols – Eagles, Hawks and Kestrels.

Over half of the Scouts attended the annual Camp, under Hugh Dent, at Lewannick, after the Troop Leader earlier in the year had said that; *"it cannot be over-emphasised that camping forms an integral part of Scouting".* The weather at Lewannick however, *"was not altogether favourable, thus giving full experience of the vicissitudes of camping under not-so-perfect conditions"*

The rain also affected the endeavours of the Wednesday afternoon tennis players. *"A reasonably high standard of play has been attained and (unofficial) House matches have been played. These matches noticeably increased enthusiasm and fostered a desire to improve one's play rather than play solely for enjoyment."* The anonymous report (by Sheere?) then went on to a familiar plea; *"It is, then, sincerely hoped that tennis will soon be made an official School sport."*

Like so many other activities, those of the JTC also fell foul of the weather that summer;

"Field Day this term (14 June) was to have included a patrol exercise and a demonstration by 27 Training Regt. RA. The Troop of 25 –pounders and an Air OP both came a considerable distance to perform on the airfield at Yelverton. Fortunately the rain just held off enough to let the demonstration of gun drills and fire control finish, although the plane was hampered by low cloud. But uniforms and spirits were very dampened by midday, and the exercise was called off."

Like so many other sections the JTC had returned to its pre-war situation; *"Captain Barnes MC, has resumed command; Captain Hill once again, has cheerfully agreed to serve as second in command. Lieut Dufton has resigned, but continues to help with musketry."*

There was one even more significant piece of news in this section though, namely that; *"The War Office has finally agreed that holders of Certificate "A" should wear their Red Star when they join the Army proper, and continue to be thus distinguished until their training period is finished. This outward and visible award for work done will also serve to indicate to instructors those recruits who have had previous training."*

"Since most boys, on leaving school," wrote Captain Barnes, *"will find themselves in one of the Services for up to two years any assistance in rapid promotion is valuable. The moral is that every boy in a school lucky enough to possess a JTC should be a hard-working member of that JTC."*

Here we had the first clear reference to the period of National Service that would be the lot of 2.5 million young Britons over the next eighteen years. Every week some 6,000 new recruits would be called up to do their bit, some more readily and more willingly than others. The clear message here from Charlie Barnes was - join the JTC at School, get your Cert.A and you'd have a head start.

And just as camping was an integral part of Scouting so too it was important to the JTC experience, and to the attainment of that Cert A. So it was a welcome move when, for the first time since 1938, Southern Command decided to stage a JTC Camp at the Royal Military College, Sandhurst.

And the verdict? *"It certainly lived up to all expectations,"* wrote HR (H Roskruge?). *"Mornings and afternoons were taken up by exercises, and marches to the training ground, in addition to Saddleback Hill, will always be remembered."*

"Captain Barnes and Captain Hill did a great deal to

make the camp a success, also CSM Harris, Sergeant Kennedy and Corporal Bell for their part. Last, but by no means least, "Pro". We really did not recognise his value until he left us – and then we saw how much we missed him: especially when it came to cleaning rifles."

CLB also had a few words about the rest of the JTC equipment; *"In our pre-war dress our original association with the 60th Devon and Cornwall Territorials was shown by the cap badge (Devon) and buttons (Cornwall). The cap badge we still wear, the buttons have gone. But it is proposed to wear a lanyard and a patch, behind the cap-badge, both of Light Infantry green."*

And there was more, later in the year; *"New equipment has been issued; uniform supply is much better, the boot problem has disappeared, and greatcoats are on the way. Financial considerations do not permit real generosity in the equipping of cadets, but with the removal of those practical obstacles and the first-rate "Q" work of Cpl Benns, one's pride in the appearance of the contingent on parade should soon be restored."*

The Corps wasn't the only area in School about to benefit from a bit of investment; *"The equipment and furniture of the school will also be improved,"* said the Headmaster at Speech Day (22 October 1946), adding the qualification; *"though affluence will not be sought".*

The incentive, and doubtless the wherewithal, for this came from an increase in numbers that Autumn term, prompting *"a bevy of new desks".*

Figures that Garnons Williams was looking towards were a maximum of 170 pupils for the Prep, in their soon-to-be-occupied premises at Hartley Road, and a proposed increase in *"the numbers in Big School by 30 a year, till the total of 520 is reached."*

"This increase," he said, *"should make possible a larger staff, with closer attention to the individual needs of pupils in the curriculum."*

The Preparatory School pose for what would appear to be their final full photograph at Ford Park before the move up to Hartley Road. John Cundy is sitting two to the left of Leslie Wills, IDW Wright is to the right of Wills, then Ian Edwards, Mrs Hill, Mr Westhead, Mr Firman, Miss Beare, 'Bill' Sykes, Mrs Court-Hampton, Mr Parks, then Mike Cundy, Gerald Pengelly and David Webb.

Speech Day, as well as being a vehicle for the Annual Distribution of Prizes and a speech by the celebrated Liberal Distributionist, Sir Henry Slesser, was an opportunity for the Head, and others, to thank Charles Serpell for his 38 years service as Clerk to the Board of Governors. Mr Serpell had started his connection with the College as a boy of nine back in 1879, when the School had been open for just two years and before the Main School building had even been completed. In 1887 and 1888, just before leaving the School, he had been editor of the Plymothian. Retaining an active interest in the School after leaving, he was elected a Governor in 1905, a post he resigned from three years later to take up the role of Clerk. *"In that role he has been associated with five headmasters,"* said Garnons Williams, *"the youngest of them has been here little over a year, but that has been long enough for him to gain some conception of what the school owes to him".*

Unusually, but by no means inappropriately, Mr Serpell was succeeded in his position by his son Roger, another Old Boy.

Doubtless both Serpells, senior and junior, would have enjoyed Sir Henry's speech, homing in, as it did, on the virtues of the study of History, *"and with it, Philosophy ... a subject which, apparently the ordinary man could very well do without."*

From his early appointments, from his choice of speaker and from his involvement with particular, extra-curricular activities at School it was apparent that Garnons Williams was cast in the mould of a true Classicist.

A couple of visits from the Lord Mayor, Isaac Foot, one of the most inspired and inspiring local figures to wear that chain of office, helps confirm that picture as do his chess exploits.

The recently-departed Mr Gould had revived chess in the School on his arrival in 1940 and Hugh Dent, writing from his Services outpost, had expressed support for it.

Now, back at School, Dent was keen to take the club further and *"an eight-board match was arranged with the Ford Park Amateur Chess Club, which the School team succeeded in winning by five games to three".*

Significantly both Dent and Garnons Williams were in the Ford Park team, with the Head being one of the three members of the opposition to register a win. Mr Dent lost to Lean. *"Thus we avenged the defeat we suffered at their hands last term,"* wrote the Hon Sec, DG Sheeres who was the Head's opponent.

The School were also successful against Devonport High School, *"whose Chess Club, like our own, has only recently started."*

In the terms that followed Mrs Dent and Mr and Mrs Roger Serpell appeared within the ranks of the Ford Park Amateurs, along with Mr Barnes and Dr Ellingher.

Further matches were arranged with DHS and Sutton High School, however, as the new academic year started, and although a high level of enthusiasm was maintained, the standard of play slipped a little. In three eight-board matches the School only won four games, a young TEJ Savery being the only one to be unbeaten in two games.

Staff members Meek and Dufton, as Chairman and Guest Speaker respectively, lent their support to the Philatelic Society. Mr Dufton *"gave a most interesting talk and exhibited his stamps to the Society",* in the Spring term. Later that year, in the Autumn term, the newly-elected Chairman, Dr Ellingher, entertained members with a talk on *"collecting stamps on covers".*

Numbers were up in the new School year and young members were no doubt encouraged by the presence of the new President of the Philatelic Society, Mr Garnons Williams himself.

Across the board generally, not just the chequered, chess variety, the new Head was seen to be taking a very visible part in the School's extra-curricular activities, so too was the Prep Head with the new media playing a prominent part. Musical Appreciation Evenings

were inaugurated in Big School courtesy of the new art master's apparatus for playing gramophone recordings. *"Things To Listen To This Week"* was another innovation, with boys flagging up what was worth tuning in to on the wireless each week. CF Davies was the first editor and reported that *"odd questions at odd times to this one and that one have proved that boys are listening".* Rediffusion was installed that spring and *"used regularly ... It is an asset, and the musical lessons are good, the travel talks most interesting and valuable."*

Television was still some years away from the westcountry, but the role of film was becoming increasingly difficult to ignore.

"It was a matter of some interest to read that at a conference of educational bodies in February of this year educational film policy was discussed in a lively fashion. Broadly speaking it was maintained that there should be a yearly programme, and that the business should receive State subsidy. The British Film Institute indicated its attitude by maintaining that not only would films be made under direct Governmental sponsorship but that valuable films would be made by some of the great industrial concerns and commercial companies."

"As with other mechanical aids to education, so with the cinematograph. Unless it is used widely and hand in hand with the more usual methods of attack, it is valueless. In the Junior School in general, and in particular in the Preparatory School here, a projector would be of greatest value. To be able to make use of films, such as are going to be available, could only have one result – a more lively interest in the subject."

"Apparatus is at present very hard to get, although, even now, films are available. One ventures to write this in the hope that there may be someone who may be able to assist in getting hold of a projector. One is seeking co-operation in a matter which is considered to be of great importance – particularly at the beginning of what seems to be a new educational era."

Plymouth College.

Oct 1946.

Whatever the technological advances that were being made in the classroom there could be no doubt that a new educational era was dawning for the Prep. However, the path to the Mount House site was proving to be far from smooth. The field there was still churned up and there were unforeseen last-minute delays with regard to the move, although not with regard to the development of the School itself. Indeed the programme of development for the lower school meant that by the spring term of 1946 the pressure on space had forced expansion of the Prep into Shaftesbury Villa *"where Div. II has its classroom, and it is prophesied that another form, Div I, will be in that building in September"*

At the same time it was hoped that Munday House (as the Mount House site was now known) might be ready for occupation by September. However, despite the fact that the Admiralty had at last vacated the premises it still wasn't ready in time. Moreover, *"in view of the food situation, it has been decided to allow the playing field there to continue to be used for allotments"*.

The Spring term found the Prep still at Ford Park, it also found a number of other unforeseen problems; *"Snow, frost, rain ... measles and chicken pox. Such things in succession are enough to make any Winter Term a poor one, but they make the so-called Spring Term just shocking. The Spring Term is never a good one, but the 1947 flavour to it will not be forgotten in a long time."*

There were other problems caused by the cold snap, among them those occasioned by the attendant fuel crisis; *"two recitals of records have had to be postponed till next winter: one by Mr Wills and one "A Boy's Choice"."*

Mr Firman's Prep notes then took a more positive line; *"This is the last term for the Preparatory School in Ford Park. To some of us it will be very odd to be outside the School precincts. But the change of surroundings, more spacious class-rooms, and a hundred other*

things, not to forget our own swimming bath – these are all things, I think, to which we look forward. Work at Munday House is going on apace, so that next term we may open there on April 26th. Architects, builders, and myself all hope that there will be no delay in beginning term. We hope to be working in Munday House by the time this is published."

They weren't. The move therefore was to come too late for Mrs Hill, who had left the Prep when she had married in 1938, only to return to the Staff at the outbreak of war. Now she had decided to give up teaching altogether; *"It is with very great regret that we bid her farewell. Her patience is proverbial, her technique unsurpassable, and her forbearance with Division III never to be equalled."*

Her departure opened the door for Mr Kirke. Fresh from war service with the RAF, Kirke was a former pupil of Sherborne and student from Keble – where he was *"Coxswain of the Oxford University Eight in 1937"*. In his first term *"he has been doing some very hard and most useful work with Remove "A" and "B" boxers."*

At the beginning of the Summer Term, Mr LSR Coombe joined the Prep staff. A Cambridge graduate, Coombe had previously been teaching at King Edward VI Grammar School in Totnes.

With pupil numbers at both the Prep and the Main School increasing, pressure on the existing playing fields was also bound to be on the increase.

"The static water tank has gone," the rugger report read that winter, *"but limitations of time and space still made it hard to give the mass of boys as many games as we should like."*

Clearly this had been partly why the OPMs had found themselves a new pitch at Elburton. However the School's first game of the 46/47 season, saw the OPMs at Ford park once more.

Played on the 28 September, *"in summer weather"*, the teams *"stood in silence for a minute in memory of the*

OPM players who lost their lives in the war".
"The few experienced players in the School XV played well, but the newcomers were obviously a little bewildered by the speed of the game."

Plymouth College 1st XV - 1946-47: Back, CE Blackler, SP Hopkins, AP Helsing, HW Roskruge. Middle; DG Rice, TN Storey, FR Webber, TI Adams, JW Ricks. Front PWJ Luddington, P Berryman, DG Sheeres, P Chislett, DEG Perry.

The School lost 35-3 in a game sadly indicative of the season to come, with more than four points conceded for everyone scored. Once again there was a shortage of older boys and players were often snatched from the seconds who in turn had a severe shortage of fixtures – only three games were played. Meanwhile the 1st's won only two of their eleven matches, against Launceston and Sutton, but lost key home games to DHS, Hele's (Exeter) and Shebbear, and only managed a draw with Kelly. Sheeres, the Captain, Berryman and Roskruge were among the stars, and had Rundle not been called up early in the season things might have been a little different. Indeed some games were very close, but on five outings the firsts failed to score at all and the season was a disappointing one.

So it was to be, too, for the Hockey team, which also suffered from the, albeit temporary, loss of their Captain, through injury, for the opening games of the season. Like the contemporary rugby side only two wins were managed all season, but this was the second youngest side of the forties to date and the season was badly affected by the weather.

Plymouth College Hockey 1st XI - 1947, Back; M Lunn, AP Hesling, TI Adams, RE Benns. Middle; HW Roskruge, CB Arscott, P Berryman (Captain), GA Rogers, PM Dunkley. Front; GR White and DEG Perry.

In the event only eight games were played, the lowest number in seven seasons, and yet the six defeats suffered represented the highest number of losses in that time. The two inter-school games though, against Plympton and Kelly, were both won and in fairness the other matches were all against older more experienced sides – the Old Boys among them. The last game of the season this Past v Present fixture was staged for the first time in seven years and Eric Holman arranged a convivial tea afterwards. The Old Boys, whose ranks included recent leavers Skinnard and Palk and a couple of older old boys like Snell and Annear, who had left in the twenties, won narrowly, 3-2. Berryman, Rodgers, Dunkley, Roskruge and Perry all aquitted themselves well, but it wasn't just inexperience that had an impact on play and performance. Fixtures for all teams were extensively curtailed by the snow that fell in the early part of 1947. Many games were simply cancelled, one

or two perhaps should have been, viz the 2nd XI match against Tavistock Grammar, at Tavistock on January 29.

"Most of the game was played in a blinding snowstorm, and while thoroughly enjoyable to both sides and freely enlivened by comedy, provided little or no test of hockey". The school lost 4-3, incidentally.

The snow wasn't confined to the Westcountry either and both the Oxford and Cambridge letters made reference to how *"our native clime ill befits us for such Arctic sports ... skating, tobogganing and rowing through ice-floes".*

"The snow has blanketed all," wrote a snowbound "Oxoniensis". Meanwhile, in that same issue, Plymothian editor VWG Tompkins made mention of a letter *"questioning the interest of University Letters".* The same editorial referred to a piece in The Times deploring the low standard of School Magazines generally and, somewhat tongue in cheek, Tompkins invited readers to contribute to sending a delegate to the forthcoming Annual Convention of the Scholastic Press Association in New York.

But, however it compared with other school magazines, this particular Plymothian was well up to its own standards, both in terms of society and sports reports and original contributions; although here, too, the snow made an impact:

"As I looked out on morning's light,
I saw a most surprising sight:
The snow had fallen through the night,
And covered all the earth."

Part of AJL Barnes' poem that won second prize in a Prep Poetry Competition.

"We suspect," ran the editorial reference to the white stuff, *"that the Staff really welcomed the snow for the chance it gave them to parade the exotic garments acquired in their country's service; and we understand that even Seniors, sheltered by the shadows of a friendly night, participated in a snow fight."*

A more attractive option perhaps than doing Prep, certainly it was according to the "Special Committee" reporting on the state of Plymouth College:

"The committee deplored the fact that many schoolmasters still persist with old-fashioned "Prep". It is argued that the radio has supplanted "Prep" just as the cinema replaced the penny reading. The modern master should "set" Dick Barton as regular homework, and test his pupils each morning by a "Quiz" with the usual cash prizes. It is visualised that in the near future "Itma" will be accepted as a main subject in the School Certificate, with "Merry-Go-Round" as a "subsid"."

From the golden age of radio BBC's forties favourites Dick Barton with Noel Johnson the first in the title role in October 1946 and ITMA with Tommy Handley and Hugh Morton.

This same theme was revisited in June when a Quiz was held in Big School *"on some pretext connected with Hospital Week".*

"The audience was lively and co-operative, and sang with evident appreciation the song which enjoined them to "Forget its wet, ignore the prep., and try to win the dough, Have a Go, Have a Go"!"

"The first item was "Twenty Questions". This enabled Mr Barnes to draw on the board a famous pipe, a certain scout hat, and a Pavilion Lunch. This was followed by the Quiz proper. The inquisitor was no Wilfred Pickles, and relied on a slight extension of the peculiar technique which he has evolved in the attempt to inculcate Latin Grammar into IVa, brow beating

and at times hand beating his victims, and showing an undue interest in their private diversions."

"He met his deserts when Mr Mercer, a recalcitrant victim, seized him by the neck and questioned him instead. Dissatisfied with the replies, Mr Mercer ordered him to sing like Bing Crosby, and then to imitate a ventriloquist, with a boy as the dummy."

After more questions and more singing, "The Quiz finished with the singing of the "Quiz Song". Big School may have heard nobler utterances and sweeter music, but not for a long time has it resounded with such hearty laughter, and thanks are due to all the masters concerned for providing an hour's good entertainment."

The return of Mr Mercer was a welcome one across all aspects of school life, especially the sporting life, which, did not, on the face of it, look too good, and at this distance it would appear to have been enough to make any Games Master weep, but Ted Mercer was not just "any Games Master".

"The last of the staff to return from military duties" the delayed reappearance of Mr EC Mercer meant that two men, both OPMs, had spent a term each temporarily at Plymouth College; JC Read in the Winter Term (1946) and JW Trobridge, Spring Term (1947 – having just returned from Italy he was filling in part of his demob leave and was about to take up articles with Norman Sitters' law practice), but now the much respected master was back and in the Summer Plymothian he set out his stall in a way no other master had done before (with the possible exception of the recently appointed Art Master, Mr Wills).

"First of all I should like to pay tribute to the work of my colleague, Eric Holman, who acted as Games Master from 1940 until the early part of this year. The difficulties of his office during these years require no emphasis, and it follows that it would have been something of an achievement to have merely kept the engine turning over; but to have run the engine at full speed and enhanced the good name of the College in all spheres of athletic activity is an achievement of which he can be justifiably proud, and one which I personally can but wonder at. To his name must be added those of the members of the Staff and Ground Staff, and, indeed, those of the boys who supported him. The School has been described as an oasis of sport in Plymouth during the war years; it is fitting that it should have been so."

Referring to an apparent lack of success in the current academic year he continued;

"It should be noted that the number of pupils who entered the School in 1940/41 was a third of what it now is to-day, and this happy band now constitutes the senior school. As a result we have had to call upon a number of boys for the first XXII who would normally have been distinguishing themselves as members of the "Colts" XI's. The senior sides have therefore lacked experience and, in some cases, stamina, and the junior sides have been diluted. I offer this as fact, not excuse, for it is doubtful if the school sides have ever contained a set of cricketers with more natural ability. In these circumstances it is reasonable to look to the future with a large measure of optimism."

"Our object," continued Ted, "is not to produce four School XI's that will win all their matches and establish a reputation for doing so, but rather to teach all boys the elements of the game as best we can, contribute to their physical development and enable them to enjoy their cricket at school and in later life."

"To this end," he announced in a triumphant tone, "I am happy to report that the Headmaster has arranged for all boys in the First and Second Forms to play games for an hour and a half each week during what has previously been regarded as "school time", it is still, with a difference."

"By next season, I hope that we shall have the facilities and equipment to give all boys in the remainder of the school at least one evening in the nets every two weeks, and thus offset the concessions to the Junior School."

"I extend a very cordial invitation to Parents, Old Boys and other friends of the School to come along and help us with the coaching, umpiring, refereeing, etc. Please let me know when you think you can come along; a verbal message and short notice will suffice. I don't think that we see nearly enough parents of boys in the School watching and encouraging their sons. (Will all boys please ensure that my remarks "go home"?). Next year I hope we shall be in a position to offer a little more hospitality, but we should like to meet you anyway. In the interim, if you want to take a part in the harmonious physical development of your son, encourage him all you can. Buy him bats, balls, footballs, books on games, etc., etc., and play with him. A cricket bat is rather like a packet of "Smith's Crisps" – no picnic basket is complete without one. Don't get alarmed at a few broken windows; there are more open spaces and less windows in Plymouth than there were, and the Chief Constable is a keen cricketer himself. All this may seem a little undignified, but I hope that I have given you the germ of an idea. One of the best ways of keeping fit and alert is to play games, and the way to become a cricketer is to play cricket and watch good cricket. The way to be young is to be with those that are young."

Ted Mercer, the man who won a little Ford for his slogan for Sharp's Toffee, returns to Ford Park after war service with both barrels blazing, as he aims to get School sport back on track.

Thus ended the persuasive prose of the then 37 year-old Games Master. It was a message that rings as true now as it did then, although the *"broken window"* bit may raise a few more eyebrows today! Nevertheless anyone reading it would have been in no doubt that Sport at the School was in truly passionate – and capable - hands.

The first XI won one, lost one and drew two of their four inter-school fixtures *"and showed up well against older and more experienced players"*, although they were well and truly hammered by the "Staff and Gound" team. In what was the opening match of the season for the firsts, Mr Radford hit an unbeaten 49 and Mr Barnes knocked up 36 as the side coasted to 151 for 2. The School, for their part. struggled to reach 27 with Mr Mercer returning figures of 3-5 and Mr Bonser 2-4.

The blow to the boys pride must have been softened a little by the observation at the end of the report that *"the Staff XI must now be one of the strongest in the district"*.

Once again the pre-war ploy of playing staff members in School, or rather "Club", sides was practised. Messrs. Mercer, Radford and Pro Heywood were among those who made notable contributions, with the first two scoring 35 and 88 in the school's seven wicket victory over Liskeard, and Ted taking 6-39 in a game that the RN Barracks team won by just one wicket. Among the boys, Dunkley, Lunn and Gosling all had five-wicket hauls, with Dunkley and Perry both hitting 50s in the School's comfortable win over the City Electricity Club.

More than any other sport, perhaps, the sounds generated by a cricket match, although punctuated by large periods of silence, seem to carry further than most; the thwack of leather on willow as the red ball is middled or the enthusiastic appeals of a fielding side, cut through the air and open windows.

"For hours imprisoned at my desk I am,
Forced to read Ovid's classics, line by line,

His tales of Hercules, who held the sky,
From Cacus captured back the stolen Kine ...
Outside the room, the sky is bright and blue,
And cricketers are playing happily,
This Ovid tires me; cannot I play too?
Tomorrow I shall do it easily.
"No! Vile Procrastination, I will not give way;
Back to my Latin Verse – cricket another day!"

The Summer of '47 Charles Arscott and his chums pose outside Big School, among them Palmer, Hemer, Luddington, Thorpe-Tracey, Berryman, Dunkley, Bennett, Thompkins and Coyte.

These frustrations, of course, were exacerbated if this was the big exam term for you;

"The summer sun is shining bright,
The grass is soft and green,
The water in the swimming bath
Is fresh and cool and clean.
For other boys the Summer Term
With fun and games is crowded,
But for the School Cert. Candidate
The sky is always clouded.

Behold him in the swimming bath
The poor, benighted lad;

He quite forgets to shed his clothes
And dives in fully clad.
Assail him not with ribald cries:
His mind, if you could see
Is full of contexts from Macbeth
And U.S. History.

Or else, on Wednesday afternoon,
When down to play at cricket,
He interposes not his bat,
And throws away his wicket.
Alas! Forgive the wretched youth,
Forget he made no score:
His mind was on the properties
Of H_2SO_4.

And if a fives ball comes at him,
Oh, do not start to grin
If he forgets to hit it back
And tries to head it in.
His thoughts, perhaps were dwelling on
The measurement of diameters,
Or else upon the scansion of
Ovidian Pentameters.

And when at last the term is done
Don't think that he's in clover,
That he can have his bit of fun,
His grim ordeal now over.
How little can you understand!
His worst woe is the last.
All through the holiday he'll fret
To know if he has passed."

This last work was signed *"Ovum"*, while the previous poem was credited to *"GM"* and both were indicative of the quality and character of the post-war pieces that were percolating into the Plymothian. Some were more original than others;

"I sprang from the Cow-Shed, and Cutler, and he;
I galloped, Steve galloped, we galloped all three.
"Good Speed!" cried the Marker as past him we sped;
"Same to you!" answered Butcher, "but I'm nearly
dead".
Then next we passed Norris, perched up on a gate,
Who said, "My young friends, this will get down your
weight".

"My goodness!" said Skinnard, "just look at my
boots!
Do cows have to be such insanitary brutes?"
At the archway quoth Goatley, "Your running's not
bad,
But hurry, or you will be beaten, my lad."
Just then I saw Allgood a furlong ahead,
And after him down 'cross the ploughland I sped.

At the fourth field, friend Goodenough turned round
and said,
"I've just seen old Polkinghorne three fields ahead.
If we don't put a spurt on and keep him in sight
We'll be running this blighted race all through the
night."
Then through a farm gateway, with mud to the knee,
Steve wallowed, I wallowed, we wallowed all three.

Then all I remember is friends flocking round,
As I sat with my head 'twixt my knees on the ground,
But no voice was praising my effort or his,
And nobody thought to revive us with fizz.
Next year, if old Martin wants me to run,
He'd better arrange for some tea and a bun
Only then to his pleas will I graciously yield
If I'm promised an ambulance home from the field."

Entitled *"How We Ran The Good Race (with apologies
to Robert Browning)"* this entertaining account of the
1947 Cross Country told us that at least it was across

country once more. It was run near Marsh Mills in
fact and the aforementioned Polkinghorne was the
fastest Junior. Both age groups completed the same
three-and-a-half-mile course, "old" Martin finished
fourth in the Seniors, which was won by Rogers of
Sargents, but with Martin, Polkinghorne and Palmer
(2nd in the Seniors) and Trewethan (Price Cup winner),
Thompsons emerged overall winners. The weather,
incidentally, was fairly foul - *"a thick mist hung over
what turned out to be a very wet run".*

*Athletics Team 1947. Back row; PD Smith, JW Ricks, AR Martin,
NT Ross, LG Pomroy. Seated; TN Storey, GA Rogers (senior Cross
Country winner), P Berryman, DEG Perry, TI Adams. Front ; R
Polkinghorne (junior Cross Country champion) and MA Congdon.*

The weather also had an adverse affect on the School
Fives and the team's opportunities for practise. A
match with the Staff failed to happen, while in the only
Spring Term fixture that was fulfilled the School again
found it difficult to adapt to the fuller court that Kelly
were used to.
Kelly also had the upper hand in the inter-school boxing
contest, staged in the School Gym on 11 March. *"Our
opponents showed themselves superior in both fitness
and training and won nine bouts to three".* Cutler,
Vaughan and Turner were the three School successes,

with the latter two both winning their respective weights
in the Inter-House Competition staged the previous
month. But it was the Inter-School contest that created
the most interest;
*"Although we were beaten, this match at least served
to focus the attention of every member of the School
on the sport, and should stimulate a far more active
interest than was apparent before."*
*"We greatly appreciated the presence of Mr RVH
Westall, the Headmaster of Kelly College and also that
of our own Headmaster and his wife."*
Other highlights that Spring Term included the success
of the Shooting VIII who, having won 15 out of 18
matches, finished equal in points with the winning team
in the Plymouth and District Miniature Rifle League,
"but were placed second on aggregate scores."
Asser (the Captain), Greasley and Chesterfield were
the most consistent, with team Secretary, Storey, not
far behind them.
Of the non-sporting activities Friday evenings at 8pm
saw regular meetings of the Literary and Debating
Society under the "energetic" Chairman, WGM
Jones. Among the motions carried; *"Recent British
domestic policy is not to be admired"; "Progress is
not necessarily synonymous with Happiness"* and
"England is on the down-grade". MD McKee was
the successful candidate in the March mock-election
and *'The Living Room',* by Esther McCracken, was the
subject of the Play-reading.
Another increasingly popular, extra-curricular, activity
was the Chess Club, membership of which *"has
increased considerably since permission was granted
for those interested to remain after School hours"* in
Room 5.
Meanwhile, despite the difficulties in obtaining film,
*"several enthusiasts (from the Photographic Society)
captured interesting and unique views of the School
under snow."*
Among the many victims of the severe weather that

term was the School Sports. Preliminary events were run off by Wednesday 26 March but with the term ending two days later it became necessary to postpone the finals until the first Wednesday of the Summer Term – 30 April.

Rice and Pomroy were the Senior stars - Polkinghorne and Hick, the Juniors. Rogers and Storey both won more than one Senior event and although no track or field records appear to have been broken, there was one new School Sports milestone set;

"It was a happy inspiration to invite Mr H Sargent to present the prizes; the Grand Old Man of Plymouth College needed no introduction to his audience, and his claim that he has seen every Sports Day at the College for the last forty-nine years surely establishes a record which only he himself is likely to better in the future. His reminiscences of earlier days were much appreciated."

Sadly Sargent's House was the least successful of the four on the day, Thompsons, finishing ahead of Palmers and College.

The following month the annual Inter-School Sports was held, once again at Kelly. With a record entry of sixteen schools taking part, here new records were set; a throw of 118ft 4ins in the discus (Kelly) and a distance of 41ft 8ins in the Hop, Skip and Jump (a pupil from Hele's). A Dartmouth boy also equalled the 100-yard record time of 10.4 seconds. Although the School only achieved one top three placing in any event (Rogers' runners-up slot in the mile) Plymouth College finished a creditable seventh overall, but a considerable way behind the winners, Dartmouth, who comfortably knocked Kelly into second place.

In the Pool, in June, the School won three Swimming Galas including two victories over a Plymouth City Transport side that on one occasion at least were *"much strengthened by members of the Tinside Club"*.

Bennett and his team, however, were less successful in an earlier encounter with an RNEC side at the Royal Naval Barracks, who had the better of them both in the individual events and in the Water Polo.

The future of Swimming at Plymouth College had never been brighter though, with the bringing into service of the *"swimming bath"* at Munday House. *"A more pleasant place in which to learn how to swim would be hard to find. Situated as it is in a sheltered corner of the highest district of Plymouth, and surrounded by a garden of flowering trees and shrubs, the atmosphere is one of charm and invigoration, and the opportunity one that may well produce the life-savers and Channel aspirants of to-morrow"*.

"Each division gets at least one swimming lesson per week, which is the most popular part of the School curriculum, if the rate of striking between Ford Park and Munday House be any indication, and a class of some twenty accomplished swimmers has an "extra" after school on Monday afternoons."

"The shortage of trunks was a bit of a problem at the beginning of term for large and small alike, but a little improvisation at home soon found something to suit the purpose, and it is hoped that by the end of term every boy will have raised his standard in varying degrees, whether it be from a width to several lengths, from the breast stroke to crawl, or from just sinking to floating."

Clearly the hope had been that the Prep would be based at Hartley Road by then, but it wasn't hence the need to troop up there. But move they finally did that summer.

"We returned in September to find that our fledglings, the Prep., had forsaken their old haunts. We miss their gravity and decorum, which so often seem to reproach the levity of their Seniors; we wish them happiness and prosperity in their new roost among the trees of Hartley."

Thus did the editors of the Plymothian record the event; in the Prep notes the account ran as follows;

"Saturday, 20th September, 1947, was a red-letter day in the history of the Prep. On that day we moved at long last from Ford Park into our new premises at Munday House. There was no ceremony to mark the occasion. Indeed so smoothly was the changeover effected, we seem to have slipped away unobserved like the hosts of Midian from the precincts of the Main School, and to have just as unobtrusively entered our present buildings. No internal revolution behind the closed doors of cabinets or in the secret chambers of court circles was ever more unostentatiously carried out. No hiatus, in fact, interrupted the life of the school."*

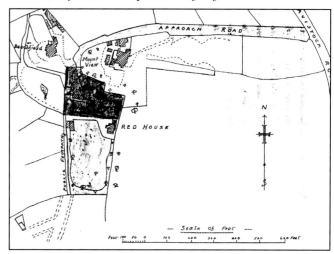

Saturday 20th September 1947 - "On that day we moved at long last from Ford Park into our new premises at Munday House".

"We are naturally proud to possess our own school. Few schools, we are sure, are situated in such elevated, pleasant and secluded surroundings, and can at the same time boast of such tastefully decorated classrooms and of so many varied amenities. Organisations like schools, however, do not depend entirely on environment for their success. Few, of course, would deny that beautiful surroundings may act as an inspiration. Hence the interest in Town-Planning, and the scheme for a better Plymouth."

This interest, incidentally, had been recently stimulated by the visit (on 29 October 1947), of King George VI and Queen Elizabeth who came to dedicate the replica of Drake's Drum, in which the Civic Flagstaff was planted at the crossing of the two great axes of the Paton-Watson, Abercrombie Plan – Royal Parade and Armada Way - both of which were officially named in the same ceremony.

George VI and Queen Elizabeth in Plymouth to name Royal Parade and Armada Way, launching the rebuilding of the City Centre.

"The first section of the new Plymouth has been set down," ran the Plymothian editorial that term. It went on, "Forlorn and inconsequent as the first piece of a jig-saw puzzle. We wait eagerly for the completion of the picture. Grass plots and tidy roads give the new area the look of a well-ordered cemetery; but we urge the City Fathers not to let too much grass grow under their feet, but to let us see the heart of Plymouth beat and throb with life."

Earlier in the year Joe Egg (a name apparently borrowed from Frank L Baum's Wizzard of Oz character) had earlier, independently, "reported" in the Plymothian on "Professor Atombombie's magnificent Plan for Plymouth College":

"The central feature is the Parade Ground for the JTC occupying most of the present playing-field, with an impressive vista of the swimming-bath. The main building will be demolished; on its site will be erected the Milk Distribution Centre, the Savings Bureau, the Dining Room and Youth Group Club Rooms. A ring road will be driven round the field, from the BR (British Restaurant) to the Empire; on this class rooms may ultimately be built, if the need is felt."

The number of literary contributions to the Magazine certainly appeared to be healthier than it had been for some time, but clearly the editorial staff would have welcomed more, and were impressed by another in-school publication;

"We have read with interest "The Forum", a magazine produced by members of the present 4a, and we envy the editor who can command such a wealth of articles from such well-informed and graceful contributors, dealing with Cornish Wrestling, Snakes, Horse Riding, Cockling, Church Architecture and Calf Rearing. How can we hope to include items written in French, in Greek, in Latin, and in Russian."

The newly moved Prep was also contemplating its own periodical, "Perhaps it may seem odd that we do not possess our own magazine. Nations in the first flush of newly won freedom are usually anxious to complete their independence by severing all links with the country which nurtured them to maturity. But the cost of a separate publication would be high and besides, we feel that there is still room for sentiment in this war-weary world. We are proud to preserve as many links as possible with the Main School and the Plymothian should enable us to maintain our interest in each other's activities."

And actually the Prep's activities at this time were particularly interesting, especially the "Experiment in Democracy". Essentially this saw the junior school electing a council of boys drawn from their own ranks to represent them on a body that met every fortnight … "with members of the staff acting as chairman and vice-chairman".

"It considers proposals which members of the school have submitted in a Suggestion Box. The first meeting dealt exclusively with questions of procedure; but at later meetings, subjects have included almost every aspect of the Prep. The difficulties of some boys travelling to and from the school, organized games in the "break", the appointment of prefects, half-holidays, school societies, film shows: all these have been referred to Higher Authority. And, of course, there was a spate of proposals that homework should be abolished on Guy Fawkes' Night – a request that was promptly granted."

Sixteen candidates put themselves up for election to the School Council and six were duly returned, among them the newly-appointed Head Prefect of the Prep, Arthur and three of the sub-prefects, Robinson, U'ren and Canniford. Bird and Cole were the other two, while Maxwell was appointed the first clerk and Gaussen and Erlich I, were made mace-bearers.

All terribly formal and designed to give what was effectively a new school, the best possible start; "Schools are made or marred by the boys that attend them. Each member of the Prep. can help to build our school's reputation. Work hard, and play even harder; we want no spivs or drones. Always take pride in your school. For it is your school: and its future lies in your hands."

The realignment of Plymouth City Centre begins.

The use of the two words *"Spiv"* and *"Drone"* here were interesting, indeed the opening paragraph of the Plymothian that winter referring to this *"remarkable term"* noted that it was the term *"which has seen the word "Spiv" pass into our language, and the word "Spud" threaten to pass out of it."*

Undoubtedly the word *"Spiv"* was on everybody's lips; in August, in the House of Lords, Lord Parkenham replying to Lord Amwell on the subject of slackers said that no doubt he had *"spivs and drones"* in mind. On the same day, in the House of Commons, Mr Atlee stated on behalf of his party that *"we shall take all action open to us against spivs and other drones"*. Stereotypically turned out in *"Padded shoulders, diagonally woven suit, spear pointed collars and dazzle tie"* the Spiv was deemed by some to be a post-war product of rationing and the *"illegitimate child of the Labour Government"*, a downmarket entrepreneur with an eye for the easy opportunity. But, in reality, they'd been around for years, it's just that there had never been such a good word to describe them;

"The Spiv! The Spiv!
Oh, how does he live?
How he makes all his cash, I can't think.
He rides in Rolls Royces,
His girl-friends wear Joyces,
Full-fashioned sheer nylons, and mink."

These were the opening lines from a Plymothian poem that term by "Quarterbarnes" (AJL Barnes?) who followed on with a verse about;

"The Drone! The Drone!
Oh, why should he moan?
He's the laziest lump in the hive,
With his hat over his eyes,
And his rainbow hued ties,
And a walk twixt jitter and jive."

There can be little doubt that the Magazine Editors would have been delighted to have such a topical

contribution from Ford Park. They seem to have been equalled pleased to hear from other, older, scribes;
"CJ Palmer was married at Monken Hadley, Herts. We have special interest in him as he used to write these notes in pre-war days. He is now on the editorial staff of the Daily Mail in London."
"KW Doble has returned to the Western Morning News. Another journalist is GC Ross, who is working on the Middle Eastern Mail in Cairo," while JR Harvey *"has written a number of agricultural books and pamphlets during the last few years"*.

The offices of the Western Morning News and Evening Herald were the sole survivors in redevelopment of the Frankfort Street, however in 1947 the old Regent/Odeon was still doing good business - although its days were numbered, as were those of the market.

Doubtless one or two of these OPMs would have been using typewriters, maybe even all of them. Back at school however, proper pens, not biros, rolling balls or gel sticks were still the order of the day.
"This term saw the revival of the ancient Ink Testing Ceremony, last performed in 1939. Tradition requires that this old rite be carried out by one candidate for HSC, one candidate for School Cert., and a figure called the "Blot King", being the boy with the grubbiest fingers

in Form 1A. They march in procession along the lower corridor, and knock at the door of the Porter's Lodge, calling out;
"Porter, Porter, come outside,
Fetch you ink for to be tried"
"The Porter then "blows" a measure of ink for each of them: this is solemnly tested for its capacity to make nibs corrode, to cause fountain pens to seize up, and to produce expansive and persistent blots. If the ink passes these tests, the Porter is then given a Diploma, to certify that he "do make good ink". The part of the ceremony in which a measure of ink was quaffed by a boy in the Prep. to test its merit as a beverage, was omitted this year, upon an order from the Ministry of Food."

Anyone who remembers using an ink well in that dark-stained hole in their old wooden desk will have their own memories of *"ink testing"* and of that oft-unsung hero the School Porter. However, few School support staff over the years can have come anywhere near holding the degree of respect and affection that generations of boys had for the man mentioned in the Autumn 1947 edition of the West Country Magazine;
"Ford Park, the home of Plymouth College cricket of rich vintage, is inevitably associated with the name of Bill Heywood, known only – though affectionately – as "Pro" to hundreds of boys who have gleaned their cricket from him, and gleaned it well, during the last quarter of a century or so. "Pro" has fashioned enough players to build up several county sides, and he promises to carry on his noble and enthusiastic work for many years still to come."

Curiously enough, in that same Plymothian there was news of the death of the first games master Pro worked with at the School – Arnold Lingley. "Shanks", as he had been known, had not long since celebrated his seventy-seventh birthday when he died in Winnersh, Berkshire, in November 1947. He had retired in 1935 around the time that one of the staffroom's newest recruits, H Samuel Rendle, had moved up to the Main School from the Prep.

The beginning of the new academic year, 1947/48 saw three new faces in the Ford Park staffroom, Rendle, Scott and Hills-Harrop.

Sam Rendle, OPM and Francis Scott arrive at Ford Park.

Rendle, at twenty-three, was the youngest of them and not surprisingly instantly became the youngest member of staff too. An old boy of the School (1931-42) he was known to all but a few of the staff and came back to Plymouth College, fresh from Bristol Grammar School, via Cambridge, where he had read mathematics. Hills-Harrop and Francis Scott were also Cambridge men; the former being a thirty-one year-old linguist who had previously taught at Colyton Grammar School; the latter, a year older, and a history master who had been teaching in his varsity town, at Cambridge High School for Boys.

Scott arrived as a replacement for Wilfred Savage, while the other two apparently came to boost staff numbers in response to increased pupil numbers and brought to ten the number of new faces that had joined (as opposed to re-joined) the common room since the

end of the war. In his report that term at Speech Day the Headmaster reported that with the *"Third Stream now in its second year the Main School now numbers 420 boys and we have taken over the old premises, now known as "Valletort" which the Prep School vacated on their move to Munday House."*

"The increase in staff attendant on this offers large possibilities of providing a more expansive curriculum to meet more closely the special needs of pupils."

The Head also spoke of his delight in the increase in boarding numbers, made possible by the extension of the Boarding House.

"Boarders, particularly when they come from the country, enrich the life of the school and do much to prevent the "provincial" outlook," he said.

Mr Garnons Williams then launched a brief attack on the proposed abolition of the School Certificate Examination and hoped that *"there might yet be time for a reprieve to prevent this judicial murder."*

Sir George Schuster presented the prizes that day, four of them going to the star fifth-form linguist MD McKee who, somewhat unusually bagged the English, French, Greek and Latin prizes.

Another talented languages student was Higher School Certificate achiever PWJ Luddington, who won the Sixth Form Art prize as well as the French and German prizes. Not surprisingly, Luddington later gained an Open Scholarship in Modern Languages at Brasenose College, Oxford.

Interestingly enough, after the recent questioning of the value of the Oxbridge letters, both were a little shorter than usual in the winter '47 Plymothian. Even more remarkably the Cambridge missive was written in rhyme;

"There was Josh and Jim, and Jonny and Tod
And (snaking his hips a la Conga)
Last in that motley procession came Dodd
Taking lessons from Madame la Zonga"

Six Lessons from Madame La Zonga was a popular hit

song of the day, incidentally, while Josh, Jim, Jonny and Tod were the first names of Cambridge-based OPMs Piper, Ivory, Trevaskis and Lawry respectively – *"It is always advisable to know the Christian names of the great"*. Perhaps so, but it was most unusual at that time to find any first names in the Plymothian.

And there was more;

"Then Nob sang a song to the sound of a gong
Which the Master of Trinity beat,
Which the Dean of St John's, and four or five dons,
Rhythmic'lly shuffled their feet.
NOB'S SONG:
I'm comical Nobby,
I'm Clarke (with an "E")
I'm adept at Hockey,
As people can see
(For I've frequently played for the Varsitee)

This too was true as centre-forward Clarke not only obtained his Blue for Hockey, but *"his vigorous play in the Varsity match helped to secure their victory over Oxford"*

The final verse of this entertaining epistle also contained more sense, and valuable information, than it appeared at first glance;

"As the moon lightly played on the spilt lemonade,
And hung like a cheese over Caius,
The party dispersed, while a whimsical blade
Sang the "Carmen" in bad Japanese."

The key here being that *"Caius"* is pronounced *"keys"* and the *"whimsical blade"* in question was Geoffrey Sargent *"the first student ever to sit for the Japanese Tripos at this ancient university."*

Notwithstanding his attempts to translate the Carmen, Sargent was truly a pioneering pupil at Cambridge, and a decade later his PHD *"The Japanese family storehouse"* or, *"The Millionaires' gospel modernised"*, would become a seminal academic text.

By a strange coincidence in the OPM notes at the back of that particular issue of the Plymothian, there was a

letter from Wing-Commander EC Harding, who had left Plymouth College in 1931, and was now based *"at Iwakuni, an airfield on the eastern coast of Southern Honshu."*

Harding wrote at length about life in Japan;

"Except in or near large towns, roads are shocking, and even the versatile jeep groans in agony when driven over them..."

"As for the people, the men are polite and give little trouble, but one is not deceived by their "correct" manner and watches them carefully. The women are, however, a potential force in the re-education of the Japanese Nation. They make excellent servants and possess a high degree of loyalty, are very honest and cheerful workers."

The RAF man then concluded with the observation that;

"Major disasters are taken fairly calmly in Japan, where earthquakes (not to be recommended at 4am!!) typhoons, floods, fires and eruptions are liable to occur at intervals throughout the year. It is not surprising therefore, that survivors of the Atomic Bomb are philosophical about their personal injuries or losses."

The fallout of the war was still at the forefront of many peoples mind in all parts of the world. In Plymouth it was particularly so with the massive rebuilding programme going on around the City, especially as some of that work was being carried out by German prisoners of war.

Another OPM, Captain JL Webber, was *"interpreter officer at Plympton prisoners of war camp"* and when he got married earlier that year in Yealmpton, *"music was supplied by German instrumentalists"*

A year or two down the line and he could possibly have roped in the services of School instrumentalists. Writing in his first report on the School's musical activities the recently appointed John Bill reported that a *"School Choir of about sixty voices had been formed during the summer term and gave its first public performance on Speech Day, when the "Strange Adventure" Quartet* from Sullivan's "Yeoman of the Guard" and the Soldiers Chorus from Gounod's "Faust" were sung, together with "Brother James's Air"."*

"The choir managed to overcome the difficult acoustics of the Central Hall very well," enthused the new music teacher, adding; *"I should like to close this first report on the School's musical activities by expressing my appreciation of the Headmaster's unfailing support and encouragement in musical matters."*

Another new teacher making an extracurricular mark was Francis Scott who found himself instantly appointed chairman of the Dramatic Society and working with Messrs Jackson and Dundas to produce suitable End of Term and Yuletide fare.

And very well they did too; *"Earnest histrionics were not attempted, but laughter abounded ... The excellent singing of the Choir in their short programme did give some balance to the occasion. As for the plays, the audience seemed to regard the first two items as mere preliminary bouts, and reserved its real attention for the big event."*

"The Man in the Bowler Hat" and *"The Police Court"* were those first two items and the "Big Event" – that was *"Strength Through Joy"*.

"Both in performance and in reception it was beyond all anticipation. The plot mattered only as the occasion for presenting Mr Dent in a Norman Hartnell creation, Mr Hills-Harrop as a voracious Vicar, and Mr Davies as a Doctor whose ardour was not yet subdued by nationalisation. Mr Rendle, as an Undertaker, looked like a business associate of Dracula and Frankenstein. Miss Hunt gave a valiant performance as Charley's Wife. But the outstanding performance came from Mr Mercer. With tremendous vigour and sustained effort he rode the whirlwind and directed the storm from his bath-chair, adding musical honours on the trombone. The elaborate setting, dominated by Mr Wills' "Family Portraits", contributed much to the effectiveness of this domestic nightmare."

Co-producer of the evening's entertainment, Ernest Dundas, was also a stalwart of the L&D, another area that the Head was keen to develop, indeed he successfully led the opposition to Mr Dundas' motion that *"Civilisation was in Decay"*.

Interestingly enough the motion put before the last meeting that term was that *"This House deplores Compulsory Military Service"*.

Interesting because one of the prime movers, and the secretary, of the Dramatic Society was also captain of shooting and senior member of the JTC, Sergeant RK Asser, and the JTC was doing very well, its members well aware that success at school made for a more successful path through Compulsory Military Service.

Army Camp that winter was at Tweseldown, near Aldershot and was by all accounts *"a grand time"*, while Field Day was near Clearbrook.

The Scouts meanwhile staged their Field Day between Roborough and Yennadon, with their summer camp once again at Werrington.

For the younger boys of the Prep school interest in matters military was fostered by a visit to the RAF Wireless Station at Mount Batten;

"We set off in high spirits in spite of pouring rain and proceeded by 'bus to Hooe; here we were met by one of the parents, who kindly placed his car at the services of the party, and were taken in small groups to the Wireless Station at the top of the hill."

There the boys were shown the Control Room;

"Here was a vast conglomeration of highly polished metallic objects, an unforgettable sight. There were weird electrical apparatus, protected by thick wire gauze and neatly spaced at regular intervals every conceivable kind of lights facing the ceiling so as not to dazzle those working below. It would have needed a Jules Verne or an HG Wells to describe the scene. The boys were rendered speechless by the sight ... It was unanimously agreed that the afternoon had been a "wizard prang"."

RAF Mount Batten with its Airmen and Flying Boats held a fascination for local schoolboys throughout the forties.

Not too sure if the boys fully appreciated the use that the RAF chaps made of that expression in the early forties though.

Incidentally with the Prep now relocated at Hartley Road and the playing fields there at long last serviceable, a decision was made to revive inter-house rugby matches there.

Back at Ford Park that same term the 1st XV under Adams, with their secretary Roskruge, got off to a flying start, winning their first four matches – against Launceston College, Shebbear, Sutton High and Hele's (Exeter). However after a drawn game against Truro School the winning form all but evaporated and an away defeat at Kelly was followed by home setbacks at the hands of DHS, and Truro Cathedral School, and further away disappointment at the hands of Hele's, with only victories against Exeter School and RNC Dartmouth lifting the gloom. Rice, Berryman, Perry and Dunkley were among the others to make a mark and overall their success rate was greater than those of the teams further down the school.

Plymouth Cillege 1st XV 1947: back; RK Asser, SP Hopkins, CE Blackler, EH Griffin, TN Storey, RB Storey. Seated; DG Rice, JW Ricks, HW Roskruge, IT Adams (Captain), P Berryman, PW Luddington, DEG Perry. Front; PM Dunkley, and PM Vaughan

The 2nd's won three of their four home matches but lost all of their away games; the Colts won their first match, but lost the next six, failing to score four times and on one occasion conceding 92 points, while the Junior Colts lost every game, failing, like the Colts, to score more than nine points in any game, unlike their opposition who managed it every time.

It was not a happy state of affairs for the Games Master but he did have a master plan. "Vols" – voluntary games - were abolished and a *"new system in which the whole school from the Third Forms upwards played in special age groups"* was instituted in its place.

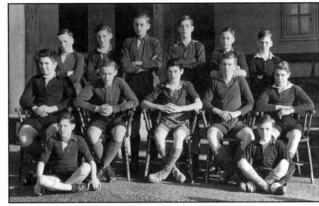

Rugger for everyone - Sargents House Junior Rugby 1947: Back; RD Keast, JK Reynolds, JR Quick, CR Turner, AR Harvey, MA Jackson. Seated; RH Curson, AS Lewis, GR Tucker (Captain), CJ Ackford, PE Coleman. Front; DE Algate, JW Watson.

"Combined with the normal training of First and Second Forms during games periods, this should eventually result in a marked improvement in the standard of Rugby throughout the school."

… And beyond it, with a bit of luck, for OPM Rugby was in no happier state;

"We hear that the rugger club is in some difficulty. Once a section of the club no longer interests the members, that section should drop out. An attempt to disband the rugger club would soon raise a loud protest, but might assist in getting a few playing members."

"How different the cricket club, which has to turn away players. We hope their idea of a North Devon tour won't be forgotten."

In the meantime it was the Hockey season once more and thanks to being *"more than usually favoured by the weather"* and the *"moving of the Athletic Sports to the Summer Term"*, hockey was played throughout the term and *"a full programme has resulted."*

Berryman, Perry, Dunkley, Roskruge and Lunn all earned their colours, with the Captain, Berryman, and the free-scoring Perry both being selected to play for the Devon Public Schools side against a County XI.

Games against other school sides - Kelly, Plympton and Plymouth Technical School - were all won and against older, more-experienced sides, the team acquitted themselves well, winning some and losing others. The OPMs got the better of them twice, as did the Royal Naval Barracks side, but RNEC 2nd's were beaten twice and a home match against RNC Dartmouth was also a comfortable success.

The School 2nd's had a mixed and lively time, winning three, losing three and drawing one, and with the exception of that one drawn match, every game saw four or more goals scored or conceded, as the final figures showed 20 goals netted in the seven games with 25 conceded.

Sargent's Junior Hockey XI 1948: Back; RD Keast, MA Jackson, RJ Quarterman, PR Lewis, DM Webb. Front; DE Algate, CJ Ackford, AS Lewis (Captain), GE Tucker, JWL Watson.

In the House Hockey, Thompsons, with both Berryman and Perry, and three other first eleven players were convincingly champions and looked on course to retain the overall Cock House trophy for a fourth successive year. Eighty boys and a dozen masters attended a dinner to celebrate the third win, the then soon-to-be-married, WGM Jones co-ordinating the proceedings. Among Mr Jones's many other extra-curricular activities he was again *"untiring"* in his efforts to make the Literary and Debating Society evenings a success. Of the various motions before the house that term, one, successfully carried, was proposed by him – and opposed by Mr Scott. The proposition? That *"this House supports Mr Bevin's suggestion for a Western Union"*.

This debate, incidentally, took place just three weeks after Ernest Bevin's Western Union speech in the House of Commons, a move which, in turn, set the ball rolling for the formation of NATO the following year.

Among the other topics discussed that term; *"Politics corrupt the nation"* proposed by Newcombe and Lander and unsuccessfully opposed by Jervis and TEJ Savery; *"This House deplores the raising of the school-leaving age"* – defeated; while the suggestion that *"This House deplores the principle of Universal Suffrage"* was carried at the inter-school debate, in February.

Debating Chambers disagreeing with Parliamentary proposals was common enough in student circles, though, and the Cambridge Letter that term noted that; *"Life persists in its age old habit of going on, with bumps being made on the river and the Government regularly being defeated in the Union."*

The Oxbridge letters this term, although a little cryptic resumed their formal nature. There were, at the time, nine old boys at Cambridge, but remarkably there were eleven at Exeter, where the overall student numbers were less, but, the OPM presence was greater than it had ever been before;

"This present session at the University College of the South-West has seen another large increase in numbers, a factor which has not tended to lessen the complications of life to-day; there are now nearly eight hundred students here at Exeter, over half of whom have to fend for themselves in lodgings and therefore miss many of the advantages of a communal life in Hall; some might indeed count this a blessing. There are still a considerable number of ex-Service students (all of the OPMs here have done war service of some kind), but from now on their numbers will decrease, and the responsibility for College affairs will fall once more upon the shoulders of those straight from school. Whether the present comparatively serious tone which the older students have undoubtedly introduced into College life will remain or not, one can only conjecture; but it is hoped that some trace of it will stay, for within the next few years College expects to receive her charter and to assume her new status of University."

Among those OPMs making a mark for themselves at Exeter we read that; *"Lyon was chosen as full-back of the Univeristies' Athletic Union Rugby touring team, Jolly had been picked for the Devon Hockey team"* while *"in other spheres "Summers has proved a most enterprising President of the Musical Society, AR White is President Elect of the Debating Society, VB Wilson has displayed his talents on the stage and RM White has edited a very fine "Rag Mag"."*

From a little further afield there was news of another OPM whose interest in the dramatic and literary arts was becoming very well known;

"JC Trewin (1920-25) whose dramatic criticisms appear in The Observer and other famous weeklies, has published a remarkable book on "The English Theatre" – sound judgement and a nice gift of phrase are in evidence throughout."

In the next breath we learnt that; *"A contemporary of his, John Rowland, writes on "Atoms, Electrons and Rays" in the same series."*

With two more volumes due from Trewin later in the year the library of OPM books was growing at an impressive rate, as indeed, at long last, was the School Library.

"Most people know that the aim of the War Memorial is to establish a collection of books worthy of the School in a room worthy to commemorate those who served in the war. At present we cannot fulfil the latter half of our project; handsome shelving cannot be obtained; the cost of developing Room Nine is absurdly high. The importance of having immediately a collection of books and a reading room in Shaftesbury as a temporary home, and, with no fanfares, no official opening, a boy in IIa borrowed 'William and the ARP' and the Library began its full existence."

Richmal Crompton's ever popular creation William Brown branches into film for the first time in 1948 with William Graham playing William in Just William's Luck, Brian Weske and James Crabbe are his chums Henry and Douglas.

"At present it consists of 1,800 books, of which 418 are classed as Junior Fiction; and 201 borrowers have taken out 833 books in eight weeks. All members of the School are automatically members of the Library and there is no entrance fee; at present half the School are taking advantage of it. The time given by the assistant librarians is their own spare time."

The books came from many sources; "Mr Bill told the Librarian to choose almost what he wanted from his own shelves; the City Librarian gave us a hundred and thirty-four volumes from surplus stock; the Headmaster," and so on, "... we welcome more gifts of books, or of money to buy them."

"Already there are many," wrote the Librarian, Hugh Dent, "who have found the Library something more than a place where one goes to borrow a book when one is bored ... The increasing numbers who go in to read the books and magazines show the value of a quiet room which has not the atmosphere of a class-room. By next term the catalogues will be complete and it will be possible to find books by subject as well as by author."

"One could," he added, and obviously did, "feel well-satisfied with this scene. Time: 12-45 one Thursday morning. Eight boys are exchanging books, and it happens that all six forms are represented. A Sixth-former is looking up a mathematical problem in the Encyclopedia Britannica: two fourth-formers are investigating "guncotton" in the Universal Encyclopedia; the bottom boy in 1c is reading an article about the "origin of coinage"; someone else is disagreeing with a pamphlet on how to do the "Crawl"; another is looking at pictures of "Wild Geese on the Severn" in the London news. One wondered how we had existed so long without a library."

Mr Dent had been trying to secure a dedicated library area since he arrived at the School over a decade earlier, and it's interesting to note that in the pages of that same year's Plymothians there were mentions of other media that would increasingly come to shift the focus of popular attention away from books;

"Thanks to the Central Office of Information, who have provided both operator and apparatus, films have been shown this term to all the School except the Fifth." Among the films shown were; "The Valley of the Tennessee" a documentary about life in America; "In The Beginnings of History", "A Cornish Valley" and "Instruments of the Orchestra".

Meanwhile up at Hartley Road we learnt that a decision had been taken at the Prep to allow "the use of the wireless during the lunch-hour". Curiously enough, later in the same piece we find, following the words "the shape of things to come", not a few words on the new media or technology but the new Prep site's garden which had been pruned and pollarded;

"If one recalls that in an effort to reach the swimming bath last summer one had to force one's way through conditions that resembled a Burmese jungle more than a school garden."

Clearly the move away from Ford Park was proving to be an all round success, with a straw poll on the matter finding almost unanimously in favour of Munday House. The one boy who preferred being at Ford Park said he did so because he now had to spend 4d in bus fare everyday.

"The reason for the popularity of Munday House, however, vary greatly. The older boys prefer it on aesthetic grounds. Nearly all of them evidently appreciate the brighter classrooms, with their green and cream-coloured walls and their fluorescent lighting. Many emphasised the fact that Munday House has a better approach and superior surroundings; they like the drive and garden and apparently have much feeling for natural beauty."

The survey came from the questioning of two Prep forms and there can be no doubting that another prominent feature of the new-look Prep was its democratic approach to life. The newly-appointed School Council had just been augmented and was currently busying itself with the compilation and codification of a list of School Rules. A Chess club was also formed at the Prep as this game continued to gain in popularity on both sites, particularly with the arrival at the Main School of "the much-longed for equipment" which meant that the Chess Club "was now in possession of eight club sets".

The term also saw a visit from Mr Goodman of the Plymouth Chess Club, who played a number of games and won them all except for his matches with the Headmaster and TEJ Savery. There was one inter-school fixture, with Sutton High School, which was narrowly lost 3½-4½.

In the boxing ring there were narrowly-lost fixtures against Kelly, in the Kelly gym, and Virginia House, at Ford Park, while a contest against a side, St Michael's Boxing Club, brought here by an OPM, the Reverend AF Martin-Langley, who had left School over a decade earlier, was comfortably won. Mr E Self was the newly appointed Boxing Instructor and star protégés Cutler, Cload and Turner were unbeaten in all three fixtures and not surprisingly also won their respective weights in the School Competition. Turner, the Captain of boxing, was the most senior of the three, finishing Welter Weight Champ, with Cutler and Cload, Gnat and Mosquito Weight respectively. All three won School colours along with Hopkins, Flanders and Allgood.

1948 School Boxing featuring Cutler, Cload and their Captain Turner, all three unbeaten in the three fixtures arranged for them.

Thompson's and Sargent's shared the honours in the inter-house boxing, and a couple of weeks later they finished first in the Cross-Country too, this time just ahead of Palmers whose boys, Newcombe and Bounsall, put in the best times at Senior and Junior level. However, Perry and Congdon, both of Thompsons, were close behind them in second place in each event and Thompson's overall had greater strength in depth. The race this year *"was not run over the Marsh Mills course, mainly because of difficulty of transport and the lack of suitable changing facilities,"* consequently *"the course chosen was one of some three miles round Central Park – entries from the Senior School were not excessive, but eighty Juniors completed the course."*

Thompson's were clearly well on course to be Cock House again, something that rankled particularly with the Head Boy, DM Griffin, a Palmers boy, who wrote in that term's House notes;

"Most members of the House, and in fact of the School, have in the past tended to think that to belong to a House is a necessary evil rather than an outlet for enthusiasm. It is to combat this attitude that the experiment has been made. Each individual member, however small or insignificant, has his part to play in making this House Cock House once again."

The experiment in question was to form a House Committee *"consisting of one member from each set of forms, designed to run the House on progressive lines".*

The same across-the-School-years approach was advocated by Griffin in his Natural History Society notes;

"If they (the senior members of the society) would be willing to invite occasionally a very small number of the younger members to accompany them on their expeditions, there would be an all-round increase in interest and efficiency."

Griffin was largely responsible for the reformation of the Natural History Society, although with the Headmaster consenting to be President of the body his influence was doubtless significant, as indeed were the *"numerous requests from all parts of the School".* Mr McD Porter was made Chairman and Mr Rendle the Treasurer and with around seventy members, talks by HG Hurrell – *"What the Naturalist Sees"*, WH Jeffrey – *"Days With A Butterfly Net"*, and Griffin himself – *"Songs of Birds"*, were all well attended.

The following term Mr Dent gave a talk on "*Wild Flowers",* two films *"Marshland Birds"* and *"Life in the Hedgerows"* were shown and there was a visit to Mr HG Hurrell's Fox Farm, at Moorgate, Wrangaton, where members were shown *"foxes, pine martins, and many birds, both captive and wild".*

Curiously enough, in the same term that this Society was revived, conjuring up editorial images of boys on Field Day *"with Butterfly Nets at the alert and Glass Bottles slung at the side",* there was a charming, lengthy and anonymous piece in the Plymothian on *"The Moor";*

"There is an old saying to the effect that if you scratch the Moor's back, it will pick your pocket. The truth of this is very evident in the tales of many commercial ventures launched, and much good money thrown after bad..."

"Men say that those who stay upon the Moor for any length of time take the "Moor Madness" and never want to leave; and certain it is that those who really know her in all her changing moods, do acquire a strange longing, and will deny that any place in the world can compare with their beloved "Dartymoor"."

"Snark" was the code name for the JTC Field Day held on the edge of the Moor, on Roborough Down that term; the June exercise was at Wigford Down, while the summer camp was at the School of Infantry at Warminster. The Lancashire Fusiliers hosted the week, which by all accounts wasn't long enough – *"a month there would not have seemed long,"* reported CSM Chesterfield.

The Scouts, meanwhile, with Griffin their troop leader, were back at Werrington, where Mr Dent led *"a most enjoyable midnight walk"* and *"Spike Burt and his Bottle Bashers"* were among the impromptu cabaret acts.

CSM Chesterfield, along with Sgt. Asser, the team Captain, was part of the very successful School Shooting team that year who finished winners of the Plymouth Small Bore League Div II, losing only one of their fourteen fixtures. Storey, Greasley, Pryor, Cummins and Hopewell all gained their full colours with Chesterfield and Hopewell both gaining places in the City team. A School eight also competed in the Devon Public Schools' Shield and Buller Cup, coming third behind Blundell's and All Hallow's.

Plymouth College Shooting Team 1948 – winners of the Plymouth Small Bore League Div. II: Back; PC Hopewell, N Cummins, M Lunn, PC Popplestone. Front J Greasely, J Chesterfield, RK Asser (Captain), TN Storey and AEM Pryor.

Markedly less successful was the School's Five's Team, whose number also included Asser, and who, once again, were soundly defeated in their annual visit to Kelly. Their captain, PWJ Luddington, made the usual and *"time-worn plea that something be done about the condition of the courts by next season".*

Lunn was another member of that weary team and he would doubtless have preferred to recall his prowess that summer with the Discus in the School Sports, an occasion that was dominated by Ricks and Storey, who between them managed to finish in the first three in every event except the Discus, the Javelin and the Half Mile. Athletics Captain DEG Perry won the Quarter, Half and Mile events, setting a new record of 2mins 10.4 secs in the Half Mile, while MA Congdon finished Junior Victor Ludorum narrowly ahead of CJ Ackford.

Athletics 1948: Back; NT Ross, PD Smith, DJ Price, AR Newcmbe, M Lunn. Seated; TI Adams, JW Ricks, DEG Perry (Captain), DG Rice, TN Storey, Front; AV Cawley, RJ Stephens, CJ Ackford.

At the Devon Public and Grammar School Amateur Athletic Sports at Kelly four weeks later, Storey bettered his own long-jump feat from Sports Day, and that of Rice, by jumping over the 20ft mark to win his event. However no-one else managed even a top three placing and the School once again finished sixth – *"Although other members of the team were winners in the school sports, they found the competition too exacting."*

Blundell's won the event and Kelly were second, and later that summer both of these Schools again had the better of Plymouth College, this time in the Swimming Pool. The fixture with the former was a first and although *"we received a thorough drubbing ... there was not such a great difference in the standard of the two teams as the points might suggest."*

But there were home gala wins over Plymouth City Transport and RNC Dartmouth, the later being a narrow but worthy victory;

"We sympathised with our visitors over the drop in water temperature from 75 degrees, to which they are accustomed, to our 62 degrees, but a warmed indoor bath means greater training facilities than are available in Plymouth and the team deserves credit for its win."

Within the School itself the Aquatic Sports were the subject of a major rethink that year with a sub-committee including Mr Davies, Mr Spear, NK Bennett, the Captain of Swimming and P Berryman, considering suggestions for a revision of the events and the points awarded for them.

Furthermore, Berryman and Mr Rendle undertook a thorough review of all the previous accounts of the Aquatic Sports since the completion of the Bath in 1902 to come up with a definitive list of record times;

"Publication in the Plymothian would appear to be an essential qualification for a record, since no other satisfactory method of verifying times suggests itself."

The 1948 School Water Polo team.

The earliest, unbeaten, records that presented themselves, under these guidelines, both belonged to FWB Blight from 1932 and 1934, while Tuckett's 100-yd time from 1935 was also listed. His 50-yd time

from the same year, however, was bettered at the 1948 Sports by NK Bennett, who also set what appeared to be new records for the 200-yds and the 50-yds backstroke (beating his own record from the previous year).

LF House posted another new record time in the 50-yd breaststroke that summer. But it was Bennett, with six wins in eight events, who was Pool Champion, although there must have been a few who sympathised with Ellis who finished second in seven of those eight senior events. Berryman, incidentally, finished third in five of them. A less-serious, but just as hotly competed for victory was the Past v Present Water Polo match played that day and featuring three Spears in the old boys' side.

While all of them still took to the water like proverbial ducks there were too many ducks for Gamesmaster's liking that season on the cricket field;

"The freak weather in May resulted in hard fast wickets and these proved to be our undoing".

It wasn't until the last Inter-School Fixture of the season that the First XI managed a win against a peer team, with Gosling finally finding his best bowling form with 6-14 and Dunkley hitting the only home-grown half century of the season with an unbeaten 51. White, meanwhile, topped the bowling figures (he logged an impressive 7-14 against Truro) and was just behind Dunkley in the batting stakes, while the Games Master, himself, managed 51 for the Club XI (School and Staff) that comprehensively beat Plymouth CC, with Mr Bonser taking 7-28.

Mr Bonser was also on fine form when a Club side (two from the 1st XI, two OPMs and seven staff and groundstaff) nearly beat Bolton Cricket Club, with a line-up that included bowlers who had played for Lancashire 2nd XI that summer.

Lower down the School, in the Colts U14 side, Cawley put on an impressive show against Sutton when he top-scored with 47 not out, having already taken 8-29. Earlier in the season Greenaway took six Saltash wickets for no runs as the visitors were skittled out for 23.

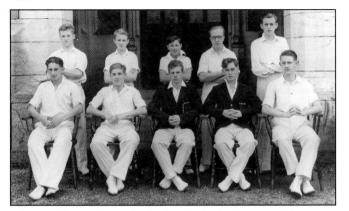

Sargents Senior House Cricket XI: Back; JH Benney, LK Dawson, DE Algate, B Coombes, JR Quick. Front; JW Ricks, K Pring, PM Dunkley (Captain) PH Flanders, NT Ross.

However *"no performance this term, on the field or in the bath, has surpassed in interest that of the School Orchestra in their first concert. They cannot as yet, blow their own trumpet, so we provide this fanfare for them:*
They nothing common played, or mean,
Upon that memorable scene.
Inwardly the fiddles may have been unstrung, the cornets breathless, and the reeds shaken in the wind, but, responded unfalteringly to the demands of their conductor, who to have produced so respectable a body in so short a time, must also be something of a conjuror."
The conjuror in question was John Bill and Messrs Dundas (clarinet), Porter (cello) and Hills-Harrop (piano) were among the massed ranks of the orchestra. Foremost among the boys was BJ Wotton who played three clarinet solos on the night. As an ensemble the orchestra played selections from Bach, Haydn and Handel. With the Choir they added selections from Handel's Messiah, concluding with Vaughan Williams' Linden Lea, then Early One Morning, Widecombe

Fair and inevitably the Carmen. A fitting climax to an *"evening memorable in the history of the school"*.
Although, strictly speaking, it wasn't the first ever Plymouth College School Orchestra, there was perhaps a feeling that this time, in the hands of an enthusiastic thirty-seven year-old, that there might be a stronger foundation to build upon. Such feelings were further enhanced when the new modern languages master, starting that September, was made Assistant Music Master before the end of his first term. Arriving at Plymouth College after two years teaching at the Lycee Montaigne, Paris *"where he also studied music at the famous Conservatoire"*, the new master had done his first degree in Exeter and was another former pupil of the School. The appointment of Harry Trevena that Autumn brought the number of OPMs on the staff to five (John Dufton, John Spear, Sam Rendle and Stafford Jackson were the others), and at 25 Harry was not quite the youngest of them - he'd been the year ahead of Rendle. He was, however, considerably younger than the other new master who arrived at Ford Park that term – Mr Gander, or rather Staff Instructor Commander (RN retd.) BV Gander, MBE.
Bernard Gander came to teach science and he came *"with a long record of service in the Royal Navy, and was for several years on the staff of the RNE College, Keyham, where he specialised in Metals and Fuel."* At the age of 54 Gander was only younger than Guy Hill, John Dufton and Eric Holman, all of whom, curiously enough, would still be on the staff when Gander himself came to leave two years later, but we are jumping forward.
The two appointments were symptomatic of the new growth at Plymouth College, growth that was spectacularly highlighted at Speech Day in Central Hall that October.
The guest speaker was Sir Alexander Maxwell, another old boy, only Sir Alexander had left the School the same month that the oldest member of staff, John Dufton,

had been born, in July 1892. At that time there were just 133 boys in the Main and Preparatory Schools – now there were 640, of whom 460 were in the Main School.
Attendant on these increases were not just added demands on staffing, but also, notwithstanding the Prep's move to Munday House, on playing fields. *"If necessary these will have to be found outside the city"*, said Mr Garnons Williams, who closed his speech with a reference to the history of Plymouth College which Mr CR Serpell was engaged in writing.
For his part Sir Alexander Maxwell provided an interesting insight into one of the more colourful characters in the School's history, his own headmaster, Francis Colson, who he said was famous for his wonted rebuke; *"Oh, do not try to be more of a goose than you can help!"*
"A phrase," he added, *"which has served me well as warning against specious phraseology or irrelevant evasion in dealing with any problem."*
Sir Alexander Maxwell had entered the Home Office back in 1904 and truly was one of the top Civil Servants of the day; *"Few men have had a longer record of service in Whitehall, and none a more honourable one"*, was how his career was summed up in the Spectator. *"Though he reached pension age eight years ago, he remained at his post through the arduous years of the war and its aftermath and goes now only when the Criminal Justice Act is safe on the statute book"* – Sir Alexander had played a large part in the preparation of that particular bill, and over the years had given *"loyal and invaluable service to Mr McKenna, Mr Churchill, Lord Samuel, Mr Clynes, Lord Templewood, Mr Morrison and Mr Chuter Ede."*
Meanwhile among those who the distinguished public servant presented prizes to that day was head boy DM Griffin, who won the Murch Memorial Prize for Science and, more importantly, a State Scholarship in Natural Science to Emmanuel College, Cambridge.

Griffin, having earlier exhorted his fellow Palmer's house members to take their House responsibilities more seriously, was instrumental in organising *"the highlight of the term's activities, the end-of-term House party, the first to be held since the war, in the School Gymnasium"*. A happy occasion, it also served as a fitting farewell for Griffin – *"a tower of strength to the House in general"* – who was off to Cambridge, via a spell of National Service.

"Sir Alexander Maxwell, an old boy of the school, who distributed the awards at Plymouth College speech-day yesterday, presenting the Murch Memorial prize for science to DM Griffin, head prefect." (Western Evening Herald).

Latterly one of his joint Palmer's House Captains was MJ Quantick, a keen member of the Literary & Debating Society, who that term unsuccessfully led the opposition in a debate deploring blood sports, and on another occasion, with F Davey, failed to convince the House that the BBC *"gives good value for the listeners money"*. Other issues raised that term included the projected Channel Tunnel, successfully opposed by Northcott and Savery. Interestingly enough, the future City Council leader and Chairman of the Governors,

Savery also seconded the successful motion *"this House deplores party politics in Local Government"*.

The big debate of the term though was the inter-school Diamond Jubilee Debate in which the motion before the three-hundred-plus pupils packing Big School was that *"This house has full confidence in the domestic policy of this Government and its ability to conduct our domestic affairs"*.

For this special occasion the main speaker on either side was not a local schoolboy – or girl - rather the motion was proposed by the Labour MP for Broxtowe, Mr Frederick Seymour Cocks, who was, as it happened an OPM, and therefore very familiar with Big School. Opposing the motion was Parliamentary prospective candidate for the Conservative Party, Mr JJ Astor.

Clearly the year had been a major one in domestic politics. On July 5th 1948, the Industrial Insurance Act, the National Insurance Act and the National Health Service Act had all become law;

"Mr Seymour Cocks gave brief details of these benefits. The expectation of life for a year-old child today," he said, *"was sixty years, the housing problem was being tackled, many houses were being built and the minimum floor area had been increased to 900 square feet. In the old days, no help had been available for secondary schools, today every child could have secondary education. The school leaving age had been raised to fifteen and half the undergraduates were now assisted from public funds. Four million children had free milk daily, and two and a half million would soon enjoy free meals – eight hundred new school canteens were being opened in 1948. The Government,"* he told his audience, *"believed in State ownership and the control of certain industries. It aimed at full employment. The Bank of England had been nationalised and so had the mines; the latter just in time, for they had become a seething hell of discontent. Gas, electricity, cable and wireless and railways had all been nationalised – and steel would be."*

"Labour," said Seymour Cocks, *"was leading the country to the sunlit heights – a social revolution had been carried out without a shot being fired."*

Jackie Astor's main case opposing centred around the contentions that no one party had *"a monopoly of knowledge with regard to the poorer classes, that British Empire was nothing to be ashamed of and that the standard of life in Britain in 1939 had been nothing to be ashamed of either."*

As Astor saw it the country was headed for bankruptcy and the assembled students largely tended to agree with him voting 251-62 against the motion.

But whatever the public opinion, from whatever quarter, there was no denying that this was a time of great social changes, right across the social spectrum. Indeed it was this year, as noted in that term's Cambridge Letter, that women were at long last accorded the status of full members of the University. There had been women studying and lecturing there before, but they were not given official recognition. In practice this meant that a female archaeologist appointed as a professor ten years earlier - Dorothy Garrod the first woman to hold an Oxbridge chair – was not able to speak at meetings of the top legislative body there, even on matters concerning her own department.

To mark the new ruling Her Majesty the Queen visited Cambridge to receive a degree and among those detailed to welcome her was the pioneering student of Oriental studies, GW Sargent, OPM.

Thousands of undergraduates turned out to see their Queen, while over at Queen's College, DF Pring was, we read, *"brought down to earth on many occasions, one of which was the Freshman's Rugger Trial."*

Back at Ford Park the rugger season got off to a good start with wins against Fisguard and St Boniface College, and then after an away defeat against Sutton they came back to beat Hele's, Exeter, at Ford Park and Wellington School at Wellington for what was, apparently, the first time ever.

Above; Sections from the whole school photograph taken in October 1948, just two years after the previous session. Below, a group of boarders pose outside Thorn Park.

Right, on a rainy sports day, at Ford Park, Pearse hurdles the high jump rope, held loosely between posts placed none-too-invitingly infront of the long-jump sand pit.

Captain Roskruge, despite being severely injured on more than one occasion, kept coming back for more. Asser made a fine job of leading the pack, Berryman was stout in defence, whilst occupying the fullback position was Ackford *"well built for the job, most promising"*, despite being *"very young to be playing with the 1st XV."*

Plymouth College 1st XV: Back row; TT Hocking, PD Smith, M Lunn, NT Ross, CJ Ackford, C Squance, PC Popplestone, MJ Quantick. Seated; DEG Perry, RK Asser, HW Roskruge (Captain), P Berryman, JW Ricks. Front; DG Price, PM Dunkley.

There were clearly a number of talented youngsters further down the School and the Senior Colts (the new side – U16 – which had only come into existence the previous year and had started with just two fixtures) started their season with an unbeaten run of four matches, double the number of fixtures they had had in their first season.

Amongst those encouraging the boys that term had been *"Messrs RH Sparks, E Stanbury, B Evans and J Hanley – all England forwards ... who have been kind enough to come along and coach or referee."*

The refereeing situation raised an important issue in another School sport – boxing;

"Boxers in the School should note that an important change has recently been authorised in the running of competitions. In future there will be three Judges and one Referee, and bouts will be decided by the Judges."

"There has," wrote Allgood, the boxing secretary, *"been a considerable revival of late in schools' boxing, and the Club is now affiliated to the English Schools A.B.A."*

"It is hoped that canvas flooring will be available for the ring by the time of the House competition at the end of February."

Ford Park Corner in the forties - familiar ground for many boys.

The biggest revival of interest in any one area at Ford Park, however, had to be in the Natural History Society;

"Within a year of its inception this Society can now, we believe, claim to be the biggest in the School, with over one hundred and thirty members, drawn from the highest to the lowest forms. One hundred and twenty of these attended the last meeting, filling the Lecture Room to its fullest capacity."

"Not a little of this success is due to Mr HG Hurrell and Mr AE Capps. Mr Hurrell gave the first lecture of the

term, showing a number of his very beautiful coloured films on aspects of Dartmoor Natural History."

Films were also shown on such divers topics as *"The Tawny Owl, Tadpoles, the Ecology of Dartmoor and the Birds of the Farne Islands."*

There were also *"two widely different films, each a classic in its own sphere, shown to the sixth form;*

"Song of Ceylon suffered from a harsh sound track, which distorted music already sufficiently unorthodox, and from the fact that its pioneer technique has been largely applied to later films of its type. One recognized, however," wrote VWG Tompkins, *"Its skill and beauty in portraying the customs and scenery of Ceylon".*

The other film though was an unqualified success - Lawrence Olivier in Henry V.

Laurence Olivier breathing life and passion into Shakespeare.

"The response to the battle of Agincourt was obvious and it left one longing to see Olivier's presentation of Hamlet in the same medium".

Other films shown to the lower forms, again with a projector provided by the Central Office of Information, included Medieval Monastery, Sizal, the Wealth of Australia and Downlands and Fenlands.

Tompkins, incidentally, was also the Senior boy in the Cadets, indeed he had just been promoted to the rank of Under Officer – "the first to hold this rank in the Plymouth College JTC". Storey was not far behind him though.

The increase of interest in film did not however, at this stage have a detrimental effect on the activities on the School stage itself; indeed the Christmas Entertainment that December "employed a greater number of boys than any previous production we can remember".

There were four small plays - reduced in number to three on the second night in order to make the entertainment a more acceptable length – with musical interludes from a School Septet (Messrs Gander, Trevena, Porter, and the boy Wooton playing, with Messrs Davies, Radford and Hills-Harrop singing).

Rather ironically Refund was the title of the play that extended the first night's bill of fare, while the three that had two airings were Pyramus and Thisbe, Thirty Minutes in a Street and Truth is a Beauty - "the new creation run up for us by "Haberdasher"that scored heavily with its audience."

"It was acted with such polish and assurance by Mrs Porter, Mr Davies and Algate, that it attained almost to high comedy, and it was difficult to adjust oneself after it to the broader humour of Mrs Scott, Mr Mercer and Asser.".

As it transpired it was to have been just about the last thing Alaister Davies did at the School – he left that month to take up a post at Wellington School; "His cheerful vigour in the class-room, in the swimming bath, and at the wicket, are well-remembered."

Davies' two-year stint at Ford Park, brief as it was, will have made more of a mark than the time spent by Messrs BH Pollack and CJ Yelland who both spent the following term, Spring 49, at the School "in preparation for their future career as Schoolmasters." But both "entered very fully into our activities" and will doubtless have registered with one or two pupils from that time.

Clearly there was plenty of good humour around that December, as that difficult decade came to a close, a feeling that was undoubtedly enhanced by another of Mr Bill's initiatives;

"The Carol Service held in St Gabriel's Church on Monday, 13 December, was much more than an evening of agreeable melody. It established itself as a new and significant occasion in the school calendar, and all will look forward to its repetition in future years."

"It is not merely that the traditional tunes, so roughly handled in the streets, are heard to more advantage inside a church. Combined with the reading of the Christmas lessons, they are restored to dignity and their meaning is enhanced as they serve to illuminate the message of Christmas with their own grace and beauty."

Once In Royal David City, I Saw Three Ships, O Little Town of Bethlehem, God Rest You Merry Gentlemen, The First Noel and Adestes Fideles were among the carols sung that night, while the lessons from the Scriptures were read by Mr Garnons Williams himself. With moving pictures, music and the dramatic arts making an ever-increasing impact on School life, it was refreshing to see that another area of promise that year was the literary output of IVb. Their – pressed –contributions for the Plymothian included essays on activities as varied as those of the Plymouth, Devonport and Stonehouse Cycling Club, Bird Watching and "the bus fancier who puts in happy hours at the Milehouse Depot, or at Brislington Shed, Bristol". One of them also, found "an interesting milk bar in Totnes".

A number of older boys, meanwhile, were venturing even further afield than Bristol or Totnes, thanks to the good natured Dr Ellingher and Mr Dent who took a "weirdly dressed assortment of twenty boys between fourteen and eighteen" on a Swiss holiday;

"First the thrill of being picked to go, followed by nervous excitement: we had never been abroad, we had never been on skis, we had not lived together at close quarters; would it turn out to be all that we expected?"

"We were in the train; we were sleeping, packed like sardines, in an air raid shelter in Clapham, on the Channel; a third class train leaving Calais ... the long climb up to Hotel Halde. Too tired to eat the biggest meal we had seen for years, we went to bed."

"Next day ... we quickly settled down to our elongated feet and found that some are born skiers (Hose and Algate), some attain ski-ing (most of the rest), and some (Gran Sherriff upside down in the snow) have skis thrust upon them."

Christmas 1948 Mr Dent and Dr Ellingher and the Swiss trip party.

Happy memories for *"twenty-two random-selected people, full of the health of that high air and the joy of learning a new art, the happiness of being together, master and boy, in scenery whose glory we remember all the more vividly now that we have left it."*

The following term there was another foreign adventure led by Mr Jackson; *"Paris, with its magnificent buildings and splendid tree-lined boulevards could not fail to impress us ... The traffic, unhampered by any speed limit, also impressed.*

Scratch Jackson's 1949 school trip to Paris, above TEJ Savery & Co. congregate outside a Parisian gallery and below the party visit the splendid gardens of Versailles.

Many times we thought our last hour had come ... We did not however, spend all our time admiring the glories of Paris. Certain members of the party were observed to be by no means adverse to the sparkle of French wine, and made full use of their opportunity of imbibing a large amount at little cost. A pleasant afternoon was spent at Versailles where Mr Dundas thought he was going to be arrested by a gendarme, but this time his captor turned out to be only a guide."

As it was, it turned out to be one of the last beanos that the OPM French master led the boys of Plymouth College on, meanwhile the Old Boys themselves were looking for a bar of their own, or at least a base of some kind;

"Attempts are still being made to find a headquarters incorporating a sports field, and it may be possible to report some progress on this in the near future", was how the report read.

OPM Cricket and Hockey was thriving, with 24 cricket fixtures being fulfilled that summer. The annual dinner was booked for the Grand Hotel on Wednesday 29 December, the tickets were 11s/6d each and there was a drive to recruit new members.

As the OPM's searched for a playing field of their own, the Prep now had one;

"In the past the Prep. ceased work on Tuesday and Thursday afternoons, and there was a general exodus from Munday House in the direction of the Main School playing field. Crossing Hyde Park Road was a major operation. We felt rather like the Israelites crossing the Red Sea while the waves of traffic stood stationary and motionless on either side."

"Such peregrinations, however, are no longer necessary, and instead of devoting whole afternoons to Rugby and arranging the time-table so that nearly every Form might be free to play games on certain prescribed days, the games periods can be spread over the whole week without upsetting the balance of the time-table and the normal sequence of lessons."

The new site was fully coming into its own now; the walls of Munday House were lavishly decorated with pupils' works and almost every class was relocated in a bid not to overcrowd the new site as the planned maximum Prep number of 180 boys suddenly had become 194 boys – *"only Division I and Division V stayed put".*

However while there may have been significant disruption at the beginning of the 1948-49 school year for the Prep, the middle part of that year went surprisingly smoothly;

"Usually there is a distinct cleveage or hiatus between the beginning and ending of a Spring term; there is a gap or period during which, owing to climatic conditions, the life of a school almost comes to a halt. The field is out of commission and absenteeism on account of illness is so widespread that the work is seriously interfered with. At no time, even for a brief period, has that been the case this term."

The unusually fine weather had a knock-on effect at the Main School, too, where, *"captained by Mr Dundas, the Staff were encouraged to take to the Hockey Field, where they have maintained an unbroken record against the Senior Colts, the Second XI and the First."*

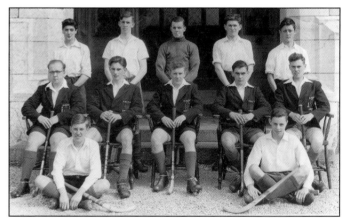

2nd XI Hockey: Back JA Greasely, CJ Ackford, P Howard, AV Cawley, DR Ellis. Seated; R Coombes, JW Ricks, R Polkinghorne (Captain) BJ Gosling, J Brownrigg. Front; RW Viant, KEP Wall.

It was a white Christmas for the "wierdly dressed assortment" of twenty-two randomly selected boys who accompanied Mr Dent and Dr Ellingher to Switzerland at the end of 1948.

The Firsts themselves won their first three games, but then failed to live up to the expectations of them, with nine of the previous season's eleven in their side. Nevertheless Berryman, Dunkley, Perry and Bennett all played in the Combined Schools XI against the County side and acquitted themselves well. The team did well too in a new fixture – against the University College of the South West – although they lost 4-2. They also lost the services, prematurely, of Berryman who, although ultimately bound for Oxford, was called up for National Service before the end of the season. Berryman, incidentally, was also chosen to play in the English Schools Rugby trials.

The fine weather that ushered in 1949 also saw more than the usual amount of activity in the Fives' Courts, following the refurbishment of one of them during the Christmas vacation.

The sun shone too on the Cross-Country run, which *"by careful planning and with the aid of a dozen markers"* saw an extension of the previous year's course around Central Park, from three to four and a half miles. Although clearly it was a cold day, that didn't stop a record number of entrants taking part – sixty seniors and two hundred and twenty juniors.

Boxing Team 1949: Back; RJ Williams, K Pring, HJL Jory, JB Lewis. Seated; BHR Mahoney, DJ Allgood, PH Flanders (Captain), C Lean, AR Harvey. Front; C Cload and DS Cutler.

Lewis finished ahead of the pack for the juniors, while in the seniors race, the favourite, Newcombe, was pipped by K Pring.

Pring was not so fortunate in the ring however and he lost out to Mahoney for the School Middleweight title. In the heavyweight contest Squance beat Savery, while in the most keenly-contested weight – Welterweight – Lean beat Allgood in the final. Allgood though won all three of his bouts for the School team, against DHS, St Peter's Scouts and Kelly, as did Cload. No-one else managed three wins, indeed Mahoney won none, but nevertheless *"gave outstanding evidence of how to box hard – and lose"*.

The newly-promoted Shooting Team also learnt to lose – *"We have discovered that matches are more difficult to win in Division I"*, wrote Hopewell in his report. There were some encouraging signs though as after six straight defeats the team managed three consecutive victories and both Hopewell and Chesterfield managed top scores of 100 during the season. Chesterfield was also chosen to represent the CCF in an Inter-Services Postal Match in March.

The OPM Shooting Team meanwhile finished second, by two points, to Alleyne's School in the Public School Old Boys' Match, competing for the Fletcher Trophy. What was particularly novel about the School shooting situation, however, was the banner under which they were shooting – the CCF; this was *"a new comprehensive name for pre-service units to combine them for the purpose of administration"*. The new initials stood for Combined Cadet Force and as if to commemorate this innovation the term saw *"a much-needed reorganization of Q by CQMS Sherriff and several senior NCO's who redecorated the Stores during the Christmas holidays."*

Furthermore it was announced that all cadets over fourteen were issued with uniform although it was noted that *"smartness on parade is still not instinctive among cadets"*.

But it was a good term for the Corps nonetheless; *"the mild winter has given great scope for outdoor instruction"* and further *"enabled us to enjoy Field Day on 11th March"*. The day itself was spent on Ringmoor Down and CSM Newcombe thanked the Commanding Officer of the Plymouth Garrison for the use of six Army trucks *"these saved valuable time in conveying us quickly to Ringmoor"*.

This facility was again made available in the Summer term, by which time there had been a noticeable improvement in the drill and general turn out of the Corps. Indeed so impressed was Major-General CFC Coleman DSO, OBE and OPM (then the General Officer Commanding the SW District) when he visited the School for an Inspection on 9th June that the Headmaster awarded the Corps a half-holiday.

The Corps, that summer, was bigger than it had ever been and every Friday they paraded – *"four platoons, in uniform, and two platoons of enthusiastic recruits"*. There were excursions to Down Thomas and Warminster, in May, for a variety of demonstrations, and in August to Warminster again for the Annual Camp (with fifty-nine cadets making the journey). There was limited success for the Shooting Team, as they finished third at the Devon Public School's Shield competition at the Rippon Tor, near Ashburton, with Greasely dropping only four points at 500 yards in a strong cross wind.

The Scouts, meanwhile, although celebrating the fifth anniversary of their first Field Day, were, nationally and locally, struggling for funds – *"which suffered by lack of donations during the war"*. Consequently the Troop Leader was appealing to parents to be sympathetic *"if requests for paid jobs are made during the "Two-Bob-a-Job" Week"* that April. Just as for the CCF, the Scouts, thanks to the efforts of MGW Burt, had put their Quartermaster's Stores in order and *"were looking forward to a Bacchanalian orgy at Camp"*, where again, like the CCF, a record number were expected to attend that summer.

The CCF *"in their Brass and Blanco"* clearly made quite an impression on the editors of that term's one-and-thruppenny Plymothian. But then there was little else that was especially noteworthy, apart from the disruption occasioned by the creation of the new Dining Hall *"when Valletort is being shaken at its foundations"* and the *"Terrors of the Gym"* ... *"with the ceiling falling piecemeal on those below."*

It had been hoped that the conversion of Valletort's basement into dining-rooms and kitchens, would have been finished earlier, but a shortage of steel supplies delayed the work. One of the upstairs classrooms of Valletort was converted at the same time – *"so as to be able to take a whole form."*

Valletort, incidentally, was also where all the Careers books – overflowing from the "new" library – were kept. The library itself was going from strength to strength. *"Our biggest expansion has been in books for scientists, ranging from things with titles like "Excursus on the Co-ordinates of Differential Integers" to "Model Deisels" and "Fun with Chemistry"."*

"W.E.Johns has passed Richmal Crompton as the most borrowed author," while the *"record for the most borrowing is held by a boy in 3b; JD Vittle has borrowed an average of two books every three days over the last six months."*

Clearly there was an impressive appetite for the printed word, however, the winds of change were blowing harder than ever before. A Prep School excursion to the City Art Gallery that year had given a number of boys the opportunity to witness a Children's Hour Broadcast with "Uncle Mac" as part of a *"B.B.C. at Work"* exhibition being staged there.

The broadcast was, according to Uncle Mac (Derek McCulloch), unprecedented in as much as the programme had never had *"such a vast visible audience before and from the City where he himself had lived as a boy."* Born in 1897, near the Hoe, and baptized in St Andrew's he could remember Spooner's fire

and the old Market and he had been with Children's Hour since the beginning in 1922, when the BBC first started. At the end of the broadcast there was a rush for his autograph but generally there seemed to be a *"complete lack of curiosity and enthusiasm. In fact"* wrote our anonymous Plymothian reporter, *"one began to wonder whether the Children's Hour programme still has such wide appeal. Perhaps Dick Barton knows the answer."*

1949 saw the fourth *"Dick Barton ... Special Agent"* series hit the airwaves, with a new man, Duncan Carse, taking over from Noel Johnson in the title role. The Devil's Gallop still conjuring up the initial excitement as the signature tune.

There was even more excitement at the Prep, however, as *"after a delay of nearly two years, we have this term at last been able to have a regular series of weekly film shows."*

There was some concern that, without commentary *"historical films are probably meaningless to the very young"*. *"Nevertheless the films shown to date have on the whole been well received by their enthusiastic, if not too critical, audience, and the "box office returns" show no sign of flagging interest."*

"Films on nature rarely fail to appeal; boys love these just as much as animal stories. Geographical films too usually capture their interest; in fact "The building of an igloo" is regarded in the Prep as "the film of the term" and has been "awarded an Oscar"."

"Films shown this term have included "The Royal Tour of Africa", "Our Feathered Friends", "Irrigation in Egypt", "Pollination" and "The Life of a Fern"."

Generally it was a vintage year for British films, with *"Hamlet"* and *"The Red Shoes"* both winning real Oscars. *"The Third Man"*, *"Oliver Twist"*, *"Kind Hearts and Coronets"* and *"Whiskey Galore"* were other home-grown favourites. But it was not all good news for the industry, as the Rank Studios at Lime Grove were purchased by the BBC for television use

and a total of 1,500 British film industry workers were laid off in the year.

Television was still a few years away from the Westcountry though and the *"weekly cinema list"* was still a pin-up feature of the trendy Oxford undergraduate, with his *"fluorescent lighting, modern furniture and electric fire."*

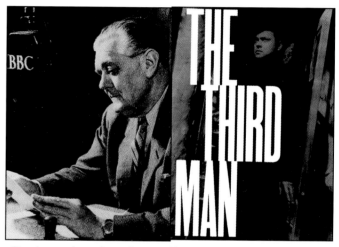

Two icons of popular culture in 1949, Plymouth-born Derek Mc-Culloch - Uncle Mac - from BBC radio's Children's Hour and Orson Wells in Carol Reed's classic movie The Third Man.

Back at Big School more films *"from the Central Office of Information"* (remember George Orwell's 1984 was published that summer) were shown to the bigger boys, among them; *"Cyprus is an Island"*, *"Latitude and Longitude"*, *"Fenlands"* and *"The Fishing Industry"*. The Natural History Society also staged a couple of film shows, and a talk about Oology – *"illustrated by eggs from the Montague-Evans collection."*

Numbers were reasonably healthy, and twenty-three members of the society went to Newton Ferrers to study the natural life of the estuary. However numbers attending the Literary and Debating Society were so low that several meeting had to be cancelled. On a brighter note, the standard of speaking at those meetings that were held was *"higher than usual"*.

More positive notes were struck at the second concert given by the School Orchestra and Choir. *"The hall was packed to the last seat." "The programme was mainly classical ... after two beautiful German folk songs, faultlessly sung by the Choir, Mr Trevena played Chopin and brought the house down with his brilliant interpretation of the difficult work."*

Meanwhile, *"the last item on the programme was of particular interest because it revealed Mr Bill from a new angle – as a composer. It was a very effective song with a fine passage for the tenors and basses, well done by them."*

Mr Bill's song was *"The Rolling English Road"*, a musical adaptation of GK Chesterton's celebrated poem from 1914 ... *"a merry road, a mazy road ..."*

Poems were thin on the ground in that term's magazine; one of them, by Head Boy, MI Lander, was entitled – *"A Prefect's Daymare"*;

"It chanced upon a summer day
(A master present sad to say)
In dreamy sleep I fell:
And as in slumberous bliss I lay,
There sounded, tolling far away,
The early morning bell."

I sprinted down the corridor,
For I was thinking "It is Moore"!
It would not do if I was seen
To come to prayers at 9.15!
How would it be if it was said,
"HE entered prayers behind the Head"?

And then, just as the masters do,
Nine turtles entered, two by two.
One said, "I will take prayers today,
Your usual masters are away".
We sang a hymn, without a tune, of some peculiar number.

It started off like "Bless 'em all" and ended with a rumba.

Then said a turtle loud and clear,
"A notice to the prefects here!
You prefects now are getting old
And many boys you've beaten.
My colleagues here agree it's time
That you were cooked and eaten".
I rushed, with mind distraught from School,
And tumbled in the swimming pool.

A voice beside me said, "I think
You've put your finger in the ink".
Thus waking, I, a little shaken,
Continued writing notes on Bacon."

Activity in the School pool that summer incidentally yielded not a lot to shout about, Mr Spear joined the Water Polo team against the Plymouth Police and played alongside Richards, Pring, House, Smith, Wright and Bennett. The last was clearly a star with his backstroke, while overall the introduction of Swimming Leagues *"in which the various forms have been competing with one another for the highest percentage of swimmers and also for the greatest average distance covered per boy"* meant that total distance swum by the School *"has been increased from 24 miles to 55 miles in the course of six weeks."*

Perhaps the most memorable aspect of swimming that year was the temperature of the water – up to 76 degrees ... *"and led to the question of whether this was a record or not. Personally,"* wrote JRS, *"I have some recollection of the figure 80 being reached in the days when the water was changed once a fortnight, but of one record I am certain, more boys have used the Bath during the last fortnight than in any other similar period in the Bath's history; no wonder so much water used to overflow into the "quad" during peak periods."*

Like the swimmers, the cricketers too were not quite *"as bright as the June sunshine"*, but *"they never depressed us and their full record is at least moderate."*

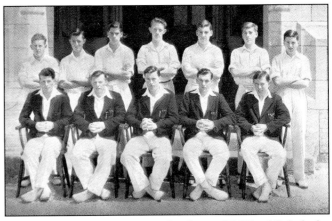

Cricket 1st XI 1949: Back; R Polkinghorne, DR Ellis, J Balmforth, NT Ross, C Squance, K Pring, B Porter. Front; MJ Quantick, DEG Perry, M Lunn (Captain), BJ Gosling, GR White.

Watching from the wings Bert Sargent thought the teams of old were better. Ted Mercer, however, felt that the bowling was easier in the good old days. Lunn, a fine swimmer, proved himself a useful cricketer too; he and Perry scored the only half-centuries and he also returned one of the tidiest bowling averages. Balmforth took three wickets in his first over against Exeter School, while Gosling too proved to be useful with the bat and ball. Mr Radford scored the summer's only ton – 131 against the City Police for a Staff and Ground XI – while Mr Mercer was also among the runs.

Lunn's overall athleticism, incidentally, saw him set a new javelin record (132ft 6in) in the School Sports, while JW Ricks' 39ft 4in was a new Hop-Step and Jump record. Ricks it was, with wins in Long Jump and Hurdles and second placings in the High Jump and 100 yards, who finished Victor Ludorum with Newcombe, who finished ahead of him in the 100 and 440 finished second overall and second to Pring in the 880 and mile.

At the invitation of Plymouth Technical College the School entered a team (Price, Ricks, Newcombe and Benney) in the Plymouth and District Inter-School Relay at Marsh Mills and won it – by five yards.

Later that summer Sandhurst-bound Under Officer Newcombe, travelled with his fellow CCF troops to Warminster, to enjoy annual camp in a brown Bell tent. Whilst there, five *"lucky cadets toured the Royal Military College of Science at Shrivenham, where they saw the most up-to-date artillery: the recoiless gun, the V-2 rocket projectors, the Link trainer and Radar."*

The Scouts, meanwhile, had their annual summer sojourn at Werrington Park, where a couple of OPMs – ' Jan' Easton and Peter Hoare – gave a hand. *"I hope they have created a precedent which other old Scouts will follow if they have the good fortune to enjoy a long summer 'vac',"* wrote John Spear in his annual review. JRS himself had been similarly helpful in his younger days, he'd also been a star in the School pool. This year however there was a star there who outshone all others, as Mr Spear described NK Bennett as being **"the best all-round swimmer the School has produced"**.

Bennett had been Captain of Swimming for four years, and that summer he took the title of Victor Ludorum for the fourth time, leaving a frustrated Pring, with six second placings, his Proxime Accessit. Bennett left the School with five swimming records to his credit *"and a high degree of proficiency at Water Polo."*

Water polo doesn't seem to have played too much of a part in the sporting calendar that year. However, encouraged by Sam Rendle, an unofficial tennis team was formed and undertook a fixture with "Sam's Sloshums" and although they were narrowly defeated *"the possibility of more matches of a similar nature is undeniably encouraging."*

As their Captain, Price, ruefully observed, however, *"We have not, unfortunately, been able to obtain fixtures with any recognised school teams due to the unofficial nature of the club."*

On an even sadder note, the death was noted of the recently-retired clerk to the Governors Charles Serpell. The 79 year old OPM had joined the School in 1879 and had only just completed a *"short historical sketch of the School"* which as yet had not been published.

Cover detail from Serpell's 20-page, Plymothian-sized historical sketch of the School, published posthumously the following year.

"There could be no more fitting memorial to him," ran the Headmaster's tribute to him. One of the first ever editors of the Plymothian, Charles Serpell had joined the Governing body not all that long after leaving School and on his retirement had been succeeded as Clerk by his son Roger, who, like his distinguished brother, David, had also been educated at Ford Park.

Another great OPM to take leave of this mortal coil that year was Lieut Coll William Drury CBE, a distinguished Royal Marine, a former Mayor – and Freeman - of Saltash, and author of *The Flag Lieutenant* and *A King's Hard Bargain*. Drury had been a founder pupil of the School just two years before Serpell in 1877.

A less drastic departure saw Mr Kirke, one of the most recent Prep staff appointments (Spring '47) move on to take a post at Somerset County School, and in his place Mr Martin-Smith, from Lansdowne School, High Wycombe, arrived to take on Division II and PE duties. At the same time, reflecting the increasing Prep numbers, Miss Jane came as Form Mistress to Division III – the Senior Division of the Lower School. Miss Jane had previously spent some time as Headmistress of Noss Mayo School.

Before the year was out there were staff changes too at the Main School as two linguists left for fresh pastures.

Like Kirke at the Prep, George Hills-Harrop had only been at Plymouth College since '47, but he left to take up the post of Senior Spanish master at Launceston College. Stafford Jackson on the other hand had been at Ford Park some seven years as a staff member and a similar length of time before that as a pupil. The comparatively short Jackson was not however, particularly well-suited to the profession. Control in the classroom did not come easy to him and he would regularly sit in front of his class, head in hands, fingering his eczema encrusted face. Nicknamed Scratch Jackson, accordingly, he was regularly "played up" and on one occasion somewhat unwisely physically grabbed and shook a lad in a class of pellet-firing miscreants. The lad was the son of the City Engineer and his parents lived near the deputy head, another OPM, John Dufton. The mother of the "abused" lad was very friendly with Mrs Dufton and, it would appear, that her complaint led to summary dismissal of Jackson by the *"fiery but fair"* Garnons Williams.

Meanwhile, missing most of the term, but not planning to leave was classics master Ernest Dundas who was indisposed through illness.

When the new academic year began that September there were a few new faces at Ford Park - two of them arriving to shore up the moderm language department. Philip Coggin, came fresh from the Royal Naval College at Dartmouth to take over as senior French master.

At 32 Coggin was still quite young, but then this was a pretty youthful department and the Cambridge graduate that arrived with him to teach French and History – Roger Elliott - was the same age as musician and modern linguist, Harry Trevena, who had, of course, just come back to his alma mater the previous year.

M. Elliott sans moustache

Hubert Hall, another historian, was, at 28, just a year older than those two, while David Lindley, a geographer, at 25 was younger still. All four new men were Oxbridge graduates and the School was quick to find them extra-curricular responsibilities.

Lindley, overnight, became College Housemaster, he also got involved with the Philatelic Society and joined the Scouts as Assistant Scoutmaster; Lieutenant Hall, an expert in map-reading, joined the CCF and was an instant help for those looking to pass their Cert A's, Mr Elliott threw himself into coaching the Shooting team, with almost instant effect, while Mr Coggin found himself in Thompson's as one of the housemasters there - he also found himself agreeing to take a party of about twenty boys to France before his first year was completed.

The Plymothian's School Notes at the start of that winter term also informed us that the two, single, OPM staff members were to be married; Mr Rendle to Miss Betty Tucker and Mr Trevena to Mlle Michelle Renard - in Paris, over the Christmas holidays.

Mr Trevena was amongst those who made the short trip up to Thorn Park on the odd occasion to entertain the boarders; *"we envy the facility with which he can move from the turn-table to the piano-stool"*.

"Joe Egg was always a welcome visitor for a sing-song too," recalls Colin May, *"his 'Plymouth College boarders, happy boys are we; Dr Battrick's orders, keep us healthy and free,' to the tune of Land of Hope and Glory, had memorable verses!"*

Mutley Plain on a quiet Sunday in 1949

There was plenty of music at Ford Park too … and dancing; *"Dancing classes have been, for some two years now, a welcome and popular activity among the senior forms, though we can recall no mention of this in the Plymothian. But we are pleased this term to record that a new class, in Folk Dancing, has been started, and is held under our own roof. We had not quite expected that it would appeal so strongly to the Rugby players among us, and particularly to those in the Science Sixth. The Rugger player may feel more at home in "Rufty Tufty" than in the Slow Fox-Trot, and the Scientist no doubt seeks some compensation for the drabness of life among the bottles. Perhaps, when they become proficient in the gym, they will venture out of doors and celebrate a victory with a Gaillard, or lament a defeat with a solemn Pavane."*

Sadly there were more defeats than victories that term as only five of the eleven fixtures were won. *"In fairness to the boys I must record that an unusual number of players have been incapacitated for long periods through illness and injury."*

1949 - the 1st XV in informal mode, pose on the Pavilion steps.

"As a pair, Price and Pring are probably the best centres that we have produced for some years," but *"their joint appearances were limited to four games."*

1949 Junior Colts XV: Back; CR Cload, JR Cundy, D Bowles, GP Stephens, NR Napper, MJ Hooper, GC Blight. Seated; NV Blackler, RJ Stephens, DS Cutler (Capt), A Richards, IDW Wright. Front; RK WIlley, CH Gullett.

Price suffered a troubling knee injury while Pring broke his collar bone in the first half of the term. In the seconds Williams and Wyman both missed matches on account of injuries, and an inevitable side-effect of all this was that no less than eight players were pulled at one time or another from the already stretched Senior Colts side to fill out the firsts and seconds. Not surprisingly, therefore, they lost five of their six fixtures, just winning the last by the narrowest of margins (3-0).

1949 Senior Colts XV: Front; BJ Francis, RD Mitchell, AV Cawley, HJL Jory, BW Richards, DP Rowe, JD Stitson, DC Chubb. Seated; MA Congdon, DH Voisin, RJ Booth (Captain), AR Harvey, JK Reynold. Front; JWL Watson, DE Algate.

Above, no more schoolwork for this happy band, on their last day at Plymouth College ... as pupils. Below - Armada Way begins to take shape, and the days are numbered for the Prudential Building (right) and Russell Street.(in the centre).

Thorn Park boarders 1949. Back; Anon, L Harvey, J Battrick, H Mitchell, J Ricks, H Jory. Middle; R Bidder, M Dean, A Beard, R Allgood, G Greenway, P Lewis, C May, J Shelton, B Luckham. Bottom; J Balmforth, A Lewis, J Benney, Mrs Kitty Battrick, Dr W Battrick, D Allgood, A Arthur. Seated;J Dawe, Allgood iii, Spot, C Matthews.

"Prior to the arrival of 'Perse' Battrick, the boarding house was run by Mr & Mrs Holman. Austerity was the order of the day - rationing and discipline were strict. One pot of jam per month, 40z butter and a small pot of sugar were issued, weekly, to each boy."

"A shop-bought pasty, bread and tea constituted a regular evening meal. Entry was via the back lane, shoe-cleaning was a daily chore and there was no radio, TV or recorded music ... but we didn't miss it as we never had it."

"After Dr & Mrs Battrick took over numbers increased. They ate with the boys and as rationing eased so the food improved. The top dorm, an unheated attic, held twelve, with 'baby' and 'senior' dorms of four to six on the floor below."

"Perce, a triple AAA Champion, who (reportedly) narrowly missed out on Olympic selection before the war, encouraged participation in all sports. He ensured fitness with Sunday walks; a bus to Yelverton and a walk home along the Plym Valley, and to ensure no slacking , he came too."

"After lunch it was letters home, then the march across to Emmanuel for the Evening Service - the second opportunity of the week to see girls. The big highlight though was the hour at Dancing Class at PHS - and some boarders never learnt to dance! No other outings were permitted - no wonder the boarders enjoyed away matches!" Colin May.

There was better news though lower down the School where the increase in numbers was having a positive effect on the potential of Plymouth College.

Another 'casual' rugger shot from 1949 - this time on the field.

"*This is the side we have been waiting to see,*" wrote Hugh Dent, of a Junior Colt team that only lost one game (6-3 against Truro), and scored 173 points in their other seven matches, only conceding more than three points on one other occasion.

"*In Southern we have a centre with a real sense of the game. One would say the same of Stevens if he could kill an insane desire to score tries instead of making them.*"

The OPM's too were enjoying some success, their most successful season since the war in fact, "*in spite of a rather more formidable fixture list.*" The newly-arrived teacher, Mr Hall, was quick to don an OPM jersey as the Club secretary noted that "*as usual we are popular opponents, well-known for playing football of a high, clean standard.*"

Both the School and the Club however were facing a major problem with regard to pitches; "*We urgently need more playing fields if we are to develop their talents to the full, and I sincerely hope that the requirements of the School and the OPM Clubs will be met by a vigorous and concerted effort before we have gone far in the second half of the 20th Century.*"

OPM RFC 1949-50: Rear; P Berryman, F Westlake, D Pring, O Daw, H Williams, J Hamley, L Daw, L Sherriff. Centre; R Pratt, P Vittle, R Priest, D Smale, A Baxter, J Beamish, JF Spear. Front; T Mutton, N Elliott, A Squire (Captain) A Northcott and H Rendle (Vice-Captain and then current member of staff).

On the House Rugby front, "*the victory of Palmer's Senior Rugger side over Thompsons enabled Palmer's to become Cock House for the first time since 1939.*"

A Cock House supper, '*a Gargantuan Feast*', was held at Goodbody's with an after-dinner entertainment, "*an opera written and produced by Mr Dundas, masquerading as a more southerly egg*", on 15 December.

A few days later, Palmer's House Captain, Hewlett and House Master, 'Joe Egg', were back in the gym again and "*with topical knockabout this year relegated to House Christmas parties, the stage was left clear for a concert of serious music and straight comedy.*"

Miss Hannaford led the orchestra in the former and dramatic entertainment came in two pieces; The Pen Is Mightier, produced by Mr Barnes and Sheridan's St Patrick's Day, produced by Mr Coggin. Of the latter Mr Dent observed that, head boy Hewlett's Credulous "*would have done credit to any amateur stage*", while Jervis's "*few minutes on stage were as hilarious as any we have had*".

"*The gym was filled for three nights, and Mr Barnes used all his ingenuity in packing sardines into one small tin three times.*"

1949 - scene from a school dramatic production staged in the gym - below, the entire cast assemble on stage. .

Hewlett was also involved dramatically with the Plymouth Shakespeare Society and for them produced Keith Bryant's The Psychologist with several boys taking part, meanwhile an old boy, ID Lodge "*enlisted several of our players to present the sophistications of Noel Coward and Agatha Christie to the rural innocents of Egg Buckland.*"

Daphne du Maurier's Rebecca was the subject of the play reading that term for the Literary and Debating Society, which again enjoyed "*quite a successful term*" ... "*but we have had to compete against counter-attractions, particularly the dancing classes at the High School.*"

Based on the debates that term it emerged that this house did not in fact *"support devaluation of the £"*, or the *"abolition of vivisection"*, however suggestions that *"the average individual does not appreciate free benefits supplied by the Social Services"*, and *"that longer working hours are essential to the country's recovery"* and *"that severer punishment should be given to juvenile delinquents"*, were all favourably received.

WGM Jones continued to oversee L&D activities while their secretary, McKee, reminded the School that *"Debating is not only an extremely interesting and amusing pursuit, but is a basic feature of democratic public life, and one's views derive great benefit from being brought into violent contact with someone else's."*

Clearly one other way of encountering other people's view was via the literary world and for the benefit of those who hadn't yet ventured into the School Library it was noted that among the periodicals regularly available there were;

"The Illustrated London News, Manchester Weekly Guardian, Children's Newspaper, Listener, New Statesman, Economist, Leader, Motor, Motor Cycle, Reader's Digest, Blackwoods, Practical Wireless, Collins Children's Magazine, two stamp-collecting and two railway papers, apart from all sorts of periodicals which we were given from time to time."

It was also noted that *"one of the competitions in Collins' has been won by P Hutchinson, who has been invited to illustrate one of their stories."*

The overall standard of visual awareness at School was clearly improving; Mr Wills himself had designed a new cover – featuring a silhouette of the main building – for the Plymothian and in his address at Speech Day the Headmaster had informed parents that *"the teaching of Art had advanced sufficiently to allow boys to offer it successfully as an examination subject ... and it is hoped that the same would happen with Music."*

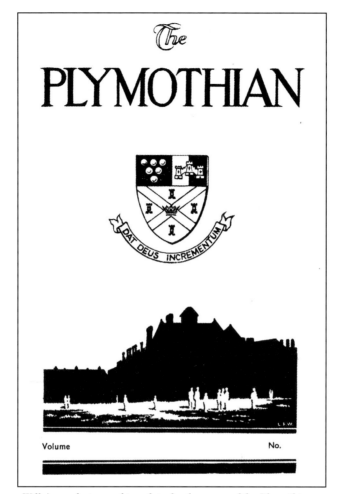

Wills' new design and template for the cover of the Plymothian.

Of course as far as school examinations generally were concerned, the Country as a whole was about to face a major new challenge.

Referring to the new General Certificate of Education that was to be introduced next summer, Mr Garnons Williams, at that same Speech Day in Central Hall said that *"it is best to accept it now as a thing decided and to make the best of it."*

"It would," he added, *"be less hard on us than on smaller schools."*

The Head then went on to emphasise how increased numbers had *"strengthened our position as a school, but they have not always increased our comfort. There must be considerable renovation of School property,"* he said, *"and there is urgent need of more space for games."*

The Head was delivering his address before an audience that included two of his own previous headmasters, one of whom, GC Turner, was to present the prizes. In his opening remarks the Charterhouse head said he would mention *"only two qualities I admire in Mr Garnons Williams – his devotion to cats and his propensity to compose Latin verse."*

Garnons Williams, in his speech had talked of the ultimate test of a school as being *"not its honours list, its certificate results, its games record, or anything else that can be judged by arithmetic. It is simply the question, "Is it a good place in which to grow up"."*

For his part Mr Turner said that he didn't feel qualified to describe what made a school a good place to grow up in, but *"a walk through Plymouth, in its present state, recalls forcibly the truth of the ancient words "It is men, not walls, that make a city" and we can learn nothing better at school than a readiness to help without question anyone who needed our help."*

Curiously enough a few boys from the School had been doing their bit for the City, *"through dabbling in first-hand historical research for the Historical Manuscripts Commission."* During the post-war salvage drive *"it was discovered that a great many documents of historical value were lying about, unexamined and unrecorded, and that there were many being thrown away."*

"The fact that many of them are in apparently illegible hands deters no schoolmaster or boy; the difficulties caused by language, for many are in Latin, can be overcome; and the decoding of some of the conventional abbreviations is fun for those who have the crossword mentality."

"As a result of the work by the School party four hitherto unknown Mayors of Plymouth have been added to the fourteenth and fifteenth century annals of the City, and many details of early social history have been recorded or confirmed."

There can be no doubt that as the forties drew to a close the young men about to leave Plymouth College had a perspective on life in the City, and at Ford Park, that was quite different from that of any previous – or subsequent - generation;

General view of the School Field at the end of the 1940s.

"During the past eight years we have seen the School pass from war to peace. The barrage balloon at the edge of the quad, the airman's huts near Shaftesbury, the AFS using the swimming bath for storage, the huge water-tank which claimed the end of the First XV pitch, and the two ack-ack guns mounting guard, are all things of the past, but were at the time, constant reminders of war. We see again the American invasion of Plymouth when over the Pavilion swarmed those barbarians who taught English cricketers to play baseball."

"The members of the Corps, training and learning what they would soon have to put into practice in earnest, were filled with a sense of urgency. The air-raids and the quick dash for cover to the air-raid shelters or the basements of the School were part of our daily routine. Ever present was the fear that the next morning would find the School a blistered shell

or a heap of broken ruins."

"How vividly was impressed on each one of us the terrible toll of war, as year by year the list, which was read to us on Founders' Day, of the names of Old Boys of the School who had made the supreme sacrifice, increased in length!"

November 1949 and outside the Guildhall the City of Plymouth observes a minute's silence for those who fell in the two World Wars

"Who can forget "VE" Day and the feeling of relief? Then came the thrill of anticipation as we heard that members of the Staff, who had heretofore been names only, were returning. Would they prove as strict as they were pictured? They returned, and the ladies who had joined the Staff during the war, and who had played their part in our school life, departed. Soon we were told that our Headmaster intended to retire, and in the September of 1945 our present Headmaster was welcomed to the School."

The Plymothian editor and winner of a State Scholarship in Classics at Oxford, F Davey, then wrote; *"we remember more personal events: the first Latin, French and Greek lessons – "Ou est le tableau noir?" and "Britannia est insula" – followed by paradigms and principal parts. The examinations loomed ahead. Then the Sixth Form and a sense of responsibility.*

Proses and Verses ... "Has anyone a 'Vix'?"
The easy style of Davy's prose and his experiences as editor made him a natural candidate for future Oxford letters, it was, after all a task few undergraduates ever seemed happy to be charged with;
"I'm not writing it," said the Third man, forcefully. "Thanks for the drinks," and, picking up his beer-stained zither, he was gone, leaving behind him the faint aroma of stale tobacco."
"Nightmare memories of Anton Karas and Housewives' Choice" were part of the cultural backdrop for everyone that term and the Cambridge letter had little to add, save that *"Things ain't what they used to be"* and that Guy Fawkes night had passed quietly and Hon Sec and Treasurer, Derek Pring *"has still omitted to get his hair cut."*

His younger brother, soon to be joining him at Oxford, was still making his mark at Ford Park and was taking a keen interest in the one boxing fixture staged that term. Fought against DHS in their gym in Stoke, it wasn't a particularly successful engagement, with Turpitt, Hewitt and the club Captain Allgood winning their bouts, and six others losing.

Altogether more successful were the shooting team. With a fresh injection of coaching and enthusiasm from the newly-arrived Mr Elliott, the team entered for Division II of the Plymouth and District Small Bore League, won their first four matches and were leading the league. The team, led by Greasley, were also doing well in their Postal matches, having set a new School record in their first shoot. AR Harvey was a particular star, becoming Junior Champion of Devon, and maintaining "champion's" form with the best average in the team – 97.

Another area where the level of competition was on the up was in the Philatelic Society. Here the highlight of the term was the Stamp Arranging Competition and *"all the entries showed great care and were of a far higher standard than those shown in 1947 and 1948".*

The Ford Park site from the air - 1950 - note the School Field is marked out with four hockey pitches.

The largest Society in the School however was the youngest – the Natural History Society, which celebrated its second birthday with a membership of over a hundred. The term's programme included *"a most interesting lecture on "Fish and Fishing" given by Mr GN Radford,"* while *"a visit to the Tavy estuary attracted twenty-one members"*.

Mr AE Capps gave freely of his time – and projector – and films on Animal Movement, Wood Ants and the Woodlands were among those shown.

The boys of the Prep were also treated to a number of Natural History films too, such as *Life in the Hedgerow, Washing Time at the Zoo, and Fruits broadcast by the Animals"*, there were also some Geographical features – *"The Manchester Ship Canal, London's River and the Building of A Dock"* and one historical production *"Land of Drake"* – *"which contained some good shots of Devon scenery."* Not all these were deemed successes however; *"the gap between the film producer and the teacher has been too wide and has existed for too long – that is one reason why we saw so many unsuitable films last term."*

Garnons Williams greets Douglas Marshall, OPM and guest speaker at the 1949 OPM dinner in Plymouth, Chairman of the OPM Club, Arthur Lyddon, looks on.

A gap, or rather span, of some forty years was represented by the four surviving Plymouth College headmasters who descended on the London Dinner that October; as Messrs Chaytor, Dale, Ralph and Garnons Williams were among the thirty or so at the Holborn Restaurant supporting the welcome post-war revival of the London Section. Arthur Lyddon, Club President was there too and doubtless reported favourably on the section of the club closest to his heart, the OPM Rugby XV who were enjoying their most successful season since the war. Meanwhile the OPM Hockey team were having *"what looks like being its most successful season of the Club's history."*

"With the acquisition of the ground at Peverell Park and the presentation of a set of goal posts and boards by Mr TA Wakeham, the club has returned to its appropriate status in local hockey circles."

Given the resurgence of club activities and the ever increasing amount of space devoted to OPM affairs it was perhaps not altogether surprising to find most of the Spring term editorial given over to the Old Boys;

"Many OPMs afflicted with ennui tell us they would give their all to have the power of returning to the energetic bustle of School life, prep, included. Let us then, spare a though for them, scattered as they are throughout the world, some in the dank jungle of Malaya, others in the lonely desert of Abyssinia, more in the humdrum banks and offices of the city. All have one common link, the OPM Club, which supplies them with copies of the Plymothian. Every member of the School will become an OPM sooner or later; he can render no better compliment to the College when he leaves it than by joining the Club, this showing that he wishes to remain in touch with School affairs."

"However we feel that we must interrupt this eulogy by voicing one small complaint. We praise these OPMs, shower hospitality on them when they revisit us, and generally make ourselves thoroughly agreeable. In return they give us an annual thrashing at hockey. There's gratitude for you."

Certainly the OPM Hockey side was the strongest it had been for some years; Garnett, the club captain, was a regular member of the County side and half a dozen of his team mates had also represented Devon. But there was undoubtedly an element of uncertainty in the air, for just as the spirit of 'resurgam' was resounding around the City, so the clouds of war were gathering once more in the Far East.

Clearly the most conspicuous signs of the rebuilding of Plymouth were evidenced in the City Centre and as the New Year dawned it was revealed that the restored St Andrew's Church was to be 18" higher than before, the foundations were laid for the new Prudential Building and drawings for the new Plymouth Co-op appeared in the Western Evening Herald.

1949 - Royal Parade takes shape and the redevelopment begins.

However 1950 was also to see major changes on Mutley Plain; in January the plan to create a dual carriageway with bus bays outside the Swarthmore and Hardings was announced and the council bought up 11 Mutley frontages. Work was scheduled to start on creating a roundabout around the Hyde Park Hotel in July, with a new roundabout at the other end later in the year and then in November a specialist firm agreed to install fluorescent lighting along the Plain – at no cost to the Corporation. It was the beginning of the end of the gaslight era … although the gas companies were still fighting their corner. Before the year was out however it was announced that *"fluorescent lighting may extend to the City Centre"*.

1950 - Mutley Plain becomes the first part of Plymouth to be lit with flourescent lighting.

Dominating the local and national headlines early that year though was the General Election. Called by Atlee on 10 January, it was set for 24 February. Ford Park followed suit and a Mock Election date was set for the day before the call to the nation – on 23 February.

"It was preceded by an extremely lively campaign. The lower corridor was covered with the posters of the rival parties, and some of the meetings were far from peaceful. Nevertheless few tempers were lost, and although they were vigorously heckled, the candidates came through unscathed. The verdict of the electorate, which consisted of the Sixth, Fifth and Fourth Forms, was as follows: TEJ Savery (Conservative), 97; JM Waterhouse (Liberal), 55; DJ Price (Labour), 19; GF Morrish (Independent), 3."

MD McKee was the Returning Officer, DL Farmer, his Assistant and the votes cast represented an impressive 87.2 % of the electorate. The result was perhaps not altogether surprising in the context of the School and coming straight off the back of three School debates during the course of which it was agreed that the execution of Charles I was completely unjustified, but not agreed that the Communist Party should be banned or that the Liberal Party offered the best solution to our present difficulties.

Nationally it wasn't deemed to offer the best solution either, neither was there clear confidence in the ability of the Government - the nation wanted National Service but they weren't keen on devaluation nor the Government's handling of the economy.

On 6 February Winston Churchill came to Plymouth to rally the Conservative rank-and-file and to muster support for his son Randolph, but two weeks later, when the votes were cast, Randolph trailed Michael Foot by some 27,329 votes to 30,812 in Devonport, with AC Cann polling just 2,766 for the Liberals. Meanwhile Lucy Middleton had just a three-figure majority over Nancy Astor's son JJ in the Plymouth constituency, with the Liberals again trailing considerably.

Across the country the margins were similar and Labour scraped home with 315 seats to the Tories 298, the Liberals 9 and the others 3. Among those to be successfully re-elected were F Seymour Cocks and Douglas Marshall both of whom had spent happy years at Plymouth College, as indeed had H Wilson Harris who did not actually seek re-election *"owing to the disappearance of his constituency under the recent Parliamentary Act."*

1950 General Election group with Labour's Lucy Middleton (2nd left, & Michael Foot (6th left) who spent a year or two at the Prep.

Generally it had been a nerve-wracking night for the party leaders, but an opportunity for sport for others. The Oxford Letter was little more than two pages of rambling notes on a boozy, all-night, election party listening to the wireless and gambling on the outcome. A rare epistle from Bristol noted that *"now the General Election has passed, with the loss of few lives and many reputations we presume that life at other universities will return to its normal pace"* a sentiment endorsed by the letter from Cambridge which used exactly those terms to describe life now that *"canvassers, posters and loudspeakers have disappeared."*

Meanwhile back at Ford Park there were a number of more everyday matters making little ripples – like the Public School Hymn-book which came into use at the beginning of the Spring Term;

"Several hymns and tunes have already been adopted," wrote John Bill, *"and the wider choice is most welcome."* Edited by Craig Sellar Lang, a former pupil and teacher at Clifton School, who had retired to concentrate on composition and examinations, this was the Third Edition of the book, the second appearing thirty years earlier, in 1919 and the first in 1903. Mr Bill continued; *"The book itself, apart from a rather large number of misprints, is a well-balanced selection of words and music. Most well-known hymns are set to the tune or tunes which have established themselves as appropriate. Very few entirely new tunes appear, except for the contributions of the Musical Editor. New hymns are now practised with the choir and in singing classes, as well as at the congregational practice on Saturday mornings."*

Mr Bill's contributions to the musical life of the School continued to open new doors and on Monday March 27 there was a concert evening in Big School with *"a programme of solo and concerted items by members of the School"* the like of which had not been presented before and *"it is a pleasure to record that it was highly successful."*

Mr Bill rehearses the senior School Orchestra in the gymnasium.

"All who took part deserve our praise, but we should like to mention particularly the warm tone of Owen's violin-playing, Canniford's clear and and fresh voice, the control and delicacy shown by the youthful Jenkins, the spirited rendering of the Prelude to Carmen, and the excellent concluding items in which Mr Radford's bold, dramatic singing was greatly appreciated."

AE Beard and TJ Stevens were among the other notable contributors, while the whole evening was concluded with the singing of the Carmen and the National Anthem.

The following three days, the last three days of what had been a short but busy term, saw the Dramatic Society stage As You Like It in the gym. Mr Coggin produced, Mr Bill's choristers sang, Mr Porter's quartet played in front of the curtain, *"Mr and Mrs Dent discoursed sweetly on recorders behind the scenes, Mr Will's brush evoked a disciplined riot of leaves and branches about the stage"* and even Mr Edwards lent a rare extracurricular hand as he helped stage *"a most realistic bout between Orlando and Charles, with a spectacular throw to finish the contest."*

The very versatile School Gymnasium in use as a gym, rather than an orchestra rehearsal space, examination room or concert venue.

There was nothing choreographed about the earlier bouts held in the gym the previous month though, as Valentine's Day 1950 saw the staging of the first part of the House Boxing Competition. The number of boys participating was lower than usual (maybe if Freddie Mills had beaten Joey Maxim for the world light-heavyweight title in January it might have been a different story) and in this, the seventh season of sports since its revival, it was not possible to stage a contest with another school. Nevertheless the quality of boxing was reckoned to be *"well up to standard"* and Branch, Turpitt and Pring helped win the inter-house trophy for Sargent's, while Allgood, Cload and Erlich steered Thompson's into second and Southern and Hannaford did their bit for College.

Pring, incidentally, in a rerun of his feat the previous Spring, was also Senior Cross Country Champion again, over a course that *"was slightly extended from four and a half to five miles around Central Park."*

On a fine but cold day Mrs Garnons Williams started the races and, on account of the much larger entry this year the race was run in three separate sections rather than two, corresponding to the three age groups. Consequently P Harrison won the Juniors and Pomroy the "sub-juniors".

The clement weather however was missing for most of the hockey season, with that one *"fine but cold"* day being a notable exception. This saw the last game of the season and was against the Staff;

"A very keenly fought struggle which ended suitably enough (1-1) with honours even. If the Staff did rather more of the attacking, it must be remembered that several key members of the School side had already run a gruelling cross-country race in the same afternoon."

Polkinghorne Captained the side *"with great credit"* and Pring, who had moved up from the back, was the frustrated Secretary. The latter was in the thick of the action on another occasion during the term when *"Messrs Radford, Mercer and Dent, with Gosling,*

Pring and Fedrick I, played a Kelly side strengthened by their Fives master." Hardly an unfair advantage you would have thought when both Messrs Radford (a Kelly old boy himself) and Dent, were effectively the Plymouth College coaching team. *"In the future we hope to revive the annual Kelly match,"* recanted Hugh Dent, *"but we shall never win it till we have built up a tradition of good hard-hitting play amongst the Juniors."*

Mr Dent was also trying his best to get the whole school swimming too;

"Most non-swimmers," he wrote, *"are still frightened of trusting the water, and this is a natural fear. To overcome it, be honest with yourself, admit the fear, and don't invent for yourself forty good excuses for missing lessons, but trust your instructor, who won't let you d(r)own, learn the strokes on dry land, and you will probably find it easy."*

The other big, extra-curricular area of Mr Dent's wide and tireless interest was the Library and this term saw the introduction of a bookplate, designed by Mr Wills and *"in the books of permanent value. Users have,"* he added, *"expressed their appreciation of the design."*

Among the newly-acquired books that term were Second Innings by Neville Cardus, The Big Fisherman by Lloyd Douglas and a new set of Conan Doyle's Sherlock Holmes books.

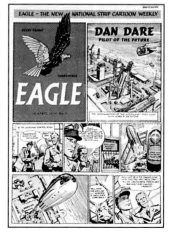

Meanwhile among those publications vying for the attention of schoolboys up and down the country that year was a brand new title in the comic canon – The Eagle. Launched during the Easter holidays, and priced fourpence, it featured, among others the heroic exploits of Dan Dare.- Pilot of the Future.

Not quite so likely to grab the schoolboy imagination but reminding us that all schoolboys grow up, there were at the back of that term's magazine a list of recent OPM publications, among them RF Tuckett's book on *Linear Polymers*, JR Brazier's *Chronology of Faust* thesis and PJ Hilson's paper *On Overpotential and the Photovoltaic Process at Polarized Electrodes*, that had just been published in the Proceedings of the Royal Society.

Closer to home there were proposals by a couple of old boys to form new OPM sporting sides, LRF House was looking for anyone interested in *"swimming, polo and other aquatic sports"*, while those who fancied joining others on the golf course were urged to contact either HR Lawry or Club President GL Wakeham.

An older old boy again was RR Brown and this term saw him become the first OPM to Chair the Board of Governors. RR Brown was one of the five Browns at the School at the end of Queen Victoria's reign and had left the School in 1900. After a few years at Oxford he had gone into the Indian Civil Service, then, in 1934, when his father was still Chairman of Governors, he too joined the Board, becoming Vice-Chariman on his father's retirement and Sir William Munday's succession, in 1936. He has, said the School Notes, *"an unrivalled knowledge of the affairs of Plymouth College"*.

He also would appear to have had ideas about the future of the School too and it is perhaps no coincidence that later that term we discover plans for the Prep to have its own Open Day and, more significantly, its own Speech Day. Whether these were the actions of a new broom or not is difficult to tell, but we do know that actions at the Prep each day were to be controlled by a new bell; *"A transmitting set has been installed in Remove B classroom. Each morning at nine o'clock a record of a peal of church bells is played and the sound immediately issues forth from the loud-speakers in all the other classrooms, summoning all to prayers."*

A Prep Classroon, Hartley Road.from the 1950 School Prospectus

Open Day was scheduled for the last Wednesday of term and boys were *"busy building models and making other preparations"* – *"tray models and weaving keep Div III very busy; plasticine modelling keeps Div IV and V busy"*.

Back at Ford Park, philately continued to be a popular hobby and two boys, CH Gullett and DG Carter came first and third in the Stamp Display organized at the Schoolboy's Exhibition by the Plymouth Philatelic Society. While showing that it was not just a boy's pursuit *"Miss Christine Holman* (Eric's daughter) *gave a short talk on Switzerland and showed her fine collection of its stamps."*

Meanwhile members of the Natural History Society began a major survey of the School grounds. Thanks to the arrival in its ranks of Mr Lindley, the Scouts started a meteorological class, while the CCF celebrated the success of HGC Scott *"who shot well enough to be selected for the England CCF team"* but bemoaned the absence of Lieut FW Scott *"on extra regimental employment"*..

Mr Scott having been awarded the Page Travelling Scholarship, was on a month's visit to the United States, Mr PH Williams, from New College, Oxford,

covered his class teaching, while another temporary face around the campus that term was that of Mr GA Wright who was down from Exeter, doing a term of teacher training.

Come the summer term Scott from America has returned; *"America is an education in itself: the rectangular layout of the towns, the parkways designed for speedy long-distance traffic, the kitchens complete with washing-up machines, centrally-heated rooms opening up one into another, and the many bathrooms."*

So began Francis Scott's tale of Transatlantic Travel, written at a time when a national survey of Britain revealed that only 46% of houses had even a single bathroom and household gadgets were few and far between – but the times here were a'changing as that summer British production of television sets increased by 250% and the first self-service store opened in London.

As the western world took its lead more and more from that large continent on the other side of the Atlantic, Scott's account was both timely and prophetic;

"In America they are making History, so naturally they teach it; but they regard it as a much more useful subject than we do. It is part of a Social Science, just as Education is a kind of Social Engineering. Nor is there a great gap fixed between where History ended and present things began, so they will always mention present implications, and current affairs, and modern problems come earlier and more frequently into their courses. Their teaching is more verbal, their text-books more voluminous, and pressure from home and school most unusual. Academically they are years behind our contemporaries, but then they do not put the bright and the slower boys in the different forms to proceed at different paces – that would not be democratic – and anyhow there is not the hurry because most stay on to 18, very many go on to College, and more stay at the University to specialise after getting their degree. Conscription does not loom before them."

Scott's itinerary took him to the New World on the Queen Elizabeth. Arriving in New York he travelled by railroad to Boston, by air to Chicago then Pittsburg and then *"a day on a train crossing the Appalachians to Washington, and from there I returned to New York."* During the course of it all he was met by *"professors, teachers, educators, and members of the English Speaking Union"* ... *"it was a very pleasant experience to visit so many American homes and talk with cultured and informed Americans."*

The young Plymouth College history master also *"visited as great a variety of schools as I could in the time, including "mixed Senior High Schools with several thousand pupils between fourteen and eighteen"* - a marked contrast indeed to the numbers at Ford Park for all the recent increases at the Main School and Prep.

Incidentally, although it may have been mere coincidence the Prep School notes that term also flagged up a contrast between the two countries separated by the Atlantic; *"The weather is always a safe topic with which to introduce oneself. Like the cigarette and the proverbial half-pint of beer it is an aid to social intercourse and puts both parties immediately at their ease. Herein lies a subtle psychological difference between the average American and a typical Britisher. Leaning against a bar counter the average American tries to start a conversation by showing photographs of his family – "Here's my poppa, and here's my momma, and, gee, here's my kid brother." The Britisher, however, rarely introduces himself or his family; he prefers an impersonal subject of conversation like the weather. Indeed he has made a philosophy of our notorious British climate; it has been pointed out, more than once, that most English proverbs are connected with the weather or with thrift – an interesting commentary on British character."*

And an unusual way to open the Prep account that term, but then unusual things were happening at the Prep that summer.

Big School - the Main Assembly Hall from the 1950 Prospectus.

The planned Open Day was re-styled *"Parents' Day"* and was *"to use a much worn phrase, an unqualified success"* and then *"history was made and a new precedent was created on 5th July when the Prep held its first Speech Day in the Main School Hall. This event, unparalleled in the sixty years since the Prep first came into existence, was attended by a very large audience ... the Hall was in fact filled literally to the point of overflowing."*

The National Anthem was sung, the Rt Rev Bishop of Sherbourne was welcomed in verse by the Prep Captain, MD Spear, and then Mr Firman gave his address.and this in itself turned out to be quite historic. A change in the Entrance Exam arrangements had altered the situation at the Prep a little and while this was no time for *"revolutionary and foolish experiments which might lead to disaster ... it had now been found possible to make certain relaxations this year and homework now was definitely abolished."*

"The Prep," he added *"is also aware of trends in modern education ... the need, for example, of co-relating hand and brain at all stages in primary education was widely believed nowadays, and certain boys have spent many evenings making models."*

Little could Mr Firman have imagined the reaction to his homework ruling - it was both widespread and *"in some quarters misgiving."* An indication of just how widespread is that it not only attracted the interest of the National Press, there was even an enquiry from an American asking for further information. The news was, however, that there was *"no deterioration in the standard of work."*

Meanwhile, as the Main School geared up for major changes to its examination system, there was another staff change as Commander Gander announced that he was heading off to take up the post of Senior Chemistry Master at the King Edward VI School in Chelmsford – *"we wish him every success and thank him for his help on the hockey field ... as the Orchestra's principal flautist he will be greatly missed."*

56 year-old Gander had only been at the School a couple of years and his departure was to make way for a much younger man. Meanwhile the Orchestra was going from strength to strength and that summer a School Concert saw an Old Boy *"who has been out of touch with School events for sometime"* return to Ford Park. Frederick Harvey was a baritone of national standing and was a regular broadcaster on the BBC, his appraisal of the School Choir was extremely favourable; *"If this is a sample of what the School usually produces, it augurs well for the future, and I for one shall look forward to attending many more such occasions."*

Messrs Bill and Trevena were their usual competent selves, Miss Hannaford was once more singled out for praise, as indeed were CW Jenkins for his Brahms solo, and JHL Owen for his violin pieces – one of them a piece by Bach whose bi-centenary was being celebrated at the concert.

Frederick Harvey was not the only one with BBC connections at that time, a few weeks after the concert, Mr Coggin gave a talk on the BBC West Region Home Service called *"Twelve for an Alibi"* – it was his third such broadcast.

That Easter, incidentally, Mr Coggin fulfilled his original promise to take a party of boys (twenty-one of them) to France. Crossing from Newhaven on the Boat Train, SS Arromanches, the party met up with another group, from Wellington School, in Paris. Brittany, St Malo, Tours, Rennes, Chateaubriand and Chartres were among the places visited, and *"in the words of the well-worn (but wholly inadequate) stock phrase, "a good time was had by all"."*

Another phrase, not quite a stock one, but one that nevertheless appeared several times in that summer's Plymothian, concerned a certain oral activity. The author of the Cambridge letter *"chewed his pen top vigorously"*, the scribe of the Oxford missive exhorted his readers to *"suck your pen and think"*, while the Editor himself, who had complained in his editorial about the lack of original prose or verse for the Magazine, spoke of *"chewing his fountain pen and staring out of the window"*. This was in his, Morrish's own prose piece for the periodical, he also penned a poem on the joys of Spring.

In spite of his most earnest appeal, however, Morrish's personal contributions were the only ones not related to a specific School activity as the details of another summer term unfolded.

In the athletic sports *"general standards were much as usual, with the winners of the Senior flat races coming close to record times. Mr JR Spear's 1933 shot-put record still stands, after the closest approach since it was made: Jervis, coached by the holder, was four inches short of it."*

There was, however an interesting *"and most successful"* innovation at that sports day, as noted by the Athletics secretary Price, *"Mr Trevena used a microphone very effectively to let the watchers know what was happening. And how valuable an impersonal gadget is the loud-speaker which can look one way and ask someone in the other direction: "Please keep the track free"."*

Not all the messages broadcast in this way were intended to be, however. A local newspaper reporter attempting to extract useful quotes from the Headmaster, was rounded on by an irritated Garnons Williams who boomed *"Go away you silly man, can't you see I'm busy!"* Unfortunately the Head was within range of the microphone and the words echoed around Ford Park for all to hear!

Greasely was the Senior Victor, with the sprinter Benney his proxime accessit, just managing to thwart the mile and half-mile champ Pring, and the discus and javelin star Prynne. Battrick was the junior champ, with Reid, second to him in the main three sprints and first in the 880 finishing second overall.

Battrick, with three firsts was one of the stars of the Junior Athletics team who competed in an inaugural inter school event at Kelly and shared first place with the Tavistock boys, while the senior competing at Blundell's finished seventh overall, with Prynne and Jervis, while not actually winning their events both bettering the school records in the Javelin and Weight respectively.

While little, if any, mention was made in the magazine of the London Olympics in 1948, Ted Mercer, in his cricket report that summer (1950), was aware of the increasing influence of the modern media over the traditional summer sport;

"The detailed broadcast accounts of first-class cricket matches, the instructional films and the spate of cricket literature which appears these days are not without their effects on schoolboys. They stimulate interest, but the effect on bowling is not always to the good. We note Bill Bodkin of IIb Gentlemen turn to his Captain and remark: "I think I'll cut out my in-swingers and try him with my wrong 'un." Ask the batsman to stand aside and tell Bill to try six balls aimed at the wicket. He couldn't hit the sightscreen if it were there, let alone the stumps! It may therefore be of value to quote the Yorkshire Captain who accounted for the continued

success of his side quite simply: "We just bowl at the wickets and hold the catches." If the 1st XI had done just that they would have been a far better side."

As it was the team won just three of their eleven games, with Fedrick top scoring with an unbeaten 45, Squance and Pring bagging the most runs overall and Congdon and Burt the most wickets. Pashley took five wickets for just seven runs against Plympton but his *"batting has been disappointing ... although one or two of his off drives were on a par with those that one saw flash from the bat of his uncle, the late Roy Kilner, the best cricketer this writer ever saw."*

A comment that prompted the Headmaster to add a comment: *"Did you Yorkshiremen ever see much of Frank Woolley?"* Roy Kilner was a star all-rounder for Yorkshire, taking over 1,000 first class wickets and scoring over 14,500 first class runs – he also played a number of tests matches for England, his brother Norman, also represented his county, as did their uncle Irving Washington.

Right: Pashley's uncle Roy Kilner.

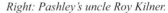

Those were the days when you had to be a Yorkshireman to play for the County – and proud they were of it too, as were the Yorkshiremen in the Plymouth College staff room - Ted Mercer, from near Batley, Hugh Dent, from Leeds and Francis Scott, from Hull – hence the former Winchester scholar, Garnons Williams's pointed postscript – a postscript, incidentally that suggested that the Head vetted the periodical prior to publication!

Keen as they were, the aforementioned Yorkshiremen didn't all appear to share the same degree of fanaticism when it came to sport – Francis Scott once incurred the wrath of Ted Mercer by giving three LBWs in a Staff

1950

v School match – *"I thought the masters were scoring too many runs!"*

It wasn't an issue that summer though; the Staff dismissed the School for 110 and passed that total with the loss of just two wickets, Nigel Radford hitting 43.

Plymouth College 2nd XI 1950: Back; GH Davies, A Richards, AV Cawley, RJ Williams, G Friend, CRS Cload. Front; DE Algate, IK Dawson, R Polkinghorne (Captain) BL Varcoe, DS Cutler.

The 2nd XI also won just three of their matches, one of them thanks largely to the singlular efforts of Richards who scored an unbeaten 66 against RNC Dartmouth's U16s and then took 5 for 26, as the naval lads were dismissed for just 67.

Unbeaten Junior Colts 1950: Back; CV Denning, RJ Morrish, JR Tredinnick, RJ Passmore, PH U'ren, DS Bird. Front; MC Turpitt, RE Southern, TJ Stevens (Captain), JM Hewitt, MJ Cowan.

The Under 14s by contrast were unbeaten in their nine matches, with Southern, Stevens and Turpitt among the stars, with one team, Plympton, being skittled out for just 20.

The School Pool - very busy across the summer term of 1950.

In the School pool IVb topped the swimming league with each boy swimming an average of 603 yards across the term. At the bottom of the table, and possibly the pool, were the Classical VIth whose six members managed to swim just fifty yards between them!

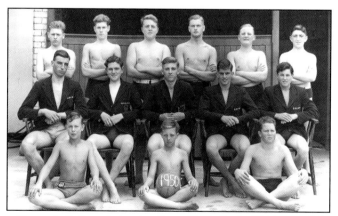

Plymouth College Swimming Team 1950: Back; JH Davies, JM Wilkins, RT Booth, CF Kenshole, PI Palmer, DM Webb. Middle; MA Jervis, DC Searle, K Pring (Captain), IDW Wright, DE Algate. Front; HJ Heath, AJ Hannaford, GC Blight.

Two days before the end of term a dripping Pring emerged Senior Victor from the Pool on a pleasant

Wednesday afternoon, while for the Juniors, Hannaford, Stott and Palmer all set new records although none of them claimed the overall title of Junior Victor – that went to HJ Heath.

Sargent's House Swimming Team – House Champions, 1950: Back; RFCrimp, CJ Ackford, DM Webb, WJ Hart, C Matthews. Front; DE Algate, MA Jervis, K Pring (Captain), IDW Wright, HJ Heath.

On the Water Polo front the results were patchy. The OPMs, in their first game together, were beaten 4-0 by the School, but in their four inter-school matches the boys, most of them from Sargents, were less successful, finding the 33-yard bath at Blundells a particularly difficult challenge.

The OPMs, led by House, contested two other fixtures in their first "season" winning one and losing the other – there were plans for a swimming "club night" through the winter, and there was a floodlit match on the evening of the 'At Home' held at the School during the course of the Past v Present cricket match. There was also a Dance held at the School on the same night, and the Club were eager to express their thanks to Mr & Mrs Garnons Williams for their help and co-operation. So successful was the event that it was decided to revive the winter dance as well.

The OPMs generally were looking to expand their range of activities and across the board there was evidence of reigning in the services of past pupils, from the musical contributions of Frederick Harvey, the booking of Canon Caley OPM, Rector of Stoke Damerel to preach the sermon at the Commemoration Service, H Wilson Harris, OPM and editor of the Spectator, to present the prizes, Air Commodore AP Revington CB, CBE, OPM to talk to the Sixth Form on the RAF and Colonel RA Bishop, Commanding 26 Group RE, OPM, who, on 6th June, came as the Inspecting Officer for the CCF's Annual Inspection.

There was a change to Field Day that term, incidentally, with all the cadets over 14 visiting the Royal Marines at Lympstone. There was a change too in the venue of the Annual Camp, which was held in the grounds of Eaton Hall, Chester, an Officer Cadet's Training Establishment. Held during the first week of August, in *"far from perfect weather"*, *"the cadets occupied ridge tents, rather larger and probably more comfortable than the customary bell tents – cadets can never arrange themselves satisfactorily in a bell tent."*

Eaton Hall also benefitted from a much more hands on approach than the cadets were previously used to;

"newly commissioned officers directed all training which was very much more personal than before. There was only one large-scale demonstration, that of a Platoon attack. All other training involved cadets, either as demonstrators or participants. This is a much better arrangement than merely allowing cadets to watch the motions of supposed experts."

There was another *"pleasant innovation"* – *"the introduction of a comprehensive transport service. This made it unnecessary for cadets to march at any time more than four miles in getting to, and returning from, their training each day."*

One drawback, however, was that Chester was a long haul from Plymouth and the train journey took some ten hours; *"the fact that the contingent was concentrated into one "restaurant car" type carriage enabled authority to be exercised with ease, and any embryo mutinies were stifled at birth. The journey was,*

therefore, abnormally peaceful, with the tenor of events only broken by the sight of a certain sergeant, who shall remain nameless, standing on Bristol station, a glass of liquid (also nameless) in each hand, watching the train leave without him."

Plymouth College Shooting VIII – 1949-50: Back; D Hooper, JK Reynolds, RW Viant, DE Algate. Front; AR Harvey, HGC Scott, JA Greaseley (Captain), TAL Prynne, AD Rowe.

Joining in with the School party at Eaton Hall was *"one OPM now at Sandhurst"* (Newcombe), there were also a couple of OPMs at the summer scout camp, held, for the third year in succession, at Werrington. And, despite the almost continual rain these two, *"hardened survivors of unnumbered camps"* were *"heard to agree that this year's was the best they had ever known."*

"There are of course, certain details which stand out; the ebullient energy of Mr Lindley, who never seemed to tire of chopping wood, the genial figure of a now happily-recovered Mr Dundas going around the patrol sites, instructing novices in the arts of tea-making and egg-frying, Mr Dent's recorder group which accompanied the songs we like to sing while drinking our cocoa before sprawling into our sleeping-bags, the rainproof headgear which Mr Spear produced from a margarine box and the impressive medicine chest with

which Lander cured our aches and pains."

"yet perhaps the most memorable feature of the camp was the performance at our last camp-fire of the Maestro Josef's opera "Trial by Prefects," produced by the composer under licence from Palmer's House."

Sadly for the School Troop, Mr Spear had officially left the Scouts that summer term, but his presence at camp was surely an indication that he was still around to offer help now and then. Meanwhile among Mr Dent's many other extra-curricular activities was the production of the Dramatic Society's plays. This summer, however, he handed the reins over to AG Stevens of the Modern VI whose directorial debut saw Jervis, Hesletine and co. take the stage of the Virginia House Settlement with a performance of Bernard Merrivale's *"Happy Landings"*. And very well received it was too.

As was another, out of Ford Park, School activity. This time Beaconfield Road was where we found the Auckland Tennis Courts, and here *"boys over 16 not required for cricket"* were able to play the racket game. The standard of play that summer was well up on the previous year and a singles tournament was started and with Greasely as the captain, and Polkinghorne the secretary, a match was played against Sam's Sloshums and a further fixture was arranged with a Plymstock team.

When the new academic year started in September Polkinghorne had put his racket back in its frame and assumed new responsibilities as Head of the School and Captain of Rugger. The summer was over, but certain events of the holiday period cast a cloud over many parts of the country, especially in this Services City and in the Sixth Form of Plymouth College;

"It is rather sad to read over the Editorials of this magazine written four or five years ago. The war, with its terrible strain on the School, and its even more terrible toll of the lives of OPMs was over at last; the horror and suspense of the ugly conflict were dispelled in a wave of cheerful optimism. This optimism was

clearly reflected in the columns of the "Plymothian". Many were the sentiments of confident hope expressed in them. Some of those hopes have been fulfilled; hopes about the prosperity and expansion of the School, these have not been disappointed. Others, however, looked forward to equal prosperity in the international field. They saw with shining eyes the dawning of a new era of perpetual peace; the war had brought all wars to a final and everlasting end."

"Today the boots are marching again. Incessantly the armaments factories are turning out a myriad of devilish weapons that are not intended to be laid aside to rust. On every side there is talk of war; and as day follows day we seem to be sliding inch by inch down as abyss towards irreparable disaster at the bottom. A school is far too busy with its own affairs to take a great deal of notice of such matters; but it is a sobering thought that if war does come, it is likely that many of our seniors will never return. Whatever the cost, we must climb from the abyss. Every other consideration must be subjected to this object. The fight for peace is as arduous as was the fight for victory; let us hope that at least partial success will have been attained when next year we repeat our annual greeting: A MERRY CHRISTMAS AND A HAPPY NEW YEAR."

Written towards the end of the winter term of 1950 this editorial of GF Morrish, still in the Plymothian hot seat, expressed the fears harboured by many older boys. Curiously though, just as the references to the two World Wars had often been thin on the ground, there was little direct reference to what and where the conflict was. For this we had to look deeper into the magazine, and there tucked away in the Literary and Debating Society notes is the answer, buried in the Proposition put forward by Morrish himself ; *"That this House deplores the crossing of the 38th Parallel by the United Nations forces in Korea."* Falmer seconded and Jeffery and Cutler opposed, unsuccessful as the motion was carried 21-4.

The debate was held on Friday 6th October, less than a week after the Americans had reached the 38th Parallel and General MacArthur had told the North Koreans to cease hostilities. American troops had first seen action back in July and in August British forces had joined the West's offensive.

A fortnight later, the Rev Canon Caley OPM addressing the School at the Commemoration Service in St Gabriel's spoke of *"many similarities existing between the School as he knew it and the School as it is today. At the same time,"* he added, *"those were days of peace and security, and the present tension between the Western Democracies and the Iron Curtain did not exist. The present problem was to find the path to peace, as General Marshall had recently said. Every boy would soon be taking part in the fight for peace, and he would have to decide on what principals his actions were to be based. General Smuts,"* he said, *"had declared at the end of the last war that we should hold fast the eternal message and follow the greatest light which had ever risen on the human horizon. Jesus Christ was still the one and only leader."*

In the pages of that term's Plymothian the only other piece of politicking came from Morrish's seconder, Falmer, who produced a two and a half page essay on *"Western Europe in 1950"*, at the end of which was appended *"Publication of this article is not to be interpreted as agreement with any of the views expressed in it".*

It was, as it happened, one of only two pieces of student writing, other than House or Society notes, that was not written by the editor, the other being Dunne, of 3b's unusual account, of being bitten by a viper at Postbridge during his summer holiday. Morrish's own contribution was another, rather wistful, poem *"Summer Vision".*

New literary additions to the Library included *"The Kon Tiki Expedition"*, *"Elephant Bill"*, Kafka's *"The Castle"*, Bryant's *"The Age of Elegance"* and several novels of Graham Greene. New plans (by Mr J Leighton Fouracre OPM) for the Memorial Library were also unveiled; *"With adjustable shelves it should be possible to have the collection arranged on the Dewey system in use in nearly all great libraries now, so that practice in our own will enable boys to find their way about any of the libraries of the world without having to waste time by looking in the wrong place or asking assistants."*

"Heating will be automatically controlled, the shelves lit from above, the reading-desks lamplit and well-spaced, the librarian's desk and catalogue stand designed for their purposes."

"A central feature of the new Library," revealed the Head that Speech Day, *"would be a memorial board containing the names of the 67 boys who died during the war of 1940-45* (sic)." Mr Garnons Williams also informed parents and pupils on Speech Day (20 October) in Central Hall, that *"the basement of No.1 Shaftesbury Villas is now being used by the Scouts, and their old room is what is proposed as being the new Library. The TA,"* he added, *"have presented the School with a hut for the use of the CCF contingent and this has enabled two rooms to be used as classrooms ... whilst a third is now available for the housing of stage properties."*

The problem of playing fields had been temporarily solved thanks to the OPMs and Argum who provided pitches at Elburton and Roborough, *"but the Governors are on the look out for first class playing fields outside the city."*

Back at Ford Park and the new green and cream school canteen was now serving 300 meals a day. Among the new faces using the facility, over and above the 49 new first formers, were three new staff members, all of them, strangely enough, Yorkshiremen; David Whitman whose school and university life had been in Sheffield, and who had been in the Meteorological Branch of the RAFVR during the war; Alan King, a Cambridge graduate from Bridlington, and Arthur Addis who was educated at West Hartlepool Grammar and Durham University. Maths, Music and Physics were their specialist subjects and all three had done War Service and were in their early thirties.

Arthur Addis and Alan King take their places in the staffroom.

It was significant that only one member of staff had left at the end of the previous year, and interesting that he had written, after leaving that, although he had only spent two years at the School, after a lifetime in the Royal Navy, he *"had never been in any ship or establishment involving a better "ward room" spirit than that which existed in the School's common room"*.

The Headmaster quoted those words at Speech Day and happily concluded that *"if all was well there, nothing very much could go wrong with a school."*

Presumably the Headmaster himself did not spend too much time in the staff room, as it would appear that while the staff generally got on with each other, they didn't all warm to Garnons Williams himself – neither, apparently, did many of the boys; *"One of the worst aspects of my otherwise happy time at Plymouth College*

was having Garnons Williams as a Headmaster," recalls Colin May who that term, along with JE Taylor, was selected to play U15 rugby for Devon.

Back in the staffroom, all was not particularly well, for in truth teachers were very unhappy with their pay; *"considering all things, teachers are among the most underpaid men in the world,"* said their supportive Headmaster that Speech Day.

Sentiments echoed by George Riding, a former Headmaster of Warwick and Aldenham Schools. Riding was also critical of Lord Verulam's recent pronouncement that the teaching of French was *"the biggest national waste of time"*. There to present the prizes, Riding said that *"whatever subjects are taught, the important thing is that boys should follow their own bents and should always be enthusiastic. Jobs in which the boys' natural inclinations are thwarted are to be avoided,"* he added.

If the members of the School's Literary and Debating Society were anything to go by, entry into the job market was not something they were in a hurry to avoid, as the proposal that the school-leaving age should be raised to sixteen was roundly defeated 22-2, those two votes presumably coming from Richards and Jolly who proposed and seconded the motion.

There wasn't much more support either for the suggestion that the country needed a coalition government, Savery and Spencer successfully opposing that one. Hesletine's proposal that *"the standards of music and literature were now lower than ever before"* was also thrown out by a 19-5 majority, while there was a small balance in support of the motion regretting the *"TUC decision to end the wage freeze."*

Other issues debated that term included the 'Colour Bar' and the 'Supernatural'. Jolly and Richards, incidentally, with Goodman were a major part of Mr Coggin's junior team that played out the dramatic element of the Christmas entertainment on 19, 20 and 21 December. Performed in panto-style and helped

in its setting by a back wall of *"pantomime forest ... by Disney? Rackham? Certainly Wills"* it featured a *"well, so realistic that we are constantly expecting to find a pussy down it."*

The Orchestra also played. The choir sang carols and Mr Trevena played Mendelssohn's Andante and Rondo Capriccioso. Messrs Trevena and Wills also entertained the boarders that term at Thorn Park; the former with his music the latter with his puppets.

Meanwhile … *"the most significant event of the term has been a wild outbreak of Chess Playing. Their minds sharpened by prep., the boarders set out their chess men with eyes sparkling and hands shaking with excitement; there is a chess league, headed at present by Harvey v, and games will continue to be played, for it is notorious that anyone who has once tasted the blood of a pawn can never be rid of the craving."*

Another of the term's great talking points was the visit of the man with moving camera; *"The recent expansion of our numbers was much in evidence on the occasion of the School photograph. We can no longer accommodate ourselves on a few chairs and tables; we need now an imposing erection of tubular steel, and a photographer who will marshal us like a De Mille directing a crowd scene in some epic of life in the Circus Maximus."*

"The School, indeed, was literally on tenterhooks as it awaited the slow and supercilious sweep of the camera. The photograph itself is, we consider, a triumph. Avoiding dull uniformity and monotonous regularity, it presents a pleasing variety of posture, and countless felicities of detail. We regret, however, that no one attempted the legendary feat of the boy who, having been photographed at one end of the group, ran round the back in time to be photographed again at the other end."

One off-beat highlight that term included *"a somewhat different sort of music being played somewhere in Hartley, by past and present members of the College".*

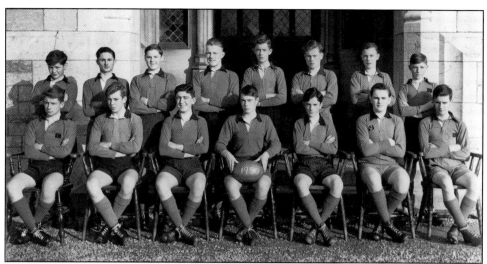

Above - purveyors of a new king of music. Above right, hockey action on the field. Right; Unbeaten Plymouth College Colts Rugby 1950: Back; DC Robinson, P Harrison, FS Furze, R Kerley, DL Brown, BA Reynolds, JHJ Heath, JM Hewitt. Front; BN Williams, TM Warren, DM Webb, DG Porter (Captain), TJ Stevens, JE Taylor, JW Reid. Below section from the whole school photograph from October 1950.

"It was the week when the music publishers wanted us to like a tune called "So Ends My Search for a Dream", and we remember a pleasant "Summertime" with muted trumpet and closed window, a rhythmic "Mule Train", a frenzied rumba at the piano, and a well-pointed vocal of "Rag-Map"."

References to young people stepping outside the classical and traditional to make their own music were rare up to this point in time, but here we were at the dawn of a new decade and who knew what the future had in store?

Clearly there were indications that not all teenage boys wanted a diet of so-called intellectual music and one of the short debates that term was *"that the third programme should be abolished"* – however Lethbridge and Greenaways motion was defeated by Farmer and Truman. DL Farmer clearly enjoyed the service that the BBC had started in September 1946 and his classical music and twice that term he brought his gramophone into school and some of his *"new 'long-playing' type records"*. The musical fare, served up on LPs for these "Gramophone Recitals" included music from Mendelssohn, Verdi, Prokoviev, Tchaikovsky, Delibes and Bizet.

With their love of the past Farmer and magazine editor Morrish seemed less certain about the future and between them they proposed and seconded the motion *"that the Festival of Britain is a waste"* (it was defeated), while Morrish later that term seconded a motion in the inter-school debate suggesting that *"the modern generation is more degenerate than its predecessors"*. That too was successfully opposed – by TM Bossom of DHS and Miss B Smith of St Dunstan's – the votes cast 34 for, 50 against.

Another of Farmer's passions apparently was Badminton and under that heading he informed Plymothian readers that *"certain Senior boys have been playing Badminton in the School Gymnasium for what seems to be the first time in living memory."*

Mr Barnes had agreed to supervise *"and several other members of the Staff have agreed to help in coaching"*. Meanwhile *"to cover the cost of providing shuttlecocks, a charge of sixpence per night has been imposed on players."*

Then he added, *"it is hoped that a School team will be playing in the local League in the not too distant future."*

Indeed it may well have been the first time that Badminton was ever, formally, played at School, certainly it appears to be the first time that the sport had received any sort of mention in the magazine. Significantly enough this particular edition of the magazine was a milestone in other respects too;

"With this copy the Plymothian enters into its 300th issue. What will be the world's reaction to this breath-taking achievement we know not and care less; we do not publish the Plymothian for the benefit of the world at large, and though it may occasionally turn up as a mental sedative in a dentist's waiting room, or even as a wrapping for fried haddock, these are not the destinations intended for it. It is printed solely as a faithful record of the School's activities and achievements and if the public would like to see, at our tercentenary, an extra-large issue containing crossword puzzles, soap advertisements and slimming recipies, the public is due to be disappointed. We have retained the time-worn and approved features of the past 299 publications, introducing no revolutionary changes, unless the printing of a chess problem can be brought under this heading. We are not ambitious, and in our very stolidity lies the firm hope that the principles of the past half-century will be retained during the next. Is this too much?"

The ubiquitous Farmer also had something to say about the Tercentenary and looking back to the first ever issue in 1883 he noted the music master's plea for a School Song;

"The contest, strangely enough was won by the

Headmaster with the immortal paean, known as *"Carmen Collegii Plymothiensis"*. In its original form, it boasted five verses; we can only regret that we no longer sing the verse which includes the lines:
"Hic palaestrae motibus
Membra nunc pulsantur"

"The Plymothian in its youth was also fond of printing "Letters to the Editor," added Farmer who was Assistant L&D Secretary to Morrish who was also, of course, the current Plymothian editor. And apart from Farmer's piece, and a poem of his own (about fish), he was desperately short of the sort of original contributions he, and any number of his predecessors, had been hoping for.

Morrish was altogether more successful in the Latin Reading Competition held by the Classical Association at the University College, Exeter that term. By a strange coincidence, perhaps, the School had a young student teacher doing his teaching at Ford Park that term who was from University College, Exeter – he was also an OPM – DC Henwood.

Joining the staff on a full-time basis that term was Angus Rose, who arrived in January to teach English and Maths. Educated at Peter Symond's School, Winchester, and Queen's College, Oxford (where he read English), 25 year-old Rose was one of that generation whose education had been interrupted by the war - he'd been commissioned in the RNVR and had served with light coastal craft in the Mediterranean.

New staff member Angus Rose.

Rose's naval perspective was a comparatively unusual

one in the staff room and before the year was out it would be called upon to help create a major new initiative for the School CCF. In the meantime the existing Cadet Force, particularly those interested in shooting, were benefitting enormously from the enthusiasm of another young member of staff, Lieut R Elliott, *"who has thrown himself wholeheartedly into the task of Master i/c shooting."*

This eventuality was occasioned by the retirement, from that office at least, by Mr Dufton, *"who has been Shooting Master since the VIII was formed."* Mr Dufton has during the last eight years *"unstintingly given up a great deal of his spare time to coaching and encouraging the team. He is still Captain and a leading shot of Ford Park A."*

The impact of the team's new mentor appeared to be instant; *"The standard of the VIII this term has improved out of all recognition, the most notable total being 587 which is a new School record. The individual scores for this match were: Harvey, AR, 100; Reynolds, JK, 99; Cowan, M, 98; Hooper, D, 97; Turpitt, MCC, 97; and Turpitt, DEE, 96. The previous record of 585 was set up on the 11th November, 1949."*

It had been a fairly wet winter though and *"in a drab term, open and closed range shooting"* had been *"a main activity, under Lieut Elliott's aegis."*

"The foul weather this winter has (also) given a fillip to Chess, and the results of the huge number of games played in Room Eight will tell when the second and first form boys are at the top of the School."

The younger boys, however had a tendency to rush and as well exhorting them to slow down there was some sound advice; *"The habit of never allowing yourself or your opponent to waive the touched-played rule soon teaches care; the wise beginner always plays with his hands under the table."*

"In School matches, Plympton proved superior, Sutton elusive, and Devonport for once not up to us. In a practice match, the Headmaster maintained his unbeaten record against boys at the School after a long struggle against Harvey (LR), and Mr Martin, of Plymouth Chess Club, fell to a wily and complicated attack by Morrish."*

Morrish was also in action, albeit in a minor way, in the Dramatic Society's production of Shakespeare's Scottish play; *"To produce Macbeth is a formidable task, and that failure in it is more likely than success, cannot be doubted,"* wrote the Headmaster, in his appraisal of the end of term (Saturday 31 March, April 2nd and 3rd) presentation.

Having said that though, Mr Garnons Williams considered the School's production a success, with Head boy, Hesletine, *"who doubled the parts of Banquo and the Doctor, outstanding"* ... *"But, when all is said and done, the play does depend largely on Macbeth and Lady Macbeth; and here it was well served indeed."*

Stevens and Shepheard took on those two roles, Mr King composed music especially for the presentation and Mr Coggin provided *"the touch of the master hand"* on production duties.

Two days before the staging of Macbeth, the Music Society had their share of the limelight, in Big School with an Easter Concert. The evening featured a number of solo and ensemble contributions, including no less than four piano duets; Mr Trevena and Mr King; Mr Bill and CW Jenkins; RJ and R Quarterman and RC and GC Fedrick.

Among the highlights, *"JE Dykes must be commended for his trumpet playing in Purcell's Cebell,"* while the evening was brought to a close *"by a song different in vein from anything which preceded it – with Mr Radford giving a vigorous performance of Wilfred Sanderson's "Drake Goes West"."*

The poor weather was also good news for other indoor events and that term there were a series of Sixth Form Lectures from a number of local worthies including; Mr D Childs, the City Treasurer; Dr GB Carter, the Deputy Medical Officer of Health; Mr E Foulkes, Clerk to the Plymouth Magistrates; Col JF Skittery, the Chief Constable, who advised that a career in the Police was only for the keen - *"promotion is slow and not automatic"*; Mr JC Trewin OPM, well-known drama critic, who maintained that the *"only practical way to success in journalism as a career, was to start on a local paper"* and Mr J Paton Watson, the City Engineer. At a time when the first major post-war store in town – Woolworths - had only recently been completed, the softly spoken Scotsman outlined the aims and achievements of the Plan for Plymouth (which he had co-authored), especially with regard to the rebuilding of the City Centre. *"He demonstrated, with the aid of maps, how the new estates had been planned as communities to conform with the topographical layout of the city, and, taking Ernesettle as his example, Mr Paton Watson showed how factories were being built near the Housing Estates, which would enable more married women to enter industry."*

The first new store in the City Centre, Woolworth's, opens - 1950.

There was also a talk by the Rev W Pile, OPM. With many years' experience there as a missionary, the Rev Pile gave an eyewitness account of the changed conditions in China;

"He described these changes and the efficiency and indoctrination practised by the new regime, while also remarking on the curtailment of personal freedom."

For all these indoor activities and for all the terrible weather, there was some sport played; however to give some indication of the scale of the problem *"no less than nine first eleven fixtures were scratched out of a total of sixteen,"* and *"less than half the second eleven fixtures",* with *"the opportunities for practice almost nil."*

Plymouth College 1st XI, 1950: Back; DS Cutler, DH Voicin, RC Fedrick, MA Congdon, IK Dawson, RJ Stevens. Front; RW Viant, BJ Porter, CJ Ackford (Captain), C Squance, AV Cawley.

Plympton Grammar were the only regular school side encountered, while the fixture against OPMs was one of only two won by the firsts. Ackford and Porter were selected to play for a Combined Schools XI against a Devon County side and Squance distinguished himself in goal. The seconds too only won two matches, but significantly they were the only two played against school sides, away to Kelly and at home to Plympton Grammar. Both the Staff and the OPMs scored five or more against them. Meanwhle the colts' only official fixture was cancelled, but two members of the side, May and Stevens, both won Final Order Colours for the 2nd XI.

Hockey 2nd XI, 1950: Back; TJ Stevens, RJ Quarterman, C May, JWL Watson, RK Willey. Front; GF Greenway, LR Harvey, MW Burt, AJ Goodenough, A Richards. (absent J Wilkins, Captain).

Junior Colts Hockey XI, 1950: Back CJ Batty, PE Branch, DS Bird, J Chown, K Erlich. Front; EA Chapman, MJ Barrett, MCT Turpitt (Captain), RJ Bidder, PJ Pomroy.

Happily the grey skies cleared for the afternoon of March 7th and the sun shone on the annual Cross Country race, however, *"the rain which had, until the day, been almost incessant, made an absolute morass of the School field, and by the time the Senior Race started, with one and a half laps of the field to wade through, the general feeling was that Wellington boots would have been infinitely preferable to the slippery gym-shoes which were used by everyone."*

The conditions, however, did not appear to deter any of the participants, indeed according to the Hon Sec,

Hesletine, *"there has never been such a large entry".* There were 42 Seniors, 99 Juniors and 137 Sub-Juniors, representing something like half of the entire school. Mrs Garnons Williams started all three races and of the seniors Greenaway finished first, ahead of Hesletine. May was the first junior home, while Doidge headed the sub-juniors, with PJ Brokenshire winning the Price Cup.

With the field a muddy mess it was timely that the term saw the re-surfacing of the quadrangle, and the laying down of three concrete cricket wickets.

Not surprisingly OPM hockey was just as badly affected by the poor weather, the oval-ball boys, however, were undeterred by the mud and rain and after a slow start won over half of their games with Peter Vittle looking set to break Bob Pratt's individual scoring feat of the previous season of 108 points.

Interestingly enough the OPM notes in this particular issue of the magazine were more extensive than ever before and bear the hallmark of John Spear who would go on to expand on this feature over the next few decades. One suspects that he was spurred on in this by the comments of the Club Treasurer who at the AGM *"drew attention to the strain on the funds of the Club caused by the present system of the issue of the Plymothian. The cost is very high and the income of the Club must be increased by additional membership or the numbers of the issue of the School magazine reduced."* A discussion followed in which it became evident that members appreciated receiving their magazine and were keen not to lose that link with the School. *"It was subsequently resolved to continue the present practice for at least another year."*

On the membership front there were very encouraging signs, with *"some two hundred members and their friends meeting at the Duke of Cornwall for the revived Annual Ball"* and a successful dinner being held at the Lockyer Hotel. Mr Dale was the principal guest and it emerged from the evening that he and Mr Garnons

Williams had met in '39 when the City of London School had been evacuated to Marlborough. Sixty-three year-old Dale had been gone from PMC for some twenty years, but *"one felt he had lost none of the presence which made one scared stiff of him in the lower forms when he told us to "Abi Romam" – an awe which turned to admiration as one reached the top half of the School."*

Another master mentioned in JRS's notes was DI Davies, the only staff member who went off to do war service and didn't come back to Ford Park. *"I saw him about a year ago, he is now teaching at St Alban's Grammar School and I am sure all Old Boys who knew "Di" will be sorry to know that he and Mrs Davies had just lost their only son after a very short illness – at the age of eight."*

Meanwhile, reaching the age of 80 that April was a special favourite of John Spear, Bert Sargent, *"recently severely handicapped by arthritis"*. Sargent was still living close to the School and was a regular visitor. Other past staff members and old boys popped in from time to time, including one that Plymothian editor Morrish (in the hot seat for the final time) recalled as *"a towering prefect when we were the lowest of the low."*

"We awaited with interest his reaction to the sweeping changes of the past few years. His comment was surprising. "The old place hasn't altered much," he said. "Oh," we exclaimed, "but when you left the School was only half its present size; there was a barrage balloon on the field, and there were mistresses on the Staff; there was no canteen, no Valletort ..."

"Well, you know," he replied, "when you come to think over your schooldays you don't remember the more obvious things so vividly. You think more of the humdrum, everyday scene, and picture the faces of boys walking eagerly about the corridors, or singing full-throatedly in prayers, or dispatching the cricket ball with a satisfying click. That hasn't changed, and never will."

"And so it is. Soon – some sooner than others – we will all be Old Boys ourselves; and many of us will return after long absences in distant parts of the globe. There will inevitably be changes; perhaps a new wing in the Main School, or tennis courts on the field; but they will not disturb us unduly. Sauntering through familiar places packed with memories, we will glance into the rooms we knew so well ourselves, and listen to the chatter and bustle of which we once formed a part; and then we will smile, and shake our heads wisely, and say to anyone who cares to listen: "The old place hasn't altered much."

So ran Morrish's last and most wistful editorial. Certainly his had been among the more mature and interesting of such contributions over the years and his equally dewy-eyed "Summer Lyric" – celebrating the *"Voluptuousness of summer-sated hours"* – oozed a similarly timeless charm.

The boys of summer *"... dispatching the cricket ball with a satisfying click. That hasn't changed, and never will."* The Plymouth College 1st XI take the field for a fixture with Sutton High School during the summer term of 1951.

Still looking over his editorial shoulder and eager to inflict his opinions on all readers Farmer produced that summer a celebratory review of *"Recent British Music"*.

"A bloodless revolution is even now taking place in this country, a revolution of which the vast majority of our people is ignorant, but which conceivably will mean more to mankind in three centuries than the troubles which are at present disturbing the world."

This was no tribute to Ted Heath or a look at be-bop or swing, rather it focussed on *"that Grand Old Man of British Music, Ralph Vaughan Williams, second to no living composer save, possibly, Sibelius."* Delius, Ireland, William Walton and Benjamin Britten were also singled out as *"the leaders in this great revival if British music, men whose work will outlast the transitory troubles of the world in which we are living, men whose music is superior to that produced in the other great period, the Elizabethan and Stuart ages, men who are indeed, worthy successors of Byrd, Morley, Tallis, Lawes and Purcell."*

It was one of only three original contributions to the Summer 1951 Plymothian (not counting a second Chess Problem set by Morrish), the third being DSC's rhyming *"Guide to the School Rules"*;

"If you wish to be accounted as a really model chap, You must never eat in public and always wear your cap. You must reverence all prefects with a deferential bow; And act with due decorum, and never make a row, You must move about the corridors with slow and stately pace, And regulated footsteps – you must never, never race. And in the "quad" each morning you can have a lot of fun. Provided always that, of course, you do not fight or run."

A reference in the last few lines to the Jew's harp gave an indication of what was capturing certain young boys musical fancy at the time, notwithstanding the efforts of Mr Firman at the Prep to get all boys *"while you are young and eager to play either the piano or violin – preferably the piano"*.

"To be able to play the piano is a great asset in later life and it is worth what young folk call the "drudgery of practice"."

Of the boys then in School, Clive Jenkins was probably the most accomplished pianist and certainly his skills were to stand him in good stead. That summer young Jenkins played *"a gymnastic Gavotte,"* the only schoolboy solo contribution to the School Concert, while the aforementioned Farmer was one of the two clarinettists playing Mozart's Trio for Two Clarinets and Bassoon – the item that Mr Coggin, in his review, *"enjoyed most among the smaller pieces".*

Mr Trevena also entertained with his Chopin Ballade in G Minor, although he deferred to Mr King on keyboard duties in the orchestra, where he played horn. Mr Radford was the centre pin of the Choir and Mr Bill conducted as usual. Messrs Ward, bassoon, McD Porter, cello, Rose, recorder and Dundas, clarinet, were among the other staff members bolstering the ranks of the orchestra.

Meanwhile, missing from the staffroom during the latter part of term was the Senior Master Mr Dufton, absent through illness. At 58 John Dufton was both the oldest (a few months older that Guy Hill) and the longest serving full-time member of staff (the part timer, Rev Benskin was older). He predated both Dale and Ralph, both of whom were in Plymouth that year; the latter presenting the prizes at the Athletic Sports on 12 May. It was his first formal visit to the School since his retirement and *"he rejoiced especially to see the field freed from its war-time encumbrances and restored to order."*

The weather was fine, the running was keen and Willey and Greenway were the fastest boys on the flat. However, Ackford impressed across a range of events – he won the Hurdles and Weight and was second in the High Jump and third in both sprints - and thus picked up the Victor Ludorum cup. Scott was his Proxime Assessit. Among the Juniors, Barrett was unbeaten in all four distances and Southern excelled with the Javelin, did well with the Discus and came third in the quarter-mile to finish Junior Proxime to Barrett.

Kelly, once again, was the venue for the inter-school Athletics and the School were fifth of fourteen in the Senior event on 26 May and second, to Kelly, in the Junior competition, three days earlier. Southern won the Junior javelin, while the Captain of Athletics, Ackford, later won the Devon Junior Championship shot put with a record heave of nearly forty feet.

Theoretically, of course, having more boys at the School meant there should be more chance of finding star athletes and to that end Mr L Williams, the local AAA coach, was brought in to help with training.

Meanwhile, Mr Mercer, in a similar vein in his report, noted that *"the increasing number of boys is placing a great strain on our resources and on Heywood in particular. He has now completed twenty-six years as a Professional here – a remarkable record – but, to judge by his bowling for a Staff XI against a London touring side, he is as good as new, or very near it. He has now been joined by Mr EM Glover, the Soccer international, who played a number of games for Glamorgan under the late Maurice Turnbull. His enthusiasm is unbounded, and we are very happy to have him with us."*

Although not an official game at Plymouth College for many decades, there's always a game of football at some point in the season, here Fedrick and Jervis are at play in Central Park - 1951.

Glover had played football for Wales – and Grimsby – and had come to Plymouth just before the War – indeed he played in all three league games of the 1939-40 season before it was abandoned - he scored once. Apart from a knee injury, and the War, he might have become a true Home Park legend – but it wasn't to be. Glover's first season at Ford Park, however, saw the new concrete wickets with "Ruberoid" covering and Ted was able to report that the cricket standard throughout the School *"is very much higher than it has been for a number of years and is likely to improve further."*

Captained by the "genial" Squance, the team had a reasonable season although there was a memorable, and diabolical, collapse against Truro when, needing just thirty runs with six wickets left, the last four wickets conspired to fall in four balls!

Fredrick had already taken 5 for 10 and Cutler 5-35 in that match and all had looked rosy. The team's successes owed much to Cutler's slow leg spin, particularly his 6-22 against Plympton and 7-35 against Dartmouth. With the bat, Congdon was the most consistent, his 229 runs coming at an average of almost thirty despite never scoring more than 42, while Harvey hit an unbeaten 63 in a drawn match at Kelly.

Plymouth College 2nd XI, 1951: Back; BN Williams, DGF Porter, BL Varcoe, C May, DM Webb. Front; AJ Goodenough, IK Dawson, DH Voisin (Captain), JC Friend, A Abburrow. Absent AV Cawley.

In the 2nd XI Goodenough bagged a remarkable 8-12 against Plympton. The Colts beat Kelly at Tavistock but lost at home, while for the U14's Fedrick was impressive with bat (two fifties) and ball.

Plymouth College Senior Colts, 1951: Back; DJ Bird, JR Tredinnick, CJ Batty, MJ Cowan, RJ Passmore, RJ Morrish. Front; MC Turpitt, JM Hewitt, TJ Stevens (Captain) RE Southern, R Arscott.

With more boys than ever at the School all sports records were ripe for improvement and at the Aquatic Sports on the last Saturday of term AJ Hannaford set two new records in the Junior sprints and Buckingham set a new benchmark of 49ft 9in in the Senior Plunge. However while Hannaford easily won the Junior title, Heath and Goodenough battled it out for the Senior title with the former having the edge overall. The two were described by JRS as both being "*above average for their age*" and Goodenough scored freely in the numerous Water Polo encounters, the first six of which were fairly comfortable victories for the School.

By the end of that term over three-quarters of the boys in the School (330 out of 499) were "swimmers" with Vb becoming "*the first form in many years to have no non-swimmers in their ranks.*" Thus it was not greatly surprising to find JRS suggesting that "*for the first time in the School's history we have produced a 2nd VII at water polo.*"

Over and above the sporting life of the School the hike in pupil numbers had a variety of other implications, particularly for those who not only enjoyed splashing about in the water but who fancied a life on the ocean waves;

"*As from 1st September,*" ran the announcement in the Plymothian, "*the contingent will justify its title of Combined Cadet Force by forming a Naval Section. Living in Plymouth, and sending so many boys as we do to the Navy, this is a logical and desirable development. We have been granted the services of an ex-Naval officer with the capabilities and willingness.*"

"*It should be made clear that this section is for boys who intend either to make the Royal Navy their career, or to be in the Volunteer Reserve: and to have a certainty of National Service with the Navy such boys must join the RNVR, Schools and Universities list.*"

"*Cadets who wish to join the RN Section should be able to swim and willing to sail, an activity in which it is hoped that some Senior Army Section cadets may join.*"

AR Harvey was the most senior boy with the CCF that summer, Wigford Down was the back drop for Field Day, Warminster the setting for camp and Col Sir John Carew Pole, Bart., DSO, inspected the contingent on 4 June;

"*During the war he commanded battalions of both our parent Regiments and it was satisfactory to hear him comment favourably on the turn-out and steadiness of the parade.*"

All was not necessarily as it appeared however and a terse note about Field Day suggested that "*once again quite a short march left one doubtful of boys' physical fitness and sure that insufficient care is taken of boots, socks and the fitting of equipment.*"

No marching for the shooting team on their travels though, instead "*luxurious transport in the form of a private bus to Shillamill.*" Most of the shoots were at Shillamill, with Wednesday afternoon practices

at Cleeve and an Inter-School Shoot at Rippon Tor "*shot in wet and windy conditions*". The School did moderately well, but the real breakthrough that season came at a time when, in the past, all full-bore activities had ceased, and the Shooting team not only continued to practice, but they also had a match against the City of Plymouth Rifle Club "*which we won by two points*". During the match the team shot at 600 yards for the first time.

"*A serious occurrence during the term was mutiny of the markers, who, on finding that markers for other teams were paid for their labours at the rate of three shillings (15p) an hour, decided that they should be similarly rewarded, and promptly went on strike. Needless to say, the mutiny was ruthlessly crushed with bribes and promises of payments on future occasions, so we still wish to thank Messrs. Booth, Squance, Pallett, Goodenough and McGinnes for their very efficient marking in the butts.*"

With the hitherto unprecedented enthusiasm for shooting it was no surprise to find that "*house shooting is being reintroduced ... it will be shot as follows: (a) teams of four, consisting of two Seniors and two Juniors; (b) rifles will be .22 Mosbergs, fitted with slings: (c) targets will be 25 yard NSRA, five decimal bull, tin hat, and (d) ammunition "as issued" to the CCF. Houses will have adequate facilities for training.*"

For those sufficiently interested there were other opportunities too and in a competition held at Lee Mill by the Stuart Road Rifle Club, the results, from the School's perspective "*were most gratifying. AR Harvey receiving no less than eight prizes in the 'A' Class, while JK Reynolds won four prizes and D Hooper two in the 'B' Class.*"

Doubtless all three boys and those others of the CCF read the notes of their own exploits with a certain amount of satisfaction, and in the same issue they would also have read the latest news of an Old Boy who had left Ford Park seventeen years earlier. Major ED

(Edgar Denis) Harding was serving with the Gloucester Regiment in Korea and had been reported *"missing, 26 April 1951"*.

"So far there is little we can add. Group Captain EC Harding (24-31) his brother, has written to say that so far as is known, he was wounded in the hand, returned from the FDS to his Company, and was seen with some of his men after the main battle. Since then the Pekin (sic) radio has announced that there were three majors captured with the CO of the Battalion."

Later awarded the DSO for his heroic part in the Battle of the Imjin River – *"his exemplary conduct sustained the morale of his men under exceptionally testing conditions"* – Major Harding was captured soon after the encounter (which had taken place between 22-25th April). During his incarceration Harding and his commanding officer, Col JP Carne, were accused of *"disrupting the study programme"* and of having *"a generally hostile attitude towards the Communists"*. For three weeks the two men were kept in small cells with only sorghum to eat twice a day, while their Chinese captors searched for evidence of their 'misdeeds'. Both were sentenced to six months in prison.

Following on where the previous issue left off the Old Boys section was again extensive and among the many mentioned we read that VJ Boatwright (27-37) had been ordained after the war service with the RAF and was married and living in King's Lynn; MT Parker (26.34) *"is now teaching at Brentwood. A bachelor gay, he still plays hockey and cricket, and next year will be spending much of his time teaching Biology"*; JR Hamley (36-45) *"is now travelling for a tobacco firm – he has also been acting for the BBC in 'At the Luscombes'."* Having started three years earlier on the West of England Home Service, this pre-Archers radio serial set in a West Country village, would run for many years – Pop Luscombe's favourite and oft recounted phrases being *"cor, dash my buttons Flo!"* and *"stretch a long arm for the teapot Harry"* – halcyon days!

The cast of the long-running BBC Home Service radio series At the Luscombes which was set in the village of Dimstock, which was loosely based on a place called Wylye somewhere between Salisbury and Warminster.

Congratulations meanwhile were offered to G Creber (27-34) on his election to Plymouth City Council and to the OPM treasurer, S Edgcumbe (27-33) on his election as President of the newly-formed Junior Chamber of Commerce – *"incidentally quite half the committee and officers of the Junior Chamber seem to be drawn from OPM ranks"*.

"A younger OPM to gain distinction locally, was B Williams (49-50) who is training to be a chef. His entry, a fruitcake, for the "Festival Faire" competition, led to most complimentary remarks from the judge and Lady Astor."

The old School tie was not without its impact around the world either *"an OPM tie led to the recognition of J Miles (46-48) in the Merchant Navy, by EN Lake (32-39) in Nigeria."*

JRS also reported that *"the present Resident Governor and Major of the Tower of London – also Keeper of the Jewel House, is an Old Boy of the School, Colonel EH Carkeet James (01-04). He took part in both World Wars, he lost an arm at St Eloi, in 1915, though back in France before the end of the same year; at the end of the War his decorations included an OBE and MC, three mentions, and the French and Belgian Croix de Guerre. He was one of the first British officers to enter Paris in September 1944."*

Carkeet James had recently written a History of the Tower too, while another OPM, First World War veteran WF Roper (13-16), who had devoted his later life to medical work in prisons, had just published a paper on the psychiatric treatment of criminals. The Telegraph

had recently devoted one of its leader columns to his work.

There was news too of Stafford Jackson OPM whose sudden departure from the staff was still fresh in many minds; Scratch Jackson had apparently left the profession and was *"now working with a new team in the Travel Bureau line and I understand several very complimentary testimonials have been received from "travellers" who have passed through his hands."*

Former headmaster Rev HJ Chaytor was also mentioned – the eighty-year-old Oxford man had just been appointed Warden of All Souls' Cambridge.

DR Colwill receiving his prize from Mr LHA Hankey, Headmaster of Clifton at the Prep Speech Day - held in Big School 4 July 1951

Another former headmaster FR Dale, meanwhile had been one of the many visitors to the Prep that term. It was the headmaster of Clifton, Mr LHA Hankey, however who presented the prizes at the Prep Speech Day. Mr Firman used the occasion to publicly point out that the recent abolition of homework had been *"no stunt, although the national press had tried to sensationalise it. There has been no deterioration in the standard of performance in either work or games, and examination results have varied very little,"* he said.

Central Methodist Hall - Main School Speech Day 1951, with Headmaster Garnons Williams centre stage.

1951

Certainly the parents seemed to be happy and Mr Firman concluded his speech with a reference to the *"big expansion"* that was due to take place in September *"when room has to be found for three new forms".*
Meanwhile, back at Ford Park, that summer term witnessed *"the birth of a new Club within the School's precincts – the Plymouth College Lawn Tennis Club, which is being run on highly constitutional lines, with rules and a very select committee under the chairmanship of HS Rendle esq."*
"Games of tennis have been planned every week to give as many boys as possible a chance to exhibit their prowess, be it for clowning or for tennis."

Tennis proves popular for both sexes locally in the early fifties and here we see Tim Wall in his school cap, and a number of tennis playing friends and sisters and Moorland schoolgirl and future Wimbledon Champion - Angela Mortimer

That said, and despite unfavourable weather that term, the team, led by HGC Scott, still managed to register a win over the St Boniface boys in their only fixture.
The prospect of matches with OPMs must also have been a consideration as the club continued to thrive, and the oval ball boys held a *"highly successful"* Rugger Ball at the Duke of Cornwall. Making strides forward on

one hand the team, looking over its collective shoulder, was however still finding it difficult to *"revert to the pre-war hoop shirts".*

OPM RFC 1951-52: Back; F Westlake, R Priest, P Vittle, J Hamley, J Spear, E Elliott; Third row; G Blight, D Smale, L Sherriff, L Daw, N Ross, K Pring, H Roskruge. Second row; R Keast, R Pratt, S Loe, M Hooper, D Pring, R Turner. Front; T Mutton, N Elliott, F Axworthy (Captain) J Northcott, J Beamish (Vice Captain).

Nevertheless that winter a new set of shirts and badges did arrive and the team looked *"well turned out"*. There was a good turnout too for the cricket team's Flannel Dance on the occasion of the Past v Present match that summer, and for the London Dinner, which Garnons Williams, Ralph and Dale attended.
The London Branch had now gained sufficient momentum for RG Hutchings, the London Secretary, to announce his intention *"to be at the 'Pillars of Hercules' – a tavern in Greek Street, Soho – just behind Foyles, on the second Tuesday in each month, from 6 to 7pm, in the hope that a few OPMs will join him for a drink, not necessarily alcoholic, and a chat."*
Meanwhile the London Dinner must surely have come as a welcome respite for Garnons Williams, coming as it did on 12 October, just a couple of weeks before the School was due to have its first full inspection in thirty years.

At the start of that new academic year pupil numbers were at an all time high with exactly 800 boys on the School Roll – 261 at the Prep and 539 at the Main School. The sixth form, with 80 boys, was looking particularly healthy and the 20 boarders also represented a new 'record'. These boys incidentally were all housed in the expanded (in 1947) property – No.12 Thorn Park. Boarding had moved from Ford Park during the war and would probably have moved back at the end of hostilities had it not been for the reluctance of the Inland Revenue Department to move out of No.2 Dunkeld Villas, where the boarders had been. Only five of the 800 boys were from outside Devon and Cornwall, with the vast majority – 558 – were from Plymouth. Of that Plymouth contingent just over 100 were on free places, with a further 55 coming in that way from Devon and Cornwall. Of an anticipated new entry of 90 boys into the Main School it was estimated that just under half of them would come up from the Prep, about a quarter would come in on free places and the remainder would be drawn from primary schools, maintained or private, in the area.
When it came to leaving the School the statistics were even more interesting. In the previous three years it was calculated that of some 173 leavers, 27 had gone on to University, 24 to other further education, 23 into the Forces, 16 into "the Professions", 30 to business, 15 Agriculture, 12 Civil Service, another 12 into "the Sea" and 14 were given as "Miscellaneous".
Financially, after taking account of essential repairs, the School made a slight loss on the previous year's operations (income from fees was just over £20,000 with Ministry capitation grant on top yielding a further £10,000 – the boarding house itself made a surplus of £200 in the year 1950/51. The principal item of expenditure, inevitably, was teacher's salaries which accounted for a little over £16,000 – that was the combined total for all 28 full-time assistant Masters, the Headmaster and two part-time members of the

Far right: 1951 Rugby 1st XV; Back; BN Williams, JE Taylor, JR Cundy, DL Bowles, C May, IDW Wright, AJ Lander. Seated; AR Harvey, JC Battrick, CJ Ackford (Captain), NV Blackler, RJ Stephens. Front; CH Gullett, RK Willey. Absent BJH Porter.
Right: In Plymouth City Centre the new Marks and Spencer building starts to take shape.
Below: 1951 Plymouth College Lawn Tennis Club: back; J Guy, DG Carter, CV Denning, MF Pearse, C Dean. Front; JR Tredinnick, JM Hewitt, A Aburrow (Captain), HS Rendle (OPM) master i/c, MJ Cowan, EA Chapman.

1951

Main School and eleven full-time members of staff (six men, five women) at the Prep. The inspectors only identified one weak teacher, although they did note that the post-war expansion had led a relatively large number of *"younger men with limited experience"* being on the staff. They also felt that one or two of the older members *"would profit by a refresher course"*.

The overall impression, however, was of *"a friendly, hardworking team, on good terms with the boys and with one another and giving much to the boys both inside and outside the classroom."*

Mrs Garnons Williams was singled out for particular praise for her *"energy and cheerfulness"* and for her role in *"organising and directing the service of the mid-day meal under most trying conditions and her genuine interest in the welfare of the boys."*

Dining Room staff - "Mary, G Ray, A Ray, Dunleth"

Nearly 60% (around 300) of the boys in the School stayed for dinner, *"served in three sittings in the remarkably short time of an hour and a half."* Bearing in mind that the Valletort basement had just been refurbished to accommodate this activity it must have been a bit disappointing for those concerned to see that the Inspectors thought that this was *"a poor setting for what should be a dignified occasion in the school day ... It is hoped, however, that future extensions to this School will include a more spacious and pleasant dining room and kitchen."*

Doubtless part of the success for the smooth running of this operation was due to the involvement of School prefects and one fascinating aspect of Inspections is for any School to see how, according to the Inspecting team at least, it stands in relation to its peers. Here at least was one area where, even in 1951, a collective eyebrow was raised by the situation at Ford Park; *"The School prefects are responsible for the usual routine duties in the maintenance of discipline. It is, however, somewhat unusual and surprising in these days to find that all prefects have the right to administer corporal punishment, though prospective victims have the right of appeal to higher authority."*

The Inspection was also interesting for its review of Curriculum, which in forms I and II was then identical across all three streams. Scripture, English, History, Geography, Latin, French, Mathematics, Physics, Music and Art were studied by all boys, with a third language – Greek or German – coming in during the third form at the expense of Art, although boys could do an after-school art class if they wanted to.

"All boys in Forms III start chemistry. In Forms IV the curriculum remains as in Forms III except that (a) class singing ceases, (b) the B boys who may do Greek or German resume History and drop chemistry (c) the A and B Forms are 'setted' for Mathematics. In Forms V the main division into Arts and Science 'sides' occurs: boys who choose to continue the study of a third language in VA give up all Science and vice-versa: History and Geography become alternative in the same Form, and also in VB for those boys who continue their study in Latin. The boys in VB who drop Latin (this year 17 out of 30) take both History and Geography. Setting in Mathematics continues and there is a certain amount of cross setting between the A and B Forms in Science, History and Geography, though not for all the lessons in these subjects. The curriculum of the C stream undergoes little change after the third year (IIIC)."

"Boys in VA and VB take the Ordinary level papers in all subjects which they study, while VC moves up into Remove for a sixth year and takes Ordinary papers at that stage. Those in the A and B Forms who are too young to be official candidates for the examination take the same papers as the others and these are corrected internally."

Generally the Inspectors seemed happy enough, but they did have some comments to make – comments that would have specific implications for the School; it was felt, for example, that much of the work of Form IIC in Latin *"is without profit"*; that the amount of English in IVA was not enough to *"enable even able boys to read widely or deeply in English literature"*; and that *"the load of three foreign languages and two sciences carried by all boys in Forms IIIA and IVA is exceptionally heavy"*.

The main criticism, however, revolved not around what was being taught, but what was not being taught. *"Because of the lack of a laboratory no biology is taught at all and this is a serious deficiency in the School's curriculum."*

Whether this was about to be addressed or not, is not clear, but the success of the Natural History Society must have shown the Headmaster that the demand was there already and perhaps it was no real surprise to find the Inspectors noting *"from discussions held at the Inspection it is likely that biology will soon find a place in the School."*

And so it would. In the meantime it was suggested that there was room for improvement in the English, French and Geography departments, while *"those responsible for the recent inception of the General VI are to be congratulated"*.

Lower down the School statistics for the Prep revealed that only eight boys from there had failed the entrance exam to the Main School in the past three years, and during that same period the vast majority had made the move from Hartley Road to Ford Park with only 38 boys over that three year period going to other schools; *"eighteen on account of the removal of their parent* to other districts; one to a local Secondary Modern School; three to local Grammar Schools; three to Clifton College Preparatory School. In addition one Scholarship has been gained to Christ's Hospital, and a Bursary and Chorister's place has been secured at Westminster Abbey."

On a more mundane note some of the Prep classrooms were said to contain *"more children than is really desirable and the provision of more suitable desks is under consideration."*

"The School," said the Inspectors, *"is fortunate in having an open-air swimming pool, a radio, a gramophone, two pianos, and a cine projector."*

The Prep School's pleasantly-located open-air swimming pool.

"The School day begins with an act of worship in which the boys participate. They assemble to the peal of bells and an organ voluntary, which are relayed from the School's broadcasting station ... about 180 boys (out of 261) take the mid-day meal, which is an enjoyable social occasion."

Returning to the Main School the Inspection Report then turned its attention to each of the subjects, making a number of interesting comments along the way, with several members of staff being mentioned along the

way, but never, specifically, by name. With regard to English *"the stimulating contribution of one of the chief teachers, the School librarian, was noted".*

Hugh Dent had plenty of reason to be pleased with his new, or rather, the School's new, Memorial Library. Opened two days before the end of the summer term the fitted oak shelves and desks, would still have exuded that special newness a few weeks into the winter term. The opening had been a particularly poignant affair, with the Reverend Benskin preaching a sermon during which he recalled incidents from the school days of several of the boys who had been killed in the War – *"He showed how Plymouth College had helped to form their characters – it is for the freedom of mind and spirit that they have given their lives".* Another speaker, the guest of honour, unveiling the plaque, Major-General WHA Bishop OPM, echoed those sentiments; *"They lived up to those principles which have been taught at this school – that you think of your side and not of yourself".*

Another of Hugh Dent's passions was History and this department too was found to be *"in a very healthy state"* – *"one interesting feature is the extensive use made of local traditions, monuments, relics, sites and other matters of historical interest in which Plymouth and its neighbourhood are particularly rich."*

In this context it's worth quoting the thanks, logged in the previous term's Plymothian, of the Genealogical Society which acknowledged in its Transactions *"the work of eleven boys, and one Prep. boy in copying and recording the inscriptions on the gravestones in Charles Churchyard before it is dismantled."*

With regard to Geography, *"the lack of an advanced course has undoubtedly had the effect of depressing standards";* in French there was feeling that there was too much reliance on the text-book, particularly among the non-specialist masters; *"German",* it was noted, *"is taught by one Master, throughout the School"* (Dr Ellingher) – *"a painstaking and methodical teacher".*

"The attainments in Classics are at present disappointing ... if it were not for the extremely pleasant personal relationships between Master and pupil, Latin would be even less popular". Sadly that Master, one of a happy team of classicists, was about to leave, and it is a testament to his success that even the Inspectors were moved to write – *"his departure will leave a gap which will not be easily filled."*

Another teacher leaving at the same time as Mr Dundas, was Mr Wills, the Art Teacher, *"who holds no recognised Art teaching qualification"* but whose *"enthusiasm and determination have been largely responsible for the introduction of the subject even on its present modest scale".*

Mathematics was deemed to be *"sound"* while, with regard to Science, over and above the lack of Biology provision, and the labs in which to teach it, there was thought to be a *"shortage of apparatus suitable for class practical work."*

There was a materialistic note too on the issue of Sports provision; *"Games are restricted to the School field where the pitches are all under sized and over used".*

"Changing accommodation for Physical Training and Games adequate but facilities for washing after exercise are not." "Three Rugby Fives Courts - need reconditioning, would be of greater use if covered."

So much for the facilities, what about the PT or PE teacher himself? *"It is to be regretted that there seems to be little corelation between the work in the gymnasium and the other physical activities. One reason for this may be that the Physical Education Master is confined to his gymnasium for twenty-seven periods in the week and so has little opportunity for contact with the boys in other directions. Another reason is that the work itself, although it reaches a high standard, still follows the old form of Swedish gymnastics which alone may not provide the essentials such as good quality of movement and training in basic skills common to all forms of physical activity. The Master concerned,* who is fully qualified in his subject and has had much teaching experience, would, it is felt, benefit from attending a suitable refresher course in the more recent changes and trends in Physical Education."

Undoubtedly the fact that he was operating on his own was a problem for Ian Edwards, however he was far from being the easiest person on the staff to work with and was very much a law unto himself. Not for him the inconvenience of Saturday morning School – it interfered with his private life, not for him after-School activites – indeed most boys were aware that if they had PE last period of the day then it was quite likely that the PE Master would be on his way home once they were in the showers – some seven or eight minutes before the bell would go to signify the end of the academic day. Not really surprising therefore that he didn't get involved with team activities – as far as the School was concerned he wasn't really a team player.

Such an attitude, however, was atypical of prevailing ethos of Plymouth College; *"A good spirit pervades the classroom. To the visitor the boys gave the impression of being forthcoming, courteous, and friendly in their relations with their Masters and with one another."*

The Inspectors however did feel it was worth mentioning that some of the boys *"might with advantage be smarter in appearance"* although in fairness they acknowledged that *"the present state of the buildings hardly conduces to pride in personal appearance."* They also recognised that this situation was itself the product of *"the enforced moratorium on school building and even repairs".*

As for the future; *"the precise place which this School is to occupy in the future educational provision of the area is not yet fully determined, But as there can be no doubt of the vaulable service it has rendered in the past to the education of the boys from Plymouth and the surrounding areas, so there is firm ground for believing that, given the full co-operation of all interested in its welfare, it will continue to play an important part in the years to come."*

In the post-inspection meeting between Senior Staff, Governors and the Inspecting Team leaders, the lead inspector was asked by one of the governors if he considered the percentage of boys leaving the School at 16 (37%) to be high, only to be informed that it was about average. Another governor asked what the lead inspector considered to be the main priority – *"Playing Fields"* was the reply.

A few major issues to be addressed in the future then, most of them already more than obvious, but what of the present? How did the inspection impact on the boys?

"The General Election and the General Inspection very nearly clashed," wrote DS Cutler, for the December Plymothian – *"the former came a week before."*

"Nevertheless the change of Government did not affect the working of that body known in the trade by the name of the "Ministry". The complicated machinery, put into operation so long ago, was moving relentlessly, and on the appointed day the Inspectors arrived."

"To make the week better for the Inspectors a slight change was made in the time-table so that they might have a full day on Wednesday. It was as follows (read carefully!): Monday was Wednesday, Tuesday was Monday, and Wednesday was Tuesday. Quite simple really! As a sociological experiment it was excellent, for it solved the old problem of "that Monday morning feeling". The solution is simple, you just change Monday and Wednesday round."

And the Inspectors themselves? *"They arrived complete with brief-cases and absolutely bursting with an apparently unlimited supply of awkward questions. Rumour has it that the brief-cases contained only sandwiches, though no one knows for certain."*

"Many of the Junior School were very disappointed, for they had expected that our visitors would be in uniform – like transport or police inspectors. However, it must be stated that they were much more pleasant to talk to than their appearance at first sight suggested."

"The visit lasted four days, and all School activities came under the eagle-eye of officialdom. Even the lunches in the canteen had an official taster. But though the boys came in for a lot of grilling it was the masters who felt the strain. Many a brow was furtively wiped and many were the sighs of relief as periods ended."

As it transpired the Classics Inspector had been first to arrive … *"But no barricade of dusty tomes, behind which they are wont to hide themselves could cover the blushes of the Classical Sixth when asked: "Do you read much Latin and Greek literature for fun?""*

Plus ca change?

Incidentally the General Election, referred to by Cutler, followed Labour's narrow victory barely 20 months before - early the previous year. Mr Atlee had won that with a majority of just five and his tenure since had been a little precarious.

Eventually after much harassment from the Conservatives, particularly over the nationalisation of the steel industry, Atlee had resigned. Then in September came a fresh crisis over the balance of payments and both the Minister of Labour, Aneurin Bevan, and the President of the Board of Trade, Harold Wilson, also resigned.

Labour's Lucy Middleton on the election trail again after less than two years - this time she loses to Jackie Astor.

"A good spirit pervades the classroom. To the visitor the boys gave the impression of being forthcoming, courteous, and friendly in their relations with their Masters and with one another." The Inspectors however did feel it was worth mentioning that some of the boys "might with advantage be smarter in appearance" although in fairness they acknowledged that "the present state of the buildings hardly conduces to pride in personal appearance.". Arthur Addis (above) poses with Form 5B; Back; DW Holman, DT Parnell, PT Shipman, LW Waldron, MJ Barrett, CS Luke, GW Searle, CP Littlejohns, JR White, PG White, PA Jolly. Middle; D Hooper, JE Taylor, MC Turpitt, Mr AJW Addis, JM Hewitt, PJ Rickards, MJ Cowan. Front; PJ Richards, P Harrison, AE Beard, JR Tredinnick, DJ Pomroy, AL Cooper, CB Besant, CJ Batty. Right; Meyricke Jones poses with a similarly less than uniform group of students outside Main School.

Mr Atlee appealed to the nation to re-elect Labour with a larger majority, but to no avail - the Tories won with a narrow, overall majority of fourteen. Conservative OPMs Douglas Marshall (Bodmin) and RD Williams (Exeter) were both returned, the former for the third time, while the Socialist Seymour-Cocks was re-elected for Broxtowe (Nottingham). Locally Michael Foot who had spent a year or two at the Prep before the war, held his Devonport seat for Labour, but Jacob Astor took back Sutton for the Tories.

A debate in the new Memorial Library (a more friendly and less formal environment) two weeks before the nation went to the polls showed that the mood of the School was vaguely in tune with the electorate; a majority of ten considered that *"a new Labour Government would prove disasterous for the Country"*. But there was no mock election this time around at Ford Park however. Clearly the imminent Inspection – which started four days after the General Election - had served to focus thoughts elsewhere. The great democratic decider gave some past pupils the excuse for a good time, however, as the Oxford letter revealed that not only were there now 15 Old Boys up there but that there *"had been a few cases of mild inebriation among the older OPMs"* on the night the votes were counted. There was a similarly healthy number of OPMs (twelve) at the other place too.

Among the newest batch of Oxbridge OPMs was GF Morrish who, interestingly enough, given the transatlantic wave of anti-communist witch-hunts had just become the *"College Secretary for the Society for Cultural Relations between the Peoples of Great Britain and the Soviet Union."*

Meanwhile his erstwhile colleague on the Plymothian, DL Farmer, had, we read, been *"knocked out in a hockey match against the ladies of Sommervill. This may*," wrote Oxoniensis, *"account for his pronounced misogynism."*

Back in Plymouth the movement of a number of younger females led to the creation of much needed space at Hartley Road. *"The flight of the Busy Bees" enabled Mr and Mrs Firman to move into Red House so that all the rooms at Munday House can now be used as classrooms or in some way by the Prep."*

The Busy Bees girls school had actually moved to their new quarters in Thorn Park earlier in the year and the move gave the Prep an opportunity to reorganize. *The division between the Upper and Lower forms has been made clearer and more arbitrary. All the Lower School is now neatly and compactly tucked away in the south side of Munday House; it fills the old Division I classroom and most of the rooms formerly occupied by Mr and Mrs Firman."*

"The reorganization, however, does not stop here, and is at the moment far from complete. There had, of course, to be a corresponding increase in the number of staff, and accordingly three new appointments were made. As a result, it is impossible for all the masters and mistresses to use one small common room in comfort, and so the staff has been divided and segregated into two compartments; the mistresses now have their own separate common room".

All together outside the Prep School, Mr Firman assembles his troops for a photo session - inside however pressure of numbers mean staff are segregated into male and female common rooms.

More misogyny … or practicality? The three new appointments, plus one replacement were; *"Mr Redgrave, from St Catherine's, Oxford, the new form master of Div 1A and who has taken Mr Martin-Smith's place to teach, among other things Physical Education; Mr Baker from St Luke's College, Exeter, who is Form Master of Div IIA – he is tackling Manual Instruction with enthusiasm; Miss Bishop, who comes from St George's School, Ascot, to take charge of a new form IIIB, and is also taking all the Lower School for Art and Miss Nicholls, who for the last three years has been at Emro, now has Div IV."*

Mr Redgrave, incidentally, did not come alone – *"we welcome Mrs Redgrave, Blaize and Sarah, whom we see often – they are our neighbours in the Cottage."*

On the non-teaching side there was also *"another new appointment, that of a School Secretary … quite an innovation for the Prep."* Among the other additions at Hartley Road that term were a *"Music Room, a Manual Instruction Room and a Quiet Room, and it is hoped that in the near future there may also be a Nature Room."*

The appointment of someone who could cover art across the Lower School was doubtless partly prompted by imminent departure of Leslie Wills who had arrived to teach art, at the Prep and the Main School, in 1946.

"We shall miss his generous assistance and no less genial presence, and his wise and tolerant humanity."

Mr Wills was thanked for his various contributions; *"the present cover of the Plymothian, the bookplates for the College Library, the reproductions of famous paintings now to be seen in our classrooms and his impressive sets for Shrewsbury battlefield, the Forest of Arden, the weird wood in The Old Wives' Tale, and the gloomy castle in Macbeth."*

"Too much talk not enough action" was another verdict on the departing Mr Wills, however, and while opinion may have been a little divided there was pretty universal sadness surrounding the departure EG Dundas – Joe Egg, who had been at Ford Park since 1937.

"It is possible to be a good Sixth Form master and yet be little known outside the Sixth. Had Mr Dundas's scope been thus limited, his scholarship, his tact and his interest in his form would have justified the compliment, But throughout the School many boys with little Latin and less Greek have come to know him as a friend with a real interest in their lives and pursuits."

"His dislike of the limelight meant that much of his work was anonymous. For several years he managed the Plymothian and contributed its best articles. His acting ability was seldom seen, but every producer, scene-painter, and concert organizer, relied on him to spend hours of his time and a fund of wisdom and experience in making good acting possible."

"His entry on the variety stage of 1947 was greeted with the coo of affection which goes beyond shouts of applause. His talent include the playing of several instruments – squeeze box, recoder, clarinet – and a fluency in occasional verse and topical comedy, always lighthearted, never designed to hurt. Some of his songs will go to posterity, on buses and at sing-songs; it is difficult to imagine a Palmer's concert without him."

"In one human attribute he is lacking: he does not feel contempt, except possibly for those who don't know how to "mash the tea as they mash it in Liverpool". One remembers him at Scout camps from 1938 to 1951, forever humming songs forever new, welcome on every patrol site, helping to cook or mashing yet another pot of "Rosy Lea"."

"Quickly after his appointment, his colleagues on the Staff learnt to recognize his quiet wisdom, his shy friendliness, and his deep sympathy. Several examples of his generosity are unknown, and he would prefer them to remain unknown, but the kindness of heart which prompted them was always obvious and open to all. Between 1941 and 1946, when he served as a driver in the RASC in Africa and Italy, his rare letters were treasured; when one met an OPM an early question was always: "How's Joe Egg? When's he coming back

to Plymouth?" And after he came back, during his illness there were the same eager enquiries."

"Several members of the School have already taken advantage of his "If you ever come up Liverpool way ...", and, no doubt, many more will, for he is one with whom we will not willingly lose touch. As it says in Latin for To-day (Book 1): "Magistrum bonum semper amabimus"."

Alsop High School was 41 year-old Joe Egg's next port of call, meanwhile arriving fresh-faced from Marlborough College and Worcester College, Oxford was a 24 year-old modern languages man, WWM Philipps. Replacing Dundas, meanwhile, would be another Oxford man, a classicist with a terrible stutter, Geoffrey Suggitt.

But we're jumping ahead. The real novelty at Ford Park that autumn term was the formation of the Naval Section of the CCF *"whose appearance in the time-honoured uniform of the Senior Service has added fresh colour to our peaceful scene."*

"The School is becoming accustomed to bodies of varying shapes and sizes clad in the familiar bell-bottomed rig of the Navy," we read in the first fully-fledged RN Section report.

"Instruction has been divided between the RN Barracks and the School and we are fortunate in being able to draw upon the services of qualified instructors from HMS Drake, who visit us on alternate Fridays when we are not at the Barracks."

"Equipment has been arriving at irregular intervals throught the term, and is, at the momentm lurking unused in various quarters of the building. However, this state of affairs will be ameliorated during next term, for the section is well on the way to obtaining a hut of similar proportions to, though of greater elegance than, that belonging to the Army Section. Plans have been submitted and approved and it is hoped that we shall be in situ next January, with all our stores, uniforms and equipment under one roof."

The first RN Section Field Day was to have been spent at sea on board the locally based destroyer HMS Wizard, but, *"this proved impossible, for she was ordered to sail a few days previously, and to take up station in the Atlantic, at some point on the route followed by Their Royal Highnesses Princes Elizabeth and Prince Philip on their visit to Canada."*

"The day was spent instead in the Barracks - HMS Drake – our "first coporate taste of salt water, when we sailed and pulled our way to and fro across the Hamoaze."

All at sea - the naval section have an outing on HMS Meon.

A proper sea trip followed on 20 November when *"we embarked in HMS Meon, a modified frigate, and in murky weather, with a reasonably choppy sea. We set out to find our sea legs. Some succeeded. The ship was virtually ours for the day: as a result, blue-clad figures could be seen at odd times clinging to the rigging, exploring the radar cabinet, patting depth-charges, examining the wheelhouse, and even, at one point, slithering about on the fo'c'sle in an attempt to learn some of the intricacies of the anchor and cable."*

Back on dry land and back with the Senior Section, as far as Plymouth College was concerned, and there was a certain sneeriness in the re-styled *"Army and Basic Section"* notes;

"During the past few weeks the stores have been convulsed by the arrival of curiously-shaped navy-blue garments, anchors, ropes, pulleys and lamps. Several stores checks and the arrival of a bevy of young "persons" with a demand to be fitted with uniform for a Nativity Play have added to the gaiety."

Like that of their new Naval Cadet Force colleagues, Field Day – October 20 - didn't quite go according to plan; "Debussing at Burrator, the main body began its training by a short, mistaken, route march to Gutter Tor – and then back to its planned training area around Sheepstor."

Meanwhile the newly promoted Under Officer AR Harvey and his colleague Sgt Reynolds (Captain and Hon Sec. shooting) were able to report that the "great things expected of the shooting VIII" had come to pass. "The team's scores have on no occasion this term dropped below 578, and when it is realized that in the whole of last season's shoots we only bettered this score three times, it may be seen how improved the shooting of the team has been."

In nine shoots they were unbeaten and what's more not once in those nine matches did their opponents better their lowest score of 578. Small wonder that they were grateful to Mr Elliott, master i/c shooting, "who has unstintingly given up his spare time after school and in the evenings supervising practices and matches."

The highest score possible being 100, Harvey himself averaged 98.8 over the nine matches, while Reynolds and Prynne were over 97 and all eight over 95.

Although not quite as successful, the 1st XV nevertheless won all their home matches convincingly (always scoring 19 or more with the opposition never scoring more than 6) – away from home it was a slightly different story, but "the School was happy in its choice of Captain. CJ Ackford is endowed with the obvious qualities of leadership" and he "created a good impression when playing for the Devon P & GS XV last year and for Aberavon before this term began".

Plymouth College 1st XV, 1951; Back BN Williams, JE Taylor, JR Cundy, DL Bowles, C May, IDW Wright, AJ Lander. Seated; AR Harvey, JC Battrick, CJ Ackford (Captain), NV Blackler, RJ Stephens. Front; CH Gullett, RK Willey. Absent BJH Porter.

Meanwhile MJ Barrett and RE Southern were chosen to play for Devon Schoolboys against the Cornish Schoolboys.

As a follow up to a visit from rugby stars Robin Prescott and Vivian Jenkins on the morning of the Springbok's match, the School team landed the promise of a fixture at the Tiffin School, Kingston-on-Thames, in January on the morning of the England/Wales Twickenham game ... scheduled as the afternoon's entertainment.

2nd XV, 1951: Back; TJ Stevens, FS Furze, CE Blamey, GP Stephens, NJ Napper, JK Reynolds, TM Warren. Seated; A Richards, GR Pengelly, GF Greenway, DH Voisin (Captain), LM King, DG Porter. Front; HJ Heath, DN Brown.

Jenkins, then working as a sports journalist, was a true schoolboy's hero, having played rugby and cricket for both Oxford University and Glamorgan, he'd also played rugby for Wales fourteen times before the war. The 2nd XV, led by Voisin, was even more successful, losing only once – away to RNC Dartmouth 2nds by just three points - and annihilating Shebbear's second string side 79-0. Curiously the Shebbear boys were the only ones to beat the School Colts XV that term, although it could hardly have been closer 11-10, otherwise the Colts were successful on every occasion, home or away, registering impressive wins away at Truro, Hele's, Sutton and DHS, and beating Exeter, Kelly and Wellington at home.

Only one School beat the Junior Colts too – Sutton - both home and away. That said they had been losing several games at the half-way stage but "never admitted defeat ... a good augury for the future".

Things were looking fairly rosy, thanks to Mr Rose, with one of the non-sporting, extra-curricular school activities; "To say that the Literary and Debating Society has woken up would be to cast a slur on previous sessions, so let it suffice to say that the Society has been revitalised. For this a debt of gratitude is due to ADS Rose, Esq., the Chairman."

In addition to questioning the desirabity of a new Labour government, the House also considered, and deplored, Blood Sports, but did not deplore, by a narrow majority (13-14), "Sensationalism in the Newspapers".

The Natural History Society continued to demonstrate the likely enthusiasm for the teaching of biology, while ITM Ross and JM Wilding won first and second prizes respectively in the Senior Stamp Competition at the City Library, while JN Landeryou won second in the Junior Section. The following term the new School Library was the focus of attention for the Stamp Club who "ably" organized the first ever exhibition there; "This opens up possibilities for other exhibitions; Natural History, Model-making, Art, History of Plymouth

..." Meanwhile the School Chess team, captained by Goodman, had a mixed term, with a whitewash over Plymouth High School and a good victory over Exeter, but losing to Sutton, Public Central and Plympton.

As the term drew to a close the Choir's unaccompanied singing of *"the lovely medieval carol "Lullaby My Liking", set to the music of Gustav Holst"* was a highlight of what was only the fourth annual carol service although *"it seemed impossible to believe that it was not a tradition with its roots somewhere far off in the School's past"*. Meanwhile the Christmas Concert, which did have a bit of a history, took place on the following three evenings 18, 19 and 20 December and as well as a few seasonal musical items of its own saw Mr Rose assemble a youthful cast for the *"The Trail of Toad"* with RJ Turner as Toad. Meanwhile AG Stevens *"competently"* produced *"a very different kind of play, relying on the gentle irony of human follies"* – Clifford Bax's *"The Poetasters of Ispahan"*.

Scenes from Mr Coggin's 1952 production - a School for Scandal.

Jenkins, fresh from his performance as Silvermoon, the wealthy jeweller's daughter, in the latter was back in female attire once more in the spring term as Lady Sneerwell in Mr Coggin's production of *"The School for Scandal"*. A production that was *"enriched by a most generous loan of valuable period furniture from Mr R Andrade"*, not forgetting the costumes and wigs supplied by Doreen Erroll, the portraits lent by Mr William Turner and the sets *"built by the Stage Staff and painted by BTN Bennett Esq., AE Beard and MFP Pearse."*

"There was real artistry in Mr Bennett's "Portrait of the Nabob as a Young Man"," according to the reviewer on this occasion, Mr Dent.

Brian Bennett and Geoffrey Suggitt join the staff at Ford Park.

24 year-old Brian Bennett had arrived at Ford Park in January as the replacement for the Art Master, Leslie Wills. Bennett had already exhibited paintings at the Royal Academy and other places, but his degree from Magdalen College, Oxford, was in History and he would also teach a bit of that.subject.

Joining the Common Room at the same time was Joe Egg's successor, Geoffrey Suggitt. Suggitt swelled the ranks of the Yorkshire contingent on the staff still further – he'd been educated at Leeds Grammar School before heading off to The Queen's College, Oxford, *"where he obtained a Second in Classical Moderations and a First in Greats"*.

Unlike the younger Bennett, 29 year-old Suggitt had already taught at two other schools, Taunton and Dulwich, spending three years at each of them. Coincidentally three years was to be the duration of Hubert Hall's stay at Ford Park. At the end of that Spring Term, "Conk" decided to give up teaching and instead become an Education Officer – *"in Her Majesty's Colonial Service"*.

"During his years at the School he endeared himself to boys and masters alike, and his even temper and unfailing geniality will long be remembered." The rugby talents of the young Historian were also appreciated and on his leaving, the Plymothian, on behalf of the School, wished *"all happiness and success to him and his wife in their new life in Tanganyika"*.

Making the journey in the opposite direction, and in even greater haste, earlier that same term was indeed "Her Majesty". The Duke of Edinburgh and Princess Elizabeth were in Kenya at the beginning of a tour of the Commonwealth on 7th February 1952 when a member of the tour press informed the Duke that he had just heard on the telephone from London that King George VI had died peacefully in his sleep at Sandringham. The official news came just after that, when it had been de-coded at the British High Commission in Nairobi. The new Queen's first concern was to let people in Australia and New Zealand know that the royal tour (which her father had originally intended to have undertaken) would have to be abandoned and as dusk fell on the evening of the 8 February her plane touched down at London Airport, where she was greeted by the Prime Minister, Winston Churchill and the Leader of the Opposition, Clement Atlee.

Meanwhile, at Ford Park, *"the usual serenity of the Spring Term was shattered by the tragic news. The same depression and sense of personal loss which the* nation felt on that dreary February day pervaded the atmosphere of the School. Perhaps the one redeeming feature of our sorrow was the universal sympathy of the world at large: it proved that political schism has not yet divided the world so irreconciliably that the nations cannot temporarily ignore their differences and join unanimously in revering the memory of a great ruler and humanist."

At the Prep there was a short service a week later; "After the two minutes' silence had been observed, twelve bells were sounded on the School ship's bell in accordance with the naval tradition upon the death of a monarch. Hymns were sung and prayers said. There was a short address given by the Headmaster and the service, which was attended by the entire Staff and boys of the School, ended with the singing of the National Anthem."

Closer to home the School was to mourn a second loss that term as Sir William Munday passed away on Tuesday 15 April. Although Sir William was 87 he had only resigned the Chairmanship of the Governing Body two years earlier and had continued to appear at School functions. "His passing has meant not merely the fading of a memory but the loss of a true friend", wrote the Headmaster in his tribute.

"When I was appointed in 1945, I was able to look to the Chairman of Governors for advice which never failed in its wisdom and for encouragement in every plan. A man of remarkably wide reading and intellectual interests, he was also a notable man of affairs. A High Churchman and a strong Conservative, he was no bigot, and the respect which he felt for the views of others was matched by the respect which his piety, integrity and strong sense of duty invariably won for his own."

The darkness cast by the news of these deaths was not helped by the climatic conditions in the first half of that Spring Term and more than half of the 2nd XI hockey fixtures fell victim to the weather – "Perhaps we shouldn't expect to play before half-term".

Plymouth College Hockey 1st XI, 1952: Back; TJ Stevens, DJ May, JWL Watson, DS Cutler, C May, RJ Stephens. Front; DH Voisin, AV Cawley, MA Congdon (Captain) RC Fedrick, NJ Napper.

The firsts were a little more successful, the weather only claiming three games and only the more experienced Belair side ever really getting the better of them. They also lost to OPMs, but only just - 6-5 - the winning goal coming in the last minute of play. Stevens was the team's spearhead, while Fedrick, Voisin and Cawley all had the call to play against the County for the Devon Public School XI, while one of the lost fixtures at Ford Park was against a County side.

Of the 2nd XI fixtures fulfilled, only one was lost – away to Kelly – the others, against Tavistock, Exeter, Plympton and Saltash were all won by two or more goals, with Porter, Webb, Hewitt, Richards and Southern all winning their full colours. The seconds found matches even harder to come by, as did the junior sides.

The junior boys made up for their lack of match practice by being "brought to good trim in their outings in games periods" and thus provided a big field for the annual Cross Country on Wednesday 12 March. Barrett beat off a serious competition in the Juniors, Brokenshire in the sub-juniors, while Elliot of 1a won the Price Cup. "The Seniors were thinner on the ground: perhaps the

modern adulation of Science has spread a regard for the Principle of the Conservation of Energy beyond the Science Sixth, where it has long been held in percular regard as a guide to conduct. Reid, with a heretical disregard of such dogma, had made himself thoroughly fit and won a good race."

Watson and May were second and third respectively. May, promoted that term to Act/L/Sea in the newly constituted RN Section of the CCF, was among those to visit HMS Drake on Field Day that term; "the Waller dome teacher was placed at our disposal, together with a whaler and a Diesel picket-boat. The field gun's crews, training for Olympia, also happened to be practising. "We saw and we purred applause"."

Plymouth College CCF, Senior NCOs, 1952: Back; Sgt Wroath, Sgt. Battrick, L/S May, Sgt. Hooper, Sgt. Wright. Front; CSM Pengelly, RSM Prynne, U/O Cutler, CSM Congdon, CQMS George.

Applause was due all round too to the School's Shooting VIII; "In winning both the Plymouth and District Second Division and our section of the Devon Postal League, the VIII has had probably the best season ever." The highlights included a new match record of 589 with individual scores of 100 for both Reynolds and Turpitt. The team also came second (first of the schools) in the NSRA Junior Winter Competition. Hearty thanks were recorded for the hard work of the coaches and "Messrs Elliott and Scott's cars".

Plymouth College Shooting VIII, 1952: Winners of Devon County Miniature Rifle Associations (Winter Postal League), Undefeated Winners of Plymouth & District Small-Bore League (Div II). Back; A Richards, JM Hewitt, MC Turpitt, PV Clarke. Front; MJ Cowan, JK Reynolds, AR Harvey (Captain), D Hooper, TAL Prynne.

The House Shooting Competition, in abeyance since 1945, was also revived that term and although the standard was not high, *"the event served to widen interest and the pool of possibles"*. Sargents, with the School team's Shooting Captain and Secretary – Harvey and Reynolds – were victors. In Harvey Sargents also had one of the senior figures in the CCF and, in Watson, they had the Troop Leader of the Scouts. Watson was also one of the main contributors to the activities of the Literary and Debating Society, who that term overturned the suggestion that *"The City of Plymouth was a Deplorable Blot on the Country's Landscape"*, they were however, strangely unanimous in agreeing that the *"Moon is Made of Green Cheese"*. A very successful inter-schools debate in Big School on 4 March saw visitors from six schools consider the motion *"This House deplores Co-education"*. *"It provoked a great deal of interesting and amusing debate,"* wrote DS Cutler. *"The motion was carried by fifty-nine votes to forty-two. Afterwards a mistress from Plymouth High School said that it had been the*

best inter-schools debate she had attended."

Among those continuing their interests in the art of public debate beyond school we read that GF Morrish had *"succeeded in annoying Randolph Churchill at a meeting"* at Oxford while in the Cambridge Union, Cantabrigiensis informed us that *"JM Waterhouse continues to hold audiences spellbound with his peculiar mixture of Gladstonian thunder, Disraelian lightning and Waterhousian fog"*.

There were healthy numbers of OPMs at both places and an even healthier contingent at the annual dinner – seventy three – *"one more than what was believed to be a record last year"*. Guest speakers at the Invicta Hotel dinner were the Reverend Benskin and Major-General WHA Bishop, CB, OBE, *"one of the School's most distinguished Old Boys"* who the following day, Saturday 22 March, addressed the Sixth Forms on *"The British Commonwealth"*.

"It was," ran the Dinner report, *"particularly gratifying to find such a good number of those present who had left School recently."* Indeed some of these younger OPMs had formed an *"under 25's"* committee and were planning to hold a Flannel Dance on the evening of the Past versus Present Cricket match *"with the possibility of a special interlude for square dancing"*.

There was also talk, largely generated by SE Westlake, of trying to raise an OPM Golf team of about fifteen *"to play matches against Yelverton and Bigbury"*. *"Subject to sufficient players being available."* BW Richards was also proposing to arrange some swimming fixtures locally.

Meanwhile, on the other side of the Atlantic, a former School boxing champ in New York, JR Brazier, was finding *"the task of getting British textiles across to the Americans really hard work, but finds watching boxing either on the TV screen or at the ringside provides some consolation."*

Television had yet to arrive this far into the South West although that April an Eggbuckland man succeeded in

transmitting television pictures to Plympton and Saltash. Mr Harold Jones, a Fellow of the Television Society, and one of only three people in the country and the only one in the South West, to have been granted a licence by the Government to make television transmissions, said his work was purely experimental and he wasn't allowed to broadcast programmes or advertisements. However, according to the Western Evening Herald, he had achieved *"excellent results in his own home, televising members of his family and guests from room to room"*.

Curiously enough a group of boys from the Prep were taken to the offices of the Evening Herald and Western Morning News, in New George Street, around this time; *"The first room we visited was where the news is received from different parts of the country on a special typewriter on a continuous roll of paper. The news sheet is then sent down a tube to the Editor and Sub-Editors, who decide what is to be printed in the newspaper."*

"Next we went to see the photographs being made and then on to see the actual printing of the next edition of the paper."

"The first machine we saw was the one that makes the letters from lead. In another machine the pages are pressed on to some thick paper. This paper is then made into something like a half-round tub into which is poured a metal mixture, which forms the letters to be printed on the newspaper ..." So wrote JE Davis of Remove A, meanwhile his classmate, AG McFadyean, provided his eye-witness account of a School trip to the other media nerve-centre of the city – Seymour Road and the BBC; *"First we were shown over a room in which was a big machine. If something went wrong with it, they would alter some plugs, which would switch over to another, similar machine. Then they took us to a small room, which was used to make the voices echo. Then they took us to the transmitter room, in which was a very old transmitter and an American one, which is*

used for the Third Programme only ..."

Another Remove boy, SJI Lee, commenting on another room, this time at Hartley Road, had this to say about the Prep's new Nature Room; *"It contains a vivarium inhabited by two half-grown slow-worms, Sally and Sammy, and four younger ones; there are also two small frogs and a large toad."*

"There is a formicarium with many ants and their chrysalises, loosely called ant's eggs. There is also a caterpillar farm containing moths' and butterflies' eggs and caterpillars. We also have two fish and some water-beetles and snails."

The Prep section of the Plymothian that Summer Term was far and away the most substantial it had ever been, doubtless in part reflecting the increased number of boys at Hartley Road. Another more obvious consequence of this increased number of boys was an increase in the number of parents wanting to follow their boys' progress.

Thus it was perhaps not surprising to see Mr Firman regretting that *"Big School was not large enough to accommodate all the parents and visitors at Speech Day and that so many had to be outside in the corridor and on the stairs."* Held on a Wednesday afternoon, to avoid interfering with Main School school activities Mr Firman added; *"At once we are investigating how to avoid this in future years."*

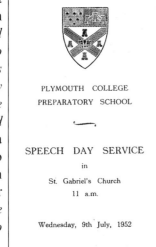

PLYMOUTH COLLEGE
PREPARATORY SCHOOL

SPEECH DAY SERVICE
in
St. Gabriel's Church
11 a.m.

Wednesday, 9th July, 1952

Like the Main School event the Prep Speech day was divided into two with a morning service at St Gabriel's and the prize giving in the afternoon. The Rev R Ball preached at the former; *"Taking as his text "Knock, and it shall be opened unto you"* the Rev Ball pointed out how commonplace and yet how important door-knockers (or their modern counterparts, door-bells) are in our lives. Almost every big event in our lives starts with a knock on the door."*

Meanwhile in the afternoon the Senior Education Officer for the County, Mr WE Philip, told the crowded Big School assembly that; *"Although he thought it likely that the Fleming report would be implemented still further, that independent schools would, in future, be more closely linked to the State system, and that more and more boys in the direct grant schools would come from the primary schools, there was, in his opinion, still a place for the independent school in English education. It had smaller classes, its staff were usually better qualified, and it was the gateway to a highway to a higher type of education and social status."*

Quite what the boys themselves made of Mr Philip's speech is not recorded, but there were plenty of other first hand accounts of Prep activity, including; the visit to the Plymouth Lifeboat at Millbay; a trip to the Danish Research ship "Galathea" (*"a former British frigate, the ship has the world's longest fishing line, 10,000 metres of steel wire"*) in Devonport Dockyard; to Lee Moor China Clay Pits; the Town and Country Exhibition at the newly opened Dingle's Store, and the Royal Show – the Show of the Agricultural Society of Great Britain, held at Stover Park, Newton Abbott – *"When the Queen passed through the streets she was dressed in a black dress and shoes and a black and white hat"*.

The extra-curricular Prep programme wasn't confined to trips away from Hartley Road, however, and that term saw the staging of a major Arts and Crafts Festival at the School, with Music, Art, Verse Speaking, Prose Writing, Prose Reading, Stamp Collecting and Modelling.

"Ships, a model of the Globe Theatre, garages, ancient castles, a toy chair, a bird-cote, a tea-tray and a mechanical man were among the variety of exhibits" and the adjudicator, Mr F Coford, said that the standard was amazingly high. It was interesting to note that the songs in the music section were chosen by WH Parry one of the group of Inspectors who had visited in October. Quite who chose the passages to be used for the Prose Reading was not recorded, it was however noted that *"Mr Garnons Williams rather hesitatingly criticised the choice of Enid Blyton's prose for such a competition."*

"It might be prejudice on my part," added the Main School Headmaster, *"for my reading of Miss Blyton's literary output is limited, and all may not be as bad as Mary Mouse."* The Head's remarks were followed by a very rare editorial comment about Mary Mouse – *"A story which is regarded by some serious critics as the nadir of Miss Blyton's works."*

Not a lot of Blyton in the Main School library then one imagines, however, Mr Dent was pleased to report that term, elsewhere in the magazine, that *"we have recently received seventeen of the most popular junior fiction books in the Library, increasing our Biggles and Gimlets to nearly fifty."*

Somewhat overshadowed by his earlier creation, Gimlet – Captain Lorrington King DSO, MC and Bar – was author, Captain WE John's response to a request from the War Office to come up with a soldier hero to complement his RAF superstar Biggles. Gimlet's first outing, in King of the Commandos, appeared in 1943 and suddenly there was a new gang, King's kittens, to inspire the nation's youth, with "Copper", "Cub" and "Trooper" - Corporal Albert Edward Collson, Nigel Norman Peters and Private Troublay. To add to his appeal in the Ford Park library it emerged that the fictional Gimlet was a local gentleman – his home address, Lorrington Castle, Devon (somewhere near Torrington perhaps? – Chichester country).

This newest set of literary acquisitions was partly made possible by a legacy from the late Sir William Munday who left £25 and *"the pick of a hundred books from his collection"*.

Mr Bill and Mr Fielding also made gifts to the Library and among the former's many extra-curicular activities that term he had the pleasure of attending the first Modern Language Evening in the Gymnasium. *"It proved to be a most varied and enjoyable programme of music and drama"*; IIB presented Le Café Cognac, a one act play, IIIC did one too, Au Chant des Oiseaux, the boys of IIA came up with a couple of sketches, there were German songs, French poems and a recital of Daquin's "le Coucou" by Mr Trevena who later led the audience in a rousing rendition of the "Marseillaise".

Ten days later – Thursday 19 June – Harry T was tinkling the ivories at the Summer Concert, again in the gym – *"it is hoped that he may, at the next concert, have a concert grand piano which will bring out more clearly the more delicate passages in any work."*

This time it was the turn of the Prep Headmaster to supply a critique of a Main School event and just as Garnons Williams had spoken his mind over the Prep Arts and Crafts event, so Mr Firman was not of a mind to just pour out platitudes; *"There is no doubt but*

that the Orchestra is established," but *"an increase in players is clearly desirable and, I would say, more stiffening from OPM players. The choir enjoys fully what it sings, and over all the tone is pleasant."*

That said Mr Firman clearly enjoyed the folk-songs, sea-shanties and madrigals and congratulated Mr Bill and Mr King on their choice. Mr King in turn was congratulated elsewhere by Mr Bill for his setting up of a recorder group – *"an excellent introduction to ensemble playing"*. Mr Bill also congratulated *"our bassoonist, JH Davies, on being selected to take part in the Summer School for orchestral players at Canford in August."*

And then there was PK Clarke's nine day spell with the 120-strong National Youth Orchestra in Bournemouth. *"The orchestra's conductor, Sir Adrian Boult, gave lectures on the art of conducting; there were private classes by our professors and classes on composition by Malcolm Arnold."*

"It is customary on these courses for the Orchestra to tackle a new composition by a British composer, and this year the piece chosen was Benjamin Frankel's "Mephistopheles Serenade and Dance". The work is most weird on first hearing, but after much work and practice one can discern its careful construction and follow the drama of the Mephistopheles story. Benjamin Frankel was a very popular figure with the orchestra, and directed us while sitting on an enormous high cushioned stool and whilst smoking a cigarette through a large crooked bamboo holder. He looked a typical musician."

Composed specifically for the National Youth Orchestra, forty-five-year-old Frankel's eight-minute epic was subtitled *"A Caricature for Orchestra"* and was recorded, and soon afterwards broadcast, by the BBC. Alas no cassette recording facility for young Clarke; *"All that I had to show to prove that it was not a dream was a programme, worn and much tougher fingers, and a much wider and deeper knowledge of*

music, its meaning and interpretation."

Clarke's piece was one of a handful of extra items in that term's magazine, among them a poem "Thoughts of an Irish Mariner" and the story of Albert the Snake, both by TJ Williams. The Cambridge letter expressed *"worried calculations as to the length of time to Tripos"* while the termly Oxford missive spoke of two distinct classes at the University in the Summer: *"those who go to the river and those who go to the Examination Schools."*

The opening of Hill Lane Tennis Courts at the dawn of the fifties - strictly for young players - did a lot to champion the sport locally.

Back at Ford Park meanwhile, as well as the newly-introduced GCE examinations there was another new "official" Summer term diversion – Tennis: *"This has been an extremely important term in the development of School tennis. For the first time in recent years the Plymouth College Lawn Tennis Club has been allowed to udertake a full set of fixtures."*

Indeed it was probably the most extensive set of fixtures ever undertaken by the School and doubtless part of the determination to see a School side established was the fact that there were a few very useful players now at the School. So good were they in fact that, despite their comparative inexperience, they nevertheless won all their matches – *"often against older and more experienced players."*

"The highlight of the term was the defeat of Kelly College at Tavistock, a performance which is all the more creditable when it is realised that our opponents have two hard and three grass courts at their disposal, and are therefore able to devote considerable time to the game. The Plymouth College team has again been forced to rely on the use of outside courts on Wednesday afternoons only, so that any form of team practice has been out of the question."

"The Singles and Doubles Tournaments are both progressing satisfactorily, with a much higher standard of play than ever before, and mention should also be made of the Spring Tournament held at Hill Lane. This was open to the whole of Plymouth and District, and Plymouth College had the honour of providing all four semi-finalists in the Boys' Singles, which was eventually won by DM Webb, after a great battle against A Aburrow in one of these semi-finals."

"Regular Wednesday afternoon play has been taking place at Aucklands, and also at Whiteford Road, where we have been greatly indebted to Mr Hamilton-Whiteford, OPM, for the use of two new courts."

Not surprisingly perhaps, Mr Rendle concluded his historic Tennis review on a very upbeat note; *"Finally, with our own membership of seventy boys over fifteen, and with many younger boys right down to the First Forms playing at Hill Lane Junior Club, there is virtually no limit to the future promise of School tennis."*

Among the scalps alongside Kelly's in the trophy cabinet that summer were those of RNEC (Keyham), HMS Fisguard, Hill Lane LTC, and DHS – *"this match held on one of the hottest days of the term lacked excitement, except for that caused by the bees from a nearby hive".* (Hill Lane, incidentally, was a young and particularly vibrant club around this time and among the girls playing there was the future Wimbledon

Champion Angela Mortimer).

The Schoolboys also beat a Staff team that included two OPMs, Messrs Rendle and Trevena; *"a very enjoyable game in which the School team appreciated the "coming out of retirement" of several members of the Staff. However,"* wrote the newly-elected Hon Sec, Lander, *"a high standard of tennis could not be obtained on the poor surface of the courts at West Hoe."*

The other masters to play on that day were Barnes, Lindley, Rose and Suggett, while Aburrow, Lander, Wright, Hewitt, Cowan and Prynne made up the three School pairs, with Webb the principal absentee.

Principal absentee at Ford Park at the end of that term, however, was someone who been a regular visitor and supporter of social and sporting events since his retirement in 1934 – Bert Sargent.

He died on 25 May 1952, just a week or so after the event he had seldom, if ever, missed since arrival in 1903 – Sports Day. Born in April 1871, his Plymothian obituary was written by the Headmaster who had been there for the last five years of Bert's teaching career – another Herbert - HW Ralph;

"Herbert Sargent would probably have regarded it as a compliment rather than a criticism to be called a master of the old school: for he had a profound mistrust, not unmixed with contempt, for anything he considered extreme in modern methods and ideals of education. The virtues he most respected and encouraged his pupils to cultivate were those of discipline and hard work: he agreed that school was a place in which to grow up pleasantly and happily, but he insisted that it was also a place in which to learn to work."

"He was a kind, hard-working and extraordinarily successful teacher of mathematics with the happy gift of extracting the best from his pupils without fuss or friction."

Remembered just before his retirement by the naming of East House (his house) after him, Sargent, in his will, left his own legacy to Plymouth College with a

bequest of £200 *"the interest on which is to provide a prize known as the Sargent Prize for Mathematics and Science."*

The death was also noted that summer of the younger brother of the late Sir William Munday, namely Major-General RC Munday, CB, OPM. Meanwhile, a new arrival at Ford Park that term was the 31 year-old History teacher Robert Blackledge. Educated at Spalding Grammar School and Keble College, Oxford, Blackledge had served in the Royal Artillery during the war and came to Plymouth College from King Henry VIII School in Coventry. He came as the replacement for 'Conk' Hall.

There was also a need generated for a modern linguist, albeit a temporary one, as Philip Coggin opted to spend a year teaching at the Lycee Janson de Sailly in Paris.

Plymouth College Athletic Team, 1952: Back; AJ Lander, JW Lethbridge, C May, AV Cawley, RC Fedrick. Front DH Japes, JC Battrick (Captain), TAL Prynne.

But we're jumping forward again. Going back to the beginning of that term a spell of English summer rain *"made mockery of set programmes of heats and caused postponement of the Sports."*

It also meant for heavy conditions when the Sports eventually, were staged in the middle of May. Nevertheless Prynne managed to set new records in the Javelin and Discus (142ft 4in and 112ft 11in respectively). Frustratingly Southern also bettered the old Javelin record and Battrick the Discus, but both were outgunned by Prynne. Battrick, however, won the Weight and the Quarter-Mile and two seconds, in the 100 yards and the Hurdles, were enough to see him pip Prynne and take the Victor Ludorum.

Bidder, with wins in the 100, 220, Long Jump and Discus was worthy winner of the Junior title, ahead of Cullen, while Mr Rendle finished ahead of Mr Spear and Norman Elliott to win the Old Boys race.

The Devon Public and Grammar School's Championships were held at the Brickfields ten days later and the School finished seventh out of fourteen, with Prynne picking up a second in the Javelin and fourth in the Discus. Japes, who along with Battrick and Prynne was the only other athlete to win School colours that summer, came sixth in both the events he had won at School, the 220 and the Long Jump.

Thompson's Athletic Team - with half of the School Team in their number they were House Champions of 1952: Back; RW Sheppard, WJ Loram, MJ Barrett, RW Maddock, CJ Foxwell. Front; C May, JC Battrick, TAL Prynne (Captain) AV Cawley. P Glover (Shield).

However, while the Athletics achievements gave little to shout about, the Cricket report for once had a happier tale to tell;

"In one school game some two or three years ago our opponents had made a score which looked like the number on a railway ticket and the School wickets were falling faster than the evening sun. It could have been one of many games about that time. I appealed to one of my colleagues for advice – "What am I going to say in The Plymothian about this?" "Say anything," he replied. "Yes, anything, anything about anything, except cricket and the 1st XI!"

"Happily, those days have ended," wrote Ted Mercer. *"I now can and must write about the 1st XI."*

Plymouth College 1st XI, 1952: Back; BN Williams, TJ Stevens, J Truman, DG Porter, A Richards, DM Webb. Front; DS Cutler, RE Southern, MA Congdon (Captain), RC Fedrick, JW Watson.

Foremost among them *"two of last year's Colts who have enjoyed more success than some of the veterans – RE Southern and TJ Stevens."* They were the only two to score more than 200 runs that season and Stevens, in addition to an undefeated 96 against Plympton, managed scores of 88 not out and 106 not out in the two games that gave Palmers the House Cricket Championship. Southern's top score of 60 came in a game that the School declared on 154-8 against Kelly at Ford Park,. Sadly, however, Kelly managed to knock the score off

with a loss of just five wickets. Truman hit an unbeaten 83 in a match tied with Truro, while Fedrick enjoyed success with bat and ball, hitting a 50 against Plympton and taking 6-41 against RNB and 5-13 against Exeter School. Cutler with 7-14 was similarly impressive against Sutton.

Cricket 2nd XI, 1952: Back; JM Hewitt, RJ Morrish, DG Bryan, DS Bird, R Arscott. Front; MC Turpitt, A Aburrow, DH Voisin (Captain), LM King, RW Sheppard, (absent JR Tredinnick).

All in all a successful season for the firsts and even more so for the unbeaten seconds who won eight and drew three of their fixtures with Turpitt, who also turned out for the firsts, returning a remarkable average of 67.5 (although his top score was only 50 not out, he was only dismissed twice in eight innings). Together with Shephard he also took most wickets, Turpitt taking 31 at an average of 5.9 and Shephard 42 at 5.4. Aburrow, who hauled a total of over 200 runs for the seconds, also represented the firsts. And with *"some promising batsmen in the colts"* it was no wonder that Ted felt that *"school cricket is in a happy position."*

The mood in the swimming pool was bouyant too, with nine records being lowered in the Jubilee year of the school aquatic sports. Prizes and certificates were awarded at the conclusion of the events by CP Brown, who had been at the school fifty years earlier when the Bath had first opened. His father, JP Brown, had, incidentally been there in 1902 too, as a school governor, proposing the vote of thanks to Joseph Thompson, whose £900 gift had enabled the building of the Bath.

The Jubilee Swimming Sports programme contained an interesting review of the sport at the School over the previous fifty years. Almost certainly penned by one of the pool's greatest advocates, John Spear, it flagged up several key dates, including the introduction of Water Polo (one of JRS's strong points) in 1924, the start of Inter-School competitions in 1937, and, just after the War, in 1946, the opening of the pool to the whole school, rather than just those who paid a subscription.

The author was also keen to point out recent improvements in standards, *"due largely to the patient and helpful advice of Mr Williams"*.

Hannaford, the junior victor, posted three of the nine new records in the five events he won, with RF Williams, finishing second to him three times and setting a new best time in the 100 yards - 71.4 seconds. In the senior events, Heath set a new record in the same event, 66.8 seconds, and finished ahead of Twigg and Skentelbery over several other distances, while Furze set a new butterfly time and Buckingham won the plunge.

While the swimming sports were *"once again fortunate with out weather"*, the much lamented rain from earlier in the year did have one positive side effect; *"the wet weather in the late spring enabled Heywood to make a first-class job of the outfield. It can have rarely been better."*

The same could be said that summer for the lower corridor which was completely redecorated over the holiday period. It augured well for the new academic year. One wonders if, at the back of the headmaster's mind, he was thinking forward to an auspicious date in the School's calendar. It certainly appeared that way from the notes of the OPM Committee that July;

"At the last meeting the Headmaster said that he would be interested to know whether any Old Boys had any

strong views for, or against, 1954 being considered as a centenary year of the School (Mannamead School being founded in 1854, Plymouth College 1877; amalgamation 1896)."

"At the moment he was quite open-minded about it, but the unusual amalgamation made it difficult to find a precedent."

If Garnons Williams was thinking quietly in terms of a centenary bash with himself at the helm, it obviously wan't at the expense of all other thoughts, for the first term of the 1952/53 School year was to be his last, but when the school reconvened after the summer break there were no obvious clues to suggest this.

There was one new staff member as the new academic year opened, 25 year-old - Frank Jeffery - a recent graduate of Southampton University, who had just completed a year's teaching practice at Brokenhurst. FJJ's arrival meant more than just a new face in the staffroom, it heralded a new subject in the school's curriculum - Biology.

The School's first dedicated biologist, Frank Jeffery, arrives.

"Garnons Williams asked me to introduce the subject from the bottom up, it was to be a gradual process starting with the first form and working the subject up as they moved throught the school."

Jeffery's appointment was in direct response to the General Inspection of the previous year which had been critical of the lack of Biology and his arrival in the staff room meant that the number of staff was now thirty - double what it had been in 1939. This, as the headmaster observed at Speech Day, meant that the common room was now much too small, but the discomfort, he hoped, would soon be alleviated. On a

more positive note; *"The more there are on the staff, the greater are the number of skills outside the classroom ... and the greater variety of character for the boys to study."*

Garnons Williams also announced to the parents, pupils and staff assembled in Central Methodist Hall that Ocotober, that he thought *"the zenith of our expansion has now probably been reached"*.

Joining the school at that same term, but only as a temporary replacement for Mr Coggin (who was taking a year's sabatical in France), was another young graduate, Roy Holmes, a westcountry boy educated at Bristol and Exeter and with a first class degree in Modern Languages from Oxford.

Holmes quickly found himself involved in extra curricular activities, not least of which was chairing the Literary and Debating Society meetings on the several occasions that Mr Rose was unable to attend. As ever the debates that term highlighted the issues of the day; *"The Modern Generation is half-baked"* (defeated 21-4), *"Shakespeare is England's greatest humbug"* (defeated 12-2 with 8 abstentions!), *"That television should be banned from the Coronation Ceremony"* (carried 13-6 - perhaps because no signal was yet available in the Plymouth area). Once again corporal punishment was deplored, but PI Palmer's attempt to convince the house that *"all forms of mass-produced entertainment"* should also be deplored was defeated 9-8.

The largely Conservative stance of the School was echoed in two debates; *"This House wholeheartedly supports the Government's policy of denationalisation"* (carried 12-6) and the OPM debate held on 12 December, when GF Morrish and Mr Trevena contended that *"the country is in its worst state ever after twelve months of Conservative misrule"*.

MD McKee and TEJ Savery successfully carried the counter view, as the motion was defeated 13-4, with two abstentions. It's interesting to note that the highest number of abstentions that term was reserved for the debate on the situation in Kenya which nevertheless successfully contended that the trouble there was *"as much the fault of the white man as of the black"*. Curiously there were no details of proposers and seconders on this one, but numbers over the term seemed as healthy as ever for this society. This was encouraging in the light of the fact that the number of extra-curricular activities was on the increase, among them the ever-expanding Natural History Society, now boosted by the creation within the School of a Natural History Museum.

With *"specimens and collections presented by the Scout Troop, the Natural History Society and individuals both inside and outside the School"*, the Master-In-Charge of this new institution was, unsurprisingly, the newly-arrived biology master, Frank Jeffery. Clearly there was a keen interest, a record membership of 156 had signed up for the Society and fieldwork - *"an essential function of this Society"* - was promised for the new year.

As for the Scouts themselves they too were enjoying record numbers - *"the total membership is now forty-eight - and a Senior and Junior Troop have now been formed"*. The year 1951-52 also saw the appointment of ten King's and Queen's Scouts in the Troop *"which surpasses by far any previous record"*.

A highlight from that winter term came when Troop were invited, on 29 October, to provide Scouts *"to line the route to the King George V Playing Fields at Elburton, when they were opened by the Duke of Edinburgh"*. There was a low point too, and that was losing Mr Lindley, ASM of the Troop for the previous three years and secretary to the Plymouth Senior Scout Association. His departure was also felt by the Philatelic Society, which he had jointly chaired with Dr Ellingher and by the various hockey and cricket teams he had worked with.

29 year-old David Lindley was off to Crewkerne School where he took up the post of Senior Geography master, meanwhile his replacement at Plymouth College was F Musgrove.

Musgrove was an Oxford graduate and a former RAF flying officer who had taught at schools at Barnard Castle and Uganda since the war.

His appointment here, however, was to prove even more of a flying visit than his previous two placements, his encouragement for open-air scouting being his main legacy over the two terms he was at Ford Park.

Musgrove's flying visit.

Musgrove's brief reign as ASM of the Scouts was mirrored, albeit in different circumstances, by Francis Scott's three terms at the head of the 290-strong College Cadet Force. Lt-Col CL Barnes had resigned his command of the CCF on 1 September 1952, a decision regretted by many, *"because we have learnt to respect him as a CO, who is our counsellor and friend - ever ready to listen to our problems or our complaints. His Field Days, his sandtable lessons and his example taught cool, calm leadership - the happy knack of managing without appearing to interfere, advising without nagging, and controlling without "flap"."*

"Many Sandhurst cadets and many boys now serving for their National Service have especial cause to be thankful for his help and advice."

Major Scott, too, was off at the end of the summer term of 1953 and a year to the day after his resignation Major Barnes resumed control of the CCF.

But we've leapt forward again, there were other upheavals in the air. As the Christmas term drew to a close a decision was taken *"with 'the approval of the Governors and the Headmaster' that for an experimental period of four years hockey should cease to be played as a School game. It is hoped that with the greater amount of rugger which will thus become possible, the standard of play will improve throughout the School. With the present restricted playing-field space, no other way of increasing the amount of rugger played can be devised."*

So ran the editorial line in the School Notes in the February 1953 Plymothian, the same magazine that opened with the paragraph; *"The change in the date of publication of The Plymothian, while it renders ridiculous any attempt on our part to wish our readers the traditional "Merry Christmas and Happy New year," does give us a welcome opportunity of expressing our appreciation of Mr BH Garnons Williams, the startling news of whose departure from Plymouth College excited our interest during the holidays."*

Certainly the seemingly last minute change in publication date took many by surprise, indeed both the College and the Sargent's House notes slipped through with *"happy and prosperous New Year messages"* and with one or two mentions of last term's magazine being the July '52 publication, one wonders at what point the Merry Christmas greetings were edited out.

Immediately below the public information piece on the suspension of hockey we read; *"It has been decided that the Plymothian shall henceforth appear twice yearly, in February and July"*.

There were grave mutterings on both counts.

"This has been the most unfortunate season in the Club's history", began the OPM Hockey report in the same edition of the Plymothian. *"The news that Hockey will cease to be played as a School game after the end of the current season, for a trial period of four years, has come as a great shock to the Club as well as to local Hockey circles. All hockey enthusiasts regret that this step has been taken."*

Meanwhile in the second of what we were told was now to be a bi-annual publication, the July 1953 Plymothian, the same one that announced Garnons Williams imminent departure, we read, in the Under 15

October 1952 and for the third time in five years the whole School lines up for a photograph - although this is just a section of it.

416

Plymouth College.

1952

417

Hockey report; *"The disappointment felt by many of the Colts at the loss of Hockey having proved unfounded, we now look to the future for rapid progress from what was undoubtedly a very promising side."*

So the decision taken *"with the approval of the Governors and the Headmaster"* was overturned and TJ Stevens, the then Secretary of Hockey, could look forward after all to leading the School side out the following Spring, albeit with a different Headmaster on the touchline.

But what of the rugby that winter of 1952? May, Battrick and Cundy led by example, each of them earning a place in the Devon Public and Grammar School trial match, with Battrick and Cundy both going on to win County caps. *"May's turn will surely come, there have been few better forwards in the School"*, was Ted Mercer's verdict on there not being a third Devon cap in the side.

1st XV 1952: Back row; BN Williams, A Richards, GC Gray, LM King, FSW Furze, GR Pengelly, JW Reid, IDW Wright. Seated; JE Taylor, JR Cundy, C May (Captain), JC Battrick, P Jolly. Front; DGF Porter, JM Hewitt.

Southern had been expected to fulfil the fly-half role but fractured his wrist in the summer holidays, and Stevens injured his hand early in the season and kept the former company on the touchline.

Kelly, the old enemy, were played for the first time in three seasons, previous fixtures having been lost to the weather and the reinstatement of the fixture brought great pleasure, particularly as the School won. The result was all the sweeter for having been the first fixture played by the School at the Sports' Stadium at Pennycross - *"The advantages of playing on a well-drained level ground were soon reflected in the open play."*

The venue was reflecting favourably on OPM performances too. After an early defeat at the hands of Plymouth Albion they went on to win a dozen games on the trot, many of them by crushing scorelines. *"The most important step towards advancing the (OPM) Club to the position it should hold in West Country Rugby has been the aquisition of a ground right in the centre of the city, at Pennycross Stadium. Covered stands, hot showers and canteen facilities make it ideal."*

Meanwhile the School 2nd XV suffered from having to replace injured members of the 1st XV, but nevertheless beat Sutton, Shebbear, Devonport and St Boniface, while the knock-on effect for the Senior Colts was such that although there was still *"sufficient talent to build up a very reasonable side ... it may prove more beneficial to the School to abolish the Senior Colts XV, substituting in its place a 3rd XV where there is no age limit."* At least that was the view of the master in charge of the side, Sam Rendle, and while the demise of hockey was **not** forthcoming the following year, the arrival of a 3rd XV was. Further down the ranks, the Junior Colts had an exceptionally fine season, scoring 51 tries in seven fixtures and conceding only three - needless to say they won all their games.

When not in his rugger kit, or indeed his school uniform, May was to be found leading the infant RN Section of the CCF, which had now grown to a body of eighteen, most of whom enjoyed a Field Day at the RN Barracks at Devonport, with an afternoon inspection of the experimental cruiser, HMS Cumberland.

The main CCF body spent their Field Day crawling through gorse at Horrabridge, while camp that summer was an *"easy"* one at Warminster; *"few long marches,*

few prolonged periods of exhausting training and unfortunately, far too few good demonstrations."

Having said that *"Lieut Blackledge arranged an extensive Map Reading scheme and an exciting "night op". Lieut Elliott organised an instructive and enjoyable morning on the .303 range - no easy task when dealing with 120 cadets."*

There was also a trip to Longleat, organised by Capt Scott, and back at camp, *"a loud speaker system blared out music continuously - the NAAFI, as usual gave excellent service."*

Mr Elliott was thanked elsewhere in respect of his efforts with gun instruction, although the School shooting side suffered somewhat this season from losing certain of their senior marksmen and from firing in a higher league, having been promoted to Division 1 in the P&D League. Mrs Elliott was thanked too for her *"provision of the necessary ingredients for brewing tea."*

Other aspects of School life that autumn term included news of the Library's reabsorption of the old Reading Room - as an annexe of the Library, now fully organized according to the Dewey system of indexing, and the addition of 300 books and *"a dozen leather-seated Libraco chairs".* There was also news of the Chess team, including a 5-1 victory over HMS Fisguard, and of the musical endeavours of the Choir and Orchestra, most of which centred around the annual Carol Service and the Christmas Concert.

The former was held at St Gabriel's on Monday 15 December, under suitable seasonal conditions - it was cold and wet - the latter in the School gym, with music by Purcell and Beethoven and words by Talbot and Shakespeare. *"Capability Bennett"* providing the landscaping for the *"box-hedge"* scene from Twelfth Night, with CW Jenkins as a *"very young"* Malvolio ... *"his affectations of manner and speech nearly always happy."*

AJ Talbot's *"The Centurion's Billet at Swacking Bulphen"* would have been more fun, according to the resident Plymothian theatre critic, Hugh Dent, if *"all the players acted as hard as Aldersley did in Astel."*

It wasn't just the strength of the acting that shone in the School's next major dramatic production in the Spring Term. "Topaze" was a credit to the School generally and it reflected well on the strength of the Modern Language department, as the production of Marcel Pagnol's French piece was *"one of the first known on the English stage"* and *"all the more praiseworthy it is that the play has been translated by boys of the school - RJA Elford, HJ Heath, DC Honey and PG White, from the original French."*

There was also the difficulty of conveying the spirit of the original ... *"for the situation which 'Topaze' demands, political and private corruption in public matters, is one which British audiences prefer to believe impossible in our own land."*

A Hosking took the title role and played the part *"excellently"* ... *"he held the play together admirably"*. While *"special honours must go to I Ritchie who, as Suzy Courtois, showed us that Shakespeare's use of boys as his heroines is not as amazing and unthinkable as some imagine."*

Among many others singled out by the anonymous reviewer for commendation were DS Cutler as the ranting spiv and W Richards, *"almost a gentleman"* crook.

Cutler, incidentally, as Under-Officer of the CCF wrote a fascinating piece for the Plymothian about his being the first boy from the School to enter RNVR and Universities Scheme - the only way to facilitate, but not actually guarantee being able to do National Service in the Royal Navy. Cutler's three week course over the Easter period was undertaken on HMS Indefatigable and was done along with 120 boys from *"the major public schools and various universities."*

Once he had got the hang of his hammock it all seemed pretty plain sailing for the School Cricket and Hockey captain. Curiously enough, after all the fuss made about the possible loss of hockey for four years, the potential hiccough went unheeded in the Plymothian reports for the 1st XI, however Cutler, along with Stevens and Hewitt were congratulated on their playing *"with conspicuous success in the Devon Schools XI against the Country XI"*. Hard to imagine that, had the sport been dropped from the School calendar.

Having said that the team, despite a *"forward line that contained some strong and skillful players"*, were *"extremely ragged"* at times, *"and the line never combined"*. Stevens *"played quite brilliantly on occasions"*, but *"at times tended to try and do just that little bit too much on his own."*

Hockey 1st XI 1953: RE Southern, GR Pengelly, C May, MJ H-Merrett, G White, A Richards. Front; DS Bird, TJ Stevens, DS Cutler (Captain), JM Hewitt, EA Chapman.

There was a similar story in the 2nd XI where *"although individually the standard appeared as good as in previous years ... the results were disappointing."*

However the 2nd XI reporter was mindful of their brush with temporary extinction; *"It is better to have played and lost than never to have played at all"*, was the apposite reworking of the Augustinian quote. Two of the heaviest defeats, incidentally were inflicted by the Staff and the OPMs, while one goal was the only difference in the two encounters with Kelly.

The OPM Hockey Captain at the time was the newly married Bryan Johnson, who with his brother Geoff, was one of more than ninety who attended the OPM Annual Dinner, held in the Connaught Rooms on Thursday 19 March. The record number of attendees included ten members of the current School Staff and this was not only the last OPM dinner that Garnons Williams attended as Headmaster, it was also one of the last major functions he would have been at - in that capacity.

March 1953, the OPM Dinner in the Connaught Rooms. Garnons Williams is just to the right of the OPM Crest and CP Brown. Charlie Barnes, third from left, proposed the toast to the Club, nearest the camera, bottom right, is George Creber.

The Club President, L Bond Spear, presented the Headmaster with *"a silver sweet dish, suitably engraved, as a mark of appreciation of Mr and Mrs Garnons William's co-operation with club functions."*

The Head expressed his thanks in his response to the School Toast, which was proposed by CP Brown. John Dufton, OPM and Second Master, was among the Staff present and he it was who would see the School through the final term of that academic year.

Strangely enough, joining the Staff that same term was another OPM, Ronald Trounson, a Cambridge graduate who had left the School less than a decade earlier. A distinguished sportsman in his time at Ford Park, Trounson came back to boost the Classics Department, although it is interesting to note that Garnons Williams' successor as Head was to be yet another classicist.

The summer term was also to be the final one for Messrs Holmes, Musgrove and Scott. Roy Holmes had been standing in for Geoff Suggitt, and was heading off to East Ham Grammar School in London, and was thanked for his part in organising the Easter trip to Paris. Musgrove meanwhile was leaving, after two terms, with not even the merest hint of faint praise. The line recording his departure merely read; *"we hope that he has enjoyed his two terms at the School."*

Someone who undoubtedly did enjoy his six years at School, and whose presence the School undoubtedly enjoyed too, was Francis Scott, who, at just thirty-eight, was leaving to take up the Headship of Batley Grammar School in his native Yorkshire.

In his six years as Senior History Master numerous History Scholarships had been won to Oxford - *"an event which before was a rarity has become almost a regular occurrence"*. Scott *"also obtained some renown as the first member of the Staff to own and sail a yacht."*

In his last year at Ford Park, Scott also took control of the CCF and had special responsibility for the School 2nd XV ... *"he takes every good wish from Staff and boys for his future happiness and success."*

Before all these departures had taken place however, Garnons Williams proposed a staff photograph. It was taken, in the early part of 1953, infront of the School and was inevitably a true snapshot in time, but who could have foretold just how many changes there would be over the next two years?

But first, the summer of '53, such as it was a summer; *"During the first half of the term the cold weather acted as a brake on the general enthusiasm of the School and the one hundred and sixty coats pegs (in the swimming bath) which replaced the rusted remnants of former years seemed a little unnecessary."*

The annual Athletic Sports went ahead unhindered however and *"were more than usually successful."*
"Three records were broken, by JC Battrick, RE Southern and JR Cundy, in the Shot, Javelin and 220 yards respectively." Battrick and Southern shared the senior Victor Ludorum title, despite fine winning performances from Cundy, in the 100 and 220, George, in the Mile, 880, and Hop, Step and Jump, and Lethbridge in the High Jump and Long Jump.

Niblett and Murton were Junior Victor and Proxime Accessit respectively and Niblett won two of his events - 220 & 440 yards - at the Junior Athletic Sports at Kelly. But still the School finished fourth out of four.

The seniors fared a little better, comparatively at least, finishing fifth out of thirteen at the Senior Inter-School Sports at Kelly, held on 30 May. *"From our point of view the meeting was chiefly notable for RF Southern's achievement in the Javelin and Discus, and the bad weather."*

PMC Lawn Tennis Club, 1953: MCT Turpitt, DG Carter, DN Axford, HJ Heath, CV Denning. Seated; JR Tredinnick, A Aburrow, DM Webb (Capt.), MJ Cowan, JM Hewitt. Front EA Chapman.

The cold and wet conditions in the first half of the term did nothing for the furtherance of the School's Tennis ambitions either, nevertheless all five matches were won, versus Plymouth High, HMS Fisguard, RNEC 2nds, the Staff and Kelly. Webb and Aburrow leading from the front, notably against Kelly, at Kelly, when they won all six of their sets against three different Kelly pairs either 6-1 or 6-2. It was however Webb's last year at School and there was no doubt the team were going to miss the young man who'd won four Plymouth titles in the last two years.

Inclement weather - heavy rain - greeted the CCF on their Field Day outing to Dartmoor, although the weather improved slightly after the comfort of the Co-op coaches had been forsaken. Still, it didn't dampen the enthusiasm of the recruits, as a record number of cadets, 125, signed up for Annual Camp, at Castlemartin, Pembrokeshire - a new location for the School.

In the meantime, as June 1953 unveiled itself in memorable fashion, with the news of Hillary and Tensing's successful assault on Mount Everest almost being buried in the media attention lavished on the Coronation, so the weather took a turn for the better. Indeed when the CCF sections lined up for Admiral Sir Maurice Mansergh on 9 June there were a few unexpected problems; *"The general turn out and steadiness on parade were excellent,"* but *"our numbers became smaller as the morning wore on and the sun became hotter"*.

The swimmers revelled in the improved conditions however and there was high praise from the man who had spent more time in the School Bath than most - John Spear; *"It is,"* he said, *"fair to say that this year's swimming team is the best the School has ever had."*
"It must be admitted that the arrival of Parsons from Malaya tipped the balance, and it was fortunate that his speciality - the backstroke - did not clash with with the three free-style specialists - Heath, Hannaford and Williams, RF., all of whom have improved on their style and times on last year's performance."

March 1953 Garnons Williams assembles the staff for a group picture: Back row; Bill Phillips, Francis Scott, Hugh Dent, F Musgrove, Frank Jeffery, Dr Ernest Ellingher, George Bonser, Roger Elliott, Alan King, Harry Trevena, Sam Rendle (behind him), David 'Slim' Whitman, Brian Bennett, Nigel Radford, Roy H Holmes, Donald MacPorter, Arthur Addis, Bob Blackledge, John Bill, John Spear, Geoffrey Suggitt and Angus Rose. Front row; Meyrick Jones, Bill Barnes, Ian Edwards, John Dufton, Garnons Williams, Eric Holman, Guy Hill, Bill Battrick and Ted Mercer.

1953

Inter-school encounters were won against Blundell's and Kelly. Dartmouth, RNEC, and Devonport RSA were also beaten, with only HMS Fisguard registering a win over the School, although the Water Polo team, who won all their matches, beat them 4-2.

In the Aquatic Sports held on the last weekend of term, Saturday 18 July, *"Heath, Williams and Parsons fourght out most of the races"* with *"Heath finally emerging as Victor Ludorum, but William's swimming over longer distances and Parson's back-stroke both deserve a mention."*

Plymouth College 1st XI Cricket 1953: Back row; BN Williams, GC Fedrick, A Aburrow, R Arscott, DM Webb. Front RE Southern, J Truman, DS Cutler (Captain), A Richards, TJ Stevens, JM Hewitt.

While Williams, RF was a star in the Swimming Bath, out on the Square it was Williams, BN who *"really deserves an article to himself ... he is a lion!"* At least according to the Gamesmaster, Ted Mercer, who produced a fullsome account of the Cricket of the *"successful and happy 'Coronation' term"*. This was the summer that *"masters in charge of the School XIs are of the opinion that the boys are keener on cricket than they ever were"*. It was also the summer that, somewhat unusually, if not unprecedentedly, team members were referred to, by a master, by their Christian names - hence we find reference to Captain and Secretary; *"David Cutler ... marked powers of leadership,"* and *"Alan Richards ... another natural cricketer."*

"The Captain," we read, *"leaves at the end of the term, and so do John Truman, David Webb and Neil Williams. They will be difficult to replace."*

With Cutler taking 7-43 against the Staff the rest of the masters might have been glad to see him go, but there was always Fedrick, Southern and Stevens with another summer to go.

Plymouth College 2nd XI, 1953: Back row; GW Searle, BK Niblett, RJ Morrish, CB Besant, JR Tredinnick, PM Gibbs. Front; DS Bird, BR Jervis, DG Bryan (Captain), MC Turpitt, RW Shepperd, MJ Hamblyn-Merrett.

The 2nd XI had another successful summer; *"any member of the team will tell you that they haven't been beaten since 1951 and they are obviously proud of this record."* Turpitt topped both batting and bowling averages, his 7-33 and 22 against Kelly helping secure a popular win, while Sheppard's splendid 7-12 against Fisguard saw the opposition skittled out for just 29.

The Colts weren't quite as strong, however *"considering the poverty of talent the actual results in terms of matches won has been better than expected."*

The same could not be said for the shooting team there *"the only interest of the term was the presentation of the Devon Pairs Handicap Trophy to A Richards and M Cowan."* Several of the regular shots failed miserably at the inter-schools .303 shoot at Rippon Tor, the side finishing seventh out of nine.

There were bigger guns in action at the Naval Gun

Shooting VIII: Back row; JM Hewitt, DS George, MC Turpitt. Front; A Richards, MJ Cowan (Captain), D Hooper, Lt R Elliott.

Battery at Wembury where the RN Section watched 4-inch weapons *"firing by radar at target aircraft"* on one of their two Field Days. Eight of the Section's Senior Ratings also spent four days at sea aboard HMS Protector, a net laying vessel. *"The remainder (of the cadets) spent a week on board HMS Verulam, a fast A/S frigate at Portsmouth."*

Annual Inspection and the Plymouth College CCF contingent parade around a largely traffic free Devon Terrace. Brigadier Bramwell-David is the Inspecting Officer.

The Section's second Field Day, incidentally, was spent at the Naval Air Station at St Merryn where *"all the cadets, including some in khaki, had flights in Sea Princes"*. Although in terms of it's brief history at the School the RN Section was by no means the Senior Service, it was undoubtedly an active one and *"several of the cadets attended the Air Course at Lee-on-Solent."* Leading Seaman Colin May was the Senior Naval Cadet and the summer term for him was a happy one, the Captain of the Rugby team later recalling that the *"worst thing about my time at School was having Garnons Williams as Head"*, a prefect in addition to his many other responsibilities, May says that his Headmaster never even knew his name!

From other quarters however tributes to the recently retired Head poured in none more fullsome than from Ralph Brown, Chairman of the Governors;

"Our late Headmaster, Mr BH Garnons Williams, came to the School eight years ago from Marlborough, with a high reputation as Master in charge of the Classical Department. When the Governors appointed him they knew they that he was a good man, but few guessed his skill as an administrator or anticipated that whereas in September 1945 the numbers in the main School were 320, there would, seven years later, be 560."

"The credit of first thinking of what had been Mount House as the home of our Preparatory probably belongs to that very devoted son of the School, Charles Serpell, then Clerk, but it was Mr Garnons Williams who saw the great possibilities involved in the transfer of the Prep from its old quarters in Valletort Villas, and set about the creation of the "C" stream which the transfer made possible."

"There were obvious disadvantages in the expansion of the School in its present cramped surroundings, but Mr Garnons Williams held strongly and convinced the Governors that the more generous staffing and more lavish equipment this made possible amply outweighed the disadvantages. Already the fruits of the expansion are visible and though there are still many needs urgently waiting to be met, for example, an adequate Assembly Hall and more playing fields, they are needs which, with patience and persistence, can and will be met."

"The expansion has meant a great deal of extra work for the Staff. They recognised however that he always treated them with consideration. He has been happy in his choice of new masters and leaves his successor a fine staff, for the appointment of about half of which he was himself repsonsible."

"The Library , small but beautiful, built as a War Memorial, owes much to his wise planning and remains as a symbol of his efforts, his very successful efforts, to raise the standards of literature, drama, music and all the arts through the School. He has been a great administrator, but he is an idealist first and realises that for a headmaster the best administration is a means to an end, and that end , the raising of educational standards. He has contributed greatly to that end, and his period of office, though short, will be regarded by the historian of the future as of the highest importance in the history of Plymouth College."

Exactly the sort of rhetoric one would expect from a Chairman of Governors, particularly one who had been appointed to his post just three years earlier. After the uncertainty and pain of the war years Plymouth was enjoying a boom time and it was not surprising to see that the School which had refused to evacuate was now prospering. The move to Hartley Road had clearly been a good one, but as Brown acknowledged that was largely Serpell's suggestion. As for being *"happy in his choice of staff"* at least a quarter of his twenty-five appointments had already moved on and within five years of his leaving another ten would be gone, leaving just nine of his selections on the staff, the same number as there would of Ralph's appointments from some years earlier.

But Brown's eulogising had not finished; *No valediction to Mr Garnons Williams,"* he continued, *"would be complete without a word of appreciation and thanks to his wife. Apart from her skill in supervising the canteen, she has been an ideal helpmeet in the dispensation of generous hospitality. The VIP called in to adorn a School function, the master, the parent and even the Governor has been sure of a warm welcome at her hands, and there must be many junior members of the Staff who remember with gratitude her kindness in allowing her house or garden to be used as a creche for the dumping of children during some School function."*

The Garnons Williams' had three children of their own, as did the man who the Governors had appointed as his successor, the man whose photograph appeared on the opening pages of that July 1953 Plymothian, Francis Lockwood.

At forty-five Lockwood was just two years younger than his predecessor, but unlike Garnons Williams he had already been a headmaster, at Queen Elizabeth's Grammar School, Gainsborough, from 1940 and from 1945, the same year that BGW arrived at Ford Park, at William Ellis School in London. And that was where he would remain until the end of the academic year 1952/53, leaving Deputy Head, John Dufton to take charge until the end of the summer.

Lockwood did however come down that summer term to present the prizes at the Preparatory School Speech Day, John Dufton was also there, as was a reporter from the Western Morning News who gave readers an early insight into the views of headmaster designate of Plymouth College;

"One of my objects will be to see that the boys are happy. Unless a boys is happy he cannot be making the best of himself."

"Boys should be made to believe that they are making a contribution to the community and they should get recognition for what they are doing. The essence of true citizenship is for each one of us to think we are doing something that matters."

"It is the people who think they do not matter, and think that the things the do, do not matter, who cause all our troubles."

Doubtless mindful of the fledgling Prep School Parents Association, he issued a similar message to the parents present; "I want you to feel that you can come along and see us without thinking that you are a nuisance. Criticism will not be resented", he said.

This seemed like the perfect cue for the Prep headmaster to voice his views on one or two issues, notably the present examination system whereby on "the result of one examination at 11 a boy or girl is judged to be fit for a grammar school type of education or not."

"I should like to see it possible for boys in the preparatory school to be judged by us, the staff, who probably had the boy for six years. We could then honestly decide who was fit to go on."

Firman also had a moan about "the lack of a gymnasium" for the Prep, a point that the Chairman of Governors was swift to address, stating that there were so many financial difficulties that it was still not possible to say when a gymnasium would be provided.

The Prep was undoubtedly, however, making good progress; the appeal for Boat's Badges earlier that year had yielded a good number of specimens which were now adorning the Main Staircase and a set of Coronation Gates had been ordered for the entrance to Munday House.

The Coronation clearly had a bigger impact on the Prep than it did on the Main School. On Friday 29 May there was a special Pre-Coronation Service "the closing event of School's day before the breaking up for the Coronation and Half-Term holiday".

"A corporate act of worship and dedication in honour of a historic national occasion," each boy was presented with a Coronation Mug after the Service by the Chairman of Governors.

Prep School's Coronation Service with the Reverend JW Molland.

New age coins, Queen Elizabeth II: Farthing, threepence, sixpence, ha'penny, shilling, florin (two bob), penny and half a crown.

Then, on the Tuesday after half-term, the School were taken to a local theatre to see the Coronation film - "A Queen is Crowned". Remember the BBC's television service had yet to reach this far west, and anyway the proceedings were bound to look more impressive on the cinema screen than they would do on a 9-inch TV

The City celebrates: Official programme, Pageant on the Hoe and one of a set of stamps issued by the Chamber of Commerce.

The following week J Pengelly of Remove II was even more fortunate as he was able to witness, first hand, the Coronation Review of Navy at Portsmouth.

Pengelly's father was the Commander of HMS Perseus and according to Pengelly junior the light fleet carrier played "a very important part" in the Review, "as she accommodated Members of Parliament and many Lords and Ladies."

In addition to all the ships present there was a fly past of "300 types of aircraft", the whole event culminating with a fine firework display. Small wonder that our man in the Remove deemed it to be a day that "will be long remembered by me".

Back at Hartley Road, Sports Day, *"in spite of all efforts by a recalcitrant climate to make this impossible"*, turned out to be a memorable one for Organ, who stole the Victor Ludorum title by just one point from Newton and McFadyean.

McFadyean, incidentally, won the newly-introduced Javelin event (he shared the title with Strevens) and the high jump, an event in which *"the out-dated "scissors" method of jumping was discarded in favour of the technically more efficient 'Western roll'."*

PC Organ jumps 12ft 2in to win the over-10 long jump at the Prep

Looking to the future, from the summer of '53, David Colwill snaps four of his form chums at the Pavilion; l-r, Roy de St Croix, Richard Newman, Brian Eames and Peter Gibbs-Kennett.

LF Paul, the Vice-Chairman of Governors and then Deputy Lord Mayor, presented the prizes, one of them going to young Newton who, before the end of term would take centre stage once more on the Hartley Road Playing Fields with his appearance in the title role of the drama group's production of Robin Hood.

Members of the cast of the Prep's first play - Robin Hood; DJ Newton, played Robin, MD Lacey - Little John, PJW Biscombe - Peter the Potter, MB Rutman - Friar Tuck, NE Carson - Will Scarlet, RW Moses - Will Stutley, RS Harding - Much the Miller, RJ Cawrse - the Sheriff of Nottingham, RG Creber his deputy and AJ Vinson one of his men.

Produced and scripted by Paul Redgrave, the show featured some *"delightful music for the Outlaw's Song,"* composed especially by Mr AB King.

A review of the Robin Hood show appeared in the local press, but was too late for the record-breaking, sixty-six page, July 1953 Plymothian, instead it appeared in the next, equally lengthy edition of the Magazine - in March 1954.

It was surely the longest interval between publication dates since the Magazine was first produced and was undoubtedly a reflection on the many changes that had been going on in the meantime. There was a new man at the helm of the good ship Plymouth College and the new broom seemed to be sweeping around every corner.

FRANCIS LOCKWOOD
AND THE SPIRIT OF CHANGE

The spirit of change was everywhere as the new school year started on Friday 18 September 1953. The Country had a newly-crowned Queen, the City had new buildings popping up all over the place and Plymouth College had a new Headmaster.

It was a fascinating time and arriving in Plymouth that summer Lockwood would have found it a very different place from that which he had known over twenty years earlier when he had been here to complete the practical part of his teacher training.

Educated at the Perse School and St Catherine's College, Cambridge, Lockwood studied classics at both Cambridge and London and gained an MA degree from each University. His formal teaching began at Wilson's Grammar School in London and he was just thirty-two when he gained his first Headship, in Gainsborough, in 1940. At the end of the war he moved to London to become Headmaster at William Ellis School. After

eight years he came to Ford Park where in 1931 he had previously been a popular trainee teacher, active both on the football field and within the ranks of the OTC (as the CCF was then).

Interestingly enough, John Dufton, the interim head in 1953, was one of just four existing staff members who the young Lockwood would have encountered during his first spell here, Holman, Hill and Edwards being the others. We have no way now of knowing whether Lockwood kept any sort of contact with the School after he had completed his training, but the Gymnasium, rooms 9,10 and 11 and the Pavilion would almost certainly all have been new to him, as indeed would the Prep School situation. In all other respects however Plymouth would have been presented a much-changed appearance. By 1953 much of the 72-acre City Centre site had been cleared for the redevelopment as detailed in the 1943 Plan for Plymouth. Royal Parade was almost complete, Armada Way, New George Street and Cornwall Street were taking shape and there was plenty of work in the construction industry with new housing estates appearing at Honicknowle, Ham, Ernesettle, Efford and Whitleigh.

Some of the more presitigious developments were being undertaken by some of the biggest names in architecture in the whole of Europe, but there was plenty of work too for the local boys;

"SR Edwards (18-25)," wrote John Spear in his OPM notes, *"was the architect responsible for the new GEC building in Union Street and IS Hodges (12-23) planned the Harding's furniture building in Old Town Street with its revolving shop window and bungalow inside."*

Elsewhere there was plenty of work in the Dockyard with some 20,000 men employed there. After the death and destruction of the Blitz, Plymouth was now booming and new incentivised industries were taking advantage of the deals offered to move here, too.

Such was the climate that Lockwood arrived into that

summer and with all the changes that were taking place in the outside world it was no surprise to find the new head making an immediate impact at Ford Park, as the editors of that March 1954 Plymothian felt duty bound to observe;

"In this, the first Plymothian since Mr Lockwood took over the headship of the School, it may not be amiss to consider the changes that have taken place at his instigation. The revised time-table, games on Monday afternoon, the New Look fixture card - these were the nine day wonders: the one vital change, the one most discussed by OPMs, the one that must have the greatest effect on the life of the School, is the birth of two new Houses."

Perhaps the editors were unaware that the last time Lockwood had taught at the School, just twenty-two years earlier there had just been three houses anyway - East, South and North Town, and that the present set up of Palmers, Sargents, Thompsons and College houses was barely twenty years old. Whatever the answer, there seemed to be no doubting that the School was big enough to support the new arrangement - Chaytors and Dales were the two new Houses - or that the new set up had *"brought about an increased competitive spirit in the school ... The old Houses have felt the challenge of new rivalry; the new the challenge of well-established traditions."*

It's not entirely clear whether it was A Hosking - Editor of "The Plymothian" writing this piece or the master whose duty it was to ensure smooth publication of the long overdue periodical, either way the writer was firmly behind the Head's new initiative;

"Healthy competition must be beneficial to the school but more important is its effect on individual boys. Rome was not built overnight and it is not yet possible to judge any such effect, but ultimately the smaller Houses will mean a greater part in the House affairs for each individual and a greater share of responsibility of running this small community, the House."

September 1953 - The City's new centre starts to take shape and a new Headmaster arrives at Plymouth College.

"Competition, the importance of the individual, responsibility - these things are sadly lacking in the modern community, the community outside school, and we are convinced that the larger number of Houses has done somthing to restore these things inside school. Bernard Shaw said that school interrupted his education, but the purpose of this editorial is not to be controversial, it is to praise a fait accompli. What Shaw failed to realise is that a sense of community which regular House Prayers help to create, a learning to live together without the hard knocks of the outside world - these things are themselves an education."

Fine words indeed, but how did the new system work in practice? Well according to its captains, Carter, Denning, Jolly and Shepheard, Chaytors *"had the happier start"*.

"We were very fortunate in acquiring the services of Messrs. W McD Porter, BTN Bennett, R Elliott and ADS Rose as Housemasters." Newly-launched into inter-house activities Chaytors won the Junior Rugger Challenge Cup and came second in the Senior Championship. The writers of the first ever Dale's House notes had little more than their birth to celebrate;

"As we pen these notes, we are making history; but history depends on tradition and a strong foundation of house spirit must be laid now if the house is to distinguish itself in later years. At present our efforts are not co-ordinated and that this probably accounts for our lack of success on the Rugger field to date."

Inevitably the creation of the two new establishments betokened changes to the existing ones;

"Business in the transfer market has been brisk," was the dry observation from Battrick, Bryan and Lethbridge, the College House Captains.

"We welcome with pleasure, the Boarding House en bloc, and especially Dr Battrick, whom we are pleased to see as house master ... We are however sorry to lose Mr Porter who has done so much for us in the past.

We wish him success, though in moderation, with his new house." Battrick senior and junior, incidentally, had come across from Thompsons, and currently the Science master's son was Deputy Head Boy and Captain of Rugger. The House won the Senior Rugger tournament and well they might observe that *"with the new faces in the house, we have achieved a nice balance of brawn and brain."*

Thompsons in turn were lamenting the loss of both Mr Battrick and Mr Jones, two long established staff figures, welcoming, in their place, three of the freshest faces in the Common Room - those of Blackledge, Philipps and Suggitt.

One suspects that Thompson's House notes were largely written by Hoskin, a House Captain in addition to being Plymothian editor, for the notes, like the main magazine editorial tackled the wider implications of the new system;

"An innovation which was greeted with mixed feelings by most people was weekly House Prayers. All doubts have now been dispelled for the regular meeting gives the house the feeling that it does exist as a separate body within the School."

The implication that not all these changes met with instant approval was also alluded to in the Palmer's House notes;

"The new "Six House" system is still in its infancy, consequently innovations and new ideas are not infrequent ... We welcome, as one of the more pleasant innovations, Mr Winterbotham and Mr King, who have taken over, together with Mr Barnes, the position of Housemasters."

Twenty-six year-old Anthony Winterbotham was one of two new staff members who joined the School as Lockwood himself arrived. A past pupil of St Paul's School, Winterbotham was, like his new Headmaster, a Cambridge graduate. So too was the other new young master, arriving at Ford Park that September - Denis Collinson.

Denis had read history at Gonville and Caius and together with Ron Trounson brought the number of consecutive Cambridge graduates to be appointed to four. It marked anouther definite wind change as six of the last seven appointments made by Garnons Williams had been Oxford men, like Garnons Williams himself.

Dennis Collinson, the only Lockwood appointment to stay beyond the 1950s.

In 1954 Lockwood would appoint two more Cambridge graduates and, as fate would have it, he would go on to become the first Headmaster of Plymouth College never to appoint an Oxford scholar.

Interestingly enough, it would appear that an earlier School Head and Cambridge man, Freddie Dale, had been instrumental in Lockwood's appointment. There had been a large number of applicants for the vacancy created by Garnons Williams departure *"no fewer than 31 who were 'double firsts',"* a situation that had posed problems for the Governors. However their task *"was made somewhat easier by the experience and advice they received from Mr Dale, whose recommendation and testimony of Mr Lockwood's capabilities had been of considerable influence."*

Small wonder therefore that Lockwood would suggest Dale's as a fitting house name for one of the two new institutions he was to create in his first term. Or that Dale was to be invited to present the prizes at Speech Day, held on *"Trafalgar Day"* (21 October) 1953.

"There is no need for me to introduce Mr Dale to you, rather might he introduce me," said Lockwood about the man who had left the School a generation earlier, back in 1929.

He then went on to talk about the *"various changes which had come, and would occur in the future."*

Lockwood hinted at *"the shape of things to come when he expressed the hope of a new large scale building project being started shortly."*

"It would," he concluded, *"be a very pessimistic man indeed who could see anything but the brightest of futures for Plymouth College."*

As if to echo just how much the two men were singing from the same hymn sheet, Dale, in his speech, said how much he disliked pessimists, furthermore, he added; *"in considering the changes which have occurred in the last fifty years, I do not see why as great an advance should not take place in the fifty years to come ... it is one of the School's obligations to make that advance."* He also expressed the hope that the House bearing his name *"would prove to be the best of all."*

Clearly there was a spirit of great optimism around and with numbers, including the Prep, up to 863, who knew what the future held?

This was up by almost forty on the previous year's tally and whilst the Headmaster acknowledged that *"there is no virtue in number as such, our increase is due to the best possible of reasons - the refusal of our senior boys to leave."*

"The Sixth Form now stands at 121. This is most encouraging, for we can do more to educate a boy during one year in the Sixth than we can in the previous five years of his sojourn in the main school. There is nothing surprising in this. Until abut thirteen a boy tends to believe most of what we tell him, though he rarely acts on it. From then until the age of sixteen he believe little of what authority has to say beyond the date of the Battle of Hastings or the meaning of Gallia in tres partes divisa est."

"After sixteen, however, he begins to think that perhaps our experience may have some value after all. Our chance to civilise the barbarian has arrived."

"How exasperating, then, if he choses precisely that moment to leave. Many of his personal difficulties, if not over, at any rate seem not entirely insoluble. He needs time to grow up in the midst of the exciting ideas of the world now opening up before him. Small wonder, then, that a gap in poise and personality seems quickly to widen between those who stay on at school and those who leave to spend their days in routine employment and bring jaded minds to the only times when they could execise their imaginations."

"Small wonder too that real responsibility tends eventually to come to those who have had the inestimable privilege of spending their most vital years in the Sixth Form of a school like this."

This great increase in sixth form numbers was due substantially to the transformation that Garnons Williams had effected before his departure whereby Plymouth College went from being a two to a three-stream school. *"This,"* said Lockwood, *"is a great achievement and leads logically to most of the changes which have been inaugurated since my appointment."* Allied to these changes the abondoning of the School Certificate; *"Personally I rejoice at the passing of the School Certificate. The freedom conferred by the new arrangements is most welcome. For once I even find myself in agreement with the Ministry of Education when they suggest that it is often a mistake to allow boys to take at O level subjects which they intend to study in the Sixth Form. Would for once that Oxford University was as enlightened; Cambridge of course is much more sensible. In certain cases O level must be taken, both to provide minimum qualifications, and sometimes as an insurance policy. Apart from that and the temporary blindness of Oxford, the examination at O level merely provides a distraction for which there is little justification in the case of the future candidate for University entrance. Furthermore, I deplore anything which causes a boy to regarnd the Fifth Form as the culmination of his school career."*

In practical terms the new arrangements also made possible the creation of "The Remove" a body of boys who weren't driven by an unduly academic syllabus.

"We were educational pioneers," recalls John Cundy, *"as C-streamers we weren't expected to do overly well in exams. The only reason that I went back for what was my last term at School was so that I could carry on playing for the First XV. Ted Mercer wanted to keep me in the side - I didn't do formal school work that term, I just helped Ian Edwards out in the gym! ... Can you imagine that now?"*

Within the Staff Room this new stream was viewed by some in an interesting light; *"Hands up all you boys in the "A" Stream,"* Eric Holman, would ask. *"You boys will do well. "B" Stream? You lads will do quite well too. Now where are all you "C" Stream boys? You're the ones I want to know - you're the ones that will make the big money!"*

Academically the School was doing quite well at that time, the broken year under Garnons Williams and the temporary custodianship of John Dufton, had been a good one and great things were anticipated for the future.

Dufton was thanked both by the Head and the Chairman of Governors at that Speech Day, as indeed was Roger Serpell, the Clerk to the Governors, for *"the great amount of work he had done in preparing lists of candidates and making the task of selection less formidable."*

61 year-old OPM John Dufton who took temporary charge of the school he had first came back to, as a teacher, in 1919.

Interestingly enough one of the names that appeared on the shortlist drawn up by the Clerk and the Governors was that of CM Meade-King, who had had been relatively optimistic about his chances - but it wasn't to be - not in 1953 anyway.

Before concluding his first Speech Day address,

Lockwood informed his audience about the decision to complete the purchase of the whole Dunkeld Villas (at a cost of £7,000), a move that would enable the boarding facilities to be brought back to Ford Park.

"It will be renamed Colson House and will ultimately provide ample accommodation for College House. Not only will we now be able to find room for all those in need in the foreseeable future, but we shall also be prepared to allow residents in Plymouth the undoubted benefit of Boarding School education."

"I myself had the inestimable advantage of crowning my school career as a day-boy with a period in a Boarding House of the same school. My development during that period both in gaining independence and, I think, the power of co-operation in a community, was inestimable. I strongly recommend that parents should consider allowing boys to have, say , their last year in the school as Boarders, to have, in other words, a period as a professional schoolboy, as opposed to the amateur that the day-boy must be."

It had been a term of many changes and announcements, the creation of two new houses had meant that more inter-house fixtures were possible, a situation that required more time - an extra half day - for games and more playing fields. Both of these issues had been adressed and along the way the School morning had been lengthened and an, in addition to the extra time for sport, an extra teaching period been created;

"I am grateful," said the Headmaster, *"to parents for having submitted with such good humour to an earlier breakfast."*

Lockwood also referred to the *"introduction of two major subjects into the Upper School. For the first time Biology now can be taken in the Sixth Form to Advanced Level, and Economics has also been introduced."*

"The need for Biology," he said, *"is self evident, I can only say that it gives general satisfaction that our Sciences are now complete."*

"The introduction of economics is more controversial,

Microscopes make work more interesting within the School's new Biology Department.. The School's first ever A Level class; Messrs Pearse, Erlich, Harper and Robinson.

but I think at a time when the very life of the country depends on an intelligent understanding of our means of subsistence, Economics should be regarded as having its place by right."

Thus it was that Brown, whose father had been Chairman of Governors when Serpell's father had been Clerk to that same body, turned that Speech Day to Francis Lockwood and said; *"I don't know if the School has yet given the Headmaster a nickname. I feel sure however, that one of Mr Lockwood's slogans must be, 'Do it now!'.* *"Mr Lockwood has,"* he said, *"already proved himself a very live wire. He obviously is not in the habit of letting grass grow under his feet."*

Just over a week later Lockwood and Dale were together again, with them, in the same room, Basil Garnons Williams and Herbert Ralph. And what was that brought these four heads of Plymouth College together? The OPM London Dinner.

Held on 30 October 1953, at the Holborn Restaurant there were fifty-six members and guests in attendance, a record for the London Branch. The occasion was presided over by David Serpell. His brother Roger, Clerk to the Governors, was also there, as was NE Waterfield who was elected President for the coming year and who had left the School the year of the merger

with Mannamead - 1896.

It was doubtless an occasion steeped in nostalgia and must have made quite an impression on Lockwood, in this, just his first term at Ford Park.

It was also of course the first term for another man with a fine grasp of historical context, Denis Collinson, the man who would turn out to be the only enduring staff room appointment made by Lockwood.

In September 1953 he was a young, twenty-four year-old, History teacher and he arrived in a school just about to celebrate a centenary of sorts with a youth culture just beginning to find its own voice, although not everyone was ready to hear it.

In the Literary and Debating Society that October the House decided, by a narrow majority, that they saw nothing in modern music and that they were looking forward to National Service.

More in accordance with the mood of contrariness, a significant number of propositions put to the House that autumn were defeated, among them; support for commercial television, the suggestion that the *"present incompetent Government should be defeated"* and the notion that *"this House is descended from the Apes".* There was, however, overwhelming support for the quirky motion to *"spoil the rod and spare the child".*

But while JD Salinger's recently published *Catcher In The Rye* was fuelling the thoughts of an increasingly disaffected fifties youth culture, at Ford Park it was still business as usual. New additions to the Library collection still merited mention in the magazine and included; *Flowering Plants, Modern Chess Openings, British Stamp Design* and Hunt's *Ascent of Everest.*

Mr Jeffery had taken on the mantle of the Natural History Society, from the man who had so successfully relaunched it after the war, Mac Porter. In his first term in charge FJJ *"showed the Society a series of slides, projected on to a screen, illustrating 'Freshwater Life' ... He made us realise that there is more life in our ponds and streams than mere fish."*

The well-known Westcountry naturalist HG Hurrell had opened the term's activities by showing some of his *"very interesting films, including 'The Flamingoes on the Carmargne',"* and in December Mr Capps brought a few more films including *'The Meadow Ant'* and *'Life in the Hedgerows'*. From among the society's own ranks JWS Dempster and GR Sloggett *"gave the first of what is hoped will be a long series of talks by Members. Their subject, 'Butterflies and Moths', was well illustrated by specimens and items of the collector's equipment and apparatus."*

Membership of this body, which now met mostly on Tuesdays after school, was healthy despite the demands of other activities and within the Society, membership of the microscope section had more than doubled. There was also an increase in the membership of the Philatelic Society which staged nine meetings that term, one of the highlights being a visit to the Main Sorting Office at Pennycomequick *"where much of practical interest to stamp collectors was shown to us."*

Also that term a new and somewhat practical innovation saw the introduction of the Plymouth College Printing Society. Instituted under the direction of Mr Coggin around twenty boys signed up for it and six formed a committee for the general running of activities, under the chairmanship of PA Jolly, with MJ Cowan in charge of machines. One of these machines was *"a new large rotary Press which can print larger pages than the original and much smaller hand-platen machine."*

It was a laborious process, as secretary GD Williams explained; *"The compositing of type is done letter by letter and takes a long time. There is room for a few more members but they would have to be keen and careful."*

"Members," he said, *"are still learning the art of successful printing,"* adding, *"there have been unfortunate cases of whole pages of type being dropped and of printing errors passing the proof-readers, but these have been few and far between."*

Notwithstanding these problems however, Williams proudly announced that the Society *"had printed the Carol Service and the End of Term Concert programmes and also the School Calendar."*

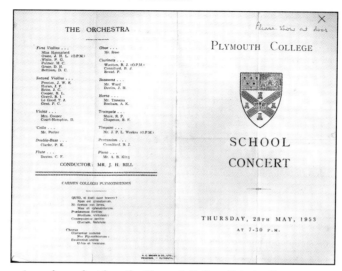

An early product from the Plymouth College Printing Society.

That particular Carol Service was, incidentally, the fifth to be held by the School and it was held, before a large congregation in St Gabriel's Church *"which does not lend itself easily to the creation of an atmosphere",* on Monday 14 December 1953.

Among the interesting features were an airing of Mr Bill's own carol composition *"I sing of a maiden that is makeless"* and the reading of *"the first five lessons by boys chosen to represent various age groups."*

"Partly through nervousness, partly through lack of an established tradition, the readers were, as a group, disappointing, only one boy making any real impact on his hearers. Nevertheless, let us hope that the time will soon come when we can compare our Carol Service with those broadcast from other schools."

Wireless broadcasts were becoming increasingly significant in academic life and the purchase that term of a school tape-recorder - not long available

commercially - had two obvious and immediate benefits; *"in the recording of broadcast talks and in voice tests".*

The ability of boys to speak clearly and project themselves well, had suddenly become an area of concern across the School and the same problems relating to vocal delivery at the Carol Service were evident over the next few days in the production in the School Gym of George Bernard Shaw's Androcles and the Lion. Mr Suggitt in his appraisal of the production complained about the *"inaudibility of some characters; the intrusion of Plymothian accents in the Roman Empire and the general lack of conviction displayed by the Christians."* But he made *"special mention"* of M Wakely, *"who was head and shoulders above the rest in his sensitive characterisation of Androcles, and of P Andrade, for the construction of so genial and benevolent a lion."*

The play, incidentally, formed just part of the Christmas Concert and there were also creditable performances by the School Orchestra and Mr Trevena, who performed Weber's *'Invitation to Dance'*.

Mr Trevena had also been prevailed upon in Lockwood's extra-curricular drive to create a School Gramophone Society, although one suspects he didn't need too much persuasion. Insituted in the winter term the Headmaster was President with Harry T as Master-in-Charge; *"Some 25-30 members have attended and all new members are welcome since only with a large audience can the atmosphere of the concert hall be captured."*

RS Davies was the Hon Sec of the new society and his notes he ruefully noted that *"owing to the formation of so many new societies meetings have to be held in the lunch-hour ... but boys for whom this time is normally inconvenient can lunch at school on the day concerned."*

Not surprisingly that first term saw all the records provided by Harry Trevena including the whole of Puccini's La Boheme and works by Rossini, Mozart,

Liszt, Chopin, Beethoven and Tchaikovsky all featured heavily.

The long-playing record was, at that time, still, of course, very much a novelty, with Decca releasing Bach's Brandenburg Concertos as the first 33.33rpm LP in this country in August 1950. Having said that Plymouth College was by no means the first School in the area to form a society dedicated to the medium as there was already, by that stage, an Inter-Schools Gramophone Society *"in which"* we read in the Easter of 1954, *"the College is increasingly taking an active part"*.

The role of Musical Appreciation was undoubtedly being thrust more into the spotlight under the new Headmaster and another change that accompanied his arrival at Ford Park was the replacement at Assembly in the morning, of the *'Public School Hymn-Book'* with the Revised *'Ancient and Modern'*.

"This change does not in practice make much difference to the hymns and tunes used, but the 'Ancient and Modern' is published in a convenient melody edition, which is useful for Trebles in the choir, and an inexpensive "words only" edition, as well as a full music edition."

The winds of change swept through the corridors of Ford Park with a strength that blew many cobwebs away that term and during the first full holiday period of the new Headmaster's reign the dusters were truly out as the top corridor of Main School was redecorated and three trees on the School Field were felled. We also learned from the School Notes, in that March 1954 Plymothian, that the School had *"acquired new playing-fields at Whitleigh and Peverell"*. There was news too of the new sixth-form periodical *The College Gazette* which had been another 1953 innovation. It had begun life as *'666'* but quickly changed its title *"thus broadening the extent of its aims and it clientele."*

The information regarding this publication appeared directly below an item about the new Printing Society

suggesting that this was another of their in-house productions. Nothing further is said about the change of name and one can only assume that while *'666'* was a nod in the direction of the expanded middle, lower and upper sixth, its association with the *'Mark of the Beast'* may have been a factor in its being dropped.

It is also not clear whether the previous Plymothian's Cambridge letter had been dropped, or had simply failed to appear, but it wasn't there. An extended Oxford missive, written entirely in lower case, in the style of e.e. cummings was the only undergraduate offering. It was no great surprise to find that in the first Plymothian under Lockwood that Cantab was back, although it would have been interesting to know how the new head responded to the comment from Oxoniensis that same issue that a highlight of the Oxford term had been a visit from DM Griffin *"of the Fenland Polytechnic"* - the dark blues' dismissive term for the light blue institution.

Colour, curiously enough, was on the agenda of some other old boys as *"after several requests by members for a less cheerful tie for wear on formal occasions the OPM committee were empowered at the AGM to decide*

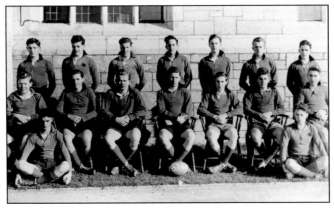

1953-54 1st XV: Back; JM Hewitt, DC Robinson, GC Gray, A Hosking, HJ Heath, R Kerley, TJ Stevens. Front; A Richards, FSW Furze, JR Cundy, JC Battrick, PB Jolly, GR Pengelly, RE Southermn. Front; CV Denning and R Arscott.

upon a plain tie with a small repetitive crest monogram or emblem."

Generally the Club was thriving; a team of Mops (an anagram of OPMs) was sent to the Hockey Festival at Paignton; Derek Pring, the Cricket Club Captain, set a club new record of 113 wickets, including four in the last four balls of a match against Torquay Corps thereby tying the game; and the Rugby Club, organised by Tommy Mutton was *"satisfied with the progress made considering the stronger opposition."*

A mix of old boys and current pupils descend on the Paignton Hockey Festival as the MOPs (i.e. not quite OPMs), among them

The Rugby Club held a Ball in the School Gym after the game with the School on the last Satruday before Christmas, with the Ladies Committee, serving and providing *"an excellent buffet"*.

Outside help was also proving invaluable to the Prep, who, having first mooted the idea of a Council of Parents back in September 1952, decided, in October 1953 to formally institute such a body. Part of the impetus for this came when *"it had been found out that 1954 was the Diamond Jubilee of the 'Prep',"* and exploratory meetings were held in January and February 1954.

The idea being that Parents might have some say in *"the invitation to Guests of Honour for Speech Day and Sports Day; arrange for entertainment of parents by pianoforte recitals, song recitals, bridge, chess etc. And in this Jubilee year consideration might be given to ways and means of raising money towards the cost of a Gym-Hall for the Prep."*

At the first full meeting, on 8th February, Ivor Thompson was elected President and it was agreed that meetings would be monthly, and the venue would be the newly-decorated Council Chamber where the School Council also met. *"The Headmaster has had a u-shaped table erected in the chamber, and this, together with the Coronation Regalia and the old School colours, adds a great deal to the dignity and comfort of Council meetings."*

This, incidentally, was by no means the only way the adult world was being brought into the Prep as we learnt from the *"institution of the new Prep Captains, and the presentation of their Caps."*

The event took place on Saturday 7th November 1953, and the whole School and Staff were present, along with the parents of the boys who were to receive their Caps. Dubbed *"the Capping Ceremony"*, it took place immediately after Morning Prayers; *"the elected boys lined up in front of Mr Firman for their institution as Prep Captains; he then fully explained to them what their responsibilities and obligations would be; each boy replied in turn that he fully understood what was expected of him, and gave his promise to fulfil these duties and obligations to the best of his ability. Caps were then presented and the assembly dispersed."*

It was clearly a very weighty moment in the lives of these young boys; *"All those who were present could not but feel that they were deeply impressed with the sincere atmosphere which prevailed during the whole ceremony."*

On a lighter note, the outstanding event of the Prep term was deemed to be the Staff Refresher Course; *"We must*

express our appreciation to the ladies and gentlemen who gave up the whole of a Saturday morning, and part of an afternoon, to conduct this Course" ... although, alas it did not go along the lines dreamt up by the event's recorder;

"Westhead, stop fiddling with that pipe" ... *"Armstrong, stay behind and see me after the bell"* ... *"Coombe and Redgrave, this is not a noughts-and-crosses class"* ... *"Baker, behave yourself"* ... *"Fry, wake up"* ...*"*

One name destined not to appear in that list, was that of Miss M Bishop; *"We are sorry to say 'Farewell' to Miss Bishop (1951-53) who has married Mr F Scott, now Headmaster of Batley Grammar School, lately Senior History Master in the Main School."*

"An impressive display of produce, given by pupils, which formed a background to the Harvest Festival Service Conducted by Rev. JWG Molland, Vicar of St Gabriel's at Plymouth College Preparatory School today." Western Evening Herald, 9 October, 1953.

Another of Prep teachers, Miss S Nicholls, was married at the end of 1953 (to a young OPM naval officer EA Prior). Miss Nicholls decided to remain on the staff *"for a time"* and the one new face in the Prep Common Room was that of Miss M Whittard. a French specialist who arrived to teach Remove I and II.

In a year that saw many innovations, both at the Main

School and the Prep, including the Main School acquisition of a tape recorder and the institution of a Gramophone Society, it's interesting to note that the Prep School Choir made a gramophone recording of Jesse Irving's 'Crimond' (aka *The Lord's My Shepherd*) and *'O Life that Makest All Things New'* in St Gabriel's Church, seventy-five of which had, within a few months, *"been sold, several finding their way into homes in various parts of the country."*

While, doubtless, not all boys were in a hurry to persuade their parents to purchase the recording, there was, in certain quarters, considerable pressure from Prep boys to get their parents spending; *"About twenty-five boys have bullied parents into buying arrows, bows and bracers on the grounds that Archery is compulsory, which it is not, and that Mr Redgrave said that they had to have them, which he did not."* And there was an identical tale to tell in the nascent Fencing arena; *"Nearly all the boys in the new Fencing Club now have their own foils, having convinced their parents that Fencing is compulsory, which it is not, and that Mr Redgrave said they had to have them, which he did not."*

The Prep wasn't the only part of the Plymouth College operation looking to introduce new sports, back at the Main School plans had been drawn up for the creation of Squash Courts on site, plans which must have both delighted and dismayed those who had been campaigning for covered Five's Courts for many, many years. Doubtless the Tennis players, currently making do on the courts at Aucklands (Beaconfield Road) and Brandreth Road, would also have had a view, but they had other reasons to be gloomy that summer as they were losing the services of Sam Rendle who was leaving to take up a teaching post in Jamaica.

Sport was clearly another area that Lockwood was looking to upgrade in his bid to increase the value-added profile of Plymouth College. In both swimming and athletics a *"new system was arranged whereby points were awarded for standards and this started a tremendous amount of enthusiasm, especially from the younger boys."*

The idea was not entirely new to Ford Park, but clearly it was some years since it had been last implemented and *"the standard of the heats and the training was high, and sports day was looked forward to with great intrest by the whole school. The sports were held for the first time on the Brickfields and two records were broken and one equalled"* ... and there could perhaps have been more had not the Captain of School Athletics, JC Battrick, pulled a muscle shortly before the big day, forcing him to pull out of the track events.

As it turned out JW Lethbridge shared the title of Victor Ludorum with RE Southern; Lethbridge it was who equalled the one record (5'5" in the High Jump) while Southern established the two new ones - 10.9 secs in the 100 yards sprint and 123'2" in the Discus. Southern also won the 220 yards and the Javelin an event which he also won at the Devon Public and Grammar Schools' Championships at Kelly three weeks later.

The School finished fourth over all - *"not as close to the winners as was expected"* and only one other event was won by a Plymouth College athlete - J Chown in the mile.

Chown, the School Cross Country Champion for 1954, had earlier won the Mile at the School Sports in a time of 4'58", bettering the previous years' time by being under 5 minutes, but some way adrift of the time set just two days earlier by the 25-year-old medical student in Oxford, Roger Bannister, who, in front of a crowd of 3,000 spectators, and ahead of a field that included Chris Brasher and Chris Chataway, became the first man to run a mile in less than four minutes. Bannister would also paste another sub-four-minute time at the 1954 British Empire and Commonweath Games (previously known as just the British Empire Games) in Vancouver that summer.

There were no British swimming champions at those games but there were silver medals in the pool for Scotland's Jack Wardrop and England's Peter Jervis, the former recording a time of 4'41" in the 440 yards freestyle, some two minutes faster than the new School record set by RF Williams. in the 450 yards freestyle event in the School Aquatic Sports that summer.

Swimming and Water Polo Team, 1954: Back row; DC Robinson, P Clemens, PL Veal, RA Williams, RF Williams. Middle; TJ Parson, GM Buckingham, FSW Furze (Capt.), MH Twigg, AJ Hannaford. Front; EJ Parnell, MD Thomas, TJ le Good.

Clearly, however, the School swimmers were hampered by a number of things, not least of which was the length of the pool (shorter and requiring more turns) and the temperature; *"the weather during the summer of 1954 will be remembered for a long time - the general absence of the sun hept the temperature of the bath well below average (about 58F), and for the non-swimmers especially it has been a very discouraging term."*

This was particularly unfortunate given the amount of effort devoted to driving swimming forwards at Ford Park. The new measures introduced included the replacement of length swimming by a system of standards, the replacement of the inter-form swimmers league with an inter-house swimmers league that counted towards the house competition, the extension of points to include acknowledgement of not just the usual 1,2,3 - gold, silver and bronze - but also of fourth

place, and the instigation of an Inter-House Water Polo competition organised on a league basis.

Over and above all these changes there was the introduction, for the first time, of a compulsory swimming period for all the first forms on either Monday or Wednesday afternoons. A consequence of all these changes was that there were several more races than usual on Wednesday 14 July when the Aquatic Sports were concluded.

Heavy rain fell during the morning but happily the skies cleared leaving a warm sunny afternoon and the sun shone especially brightly on Dales, for whom Parsons, Victor Ludorum, and Furze were particularly successful. Both were School Water Polo team players and in that capacity played their part in achieving some creditable results against a variety of adversaries although sadly the home swimming battle with Kelly, played out in front of the Headmaster and several governors, was very narrowly lost 36-34.

Incidentally, going back briefly to the athletics that summer, three days before the Senior Championships at Kelly there was a four-way Junior School event at the Tavistock-based school which Plymouth College won. Thanks largely to a stirling performance from Elliott who won the 100, 220 and quarter mile, together with other first placings - in the High Jump, Long Jump and Shot - by Organ, Harbour and Foxwell respectively.

However there was far more to the spring (*"one of the wettest and frostiest on record"*) and summer sporting calendar than athletics and swimming, indeed, before the pool was filled for the season, it was used by the hockey players for stick practice. With a late start to the hockey season occasioned by having four rugger fixtures to fit in first, and with the game so nearly having an enforced break from the school's calendar, it is perhaps all the more remarkable that the team was, according to its secretary, TJ Stevens, *"in the opinion of some of our opponents, the best we have had since the war."* Stevens, who found the net thirteen times in seven of the fixtures, was the sides' most prolific marksman and along with Hewitt and Southern was selected to play for Devon Public Schools side against a County XI at Tavistock. The game was drawn, 2-2, a better result than the 4-2 defeat that the School suffered against Kelly at Ford Park, however it was the only interschool fixture they lost and they did put eight past Plympton Grammar, six past Exeter School and five past the Staff XI.

Hockey 1st XI, 1954; Back row; A Richards, PM Gibbs, GW Searle, GC Fedrick, J Chown. Front; GR Pengelly, RE Southern, TJ Stevens (Capt.), JM Hewitt, DG Bryan. Absent, EA Chapman.

Eight of the School 1st XI also joined the Plymouth Belair side for the Paignton Hockey Festival and having restyled themselves the Specialists they lost to Exeter Exiles on the Good Friday morning, drew with the Rousdon Ramblers in the afternoon. On the Saturday they beat Southampton's Supermarines in the morning and were beaten by a Swindon side sporting six county players, in the afternoon. After Sunday's rest day, Easter Monday saw a morning defeat at the hands of the Pussdogs and an exciting 3-3 encounter with the Devon Dumplings in the afternoon. The opposition again included several county players and the international player, Wootton, and for the less-experienced Specialists it meant the weekend ended on a high note.

The massed teams of the 1954 Paignton Hockey Festival.

Seven of the School Hockey XI also figured prominently in the Cricket XI, with Richards scoring the most runs, Fredrick taking the most wickets and both, along with Stevens, Gibbs and Southern, proving themselves to be useful all-rounders - indeed Stevens, Fedrick, Southern and Hewitt were selected to play for Devon Colts, Richards being slightly too old.

In a summer where the 1sts only lost one inter-school fixture - against Truro - there were a number of statistical highlights with Tredinnick taking 5-7, including a hat-trick, against Plympton Grammar, Fedrick taking 7-17 against Fisguard and Gibbs 6-9 against Sutton High School.

Cricket 1st XI, 1954: Back row; GW Searle, JR Tredinnick, A Aburrow, R Arscott, PM Gibbs, TV Chapman. Front; GC Fedrick, RE Southern, A Richards (Capt.) TJ Stevens, JM Hewitt.

In the eight-wicket win against the OPMs Hewitt

posted the first schoolboy century for the School since the war, with an unbeaten 112, while in the enjoyable draw against Devon Dumplings, the newly-arrived history master, Dennis Collinson, in his first summer at Ford Park, scored 93 before he was run out.

The 2nd XI also only lost one inter-school fixture, when they only managed to score 33 having skittled Sutton High School out for 35. Another low-scoring encounter saw the Seconds dismissed by DHS for just 37, before the tables were turned and the Devonport boys fell for only 27. Meanwhile, the unbeaten Colts were even more successful, only West Buckland scored more than fifty against a bowling attack headed by Rouse and White, and Tavistock Grammar, Truro, Devonport High, Sutton and Shebbear were all turned over for less than 40.

With the younger lads doing so well the future of cricket at Ford Park was looking quite healthy and it was interesting to note that the game was being more heavily promoted than ever before, even further down the School, with the inception of an *"all against all"* House cricket competition at the Prep; *"This has meant much less batting practice in nets, but this has been amply compensated for by quicker fielding and throwing and much better running between the wickets. It has also meant that at least 66 boys will play five games under real match conditions. It is already apparent how much most of them have learnt about how to set about winning a game of cricket."*

Over and above such practical experience was the screening at the Prep of a number of *"Sports Films"*. Following the success of the first in the series on Rugby football, there were offerings on Athletics, Cricket and Swimming.

Made at Queen Elizabeth's School, Barnet, the characters in the films are *"members of the school performing under normal circumstances and under the supervision of their games master. This, in itself, is a good point,"* said our anonymous reviewer, *"Films* in which such maestros as Stanley Matthews or Denis Compton perform feats of wizardry or make elegant strokes with meticulous accuracy undoubtedly appeal to small boys with their natural propensity for hero-worship, but they do not cater for their immediate needs and the necessity to learn thoroughly the rudiments of the game."

One wonders, however, what lessons were learnt in 'The Pater's Match' two days before the end of term; "The amusement was provided by many of Plymouth's more distinguished citizens coping with the problem of bowling and batting left-handed."

The boys were 100 for 2 at tea and after the break "bowled sufficiently accurately and fielded well enough to dismiss the Paters for 23."

Back at Ford Park, or at least based at Ford Park, the School Tennis Team managed to complete five fixtures, while a sixth was rained off. Sadly that was the only inter-school fixture, against DHS, but nevertheless completed encounters were staged with RNEC, at Manadon, with Fisguard at Torpoint, with RNEC at Keyham and against the Staff. Aburrow, Hewitt, Cowan, Tredinnick and Chapman were all awarded their colours and Aburrow won the School Singles Tournament.

With all the existing extra-curricular groups and societies and the Headmaster's drive to increase both availability and range of these activities it was perhaps no surprise to find yet another sport on the College agenda - Golf; "Fifteen boys during the summer term took advantage of the offer made by the Golf Foundation for tuition in golf under Mr KJ Hooker, the Yelverton GC professional."

It was an OPM, Stuart Westlake, then Captain of Bigbury Golf Club, and Secretary of the OPM Golfing Society, who brought this scheme to the School's attention - he also provided "clubs for practice use". It was too soon to know how successful the enterprise might be, but there was clearly already an air of expectation for

the coming season ... "Enthusiastic members will be welcomed. Significantly, however, there was no name or set of initials at the end of the School's first Golf report and one suspects that what it really needed was an enthusiastic member of staff to truly drive it forward.

Certainly that's what had happened with regard to Shooting, with Roger (Captain) Elliott giving up "so much of his spare time and always showing a keen interest in all the team's activities."

This was another area where the School was breaking new ground in 1954; "This year, for the first time in the School's history, a team was sent to Bisley to compete with 88 other public schools for the Ashburton Shield. We were placed 62nd with a score of 478 ex 560, which was quite a creditable effort, although certainly not the best of which some of our older members are capable."

In the Devon Public Schools Rifle Shoot for the CCF Shield at Rippon Tor the School finished a disappointing sixth, but most of the team were quite young and inexperienced, although despite all that Hicks showed a great deal of promise.

Sargent's House Shooting Team, Winners of the Inter-House, Small-Bore .22 Shooting Competition, 1954. Front; B Canniford, MCT Turpitt and Macnamara.

In addition to the Shooting Team's .303 experiences, there was opportunity for all those at the CCF Camp at Windmill Hill, Wiltshire, that summer to fire either a rifle or a bren gun "and the Support Weapons Wing of the School of Infantry gave a demonstration of the 3-inch mortar platoon in action."

"Everything conspired to make this camp enjoyable. The food was good and the tents were extremely comfortable without the usual duckboards. The fine weather and pleasant atmosphere were undoubtedly beneficial to those of us who had recently finished our toils in the examination room."

The weather for the Field Day earlier in the year had not been so good, drizzle falling as 2nd Lt Prynne RM OPM met "A" Coy at the RM Commando School at Bickleigh. They enjoyed a damp clamber over the assault course. It was wet too for the Recruit's Field Day at Cadover and the Dewerstone, "yet even in those conditions the recruits swore that they enjoyed thmselves. Whether it was the fact that they had a day from school, or whether they really like crawling over wet moors in thick mist and pouring rain, I leave you to decide," wrote CSM "R" Coy.

Weather also hampered the RN Section Field Day. "It was hoped that we should be able to sail in our whaler, a brand-new white boat which has new rigging throughout. Our hopes, however, were washed away by the rain."

With nine new recruits numbers in the infant RN Section had risen to a new high of 26 and they distinguished themselves at the Annual Inspection of the CCF; "The march past was a triumph for the RN Section, some outside spectators asking if we were a special squad from the RN Barracks, so good was the marching."

There was a trip to Yeovilton for a handful of the RN Cadets during the Easter holidays, while a further thirty four CCF cadets, together with three officers, went to Iserlohn in Germany, where they had the chance to drive in Bren-gun carriers and Centurion tanks. "Two visits

John Dufton takes a class in the Physics Laboratory.

of special interest were to Moehne and Sorpe Dams, which were destroyed by the "Dam Busters" under Wing-Commander Guy Gubson during the Second World War,"

Paul Brickhill's novelised version of the story of the Dam Busters had come out just a year or two earlier and was already a schoolboy favourite while the Dam Busters film, which was already in production, would be one of 1955's biggest box office successes, so it's easy to see why this would have been such a thrill for the cadets.

Annual Inspection of the Plymouth College Combined Cadet Force. 31 May 1954. Brigadeer Creedon took the salute.

Back home and still in camping mode, Mr Bennett took the School Scout Troop to Bibury, near Cirencester, that summer; *"Although the weather was never very fine an enjoyable camp was held and every opportunity to visit local beauty-spots and places of interest was taken."*

"Undoubtedly the most important event of the (scouting) term and one which ought to do much to give the Troop a greater spirit of initiative was the acquisition of a camp-site near Plym Bridge. This site, while being well provided with wood and water, is by no means a paradise; there is a vast amount of work to be done there, clearing the undergrowth, preparing the ground and building shelters. This work provides excellent scope for the initiative and spirit of adventure that scouting is intended to produce, and it was a little

disappointing that the response to this challenge last term was not greater. Nevertheless one very enjoyable camp was held there at Whitsun, and on field-day a real effort was made to break the back of the work that has to be done."

The disappointments experienced by the scout leaders however were nothing compared to those logged by the potential producers of the *"first abortive attempt at a House Drama Competition"* which *"collapsed beneath the burden of the GCE, a dearth of plays and a surfeit of other activities."*

News of the failure of the Drama Competition was tucked discreetly away, in a couple of lines, deep in the Thompson House Notes, the information however makes sense of the page and a half of vitriol from Jenkins, CW at the beginning of the Plymothian;

"Beware, o my readers, when talking of the drama with regard to the presentation of a forthcoming play. When your associates approach you with that I-want-something-from-you look in their eyes, beware, o my readers. Say, "No", or on your own head be it."

Writing from the perspective of the *"most low of all dramatic beings - the producer"*, CWJ went on to say; *"Thinking of 'his' play was sheer delight; casting was pleasant and worthwhile"* it was the rest that was the problem; *"Every actor is firmly convinced that he has no need whatsoever to come to rehearsals; rehearsals exist purely and simply for the amusement of the producer. The night before the presentation of the play he learns his part. If the actor finds this too irksome a task he makes the play up as he goes along. This is called actor's licence or prompter's hell."*

"The producer's job in actually producing the play is easily explained. One imagines that he just sits at the back of the hall and directs. In actual fact he reads nine parts at once for the benefit of the one person who did attend rehearsal."

"It has been found from experience that that one person has to do nothing except walk on, and therefore the

producer gives a delightful monologue dashing to and fro across the stage trying to represent nine different characters at once ..."

"The drama is a religion, the deity being 'the star'. The producer is a mere third-rate priest in attendance to the Great One. If the results of the play are good, the star is praised and the now exhausted priest is ignored. If the play is bad, the star is praised and the now exhausted priest is sacrificed ..."

Our young writer/producer, and, little could he have thought it then, future Plymouth College music teacher, then concluded his piece with another warning; *"never pay any attention to the old theatrical cliche, 'It'll be alright on the night,' even though it may be of some solace to you. It never is."*

The experience was clearly a salutory one, and there can be little doubt that Jenkins was on happier ground in the School Gym that summer when he and Mr Bill *"gave a lively performance of three movements from Peter Warlock's Capriol Suite."*

The Concert was well-received - *"the standard both of presentation and performance was high"* MJ Barrett with the choir finished the evening's programme with a *"rollicking sea-shanty in which harmony and body-sway were judiciously combined. This was good stuff which set all our feet twitching and heads nodding, but surely they ought to have enjoyed it too! The trebles, in particular, perpetually have sad eyes glued to sagging copies."*

Someone who clearly did enjoy his music was the leader of the Orchestra, Peter White, who, that summer, won the *"Maud Mary Gooch Scholarship, tenable for three years at the Royal Academy of Music."*

There were also non-music scholarships for GB Williams (Classics) and RJA Elford, RJ Harvey, AW Pearce and P Shepheard.

As ever there was more to the School than Sport and the Arts, although clearly for many boys the most memorable moments of the *"Happiest Days of*

Your Life" are associated with those extra-curricular activities. Certainly there had never been so many out-of-hours sections and societies. There was surely something to cater for all tastes on the Ford Park menu in 1954, and while some aspects of the bill of fare might be more difficult to sustain than others there was clearly an appetite there.

And not just within Ford Park, as the Inter-School Gramaphone Society demonstrated, and the success of the Inter-Schools debate, and the fact that the Secretary of the School Philatelic Society - Ross - was also elected Chairman of the newly-formed, city-wide Plymouth Junior Philatelic Society.

Seventy-five boys joined the new Printing Society; the Natural History Society was blossoming and, to cap it all, there was yet another new indoor diversion;

"We had a special privilege in being the first House to win the new chess trophy which was only won after a hard and keen struggle with College and Thompsons," wrote the House Captains of the newly created Dale's House.

Incidentally, the creation of nominal houses commemorating the names of Freddie Dale and Henry Chaytor was not the only gesture the new head made in acknowledging the contributions of his predecessors, for he also had the boarding house re-christened in favour of the first of the great twentieth century School headmasters Francis Colson, as Dunkeld Villas became Colson House.

Significantly the next Headmaster in that worthy line was Herbert Ralph, who had succeeded Dale in 1929 and Ralph it was who was the guest of honour at the OPMs Annual Dinner, held, *"probably for the first time ever"* in Big School, on Saturday 20 March 1954. After the meal the 69 year-old Ralph spoke *"in a reminiscent mood of the war years ... and reminded us of the debt the school owed to the staff and boys who had prevented the incentiary from making any impression on the school premises."*

Forebodingly Francis Lockwood was *"unable to be present owing to illness"* but he *"recorded a speech on the school tape recorder"* to which Mr Dufton *"added his own comments on the school's progress."*

Doubtless the fact that the School was gearing up to celebrate its centenary had some influence on this expression of recognition of the 'whos and hows' Plymouth and Mannamead College had survived its first hundred years. And with such a profound feel for the past, and notwithstanding the changes Lockwood was currently introducing, he also had a keen eye on the future.

Before the Main School got properly down to celebrating its major milestone, the Prep weighed in with its own Jubilee Speech Day, on Wednesday 7 July. As on so many other occasions during Lockwood's first year, the event itself marked a notable first; *"For the first time in our (sixty year) history, the Prize-Giving was held on the premises, thanks to the erection on the field of an immense Marquee, spacious enough to accommodate even the large concourse of visitors who had gathered on this, the only really summer-like day for many weeks."*

Mr EW Davies, Headmaster of King's School, Rochester, presents the leadership cup to CW McFadyean. Wednesday 7 July 1954.

In his speech, the Prep Headmaster, Mr Firman, said that there were now 270 boys at the School and this was the peak of its capacity. *"Many,"* he said, *"would like to see the size of a school class limited to twelve, my own ideal figure is twenty-five, because then competition is allied to individual attention."*

Having outlined his perceived need for a Prep School Gymnasium, he went on to say that the standards of work at the School were kept as high as possible and the percentage of those passing the entrance examination into Plymouth College was 74, *"which I don't think is too bad. The future,"* he said, *"is very rosy and I have no fears of it myself."*

The prizes were presented by MR EW Davies, the headmaster of King's School, Rochester, who informed his audience that one of the great aims of education, *"in my opinion, is to enable our children to enjoy the inheritance that is theirs and so to pass it on in the course of time, to their children."*

Speech Day at Hartley Road, visitors enjoy the model yacht pond.

"This inheritance is not only concerned with science and knowledge, it also means tradition, a way of life and environment. A generation which tolerates the cheap, gaudy, and the shoddy would hand these things on; and if parents cannot rise above football pools, what hope have their children."

Proposing a vote of thanks Mr Lockwood described the Prep as "something at the top of this hill that is of great value to Plymouth as a whole."

After the prze-giving was over the school drama group presented, in the open-air, a new play by Paul - brother of actor, Michael - Redgrave, Yashmak "a light-hearted variation on a certain well-known Eastern story."

"In picturesque surroundings and ideal weather, parents watch an open-air performance of 'Yashmak' by pupils of Plymouth College Preparatory School at yesterday's Speech Day." WMN July 1954.

Incidentally Lockwood had, a couple of months earlier, attended a Special General Meeting at the Prep, with Mr Firman, to answer parents concerns, and to give "an informative address on the relationship between the Main School and the Prep", which was indeed one of the main areas of worry.

Of maginally less importance to parents, but of great importance to the boys, were the measures being taken to raise funds for the new Prep gymnasium, foremost amongst which was the new Tuck Shop.

"It was Mrs Firman who took the initiative in this project. With the active co-operation of a Committee of ladies from the Parent Association it has got off to a good start. Every morning Mrs Firman and two or three volunteers from the parents are in attendance to sell their wares to the Not-so-Simple Simons as they come out for break."

"One evening a week the School Kitchen is invaded by "Harbingers" of sweetness who produced the weekly quota of mouth-watering delicacies which will pull out the pennies from the most untidy pocket!"

"Housed in the Chalet which had previously been used as a garden and tool shed, the Tuck Shop with its red and white check curtains and shelves with covering to match is now an attractive little building and the opening on June 21st caused much excitement. I am pleased to report," wrote Ivor Thompson, "that it has done a roaring trade ever since. The boys appreciate the chance to buy bags of sweets in sizes and prices to suit all pockets. To supplement the home-made sweets there are the stock lines favoured by all schoolboys since Tom Brown's Schooldays."

"Those responsible for the scheme are to be congratulated. For those parents who may be worried about little Johnny's expanding waistline there is the comforting thought that all profits go to the Preparatory School Gymnasium Fund!"

Note there was no apparent concern over little Johnny's teeth!

Incidentally a bank account in the name of Plymouth College Gym was set up at Mutley Plain and among the first amounts deposited were £53 from Speech Day and the School Play, £20 from the Tuck Shop, £15 from a card evening and £5 from an anonymous parent who was donating the profit (about 2/6d - 12p) on each frame he made for the newly-taken Prep School Photograph. The picture, which had the boys arranged on the terracing at the north end of the Field, was taken on 21 May.

Meanwhile, on Saturday 17 July 1954, on the last weekend of term, and thus the School year, the Main School celebrated the "Centenary of the Mannamead School foundation by holding a Fete which was opened by Lady Roborough."

"The reason (or perhaps excuse) for the Fete was twofold. First to swell the balance of the Centenary Fund; second, to provide an atmosphere of festivity, where hilarity, abandon and general joie de vivre could be given a free rein. Alas this last proved predominant and we suffered, indeed, gallons of it, from about 11am. onwards."

"However, once the fact that we were in for a wet afternoon really soaked in, all the stalls which had been pitched on the field in the morning were hastily brought indoors, and promptly, at the appointed hour the Fete was declared open."

"Inside the school an astonishing transformation had taken place. Classrooms resembled fair booths, and the upper and lower corridors seemed akin to the Underground during the rush hour. Here you could find exhibitions of photographs and stamps: a display of still and mobile life in the Biology laboratory: a demonstration of live Chess: and in a marquee, an astonishing variety of goods for sale ranging from the most elaborate fancy cakes to jig-saw puzzles, and from Devonshire cream to cricket balls. All this produce for sale was generously given by parents, boys and friends of the schools."

"Other attractions were a game of push ball: a coconut shy, the attendants of which valiantly remained in the pouring rain until their prize stocks had gone: a very *popular crockery smashing stall - no prizes except the satisfaction of demolishing twelve-inch dinner plates: lightning sketches: a walking robot: a shooting gallery and perhaps the most enthralling item of all, a model exhibition"* ... *"This included two complete model railway tracks, aeroplanes ..."*

"The grand finale took the form of a dance held in the evening in the Gymnasium" and over the whole day some £300 was raised towards the Squash Courts. *"On a pouring day that was indeed an achievement."*

Fundraising begins for the proposed Squash Courts at Ford Park.

And so ended Francis Lockwood's first year in charge at Ford Park, and the first hundred years of Mannamead School - a hundred years in which *"we have built up a fine tradition that is not going to be shaken easily."*

"No, we have no outstanding academic record; no Prime Ministers amongst our old boys; no unbeatable 1st XV or XI. However we have kept going for the last hundred years, we have produced some distinguished scholars and athletes and we have had our failures."

"But let's forget the pompous talk of our "brilliant history" and rejoice wholeheartedly in Our Centenary - so here's to the next hundred years and just wait until Plymouth College catches up with Mannamead School!"

As fate would have it there were half a dozen members of staff who would still be at Ford Park twenty-three years later when that second centenary would be celebrated and another half a dozen who would retire just three years short of that milestone. Sadly, however Francis Lockwood was not destined to be a part of those celebrations in any shape or form. As the first Plymothian of new academic year went to press in October 1954 the following notice appeared;

"We announce with regret that the Headmaster was removed to hospital, where he was ordered a complete rest. We wish him a quick recovery and a speedy return to duty."

There had already been signs earlier in the year that all was not well with the Headmaster, but he rallied and he returned. On Monday 14 February, Valentines' Day, 1955 he gave one of his typically gritty and poignent addresses to the school - *"never have I heard so much put into so few words,"* recorded his obiturist in the Plymothian.

Three days later the School adjourned for half-term and on that Saturday the 47 year-old Francis Lockwood died, suddenly, reportedly of a burst ulcer. A hard taskmaster he had nonetheless *"always extracted from himself more than he asked or expected of others,"* .... and had sent himself to an early grave in the process.

And so it fell on his successor, a man who had been on the Governing Body's shortlist along with Lockwood, two years earlier, CM (Martin) Meade-King, to steer Plymouth College towards its own centenary.

As it transpired he would retire just a few years short of that milestone, but along the way he would become the School's second longest=serving Headmaster in that period.

Martin Mead-King,

And yet, as Meade-King later recalled, it so easily could have been a very different story; *"I first applied for the job in 1953. I think the Governors should consult the candidates before making an appointment, after all they have a good idea about who's best for the job. Lockwood was a lovely man, I'd have given him the job every time. When they announced the chap that had got the job we all spontaneously burst out laughing - we simply couldn't believe it - he was hopeless. Happily he had second thoughts and withdrew shortly afterwards without taking up the post and the Governors reconvened and appointed Lockwood. I think the problem was that he wanted to push new ideas through too quickly. Unfortunately he died before being able to put them into practice."*

ARY 21, 1955.

Headmaster of Plymouth College dies at 47

WAS BRILLIANT TEACHER

MR. FRANCIS WILLIAM LOCKWOOD, headmaster of Plymouth College since the autumn of 1953, died suddenly in hospital in Plymouth on Saturday morning, after being admitted the previous night.

He was 47 and leaves a widow and three children.

Mr. Lockwood suffered ill-health for many weeks during the latter part of last year, although he had returned to take up his duties at the College at the start of the present term.

Regarded with affection by members of his staff, and by parents, his death came as a shock.

He took over the headmastership of Plymouth College from Mr. B. H. Garnons Williams at the beginning of the autumn term in 1953, having previously been headmaster of William Ellis School, London. He was educated at Perse School, Cambridge, and St Catharine's College, Cambridge.

Headmaster at 32

Mr. Lockwood obtained a Second Class in both parts of the Classical Tripos and subsequently obtained his London M.A. by examination and thesis.

Mr. F. W. Lockwood.

APPENDIX
STAFF LIST 1877-1954
COMPILED BY F. J. JEFFERY

Name		DoB	Degree	Arr	From	Dep	To	Subjects	Posts
BENNETT	George L	1846	MA Camb	1877	Rugby Prep	1883	HM Sutton Valance	Lat/Fre	Headmaster
Botheras				1877				Writ/Arith	
Lohr	FN			1877		1888	Dcsd	Music	Visiting
Norman	JS			1877		1882	Kent Prep Sch		
Ritchie	FN			1877		1882	Kent Prep Sch		
Sparks	Rev Frederick			1877		1885	Oxford Military Coll	Maths	
Logan	WH			1879		1889	HM Daventry Sch		
Moore	Edward H			1883	Rugby w Bennett?	1887	Kent Prep Sch	Lat/Grk	Moore's Hse
COHU	Jean Rougier	1859	MA Camb	1883	Dulwich Coll	1884	HM Richmond GS		Headmaster
Fitch	Sgt Major			1883				PT	Visiting
Thompson	EA		BA Oxf	1884		1887	Kent Prep Sch		
BATTEN	James M	1853	MA Camb	1884	Newton C	1889	Insurance	Classics	HM
Field	CA		BA Camb	1884		1885		Classics	
Ginn	EF		BA Camb	1885		1886		Maths	Snr Maths
Bere	FW		BA Oxf	1886	Oxford Univ	1895	Solicitor	Maths	
Little	JE		MA Oxf	1887	North Allerton	1889	HM Hitchin GS	Classics	2nd Classics
Sayer	S		MA Oxf	1887	Ipswich Sch				
Neligan			BA Dublin	1887					
Keeling				1887		1890		Lat/Eng/Hist	
Richards	Rev D			1887		1892	RN Instructor		
Greenway	John Brabyn	01.08.66	BA Oxf	1889	Temp 1887	1894	Oxford Univ/student	Languages	
COLSON	Francis H	24.04.57	MA Camb	1889	Bradford GS	1908	St John's Coll	Classics	HM B/Hse
Garford	Edward	??.??.59				1903	Retd Dcsd March '04	Gymnastics	
Gwyther	George M	09.04.68	MA Camb	1890	Oxford Univ	1910	Dcsd Dec/1910	Eng/Hist/Class	Hse Tutor
Kuhne	Carl Theodore	20.05.49	CM Clgne	1890	Clifton Coll	1918	Retd.	Music	Visiting
Rudge				1890		1895		Science	
Haywood	Rev J Hirste			1891		1903	Sec. Dr Barnados	Maths	S Town Mtr
Thompson	Joseph	28.12.59	MA Oxf	1891	Truro	1919	Retd.	Lat/Mod Lang	N Town Mtr
Dequaire	M			1894					

Pridmore	WH		BA Oxf	1894	Jesus Coll Oxf			Languages	
Lake	Rev KA		BA Oxf	1895	Oxford Univ	1898			
Southby	FF		MA Oxf	1895	Oxford Univ	1903		Maths/Science	H Dept
Murch				1896	Mannamead S	1898	Dcsd	Geography	Naval Crse
Palmer	Francis B	08.09.56	MA Camb	1896	Mannamead S	1920	Retd.	Maths/Scripture	2nd M/B Hse M
Woodcock	Frank W	14.07.63		1896	Mannamead S	1909	Retd. (health)	Latin/English	O/C Cadet Corps
Thill	John A	26.11.60		1896	Heidelberg Sch	1923	Retd.	French/German	
Wheat				1896		1906			
Powell	FG			1896		1897	Almondsbury Sch	Lower School	Visiting
Babb	Ernest H	30.10.68	R Coll Art	1898		1911		Art	Visiting
Pryor	James C	18.01.79		1898		1901	Dcsd	Typewriting	Visiting
Hope	HP		MA Camb	1898	Cambridge Univ				
Treleaven	Edward	26.01.77	BA Oxf	1898	Oxford Univ	1906	St Olave's	English	
Caldwell	AFS			1899		1902		Science/Maths	Hse Tutor
White			Bsc Lond	1902	Bath Coll	1903		Science/Maths	Hse Tutor
Gardiner	Ernest A	02.08.80	MA Oxf	1903	Oxford Univ	1912	Berkhamsted Sch	Science/Maths	HD Sci Hse M
Sargent	Herbert	13.04.71	MA Camb	1903	Friars Sch	1934	Retd.	Maths/Physics	2M Hse M
Blunt	Edward J	12.02.75	Dip Berlin	1906		1920	Anitpodes	PT	
Clynic	John O	30.04.79		1906		1916	War Service	Manual Work	Visiting
Pocock	HBI			1904		1908	HurstPierpointColl		
Hodge	Rev JM			1906		1909	Retd. Ill health		
CHAYTOR	Rev Henry	10.02.71	MA Oxf	1908	KingEdwdVIISheff	1919	StCatherine'sCamb	Classcs/Divinity	HM B Hse
Dodson	Charles W	09.06.88	MA Oxf	1910	Farnham GS	1922	HM Salop	Hist/Geog/Eng	O/C Cadet Corps
Powell	John L	23.05.80	MA Oxf	1910	RGS Worcs	1912	Repton Sch	Geog/Hist/Eng	
King	James K	23.11.82	MA Camb	1912	Downside	1914	Highgate Sch	Science	
Page	Alfred H	23.09.88	BA Camb	1912	Missionaries	1915		English/Maths	
Truelove	Harold E	14.10.88	BA Oxf	1912	Oxford Univ	1914	Interned by Germans	French/German	
Gurnhill	Geoffrey D	23.03.91	BA Camb	1914	Forest Sch	1915	Red Cross - Italy	Classics/Divinity	
Martin	Rolfe G	18.12.89	BA Camb	1914	Cardiff HS	1919	Macclesfield Sch	Science/Maths	
Horrill	Arthur J	01.04.74		1916		1918	War Service	Gym/Boxing	Visiting
Meech	William H	16.03.82		1916		1936		Handwriting	Visiting
Stansfield	Wilfred W	22.04.83	BA Camb	1916	Ramsgate Cnty S	1918	War Service	English/Maths	
Williams	Arthur S	27.07.85	BA Camb	1916	Victory Coll, Jersey	1917	War Service	Classics/English	B Hse M
Lingley	Arthur G	26.07.70	MA Camb	1917		1935	Retd.	English	B Hse M

Trenchard	Alice M	24.10.90	BA Lond	1917	Clarehouse Sch	1919		French/German	
Anstice	Edmond H	01.07.94		1918	War Service	1919		Form Subjects	
Cairns	George F	01.04.71	MA Edin	1918	Taunton Sch	1931	Retd.	History/Maths	FM 1A
Johnston	Rev Samuel	23.03.69	DSciEdin	1918	Huish's Sch	1919		Science/Maths	
Wylie	George M	06.01.91	MA Camb	1918	KingWm'sColl IoM	1920	Nuneaton Sch	Classics	
Dufton	John T	16.07.92	MA Camb	1919	War Service	1956	Retd.	Physics/Maths	HD SM
House	S	01.03.89	Bsc.Lond	1919	War Service	1920	Finsbury High Sch	Science/Maths	
Richardson	Denis J	08.09.88	MA Camb	1919	War Service	1923		French/German	FM Hse M
Beaumont	Henry F	24.09.90	BATrCollDb	1920		1925	Vicar Yelverton	Classics/Scripture	
DALE	Francis R	07.03.87	MA Camb	1920	Leeds GS	1929	HM CityLondonSch	Classics	HM
Dobson	Hubert	16.06.84		1920	RussianOfficer'sCamp	1929		PT Swimming	Gym
Dodd	Rev Henry	17.12.87	MA Oxf	1920	Madras Univ	1922	Parish Birmingham	Classics/Scripture	FM
Highatt	Frederick W	24.10.84	BA Lond	1920	Rutlish Sch	1921		History/Maths	FM
Mayne	Gerald W	24.09.84	DipSupParis	1920	PangbourneNautColl	1924	Cheltenham	ModLang/Latin	
Osmund	Charles W	02.01.83	BscDurhm	1920	Haberdashers Sch	1933	Dcsd.	Chemistry/Maths	SnrSciM
Gingell	Walter C	05.04.89	MALlbCamb	1921	S.Cyprian'sSch	1933	Dcsd.	Maths/English	FM
Naish	Walter V	06.05.92	BA Oxf	1921		1924	Bournemouth	Latin/English	FM
Benskin	Rev Bernard	01.09.83	BA Oxf	1922	Stamford Sch	1937	Vicar S.Anthony	Hist/Geog/Script	FM
Lord	Lionel C	25.12.98	BA Camb	1922	Cambridge Univ	1937	HM Bury GS	Classics/ClclHist	HseM(NT)
Holman	Eric JL	21.02.97	Msc Birm	1923	Birmingham Univ	1962	Retd.	Chemistry/Physics	BHseM 2M
Rutherford	Richard V	27.09.98	BA Camb	1923		1924		German/French	
Coggin	Maurice E	11.10.92	MA Camb	1925	Koningsberg Univ	1925	Denmark	German/French	
Davies	David I	14.01.98	BA Wales	1924	St.Barts GS	1940	War Service	French/Latin	HseM
Adams	Walwyn T	11.09.94	BA Camb	1925	Nottingham HS	1926			FM
Woodcock	William W	05.10.99	MA Camb	1925	Romford	1945	ControlCommission	German/French	FM
Hill	Guy M	06.11.92	MA Camb	1926	Alsop HS	1956	Retd.	Greek/Scripture	FM HseM
Dawes	Rudolph V	06.05.96	MA Camb	1927	Nantwich GS	1935	HM DonningtonGS	Maths/History	FM
RALPH	Herbert W	24.05.85	MA Camb	1929	HMKing'sS Chester	1945	Retd.	Classics	HM
Edwards	Ian S	08.08.01	Dips	1929	PlymEducC'ttee	1966	Retd.	PE Art	HD
Price	John A	25.05.07	BA Oxf	1931	Oxford Univ	1933	Sydney NSW	French	FM
Batrick	William E	11.06.08	Phd Lond	1933	PlymCorporationGS	1972	Retd.	Chemistry	B Hse M 2M
Blatchford	Alfred H	01.11.08	Bsc Redng	1933		1934	Agricultural College	Form Subjects	FM
Barnes	Cyril L	07.01.10	MA Camb	1933	The Hall School	1974	Retd.	Latin/French	FM 2M HM
Mercer	Edward	12.12.09	Bsc Drhm	1933	Cambridge Univ	1974	Retd.	Maths	FM Games M

Bonser	George H	29.10.08	MA Camb	1934	KingEdwdVINuneaton	1974	Retd.	Maths	FM HD HseM
Jones	WG Meyricke	06.04.09	MA Oxf	1934	Columbia's Coll	1975	Retd.	English	FM HseM
Dent	G Hugh R	17.02.12	BA Oxf	1935	Oxford Univ	1966	Retd. (health)	English	FM HD HseM
Porter	William McD	14.01.07	Bsc Lond	1935	Sandbach School	1972	Retd.	Geography	FM HD HseM
Dundas	Ernest G	06.03.10	MA Camb	1937	Oulton High School	1951	Alsop High School	Classics	HseM
Hill	Charles P	29.12.14	BA Oxf	1938	Oxford Univ	1940	Warwick School	History	
Meek	Horace L	12.11.02	BA Lond	1939	Llandou College	1946	Brentwood School	Maths	HseM
Goad	Kathleen	10.06.00	BA Lond	1940	Headland College	1944	New post	English/French	
Gould	Herbert W	30.10.02	Bsc Lond	1940	Loughton School	1945	Portsmouth LEA	Maths	
Jackson	Stafford B	23.06.19	BA Oxf	1940	Oxford Univ	1949		French	
Rigby	Richard	10.12.89	MA Liverpl	1940	Brentwood Coll	1944	Dunstable	French	HseM
Butcher	Nelly O	08.06.95	BA Wales	1941	Home	1946	Home	English/ModLang	
Savage	Wilfred H	16.04.04	MA Oxf	1941	KingEdwVIISheffield	1947		History	HseM (P)
Drew	Douglas L	27.02.90	MA Oxf	1942		1945		Classics	
Sykes	Marjorie	01.02.01	BA Lond	1944	Home	1946		English/History	
Ellingher	Ernest	28.03.08	DrJr Vienna	1945	London	1961	Retd.	German	
Coulthard	Pamela	23.07.23	BA Oxf	1945	Heathfield School	1945		English	
GARNONS-WILLIAMS	Basil H	01.07.06	BA Blit Oxf	1945	Marlboro College	1953	HM Berknhampstead	Classics	HM
Radford	G Nigel	13.08.14	BA Oxf	1946	War Service	1979	Retd.	Latin/History	FM BHseM SM
Spear	John R	22.06.15	BA Drhm	1946	War Service	1975	Retd. (health)	History/French	FM HseM LSM
Bill	John H	30.05.11	MA BMusOxf	1946	War Service	1974	Retd.	Music	HD
Davies	Alastair L	06.04.15	MA Oxf	1946	War Service	1948	Wellington Coll	History	
Wills	Leslie F	02.02.00		1946		1952		Art	Main & Prep
Hills-Harrop	George D	14.05.16	MA Camb	1947	Colyton GS	1949	Launceston Coll	Mod/Lang	
Rendle	H Samuel	18.03.24	BA Camb	1947	Bristol GS	1954	Jamaica	Maths	
Scott	Francis W	08.06.15	MA Camb	1947	Cambridge HSB	1953	HM Batley GS	History	HD
Gander	Bernard V	23.01.94	Bsc Lond	1948	Royal Navy	1950	Colchester GS	Science	
Trevena	Harry	12.11.22	BA Lond	1948	Paris	1982	Retd.	Mod/Lang	FM HD
Coggin	Philip A	20.07.17	BA Oxf	1949	BRNC	1955	HM Brampton School	Mod/Lang	
Elliott	Roger	07.03.22	MA Camb	1949	Cambridge Univ	1987	Retd.	History/French	O/C CCF
Hall	Hubert T	18.06.21	BA Oxf	1949	Oxford Univ	1952	Africa	History	
Lindley	David	11.07.24	BA Camb	1949	Cambridge Univ	1952	Crewkerne School	Geography	
Addis	Arthur JW	17.02.21	Bsc Drhm	1950	Durham Univ	1981	Retd.	Physics	FM HD SM

King	Alan B		MusB Camb	1950	Cambridge Univ	1969	Bridlington School	Music	
Whitman	David E	25.01.18	Bsc Sheff	1950	Liskeard GS	1958	Canterbury	Maths	FM
Rose	Angus AD	02.08.25	MA Oxf	1951	Oxford Univ	1956	HM Portugal	English/Maths	FM
Philipps	W William M	01.04.27	BA Oxf	1951	Oxford Univ	1956	Pangbourne	French	FM
Bennett	Brian TN	24.09.27	BA Oxf	1952	Oxford Univ	1955	Berkhamsted Sch	Art/History	
Blackledge	Robert CR	26.10.20	BA Oxf	1952	KingHenryVIIICoventry	1957	HM Ludlow School	History	FM HD Careers
Holmes	Roy H	25.04.26	BA Oxf	1952	Oxford Univ	1953	East Ham GS	French	FM
Jeffery	Frank J	06.06.27	BscLond	1952	Southampton Univ	1987	Retd.	Biology	FM HD DHM
Suggitt	Geoffrey	27.01.23	MA Oxf	1952	Dulwich Coll	1959	G Watsons Sch	Classics	FM HseM HD
LOCKWOOD	Francis W	1908	MA Camb	1953	HM Wm Ellis School	1955	Dcsd. (19Feb)	Classics	HM
Collinson	Denis W	31.10.28	BA Camb	1953	Cambridge Univ	1978	Open University	History	FM HD BHseM
Trounson	Ronald C	07.12.26	MA Camb	1953	Surrey LEA	1958	Denstone Coll	Classics	
Winterbotham	Anthony JM	17.04.27	BA Camb	1953	Wotton House Sch	1955	Wells Theological C	Biology	
Cooke	David C	28.05.19	MA Camb	1954	HM Bahamas	1955	Forest Gate School	Maths	
Lowndes	Ashley G	09.10.85	ScD Camb	1954		1955	Probus School	Biology	Part-time
Porter	William A	24.09.26	Bsc Lond	1954	Wembley GS	1958	Evesham GS	Geography/Biology	FM